Paleobotany

An Introduction to
Fossil Plant Biology

Paleobotany

An Introduction to Fossil Plant Biology

Thomas N. Taylor

Professor of Botany
The Ohio State University, Columbus

McGraw-Hill Book Company

New York   St. Louis   San Francisco   Auckland   Bogotá   Hamburg
Johannesburg   London   Madrid   Mexico   Montreal   New Delhi
Panama   Paris   São Paulo   Singapore   Sydney   Tokyo   Toronto

This book was set in Times Roman by Black Dot, Inc. (ECU).
The editors were James E. Vastyan and James S. Amar;
the production supervisor was Dominick Petrellese.
The drawings were done by J & R Services, Inc.
The cover was designed by Elliot Epstein.
Fairfield Graphics was printer and binder.

Cover: Cellulose acetate peel from a Lower Pennsylvanian coal ball collected in eastern Kentucky.

PALEOBOTANY
An Introduction to Fossil Plant Biology

1 2 3 4 5 6 7 8 9 0 F G F G 8 9 8 7 6 5 4 3 2 1

Library of Congress Cataloging in Publication Data

Taylor, Thomas N
    Paleobotany: an introduction to fossil plant biology.

    Bibliography: p.
    Includes index.
    1. Paleobotany. I. Title.
QE904.A1T39   561   80-23958
ISBN 0-07-062954-4

For Timm

Contents

Preface

Despite the antiquity of the materials with which the paleobotanist works, the discipline is changing rapidly. New discoveries are being made that influence not only the study of all fossil organisms, but many areas of contemporary biology as well. In general, there are two primary reasons for this increased activity. One involves the utilization and incorporation of new techniques in the study of fossil plants. Such approaches as scanning and transmission electron microscopy, laser pyrolosis, computer-assisted modeling, microprobe analysis, statistics, and geochemistry represent but a few of the contemporary biological techniques used today to solve problems in the field of paleobotany. Second, and of far greater importance, is what may be regarded as the broader biological and geologic training that is being received by paleobotanists entering the field today. This training not only involves the basic disciplines of botany and geology, but also includes many other areas of the biological sciences. The combination of new techniques and broader training has resulted in paleobotanists today viewing fossil organisms not as static imprints or coalified relics of the past, but rather as once living, dynamic organisms. This approach, which is sometimes referred to as whole-plant paleobiology, promises to provide even more insight for the solutions to the many problems that will be encountered in the study of fossil plants in the future.

Palynology is a rapidly expanding and developing subdiscipline of paleobotany that concerns itself with the study of pollen grains and spores. Traditionally there have been two principal approaches to the study of fossil pollen grains and spores. In one method, the grains are used as index fossils in order to provide a method of determining the relative stratigraphic positioning of the sediments in which they are found. The other approach, and the one used predominantly in this book, views the grains as component parts of the life history of an organism. Although the stratigraphic value of pollen and spores is considered, the primary emphasis in terms of these palynomorphs is in the context of whole-plant biology.

This book is designed for use by upper-division undergraduate and graduate students in the biological sciences, as well as students whose primary focus is in the geological disciplines, but who may have a minimal background in areas of plant biology. In this regard, a considerable amount of information about living plants has been incorporated in the introduction to each of the major groups of plants. In addition, one chapter has been devoted to basic structural and morphologic features of living plants. It is anticipated that the serious nonbotanist will utilize this knowledge as an introduction, seeking supplemental information from textbooks and reference books specific for a given subject. To further assist the nonspecialist, a comprehensive glossary has been provided.

The chapters have been arranged in what might be regarded as a traditional classification of plants. There has been a conscious effort to provide a reasonable balance in subject matter and detail for all areas of paleobotany and major groups of plants. Because of the numerous advances made in recent years in understanding of the earliest forms of life, a chapter has been devoted to the biology of Precambrian organisms. In discussing the evolution of plants through time, the author has been concerned with providing enough factual information about the individual plants so that concepts and ideas about their evolution can be evaluated. In addition, an effort has been made to discuss some of the more biological aspects of fossil plants, such as their development, reproduction, and ecology.

There has been an attempt to reduce to a very minimum the number of references that occur within the text so that the reader will not be continually interrupted by the references and taxonomic citations that often accompany a book of this nature. The bibliography has been arranged by chapter and, in most instances, by a further subdivision of the citations according to the classification used in that chapter. It is hoped that this arrangement will facilitate an opportunity for the reader to obtain additional information on a particular subject or to search out the original reference for a specific topic.

In a discipline such as paleobotany photographs are especially important, because one fossil may represent the only information known to exist about a particular plant or plant part. It is for this reason that I am deeply appreciative to my many colleagues who have so graciously provided illustrative material or allowed me to photograph specimens from their collections. All these colleagues have provided the necessary stimulus for this book through their devotion to the study of fossil plants. Many have aided in their willingness to discuss current research ideas and to read and critically evaluate some of the chapters. The assistance of the following people is greatfully acknowledged: Elso S. Barghoorn, Harlan P. Banks, R. A. Baschnagle, James P. Basinger, Robert W. Baxter, Charles B. Beck, Harold C. Bold, Patricia M. Bonamo, Édouard Boureau, David F. Brauer, Jack D. Burgess, William G. Chaloner, William L. Crepet, Rudolf Daber, Charles P. Daghlian, Roger J. Davey, Theodore Delevoryas, David L. Dilcher, William A. DiMichele, Jeffrey B. Doran, James A. Doyle, Dianne Edwards, Donald A. Eggert, Graham F. Elliott, Gary L. Floyd, R. Förster, Jean Galtier, Patricia G. Gensel, Charles W. Good, Rodney E. Gould, Jane Gray, James D. Grierson, John W. Hall, Christine M. Hartman, Leo J. Hickey, Llewellya Hillis-Colinvaux, Harold J. Hoops, Francis M. Hueber, James R. Jennings, Andrew H. Knoll, Valentine A. Krassilov, Albert G. Long, Jacob Lorch, Hari K. Maheshwari, Sergius H. Mamay, Steven R. Manchester, Lawrence C. Matten, Sergei V. Meyen, Michael A. Millay, Charles N. Miller, Jr., Marjorie D. Muir, Karl J. Niklas, Matthew H. Nitecki, Virginia M. Page, Hans D. Pflug, Raymond N. Pheifer, Tom L. Phillips, Gar W. Rothwell, Jeffry T. Schabilion, Stephen E. Scheckler, J. William Schopf, Rudolph Schuster, Hans-Joachim Schweitzer, Andrew C. Scott, Judith E. Skog, Edith L. Smoot, Satish K. Srivastava, Wilson N. Stewart, Benton M. Stidd, Ruth A. Stockey, William D. Tidwell, Robert H. Wagner, L. R. Wilson, and Joseph M. Wood.

I am especially appreciative to my student Edith L. Smoot and colleague Michael A. Millay for their valuable suggestions and the numerous ways they assisted in the development and completion of this book. Much of the initial planning of this book was carried out in collaboration with Ted Delevoryas, who not only was responsible for my initial contact with paleobotany, but who has continued to serve as a source of inspiration through his friendship and his dedication to the study of fossil plants.

Above all I wish to acknowledge the loving support of my wife Judith and my children, who have been so very understanding and tolerant each time the "crabby" book was being worked on.

Thomas N. Taylor

Paleobotany

An Introduction to
Fossil Plant Biology

Chapter 1

Introduction

The earth is a vast cemetery where the rocks are tombstones on which the buried dead have written their own epitaphs.

Louis Agassiz

The only method by which a history of the plant kingdom can be reconstructed is by a study of fossil plants found in the rocks of the earth. Paleobotany is the science of fossil plants, and through the efforts of paleobotanists, we are gradually piecing together the complicated picture of vast changes that have taken place in the plant kingdom. It is natural for a nonspecialist to wonder where fossil plants occur, how they were formed, how one knows where to look for them, and what to do with them after they have been collected.

HOW PLANT FOSSILS ARE FORMED AND STUDIED

Actually, plants were preserved in the earth's crust in a variety of ways. Different kinds of physical and chemical processes were involved at the time of preservation. Moreover, different kinds of environmental settings and depositional processes also resulted in fossils that occur in a variety of forms. Because of the different kinds of preservation, the paleobotanist must employ different types of techniques to extract the maximum amount of information from the fossils.

Fossil plants are found in almost all regions of the earth, the most notable exceptions being recent volcanic islands. Otherwise, where sedimentary rocks occur, there is a good chance that fossil plants will be found in them. Sedimentary rocks are those formed by the accumulation of rock particles. These particles are derived from the weathering and mechanical abrasion of existing rocks. The breakdown of rocks into smaller units also may occur by chemical weathering, with rock components being released into solution, later to resolidify at some other place. Typically, then, plant parts are fossilized in areas where sediment is accumulating. Such a situation could conceivably involve a delta, where the course of a river constantly shifts, where channels are abandoned and new ones initiated, where natural levees are destroyed during flooding with new ones being built up later. An example of how plant parts may become fossilized might involve a delta levee, undisturbed for some time, that develops vegetation. Associated with the deltaic system are abandoned stream channels, often referred to as "oxbow lakes." A flood would destroy the levee, knocking down trees and other plants growing on it. These plant parts would then be carried to abandoned channels and other places where a high concentration of sediment would bury the plant fragments and fill in the oxbow. As might be expected, those plant fragments carried for great distances would tend to be tattered and shredded, and those deposited close to where the plants were growing would be less distorted. As sediments accumulate, water is squeezed out of them, so that they become much more compact and plant fragments contained within become flattened. Internal structure is obliterated as the cells become squashed, and frequently all that is left is a thin carbonaceous film that conforms to the original outline of the plant part involved (Fig. 1-1E). This type of fossil is called a compression, and it is probably the most common type of plant fossil. As one might predict, if the sediment grains that bury the plant parts are large and angular, the resulting compression shows less clear detail than if the sediment particles were smooth-edged and fine. Actually there is a vast range of sediment size and structure, with plant parts even preserved in conglomerates, rocks with variously sized particles.

Compressions are not always formed in deltaic systems; they may be formed in lagoons, along meandering rivers (not necessarily near deltas), and in ponds, swamps, or other situations. Most often a terrestrial system is involved (as opposed to a marine environment), although there are even some instances in which plants are preserved in marine limestones. Most well-preserved compressions are found in clay or shale, the latter derived by pressure and dehydration.

In certain instances, plant compressions are found in consolidated volcanic ash. These would have come from plants growing near an area where there was volcanic activity, with clouds of ash being spewed into the air. Often there is severe atmospheric turbulence near a volcano, with thunderstorms developing as a result. The water from the rain and the ash make a fine-grained mud that cascades down the hillsides, picking up and burying plant parts as it goes. When the mud hardens, it entombs pieces of plant material within it.

Figure 1-1 Types of fossilization. A. Petrifaction and partial cast of *Lepidostrobus fayettevillense*. ×1.2. B. Impression of *Macrotaeniopteris magnifola*. ×1. C. Silicified cone of *Araucaria mirabilis*. ×0.4. D. Surface of coal ball showing portion of *Lepidostrobus* cone. ×0.4. E. Transfer from compression of *Oligocarpia brongniartii*. ×0.9. *(A from Taylor and Eggert, 1968.)*

A very unusual kind of matrix in which compressions occasionally occur is a rock formed from the siliceous shells of microscopic plants called diatoms (see Fig. 4-4A). The rock that results, diatomite, is especially fine-grained, and preservation of plant parts in it is often superb. Since the diatom frustules, or shells, are acutally microscopic plants (algae), in this method of preservation one plant is serving as the matrix for another plant.

Leaves are the most commonly preserved plant parts, and in many instances, the rock containing them has many layers at close intervals. These leaves are deposited along bedding planes, and to uncover them, one attempts to split the rock along the bedding planes with a knife if the matrix is clay or a hammer and chisel if the rock is harder. Sometimes the paleobotanist must resort to sterner measures, such as using a jackhammer or even dynamite.

Most compressions are of value in showing surface details. Such features as leaf shape, presence or absence of a leaf stalk or petiole, blade margin, and pattern of veins (venation) are readily discernible. When there is an abundance of leaves from one kind of plant, it is possible to determine the degree of variability exhibited by the leaves of one species.

The best kinds of compressions for easy study are those preserved as a relatively dark carbonaceous film on a matrix of light color. The contrast makes examination and photography relatively easy. At times, however, the matrix may be quite dark, almost the same color as the compression. Photography is then difficult, but details may be enhanced by submerging the fossil completely in water or a liquid such as xylene.

In a few instances, compressions were preserved under low heat and pressure such that all cell contents were not obliterated. In one recently published study (Niklas et al., 1978), compressed angiosperm leaves of the Miocene Epoch were embedded and sectioned so that structures inside the cell could be examined with the aid of the transmission electron microscope. The preservation of these fossils was so exquisite that the cellulosic microfibrillar organization of the cell walls could be examined. Even more astounding is the fact that such cell organelles as chloroplasts with grana stacks and starch, nuclei with condensed chromatin, and plasmodesmata were preserved within the mesophyll cells of the compressed leaves.

Although most compressions show only superficial details, in some instances it is possible to learn a great deal about cellular details of the epidermis. Aerial parts of all land plants are covered with a thin film of waxy material, called cuticle, that prevents excessive water loss from the surfaces of the plants. This cuticle is not a layer of cells, but an amorphous material that conforms to the contours of the cells at the surface of the plant organ. It is possible to remove the cuticle, either mechanically with a needle or a brush or chemically by dissolving away the matrix. Pieces of cuticle retrieved in this way can then be bleached and stained with certain common biological stains (see Fig. 1-4F). When mounted on a slide and examined with a microscope, these pieces of cuticle reveal considerable epidermal detail. Shapes of cells are apparent, along with the structure of the stomatal complex (the cells associated with pores in the leaf), distribution of stomata, presence of hairs or glands, and other distinguishing features. The cuticle in fossil plants is very much like fingerprints, with many species having distinctive epidermal features that are often useful in identification. Furthermore, it is often possible to determine that scattered plant fragments, such as leaves, flowers, seeds, etc., actually belong to the same kind of plant because the cuticle is identical among all the parts.

In recent years, paleobotanists have routinely employed scanning electron microscopy as an aid in greatly magnifying minute structures of fossil plants and plant parts (Fig. 1-2). In some instances, cuticular fragments can be examined directly with the scanning electron microscope (SEM). In other cases, it is necessary to make latex replicas of the plant surfaces in order to interpret complex structural details. In many areas of paleobotany, scanning electron microscopy has become a routine method of illustrating such plant parts as pollen grains and spores because of the tremendous range of magnifications available (up to 100,000 ×) and the extreme depth of focus.

Another method of studying cuticular or epidermal features is to transfer the compression from the rock matrix to a transparent film that may be examined with a microscope (Fig. 1-1E). Such a film can be made by pouring on a liquid-plastic substance (clear fingernail polish, for example) and then separating the film, with the cuticle adhering to it, from the rock matrix. A similar technique is to embed the surface of the fossil in liquid plastic (such as that used for preparing biological mounts) and then to dissolve away the rock. The surface layer of the fossil will adhere to the plastic, and it may be examined by either reflected or transmitted light.

Although x-ray analysis has been used for many years by paleontologists working with animal fossils, only recently has this technique been successfully employed in the study of fossil plants (Strümer and Schaarschmidt, 1980). X-ray analysis is especially valuable for studying specimens preserved in highly metamorphosed shales where much of the specimen is covered by the matrix. This technique not only provides details that cannot be obtained with conventional techniques, but also makes some reconstructions possible through the use os stereoscopic x-ray analysis.

Technically, coal would come under the definition of a compression fossil. It is formed from an accumulation of plant material that became crushed from

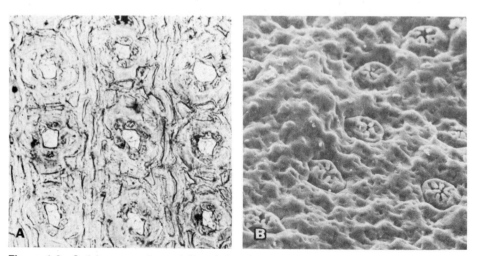

Figure 1-2 Cuticle preparations of *Pseudofrenelopsis varians* from the Lower Cretaceous of Texas. A. Transmitted-light photomicrograph of cuticle surface showing stomata. ×200. B. Scanning electron micrograph of surface showing stomata. ×210. *(Courtesy of C. Daghlian.)*

overlying pressure. In general, the less metamorphosed the coal is, the more detail one can see in the plants comprising it. Lignites, for example, represent an early stage in coal formation, with plant parts not excessively crushed and easily recognizable. In some lignites it is possible to tease apart the plant fragments and make whole mounts of various structures. Bituminous coal is more metamorphosed, the plant parts being considerably more flattened, but it is still possible to study plant fragments in it. Anthracite coal, the most highly metamorphosed type, is altered to such an extent that little of the original plant material is recognizable. Some coals can be sectioned thinly for microscopic examination, and pollen grains, spores, and fragments of cuticle can be discerned. Coal also can be macerated using chemicals that break down the solid coal and release the plant fragments. It is possible to recognize cuticle, pieces of bark, bits of wood, solidified resins, and especially spores and pollen grains (Fig. 1-3). Examination of these parts allows one to determine the kinds of plants that were growing in the ancient swamps where the coal was formed.

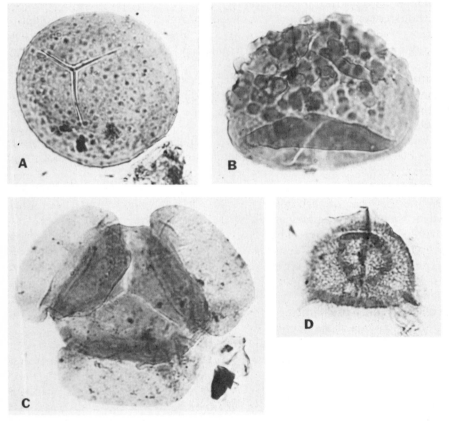

Figure 1-3 Carboniferous palynomorphs from the Schultztown Coal, western Kentucky. A. *Punctatisporites* sp. B. *Schopfites colchesterensis*. C. *Alatisporites varius*. D. *Cirritriradites annulatus. (From Gray and Taylor, 1967.)*

In rare instances, a coal is formed that consists entirely of cuticular fragments and amorphic organic material. The cuticle is so abundant that it can be peeled off in thin layers. This type of coal is called paper coal, alluding to its papery appearance, and is known from just a few localities. It is a simple matter to isolate these cuticular fragments by using a base such as potassium hydroxide. The cuticle can then be washed and mounted directly on slides for examination.

If a paleobotanist splits rock that contains fossil plant fragments along bedding planes, when the rock splits, he or she will see a carbonaceous film, the compression, along one face. Often the opposing face will reveal a negative imprint of the plant part, with little or no carbon adhering. This "negative" will show all the surface details of the compression, such as leaf shape, venation, etc., but there is no actual plant material involved. This type of fossil is called an impression (Fig. 1-1B). The process involved in the formation of an impression is analogous to the frequent occurrence of leaf imprints in concrete sidewalks. These imprints are formed when leaves fall and settle into the wet concrete just after it is poured. After a time, the concrete hardens, conforming to the contours of the lower side of the leaf that rests on it. Eventually the leaf will disintegrate and blow away, and a negative replica of the actual plant part remains on the hardened concrete. If you have ever put your initials in wet concrete, you have formed an impression.

Although no cellular details can be seen on an impression because there is no adhering organic material, in some instances, especially where the matrix is exceedingly fine-grained, a replica of the impression can be made with latex or some other similar material. This replica reproduces faithfully whatever surface details were on the impression. Examination of a fragment of the replica with a scanning electron microscope might reveal, for example, epidermal patterns with great clarity.

In some instances, three-dimensional plant parts, e.g., stems or seeds, are carried into the basin of accumulating sediment and buried. After a time, they are crushed, in which case they are preserved as compressions and impressions. However, there are times when the sediment surrounding these three-dimensional plant parts hardens before the plant fragment is crushed; the sediment then forms a three-dimensional negative of the plant fragment. If the plant material eventually disintegrates, the hollow that remains in the sediment is called a mold. The mold may reproduce faithfully the surface features of a particular part, such as characteristic leaf bases on a stem (see Fig. 8-8A) or the ornamentation of seeds and fruits, but no organic material is normally involved. Subsequently, if other sediments wash into the cavity of the mold and solidify, an actual three-dimensional positive replica (cast) of the original plant material forms. Again, no actual part of the plant is involved, but surface contours are the same as those of the original plant material. This process parallels the method by which a sculptor creates a bronze statue. He or she does not carve directly on a block of bronze, but creates the original with some other medium—wood or wax, perhaps. The sculptor then constructs a mold around the original sculpture, and when the mold is complete, the original is removed in some fashion (disassembling the mold temporarily, or melting the wax and allowing it to escape). When the mold is reassembled, molten bronze is poured into it, and an exact replica of the original sculpture, but one that involves none of the original material in that sculpture, forms. Rates of sedimentation in certain areas where molds and casts were formed must have been spectacular. As an example, the sea cliffs at Joggins, Nova Scotia, reveal exposed casts of tree trunks 3 to 8 m tall. The trees must have been buried quite rapidly in place. Sediment hardened and the trees died, leaving hollows in the hardened rock that were subsequently filled with other, more recent sediments. Molds and casts are important in showing the external form of plant parts in a three-dimensional fashion (see Fig. 9-6A).

With very few exceptions, none of the preceding types of fossils permits an examination of internal structure. There is one type of fossil, however, that is important because it allows sectioning and examination of the tissues of the plant part. This type of fossil is called a petrifaction (sometimes referred to as permineralization). A petrifaction is formed when a plant part is completely immersed in water containing dissolved minerals. The plant part (a log, for example) gets thoroughly waterlogged, with water and dissolved minerals permeating all the cells and tissue systems. The dissolved minerals may be silica compounds (Fig. 1-1C), carbonates, oxides, or some other types of chemicals. At this stage it is unclear what happens, but something triggers precipitation of the dissolved mineral (e.g., change of pH) so that it hardens within the plant fragment as well as at the outside. When the mineral is completely solidified, the plant fragment, in effect, is entombed within solid rock (see Fig. 1-1D). Most often only cell walls are preserved, with the mineral filling the spaces within the cell walls as well as intercellular spaces. Sometimes, however, some of the cellular contents are preserved.

An analogy of this process of petrifaction is the technique used to embed and section living biological material. For example, a piece of plant is killed and fixed in the appropriate chemical. It is then run through a series of alcohols to dehydrate the tissue. Finally, it is transferred to molten paraffin (or a similar kind of material). When the paraffin is cooled, the plant part is completely embedded in it—paraffin is within the tissues as well as around them.

To study petrifactions, it is necessary to prepare a section thin enough to allow the passage of transmitted light. Essentially the same technique that geologists employ for making rock sections is used to section petrified plant material. Special saws are available that can cut through most petrified material. These saws have flat, steel-disk blades with diamond dust pressed into the cutting edges. Oil or some other coolant is used to keep the blade from getting too hot as it slices through the rock. Sometimes saws with blades covered with particles of silicon carbide or some other abrasive may be used to cut through softer material. The portion of petrified material in which one is interested is cut out with a saw, and the surface where the section is to be made is polished until it is smooth. That face is then fastened to a piece of glass with one of a variety of adhesives. After the adhesive is hard, the glass slide with the piece of petrified material is placed back into the saw and the rock matrix is cut as thin as possible. At this point, the rock is still opaque. The next step involves grinding the surface of the petrified material (some machines can perform this step automatically) so that more and more light can pass through. Eventually the sliver of plant material is thin enough to be examined with a microscope. Sometimes the piece of glass on which the petrified material is fastened is the actual slide used for study. In these cases, a permanent adhesive, such as epoxy resin, may be used. Some people prefer to transfer the ground thin slice to a clean piece of glass. In those instances, a cement that can be remelted is used. However, before the thin section is lifted off, it is coated with a transparent plasticlike material that serves to keep the section intact. The thin slice is then placed on a clean slide with a natural or synthetic mounting medium and covered with a cover glass. When the medium has hardened, the slide can be examined with a compound microscope.

Sometimes calcium carbonate is the petrifying mineral. Structures called coal balls are the best-known examples of such an occurrence (Fig. 1-4E). Coal balls are variously shaped nodules (some of the first ones found in England were nearly spherical, hence the name coal "ball") that occur in bituminous coal seams (Fig. 1-4D) and contain within them fragments of plants generally preserved with cellular details and little crushing. While to the coal miner they represent impurities in the coal and are often termed "fault," to the paleobotanist they provide fascinating information about the kinds of plants that lived during the Carboniferous. It is assumed that the plants involved were growing in low-lying, swampy areas not far from coastal regions. Periodic storms washed water rich in carbonates from the sea into the freshwater swamps, and this mineral-rich water was the source of the carbonates that precipitated within and around the plant parts. The petrified plants may be sectioned and examined with the microscope for details.

There is a simple technique for preparing sections of petrified materials, but it is most typically associated with the study of coal balls (Fig. 1-5). Coal balls are sliced with a diamond saw (Fig. 1-6A), and then a slab is polished, first with a coarse abrasive (such as silicon carbide) on a rotating lapidary wheel and then with abrasives of progressively finer grain sizes (Fig. 1-6B). This polished surface is then etched in a dilute solution of hydrochloric acid (Fig. 1-6C). Because the acid reacts with the carbonate and not with the organic remains within the coal ball, the calcium carbonate is slowly etched away, leaving cell walls (and cellular contents, if present) that project in relief from the surface of the coal ball (Fig. 1-6D). After the surface has been washed and dried, it is ready for section preparation. The etched surface should not be touched at this stage because the cell walls are very delicate.

Acetone, an organic solvent, is then poured on the etched surface, and before the acetone evaporates, a thin sheet of transparent cellulose acetate is carefully rolled on the surface (Fig. 1-6E). Acetone will partially dissolve the lower surface of the acetate sheet, converting it to a liquid that flows in and

Figure 1-4 A. Collecting coal balls from a stream bank in eastern Kentucky. B. Collecting compression fossils from Carboniferous shales near Murphysboro, Illinois. C. Impression of the trunk of an arborescent lycopod *(Sigillaria)* in the shale of a coal mine near Lock Haven, Pennsylvania. D. Collecting coal balls from the Herrin no. 6 coal, Sahara Coal Company Mine near Harrisburg, Illinois. E. Coal balls in place in a bituminous coal seam in Illinois. F. Preparing cuticle mounts of Eocene angiosperm leaves collected in Tennessee. *(F courtesy of D. Dilcher.)*

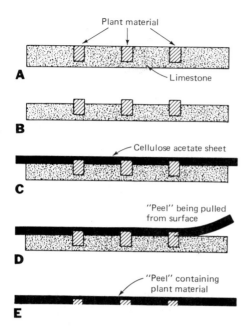

Figure 1-5 Diagrammatic representation of the peel technique. A. Calcium carbonate matrix (coal ball) containing plant material (crosshatched). B. Coal-ball surface after etching, exposing the plant material. C. Etched coal-ball surface with cellulose acetate sheet in place. D. Cellulose acetate sheet being pulled from surface with adhering plant material. E. Section of peel containing plant material. *(Modified from Banks, 1970.)*

around cell cavities and intercellular spaces. Because acetone is quite volatile, it evaporates readily, so the lower surface of the acetate sheet once more becomes solid, trapping the cell walls projecting from the surface of the coal ball. When the film is completely dry, it is carefully pulled from the surface of the coal-ball slab, taking with it the portions of the cell walls that are embedded in the lower surface (Fig. 1-6F). Many more sections can be made after fine-abrasive polishing, etching, and repeating the process. This "peel" technique also can be used for petrifactions other than coal balls, but when the matrix is something other than calcium or magnesium carbonate, a different kind of acid must be used. For example, hydrofluoric acid is used when the plant material is petrified with silica.

When the peel technique was initially devised, preformed sheets of cellulose acetate were not used; rather, a solution made of parlodion, butyl acetate, amyl alcohol, xylene, caster oil, and ether was poured on the surface and allowed to dry. This resulted in peels that were not uniform in thickness and were sometimes difficult to mount on microscope slides. Another drawback was the extensive amount of time required for the poured peels to dry on the coal-ball surface as compared with the approximately 20 minutes required for cellulose-acetate-sheet peels to dry. Despite these drawbacks, the poured peels are still useful, especially when examining very delicate structures.

The degree of preservation afforded by petrifactions is truly outstanding, with such delicate structures as nuclei, various types of membranes, tapetal deposits (see Fig. 13-30B), and certain cells of seed-plant microgametophytes

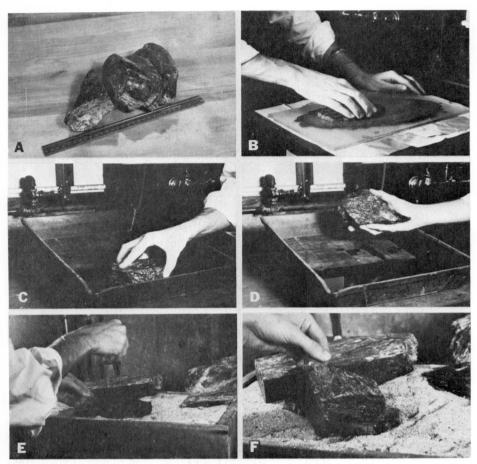

Figure 1-6 Steps involved in the preparation of cellulose acetate peels. A. Sectioned coal ball. B. Grinding the surface of the coal-ball slab with silicon carbide (carborundum) powder. C. Etching the polished surface of the coal-ball slab in dilute hydrochloric acid. D. The etched surface, revealing various plant organs. E. Applying the preformed sheet of cellulose acetate to the acetone-flooded surface of the etched coal-ball. F. Removing the peel from the coal-ball surface.

commonly preserved. Figures 1-7 and 1-8 illustrate some of the exceptionally well-preserved plant structures recovered from petrifactions.

In some instances, the matrix is too crumbly to allow preparation of ground thin sections and therefore does not lend itself to the peel technique. In such cases, it may be necessary to resort to examining the cut and polished surface with reflected light. If a series of sections is necessary, one must make a photographic record or a series of drawings, because the specimen is continually being ground away, leaving no actual record of each face examined. This technique also can be used when there is a limited amount of material resulting in drawing or photographing the surface during the intermittent stages of grinding the specimen away.

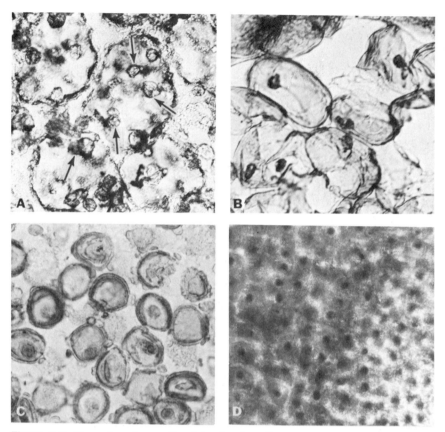

Figure 1-7 Examples of exceptional levels of petrifaction preservation. A. Starch-filled cells *(arrows)* in the megagametophyte of the Carboniferous seed *Cardiocarpus spinatus.* ×275. B. Nuclei in the monolete spores of *Peltastrobus reedae.* ×600. C. Stages in microgametophyte development in the pollen grains of *Lasiostrobus polysacci.* ×600. D. Inclusions in the megagametophyte cells of *Pararaucaria patagonica* that are believed to represent nuclei. ×300. *(A and B courtesy of R. Baxter; C from Taylor, 1970.)*

Sometimes plant material is deposited in an area in which very fine-grained sediment is accumulating, and as a result, there may be little subsequent compression or degradation by microorganisms. Some water may be squeezed out in the process, however. The fossils that result are found in a relatively unaltered condition. Internal structures are evident, but there is no mineral matrix embedding the plant parts. Leaves, stems, fruits, and seeds are occasionally found in such an unaltered state, and these can be sectioned by the same techniques employed for sectioning tissues of living plants. An initial treatment with hydrofluoric acid is sometimes used to dissolve any adhering sand or clay particles so that the knife of the microtome will not be damaged.

Peat is another example of relatively unaltered plant material. Plant parts fall into peat bogs, and because of the high acidity, microbial activity is greatly reduced, so that little or no decomposition occurs. The accumulated plant debris

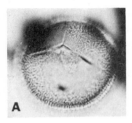

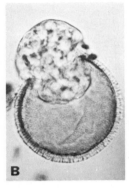

Figure 1-8 *Kollospora extrudens* (Upper Cretaceous). A. Proximal surface of spore showing trilete suture. ×425. B. Spore with gelatinous contents (cytoplasm?) extruding from proximal surface. ×425. *(From Hall, 1971.)*

builds up to considerable thickness, and while there is some breakage of plant parts and some flattening, the bits and pieces preserved can be handled just like pieces of existing plants.

In a sense, diatomaceous earth, formed from the countless silica cell walls of diatoms, might be considered unaltered plant remains. While the cell contents are gone, the silica cell walls are intact and are preserved in such fine detail that the exquisite sculpturing can be detected with a microscope.

Another example of unaltered plant material is amber, a name typically applied to a wide variety of fossilized plant resins extending from the Carboniferous to the Pleistocene; most have been reported from Cretaceous and Tertiary strata. Ambers are produced by a large number of plants, including many angiosperms, conifers, and other seed plants. In recent years, phytochemistry, infrared spectrophotometry, and X-ray diffraction have proven to be important analytical tools in determining the botanical origins of fossils resins.

While these are the most frequent ways in which plants become fossilized, there are other forms as well, or combinations of some of the fossil types just discussed (Fig. 1-1A). For example, there are times when casts of stems are encountered that contain faint outlines of the conducting system in the center. In these cases, the cast is not simply a three-dimensional replica of the original plant part, but contains some components of the original plant.

Certain algae are recognizable as fossils not because any of the original organisms are present, but because of peculiarities of their metabolism. Such algae somehow induce precipitation of calcium carbonate around the contours of the cells (see Fig. 4-1), and often this deposit builds up to a considerable thickness. Subsequently, when the organism dies, the calcium carbonate deposited around it persists, often for millions of years. Sectioning of these calcium carbonate residues allows one to reconstruct the three-dimensional aspect of the plant by following the configurations of the hollows within the calcium carbonate sheath. These lime-precipitating algae play a very important part in the building up of coral reefs; most of the bulk of the reef is produced by accumulation of calcium carbonate precipitated by algae rather than by the corals living on the reef.

Another example of an unusual kind of fossil is wood that was exposed to colloidal silica; the silica permeates the cell cavities, but somehow does not fully impregnate the cell walls. After precipitation of the silica within the cell cavities, the cell walls disintegrate. All that is left are casts of the cavities of the wood cells (Fig. 1-9). These cell casts have the negative contours of the insides of the cell walls and show counterparts of specialized wall structures called bordered pits.

Spores and pollen grains are represented in the fossil plant record in great abundance. The coat of the spore or pollen grain is composed of an especially resistant material called sporopollenin. Frequently, even when there is no evidence of any other part of a plant in sediments, spores and pollen grains are

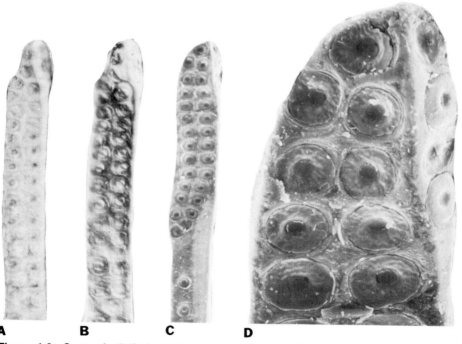

A   **B**   **C**   **D**

Figure 1-9 Casts of silicified conifer tracheids. A. Tracheid cast viewed with conventional transmitted light. ×240. B. Same cast as in A viewed with Nomarski interference microscopy. ×240. C. Tracheid cast as seen via scanning electron microscopy. ×240. D. End of tracheid cast showing detail of bordered pits when viewed via scanning electron microscopy. ×1000. *(Specimens courtesy of T. Delevoryas.)*

quite obvious. It is possible to isolate these spores or pollen grains from the surrounding sediment and mount them on microscope slides. Characteristic features such as sculpturing on the wall, shape, presence or absence of pores, furrows, ridges, or many other kinds of structures make it possible to distinguish among grains of various kinds (see Fig. 1-3; App. 2). The science of palynology is devoted to a study of spores and pollen grains, and it has become a specialized field in itself. Palynology has greatly benefited by the introduction of SEM techniques, whereby certain complex external features of grains are made clear. In addition, even certain developmental stages may be observed, especially with those reproductive structures which produce a large number of spores or pollen grains in a sequential manner. In addition, palynology plays an important role in stratigraphic studies. The pollen and spore record reflects changes in kinds of plants through time, and recognizing certain spore or pollen assemblages sometimes makes it possible to identify the age of the sediments bearing them. Palynology is also useful in attempts to reconstruct climates of the past. Changes in assemblages often reflect changes in climatic conditions, and the appearance or disappearance of certain forms vertically in the geologic column allows a fairly accurate protrayal o ' such climatic shifts.

THE OBJECTIVES OF PALEOBOTANY

At this point it might be useful to review the aims of the paleobotanist. How does the paleobotanist go about interpreting the record of the plant kingdom in the rocks, and what kinds of information is she or he seeking? As curious human beings, we are all interested in the earth on which we live and all aspects of it. It is natural to wonder about the existence of plant fragments buried deep below the earth's surface. The principal aim of the paleobotanist is to attempt to reconstruct the history of the plant kingdom. In a sense, the paleobotanist is a plant historian. Fossils from one part of the geologic column are different from those from another part. Because there are differences, the logical interpretation is that there were changes in kinds of plants through time. Unless one believes that there were practically an infinite number of "special creations," the conclusion is that new plant forms are derived from changes in preexisting forms. By studying the fossil plant record, it is possible to recognize the time at which various major plant groups originated, the time each reached its maximum development, and, in the case of some groups, the time they became extinct.

One recently developed approach to the study of fossil plants involves an analysis of the coal-forming components of the swamp vegetation during the Pennsylvanian Period (Phillips et al., 1974). This technique has been especially valuable in the Illinois Basin, where there is not only an abundance of coal-ball horizons, but a precise stratigraphy that has been correlated according to coal palynology. Inhabiting these peat-forming swamps during the Pennsylvanian in Illinois were five major groups of plants, including lycopods, ferns, sphenophytes, seed ferns, and cordaites. Their succession in the swamps provides an interesting account of the dynamics in progress for a fixed amount of geologic time within a clearly defined geographic region. Moreover, they found that the swamps were dominated by arborescent lycopods that gradually gave way to tree ferns and calamites. Palynomorphs and megafossils indicate that this stage was followed by a resurgence of tree-sized lycopods and, to a lesser extent, secondary elements of cordaites and ferns. Lycopods continued as the primary swamp inhabitants during the later phases of the Desmoinesian, with seed ferns and true ferns becoming important members of the swamp community. These researchers also determined that during the later part of the Pennsylvanian, the tree ferns became the dominant vegetation, as indicated by many coal floras. Although the plants preserved in coal balls have been rather extensively studied for many years, only recently have these fossilized peats been examined in detail relative to the paleoecology of the component plants. Questions of basic biological significance, including the anatomy, morphology, and evolutionary history of the plants, will continue to be important areas of paleobotanical inquiry. The answers, in turn, will provide an opportunity to formulate broader-based questions relating to the analysis of vegetation patterns and the succession of plant types through time.

The analysis of vegetation patterns within Carboniferous sediments, especially coal-ball profiles, is providing important new information about the complete plants. This is especially important in studies that are directed at determining what reproductive organs were borne on a particular plant. For example, recent studies by DiMichele (1979) suggest that the distribution of *Lepidodendron dicentricum* closely correlates with reproductive organs of *Achlamydocarpon varius,* which may represent the fructification of the plant. Still another area of inquiry concerns the relationship of the swamp inhabitants with other plants that grew in slightly different environments away from the peat-forming swamps. For example, in northern England and southern Scotland, the Coal Measure landscapes and plant communities of the Westphalian B horizon were critically analyzed (Scott, 1979). Data gathered from this study suggest that the floodplain supported a flora rich in pteridosperms, ferns, lycopods, and sphenopsids, while seed ferns grew on the levee banks of meandering rivers. Various arborescent sphenopsids grew around lakes and on point bars, and lycopods appear to have dominated the peat-forming (coal) swamp. The possibility exists that some cordaites and conifers inhabited upland sites at this time.

In addition to these questions, other, more economic questions have resulted from the analysis of Carboniferous peats. These include the relationships between the types of coals and the plants from which they were formed, including the potential for predicting coal characteristics. In addition, information about the vegetational community will be important in the identification of desirable coals and in wide-range mapping. The paleoecology of Carboniferous peats and the dynamics that were in progress in the coal-forming swamps represent a new dimension in the study of coal balls, and this promises to play an increasingly important role in the study of fossil plants in the future.

Fossil plants tell us many other things as well. We can deduce certain aspects of climatic changes; it is possible to reconstruct ancient environments and show changes in them; and we can learn about the relationships among plants and animals that inhabited these environments. By studying fossil plants it is also possible to infer how various types of plant organs, such as leaves, seeds, and roots, evolved. With the continued use of more sophisticated types of instrumentation, such as electron microscopy, and a variety of methods for identifying fossil chemicals, paleobotanists will make further contributions to the ontogenetic study of certain fossilized plant structures. In this way it is possible, for example, to discuss how various tissue systems developed in a plant that is millions of years old. On a more popular note, museums throughout the world contain diaramas of past ages that show various kinds of ancient plants and animals. These reconstructed landscapes contain plants that are not just idealized plants, but rather are close approximations of the vegetation that actually existed during past ages.

Where does one look for fossil plants? Most often they are found in places where strata containing them have been exposed in some way. Frequently these exposed strata are accessible along streams or rivers that have cut through rocks. Erosion by water in many other places also exposes fossil-bearing rocks (Fig. 1-4A). Often it is possible to find plants in eroded cliffs along seashores. In addition to the natural exposure of plant-bearing strata, excavations are frequently the source of many fossils (Fig. 1-4C). Road cuts (Fig. 1-4B), for example, often reveal fresh surfaces with unweathered rocks that contain well-preserved fossils. As might be expected, quarries and mines are rich sources of fossil plants. These excavations go deep into the ground, revealing rocks that would otherwise have been inaccessible. Coal balls are frequently encountered in coal mines, and often the shales immediately above the coal seams in such mines are rich in fossil plants (Fig. 1-4D). Quarries in which clay is being excavated for bricks, tiles, or pottery are other excellent places in which to look for fossils. In fact, any massive construction site, such as for a dam, a hydroelectric plant, or a building with a deep foundation, can yield an abundance of fossil plants.

RADIOMETRIC DATING AND GEOLOGIC TIME

One of the most frequent questions a paleobotanist hears concerns the method for dating fossil plants. At the present time, most paleobotanists are well-acquainted with the various groups of plants that inhabited the geologic past. Consequently, when faced with an assemblage excavated from the earth, they usually recognize the age immediately. However, such has not always been the case. Present knowledge is based on a long series of efforts to date the ages of various rocks. At the present time, the best absolute dating involves the use of naturally occurring radioactive isotopes contained in various minerals that make up a rock. These radioactive isotopes are sometimes referred to as "geologic clocks." They undergo a series of complex transformations (decay) that leads to stable isotopes, and in the process, they release energy. The rate of decay λ for a radioactive isotope of a given element, sometimes called the half-life, is constant ($t^{1/2} = 0.693/\lambda$). Therefore, by measuring the present amount of the radioactive isotope and the present quantity of the stable product, one can calculate how much time has elapsed since the minerals in the rock formed. For example, it is known that the uranium isotope ^{238}U decays to ^{206}Pb and has a half-life of 4.5 billion years. Consequently, by measuring the relative quantities of ^{238}U and ^{206}Pb, it is possible to determine the length of time the decay has been going on and thus the time of the formation of the rock. Other radioactive isotopes can be used, but they differ in their half-lives, for example, ^{87}Rb (rubidium), 48.5 billion years; ^{40}K (potassium), 1.25 billion years; and ^{235}U (uranium), 0.704 billion years. One difficulty in employing these dating techniques is that radioactive isotopes occur more commonly in igneous and metamorphic rocks and most fossils occur in sedimentary exposures. Today direct isotopic dating for sedimentary rocks is possible, but only when they contain minerals that have crystallized in the environment of deposition at or near the time they were deposited. One of these is glauconite, a silicate mineral that contains potassium. Since the potassium in part contains ^{40}K, the potassium-argon method can be used. Rubidium-strontium dating of some very fine-grained sedimentary rocks also has been successful, but the procedure is difficult and not routinely possible.

A technique has been developed whereby dating of actual fossils can be accomplished. In the upper atmosphere, cosmic rays bombard ^{14}N (nitrogen) isotopes to form an isotope of carbon ^{14}C that is radioactive. This carbon unites with oxygen to produce carbon dioxide. Plants assimilate this carbon dioxide along with that containing the more frequent isotopes of carbon, ^{12}C and ^{13}C. Carbon dioxide is continuously assimilated during the lifetime of a plant. When the plant dies, however, it no longer exchanges carbon dioxide with the atmosphere, and thus the ratio of ^{14}C to ^{13}C or ^{12}C is fixed at that time. From that point to the present, the ^{14}C decays back to ^{14}N with its characteristic decay rate ($t^{1/2}$ of ^{14}C is about 5710 years). For this reason, the ratio of ^{14}C to ^{12}C or ^{13}C is proportional to the age of the plant (or in other words, the time elapsed between the death of the plant and the present). An age limit of about 60,000 years applies to this technique because of the short half-life of ^{14}C. This technique obviously has somewhat limited usefulness in paleobotany because the bulk of the fossil plant record is much older. Human influence on the earth has even altered the usefulness of the ^{14}C dating method because combustion of fossil fuels and nuclear testing have artificially altered the ^{14}C content of the total carbon reservoir, and this has caused problems in maintaining reliable modern standard samples of carbon. Loss or addition of ^{14}C to specimens and apparent fluctuations of past atmospheric ^{14}C abundance also impose limitations on this dating method. Recently, however, new analytical techniques have been developed that allow direct detection of ^{14}C atoms using high-energy accelerators (Bennett, 1979). This technique is especially important because it requires less than 1 mg of carbon as opposed to more than 1000 mg in the conventional methods, because dates can be determined in hours rather than days, and because sensitivities are sufficiently high to allow high-precision dating back to about 70,000 years.

Frequent references will be made to the geologic time scale in succeeding chapters. Included here is a summary of geologic time (Fig. 1-10). In spite of the fact that sophisticated dating techniques have been developed, occasionally there is a discrepancy in findings among different workers. These differences, however, are not major, and the time scale included here represents a kind of

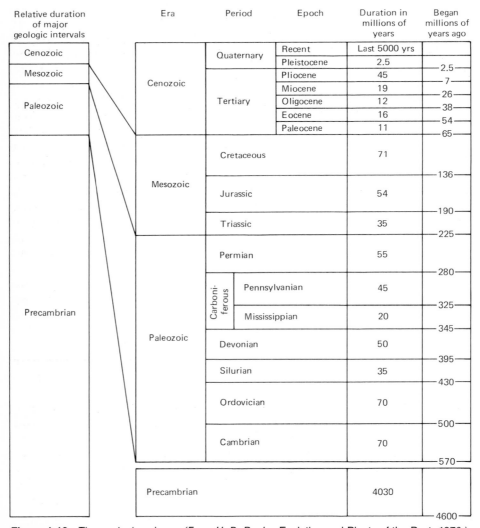

Relative duration of major geologic intervals	Era	Period	Epoch	Duration in millions of years	Began millions of years ago
Cenozoic	Cenozoic	Quaternary	Recent	Last 5000 yrs	
			Pleistocene	2.5	2.5
Mesozoic		Tertiary	Pliocene	45	7
			Miocene	19	26
Paleozoic			Oligocene	12	38
			Eocene	16	54
			Paleocene	11	65
	Mesozoic	Cretaceous		71	136
		Jurassic		54	190
		Triassic		35	225
	Paleozoic	Permian		55	280
		Carboniferous Pennsylvanian		45	325
Precambrian		Carboniferous Mississippian		20	345
		Devonian		50	395
		Silurian		35	430
		Ordovician		70	500
		Cambrian		70	570
	Precambrian			4030	4600

Figure 1-10 The geologic column. *(From H. P. Banks,* Evolution and Plants of the Past, *1970.)*

assimilation of various authors' work. A more detailed stratigraphic column may be found in App. 1.

BIOLOGICAL CORRELATION

Because radiometric dates are not available for all sequences of rocks in specific geographic regions, it becomes necessary to be able to position a given rock unit accurately relative to its absolute age. One means by which a given sequence of sedimentary rocks can be grouped according to age is through the use of index fossils. Typically, an index fossil should be (1) distinguishable from other fossils and easily identifiable, (2) have existed during a relatively short period of geologic time, (3) be abundant, (4) be widely distributed geographically, and (5) have lived in different sedimentary environments so that it may be preserved in differing sedimentary rocks. Obviously, not many fossils fulfill all these requirements, and assemblages of several fossil taxa are typically more useful than a single species. Generally, the most useful organisms for correlation are those which lived in ancient seas. This is so because, most fossiliferous sedimentary rocks accessible on the continents are from shallow-water marine deposits. Pelagic organisms provide the best long-range correlations because of their worldwide distribution, at least within certain climatic zones. These organisms include such planktonic forms as diatoms, foraminifera, silicoflagellates, and coccoliths, and they are especially important because their skeletal remains are so small that a large number can be concentrated in a small sample, such as the cuttings obtained from a well boring. Other organisms, such as those which inhabited the ocean floors (benthic), typically have a spatially restricted distribution that enables them to be effectively used in correlations of a more local extent.

Some of the best types of plant index fossils used across different facies are pollen grains and spores. Their value lies in the fact that they can be carried long distances by wind and, consequently, can be deposited in a wide variety of sediments. Some of these palynomorphs are therefore especially important in providing correlation between marine and nonmarine sediments.

In recent years, plant megafossils from some geologic periods have been useful in biozonation when used in the formulation of assemblage zones. Noteworthy among these are a variety of Carboniferous foliage types that have proven useful in establishing stratigraphic sequences in clearly defined geographic regions (Wagner, Higgins, and Meyen, 1979). For example, Paleozoic foliage types are being evaluated as a basis for delimiting biostratigraphic zones in the proposed Pennsylvanian System stratotype in North America (Gillespie and Pfefferkorn, 1979). In this case, the megafossils may prove to be far more reliable because the more abundant palynomorphs are often difficult to extract from the high-rank coals that comprise some of the stratotype section. In other instances, the identification of particular taxa has been useful in precisely dating sediments associated with intricate, tectonic structures, such as those confined to the Upper Carboniferous folding phases in northwestern Spain (Wagner, 1966). There can be little doubt that as fossil plants are better understood, they will become increasingly important as stratigraphic markers in biozonation and correlation.

CLASSIFICATION OF PLANTS

In this book the emphasis will be on the origin and evolution of individual groups of plants rather than on a discussion of floristic changes through time. For convenience, a classification of the plant kingdom is presented here; this classification is to most major groups only, and discussion of smaller categories is included in each chapter. Classification, obviously, in spite of long study and refinements in techniques, is still a subjective exercise. Each author has his or her own ideas concerning the way the plant kingdom ought to be divided, or whether the plant kingdom is indeed a single kingdom at all. Realizing this, the following classification is presented as a guide to the major groups. Some readers may wish to adapt the plant groups presented in the following chapter to a system with which they feel more comfortable.

Fungi

The term fungi does not refer to a formal category of plantlike organisms that lack chlorophyll. Some workers prefer to recognize a separate kingdom for the fungi. Other organisms that have been traditionally placed with the fungi (i.e., slime molds and cellular slime molds) are now recognized by most as belonging to a separate kingdom, Protista. The remaining fungi may be subdivided into the following five divisions.

Division MASTIOGIMYCOTA. These fungi are typically aquatic and have flagellated spores; the mycelium or mycelial thallus is coenocytic.

Division ZYGOMYCOTA. The perfect stage of these fungi is the zygospore produced by gametangial fusion. The mycelium is predominantly septate.

Division ASCOMYCOTA. The fungi in this group have a perfect stage with the ascospores (usually eight) produced internally in an ascus. The mycelium is septate except in some yeasts.

Division BASIDIOMYCOTA. These fungi have septate vegetative mycelia and produce spores (usually four) externally on a basidium.

Division DEUTEROMYCOTA. Members of this group, sometimes referred to as the Fungi Imperfecti, lack a perfect stage. When the perfect stage is discovered for an organism, in most instances the fungus is transferred to Ascomycota.

Algae

As with the fungi, the term algae includes a large group of probably unrelated forms, and the name does not refer to a natural grouping of plants.

Division CYANOCHLORONTA. These are the blue-green algae, which may occur as unicells, colonies, or multicellular organisms. The cells of these algae have no organized nuclei (in the sense that no membrane surrounds the nuclear material), nor are the pigments in membrane-bounded organelles. The pigments include chlorophyll a, ß-carotene, xanthophylls, phycoerythrin, and phycocyanins. Usually food is stored as glycogen. Neither sexual reproduction nor the presence of motile flagellated cells has been observed. There is considerable structural similarity between the Cyanochloronta and bacteria; in fact, many workers prefer to include the blue-green algae with the bacteria.

Division CHLOROPHYCOPHYTA. These are the green algae, which may be unicellular, colonial, or multicellular. Their pigments include chlorophylls a and b, carotenes, and xanthophylls within chloroplasts. Most forms are believed to have cellulose cell walls. Food is stored in the form of starch. Reproduction is variable, but involves both sexual and asexual means.

Division CHRYSOPHYCOPHYTA. This division includes the classes of golden-brown algae, yellow-green algae, and diatoms. Pigments include chlorophylls a and c (some forms may have chlorophyll e in addition), ß-carotene, and xanthophylls. Food is stored in the form of oil or a carbohydrate called leucosin.

Division PHAEOPHYCOPHYTA. These are the brown algae, which are the largest and most complex algae, ranging from unicellular forms to massive plants exceeding 60 m. Chlorophylls a and c, ß-carotene, and xanthophylls are the principal pigments, and food is stored in the form of polysaccharides, alcohols, or oil droplets.

Division RHODOPHYCOPHYTA. These are the red algae. They are mostly multicellular, with plastids containing chlorophylls a and d, carotenes, xanthophylls, and phycoerythrin. There are no flagellated reproductive cells.

Division PYRRHOPHYCOPHYTA. These are the dinoflagellates, which are unicellular, motile organisms with two flagella and cells covered with a number of platelike structures. Their principal pigments are chlorophylls a and c, ß-carotene, and xanthophylls.

Division EUGLENOPHYCOPHYTA. These green organisms are generally unicellular or colonial and swim by means of anteriorly placed flagella. They lack an organized cell wall, but instead have helically arranged, largely proteinaceous strips of material which, with the plasma membrane, make up the pellicle. Chlorophylls a and b and ß-carotene are the pigments contained within their plastids. Food is stored in the form of a carbohydrate called paramylon. Sexual reproduction is unknown among the euglenophytes.

Lichens. The organisms known as lichens consist of an algal and a fungal component that grow together to form a unique plant body. Lichens are typically not classified as a separate division because the two component organisms are members of other divisions.

Land Plants Lacking Vascular Tissue

Division BRYOPHYTA. This division includes mosses, liverworts, and related forms. They are multicellular, with an alternation of multicellular haploid and diploid phases in the life cycle. The haploid phase that bears the gametes is usually the more dominant phase. There are several cogent reasons why mosses and liverworts should be placed into separate divisions.

Land Plants with Vascular Tissue

Division RHYNIOPHYTA. Members of this division are extinct. Rhyniophytes had slender, dichotomously branched, leafless axes (spines may have been present), with sporangia borne at the tips of branches.

Division ZOSTEROPHYLLOPHYTA. Zosterophyllophytes are extinct plants that generally had dichotomously branched axes, many having borne spines, with sporangia situated laterally along the sides of axes. Primary xylem, when known, was exarch.

Division TRIMEROPHYTOPHYTA. Trimerophytes are also extinct plants that were generally leafless, with smaller, lateral axes branching from larger, principal axes. Sporangia were terminal, and xylem was centrarch.

Division LYCOPHYTA. These are the club mosses and their relatives, which are leafy plants with closely spaced leaves. Sporangia are borne on the upper surfaces of leaves or in the angles between leaves and stems. Modern lycophytes are characteristically herbaceous, but in past ages, many members of the group were arborescent.

Division SPHENOPHYTA. This group includes horsetails and their relatives, and they are characterized by leaves and branches borne in whorls at distinct nodes. Sporangia are borne terminally on specialized branches that are typically recurved and clustered into a conelike structure called a strobilus. Sphenophyte stems often appear jointed.

Division PTERIDOPHYTA. These are the ferns, which often have large and compound leaves (although some are simple), with sporangia generally located on the undersides or margin of the leaves. Their stems may be elongated and either horizontal or erect.

Division PROGYMNOSPERMOPHYTA. The progymnosperms were probably the precursors of the seed plants and are known only as fossils. They produced abundant secondary vascular tissues and were frequently heterosporous (producing spores of two types). Their branches were often flattened into complexes resembling fern fronds.

Division PTERIDOSPERMOPHYTA. These are extinct seed ferns that resembled small tree ferns in general habit, with microsporangia and seeds borne on the leaves.

Division CYCADOPHYTA. Cycads generally are squat plants (some are arborescent) with woody stems and a crown of typically pinnately compound leaves (some of the fossil forms have entire leaves). Seeds and pollen-bearing organs are borne on modified leaves that are typically aggregated into cones.

Division CYCADEOIDOPHYTA. These extinct plants superficially resemble cycads in that they have pinnately compound leaves. Seeds and pollen-bearing organs were borne on complex structures that may represent aggregations of leaves.

Division GINKGOPHYTA. This division is represented today by a single species, a tree with abundant secondary xylem, fan-shaped leaves, and naked seeds borne on elongated stalks.

Division CONIFEROPHYTA. The conifers are quite variable. Most of them are trees with simple leaves that may be small, scalelike structures, needles, or flattened and broad structures. Seeds are typically borne on the surfaces of hard, woody scales that are probably derived from modified branches and are aggregated into cones.

Division ANTHOPHYTA. These are the angiosperms, which are the dominant plants in the world at the present time. They typically produce flowers with structures called carpels surrounding the potential seeds.

Throughout earth history, other groups of plants have appeared and then become extinct. Many of them can be regarded as minor "experiments" that had only limited success with respect to long-term survival. These groups will be discussed in various places throughout this book.

CLASSIFICATION THROUGH THE LEVEL OF ORDER

Division

MASTIGIOMYCOTA	
ZYGOMYCOTA	
ASCOMYCOTA	FUNGI
BASIDIOMYCOTA	
DEUTEROMYCOTA	

Division

CYANOCHLORONTA
CHLOROPHYCOPHYTA
CHRYSOPHYCOPHYTA
PHAEOPHYCOPHYTA   ALGAE
RHODOPHYCOPHYTA
PYRRHOPHYCOPHYTA
EUGLENOPHYCOPHYTA

Division

BRYOPHYTA
HEPATOPHYTA   BRYOPHYTES

Division

*RHYNIOPHYTA
*ZOSTEROPHYLLOPHYTA   EARLY VASCULAR PLANTS
*TRIMEROPHYTOPHYTA

Division

LYCOPHYTA

   Order

   *PROTOLEPIDODENDRALES
   *LEPIDODENDRALES
   LYCOPODIALES
                                                   LYCOPODS
   SELAGINELLALES
   *PLEUROMEIALES
   ISOETALES

Division

SPHENOPHYTA

   Order

   *PSEUDOBORNIALES
   *SPHENOPHYLLALES   ARTICULATES
   EQUISETALES

*Known only from the fossil record.

Division

    PTERIDOPHYTA

      Class

           *CLADOXYLOPSIDA
           *RHACOPHYTOPSIDA
           *COENOPTERIDOPSIDA
           FILICOPSIDA

          Order   FERNS

              MARATTIALES
              OPHIOGLOSSALES
              FILICALES
              MARSILEALES
              SALVINIALES

Division

    *PROGYMNOSPERMOPHYTA   —— PROGYMNOSPERMS

Division

    *PTERIDOSPERMOPHYTA

      Order

           LYGINOPTERIDALES
           MEDULLOSALES
           CALLISTOPHYTALES
           CALAMOPITYALES   SEED FERNS

           CAYTONIALES
           CORYSTOSPERMALES
           PELTASPERMALES
           GLOSSOPTERIDALES

Division

    CYCADOPHYTA   —— CYCADS

Division

    *CYCADEOIDOPHYTA   —— CYCADEOIDS

Division

    GINKGOPHYTA   —— GINKGOPHYTES

Division

CONIFEROPHYTA

Class

Division

ANTHOPHYTA —————ANGIOSPERMS

Consistent with the most recent International Code of Botanical Nomenclature, the following endings for various categories of plants will be used throughout this volume:

Category	Algae	Fungi	Bryophytes and vascular plants
Division	-phyta	-mycota	-phyta
Subdivision	-phytina	-mycotina	-phytina
Class	-phyceae	-mycetes	-opsida
Order	-ales	-ales	-ales
Family	-aceae	-aceae	-aceae

Precambrian Biology

The sphere of paleobotany properly accommodates a discussion of the earliest evidence of life on earth. Admittedly, the first "organisms" may have been neither plant nor animal, but it was from such simple biological systems that more complex types of plants later originated. The actual time of origin and the nature of the first living systems are still uncertain, but as work on ancient sediments continues, it is becoming increasingly apparent that some types of organisms existed very early in the history of the earth.

In paleobotany, the history of the earth is divided into two major eons: the Cryptozoic (literally "hidden life") and the Phanerozoic ("visible life"). The age of the earth is estimated to be between 4.5 and 5.0 billion years, and the span of time from the beginning of earth history to about 600 million years ago is designated as the Cryptozoic Eon. Frequently, all geologic time before the Phanerozoic Eon is spoken of as the Precambrian Era, i.e., the time before the Cambrian Period of the Paleozoic Era. The oldest known sedimentary rocks date back 3.75 billion years, and there is evidence in slightly younger rocks that life existed on the earth around that time. Some of this evidence is indirect, in that there are no actual fossilized remains of organisms, but the distinctive nature of some of the rock features makes it difficult to interpret them as anything but biogenic in origin.

Very compelling evidence of early life occurs in the form of structures called stromatolites (Fig. 2-1). (Several recent papers can be found in the book edited by Flügel, 1977.) Stromatolites are laminated deposits of calcium carbonate that are built up by algae. Probably the best-known site where stromatolites are being actively formed today is Shark Bay, an inlet of the Indian Ocean along the west coast of Australia at about 26° South latitude. The algae that form these stromatolites are unicellular members of the division Cyanochloronta (blue-green algae) that live in colonies on the upper surface of the accumulating calcium carbonate. These algae typically have mucilaginous or gelatinous sheaths that serve to trap particles of carbonate in the seawater. Moreover, as a result of the photosynthetic activity of these organisms, the carbon dioxide surrounding the algae is removed from the water, causing the precipitation of calcium carbonate. This precipitation continues in thin layers, or lamellae, as the algal colonies continue to grow on the upper surface of the columnar calcium carbonate. If for some reason the colony were to die, the calcareous structure would persist as evidence that organisms were there at one time.

The earliest evidence of fossil stromatolites is found in deposits about 3 billion or more years old, and later in the Cryptozoic, fossil stromatolites occur in far greater abundance. Their structure shows the same kind of laminations as those found in modern stromatolites: they may be columnar or pillow-shaped, and they are sometimes branched from basal portions to more distal regions. Some of these fossil stromatolites have retained their carbonate nature, and in

Figure 2-1   Sequence of hemispherical stromatolites from the Precambrian Transvaal dolomite of South Africa. Height of domes is approximately 2 m. *(Reproduced by permission of Springer-Verlag, Berlin; courtesy of R. Förster.)*

others, the carbonate has been replaced by silica. In stromatolites from the Gunflint Iron Formation (approximately 1.9 billion years old), it is possible to discern remains of matted filaments interspersed among the carbonate laminae, which suggests that unlike the Shark Bay stromatolites, which are being formed by unicellular algal forms, filamentous organisms were responsible for their formation.

One interesting stromatolite that appears to have a living counterpart growing in modern hot-spring environments is the genus *Conophyton*. This stromatolite differs from all others in that it has acute conical laminations and a distinct axial zone. Columns of *Conophyton* range from as narrow as 5.0 mm to as great as 10.0 m in diameter. In one extensively studied form from the Precambrian of the Soviet Union, both cyanophytes and eukaryotic algae were identified in the silicified lamellae.

One promising avenue of investigation involves attempts to recover organic compounds from ancient sediments. It is thought that these organic compounds result from the presence of organisms at the time the rock was being formed. Amino acids, hydrocarbons, fatty acids, porphyrins, and other organic compounds have been recovered from Cryptozoic rocks, but it is difficult to prove that these compounds did not permeate into the rocks at some later time. There exists, however, a type of organic matter, called kerogen, that is insoluble in water. Therefore, if it is present in ancient sediments, it very probably was deposited at the time of rock formation. Kerogen has a carbon-isotopic ratio ($^{13}C/^{12}C$) similar to that of organic matter known to be biological in origin and quite different from inorganically produced carbon compounds. Moreover, such kerogen has been found in rocks about 3 billion years old.

The upper part of the Cryptozoic (2.5 billion to 600 million years ago) is referred to as the Proterozoic Era, and considerably more remains of microorganisms are found in sediments of that age. There are calcium carbonate deposits in Proterozoic rocks in various parts of the world that are in the form of concentric laminations, often forming spherical or pillow-shaped masses several meters in diameter. Sections made of these calcareous masses reveal no remains of organisms, but it is generally believed that these masses were deposited by microorganisms, conceivably blue-green algae, in much the same way that stromatolites are formed. In freshwater environments today, certain blue-green algae settle on an object, perhaps a pebble, and deposit concentric laminations of calcium carbonate around that object. As the diameter of the object and deposited calcareous material increases, the algal colony grows outward, simultaneously increasing in surface area. As more and more calcium carbonate is deposited, eventually an egg-shaped mass results. Sometimes known as "water biscuits," these structures are also called loferites and thrombolites. Collectively they are regarded as crypalgal, a term for rocks, including some stromatolites, in which an algal origin is inferred but cannot be proved. It is assumed that concentrically layered Proterozoic limestones were formed by similar microorganisms. This suggestion is certainly a possibility, but the massive size of some of the ancient structures makes it difficult to comprehend how an algal colony could have persisted and grown along the entire surface of a huge spherical mass that must have weighed several metric tons. However, it is equally difficult to visualize a nonbiogenic origin for these structures. Furthermore, present-day water biscuits do show uniform development on all sides.

There are other kinds of indirect evidence of Proterozoic life that show no remains of actual organisms. For example, certain coal and graphite deposits in various parts of the world are quite likely derived from organic sources. Shales with an abundance of carbon are also known, and if they are found in Phanerozoic deposits, they are unhesitatingly considered organic in origin.

Quite fascinating, and definitely indicative of the existence of plant life before the onset of the Phanerozoic, are structurally preserved remains (Fig. 2-2D). Most of these structurally preserved organisms occur in a fine-grained siliceous rock called chert. These cherts are often associated with stromatolites. However, there are pitfalls in viewing certain of these structures as the remains

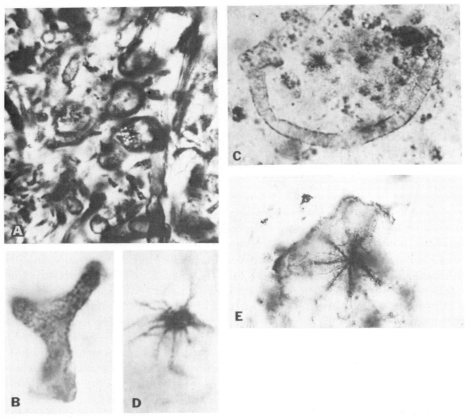

Figure 2-2 A. Filaments of *Gunflintia minuta* and sporelike bodies of *Huroniospora*. ×900. B. *Archaeorestis schreiberensis*. ×2000. C. *Animikiea septata*. ×900. D. *Eoastrion bifurcatum*. ×2100. E. *Kakabekia umbellata*. ×900. All organisms from the Gunflint chert. *(Courtesy of E. Barghoorn.)*

of plants or other microorganisms. For example, spherical bodies occur in relative abundance in rocks more than 3 billion years old, but little structural detail is discernible among these spheres, and their sizes vary so considerably that it is difficult to conclude that they are of biogenic origin. At least some of the multitude of spherical forms described probably represent colloidal aggregates of nonliving material. Although there are numerous reports of Precambrian plants, only some of the more certain and less controversial ones will be mentioned here.

Some of the oldest remains that may represent structurally preserved plants have been recovered from deposits 3.1 billion years old in South Africa. These remains contain septate filaments with occasional enlarged cells in the filament; they are thought to resemble certain blue-green algae. These deposits also contain clusters of spherical structures, and these are interpreted by investigators as possible blue-green algae.

Cherts of the Gunflint Iron Formation (1.6 to 2.0 billion years old) in southern Ontario have yielded a variety of structures, many of which appear to constitute genuine evidence of plants (Awramik and Barghoorn, 1977). There is the usual assortment of spherical and ellipsoidal forms, some of which probably do not represent plants. More convincing, however, are the filamentous forms, many of which appear to be multicellular. Some of these filaments are exceedingly slender, as thin as 0.5 μm in diameter, while others approach 10 μm in diameter. Some of the filaments (e.g., *Animikiea*) are composed of disk-shaped cells that are 7 to 10 μm in diameter (Fig. 2-2C). Others (e.g., *Gunflintia*) contain series of beadlike cells that are slightly constricted where they attach to adjacent cells (Fig. 2-2A). The remains of *Archaeorestis* reveal a nonseptate, irregularly branched organism (Fig. 2-2B) with filaments that range from 2 to 10 μm in diameter and an observed length of 200 μm. A taxon described as *Entosphaeroides* appears to be a nonseptate, unbranched filament that is 5 to 6 μm in diameter and seemingly contains spherical sporelike structures within.

One interesting organism from the Gunflint chert that shows a more complex biological organization is *Kakabekia umbellata* (Fig. 2-2E). This fossil was tripartite, consisting of a spheroidal bulb, a slender stalk, and an umbrellalike crown; some specimens range up to 30 μm long. *Kakabekia* has also been found as a living organism isolated from soil samples cultured under experimental conditions in ammonia-rich environments (Siegel and Siegel, 1968). The living species is *K. barghoorniana,* and despite information about various developmental stages, the affinities of this living organism continue to remain a matter of conjecture.

Some of the structures in the Gunflint chert may be the remains of taxa not related to any known forms, while others may not represent organisms at all. It is difficult to assign these Gunflint fossils to any group of plants with certainty. There is a noticeable similarity between some of the fossil organisms and certain algal groups. However, because modern classification systems for algae are based on more than just form, it would be impossible to categorize these fossil

organisms as algae without a knowledge of the pigments, reproductive structures, food-storage products, etc. in the fossils. Knowledge of superficial
morphology is not enough to make such a classification. Furthermore, one must
always keep in mind that some of the fossils could have come from algal or other
plant groups that are extinct today.

A report of structurally preserved microorganisms somewhat older than
those in the Gunflint Iron Formation was published after the monographic work
on the Gunflint, but plantlike organisms from this locality in northeastern
Minnesota (about 2 billion years old) closely resembled the Gunflint fossils.
Another report of fossils 1.7 billion years old from the Belcher Islands in
Hudson Bay also showed clustered unicells and filaments (Hofmann, 1974).
Some of the structures resembling unicellular algae are characterized by the
presence of an opaque spot in their centers. More about the interpretation of
these dark spots will be mentioned later.

One of the best-studied assemblages of microfossils from the Precambrian
comes from chert deposits in the Bitter Springs Formation in central Australia
(Schopf, 1968). The rich flora from these 900-million-year-old beds includes an
abundance of filaments (Fig. 2-3D) and spherical unicells. Some of the
filaments, which have been given such names as *Palaeolyngbya* (Fig. 2-3D),
Oscillatoriopsis, and *Palaeoanacystis* (Fig. 2-4D), bear a striking morphologic
resemblance to certain present-day blue-green algae. Again it must be emphasized that the resemblance is based only on superficial morphology because any
assignments to a known group of algae must be tentative unless more is known
about the pigments, cytology, and reproductive structures of these fossils.

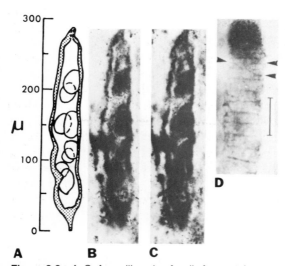

Figure 2-3   A–C. Ascuslike microfossil of uncertain systematic affinity from the late Precambrian of
Australia. D. *Palaeolyngbya barghoorniana* (scale represents 10 μm) from the Bitter Springs
Formation (late Precambrian) of central Australia. *(A–C from Schopf and Barghoorn, 1969; D from
Schopf, 1968.)*

Nevertheless, the similarities are striking. The excellent preservation of these filaments reveals the gradual narrowing of cells at their extremities, so that their tips appear pointed (Fig. 2-3D). The extreme regularity of individual component cells makes it impossible to interpret these structures as anything other than fossil organisms. Interestingly, one is struck by the extremely narrow diameters of these filaments. Most are less than 5 μm in diameter, although occasionally some reach up to 15 μm in thickness. Present-day blue-green algae frequently are just as slender, but a proportionately larger number are more robust. In fact, this same observation applies to most of the filamentous forms preserved in Precambrian sediments.

Some of the Precambrian filaments interpreted by various authors to represent blue-green algae show an occasional larger and, apparently, thick-walled spherical cell that is compared with heterocysts (literally, "different cells") in blue-green algal filaments. Such comparisons are based on superficial similarity only, and the characteristic thickened areas occurring at the parts of these enlarged cells that are adjacent to other cells of the filament have not been demonstrated in the fossils.

Of special interest are many fossilized spherical structures that resemble unicellular organisms. Most of these cell-like remains are close to 10 μm in diameter, and often, they are clustered into groups, reveal uniform sizes, and appear to have definite cell walls. As mentioned earlier, a peculiar feature of these spheres is the presence of a single, small opaque body within each. Early reports indicated that these dark structures could represent "nuclear residues," although there has been more reluctance in subsequent papers to view the presence of these dark spots as proof of the existence of eukaryotic organisms at that time in geologic history. One interpretation is that these opaque bodies do in fact represent nuclei, and that their discovery in these organisms actually demonstrates that eukaryotic organisms existed on the earth's surface close to 1 billion years ago (or even before if one considers the Belcher Island fossils). However, the dark spots could represent something other than nuclei (e.g., coagulated protoplast or a concentration of the material in solution as precipitation of silica progressed toward the inside of the cell). Because such an important event in the history of the plant kingdom is being documented on the basis of these dark spots, it is of the utmost importance that they be shown unequivocally to be nuclear remains. Electron micrographs have been made of some of these presumably petrified unicells, and there is indeed evidence of dense structures within the small spheres, along with what is called a "membrane" around the dark structures. However, in actuality, these electron micrographs seem only to magnify the unclear nature of whatever it is in these spheres that looks dark in optical section.

Certain spherical structures in the Bitter Springs chert have led to speculation and far-reaching generalizations in another direction. Occasionally one of the spherical structures has what appears to be a mark on the surface consisting of three short lines radiating from a common point. Such a three-pronged mark is a common feature on the coats of spores produced in the sporangia of vascular plants after the meiotic process. These spores result from a process of reduction division in which a single cell with a given number of chromosomes (arbitrarily referred to an 2*n*) divides within a sporangium to produce four identical spores, each with only half the chromosome number of the parent cell. Often these spores remain in a cluster, with all four cells pressed in contact with one another. Thus there are often three slightly flattened faces on each spore (representing contact areas with the other spores in the cluster) and a three-pronged mark between the contact areas. Therefore, if a spore is seen to have such a triradiate scar, it is assumed that it is the result of a reduction division in a sexually reproducing organism.

By such reasoning, it was claimed that the three-pronged marks found on some of the Precambrian spherical organisms indicate that the organisms must have resulted from reduction division and hence must have reproduced in a sexual manner. Therefore, it was announced that sexual reproduction had evolved at least by late Precambrian time, at least 900 million years ago, if not before. Caution must be expressed on this point, however. A triradiate mark may be nothing more than a peculiar wrinkle in the wall of a cell, or it may be the result of movement or concentration of cell contents before or during the fossilization process. In addition, it must be mentioned that some organisms produce cells in clusters of four, and this is no reflection at all of the sexual process. For example, several species of green algae produce mitotically derived tetrads during the formation of autospores.

In a few instances, tetrahedral tetrads (Fig. 2-4B and C) have been discovered in Precambrian sediments (Bitter Springs and Middle Proterozoic Amelia dolomite). In assessing the significance of these cell configurations, it is important to determine if they are indeed tetrahedral, and if so, whether the tetrad is original or artifactual, and whether it was produced as a result of meiosis or mitosis. In the previously noted instances, one tetrad (Amelia dolomite) is regarded as a mitotically produced algal autospore. The Bitter Springs tetrad could not be shown to have been produced during either meiosis or mitosis.

An interesting paper describing configurations formed by "stale" cultures of a particular blue-green alga contained photographs of the configurations assumed by these cells in various stages of decomposition (Knoll and Barghoorn, 1975). There was an amazing resemblance to practically every kind of "unicellular organism" described from the Bitter Springs Formation. Attempts to reply to the suggestion that the configurations of Bitter Springs organisms may be found among present-day prokaryotes have involved use of the electron microscope to examine the internal structures of the Bitter Springs unicells (Schopf, 1970*b*). However, as indicated earlier, this internal material is really no more definitive at high magnification than it is at a lower power. Therefore, no definite conclusions should be drawn from the paper that relates the strange configurations of "stale" blue-green algal cells to the configurations of Precambrian organisms. The important point is that utmost caution must be exercised in studying the remains of ancient living things. Already there is considerable

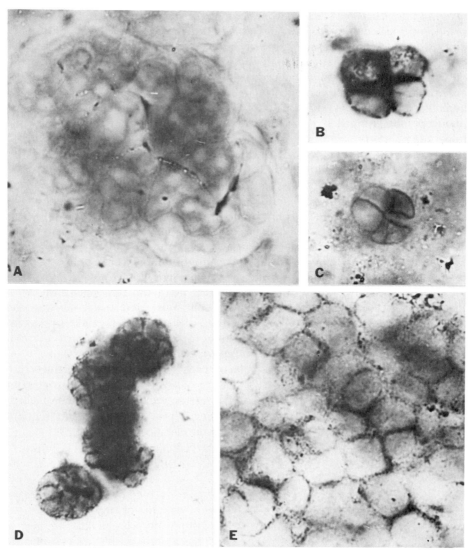

Figure 2-4 A. Chroococcacean colony of *Sphaerophycus* encased in a gelatinous sheath. ×2000. B and C. Tetragonal tetrad of *Huroniospora microreticulata*. ×2000. D. *Palaeoanacystis plumbii* in small colonies. ×2000. E. Colony of large cells of the *Myxococcoides* type. ×2000. All are from the Amelia dolomite of the Northern Territory of Australia. *(B–D from Muir, 1976; A and E courtesy of M. Muir.)*

evidence that some of the earlier work on Precambrian organisms may have been done in haste.

There can be little doubt that much of the work on Precambrian organisms is based on excellently preserved material that has received careful study (Schopf, 1970a). There is also much work, some on material with only mediocre preservation, that may be interpreted in more than one way. For example, recently compiled comparative statistical data based on populations of modern and fossil algal unicells suggest that at least some of the Precambrian spheroids probably represent microstructures of abiotic origin. Similar statistical techniques also may prove valuable in providing a basis for distinguishing Precambrian prokaryotic and eukaryotic cells (Schopf and Oehler, 1976). Generally, unicells from sediments older than 1400 million years are small (1 to 35 μm in diameter) and comparable to the size distribution of modern prokaryotes, while populations of Precambrian unicells younger than 1400 million years are statistically larger and comparable with the cells of eukaryotes. Such data may be used to provide a rational basis for establishing the point in geologic time when the eukaryotic cell type evolved.

Although there are still many uncertainties and unanswered questions concerning possible algal organisms in the Cryptozoic, it is undeniable that there were, indeed, a large number of microorganisms present in many parts of the world, that they were the principal types of organisms in existence at the time, and that they played an important part in influencing the chemistry of both the atmosphere and the medium in which they were growing. Even though more must be learned about the actual mechanisms involved in the fossilization of these organisms and the kinds of changes that must have occurred after the organisms died, it is probable that more than one group of algallike organisms was present. Moreover, it is conceivable that a high degree of internal organization had evolved before the onset of the Phanerozoic.

The recent discovery of filaments of cells collected from northwestern Australia in sediments radiometrically dated at 3.5 billion years is of particular significance in demonstrating that not long after the formation of the earth relatively complex forms of life were in existence. It is certain that in subsequent years simpler unicells will be identified in even older rocks.

Chapter 3

Fungi and Bacteria

FUNGI

Despite the rather fragile nature of most fungi, many are represented in the fossil record and may even extend back to the Precambrian. Most fossil fungal remains consist of isolated spores and vegetative hyphae; some excellent examples of reproductive structures also have been recovered. In early earth history, fungi must have played an important role as decaying organisms, much as they do today, and no doubt many of the missing parts of the evolutionary history of plants are the result of the destructive activities of fungi. Some fungi were parasitic on ancient plants, and in recent years, several life cycles have been worked out for certain fossil forms. Information about the host-specific requirements of parasitic fungi has been much more difficult to gather. Despite their long geologic history and the relatively early recognition of most of the major groups, the fossil record tells us little about the evolution of fungi. The literature on fossil fungi is extensive; consequently, only a few representative forms of some of the major groups are described here.

Many sporelike bodies and filaments in Precambrian sediments conceivably represent fungal remains. For example, *Eomycetopsis robusta* has been considered a fungus. This possible fungus from the late Precambrian (Bitter Springs Formation of central Australia) consisted of sinuous filaments with delicate external projections on its walls and internal septa. Some authorities now regard this taxon as the sheath of a blue-green alga.

Chemical treatment of a Devonian limestone revealed numerous fungal filaments of two distinct sizes. Some are about 1.6 μm in diameter, while a smaller number are about twice that size. Both fungi are estimated to have been between 4.0 and 5.0 cm long. Filament branching is irregular, but a cross wall is present at each point of branching. Many of the hyphal strands show evidence of fusion between adjacent filaments. It is important to emphasize here that one must exercise caution when working with microfossils, including such organisms as fungi, in order to be certain that what are presumed to be fossils are not existing contaminants. Such contamination can occur through secondary deposition of younger organic materials, or through the activities of organisms, such as lichens, that contain fungi and actually penetrate the rock substrate on which they grow. In the Devonian fungal filaments just mentioned, the mineral nature of the rock and the fact that fungi were approximately 7.0 cm from the rock surface suggest that the fungi were indeed of fossil rather than modern origin.

Palaeomyces is the name applied to hyphal filaments, spores, and sporangia found associated with, and in the tissues of, the Devonian vascular plants (*Rhynia, Horneophyton,* and *Asteroxylon*) found in chert in Rhynie, Aberdeenshire, Scotland (Fig. 3-1). The hyphae of *Palaeomyces* (Mastigiomycota) were typically nonseptate and branched at irregular intervals. Other hyphae were clearly septate, with the central region of the septum slightly thickened (Fig. 3-1C). At certain points along the hypha, ovoid to pear-shaped vesicles were produced that developed into large (250 μm), thick-walled sporangia (Fig. 3-1B and D). Occasionally, larger sporangia were produced, but these were not found attached to hyphae (Fig. 3-1A). Kidston and Lang (1921) assigned the binomial *Palaeomyces gordonii* var. *major* to these sporangia with stratified walls. Still other sporangia contained a variety of thick-walled spores that have been described as "resting spores" (Fig. 3-1D). It is possible that some of the species named by Kidston and Lang actually represent different developmental stages of the same fungus.

Gametophytes of vascular plants frequently contain fungal filaments within their cells. The frequent occurrence of one type of endophytic fungus in the tissues of the vascular plant *Rhynia* has been used to support the contention that *R. gwynne-vaughanii* is the gametophyte of *R. major*. In addition, the Rhynie chert fungi were present in all tissues, including vascular strands, and although some workers believe that they may have functioned as mycorrhizae, others have suggested that some, or all, of the "species" invaded the tissues of the vascular plants after they were dead or during the preservation process.

Numerous fungi representing a variety of morphologic types were present during the Carboniferous (Figs. 3-7 and 3-8). There can be little question that recognition of these fossil fungi is directly related to the extensive examination of structurally preserved vascular plants found in coal balls. In some of these Carboniferous petrifactions, there were a number of spherical, conceptaclelike structures, typically less than 1.0 mm in diameter, and most authors believe

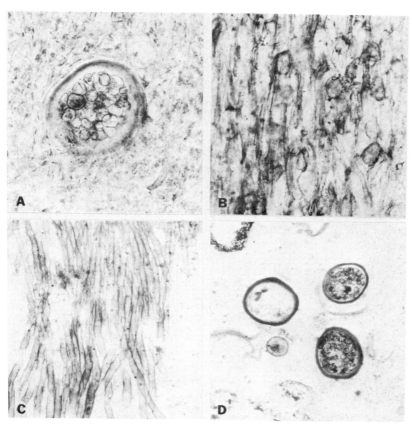

Figure 3-1 Specimens of *Palaeomyces gordonii* in Rhynie chert (Devonian). A. Large resting spore containing smaller intrusive spores in the cortex of *Rhynia major.* ×120. B. Septate hyphae with swellings and vesicles. ×50. C. Hyphae with irregular swellings. ×50. D. Cluster of thick-walled resting spores. ×50.

them to be fossil fungi. These fungi, given such generic names as *Sporocarpon, Dubiocarpon,* and *Mycocarpon,* are abundant in Pennsylvanian coal balls. In *Mycocarpon,* a common Middle Pennsylvanian form, the central cavity (550 μm in diameter) is surrounded by a wall of interlaced hyphalike cells four layers deep. Extending from the wall are numerous radially oriented spines, some with forked tips (Fig. 3-2A). Inside is an amorphous, cuticlelike membrane. In some species (e.g., *M. bimuratus*), the central cavity contains numerous small spheres.

The wall of *Dubiocarpon elegans* is constructed of club-shaped cells up to 150 μm long. Extending from some of these cells are hairs. The radiating nonseptate hyphae that comprise the walls of these structures have led some researchers to suggest that these fungal bodies represent cleistocarps or pycnidia. In addition, both the pseudoparenchymatous organization of the walls of these structures and their common association with partially decayed fossil

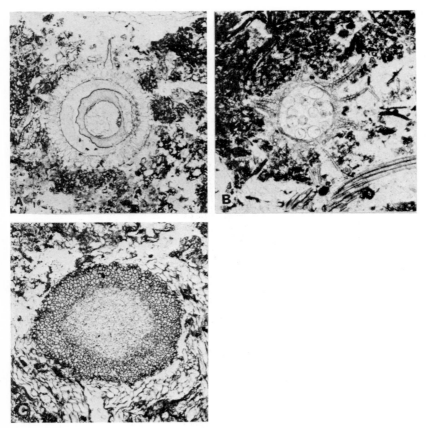

Figure 3-2 Fungi commonly encountered in Carboniferous coal balls. A. *Dubiocarpon elegans.* ×40. B. *Traquairia* c.f. *burntislandica.* ×40. C. *Palaeosclerotium pusillum* showing outer cortex and lighter central medulla of branched and septate hyphae. ×50.

plant remains are cited as further evidence that they are fungi. Nothing is known about their method of reproduction, although it has been suggested that some of these structures formed buds.

Similar bodies from the Pennsylvanian have been described under the generic name *Palaeosclerotium* (Fig. 3-2C). Each of the bodies consists of an ovoid sclerotium up to 1.2 mm in diameter. The walls of these structures are two-parted, with a central medulla of branched, septate hyphae surrounded by a cortex of pseudoparenchymatous cells. Species of *P. pusillum* are found among other plant debris. Nothing is known about how they were formed. Recent studies have suggested that *Palaeosclerotium* represented a cleistothecium that contained spores within asci. A variable number of spores (four to eight) are borne in each ascus. Clamp connections have been reported in hyphae associated with the cleistothecium, but there is no evidence that they were part of the same system. Singer (1977) has suggested that the genus could be placed within the Eurotiales of the Ascomycota.

Another Carboniferous fungus found in the wood of the fern *Zygopteris illinoiensis* is *Palaeancistrus*. In structure it compares closely with a number of existing saprophytic Basidiomycota. The septate hyphae are smooth, 4.8 μm in diameter, and follow a rather straight course within the tracheids. Both terminal and intercalary swellings, thought to represent chlamydospores, are common among the hyphal filaments. Some hyphae show incomplete clamp connections, in which the hook of the clamp does not form a complete union with the hypha. Others reveal well-developed clamp connections, thereby substantiating the existence of Basidiomycota as early as the Pennsylvanian. The saprophytic nature of *P. martinii* and the presence of clamp connections in this Pennsylvanian fossil do not support the long-held opinion that these two features are advanced and of relatively recent origin within the Basidiomycota. *Palaeancistrus* indicates that this division of fungi is far older than the fossil record demonstrates to date.

Protoascon missouriensis (Fig. 3-3) was initially described as a member of the Ascomycota, but it has been suggested recently that the affinities of this fossil are closer to some Mastigiomycota. This fungus evidences a vesicular swelling (perithecium in the original description) with a thickened outer wall and a terminal pore. The vesicle was surrounded by 10 symmetrically positioned nonseptate hyphae of varying lengths that arched up over the terminal cell (Fig. 3-3A and B). This arrangement resembles the appearance of oogonia, and when it is surrounded by antheridia, it resembles some species of water molds. This interpretation is further strengthened by the apparent penetration of the terminal cell (oogonium) by the tips of the surrounding hyphae.

Another fossil fungus that appears to have shared some features with Mastigiomycota was discovered in the ovule of *Nucellangium*. These specimens, from the Middle Pennsylvanian of Iowa, consist of thick-walled oogonia up to

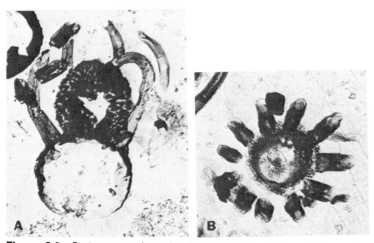

Figure 3-3 *Protoascon missouriensis.* A. Fruiting body partially enclosed by symmetrically positioned nonseptate hyphae. ×185. B. Hyphae as seen in polar view. ×185. *(Courtesy of R. Baxter.)*

100 μm in diameter. Some contained two to four inclusions that have been likened to oospheres. The oogonia, which resemble those of the existing pathogenic genus *Albugo,* are believed to have caused the irregular, proliferated masses of parenchyma that extended into the seed locule. What is most interesting about this fossil is that the structure of the fungus and symptoms it produced in the host appear to be almost identical with those of existing forms.

Yeastlike microfossils named *Ramsaysphaera* (Fig. 3-4B) and *Isuasphaera* (Fig. 3-4C through F) have recently been described from 3.4- and 3.8-billion-year-old cherts collected from South Africa and Greenland, respectively. These fossils morphologically resemble asporogenous yeasts, and they are represented as individual cells, unbranched and ramified filaments, and irregular clusters that superfically resemble the modern yeast *Candida* (Fig. 3-4A). What is perhaps most significant about these fossils is not their potential taxonomic affinities, but rather their relatively complex morphology. Here we have a relatively high level of organization in organisms that are only a few hundred million years removed from the 4.5-billion-year mark that has been suggested as the time at which the earth's crust was formed. In a recent paper, Pflug and Jaeschke-Boyer (1979) reported using microprobe analysis to correlate the morphology and chemistry of *Isuasphaera.* This technique utilizes a focused laser beam to excite the sample, thereby producing vibration spectra which are used to identify and locate the molecular constitutents of the fossil. Microprobe analysis holds great promise as a method for distinguishing specimens of abiotic origin from those that were biologically formed. Furthermore, it may provide a quantitative method for the direct investigation of chemical evolution in early organisms.

It is worth noting that an ascuslike microfossil (Fig. 2-3A through C) was discovered in late Precambrian sediments (900 to 1050 million years ago) from South Australia. The structure was about 290 μm long and 35 μm wide and contained eight ellipsoidal bodies (36 μm long) in a central cylindrical cavity. Although the structure has some superficial resemblance to an ascus, the precise biological affinities remain in question. In the absence of branched hyphae, such a structure could have represented a member of the marine algal order Chamaesiphonales, an existing group within blue-green algae.

Because of their resistant nature, polypore bracket fungi (Basidiomycota) are occasionally fossilized, and a number have been reported in sediments of the Tertiary Period. *Fomes idahoensis* is a calcified bracket fungus about 13.5 cm long and 4.5 cm wide. The upper surface is wrinkled, suggesting a series of growth increments. On the lower surface are numerous pores that represent the distal openings of the tubes embedded in the ground mycelium. A Lower Cretaceous specimen (*Polyporites*) that was initially described as a shelf fungus was later determined to be a syringopore coral.

Chytridlike (Mastigiomycota) fossils are known from Pennsylvanian sediments in association with the saccate cordaitean pollen grain *Sullisaccites* (Fig. 3-8A). These fossil chytrids consist of sporangia that are present on the surface and within the central body of their pollen grains. Internal sporangia are about 25 μm in diameter and globose in shape; those on the surface (Fig. 3-8B) contain

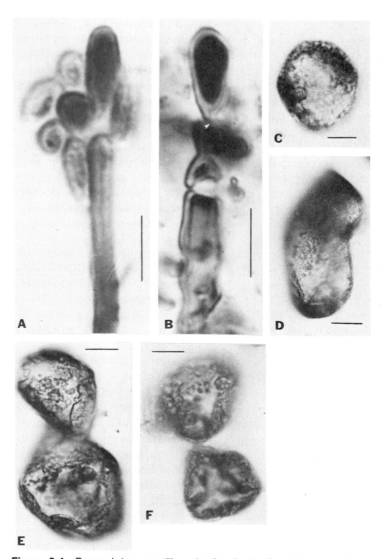

Figure 3-4 Precambrian yeastlike microfossils. A. *Candida tropicalis,* an extant yeast with a terminal bud. B. *Ramsaysphaera ramses* from the Swartkoppie chert of South Africa. Scale represents 4 μm C–F. *Isuasphaera isua* from the Isua quartzite of Greenland showing what have been interpreted as stages of budding. Scale represents 5 μm. *(A and B from Pflug, 1978; C–F courtesy of H. Pflug.)*

apical papillae, which represent discharge sites, and a swollen base, where the rhizoid is attached. Both types of sporangia contained numerous irregularly shaped dark bodies up to 2.5 μm in diameter that are believed to have been unicellular zoospores. The presence of a light refractile area in each structure is characteristic of existing chytrid zoospores.

Mycorrhizal fungi have been reported in the rhizomes and roots of a number of Carboniferous plants, and they are especially common in the lateral appendages of the lycophyte *Stigmaria ficoides* and the roots of *Psaronius.* Whether these fungi grew in a symbiotic relationship with the vascular plant or invaded the tissues after the plant died cannot be determined in most instances. It has been suggested that the relatively low degree of fungal infection, the presence of the same kinds of fungal remains both within the cells and in the surrounding matrix, and the occurrence of both septate and nonseptate fungi in the same organ would indicate that the fungi found preserved in underground parts of fossilized vascular plants most likely invaded the tissues after the plant had died and therefore were not symbionts.

Sorosporonites is a parasitic marine fungus found in the cells of the Permian calcareous algae *Permocalculus* and *Gymnocodium,* as well as in the shells of fusulinids. The fungus consists of ovoid sori that contain spherical, thick-walled spores that caused enlargement of the infected cells.

Epiphyllous fungi (fungi living on leaves of green land plants) apparently were common on many forms of vegetation as early as the Carboniferous, and probably earlier, although there are few good examples. *Stomiopeltis* is a form isolated from the cuticle of a Lower Cretaceous conifer. It consists of an extensive mat of mycelium with anatomosing hyphae up to 3.0 μm in diameter. Associated with the hyphae are dome-shaped fruiting structures that have a central ostiole. No spores were found.

The most comprehensive study on epiphyllous fungi may be found in the paper by Dilcher (1965), who described a number of species (in the orders Microthyriales, Erysiphales, and Moniliales) in leaves from the Middle Eocene of Tennessee. In several instances, it was possible to reconstruct the entire life cycle of the fungus, including both the sexual and asexual phases, thereby making assignment to modern groups more accurate. *Manginula* (=*Shortensis*) includes fungi that were epicuticular, and *M. memorabilis* is one of the most commonly encountered forms on the lower surfaces of leaves of the angiosperm genus *Sapindus.* Fungal colonies developed from spores consisting of two unequal cells. Upon germination, hyphae from the larger cells penetrated the host leaves. Mycelia developed as a result of hyphae dichotomizing into colonies up to 450 μm in diameter. Two types of fruiting bodies were formed by the irregular proliferation of cells from a short, lateral branch, and at maturity, the fruiting bodies consisted of a mass of hyphal cells with a central ostiole. The larger ascocarps produced two-celled spores (ascospores) up to 10 μm wide and 14 μm long; the smaller fruiting structures developed small, unicellular spores. These spores were oriented in chains, and upon release, they germinated to form small germinal tubes that penetrated leaf epidermis. In this genus, both the perfect and imperfect stages were described from fossil material before the life cycles of existing forms had been worked out.

Fossil fungi such as those from western Tennessee also provide a potential method for determining the paleoenvironment of the region in ancient times. On

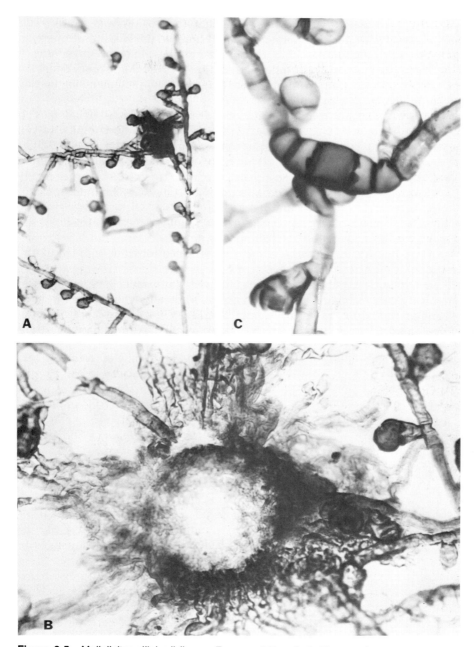

Figure 3-5 *Meliolinites dilcherii* (Lower Eocene of Texas). A. Young colony showing branching vegetative mycelium. ×200. B. Mature perithecium with radiating hyphae. ×800. C. Germinated spore showing primary hyphopodia and vegetative mycelium. ×500. *(Courtesy of C. Daghlian.)*

the basis of leaf types, it was suggested that the region was subtropical. Furthermore, it is interesting to note that the fungi, on the basis of comparison with living representatives, support the contention that the area was a subtropical, moist, low-lying coastal region during the Middle Eocene. Fourteen genera and 76 species of fungal spores were identified from sediments in the clay pits where the leaves were found.

Meliolinites dilcherii from the early Eocene of Texas consisted of colonies up to 2.0 mm in diameter (Fig. 3-5A and B). Numerous stubby, lateral, two-cell branches, one a short stalk cell and the other a capitate head cell (Fig. 3-5C), were produced along the hyphae. The latter provided the only connection between the fungus and the host cells. Existing members of the family Meliolaceae are generally parasitic and common in warm, humid, forested, tropical areas.

Silicified palm wood (*Palmoxylon*) from the Oligocene of Mississippi has yielded well-preserved oogonia and antheridia, some with contents. These fungi have been named *Peronosporoides* because of their obvious affinity to the modern genus *Peronospora* (Oomycetes).

Fungal spores represent a significant and important portion of most sediments that are examined for palynomorphs, with genera and species defined on such characteristics as size, shape, symmetry, aperture configuration, septation, and ornamentation (Fig. 3-6C through G). Although some strati-

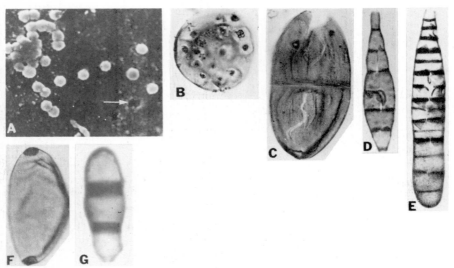

Figure 3-6 Examples of biogenic infection and Eocene fungal spores. A. *Annella capitata* (white spheres) on pollen-grain surface. Arrow indicates cavity created by biogenic infection. ×4000. B. Scattered pits indicating infection by *Annella capitata* on the Jurassic pollen grain *Exesipollenites tumulus*. ×60. C. *Fusiformisporites* sp. fungal spore with single septum. ×650. D. Multicellular fungal spore *Diporicellaesporites* sp. ×650. E. Fungal spores of the *Pluricellaesporites* type. ×650. F. Diporate fungal spore *Diporisporites*. ×650. G. Tricellate fungal spore *Pluricellaesporites minusculus*. ×1000. *(A and B from S. Srivastava, 1976; C–F from Elsik and Dilcher, 1974; G courtesy of D. Dilcher.)*

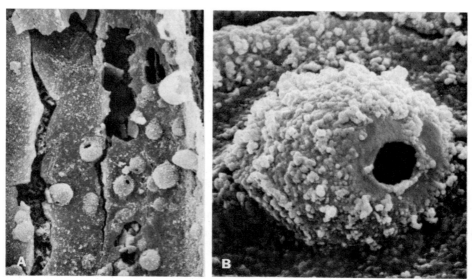

Figure 3-7 Fungal(?) bodies associated with the filicalean fern *Botryopteris*. A. Several bodies inside sieve elements. ×1000. B. Close-up of spherical body showing pore. ×10,000. *(Courtesy of E. Smoot.)*

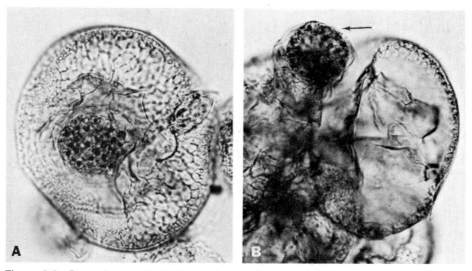

Figure 3-8 Pennsylvanian chytridlike fungi. A. *Sullisaccites* pollen grain with zoosporic fungi within the central body. ×950. B. Pollen grain with epibiotic sporangium extruding from saccus wall *(arrow).* ×950.

graphic applications have been attempted with fungal spores, their greatest potential probably lies in areas concerned with host specificity, distribution, and ecological indicators.

BACTERIA

Evidence of bacteria in the fossil record has been found as far back as the Precambrian, where exceptionally well-preserved forms have been identified with the aid of transmission electron microscopy and various biochemical techniques. All the general morphologic forms (coccoid, bacilloid, spiral, and filament) have been recognized in a variety of configurations that correspond to those of existing microbes. Fossil bacteria represent an extensive range of preservational modes, including almost all types of common mineral matrices, vertebrate and invertebrate remains, plant tissues, and coprolites.

Organisms from South African cherts about 3 billion years old represent the oldest bacterialike organisms described. They consist of isolated rod-shaped cells with slightly rounded ends and are twice as long (0.5 μm) as wide. In transverse section, *Eobacterium* is round and has a two-part wall. The outer surface is granular. Numerous pieces of evidence clearly indicate that these bacteria were fossilized when the chert was formed rather than being modern bacterial contaminants.

Fossil iron bacteria have been found in pyrite of the Middle Pennsylvanian. By means of replication techniques and transmission electron microscopy, it was determined that some of these bacteria were so similar to existing forms that they were assigned to those taxa. Other fossil bacteria have been found in Cretaceous deposits, and they have been assigned to such genera as *Micrococcus, Streptococcus,* and *Actinomyces.* Interestingly, these bacterial cells are not mineralized; they occur in plates associated with small scraps of organic matter, much the same way bacteria accumulate in lake muds today. Although it is still not known how some living bacteria became entombed in sediments, the fact that these are Cretaceous forms suggests that they accumulated in deep freshwater lakes that supported luxuriant growths of photosynthetic, presumably sulfur, bacteria. Recognition of these fossils provides an important means by which to interpret other associated fossil assemblages in the area.

Fossil sporomorphs sometimes exhibit characteristic patterns and scars that resulted from the activity of various microbes (Fig. 3-6A and B). In some instances, it has been possible to classify the patterns produced by these organisms and, by that means, to trace such degrading organisms stratigraphically. Some of these organisms were extremely specific, attacking only certain layers (nexine or sexine) of the pollen-grain walls. In others, such as the modern aquatic fungus *Retiarius,* the organism is known to be parasitic on wind-borne pollen grains that are actually trapped by short, spikelike hyphae that project from the mycelia on a leaf surface. Where the hyphae penetrate the pollen grain exine, characteristic marks are produced that can provide important information about the fungus and its biological relationship with the host. Study of such features on the walls of spores and pollen grains holds much promise as a means by which to gather information about an important group of organisms that was only indirectly preserved in the fossil record.

Probably no living organism has been as extensively studied as the bacterium *Escherichia coli*. It is an aerobic, non-spore-forming rod that is both saprophytic and parasitic, and it is a common experimental organism in many areas of modern biological research. It is curious to note that silicified cells of *E. coli* have been reported in mammalian and reptilian coprolites of the Eocene. Numerous fossil bacteria similar to living species also were recorded in Permian coprolites.

One interesting account of fossil bacteria that deserves mentioning is the report of bacteria isolated and grown from salt deposits ranging from the Precambrian to the Paleozoic (Dombrowski, 1963). Although such reports border on science fiction, the reader will have to determine whether such bacteria are actually living forms that were contaminants or, in fact, represent bacteria with biochemical pathways that became operative after many millions of years.

Chapter 4

Algae and Lichens

Like fungi, the algae have a long geologic record that can be traced well back into the Precambrian. Despite the fragile nature of most algae, there are numerous algal remains in the fossil record. Some algae have contributed to the formation of petroleum and are identified as "chemical fossils." Others are represented by thousands of feet of accumulated siliceous diatom shells. Unlike most other fossil plants, many algae were not preserved such that their histologic features could be determined; therefore, they are identified on the basis of their past activities. For example, common throughout the geologic column are the various algae that secreted calcium carbonate, in many instances forming extensive deposits. Some of these deposits, such as the so-called coral reefs, have been produced largely by certain lime-secreting algae. One such alga that is a common inhabitant of coral reefs is *Halimeda* (Fig. 4-1A), a genus that can be traced with confidence back to the Cretaceous and probably well into the Jurassic (Hillis-Colinvaux, 1980). The thallus of *Halimeda* is constructed entirely of branching filaments that are matted together (Fig. 4-1B) to form a plant body that in some species may reach over a meter in length. Since no cross walls are produced in any of the filaments, the plant may be regarded as a giant multinucleated cell. Although sections of the fossil forms rarely show any indication of the cellular details of the original organism, the activities of these

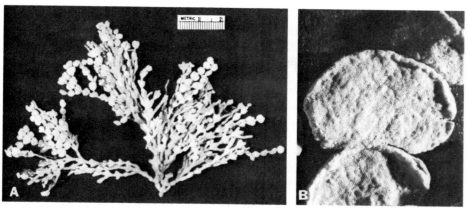

Figure 4-1 A. Habit view of *Halimeda minima* from Eniwetok Atoll. B. Segment from *H. macrophysa* from Matawei Island west of Sumatra. *(Reproduced with permission of Academic Press Ltd., courtesy of L. Hillis-Colinvaux.)*

algae can be witnessed by examining the accumulated calcium carbonate. This is not to say that cellular details in fossil algae are not common. In the appropriate depositional situations, many algae have been exquisitely preserved, just like other organisms. One need only cite the variety of Precambrian organisms, including algae, that have been preserved in cherts.

One of the difficulties in dealing with fossil algae concerns the basis upon which modern representatives are classified. In this regard, extant algae are somewhat unique in that they are classified on the basis of certain features that generally do not lend themselves to preservation or, if they are preserved, have not been identified in the fossils. Those features used to classify existing algae include pigmentation, storage products, type of flagellation if present, and degree of cellularization. Recent research indicates that mitosis, cytokinesis, spindle organization, and the method of flagellar attachment are possibly of even greater importance in algal systematics and phylogeny. Despite the obvious limitations in attempting to classify fossil algae only according to morphology, the classification of Bold and Wynne (1978) has been adopted for use here, and a few examples of fossils that may be assigned to each of the recognized divisions are presented.

CYANOCHLORONTA

Members of Cyanochloronta are prokaryotic and are referred to as blue-green algae, although, based on certain biochemical features and cellular organization, some authorities regard them as bacteria. Fossil blue-green algae represent one of the dominant organisms in many Precambrian biotas, and they include both filamentous and coccoid members. *Palaeolyngbya* (see Fig. 2-3D) is a filamentous alga from the Bitter Springs chert of Australia dated approximately 1.0 billion years before the present. Morphologically, the filaments are almost identical to the extant blue-green *Lyngbya,* which consists of a hyaline, nonlaminated sheath surrounding broad, unbranched filaments. In *P. barghoorniana,* the filaments have curved tips and partial septations near the filament ends that represent stages in cell division. Another member of the Bitter Springs assemblage is *Oscillatoriopsis,* a filamentous form morphologically identical with the living blue-green *Oscillatoria. Anabaenidium* superficially resembles the existing genus *Anabaenopsis,* but the obscured nature of a globose terminal cell makes assignment tentative at this time.

Many stromatolites are believed to have formed from the activities of blue-green algae. *Conophyton* is the generic name for conically laminated stromatolites found in modern hot-spring environments and Precambrian sediments as well. Silicified specimens from Russia contain four distinct types of microfossils, including solitary unicells up to 70 μm in diameter, colonial unicells, narrow tubular filaments (2 to 7 μm in diameter), and broad oscillatoriacean sheaths and trichomes. The identification of microfossils in the stromatolite suggests that it may have been produced by a specific type of microbial community. Information of this type may make stromatolites useful stratigraphic markers.

Four of the most commonly occurring orders of blue-green algae that are responsible for formation of modern ocean stromatolites are Chroococcales, Nostocales, Oscillatoriales, and Pleurocapsales. Coccoid cells that look similar to those of existing pleurocapsacean blue-greens have been identified in sediments 1.2 billion years old. *Palaeopleurocapsa wopfnerii* consists of ensheathed packets of cells aggregated into a pseudoparenchymatous system of dichotomous branches.

Both transmission and scanning electron microscopy have provided valuable information about the morphology and ultrastructure of several fossil blue-green algae, as well as suggesting a basis for determining stages in the growth cycle of some fossil algae. *Sphaerocongregus* is the generic name applied to three morphologically distinct cell types collected from uppermost Proterozoic siliceous shales from southwestern Alberta, Canada. One cell type, assigned to *S. variabilis,* includes coccoid cells 3 to 5 μm in diameter; another cell type is larger (5 to 6 μm) and is often arranged in chains. The third morphologic category consists of globose masses 5 to 20 μm in diameter that are composed of small coccoid subunits. Surrounding these larger cell masses is a delicate envelope. Comparisons with living blue-green coccoids suggest that the various morphologic types assigned to *S. variabilis* represent different stages in the life cycle of a single organism. Accordingly, the larger masses represent endosporangia that contain endospores, and some of the other cells represent stages in the vegetative plant body.

Blue-green algae also have been found in association with the younger (Devonian) Rhynie chert flora. *Langiella* is a heterotrichous form consisting of a horseshoe-shaped basal portion that produced a number of uniseriate branches. These filaments are unbranched and surrounded by a thin sheath. At the base of each filament is a heterocyst that is generally smaller than the other cells of the sheath; at the distal end of each filament is a hairlike extension. *Kidstoniella fritschii,* from the same locality, contains branched filaments.

Some workers believe that blue-green algae are most closely related to, and probably derived from, gram-negative bacteria. All the cyanophycean families appear to be represented in the Precambrian, with the coccoid unicellar forms known from the earliest Precambrian sediments. Based on fossil evidence to date, it can be concluded that blue-green algae diversified early, with the filamentous forms evolving from the chroococcalean forms during the early Precambrian. Because of the remarkable ecologic and physiologic flexibility demonstrated by extant blue-greens, it is not surprising that the cyanophytes were diversified early in the Precambrian and have remained relatively unchanged morphologically until today.

CHLOROPHYCOPHYTA

Chlorophycophyta, or green algae, constitute one of the major groups of algae in terms of number of genera and species. Moreover, the Chlorophycophyta may be found in a great variety of habitats and include forms that range from unicells to multicellular plant bodies. Like the cyanophytes, members of the Chlorophycophyta have been identified in the Precambrian.

Caryosphaeroides (Bitter Springs) is a Precambrian form showing spheroidal unicells that are morphologically similar to existing species of *Chlorococcum* and *Chlorella*. The cells range from 6 to 15 μm in diameter and lack sheaths; a few specimens were colonial and, in those cases, are contained in an amorphous organic matrix. Some specimens show cell contents that have been interpreted as a nuclear residue. However, as was suggested earlier, this material may represent the plasmolized cytoplasmic contents of the cell. In another Bitter Springs alga, the presence of small peripherally positioned structures superficially resembling pyrenoids has prompted some workers to suggest probable affinities with green algae. *Glenobotrydion* consists of spherical solitary cells, as well as loosely associated groups, that formed colonies aggregated into a pseudofilamentous matrix. Individual cells vary up to 12 μm in diameter, and when solitary, they lack a sheath. However, when they are colonial, a thin, nonlamellated sheath is present around the colonies.

One interesting Upper Devonian siphonous member of the Chlorophycophyta reveals a comb-shaped thallus that consists of nonseptate branching tubes. Along some of the upright tubes in *Courvoisiella ctenomorpha* are spherical structures about 200 μm in diameter, and these have been interpreted as some form of gametangium. Chemical analyses of the fossil suggest that the cell walls were composed of cellulose, further evidence supporting morphologic associations with existing Eusiphonales.

One of the most commonly encountered members of the fossil Chlorophycophyta are those forms assignable to the Dasycladales. There are more than 120 fossil genera, some of which can be traced back to the Cambrian; today the order is represented by eight genera. Morphologically, these fossil algae are radially symmetrical, with a central, nonseptate axis that bears whorls of lateral appendages, some of which are branched. Operculate cysts were produced that contained isogametes. Almost all members secreted lime around the thallus, and this greatly increased their potential for preservation.

In the Paleozoic and Mesozoic dasyclads, the primary whorled branches are irregularly positioned. These branches bear secondary and tertiary laterals. Most are cylindrical plants, although some are club-shaped, spherical, or like a string of beads. The plant was attached to the substrate by simple rhizoids. In the fossils, the encrusting calcium carbonate is sometimes so thick that several orders of branches are covered. A slightly different morphology is apparent in *Primicorallina* (Ordovician). Specimens of this dasyclad look somewhat like a fern frond with a central axis that bears tufts of four secondary branches. Another form that extended from the Ordovician into the Lower Carboniferous is *Rhabdoporella,* a type that produced only primary branches. This genus has been suggested by Herak et al. (1977) as representing a morphogenetic state in the evolution of all dasyclad algae. More highly evolved members contained greater numbers of whorls and more orders of branches. *Pianella* is a small (3.0 mm long) dasyclad with funnel-shaped branches arranged in alternating whorls. This taxon is common in the Lower Cretaceous of the Middle East, Italy, and Yugoslavia.

Recent studies by Elliott (1978) suggest that the fossil dasyclads occupied environments that were similar to those occupied by extant forms and that their adaptations to microenvironments (e.g., salinity, bottom sediment, attachments, and water energies) were also essentially similar to those of the modern forms.

Two other groups of calcium carbonate–depositing organisms are the receptaculitids and cyclocrinitids. Fossil receptaculitids range from the Lower Ordovician to the Middle Devonian. Although they are typically found associated with coral reefs, they are not regarded as reef builders, like some of the other calcareous algae. Structurally, they show a central axis with regularly arranged lateral branches (Fig. 4-2B), like the dasyclads. The ends of the branches are modified into simple heads that form an exterior wall (Fig. 4-2A). Generally, the cyclocrinids have a narrower stratigraphic range, extending from the Middle Ordovician to near the Upper Silurian. They assume a variety of shapes, and in general, the central axis has not been preserved. *Cyclocrinus* is a common Ordovician genus that consists of a club-shaped central stem with radiating primary branches. At the end of the primary branch shaft are bowl-shaped cortical cells with flattened tops, and these merge to form a reticulum of hexagonal-shaped plates perforated by regularly spaced holes. Although the cyclocrinitids and receptaculitids are now considered to be ancient algae, they were historically treated as protozoans and sponges by some authors. The reader is referred to the important papers of Nitecki (1970), Rietschel (1977), and Bassoullet et al. (1977) detailing the taxonomy of these interesting fossils.

In addition to the importance of the calcareous algae, another group of

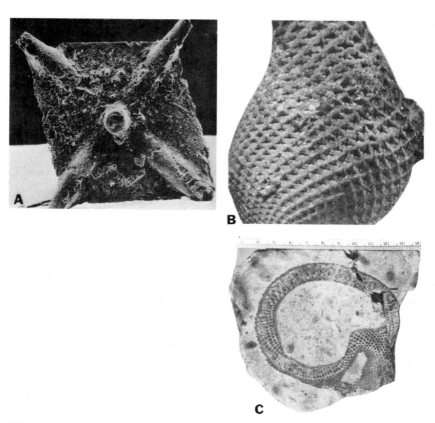

Figure 4-2 A. Ventral view of a single head of the Silurian receptaculitid alga *Ischadites tenuis*. B. Surface view of the thallus of *Ischadites koenigii* showing the surface pattern. C. *Receptaculites* sp. from the Ordovician of Canada. ×0.5. *(A from Nitecki and Dapples, 1975; B from Nitecki, 1972; C courtesy of R. Stockey.)*

greens appears to have been geologically significant. These include the algae that are believed responsible for the formation of certain types of coals and also may have contributed to the formation of some petroleum in oil shales. These irregularly shaped, yellow bodies were the result of the hydrocarbon producing alga *Botryococcus braunii* (Fig. 4-3A), living colonial green alga, that is known from both temperate and tropical climates throughout the world. The fossil colonies consisted of pear-shaped cells arranged in radial rows and surrounded by a mucilage layer that has been described as a cuticularized layer. In the fossils, the yellow bodies are thought to represent materials (paraffins and fatty acids) secreted by the cells and bound by the mucilagelike substance of the sheath. *Botryococcus* (Fig. 4-3B) colonies are known from every geologic period beginning in the Carboniferous.

Parka is the name of a slightly concave thallus ranging from 0.5 to 7.0 cm in diameter. The typical shape of this Devonian fossil is oval, with the margin slightly undulating. On the surface of the thallus are disk-shaped sporangia

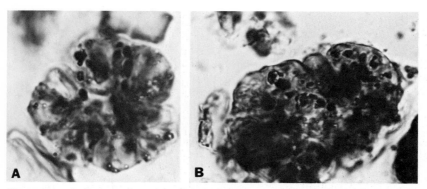

Figure 4-3 A. *Botryococcus braunii* from the Oligocene. B. Specimen of *Botryococcus braunii* from Rio Blanco Lake sediments (Pleistocene). *(Courtesy of J. Burgess.)*

containing numerous spores (42 μm in diameter) that lack haptotypic markings. *Parka decipiens* and *Pachytheca,* a morphologically similar taxon, have been suggested as representing some existing green algae (e.g., *Coleochaete* and *Phycopeltis)*. Comparison of the fossil and the living taxa is based on simulations of growth patterns and chemical analysis of the fossil specimens (Niklas, 1976).

Tasmanites is the generic name of another probable alga found in many marine facies as early as the Ordovician; specimens are commonly found in the coallike material tasmanite, as well as in some oil shales. The fossil cysts are compressed, usually ranging from 100 to 600 μm in diameter (Fig. 4-4B). Haptotypic features are absent, but the surface is covered by numerous regularly spaced punctae. Ultrathin sections of the wall reveal concentric banding and two types of pores that traverse the wall in a radiating pattern. The affinities of *Tasmanites* have remained in doubt since the original description of the taxon by Newton in 1875. However, most workers now believe that the fossil disseminules represent the cysts of such modern planktonic algae as the prasinophytes.

The genus *Pediastrum* is distinguished by disk-shaped coenobia or colonies composed of a variable number of cells (Fig. 4-4E). The cells are arranged in a concentric pattern, with each cell of the outer ring containing one to three spines. Specimens that appear similar to *P. boryanum* have been found in marine sediments of the Lower Cretaceous; others have been reported from the Miocene of Oregon and the Eocene of southern Sumatra. The Miocene fossils are 8- to 64-celled coenobia with the marginal cells bearing two spines. Today the genus lives exclusively in fresh water, and its presence in Cretaceous marine sediments suggests an early shift in the physiologic tolerance of the taxon or indicates that the genus is not as good an index of freshwater environments as was previously thought.

Thin sections of chert from the Middle Devonian of New York have produced both marine and freshwater algae. *Paleoclosterium leptum* (Fig. 4-5B) consists of solitary, elongate, lunate cells up to 46 μm long and 5 μm wide that appear morphologically similar to the extant desmid *Closterium.*

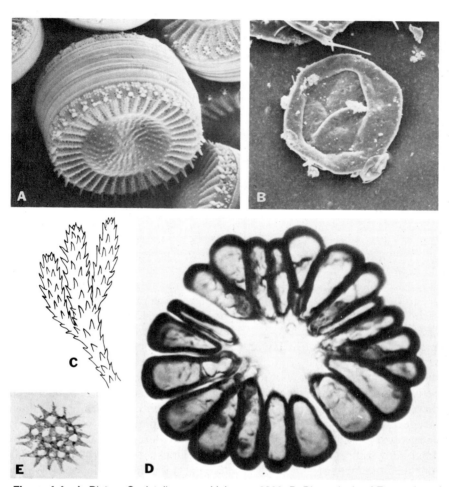

Figure 4-4   A. Diatom *Cyclotella meneghiniana.* ×3300. B. Disseminule of *Tasmanites sinuosus* from the Devonian of Ohio. ×250. C. *Caulerpites denticulata.* D. Algal specimen that resembles *Microcodium elegans.* Although found associated with shales of the Paleozoic, the specimens may represent an intrusion. E. *Pediastrum* sp. from the Kaja Well No. 1, Sumatra (Tertiary to Lower Paleogene). ×430. *(A from Hoops and Floyd, 1980; C from Parker and Dawson, 1965; D courtesy of J. Wood; E courtesy of L. Wilson.)*

An interesting fleshy member of the Chlorophycophyta that morphological-ly resembles the existing genus *Caulerpa* has been reported preserved in Miocene diatomite from California. This fossil, *Caulerpites denticulata* (Fig. 4-4C), consists of a diffusely branched plant that bears broadened ultimate segments.

Some authors treat the charophytes as a separate order within the Chlorophycophyta. However, other authors regard them as a separate division, believing that their vegetative morphology and reproduction are sufficiently

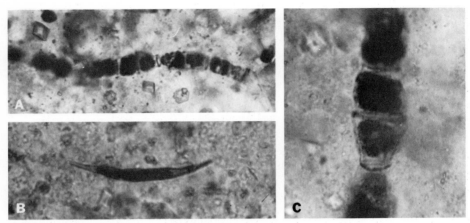

Figure 4-5 Fossil algae from the Devonian of New York. A. *Paleodidymoprium didymum* filament. ×1950. B. *Paleoclosterium leptum.* ×2500. C. Detail of *Paleodidymoprium didymum* cells. ×3750. *(From Baschnagel, 1966.)*

different to separate them from other green algae. Still other authorities regard the charophytes as a separate division of green plants. Currently, there are six living genera that inhabit mainly freshwater environments. Some forms may exceed 20.0 cm in length, consisting of whorls of laterals borne at distinct nodes. At the distal ends of the main axes are dome-shaped apical cells. The reproductive organs develop at the nodes of the branches (Fig. 4-6C) and, because of their unique organization, have been easily recognized as fossils. The charophyte oogonium consists of an egg surrounded by coiled, elongate tubes. This structure, when calcified, is termed a gyrogonite (Fig. 4-6A), and it constitutes most of the fossil evidence of the group.

The oldest charophytes are known from Upper Silurian (Downtonian) rocks of the Ukraine. Specimens of *Trochiliscus* differ from other geologically younger gyrogonites in having more than five enveloping cells that are dextrally coiled (twisted to the right). They measured about half a millimeter in diameter and are slightly longer; the base is rounded and the distal end is elongated. Surrounding the central cavity are 10 spirally arranged ridges with rounded furrows between. Inside the *T. podolicus* gyrogonite is a thin (1 μm), continuous membrane that has been interpreted as the remnant of the original oospore. In some sections, patches of disorganized cells are found associated with the membrane. The trochilisks were initially regarded as marine plants. However, it is now believed that they inhabited freshwater or brackish-water environments.

In contrast with the trochilisks, the Devonian and Mississippian gyrogonites demonstrate great structural variability, with at least six elements and an open pore at the apex (Fig. 4-6F). Near the close of the Devonian, a different gyrogonite pattern was present. It consisted of numerous elements and an apical pore, but the pattern of twisting was sinistral (Fig. 4-6D). From *Eochara*, regarded by many as the ancestral form of the modern taxa, there was a

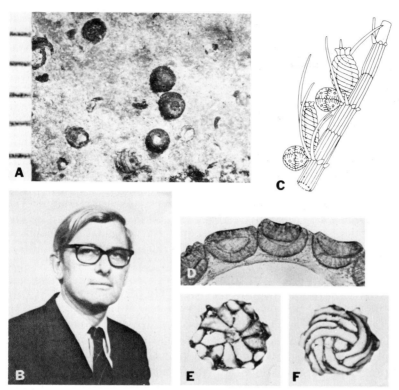

Figure 4-6 A. Several gyrogonites embedded in a Triassic shale. Scale at left is divided into millimeters. B. Louis J. Grambast. C. Branch of *Chara contraria* showing position of sex organs. D. Section through several gyrogonite tubes of *Stomochara,* a late Paleozoic form with five sinistrally spiraled units. ×200. E and F. *Atopochara trivolvis* gyrogonite casts as seen from the apex (F) and base (E). *(B from Boureau, 1979; C from Bold,* Morphology of Plants, *3d ed., 1973; D from Peck and Eyer, 1963; E and F from Grambast, 1967.)*

progressive reduction and fixation of the number of sinistrally coiled elements (Fig. 4-6F), with five (the common number in living species) established by the Upper Carboniferous. Finally, the modern forms have completely eliminated the apical pore as a result of the close association of the spiral cells at the apex (Grambast, 1974) (Fig. 4-6B).

In addition to the large number of fossil gyrogonites that have been described and used effectively in some instances as index fossils, the vegetative parts of the plant have been preserved as well. Fossils of the genus *Clavator,* known widely throughout the world, consist of strongly calcified stems with narrow internodes and six lateral branches in each whorl. The oogonia are located in a single row on the adaxial side of a branch, one per node. The spiral cells of *Aclistochara* gyrogonites are truncated at the apex. The vegetative parts of *Echinochara,* a genus common in the Morrison Formation (Jurassic) of North America, are known in some detail. The plant body reveals 12 dextrally spiraled cortical tubes constructed of elongate cells arranged in a linear series. At the distal end of each cortical cell are five long spines. Oogonia were produced in whorls of six.

CHRYSOPHYCOPHYTA

Included in the Chrysophycophyta are the diatoms, unicellular organisms that are ubiquitous in their distribution, occurring in habitats ranging from freshwater to brackish water and terrestrial to subaerial. Fossil diatoms are common in the geologic record, beginning in the Cretaceous, where the earliest forms were marine. No freshwater diatoms are known before the Miocene. Their presence as recognizable fossils is the result of the resistant nature of the cell wall, or frustule (see Fig. 4-4A), which is composed of silica with an organic coating. The glasslike composition of the wall and its inherent resistance to natural degradation have resulted in some pure deposits of fossil diatom frustules (diatomite or diatomaceous earth) that are several thousand feet thick. Diatom systematics is based on the minute sculpturing of the silica wall and, to a lesser degree, on the cell shape. For a comprehensive treatment of fossil and recent genera and species of diatoms, the reader is referred to the five-volume work of Van Landingham (1967–1971).

The coccolithophorids represent a group of unicellular algae of the Chrysophycophyta that constitutes important primary producers in the open ocean. They are extremely abundant in many Mesozoic and Tertiary sediments, but their occurrence in older rocks has not been documented. Because of their very small size and calcite crystal structure, electron microscopy represents the only satisfactory method of determining their complex morphology and structure. In most coccoliths, the crystals are rhombohedral, and when crowded together, they form a rosette or circular pattern. Their small size, abundance in Mesozoic sediments, and generally restricted stratigraphic range have made coccolithophorids (coccoliths) valuable as index fossils and biostratigraphic markers. They appear to be related to another phytoplanktonic group, the discoasters, which is entirely extinct and known only from rocks of the Tertiary.

RHODOPHYCOPHYTA

The Rhodophycophyta, the red algae, are widespread in the fossil record, extending back to the Cambrian. Extant members are distinguished from other algal groups by the absence of flagellation and the presence of certain accessory pigments, nonaggregated photosynthetic lamellae in the chloroplasts, specialized food reserves, and unique sexual reproduction. Red algae were commonly preserved as fossils because they possessed calcified skeletons resulting from calcium carbonate precipitation within their cell walls. In this feature, they differ from other lime-secreting algae that produced calcium only around their entire plant bodies.

One of the oldest (Cambrian to Tertiary) families within the Rhodophycophyta is the Solenoporaceae, a group that appeared to have its maximum development during the Jurassic. Solenoporids were nodular or encrusting marine organisms composed of closely packed radially or vertically divergent rows of elongate cells (Fig. 4-7A). Their cell diameters were almost always larger than those of living coralline red algae, which are believed to be related structurally. One of the common Paleozoic representatives is *Solenopora* (Fig. 4-7B and C), a genus established for irregularly lobed calcium carbonate masses that possessed radiating filaments. *Parachaetetes* is a Tertiary representative that is especially common in shallow-water reef facies. It occurs as bluntly lobed growths up to several centimeters in diameter. In vertical thin section, typical growths exhibit a tightly packed mass of elongate cells arranged in curved radial lines. In cross section, these cells are circular and variable in length. The cells of *Solenomeris* are polygonal in outline, with those of adjacent rows forming a zigzag configuration. What was earlier thought to represent oval, aggregate reproductive structures in the Miocene genus *Neosolenopora* is now known to be an unusual bryozoan.

The absence of reproductive structures on the geologically older members has suggested to some that they were externally produced and not calcified. Others believe that the early members produced spores in cells that were similar to the vegetative cells and, after spore production, impossible to distinguish.

A common member of the Corallinaceae, a family that includes most of the calcareous red algae, is the genus *Lithothamnium*. The genus can be traced from Jurassic tropical seas to present-day temperate and polar areas. Members

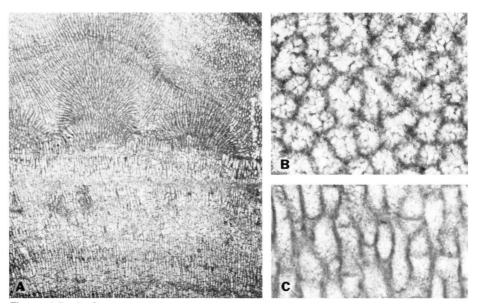

Figure 4-7 A. Section of *Solenopora jurassica* showing several zones of alga. ×14.5. B. Transverse section of *Solenopora jurassica*. ×110. C. Oblique longitudinal section of *Solenopora compacta* (Ordovician) showing cells. ×160. *(Courtesy of G. Elliott.)*

demonstrate a variety of growth forms, ranging from tiny crusts to large masses 30.0 cm in diameter. The plant body is differentiated into three distinct histologic zones. The hypothallus is constructed of loosely arranged long cells; the perithallus (middle zone), of vertical threads of cells that constitute the major portion of the thallus; and the epithallus, which represents the surface layer, of small, flattened thin-walled cells. Irregular branching is common, and includes conspicuous growth lines. The reproductive structures, both asexual and sexual, consist of conceptacles on the crust or branch surfaces, with small pores for the exit of spores.

Most of the late Paleozoic calcareous red algae grew in open-marine carbonate shelf environments, although, as a group, they tolerated a variety of environments. These wide environmental variations suggest that individual taxa may provide important clues relative to ancient environments. Far more difficult, however, is the problem of relating the late Paleozoic red algae to living groups, because the taxonomy of the fossil forms is uncertain. Wray (1977) has suggested that several of the major groups can be traced to the Solenoporaceae, the others having undetermined affinities.

Litostroma is the name applied to a small marine alga of the Pennsylvanian. Specimens consist of irregularly shaped thalloid platelets that are one cell thick and up to 6.0 mm in diameter. Variably shaped perforations appear near the margin of the thallus and the thallus shows filamentlike outgrowth. In addition, many of the cells contain shrunken cell contents or nuclei. The systematic affinities of *L. oklahomense* are uncertain, with green, brown, or red the most probable algal groups.

Another possible member of the Rhodophycophyta is *Eotetrahedrion,* a tetrahedral tetrad of spheroidal cells contained in a sheathlike membrane. It has been suggested that *E. princeps* may represent the tetrahedral tetrasporangia of some red alga. However, no multicellular thalli are known from the sediments associated with the unicells. Moreover, the fact that *Eotetrahedrion* dates from the Precambrian further detracts from its possible affinities with red algae.

Five different noncalcareous red algae have been reported from Middle and Upper Miocene sediments in California. In general, they consist of planated axes with equally spaced laterals, much like numerous members of the Florideophycidae. *Algites hakelensis* is a Cretaceous fossil that appears as a compressed, irregularly branched thallus about 21.0 cm wide. The individual blades are 12.0 cm long and about 1.0 cm wide. The taxon is assigned to the Rhodophycophyta principally on the association with living members that are common the in marine waters of Lebanon. Another species of the genus *Algites* (*A. enteromorphoides* from the Devonian of Missouri) is composed of narrow, branching filaments, and it has been suggested as a member of the Chlorophycophyta. Three other microscopic Devonian algae have been reported from marine sediments in New York. *Drydenia* consists of elliptical laminae (8.5 cm long) that are basally attached to a narrow stipe and terminate in a branching holdfast. In *Hungerfordia,* the lamina is highly dichotomous, with the distal segments lobed. Specimens of *Enfieldia* are circular (5.0 cm in diameter), with the outer margin lobed, and they are characterized by distinct reticulations. Both *Drydenia* and *Hungerfordia* have been compared with existing red and brown algae; *Enfieldia* is more difficult to systematically position, possible being related to a thalloid liverwort.

Thallites is another thalloid plant that may have been either an alga or a bryophyte. *Thallites dichopleurus* (Middle Pennsylvanian) is a dorsiventral thallus with a well-developed midrib. The undulate lamina is slightly less than a centimeter wide, with the entire thallus dichotomizing several times. Latex peels made from the surface of the specimen and examined in the scanning electron microscope show the epidermal cells of the midrib and the thallus to be of different sizes; no epidermal appendages or openings are present. Numerous other species of *Thallites* from Mesozoic rocks have been delimited on the basis of size, character of the margin, and nature of dichotomies.

PHAEOPHYCOPHYTA

The Phaeophycophyta are brown algae that range in size from microscopic epiphytes to some species of *Macrocystis* that are more than 60 m long. All are noncalcareous, no doubt contributing to the absence of a well-defined fossil record. Several of the compression-impression thalloid taxa mentioned in the preceding section (Rhodophycophyta) may be members of the Phaeophycophyta. There are numerous references in paleontologic literature to "fucoids," elliptical impressions that exhibit a morphology not unlike the thallus of the brown algal genus *Fucus*. These structures, which extend back to the Silurian, have not been demonstrated as algal in origin. In fact, most are thought to represent shell drag marks, animal traces, or a variety of sedimentary structures.

Despite the absence of clearly recognizable members of this division in the fossil record, there are a number of taxa suspected of being brown algae-like organisms. One of the most interesting of these is *Prototaxites*, a name applied by Dawson in 1859 to large (90.0 cm in diameter) silicified axes of Devonian age. Externally, the specimens range from smooth to moderately ribbed; no branched specimens are known. Thin sections of the material exhibit a pseudoparenchymatous matrix constructed of two types of elements (Fig. 4-8A). The branched smaller elements range up to about 9.0 μm in diameter and are typically longitudinally oriented. The larger tubes (Fig. 4-8B), which are fewer in number, are also longitudinally oriented and range from 19 to 50 μm in diameter. The walls are thick and striate, with the organic material forming anastomosing plates. Surrounding each tube is a hyphal sheath that is a single cell layer thick. In addition to the filaments and tubes, numerous lacunae about 0.5 μm in diameter are scattered throughout the pseudoparenchyma. These sites often contain disintegrated tissue, and occasionally hyphae, and it has been suggested that these are the result of parasites. Recently, the hyphal filaments of *P. southworthii* were examined ultrastructurally and found to contain septa or cross walls, each with a centrally positioned elliptical aperture. The septal pores of *Prototaxites* are superficially similar to the pores and pit connections of a

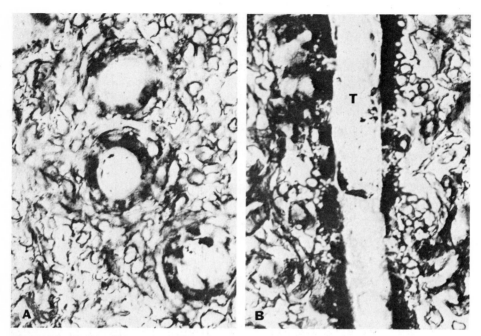

Figure 4-8 *Prototaxites southworthii.* A. Transverse section showing large and small tubes. ×440. B. Longitudinal section showing large tube (T) and pseudoparenchymatous tissue formed by smaller tubes. ×440.

number of major plant groups, including many fungi and the red algae. However, they are sufficiently different that direct comparisons are not possible. The large tubes of *Prototaxites* also have been compared with the sieve-filament elements of some browns. Although both phycologists and mycologists are reluctant to accept *Prototaxites,* recent chemosystematic data underscore an algal affinity, with the presence of cutin and suberin suggesting a terrestrial habitat. It has been suggested that *Prototaxites* may represent one of several unsuccessful algal groups that were in the process of adapting to a terrestrial habitat during the Devonian.

Another enigmatic alga common to Upper Devonian black shales is *Protosalvinia* (= *Foerstia*). These sporocarps, as they have been termed, are generally found as compressions, and they assume a variety of morphologic shapes ranging from almost circular to clavate (Fig. 4-9A). At least three taxa [*P. arnoldii* (Fig. 4-9B), *P. ravenna* (Fig. 4-9D), and *P. furcata*] have been suggested as representing different growth forms of a single biological species, with the thallus becoming more clavate-shaped and developing sporangia with tetrads of spores later in development. The surface-layer cells are uniform and, based on their arrangement, suggest that the thalli dichotomized (Fig. 4-9A). Hypodermal conceptacles (Fig. 4-9D) that contain tetrads of spores are seen in the cup-shaped lobes. Each conceptacle is slightly less than a half a millimeter in diameter and has two distinct cell layers. The spores are large (210 μm) and contain irregular punctae on the surface. Other conceptacles have been

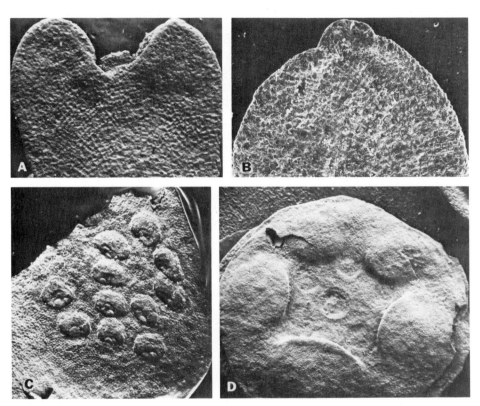

Figure 4-9 *Protosalvinia.* A. Dichotomy of the thallus of *P. furcata.* ×50. B. Specimen of *P. arnoldii* with apical dome. ×50. C. Specimen of *P. braziliensis* showing position of tetrad sites. ×50. D. Apically lobed specimen of *P. ravenna* showing lids of conceptacles. ×50. *(From Niklas, Phillips, and Carozzi, 1976.)*

described as containing multicellular clavate structures that are thought to represent plurilocular sporangia or male gametangia. They are bulb-shaped, with numerous pores on their surfaces. It is not known whether the spores are meiotic products or mitotic derivatives. Both morphologic and chemosystematic evidence suggests that *Protosalvinia* is intermediate between an alga and a bryophyte. Although several of the features point to the Phaeophycophyta, others (tetrads of cells with sporopollenin, the nature of the reproductive structures, and the large size of the plurilocular sporangia) are not found in any living brown alga. As a result, *Prototaxites* is best described as an alga that shows land-adapted features that may underscore convergent evolution at the time land plants were becoming established.

PYRRHOPHYCOPHYTA

The unicellular organisms included in the Pyrrhophycophyta are the dinoflagellates, a diverse assemblage of aquatic organisms that range from 10 to 100 μm in diameter. Most extant forms are free-living components of the oceanic plankton, but saprophytic, parasitic, symbiotic, and holozoic forms are present as well. The fossil forms (Fig. 4-10B), which can be traced from the Silurian to the Recent, evidence morphologically complex cysts (Fig. 4-10E through H). These cysts contain horns, processes, and plates, and they comprise the principal criteria for classification. Another group of closely allied organisms is the hystrichospheres, which are planktonic organisms that have had a varied taxonomic history. Some workers have argued that they are the remains of both plants and animals; others believe they represent some group of extinct algae. Today it is known that some of the highly ornate hystrichospheres, those with radiating processes, represent dinoflagellates (Fig. 4-10C) in which the outer thecal plates are not present, either lost after the death of the organism or developmentally not formed prior to fossilization. These ideas have been supported by comparison of living dinoflagellate cysts with some of the structures present in the fossils.

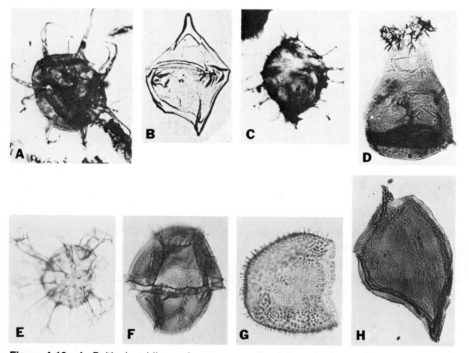

Figure 4-10 A. *Baltisphaeridium spinosum,* an acritarch from the Lower Ordovician of England. ×900. B. *Alterbia acutula,* a dinoflagellate from the late Cretaceous of the United States. ×250. C. *Danea californica* from the early Cretaceous. ×250. D. *Alpenachitina crameri,* a Middle Devonian chitinozoan. ×310. E–H. Dinocysts. E. *Systematophora* sp. from the late Kimmeridgian (Pliocene) of Surrey, England. F. *Ctenididinium stauromatos* from the early Bathonian (Jurassic) of Oxfordshire, England. G. *Cyclonephelium hystrix* from the early Portlandian (Jurassic) of Lincoln-shire, England. H. *Nannoceratopsis senex* from the early Alenian (Jurassic) of Dorset, England. *(A from Rasul, 1979; B from Whitney, 1979; C from Damassa, 1979; D from Hutter, 1979; E–H courtesy of R. Davey.)*

The remaining "hystrichospheres," those lacking radiating processes, have been referred to another group, termed the acritarchs (Fig. 4-10A), which, as the name implies, is a catchall for organisms with undetermined affinities. The widespread occurrence and complex morphology of these organisms, as well as their apparent rapid rate of evolution, have made them extremely valuable as a tool for long-range correlations and local biostratigraphic zonation.

LICHENS

Lichens are unique plants that consist of two unrelated components, an alga and a fungus, that live in a close symbiotic relationship. The lichen thallus consists of a fungal component (mycobiont), which may be either an ascomycete or basidiomycete, and an algal component (phycobiont), which may be any of a number of free-living forms, usually a member of Chlorophycophyta. In this symbiotic relationship, the alga gains mechanical protection, increased water relations, reduced desiccation, and an improved nutritional regimen from the mycelium of the fungus. In turn, the fungus gains organic nutrients synthesized by the alga.

Although the thallus organization of most lichens suggests that they would be easily preserved, there are relatively few reports of fossil lichens of any antiquity for which there is little question as to their biological identity. There is, however, one very interesting fossil from the Precambrian of South Africa that appears to have been a lichen. The fossil *Thuchomyces lichenoides* consists of a horizontal thallus with erect columns (up to 5.0 μm high) of tissue terminating in a vegetative diaspore. Surrounding each column is thin membrane. The cortical tissue of the column is constructed of several zones of branched, septate hyphae. Although morphologic remains of the phycobiont were not observed, biochemical evidence (in the form of pentose-hexose ratios) suggests that the fossil was algal in origin. Associated with the lichen was a loose network of hyphae named *Witwateromyces*. This fungus is thought to have been saprophytic because of its association with detrital carbonaceous material. The apparent symbiotic organization of *Thuchomyces* in the Precambrian is interesting in light of one theory that all terrestrial plants are the product of an ancient symbiosis involving a semiaquatic ancestral green alga and an aquatic fungus (Pirozynski and Mallock, 1975).

Chapter 5

Bryophytes

Bryophytes include mosses and their allies, the hornworts and liverworts. Some authors place both groups within a single division, Bryophyta, while others put liverworts and hornworts within another division, Hepatophyta, reserving Bryophyta for the mosses. Some authorities have suggested use of the name Atracheata to avoid confusion and to emphasize that all these plants lack vascular tissue. Studies with living members clearly indicate that two distinct groups exist. However, because many of the features used to separate Bryophyta from Hepatophyta are not easily recognized in fossils, the terms bryophyte and bryophytic will be used here, except in the few instances where assignment to one division or the other is obvious.

The bryophytes, represented by approximately 900 genera and some 24,000 species, do not represent a conspicuous portion of the earth's flora. All are small, with the largest forms rarely exceeding 60.0 cm, and many are microscopic. Living bryophytes are generally terrestrial and can be found in relatively humid environments. None possess special absorbing structures for mineral and water uptake, although some mosses have a specialized cellular conducting strand that is analogous to a vascular system.

Fossil bryophytes can be traced with confidence back to the Carboniferous, and a few have been found in sediments as old as the Devonian. In most instances, bryophyte spores cannot be distinguished from those of other early vascular plants, and it is quite probable that even some of the trilete spores in pre-Devonian sediments are those of bryophytes.

One recently described plant with possible bryophytic affinities is *Tortilicaulis* (Fig. 5-1A and B). The specimens consist of elongate, fusiform to oval bodies, thought to represent sporangia, attached to smooth, stout axes. No spores have been isolated from the sporangia. Morphologically, these late Silurian (Downtonian) fossils from South Wales appear remarkably similar to the modern bryophyte *Pellia*.

One of the oldest plants that morphologically resembles a bryophyte is the Lower Devonian fossil *Sporogonites* (Fig. 5-2). The specimens, originally found in Norway, consist of stalks about 5.0 cm long that terminate in an elongate capsule. Several elongate furrows ornament the base of the sporangium and extend onto the stalk. The sporangium is multilayered, and there is some suggestion that it may contain a central sterile zone (columella). The trilete spores are numerous and range up to 30 μm. Many specimens of *S. exuberans* are preserved with the sporangial stalks in a more or less parallel orientation, suggesting that they were produced from a common thallus; some stalks appear to be attached to an irregular carbonaceous film about 15.0 cm long (Fig. 5-2). Not all stalks bear sporangia, suggesting that they were easily detached or abscised once the spores were mature. Although the compressed nature of the specimens of *Sporogonites* reveals little about the internal organization of the tissues, it appears that vascular elements are lacking, further supporting classification of this plant with the bryophytes.

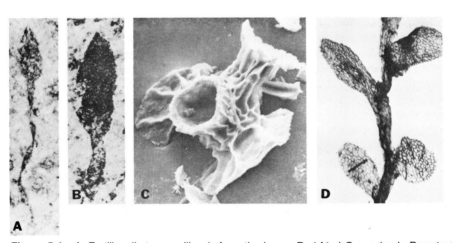

Figure 5-1 *A. Tortilicaulis transwalliensis* from the Lower Red Marl Group (early Downtonian). Small sporangium with twisted stalk. ×12. B. Massive sporangium with reticulate-appearing capsule. ×12. C. *Tetrapteris visensis* extracted from a shale sample collected from the Basement Series of the Carboniferous limestone near Caernarvonshire. ×550. D. Dorsal lobes of the late Jurassic hepatic *Cheirorhiza brittae*. ×15. (*A and B from Edwards, 1979; C from Hibbert, 1967; D from Krassilov, 1973.*)

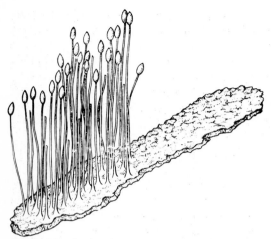

Figure 5-2   Suggested reconstruction of *Sporogonites exuberans. (From Andrews, 1961.)*

Another fossil suggested to have bryophytic affinities is *Tetrapterites,* an unusual spore tetrad isolated from the Lower Carboniferous (Fig. 5-1C). It consists of a noncellular membrane with winglike ridges that superficially resemble the spore tetrads of some hepatics.

Although *Horneophyton* is discussed in detail in Chap. 7, this Devonian plant has been regarded by some as demonstrating bryophytic features (see Fig. 7-6A). These include an avascular cormlike underground organ and columellate sporangium that has been compared to the spore-producing organ of the hornwort *Anthoceros.* A detached bryophytic sporangium also has been reported from the same fossiliferous beds that produced *Horneophyton.* It is elongate and has an apical operculum. However, it has been suggested that this spore capsule probably represents an isolated *Horneophyton lignierii* sporangium.

Several bryophytes described from early Paleozoic (Ordovician) rocks will require more detailed analyses before their biological affinities can be determined for certain. Two of these, *Musciphyton* and *Hepaticaephyton,* from the Ordovician of Poland, may represent extant plant contaminants.

Possibly the earliest record of liverworts (Hepatophyta) is the Upper Devonian (Frasnian) taxon *Pallavicinites* (= *Hepaticites*) from New York State (Fig. 5-3). The specimens consist of compressions preserved in a fine-grained shale with numerous other plant remains. They were removed by a bulk-maceration technique that involved immersing the shale slabs in concentrated hydrofluoric acid for 10 to 24 hours and then floating the thalloid specimens onto microscope slides for examination. Fossil *Pallavicinites devonicus* consists of a simple, two-parted, flattened thallus with a central midrib and marginal lamellae or wings. The thallus is dichotomously branched, and the margin of the wings shows closely spaced teeth (Fig. 5-3C). The rhizomatous portion of the plant

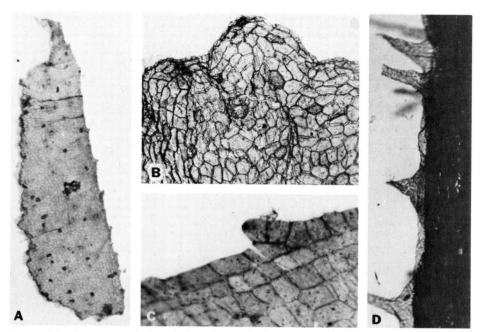

Figure 5-3 *Pallavicinites devonicus.* A. Marginal wing of thallose region of plant showing serrate margin. ×27. B. Apex of thallose portion of plant. ×58. C. Detail of marginal tooth. ×205. D. Detail of rhizoid bases. ×190. *(From Hueber, 1961.)*

consists of elongate parenchymatous cells, some with nonseptate rhizoids. No reproductive structures are known. Numerous species of *Pallavicinites* also have been described from the Carboniferous to the Pleistocene, and they have been compared with such living genera as *Pallavicinia, Metzgeria, Treubia,* and *Fossombronia.*

Muscites plumatus is the generic name applied to a small, leafy shoot preserved as an impression in rocks of the Lower Carboniferous. The axis is covered with helically arranged leaves with clasping bases. Each leaf is about 7.5 mm long and terminates in an elongate acumen. Sex organs, sporophyte capsule, and rhizoids were not present.

Despite the small number of Carboniferous mosses, numerous species have been described from post-Carboniferous sediments, including an extensive assemblage from the Permian of Russia (Neuberg, 1960). *Diettertia* is a pinnately branched dorsiventral gametophyte about 3.0 cm long. The leaves are ovate and two-ranked, attached to the axis along the upper surface, and they are uniseriate with no costae. Although superficially similar to a moss, *D. montanensis* could be assigned to neither an existing leafy liverwort or bryophyte taxon nor a previously described fossil genus. Another Lower Cretaceous bryophyte from central Montana is *Marchantiolites.* One specimen is about 4.0 cm long and contains a prominent midrib in the center of the thallus. On the lower surface are numerous rhizoids, while on the upper surface are air pores surrounded by specialized subsidiary cells. A slightly different air-pore frequency and morphology is present in the Jurassic (Sweden) taxon *M. porosus*. As the generic name suggests, *Marchantiolites* is included in the Marchantiales, principally on the general organization of the air pores, although Lundblad (1954) regards the living species as exhibiting compound pores as opposed to the simple ones found in most of the fossils. *Ricciopsis* is a rosette-shaped thallus from the same deposits, with the four main branches dichotomizing twice. Thalloid forms from the Upper Triassic of South America have been placed in the genus *Marchantites*.

Recently, a well-preserved specimen of *Aulacomnium, A. heterostichoides,* was described from deep-water varved clays (Eocene) of a freshwater lake in British Columbia (Janssens, Horton, and Basinger, 1979). The moss is irregularly branched and contains helically arranged elliptical leaves with multicellular teeth along the upper half of the margin (Fig. 5-4). Cells of the upper laminal surface are regularly isodiametric and unipapillose, while those of the basal surface are rectangular with slightly thicker walls. Based on an analysis of characteristics in existing populations of *Aulacomnium,* the fossil is believed to be most closely related to *A. heterostichum,* a living species found in eastern North America and eastern Asia.

One interesting bryophyte, *Naiadita lanceolata,* was preserved in such numbers and so many different stages of development that a wealth of information about its total biology has been assembled. The most comprehensive and detailed treatment of this bryophyte was carried out by Harris (1938) from Triassic (Rhaetic) specimens collected in Worchestershire and Warwickshire, England. The fossil plant is small (rarely exceeding 3.0 cm) and consists of an unbranched stem with helically arranged lanceolate leaves. Individual leaves are rounded at the apex and generally 1.0 to 5.0 mm long. Near the base of the stem are numerous, unbranched, nonseptate rhizoids. Located along the stem are specialized vegetative-reproductive structures termed gemmae cups. These cups apparently produced oval (about 500 μm in diameter) gemmae, which represent one of the most common components of the *Naiadita* fossiliferous beds. Some specimens possess stem-borne archegonia, which are about 300 μm long and surrounded by a "perianth" of leaflike lobes. Although antheridia are not known, numerous stages in the development of the embryo and sporophyte are preserved. The fossil sporophyte of *N. lanceolata* consists of a short foot, slender pedicle, and bulbous sporangium. The capsules are about 1.2 mm in diameter and contain spores in tetrahedral tetrads. The spores are lens-shaped, with an equatorial flange and minute grana on their surfaces. They are about 100 μm in diameter at the equator, slightly smaller in the proximodistal plane. Haptotypic features are absent.

The morphology of *Naiadita* is similar to that of a typical moss with helical leaves, but the absence of a midrib on the leaves suggests closer affinities to the liverworts. The unicellular nature of the rhizoids is also a liverwort characteristic, as are the spores. In his comprehensive treatment of the genus, Harris (1938)

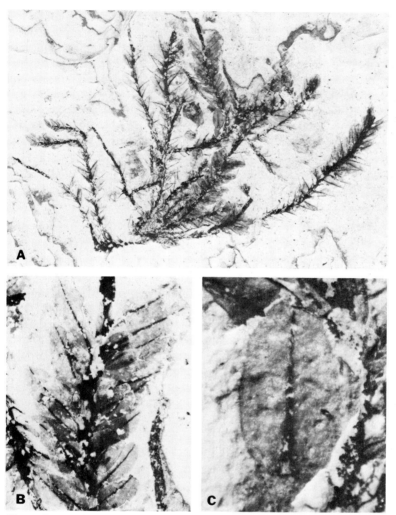

Figure 5-4 *Aulacomnium heterostichoides.* A. Habit. ×5. B. Stem with well-preserved costae. ×20. C. Leaf showing marginal teeth. ×50. *(A from Janssens, Horton, and Basinger, 1979; B and C courtesy of J. Basinger.)*

suggests that *Naiadita* was a submerged aquatic liverwort, possibly related to members of Sphaerocarpales.

Bryophytes have an extensive geologic history (see, for example, the treatments of Lundblad, 1954; Savicz-Lubitzkaja and Abramov, 1959; Neuberg, 1960; Jovet-Ast, 1967). Moreover, the fact that many fossil bryophytes are assigned extant generic names attests to their modern appearance. Almost all fossil bryophytes are represented by vegetative remains of the gametophyte (Fig. 5-1D). With few exceptions, the sporophyte is unknown, and almost no fossil bryophytes are known with identifiable sex organs. There are a number of spores that have been described as bryophytic, but in most instances, these have been recorded as *sporae dispersae* grains, which both limits their taxonomic usefulness and obscures their biological affinities. Thus the fossil record has contributed relatively little to our understanding of the origin and subsequent evolution of bryophytes.

Hornworts and liverworts commonly have been regarded as intermediate morphologic forms associated with the transition from an aquatic to a terrestrial habitat, especially given the relationship between the gametophyte and sporophyte phases in the life cycle. Some workers have suggested that these plants evolved from simple green algae; others have postulated their origin from early vascular plants of the rhyniophyte type through the continual loss of vascular plant features. The mosses also have been linked to green algal ancestors on the basis of the branching filamentous nature of their protonema. Although the fossil record today contributes little toward our understanding of the origin and evolution of the bryophytes, it does indicate that all the major groups of liverworts and mosses were clearly differentiated by the conclusion of the Paleozoic. This early differentiation has led some to speculate that the bryophytes are a polyphyletic group, with the members relatively unchanged to the Recent.

Possibly most interesting is the fact that when the earliest (Devonian) forms are examined, they demonstrate wide-ranging diversity, and this suggests that the group had already undergone division into the major orders by the Devonian. Moreover, according to Schuster (1966), they had already divided into types that superficially resemble some existing families. Schuster goes on to suggest that they originated well before the Devonian, but this cannot be proved because the earliest types are difficult to recognize. For example, it has been suggested that the earliest liverworts consisted of erect radial axes that lacked leaves and possessed relatively little morphologic differentiation.

Chapter 6

The Evolution of Vascular Plants

It is the presence of green vegetation on the surface of the earth that makes it a pleasant and interesting place in which to live. Frequently, we take this green mantle for granted, forgetting that for most of earth history the landscape was barren. Undoubtedly, algae and algallike organisms must have grown in terrestrial habitats before true land plants evolved, but surely they must not have had the same effects on the appearance of the earth as do true land plants. In the following discussion, the term land plants refers to plants with woody conducting cylinders, the so-called vascular plants. In older systems of classification, vascular plants were placed in a formal division, called Tracheophyta, and the various groups of vascular plants were included in subdivisions within Tracheophyta. As with algae and fungi, however, it appears more appropriate to consider Tracheophyta as an artificial category and to elevate what had been subdivisions to major divisions.

One of the unsolved problems in the history of plant life on earth concerns the long interval between the appearance of green photosynthetic organisms and the evolution of vascular land plants. There is evidence that autotrophic organisms existed 3 billion years ago or earlier. Plants with definite conducting systems occurred first in the late Silurian, a little over 400 million years ago. Why did they not appear earlier, and what was the stimulus that resulted in their appearance? Were there earlier, unsuccessful stages in the evolution of land plants that were not at all like those that were successful? These are some of the unanswered questions with which paleobotanists deal.

One rather recent suggestion is that vascular plants resulted from a symbiotic relationship between algae and fungi (not quite like that found in lichens, but perhaps along analogous lines) and that many millions of years passed after the appearance of autotrophic organisms before such a fortuitous association came about. There is no sound proof for this theory, and very few botanists take it seriously.

I'll say,

Even though we do not understand the events that led to the evolution of vascular land plants, there are a number of points that may be discussed in an attempt to understand at least some of the processes. We know, for example, that before vascular land plants appeared there were many algal groups in existence. Moreover, because any new group must have originated from some preexisting group, the obvious place to look for the ancestral source of vascular plants is among the algae. The logical thing to do is to examine the algal group that has the most features in common with land plants. Land plants, first of all, are typically green, containing chlorophyll pigments in specialized structures called plastids. Chlorophyll a and b are the types of photosynthetic pigments normally found in land plants. In addition, there are yellowish and orange pigments, xanthophylls and carotenes. The normal photosynthate is a carbohydrate, starch. Among known algae, only the Clorophycophyta have similar pigmentation and metabolism.

As will be discussed later in this chapter, sexual reproduction in land plants involves fusion of two dissimilar gametes. A small sperm cell unites with a larger, nonmotile egg cell. This type of sexual reproduction involving a sperm and an egg is termed oogamy. It would be logical to assume that the algal group that gave rise to land plants also was oogamous. Several algal groups sexually reproduce in such a fashion, so obviously, the type of reproduction in itself cannot be used to determine ancestry. The Chlorophycophyta show a wide range of gamete types in sexual reproduction; for example, in some, the gametes are identical and indistinguishable, and in one, separate and distinct sperm and egg cells are involved. Therefore, in addition to possessing the "proper" kinds of pigments, this plant group also contains at least some organisms with the "proper" type of reproduction.

Moreover, vascular plants reveal an interesting and regular alternation between two distinct phases of the life cycle. One phase has the diploid ($2n$) chromosome condition and produces spores, each with the haploid (n) chromosome condition. Each spore subsequently germinates to produce a small multicellular structure that bears gametes. These gametes, of course, also have the haploid chromosome condition, and when two of them fuse, the diploid condition is restored in the resulting cell, the zygote. Germination of the zygote results in the development of another diploid, spore-bearing phase. Green algae show a number of different types of life cycles, some of which are not at all like that just outlined for vascular land plants. However, such a two-way alternation does occur in many Chlorophycophyta.

Finally, land plants characteristically have a body plan that is three-dimensional and bulky. This is not the case for a large number of algae, which are often slender filaments formed by cell divisions in a single plane. Among the known groups of algae, the brown algae, Phaeophycophyta, are the most massive, and some brown algae have body types that closely approximate land-plant body structures. From a structural standpoint, the brown algae would be the most likely candidates for land-plant ancestors. Chemically and metabolically, however, there is a significant difference between vascular land plants and Phaeophycophyta. Although the majority of green algae do not have body plans that even approach those of land plants, there are some forms, such as the genus *Fritschiella,* that are constructed on the plan of a three-dimensional branching structure. It should be pointed out that although *Fritschiella* was at one time considered closely related to primitive land plants, recent biochemical and, especially, ultrastructural evidence suggests that it was probably not directly involved in the transition to vascular land plants. Two members of the Clorophycophyta, however, that may be related to land plants on the basis of similarities in mitosis and cytokinesis and in their motile cells are *Coleochaete* and *Chara.* One interesting structural feature of *Chara* is the presence of an apical cell that is similar to that found in many vascular plants.

Among the living green algae there is not one known taxon that has all the chemical, structural, and reproductive features essential to an ancestor of land plants. However, each of these necessary features is found within the division. Conceivably, therefore, the group within the green algae that may have given rise to land plants is no longer in existence.

The transition from an aquatic habitat to life on land involves a number of major modifications. The first consideration that comes to mind is the problem of obtaining and conserving water. An aquatic alga is surrounded by water, and any of the water utilized by the plant enters the plant through diffusion into the cells directly interfaced with the water. A plant growing on land is not surrounded by water, and the nearest source of water is the soil. Thus, early land plants had to evolve a system whereby water could be absorbed from the soil. This absorbing system most likely involved part of the branching plant body in the earliest vascular plants, but later plants developed a specialized root system, probably derived from the subterranean branching system of earlier forms.

Once water is within the root system, it must then be transported to aerial parts of the plant. Conceivably this process could be accomplished by diffusion from cell to cell in small plants, but such a system would not provide enough water for the ultimate parts of larger plants. Early in their evolution, vascular land plants formed a specialized conducting system, a system that involves elongated, nonliving cells that conduct water and minerals from lower parts of the plant to the tips. This water- and mineral-conducting tissue is called xylem. Because food was synthesized in the portion of the plant exposed to the air and light, and not in the underground absorbing system, some foods had to be transported to these other areas, and this was accomplished by a tissue called phloem, which is in close proximity to the xylem. As plants became progressively more adapted to the aerial environment, they increased in size, and the size increase was accompanied by an elaboration of the conducting system. Thus land plants in excess of 100 m in height (e.g., redwoods) would not have been possible without an efficient means of transporting water and minerals from the ground to the very uppermost branch tips.

The absorption and conduction of water and minerals were important evolutionary steps, but there is another consideration as well. Establishment of plants from an aquatic environment to a dry, aerial one was not simply a matter of an abrupt change. If an alga is removed from its aquatic environment, it becomes desiccated within a short time, because water evaporates from its surface. To be successful on land, plants had to evolve a system whereby water was kept from evaporating, or if evaporation did take place, it had to be controlled. The development of a thin, waxy waterproofing layer, the cuticle, kept water loss through evaporation to a minimum. Consequently, all parts of land plants that are exposed to the air at some time in the life cycle are covered with this thin layer of cuticle.

Success on land is also, to a large extent, a reflection of how successful a plant is in its reproduction. To understand this better, a schematic life cycle representative of all vascular plants will be discussed. There are, of course, individual deviations from this generalized scheme, but these are unusual or atypical.

The dominant part of the life cycle of all vascular plants is composed of cells with the diploid (2n) chromosome number. This is the most conspicuous phase of the plant life cycle and is represented by such familiar plant forms as an oak tree, a fern plant, a sunflower, or a pine tree. Because the diploid plant phase is the one in which spores are produced, the plant is called a sporophyte. A plant in this phase of the life cycle typically has a specialized conducting system composed of xylem and phloem, and the plant's aerial portions are covered with cuticle. At some point in this diploid phase, the plant develops specialized structures, called sporangia (singular, sporangium), in which spores are produced. At the time of spore formation, the potential spore-producing cells, which are diploid, undergo reduction division (meiosis), which results in a reduction of the number of chromosomes to the haploid (n) number. Each diploid spore-producing cell (sporocyte) produces four haploid spores. In the normal course of events, each spore germinates to produce a multicellular haploid plant body. This haploid phase is not conspicuous; in fact, it is not even visible in some plants without dissection of the sporophyte. In the haploid phase, vascular plants produce sex cells, or gametes, which are always dissimilar, represented by larger egg cells and smaller sperm cells. Because a plant in the haploid phase produces gametes, it is called a gametophyte. Fusion of an egg cell and sperm cell result in a diploid zygote, the initiation of the next sporophyte phase. Then the entire life cycle is repeated. Alternation of these two cytologic phases often has been referred to as alternation of generations. A more appropriate expression would be alternation of cytologic phases, because both these phases, the sporophyte phase and the gametophyte phase, often occur in the same plant; there really are no "generations" involved at all.

Botanists have long disagreed about the particulars of the life cycle of the algal group that presumably gave rise to vascular land plants. One school feels the ancestral green alga was haploid throughout its entire life cycle. The haploid plant produced gametes, eggs and sperm. These, of course, also were haploid, and fusion of egg and sperm produced a diploid cell, the zygote. But the first division of the zygote was assumed to be meiotic; i.e., four haploid cells (spores) were produced directly from the division of the zygote. Thus the only diploid portion of the life cycle was the single-celled zygote. A subsequent evolutionary change would be a delay of meiosis for a time, with the zygote dividing mitotically to produce a small diploid plant body. The meiotic division of these diploid cells would produce a larger number of haploid spores. As meiosis was delayed longer and longer, a progressively larger diploid plant body was built up. After a certain size was attained, all the cells were not involved in spore production, but only certain ones. At this stage in the evolution of land plants there was a "division of labor," with the rest of the diploid cells assuming other functions (e.g., absorption, photosynthesis, conduction, etc.). Spore formation was confined to certain restricted regions of the plant. For reasons that will be outlined later in this chapter, the diploid phase that produced spores was particularly well-adapted to a land environment, and this was the phase that assumed greater dominance in the life cycle. This theory, that the sporophyte phase originally was derived from an essentially haploid life cycle (except for one cell), is called the antithetic, or interpolation theory, and it implies that the diploid and haploid phases were quite different in origin.

An opposing view is that the ancestral algal group already alternated haploid and diploid phases and the plants of these phases were essentially similar in size and structure. After migration to land, the sporophyte phase seemed to be the better adapted and became the dominant part of the life cycle, while the haploid gametophyte phase, given the restrictions imposed by a land environment, became the less significant phase. This theory is called the homologous, or transformation theory of alternation of phases. In a sense, both might be correct in that even if the ancestral algal group did have homologous alternating phases, this condition probably was not the original one in that group and must have derived from some other condition—most probably one with a predominantly haploid life cycle.

Whichever theory is correct, both allow for subsequent patterns of evolution. Those supporting the antithetic theory suggest that the diploid phase seemed to be better adapted to the land than the haploid phase; thus it quickly overtook the haploid phase in size and differentiation, the haploid phase subsequently becoming reduced. Those proposing the homologous theory feel that although both phases were identical originally, environmental influences on each of the phases differed, and as a result, subsequent development of each of the phases went in different directions.

How is the diploid phase better adapted to the terrestrial habit? Although the life cycle of the earliest vascular plants is not known, from what we know about the most primitive of existing vascular plants, it appears that water is necessary for fertilization. Sperm cells of primitive vascular plants are motile (probably a retention of an algal characteristic) and cannot reach the egg without the presence of water. The water may be in the form of a film of dew, a swampy environment, or splashing raindrops. Whatever the source, water is essential to fertilization. After fertilization and the development of a diploid plant body, spores are produced, and they are released and carried away by air currents. Even though a smaller proportion of the diploid plant body is taken over for spore production, the absolute number of spores is increased. These spores are distributed randomly over wide areas. Each spore has the ability to germinate and produce a haploid gametophyte. Many spores will land in places that are appropriate for germination, but conditions may not be right at any given moment for sperm cells to swim to egg cells on their release. So the life cycle may be abruptly terminated at that point. However, for the spores that have landed in places that are suitable for fertilization, the life cycle continues from there. The point is, the larger the number of spores produced, the greater the opportunity for many of them to settle in places suitable for fertilization after the gametes are formed.

Ancestral algae produced spores that were motile in an aqueous environment; land-plant sporophytes produce spores that resist desiccation and can be transported great distances by wind. It will be seen in later chapters that the sporophyte phase became so dominant in vascular land plants that the gametophyte often became completely dependent on the sporophyte for its survival. It also will become apparent that more highly specialized vascular plants no longer depend on water as a medium for fertilization.

In summary, then, whether we are speaking of a duckweed, a cycad, a clubmoss, a lily, or a sunflower, each has basically the same patterns in its life cycle: a dominant, diploid sporophyte with sporangia producing spores as a result of meiosis. Each spore germinates to produce a haploid gamete-bearing gametophyte, and the gametes are of two types, egg and sperm. Fusion of two such gametes reconstitutes the diploid phase and the new sporophyte.

AN INTRODUCTION TO VASCULAR PLANT STRUCTURE

At this point it might be useful to examine the anatomy of vascular plants. Because of rigid, resistant conducting tissues and waterproofing cuticle, vascular plants are much more frequently found fossilized than are algae, fungi, and bryophytes. Moreover, the specialized conducting system makes it possible for vascular plants to reach a much greater size than do most nonvascular plants.

The conducting cylinder in the stem or root of a vascular plant is called a stele. In the center of the stele there may or may not be an area of soft storage tissue (usually parenchyma cells) called the pith (see Fig. 6-2C). Around the pith, when present, or in the very center of the axis, when pith is lacking, is the xylem, or wood. Xylem functions in the conduction of water and dissolved minerals. The actual conducting cells of the xylem are usually elongated axially, are nonliving when functional, and have walls that are heavily impregnated with an organic compound called lignin. In vascular plants, growth in length occurs as a result of division and elongation of cells produced at the tips of axes. The first-formed xylem, produced as a result of maturation of cells formed by the growing tips, is called primary xylem. The amount of primary xylem in a stem or root is generally quite small, and in many of the primitive vascular plants, the only xylem present is primary xylem. In stems, the principal food-conducting tissue, the phloem, surrounds the xylem. Phloem produced by the maturation of cells formed by the growing apex is called primary phloem. In stems that increase in diameter as they get older, additional xylem and phloem are produced (indeed, in a large tree, the principal tissue is xylem) by a layer of actively dividing cells located between the primary xylem and primary phloem. This layer, the vascular cambium, produces secondary xylem by divisions on its inner face and secondary phloem by divisions on its outer face (see Fig. 6-4A). The cells of the vascular cambium also divide radially so that the circumferential dimension of the tissue is maintained. To produce a new secondary xylem cell, a cell of the vascular cambium divides to produce two cells, one outside the other (with respect to the center of the stem). The inner one eventually matures into a xylem cell, and the outer one retains its ability to divide. Another division of the residual vascular cambium cell produces two, and again, in the case of xylem, the inner one matures into a xylem cell. After another division of a vascular cambium cell, the outer cell may mature into a phloem cell, and the inner one retains its ability to divide. It is in this manner that both additional xylem and phloem cells are produced by the same vascular cambium.

Roots generally have a similar structure. However, in roots, the primary xylem in the center of the stele very often has ridges and furrows, with the primary phloem situated in the furrows (Fig. 6-1A). Through activity of the vascular cambium in the root, additional xylem and phloem are produced, and eventually the xylem and phloem have a smooth cylindrical outline. In roots, and in stems of certain primitive plants, there is a thin layer of tissue outside the phloem called the pericycle, and immediately outside the pericycle is a single layer of cells called the endodermis (Fig. 6-1B). The endodermis may be recognized by characteristic thickenings (casparian strips) on some of its walls. A stele includes all tissue within the endodermis and sometimes even the endodermis itself.

In a young stem or root, there is a cortex surrounding the stele. Cortex is a storage tissue, although some of the peripheral cells of the cortex in young stems may be photosynthetic and synthesize carbohydrates. In addition, the periphery of the cortex in certain stems may contain strengthening cells. On the outside of all of this is a single layer of cells, the epidermis.

As a stem gets older, some of the cells in the outer cortex undergo dedifferentiation and produce an actively dividing layer of cells, the cork cambium, which forms cork, or phellem, cells on its outer face and, at times, some loosely arranged cells on its inner face (phelloderm). Cork, cork cambium, and phelloderm (when present) are spoken of collectively as the periderm (see Fig. 8-29B). As the stem increases in diameter, the epidermis is ruptured, and

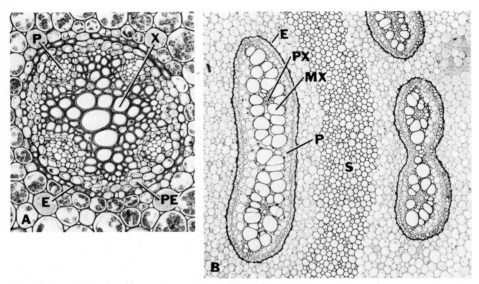

Figure 6-1   A. Transverse section of the stele of a *Ranunculus* root showing the position of the xylem (X), phloem (P), endodermis (E), and pericycle (PE). ×150. B. Transverse section through the rhizome of the fern *Pteridium* showing a medullary strand *(left)* separated from a meristele *(right)* by a sclerenchyma (S) band. E = endodermis, PX = protoxylem, MX = metaxylem, P = phloem. ×31.

eventually the periderm becomes the outer protective layer. A similar phenomenon occurs in roots with secondary development, except that the cork cambium is usually initiated in the pericycle.

The configuration of the stele may vary in different groups of plants (Fig. 6-2B and D), and progressive complexity is evident in the fossil record. The simplest type of stele is one in which pith is lacking and xylem forms a solid core in the center. Such a stele is called a protostele. Stems of many primitive plants and most roots are protostelic. A haplostele is a kind of protostele in which the xylem outline is cylindrical. In certain protosteles, the xylem, as seen in a transverse section, has armlike projections (these would be ridges in three-dimensional aspect), and the phloem occurs in the furrows. This type of protostele is called an actinostele (see Fig. 8-4). Still another kind of prostostele is one in which the xylem shows many lobes in cross section, with phloem interrupting the xylem. In cross section it appears as if the xylem is in the form of separate plates, but a three-dimensional view indicates that each of these "plates" is connected to others. This type of protostele is called a plectostele (Fig. 6-2A).

Most plants, however, do contain pith. In some of these, the xylem and phloem form a continuous cylinder around the pith. The term siphonostele is used to describe such a stele. When phloem is both on the outside and the inside of the xylem, the siphonostele is amphiphloic or termed a solenostele (Fig. 6-2D); an ectophloic siphonostele has phloem only on the outside of the xylem.

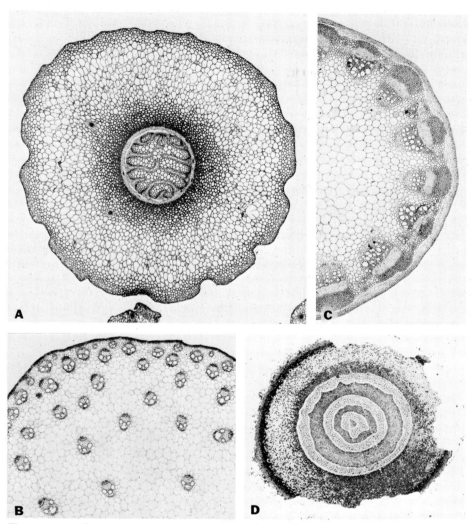

Figure 6-2 A. Transverse section of *Lycopodium* stem. ×25. B. Transverse section of *Zea mays* (maize) stem. ×22. C. Transverse section of a young stem of *Helianthus*. ×24. D. Transverse section of the solenostele of the fern *Matonia* showing three concentric, amphiphloic cylinders of vascular tissue. ×7.

Stem xylem and phloem are continuous with the xylem and phloem of lateral appendages. If one were to follow a series of cross sections in a stem from a level below that of leaf attachment to one above leaf attachment, it would appear as if portions of the xylem and phloem were pinching off from the stele and interrupting the siphonostelic cylinder. Moreover, the portion of conducting tissue that appears to have separated from the stele extends upward and outward into the base of the leaf. Such an interruption of the xylem and phloem is called a leaf gap, but it is not actually a space, as the name suggests. Instead, there is continuity of tissue between pith and cortex through this interruption. If one examines higher levels in the plant, one will notice that the edges of the "gap" appear to get closer together, and if one goes still higher, there is no interruption at all. In many stems, several to many leaf gaps can be seen in a single transverse section, so that the stele appears to be dissected into several segments. Such a dissected siphonostele is called a dictyostele (Fig. 6-1B).

The xylem and phloem of many plants are arranged in distinct strands that are separated by other tissue. In transverse section, such a stele would have the appearance of a dictyostele, in that the cylinder seems dissected, but this configuration is not related to position of leaf attachment, nor are the apparent separations due to leaf gaps. This kind of stele is called a eustele.

These types of steles are all the result of activity at the growing tip of an axis. At the very tip of a shoot or root, all the cells are more or less uniform. They are small, thin-walled, isodiametric, and undergoing divisions. A short distance behind the growing tip, some of the cells are longer and narrower than surrounding ones. These long and narrow cells are not yet mature, but they represent cells that will differentiate into xylem and phloem cells. These cells, called procambium, are arranged in a definite pattern, and this pattern influences the type of stele that will develop within an axis. For example, if the procambium is in the form of a solid cylinder, the stele will be a protostele. Sometimes the procambium is arranged in a series of distinct strands arranged in a cylinder, and such a configuration will produce a eustele.

Although individual procambium cells mature into xylem and phloem cells, their differentiation is not simultaneous, nor do all the cells in the xylem and phloem look alike. Generally the first-formed xylem cells (protoxylem) are much smaller than the later-formed xylem cells (metaxylem). When the protoxylem is situated toward the outside of the stem and metaxylem is toward the center (there is a centripetal sequence of development), the xylem is spoken of as being exarch (Fig. 6-2A). In other words, in exarch xylem, the protoxylem is outermost and the metaxylem is more toward the center of the stem or root. Exarchy is found in many primitive plants and in most roots. In another sequence of xylem maturation, the metaxylem develops both toward the outside and toward the inside of the protoxylem (the sequence of development is centrifugal and centripetal). This condition is termed mesarchy and is found in many ferns. When the protoxylem is innermost and the metaxylem develops in a centrifugal direction, the condition is called endarchy. Often the term centrarch (see Fig. 7-3A) is used if the stele has no pith and the protoxylem occurs in the very center of a solid xylem cylinder.

These various primary xylem configurations can be seen in many fossils, and often it is useful to be familiar with this information when attempting to determine relationships among groups. While it is not possible to observe the actual sequence of maturation in fossils, it is possible, as will be demonstrated in subsequent chapters, to infer what the sequence actually was.

One reason why xylem elements are so frequently preserved in fossil plants is that the primary cellulose wall is often backed by a thick secondary wall composed largely of cellulose and lignin. This secondary wall can be deposited in a variety of configurations. Often the protoxylem has a wall that is mostly primary. Secondary wall material is deposited by the cell cytoplasm on the inside of the primary wall in the form of rings. These rings are called annular thickenings (Fig. 6-3A). Annular xylem elements are often stretched in length because the protoxylem elements mature before the rest of the cells in the axis. When the protoxylem matures just after the annular elements, the secondary thickenings may form a helix (Fig. 6-3B) on the inside of the primary wall. Such helical thickenings also may be stretched to some extent.

The metaxylem of many vascular plants has ladderlike secondary thickenings. Along the edges of a given wall of an elongated xylem element are linear

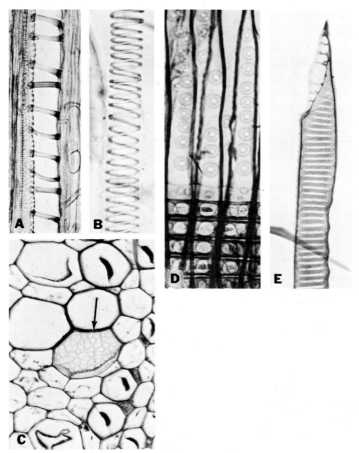

Figure 6-3 A. Annular secondary wall thickening *(Zea mays).* ×300. B. Helical wall thickening *(Helianthus).* ×275. C. Phloem of *Cucurbita* showing sieve plate *(arrow).* ×300. D. Circular bordered pits on the radial wall of *Pinus* tracheids. ×375. E. Scalariform pitted vessel of *Magnolia.* ×275.

strips of lignin connected by horizontal bars of lignin. The ladder analogy is quite striking. These characteristic thickenings are called scalariform thickenings. The ladderlike thickenings of adjacent walls are continuous, so the interior angles of the xylem elements possess solid lignin. Obviously this type of xylem cannot stretch (lignin is much more rigid than cellulose).

Structures called bordered pits (Fig. 6-3D) can be found in later metaxylem elements as well as in the secondary xylem of most existing woody plants. In these cells, most of the wall is covered with lignin and in certain places the secondary thickening is raised away from the primary wall (actually projecting into the cell cavity) forming dome-shaped structures, each with an opening at the tip. Adjacent xylem elements usually have these dome-shaped structures at the same spot, so one dome projects into one cell cavity and a corresponding dome projects into the cavity of the next cell.

Up to this point, only the nonliving conducting cells of the xylem have been discussed. Actually, xylem is a very complex tissue, often with several kinds of cells. The principal conducting cells are generally elongated axially, and the basic type of conducting cell is spindle-shaped, quite long, and tapered at the ends. This type of cell is called a tracheid. Tracheids are the predominant water- and mineral-conducting elements of the most primitive kinds of vascular plants. Tracheids can have annular (Fig. 6-3A), helical (Fig. 6-3B), or scalariform thickenings or bordered pits (Fig. 6-4D). A more specialized kind of conducting element is found in most flowering plants and in a few other groups of vascular plants. These conducting elements are lined up with adjacent elements end to end. Where one element meets an adjacent one, there is an actual perforation, so that, in essence, a continuous tube is formed. An analogy would be to compare each of these elements to drain tiles. Each element is called a vessel element, and the tube is a vessel. Unlike a tracheid, a vessel is composed of many cells. Vessel elements may have annular, helical, or scalariform (Fig. 6-3E) thickenings or bordered pits. They may be found in both primary and secondary xylem. Some kinds of secondary xylem have other elements, also elongated axially. These are thick-walled fibers that contribute to the rigidity of wood. In addition, there can be some living cells that elongate in the same direction, the xylem parenchyma cells.

Extending at right angles to these axially aligned cells, from the center of the stem outward, are other kinds of cells comprising vascular rays (Fig. 6-4C). Usually these rays are more than one cell in height and from one to many cells in thickness. The actual cells making up a xylem ray are generally elongated (at right angles to a tracheid) and most often composed of living cells (parenchyma). Certain kinds of woods have additional elements, but these are specialized and will not be considered here.

Because xylem is such a complex tissue, and because various component elements extend in different directions, to examine xylem microscopically it is necessary to use more than one plane of section. Usually three sections are made. A cross, or transverse section (Fig. 6-4A) is one made at right angles to the growing axis of a stem or root. The section exposed when one saws a tree

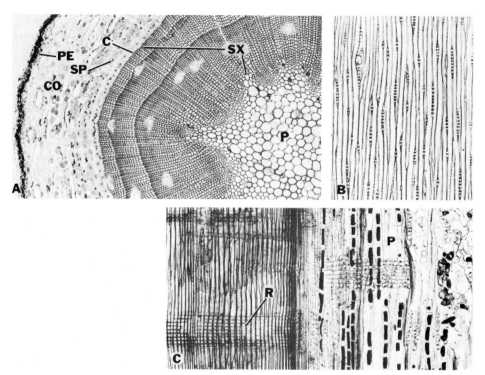

Figure 6-4 A. Transverse section of *Pinus* stem showing pith (P), secondary xylem (SX), cambium (C), secondary phloem (SP), cortex (CO), and periderm (PE). ×50. B. Tangential section of *Pinus* wood with uniseriate rays. ×50. C. Radial section of *Pinus* stem showing vascular rays (R) and phloem (P). ×50.

down is a cross section. A longitudinal, or radial section, one made at right angles to the cross section, is cut along a radius of a tree or root (Fig. 6-4C). The third plane employed in studying xylem is also a longitudinal section, but the cut is made at right angles to a radius (but not along another radius). This section is called a tangential section (Fig. 6-4B). One can also picture it as a section made parallel with a plane that is tangent to the surface of the tree (but not along a radius). A cross, or transverse section reveals the tracheids, fibers, and vessels as squares, rectangles, polygons, or circles. One would have no idea from such a section of the linear extent of these elements. Similarly, the xylem parenchyma cells appear as polygonal structures. A vascular ray, however, appears as a linear series of cells, one or more cells in width. The lengths of the component rays cells can be determined from this section.

In a radial section, tracheids and fibers appear as greatly elongated cells with tapered end walls. The pattern of secondary wall deposition can be discerned from such a section. Vessels are revealed as elongated series of cells, one above the other, with perforations where the end walls meet. In some woods, it is also possible to see that vessel end walls are oblique, and the vessel elements are relatively narrow. Other, more specialized woods have shorter, squatter vessel elements, with end walls more or less at right angles to the axis of the stem or root. Xylem parenchyma cells, which are long and brick-shaped, appear as axially elongated rectangles. Because vascular rays extend along radii, because they are many cells long (from the inside of the axis to the outside), and because they are generally more than one cell in height, a radial section of a vascular ray looks like the face of a brick wall that is many bricks (or cells) long and several bricks (cells) high. From this view, we get no idea of the number of cells that make up the thickness of the ray (or, to continue the analogy, how thick the brick wall is).

In a tangential section of secondary xylem, the tracheids, fibers, vessels, and xylem parenchyma all look more or less as they do in radial section. However, if the vascular ray is sectioned at right angles to its length, it is possible to see the number of cells in height (Fig. 6-4B) and the number of cells in thickness. In a sense, it is like viewing the end of a brick wall. We can determine the height and thickness of the wall, but not the length. In the discussion of vascular plants, there will be considerable opportunity to examine xylem in each of these three sections.

Phloem, the tissue outside the xylem, is also a complex tissue and should be studied from three planes of section as well. In most vascular plants that have tracheids as the principal water- and mineral-conducting tissue in the xylem, there are corresponding food-conducting cells in the phloem. These cells, called sieve elements, are long, narrow, and tapered at the ends. The walls evidence conspicuous thin areas, sometimes circular, other times elliptical, and still other times attaining polygonal outlines because of crowding with adjacent areas. The adjacent areas are called sieve areas (Fig. 6-3C). These thinner areas are actually perforated by strands of cytoplasm that pass from one sieve element to the next.

A more specialized system of conducting elements in the phloem involves counterparts of the xylem vessels. Most angiosperms have sieve tubes, composed of axial series of sieve-tube elements. Where the end wall of one sieve-tube element abuts the end wall of the sieve-tube element next in line, there is generally a sieve plate, composed of a few sieve areas. More primitive sieve-tube elements are long and narrow, with oblique end walls that generally possess more than one sieve area. Sometimes additional sieve areas appear on the lateral walls, but they are not actually perforated and may represent vestigial, nonfunctional sieve areas. More specialized sieve-tube elements are shorter and squatter, with end walls at right angles to the long axis of the sieve-tube element. Each end wall has a single, large sieve area (Fig. 6-3C).

In addition, the phloem of some plants contains other kinds of cells, including rays (these are continuous with the vascular rays in the xylem), fibers, and parenchyma cells. Because sieve tube elements lack nuclei when they are functional and conducting, it is assumed that narrow, nucleated adjacent cells, called companion cells, assume the function of controlling certain of the metabolic activities of the sieve-tube elements.

Phloem functions in other ways besides food conduction. In certain plants, fibers in the phloem contribute to the rigidity of the stem. Another function involves formation of the cork cambium. It was mentioned earlier that the source of the cork cambium is generally the outer part of the cortex in stems and the pericycle in roots. However, the cork, or phellem, is nonliving, and in many woody plants it ruptures as it increases in diameter. Newer cork cambia are then formed farther within the stem cortex, and the addition of more new cork cambia eventually produces the rough "bark" we see on the surfaces of old trees. Eventually, however, there is no more cortex from which new cork cambia can arise. When this happens, the living cells of the secondary phloem become dedifferentiated and form new layers of cork cambium farther in the stem. Because the vascular cambium continually produces more phloem, there will always be a source of living cells from which new cork cambia may be produced.

Obviously, all facets of the internal structure of plants cannot be covered in this brief summary. Interested students can find more details in a good general botany textbook or in a volume devoted exclusively to plant anatomy. Three excellent books are *Plant Anatomy,* 2d ed. (K. Esau, 1965), *Anatomy of Seed Plants,* 2d ed. (K. Esau, 1977), and *Plant Anatomy* (A. Fahn, 1967).

Chapter 7

Early Vascular Plants

Many researchers have speculated as to how and when plants with vascular tissue first made an appearance on land. It is generally assumed that the progenitors of vascular plants are included among the green algae, an assumption based entirely on comparative studies with living plants of both groups. Such features as the quantity and quality of the pigments and stored foods, the ultrastructural features of the cell wall, biochemical pathways, and certain aspects of sexual reproduction are often cited as features shared by certain green algae (Chlorophycophyta) and plants with vascular tissue. Despite an extensive record of certain groups, fossil algae have played a relatively minor role in explicating the transition from aquatic to terrestrial habitat. In the preceding chapter, some of the changes that had to take place in the evolution of vascular plants were considered. Although fossils demonstrating transitional phases in structure and morphology are rare, the very earliest vascular plants and their geologic position indirectly support such a sequence of evolutionary modifications.

For some time, most paleobotanists have regarded the Devonian Period as the time when this transition occurred. Others have presented evidence of vascular plants in strata as old as the Cambrian. However, some of these pre-Devonian fossils have subsequently been demonstrated to be the remains of nonvascular plants, and in other instances, reinterpretation of the stratigraphy of the fossil-bearing strata has corrected some erroneous reports regarding age. For example, for some time, the lycopod *Baragwanathia* was regarded as one of the earliest vascular plants because it occurred in the Upper Silurian deposits of Australia. It was later reported, however, that although *Baragwanathia* is in fact a bona fide vascular plant, the graptolites used to date the fossiliferous beds in which it was found were not accurately identified. Most now regard *Baragwanathia* as a vascular plant of the Lower Devonian.

A recent study describing a number of isolated plant parts from early Silurian (Llandoverian) deposits provides some interesting information about plant structures that may be interpreted as transitional between nonvascular and vascular plants. The fossils consist of megascopic compressions 6.0 mm wide and up to 60.0 mm long. Upon acid maceration, these specimens reveal a series of tubes, some of which are up to 200 μm long and 11 to 32 μm in diameter. The end of each tube tapers to a thin imperforate wall, with the inside ornamented by annular to helical thickenings. In addition, the macerates contained unbanded smaller tubes and two types of membranous cellular sheets that consist of large uniform cells and smaller, irregularly shaped cells. Several subcircular trilete spores and a number of tetrads and alete spores also were encountered. The banded tubes described from these sediments appear superficially similar to the annular thickenings of early vascular plant tracheids. The one major distinction between tracheids and the banded tubes concerns the end walls. Vascular plant tracheids have end walls that are tapered and overlap, whereas the Silurian banded tubes have end walls that vary from conically tapered to bluntly rounded. It is not known how the tubes fit together, but if they interlocked, their organization would represent a transitional status not far removed from the overlapping end walls of vascular plant tracheids. Several early plants, such as *Prototaxites, Nematothallus,* and *Protosalvinia* were discussed in Chap. 4, and the banded tubes, cuticle fragments, and trilete spores from the Silurian of Virginia may represent a similar type of plant organization. Such plants may have existed in terrestrial habitats throughout the Silurian and into the Devonian. They may represent one of several major groups that invaded the land through evolution of such features as conducting tubes, cuticle, and trilete spores, but later gave way to better-adapted vascular plants. Despite the fact that these fossils do not provide knowledge of the entire plant body, they do make clear certain characteristics that may relate directly to early vascular plants. Whether the banded tubes represent a structural cell type that parallels the evolution of the tracheid or a cell type from which tracheids have evolved can only be speculated upon at this time.

Evidence for the existence of pre-Devonian vascular plants has not come from megafossils alone, but from microfossils as well. Spores with apparent trilete sutures have been reported from some Precambrian sediments. Isolated trilete spores are probably not good indicators of the existence of vascular plants without some evidence of vascular tissue, stomata, and cuticle. Sporopollenin, the carotenoid ester that comprises the walls of pollen grains and spores and is responsible for the persistence of these structures in the fossil record, is also a component of some algal cells. In addition, triletelike marks can be produced by some algae, and they are also common on bryophyte spores. At the present time, there is no reliable method of distinguishing the spore of a bryophyte from one produced by a vascular plant. The existence of trilete spores (Fig. 7-1B) in sediments that predate bona fide vascular-plant remains but are traceable to deposits with vascular-plant megafossils has been used to support the concept that the geologically earlier spores were produced by vascular plants. A critical examination of all pre-Devonian spore types, including size, ornamentation, and morphologic type, suggests that the rate of diversification parallels that of vascular plants. These data could mean that the first vascular plants became established close to the Middle Silurian (Wenlockian).

Not everyone is in agreement regarding the stratigraphic position of the oldest vascular plants. As is often the case in paleobiology one must work with a minute fragment of the total population of organisms that lived at any particular time. With reference to early vascular plants, it is highly probable that the evolutionary process occurred among several groups and at several different times. Although the search for early vascular plants is important, what is more important is an understanding of the evolutionary level of the organs, tissue systems, and reproductive processes of these plants. The remainder of this chapter is directed toward this end.

Our understanding of early vascular plants has an interesting history that, to a large degree, has greatly influenced many areas of paleobotany. In 1859, the Canadian geologist and paleobotanist Sir J. William Dawson (Fig. 7-1A) published a report on a Devonian vascular plant collected from the Gaspé region of Nova Scotia. His reconstruction showed a rhizome bearing upright, leafless, dichotomizing axes, to which were attached pairs of sporangia. Dawson named this interesting plant *Psilophyton princeps*. However, because the plant looked so unusual, and probably because of its age, Dawson's scientific colleagues ignored the discovery. Several years later, he described some additional

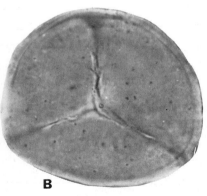

Figure 7-1   A. Sir John William Dawson. B. Proximal view of trilete Silurian spore of the *Ambitosporites* type from Gotland, Sweden. ×1300. *(A from Taxon, 1974; B courtesy of J. Gray.)*

specimens, but again, these were not seriously evaluated by the scientific community of the day. In the years that followed, other reports were made on plants with obvious vascular tissue, and gradually Dawson's initial discovery of Devonian vascular plants began to be accepted.

One of the most spectacular discoveries in paleobotany finally proved beyond any doubt that vascular plants existed in the Devonian. Beginning in 1917, Robert Kidston (Fig. 7-2) and William Lang published the first of a series of papers detailing some exquisitely preserved vascular plants collected near the town of Rhynie, Aberdeenshire, Scotland. This fossil-bearing rock consists of a fine-grained chert that is now regarded as coming from the upper part of the Lower Devonian. Most of the fossils from the Rhynie locality showed that primitive land plants did consist of dichotomizing and, in general, leafless aerial stems arising from a horizontal rhizomatous system. At the ends of some axes were terminal sporangia.

Since the discovery and publication by Kidston and Lang, numerous other presumably primitive vascular plants have been described from Devonian, and even pre-Devonian, sediments. These fossil plants are now known to represent such diverse genera as lycopods, ferns and fernlike plants, large woody trees that were probably seed-plant ancestors, and possibly the earliest seed plants. For a long time, most of these early vascular plants were placed in a single order, Psilophytales. These fossils, along with two living plants, *Psilotum* and *Tmesipteris,* made up a separate subdivision of vascular plants called Psilopsida or Psilophyta.

The continued discovery of Devonian and pre-Devonian vascular plants, some showing remarkable structural preservation, together with a reevaluation of all previously described taxa, prompted H. P. Banks to reassess the

Figure 7-2 Robert Kidston and D. T. Gwynne-Vaughan in Kidston's laboratory in Sirling. *(Courtesy of A. Scott.)*

Psilophytales. Banks proposed abandonment of the order Psilophytales, which had become a repository for all types of plants and, as such, was completely artificial. In its place he initially suggested the establishment of three subdivisions: Rhyniophytina, Zosterophyllophytina, and Trimerophytina. In this book, each has been elevated to the level of a division. —*Stockey ~ S.A level*

RHYNIOPHYTA *IN A*

Members of the Rhyniophyta represent the simplest of all known vascular plants. They consist of dichotomously branched, leafless aerial stems with terminal sporangia. When axes are structurally preserved, they contain a terete, centrarch protostele. Spores are of a single type, and the plants are regarded as homosporous. The Rhyniophyta include some of the oldest vascular plants.

Despite relatively little research with Rhynie chert plants since the original descriptions by Kidston and Lang, two of the genera, *Rhynia* and *Horneophyton,* are the most completely known members of the division. *Rhynia gwynne-vaughanii* is a fossil plant thought to be approximately 18.0 cm tall. Dichotomizing, naked aerial axes extend from a rhizome. Delicate rhizoids (see Fig. 7-5B) that both anchor the plant and absorb nutrients project from the rhizome. The stems are 2.0 to 3.0 cm in diameter, and they are vascularized by a delicate protostele consisting of only a few annular tracheids (Fig. 7-3A). Surrounding the metaxylem tracheids in *R. major* are poorly preserved cells that have been suggested as phloem; some of these cells have been described as containing sievelike areas on their walls. The remainder of the stem diameter

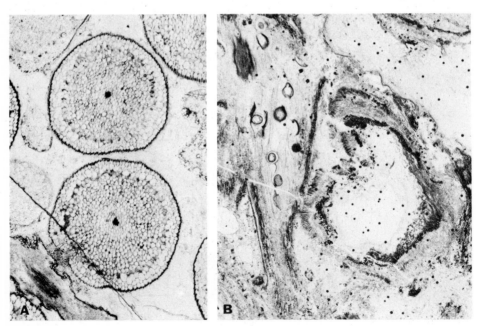

Figure 7-3   A. Transverse section of *Rhynia gwynne-vaughanii* stems. ×20. B. Oblique longitudinal section through *R. gwynne-vaughanii* sporangium showing thick, multilayered wall. ×12.

consists of a two-parted cortex. The inner zone is made up of parenchyma cells with large intercellular spaces that are surrounded by a narrower band of more tightly packed cells. Stomata (Fig. 7-4A and B) flanked by two simple guard cells and a thin waxy cuticle cover the aerial parts of the plant. Sections of the underground stems show the same tissue complement as the aerial parts.

At the tips of some branches are ellipsoidal sporangia up to 3.0 mm long. The sporangium wall is thick (Fig. 7-3B), constructed of a zone of outer palisade cells with thickened lateral walls, and it is termed a cohesion tissue. The cells opposite the region of the stomium have thinner walls. This differential in cell types has been suggested as an early type of dehiscence mechanism. Stomata

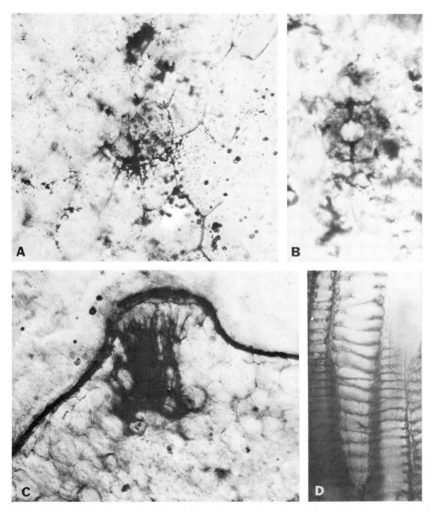

Figure 7-4 A. Paradermal section of *R. major* stem showing epidermal and guard cells of stomatal complex. ×200. B. Open *R. major* stoma and flanking guard cells. ×200. C. Stem bulge suggestive of archegonium. ×130. D. Vascular element of *R. gwynne-vaughanii* showing annular wall thickenings. ×325.

have been identified on the surfaces of *Rhynia* sporangia. In addition, the spores, some still within tetrads, measure approximately 40 μm in diameter and are ornamented with closely spaced spines. A prominent triradiate scar is present on the proximal surface of each spore.

Along the surfaces of *R. gwynne-vaughanii* stems near the plant bases are irregularly shaped protuberances that range from several micrometers to a few millimeters in length. Some of these probably represent aborted or underdeveloped lateral branches; others, the smaller ones, have been suggested as possible asexual reproductive structures similar to gemmae. Other surface projections are thought to be archegonia. Longitudinal sections of these structures do in fact suggest tiers of neck cells and a central canal leading to an enlarged cell. The

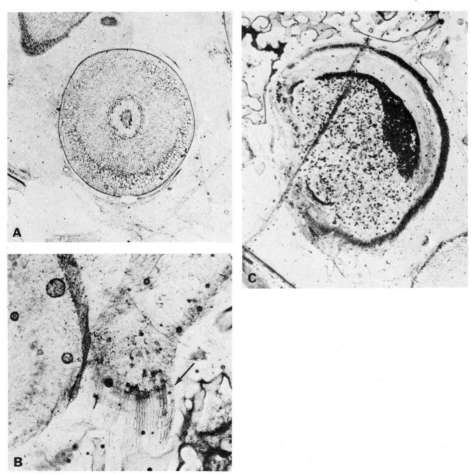

Figure 7-5 *Rhynia major.* A. Transverse section of stem showing two-parted cortex. ×7. B. Several rhizoids *(arrow)* extending from rhizome. ×25. C. Transverse section of sporangium with spores. ×9.

possibility that these structures represent archegonia cannot be ruled out. However, their organization and large size have caused some to view them as possible secretory structures or hydathodes of some type. Other cell mounds on the stem surfaces have been described as antheridia, but are far less convincing.

The second fossil species of *Rhynia, R. major,* is structurally similar to *R. gwynne-vaughanii,* but it is slightly larger (Fig. 7-5A). The plant is thought to have been approximately 40.0 to 50.0 cm tall, as determined by fossil stems that range up to 6.0 mm in diameter. Sporangia are terminal and contain trilete spores that are slightly larger than those of the other species (Fig. 7-5C). Small lateral branches and projections are not present near the bases of *R. major* axes. One of the unusual features of *R. major* concerns what have been termed the secondary wall thickenings of the tracheids. Rather than annular bands like those present on the internal walls of *R. gwynne-vaughanii* tracheids, the elements of the conducting strand in *R. major* lack clearly defined annular bands. Instead, they have a loose reticulate network of wall material. Many

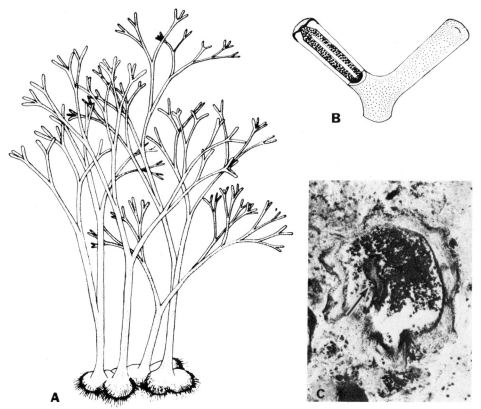

Figure 7-6 *Horneophyton lignieri.* A. Suggested reconstruction of plant. B. Reconstruction of bilobed, columellate sporangium. C. Transverse section of sporangium with spores and partial columella *(arrow).* ×15. *(A and B from Eggert, 1974.)*

researchers have suggested that these elements of the conducting strand were simply poorly preserved in *R. major*. However, recent work by David Edwards (1980) indicates that these elements were mature, but quite different from the tracheids in *R. gwynne-vaughanii*. In addition, it appears that the sporangia of *R. major* were shed at maturity.

One of the more interesting Rhynie plants is *Horneophyton lignieri* (Fig. 7-6A). This plant was initially named *Hornea* by Kidston and Lang, but that was later found to be the generic name of an angiosperm. Some features of *Horneophyton* are of special interest because they differ from those of other rhyniophytes. In *Horneophyton*, the presumably underground portion of the plant consists of a series of bulbous cormlike structures that bear numerous rhizoids (Fig. 7-7). The aerial axes are naked and dichotomously branched. Whereas the structural features of the stems are similar to those of *Rhynia*, the basal corm lacks any evidence of vascularization. Recent studies indicate that phloem cells were lost first in the more basipetal sections of the aerial stem, with tracheids losing their characteristic features in more nearly basal sections. At the transition between stem and corm, dark-colored parenchyma cells replace the tracheids and become indistinguishable in the corm proper.

The sporangia of *Horneophyton* are borne terminally at the tips of some of the aerial branches. Each sporangium is branched, consisting of two to four lobes of varying length (Fig. 7-6B). Sporangial lobes tend to be ellipsoidal to

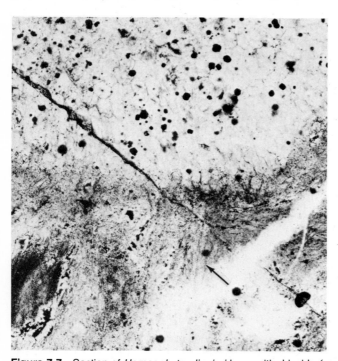

Figure 7-7 Section of *Horneophyton lignieri* base with rhizoids *(arrow).* ×60.

cylindrical in shape, with the distal end truncated. It has been suggested that sporangial dehiscence took place through an apical pore. Extending into the sporangial cavity is a column of sterile tissue around which a continuous zone of sporogenous tissue, or spores, developed (Fig. 7-6C). Both isobilateral and tetrahedral tetrads of spores are present in *Horneophyton* sporangia. The spores are radial, trilete, and irregularly ornamented by cavities that may represent levels of exine degradation, and they range from 39 to 49 μm in diameter. The plant is believed to have been homosporous.

The sporangium of *Horneophyton* is unique among vascular plants, both living and fossil, in that it consists of a branched fertile unit that resulted from dichotomies of the stem apex. Consequently, each fertile lobe was produced by its own apex, and these apices remained meristematic for an extended period of time. The sporangial organs of *Horneophyton* have been interpreted as being intermediate between the undivided sporangium with a single sporogenous cell and the synangial organization where several clusters of sporogenous cells are present. The lobed *Horneophyton* sporangium also has been interpreted as transitional, leading to a synangium in which some differentiation and partitioning of sporogenous tissue took place.

The oldest known plant on which there is general agreement regarding its status as a vascular plant is *Cooksonia*. Fossil specimens have been described from several localities, including the United States, Canada, Wales, and Czechoslovakia. Specimens of *Cooksonia* discovered in Wales are known from deposits as old as the Ludlovian of the Silurian; other occurrences suggest that the taxon ranged into the late Lower Devonian (Emsian). *Cooksonia hemisphaerica* consists of dichotomous branches up to 6.5 cm long with axes 1.5 mm wide. The vascular system consists of a slender strand of annular tracheids. The sporangia are terminal and, in *C. hemisphaerica* (Fig. 7-8B), rounded, while in *C. pertonii* and *C. downtonensis,* they are broader and longer. In *C. caledonica* (Fig. 7-8A), the shape of the sporangium is highly variable. None of the specimens shows a distinct dehiscence mechanism. Moreover, all the plants were apparently homosporous. One might suggest that the *Cooksonia* specimens described to date represent the distal branches of a much larger plant. However, the uniform sizes of the material that has been found favor the interpretation of *Cooksonia* as a small plant like *Rhynia.*

The compression genus *Steganotheca* represents a small plant approximately 5.0 cm tall that contains numerous dichotomous branches with terminal sporangia (Fig. 7-8C). Although no tracheids have been identified from the matrix, the presence of terminal sporangia and a centrally positioned striation on the axes (which probably represents the position of the vascular strand) identifies this organism as a vascular plant. The sporangia are long (2.5 mm) and truncated. Nothing is known about the sporangial contents.

Hedeia corymbosa consists of the distal end of a plant constructed of dichotomizing axes, each terminated by a long sporangium. The specimens, which are Lower Devonian, are not known in sufficient detail, so features of the sporangium and spores remain undescribed. Specimens of *Yarravia* also consist

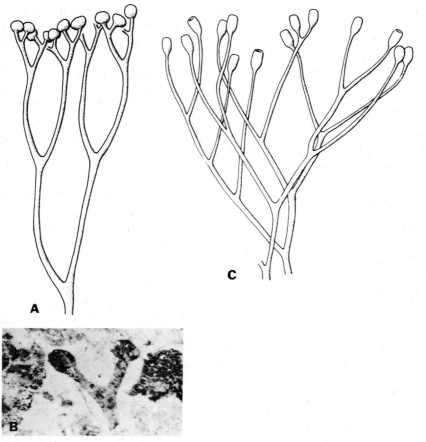

Figure 7-8 A. Suggested reconstruction of *Cooksonia caledonica*. B. Two sporangia of *C. hemisphaerica.* ×11. C. Suggested reconstruction of *Steganotheca striata. (A and C redrawn from Edwards, 1970a; B from Edwards, 1979.)*

of the distal ends of dichotomizing branches. In this Devonian plant, the individual sporangia appear to be aggregated in a simple synangial cluster.

Not all plants included in the Rhyniophyta had cylindrical axes. Some, such as *Taeniocrada* (Lower-Upper Devonian), were vascular plants whose axes appear flattened, but still demonstrate dichotomous branching. The sporangia are terminally borne and range from 3.0 to 7.0 mm long. The occurrence of this fossil in dense mats and the apparent lack of stomata on the stem surfaces have prompted some workers to suggest that it may have lived like some modern aquatic vascular plants.

Salopella is the name given to compressed, dichotomously branched axes with terminal sporangia. The stems are naked and up to 2.0 mm wide, and the spores are trilete and azonate. At the present time, the spores are sufficiently different to permit distinguishing *Salopella* from a number of other taxa included in the Rhyniophyta. The possibility exists, however, that *Salopella* merely reflects *Rhynia* in a different state of preservation.

Specimens with terminal sporangia on a dichotomously branched stem up to 10.0 cm long have been given the generic name *Eogaspesiea gracilis* (Lower Devonian). The single specimen consists of a tangled mass of axes that are believed to have been attached to a rhizomatous axis. The spores are thin-walled and probably trilete.

One plant that combines features of two early vascular plant groups and further underscores the inherent problems in classifying many of the Devonian and pre-Devonian vascular plants is *Renalia* (Fig. 7-9A). Specimens of *R. hueberi* occur as compressions from the famous Gaspé region of Quebec (Lower

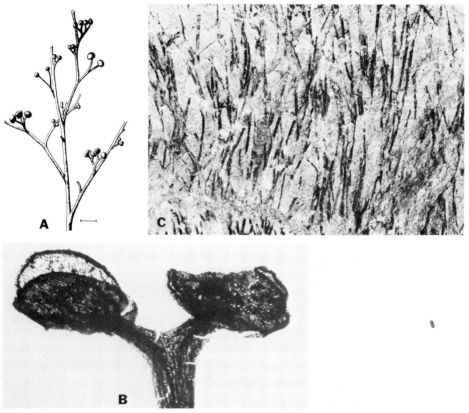

Figure 7-9 *Renalia hueberi.* A. Reconstruction of a portion of the plant. B. Half a fertile lateral branch with two dehisced sporangia. ×30. C. Portion of an exposed surface showing numerous parallel axes. ×2. *(From Gensel, 1976.)*

Devonian) (Fig. 7-9C). The largest axis is 11.0 cm long; the dichotomous branches are about 1.5 mm wide and terminate in round to reniform sporangia (Fig. 7-9B). The spores measure 46 to 70 μm in diameter and are trilete. Although a few helical-scalariform tracheids have been recovered in the macerates, virtually nothing is known about the vascular system. *Renalia* combines features of at least two groups of early vascular plants. Terminal sporangia and pseudomonopodial branching are features that suggest affinities with the rhyniophytes, but the large, reniform-shaped sporangia (with dehiscence taking place along the distal margin) are characteristics common to members of the Zosterophyllophyta.

Another Devonian plant that appears to share features with both the rhyniophytes and zosterophyllophytes is *Nothia*. The naked axes and pear-shaped sporangia were originally described as specimens of *Asteroxylon mackiei*. Today, they are recognized as the bases of a plant called *N. aphylla*. In a recent study (El-Saadawy and Lacey, 1979) it was noted that sporangial position in *N. aphylla* is highly variable, with individual sporangia being borne on adaxially recurved stalks that may range from helical to almost whorled. The sporangia are described as reniform, with dehiscence by a long, apical transverse slit, and the spores are radial and trilete. In certain anatomical features, *N. aphylla* may be compared with members of the Rhyniophyta, while the laterally borne, stalked reniform sporangia are features that suggest inclusion in the Zostero-phyllophyta. Both *Renalia* and *Nothia* underscore the belief that rhyniophytes and zosterophyllophytes were distinct groups by the Lower Devonian.

ZOSTEROPHYLLOPHYTA

Members of the Zosterophyllophyta represent some of the most interesting early vascular plants. Moreover, a considerable amount of structural and morphologic detail is known about them. As a group they also have many features in common with the Lycophyta, and they are believed to have given rise to the lycopods. Zosterophyllophytes exhibit dichotomous branching, although in some genera there is a tendency toward a pseudomonopodial habit. When structurally preserved stems have been discovered, the xylem strand is more prominent than in rhyniophytes and sometimes appears elliptical in transverse section; the xylem is exarch. The distinctive feature that separates the zosterophyllophytes from other early vascular plants is the presence of sporangia that are borne along the stem, often aggregated into terminal clusters. The sporangia are typically globose to reniform, with dehiscence generally occurring along the distal edge. Nothing is known about the vascular system of the sporangia, but all contain one type of spore, suggesting that the group was homosporous.

One of the plants that has an interesting taxonomic history and is now included among the zosterophyllophytes is *Sawdonia*. Earlier it was noted that in 1859, Dawson described a plant from the Devonian of the Gaspé peninsula under binomial *Psilophyton princeps*. In his first reconstruction, Dawson

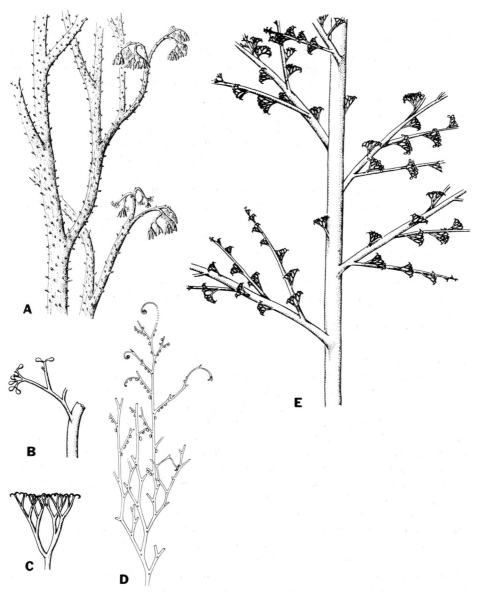

Figure 7-10 A. *Psilophyton princeps.* B, C, and E. *Ibyka amphikoma.* B. Portion of fertile appendage. C. Ultimate appendage (leaf). D. Suggested reconstruction of *Gosslingia breconensis.* E. Reconstruction of plant based on three orders of branching. *(A from Andrews, 1974; B, C, and E from Skog and Banks, 1973; D from Edwards, 1970b.)*

described a dichotomizing plant that terminated in straight or circinately curved branches. The reproductive parts were described as lateral masses. Several years later, in 1870, he modified his interpretation of *Psilophyton* by describing the reproductive units as sporangia borne at the ends of slender branches. This was followed a year later by an emended diagnosis based on additional specimens, some naked and some with helically arranged spines. At this time, some of the

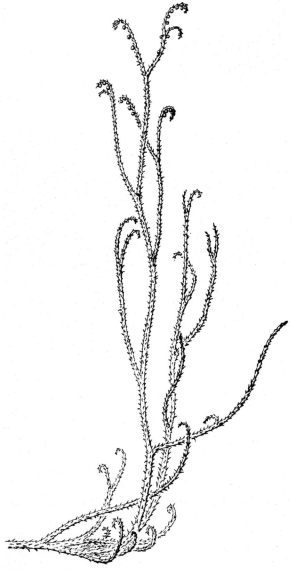

Figure 7-11   *Sawdonia ornata. (From Andrews, 1974.)*

fossils were referred to the taxon *P. princeps* var. *ornatum*. Subsequent workers were able to identify globose sporangia in lateral positions on the axes of some specimens that were referred to as *P. princeps* var. *ornatum*. The literature now contained a contradiction relative to *Psilophyton*. The *P. princeps* originally described by Dawson consisted of spiny axes with terminal sporangia, and the variety *ornatum*, which was regarded as the type species, represented a very different plant with lateral sporangia. Today the confusion has been rectified. *Psilophyton princeps* is the binomial applied to plants with naked or spiny axes that have terminal sporangia (Fig. 7-10A). Those specimens with spiny axes and lateral, globose sporangia are referred to as *Sawdonia ornata* (Fig. 7-11). For a detailed account of the historical development of the problem, the reader is referred to the paper by Banks, Leclercq, and Hueber (1975). It may be appropriate that Dawson's original description and reconstruction of *Psilophyton*, which was ignored for so many years, has today involved so many researchers and taken more than a century to comprehend fully.

Sawdonia ornata is believed to have been approximately 30.0 cm tall, constructed of pseudomonopodial axes that arose from a rhizome (Fig. 7-11). Lateral axes branched dichotomously and were characterized by circinate tips. Branches were about 5.0 mm in diameter and were covered by numerous tapered spines. The sporangia apparently were confined to the distal ends of branches, where they formed loosely aggregated spikes. Individual sporangia occurred on short, presumably vascularized stalks and were reniform in shape. Dehiscence occurred along the convex margin dividing the sporangium into equal valves. *Sawdonia* apparently was a homosporous plant with sporangia containing round to subtriangular trilete spores that were up to 64 μm in diameter. In structurally preserved specimens, the stele has a solid core of tracheids with reticulate secondary wall thickenings. Epidermal cells are characterized by centrally positioned papillae; stomata are also present on the stem epidermis, but not on the spines.

Kidston and Lang described a plant from the Devonian Old Red Sandstone Series that they felt had a tufted growth habit with predominantly dichotomous branches. Because the sporangia appeared to have been terminal, they regarded it as similar to *Rhynia*. For some time, therefore, *Hicklingia* was included in the Rhyniophyta; however, new specimens show that the sporangia were in fact borne laterally on the axes, indicating that an assignment to the Zosterophyllophyta is probably more accurate. Spores have not been recovered from the kidney-shaped sporangia, and the features of the vascular system still remain unknown.

One interesting Lower Devonian vascular plant known from a number of species is *Zosterophyllum*. It was a leafless, dichotomously branched form that produced lateral sporangia on short, delicate stalks. In *Z. llanoveranum*, from the Lower Devonian of Britain, axes are approximately 1.5 mm in diameter and consist of a strand of xylem elliptical in outline. Surrounding the stele is a cortex of three zones distinguished by the size and wall thickness of the cells. The sporangia are borne in either one or two rows at the distal ends of branches, but it is probable that this arrangement is a result of the preservation process. Sporangia vary from circular to reniform, with each borne on a small stalk that departs from the axis at an abrupt angle. Vascular tissue has not been identified in the sporangial stalk. Cells near the distal surface of the sporangium wall are elongate and thick-walled, grading into smaller, thinner-walled cells that formed a zone of dehiscence. The spores are oval and average 45 μm in diameter. In at least one species, *Z. myretonianum,* the basal region of the plant is characterized by what has been termed K and H branching patterns. Apparently, these branching patterns are the result of successive, close-order dichotomies. Branching of this type has been described in a number of zosterophyllophytes, and it is also known to have occurred in some species of the protolepidodendra-lean genus *Drepanophycus.*

Another zosterophyllophyte that is known from the Lower Devonian of Wales is *Gosslingia breconensis* (Fig. 7-10D). The plant is believed to have been approximately 50.0 cm tall, consisting of dichotomizing axes up to 4.0 mm wide in the distal regions. The base is presumed to have consisted of a rhizome bearing rhizoids, although organic attachment has not been demonstrated. Like *Sawdonia,* the specimen reveals distal tips that are characteristically circinately coiled. The aerial stems are leafless, although some specimens show small protuberances that extend from the surface only a few hundred micrometers and larger tubercles that are often identified only by their scars. These latter structures, which have been termed axillary tubercles, are vascularized by a terete trace and extend from one side of the stem just below the point of a dichotomy. Pyritized axes reveal that the xylem is elliptical in outline with annular protoxylem elements located near the periphery. Metaxylem tracheids are scalariform to reticulate. The cortex is constructed of thick-walled cells, and stomata are scattered along the stem.

In *Gosslingia,* the sporangia occur in definite aggregations in the distal regions of the plant. The sporangia are variable in shape, ranging from globose to reniform, and they are attached to the stems by slender stalks. No detailed information is known about the histology of the sporangium wall, although some spores have been recovered. They range from 36 to 50 μm in diameter and are ornamented by small spines.

Crenaticaulis is a zosterophyllophyte that is known in some detail, and it provides important information about the vascular system and sporangia of this group. *Crenaticaulis verruculosus* was described from both compressed and structurally preserved specimens collected from Lower Devonian rocks in the Gaspé region. The largest specimen consists of a 22.0 cm-long axis that shows both pseudomonopodial and dichotomous branching. The dichotomies occur at short intervals, and the distal stem tips are slightly coiled. One of the unusual features of *Crenaticaulis* is the two rows of multicellular toothlike protuberances that are nearly oppositely arranged along the surface of the stems. The teeth are triangular, and they are present on the circinately coiled stem apices as well as the stalks of the sporangia. Epidermal cells of the stem are of two types, elongate and papillate. Axillary tubercles are present in a subaxillary position on some specimens; on others their position is indicated by an elliptical scar.

The sporangia are clustered and occur in opposite to subopposite groups on the distal branches. They are pedicellate and nearly spherical in outline. Sporangial dehiscence has been termed distal, beginning on one side just above the junction of the stalk and the sporangium and arching over the adaxial face to the opposite surface. Dehisced sporangia of *Crenaticaulis* show a large abaxial and a small adaxial portion. Nothing is known about the spores. The exarch strand is elliptical in outline and composed of helical tracheids.

Rebuchia is known from Lower Devonian rocks from the Beartooth Formation of Wyoming. The specimens consist of narrow, smooth, dichotomous branches that gradually taper into blunt points. The sporangia are confined to distal branches and occur as spikes of up to 20 sporangia each. Individual sporangia are arranged oppositely to suboppositely, and they are borne on short, curved stalks, so that all the sporangia point in essentially the same direction (Fig. 7-12A). Dehisced sporangia consist of equal valves, indicating a basipetal form of dehiscence. *Rebuchia ovata* was probably homosporous. All the spores recovered are unornamented and in the 68 to 75 μm size range.

Kaulangiophyton is the name given to a Lower Devonian plant consisting of

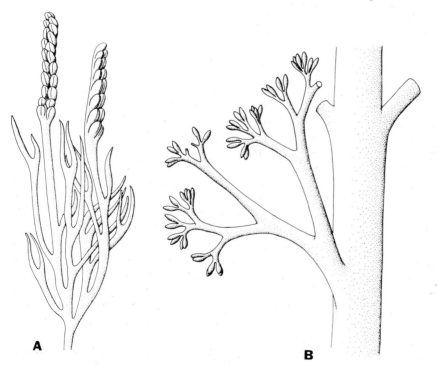

A   **B**

Figure 7-12 A. Suggested reconstruction of *Rebuchia ovata*. B. Reconstruction of a portion of a fertile lateral branch of *Trimerophyton robustius*. *(A redrawn from Hueber, 1972; B redrawn from Hopping, 1956.)*

a horizontal branching system that bears numerous, irregularly spaced, short spines. The spines are slightly curved and up to 2.0 mm long; the base is decurrent. The sporangia are borne on short stalks along the stem and appear to be interspersed among the spines, giving the plant the appearance of some species of *Lycopodium*. No spores have been recovered, nor is anything known about the vascular system. In many features, *K. akantha* is like the protolepidodendralean genus *Drepanophycus*.

TRIMEROPHYTOPHYTA

The Trimerophytophyta represent the third group that was established when Banks reevaluated all the plants included in the order Psilophytales. Trimerophytes were generally more complex than either the zosterophyllophytes or the rhyniophytes, from which they are thought to have descended. Included in this group are plants that demonstrate monopodial branching of the main axes, with lateral axes showing either dichotomous or trifurcate branching. As with rhyniophytes, the sporangia were terminal, although trimerophyte sporangia typically were aggregated into definite fertile branches (Fig. 7-12B) as opposed to strictly vegetative ones. Internally, the members of this group possessed a relatively large stele that was centrarch. Pitting on the vascular elements varied from scalariform-bordered to circular-bordered.

As indicated in the preceding section, *Psilophyton* specimens with lateral sporangia were transferred to the zosterophyllophyte genus *Sawdonia*. The remaining *Psilophyton* specimens, those with terminal sporangia, are now included in the Trimerophytophyta.

Psilophyton dawsonii is probably the most completely known member of the group. Both compression and structurally preserved specimens are known from several Lower Devonian localities. A reconstruction of *P. dawsonii* reveals a greatly branched plant in which the fertile lateral branches emerge alternately and distichously along the main axes (Fig. 7-13A). The vegetative branches are smooth; they dichotomize at right angles and terminate in slender, blunt tips. The fertile branches typically dichotomize up to six times before terminating in clusters of approximately 32 sporangia. Individual sporangia range up to 5.0 mm long, with dehiscence occurring along the lateral surface. The spores are trilete and vary from 40 to 75 μm in diameter. The spore wall is smooth, but on some grains, a delicate layer often appears separated from the spore body. If found as dispersed grains, such spores as those of *P. dawsonii* most closely approximate *Retusotriletes* or *Phyllothecotriletes*.

The vascular tissue of *P. dawsonii* consists of a centrarch protostele that accounts for approximately one-quarter of the stem diameter (Fig. 7-13C). In more basal regions of the plant, the stele has several enlarged protoxylem zones and numerous radially aligned tracheids. Traces supplying the fertile branches are initially terete, becoming more rectangular in outline at higher levels. Metaxylem tracheids are scalariform-bordered or have modified scalariform bars

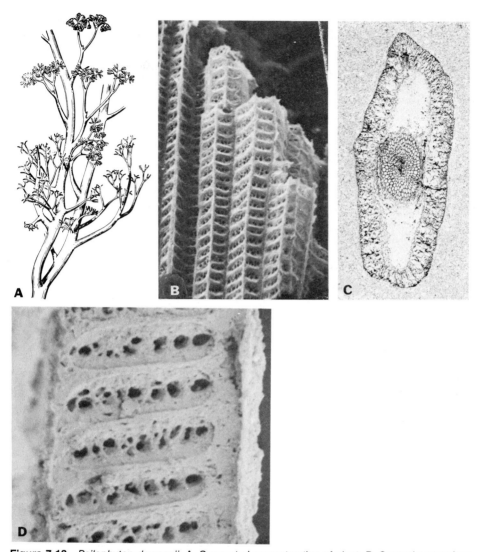

Figure 7-13 *Psilophyton dawsonii.* A. Suggested reconstruction of plant. B. Several metaxylem tracheids showing features of the pitting. ×400. C. Transverse section of stem. ×20. D. Secondary wall features showing complex nature of pits. ×2000. *(A from Banks, Leclercq, and Hueber, 1975; B and D from Hartman and Banks, 1980; C, specimen courtesy of H. Banks.)*

that resemble circular bordered pits (Fig. 7-13B and D). Surrounding the vascular system is a multilayered cortex consisting of collenchymalike cells and, toward the periphery, substomatal chambers.

In *P. princeps*, the stem surfaces are ornamented by a number of cup-tipped spines. The larger size of the sporangia and the nature of the vegetative branching further distinguishes the two species. The vascular strand consists of a solid mass of xylem that is either mesarch or centrarch.

Another recently described species of *Psilophyton* from the lower Emsian (Lower Devonian) of New Brunswick, Canada has spiny branches that dichotomize several times and terminate in rounded tips (Fig. 7-14B). Fertile branches are pendulous and, in the distal regions, covered by semicircular

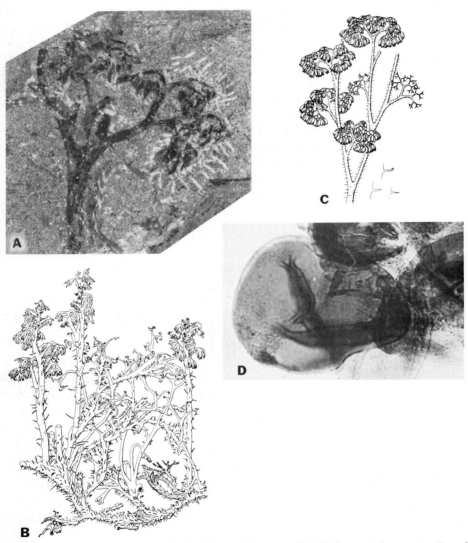

Figure 7-14   A. Fertile branch of *Psilophyton charientos.* ×3.3. B. Suggested reconstruction of *Psilophyton* sp. from New Brunswick, Canada. C. Suggested reconstruction of *P. charientos* and detailed morphology of spines. D. Spore *(Apiculiretusispora)* of *P. charientos.* ×600. *(A, C, and D from Gensel, 1979; B from Doran, 1979.)*

crenulations. The sporangia range up to 5.0 mm long and are twisted. In situ spores range from 48 to 102 μm in diameter and conform to the genus *Apiculiretusispora.*

Not all the *Psilophyton* "species" described can be included in the Trimerophytophyta. This is so because, in some instances, specimens do not reveal features of the branching pattern or possess fertile regions. There are, however, several important psilophytes that have been described. One of these is *P. forbesii,* a plant demonstrating a monopodial growth habit. The stems are apparently naked, but are marked by longitudinal striations. Ellipsoidal sporangia are borne in pairs at the tips of a series of dichotomous or trichotomous branches. In *P. dapsile,* known from the Trout Valley Formation of Maine, the axes measure approximately 2.0 mm in width; the erect plant is thought to have been about 30.0 cm tall. The stems are smooth and branched dichotomously. The sporangia are small (2.0 mm long) and are borne in dense clusters at the ends of closely spaced distal dichotomies. *Psilophyton microspinosum* is also known from the Trout Valley Formation. Fragmented stems of plants that appear to have been growing in dense stands suggest that entire specimens grew to a height of 6 dm. On the axes are delicate emergences that taper to a needlelike tip. Unlike the other species of *Psilophyton* that have been described, the sporangia of *P. microspinosum* are few in number and are borne erect rather than in the typical recurved orientation. One species of *Psilophyton, P. hedei,* was described from Silurian rocks of Sweden and is now thought to represent some invertebrate similar to a graptolite or a pterobranch. In this instance, the branched axis may represent a colony of numerous individuals that share a system of internal tubes; the characteristic "stem" spines probably represent free zooidal tubes.

Another Devonian plant that can be assigned to the Trimerophytophyta on the basis of its branching pattern and the nature of its fertile region is *Pertica* (Fig. 7-15). This genus is known only from compression remains, but they are described from at least two localities of the Lower Devonian. Extensive specimens suggest that the plant may have exceeded 1.0 m in height. Numerous side branches are borne from the main axis in an alternate, tetrastichous and dichotomous manner. The distal ends repeatedly dichotomize at right angles to each other. Like all trimerophytes, the lateral branches were either sterile or fertile. The fertile ones consist of closely spaced dichotomies that terminate in masses of sporangia. All branches are covered by closely spaced epidermal papillae. The sporangia are elliptical in outline and appear to lack any histologic evidence of dehiscence. Poorly preserved spores about 64 μm in diameter suggest that *P. quadrifaria* was homosporous.

Pertica varia was much larger than *P. quadrifaria,* reaching a height of nearly 3.0 m. The primary branches of *P. varia* are arranged in subopposite pairs, with the successive laterals decussate. Paired sporangia are erect, but the number of sporangia per cluster is smaller. Spores of *P. varia* are subcircular to subtriangular and up to 90 μm in diameter. Nothing is known of the internal anatomy of any *Pertica* species.

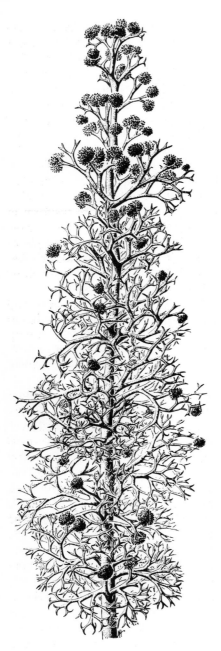

Figure 7-15 Suggested reconstruction of
*Pertica quadrifaria. (From Kasper and An-
drews, 1972.)*

Trimerophyton robustius (Fig. 7-12B), the type species of the division, was initially described by Dawson in 1859 under the binomial *Psilophyton robustius* from some fragmentary specimens collected from the shore of Gaspé Bay. The generic name *Trimerophyton* was introduced many years later on the basis of a single specimen, also from the Gaspé. The main stem of the fossil *Trimerophyton* is approximately 1.0 cm wide and consists of numerous helically arranged, trifurcate lateral branches. The first and second branching patterns of the laterals are trichotomous, with further subdivisions of the dichotomous type. All the axes are smooth, with the exception of some that are longitudinally striated. All the ultimate branches bear erect sporangia in clusters of three.

The name *Dawsonites* is a good example of a Devonian form genus that has been used by some workers for sporangia that are not organically connected to an axis or are not aggregated in large clusters. The sporangia are fusiform in shape and typically measure from 3.0 to 5.0 mm long. The genus is now restricted to terminal sporangia that cannot be identified as the sporangia of *Psilophyton*. As spores are recovered from additional fertile specimens so that comparisons can be made, many of the *Dawsonites* "species" no doubt will be placed in synonymy.

Another form genus that has been used for naked, dichotomously branched axes of the Devonian is *Hostinella*. Structurally preserved specimens consist of small fragments up to 3.0 mm wide. The xylem strand is protostelic, centrarch, and composed of scalariform-bordered tracheids. Some specimens of *Hostinella* are believed to represent an isolated branching fragment of *Psilophyton goldschmidtii*.

One Middle Devonian plant that is difficult to classify because it shares features with both the trimerophytes and pteridophytes is *Ibyka amphikoma* (Fig. 7-10E). The taxon is known from both compressed and petrified specimens and has been reconstructed as a monopodial branching system that bears lateral appendages (leaves) on several orders of branches (Fig. 7-10C). Both lateral branches and leaves are helically arranged and covered with delicate hairs. The vascular system consists of a trilobed protostele with some of the arms bifurcated at higher levels to form terete leaf traces. Protoxylem tracheids and parenchyma are present near the tips of the xylem lobes in the form of peripheral loops. The leaves of *Ibyka* consist of three-dimensional, dichotomous axes with curved tips (Fig. 7-10C). The branches that produced sporangia appear to have been homologous with the leaves (Fig. 7-10B), but have only been recorded from third-order axes. The sporangia are ovoid and up to 1.0 mm long.

The relationship between *Ibyka* and the trimerophytes and ferns includes the lobed protostele with pitted tracheids, unmodified sporangia-bearing branches, and the helically arranged leaves. Features that suggest affinities with *Calamophyton* and *Hyenia*, two genera that are placed in the Pteridophyta in this book, include the general morphology of the lateral appendages and fertile branches.

EARLY LAND PLANT EVOLUTION

The rhyniophytes represent interesting vascular plants that are both simply constructed and evolutionarily primitive. Such an interpretation is not universally accepted, because some workers believe that a plant such as *Rhynia* is the result of evolutionary reduction. The simplicity, according to this interpretation, represents a highly advanced suite of features. However plausible such an idea may be, the continued discovery of rhyniophytelike plants in Upper Silurian and Lower Devonian rocks and the absence of morphologically more complex vascular plants in older sediments continue to support the simple and primitive interpretation of the phylogenetic position of these organisms.

The simple organization of *Rhynia,* with its naked dichotomizing axes and terminal sporangia, has long been regarded as evidence of an evolutionary relationship with the existing genus *Psilotum.* Comparative morphologists cite the protostelic organization of the stems and rhizomes, the terminal sporangia, the leafless axes, and the homosporous condition as additional features that support their argument. These ideas have become firmly incorporated in morphologic thinking and are even reflected in some current vascular-plant classifications. *Rhynia* and *Psilotum* also represented interesting plant types from which proponents of the "telome theory" could "evolve" many vascular plant organs (Zimmermann, 1952). One of the characteristics used to strengthen the relationship between *Psilotum* and *Rhynia* was the absence of roots in both, a feature considered to be primitive among vascular plants. Recent developmental studies on some ferns indicate that although embryos are initially rootless, roots are, in fact, produced later, and thus the rootless condition in *Psilotum* may not be as primitive as once thought. Many workers now regard the dichotomizing axes of *Psilotum* as highly specialized fronds, a feature that further detracts from a *Rhynia-Psilotum* evolutionary relationship (Bierhorst, 1968). Finally, the absence of any recognizable fossil record of *Psilotum,* with the exception of a few nondescript spores, in the some 375 million years between the two plants, further underscores the frailty in their proposed evolutionary relationship.

One further interpretation regarding the nature of *Rhynia* must be considered. Generally it has been assumed that the leafless, dichotomizing axes (bearing terminal sporangia) of *Rhynia* represent the sporophyte phase of the plant. The presence of spores, still within tetrads, supports this assumption. With the exception of the spores, nothing is known about the gametophyte phase of the Rhynie plants. It has been suggested by several authors that the two *Rhynia* species *R. gwynne-vaughanii* and *R. major* represent different parts of the same plant. According to one interpretation, *R. gwynne-vaughanii* is the gametophyte phase, and the circular projections and reduced branches that occur near the base of the plant represent young sporophytes developing on the gametophyte. Some of the evidence used to support this interpretation includes the presence of vascular tissue in some *Psilotum* gametophytes and certain cellular details associated with the presumed sporophyte and gametophyte. A modification of this interpretation views *R gwynne-vaughanii* as the free-living gametophyte and the species described as *R. major* as the sporophyte. Although these ideas are intriguing and certainly worthy of continued discussion, the evidence suggested to date is not overwhelming. For any of these ideas to have credibility, *Rhynia* axes should demonstrate, for example, a number of intermediate growth forms, some histologic differences between the base of the sporophyte and the gametophyte to which it is attached, archegonia, and especially, antheridia that are far more convincing. In a recent report Remy and Remy (1980) described structurally preserved axes in the Rhynie chert that consist of fingerlike projections arranged in a shallow cup and are suggestive of some bryophytic gametophytes. These authors identify structures on the inner surface of the projections as archegonia and antheridia; however, the quality of the illustrations is not sufficient to conclusively demonstrate that these bulges do in fact represent sexual reproductive organs of a gametophyte.

Like *Rhynia, Horneophyton* also demonstrates some interesting features relative to the subsequent evolution of land plants. The individual columellate sporangia of *Horneophyton* have been compared with the columellate sporangia of *Anthoceros,* a living member of the Hepatophyta. In *Anthoceros,* the sporophyte is relatively simple, consisting of an upright, slender green axis that represents a sporangium. Spores are produced over an extended period of time as meristematic cells continue to produce new cells at the base of the sporangium. In *Horneophyton,* the extended sporangial lobes suggest that sporogenous tissue also was produced over a long period of time. The absence of vascular tissue in the base of *Horneophyton* is another feature that some view as hepatophytic. Although hepatophytes lack the developmentally equivalent homologues of xylem and phloem in the central region of the gametophore, recent studies clearly indicate that the hydroids and leptoids of mosses are physiologically equivalent to xylem and phloem. So convincing is the evidence that in one study, leptoids are referred to as "sieve elements." Since this information is based on ultrastructural characteristics, a direct comparison cannot be made with *Horneophyton,* although the shared features allow interesting speculation. In this context, *Horneophyton* has been regarded both as a vascular plant evolving in the direction of a hepatophyte through the loss of vascular tissue and as a hepatophyte moving evolutionarily in the direction of a vascular plant through the phylogenetic acquisition of vascular tissue. Still other workers consider it an interesting vascular plant with a base whose features are obscured by poor preservation, or they consider it a cormlike structure that lacks vascular tissue, much like the development of the sporophyte in some species of *Lycopodium* that possess an avascular protocorm.

Regardless of how the Rhynie plants are positioned into the evolutionary history of vascular plants, their excellent preservation has provided an opportunity for paleobotanists to speculate, that is generally not afforded by other fossils. This is especially important when one considers that the Rhynie flora is from the Devonian, a period of geologic time that must be close to that of the transition of plant life from an aquatic to a terrestrial habit.

The evidence appears overwhelming that the lycopods represent a natural offshoot of the zosterophyllophytes. Both groups are characterized by exarch protosteles and laterally produced, reniform sporangia. In *Crenaticaulis* and *Gosslingia,* the presence of axillary tubercles is thought to represent rhizophore-like branches similar to those of existing species of *Selaginella.* The absence of leaves in the zosterophyllophytes, although an obvious difference between the two groups, can be explained in terms of the transitional status of the Zosterophyllophyta. The zosterophyllophytes are often characterized by stems that bear various types of protuberances. These range from unicellular to multicellular spines or to multicellular teeth. The latter forms may have functioned to increase the photosynthetic surface of the stems. Generally, they were randomly scattered over the stem surfaces, although in *Crenaticaulis* the large toothlike protuberances are arranged in two rows along the stems. This tendency toward a definite arrangement may constitute the initial stages in the evolution of the microphyll. If so, the scattered outgrowths on the lycophyte *Asteroxylon* may represent a transitional stage.

In *Asteroxylon,* the stems are clothed with scalelike structures called enations. There apparently is no definite arrangment to these structures, and stomata are absent from both surfaces. Vascular traces that extend out from the actinostele terminate in the cortex near the bases of the enations. The arrangement of the vascular tissue in *Asteroxylon* also provides a clue to the evolution of leaves. With the increase in emergences that characterize the zosterophyllophytes, some modifications would have to have occurred in the arrangement of the vascular tissue. One way to increase xylem surface area would be through partial dissection, or lobing, of a protostele. The actinostelic configuration of *Asteroxylon* represents an increase in the stelar complexity over the simple protosteles of the rhyniophytes, which lack any form of stem-borne emergences.

It was noted earlier that some workers view the rhyniophytes as vascular plants that evolved a level of simplicity from more complex ancestors. Although the fossil record contradicts this appraisal, there are those who view the evolution of the microphyll as the end product of a reduced branch. In this regard, the vascularized microphyll of a lycopod may be homologized with the ultimate dichotomy of a plant such as *Rhynia.* The continued foreshortening of selected telomes (the end of a branch after the dichotomy) would result in vascularized units that, if flattened, would resemble microphylls. There is good evidence that megaphylls have evolved from reduced and planated branching systems, and the possibility remains that not all microphylls had a common morphologic and structural origin.

The zosterophyllophytes also demonstrate several stages in the evolution and organization of sporangia. These may include forms such as *Kaulangiophyton,* in which sporangia are presumably helically arranged over the stem surface, to intermediate forms such as *Gosslingia,* in which the helically arranged sporangia are aggregated into definite spikes. A further modification might result in the arrangement seen in *Rebuchia,* where sporangia are organized into definite spikes, with the individual sporangia dorsiventral in arrangement.

Sporangial dehiscence within the zosterophyllophytes typically divided the sporangium into valves of equal or nearly equal size. The one notable exception appears to be *Crenaticaulis,* in which dehiscence divided the sporangium into unequal valves. This feature may become more important as additional information on sporangial dehiscence is determined for Devonian plants. Such a condition may have evolved as a protective device or as an adaptive passive mechanism that facilitated the dispersal of spores by air currents or even raindrops.

The Trimerophytophyta demonstrate a more complex organization than that of the rhyniophytes, their presumed ancestors. In the trimerophytes, the primary axes are monopodial or pseudomonopodial. Laterals were produced in a variety of patterns, including helical (*Psilophyton* sterile branches), alternately and distichous (*Psilophyton* fertile branches), tristichous (*Trimerophyton*), and tetrastichous (*Pertica*). In *Pertica,* for example, the laterals tend to be produced in fours along the stem, with the ultimate branchlets consisting of slender, three-dimensional dichotomizing structures. It has been suggested that the planation of these lateral branches provides the morphologic equivalent of the megaphyllous leaf type. In some members of the Aneurophytales, a group of Devonian plants referred to as progymnosperms (Chap. 11), laterals are planated, while in others, the branching system is still three-dimensional.

Within the trimerophytes there is the beginning of a distinction between the central axis and the lateral branches, and this represents the precursor of a frond or leaf-bearing system. Trimerophytes also demonstrate a modification in the manner in which sporangia are borne. In rhyniophytes, sporangia are terminal at the ends of dichotomizing axes. In some species of *Psilophyton* (e.g., *P. microspinosum*), the number of sporangia is small, while in others (e.g., *P. dapsile*), numerous small sporangia are clustered. One possible evolutionary line might involve *Pertica,* with its massive clusters of densely packed sporangia, leading to some Carboniferous ferns, such as some species of *Botryopteris* and, possibly, one species of *Ankyropteris*. The other line might lead to the progymnosperms via such a plant as *Tetraxylopteris*. One recently described Middle Devonian plant that might bridge the evolutionary gap between trimerophytes and progymnosperms is *Oocampsa* (Andrews, Gensel, and Kasper, 1975). Specimens of *O. catheta* consist of closely spaced, helically arranged branches up to 7.0 cm long that were produced from a primary axis. The lateral branches divide pseudomonopodially and dichotomously and terminate in elongate, erect sporangia. The sporangia dehisce longitudinally and contain large (96 to 120 μm), trilete miospores. The spores are interesting in that they appear to have some separation between the wall layers, suggesting a pseudosaccate morphologic type. *Oocampsa,* with its helically arranged primary and secondary branches that bear erect sporangia, may represent an intermediate form between that of such trimerophytes as *Trimerophyton* and *Pertica,* on the one hand, and that of *Tetraxylopteris,* with its pinnate arrangement of ultimate segments, on the other. Such a view is supported by the stratigraphic occurrence of the taxa listed.

Of the trimerophytes known to date, only two species of *Psilophyton* come from structurally preserved material. In both, *P. dawsonii* and *P. princeps,* the basic organization involves a simple protostele, but one that is more massive than any known for the rhyniophytes. Secondary wall thickenings in the rhyniophytes are characteristically annular to scalariform. In *Psilophyton,* there is an obvious modification of the scalariform wall thickenings in which secondary wall material is deposited between the scalariform bars to form scalariform and circular bordered pits such as those of both ferns and gymnosperms.

The Trimerophytophyta are represented by relatively few species. Nevertheless, there are some apparent trends within the group that involve the evolution of one type of leaf, the modification of tracheidal pitting, and possibly the early stages in the evolution of saccate pollen. As additional specimens are discovered and described from Devonian and possibly even Mississippian rocks, there can be little doubt that this group will play an increasingly important role in our understanding of the evolution of vascular plants.

Chapter 8

Lycophyta

The Lycophyta (sometimes referred to as Microphyllophyta) have an extensive geologic history, extending back into the Devonian or, conceivably, earlier. They were widespread during the Carboniferous, representing the dominant vegetation type at that time. The extensive coal-mining operations that routinely uncover Carboniferous rocks throughout the world have been responsible in large part for the many excellent specimens of this group that constitute the focal points of reconstructions of ancient landscapes in museums around the world. In addition, the extensive Carboniferous swamps from which much of the mineable coal resources of the world have come were dominated by members of the Lycophyta, and it is apparent that much of the coal itself consists of lycopod remains.

Evidence seems to suggest that the Lycophyta could have originated in the early Devonian (or, conceivably, late Silurian?) from the Zosterophyllophyta. From these beginnings, the group radiated extensively during the Carboniferous and then began to diminish in numbers of taxa and individuals toward the end of the Paleozoic. Today the lycophytes are represented by five genera of which two, *Lycopodium* and *Selaginella,* contain most of the 1100 species. The extensive geologic history of the group and numerous exquisitely preserved specimens have provided paleobotanists with the opportunity not only to trace the evolution of the lycophytes, but also to investigate some basic facets of plant biology.

The Lycophyta are characterized by either dichotomous branching or a combination of dichotomous and monopodial branching. Their stems are densely covered with true leaves, termed microphylls. The leaves of microphyllous plants tend to be small, except in some of the arborescent members, helically arranged, and vascularized generally by a single bundle that does not produce an interruption (leaf gap) in the stele of the stem when it separates. The roots of Lycophyta tend to be adventitious. One of the most important characteristic features of lycophytes is the position of the sporangium, which is borne in the axil or on the upper surface of a leaf called a sporophyll. Sporophylls may be interspersed among photosynthetic microphylls, or they may be nonphotosynthetic and aggregated into loosely constructed strobili or cones. Most species produce only one type of spore and are therefore regarded as homosporous. In some lycophytes, however, two types of spores are produced, and they not only look different, but also function differently in the life history of the plant. The small spores (microspores) produce the male gametophyte, whereas megaspores germinate to produce the female gametophytes. Living heterosporous members of the Lycophyta produce both types of spores in the same strobilus; in some fossil heterosporous representatives, microspores and megaspores were produced in different cones. Most lycophytes are herbaceous, although some fossil forms are known to have been arborescent. Despite the large size of some of the arborescent members, the amount of secondary vascular tissue was small compared with the total stem diameter. Maturation of the primary xylem in lycophytes is exarch in most forms, with scalariform wall thickenings on xylem elements the common type. Vascular organization ranges from protostelic to siphonostelic. Although leaf gaps are not produced, interruption in the vascular cylinder occurs when branch traces are given off.

The following classification is intended to provide an appropriate framework within which to base discussion of this interesting group of plants, although, admittedly, there are a few enigmatic forms that may not fit precisely into the scheme:

Protolepidodendrales: Devonian to Mississippian
Lepidodendrales: Devonian to Permian
Pleuromeiales: Triassic to Cretaceous
Isoetales: Cretaceous to Recent
Lycopodiales: Pennsylvanian to Recent
Selaginellales: Pennsylvanian to Recent

PROTOLEPIDODENDRALES

Included in the Protolepidodendrales are the oldest lycophytes. They are represented by a diverse assemblage of presumably herbaceous plants or small trees, although anatomic details and complete specimens are not known for all taxa. Leaves were borne helically on upright dichotomizing stems or sometimes appeared to approach a whorled pattern. Anatomically preserved specimens suggest that maturation of the primary xylem was exarch or, in a few instances, mesarch. Fertile specimens indicate that sporangia were not aggregated into cones, but rather were interspersed among the microphylls. All protolepidodendrids appear to have been homosporous. As the name of the order suggests, some members have been regarded as progenitors of the Lepidodendrales. However, recent studies suggest that by the Middle Devonian, at least two separate lycophyte groups had been established. One group is believed to have given rise to the arborescent forms of the Carboniferous (Lepidodendrales), and the other, the modern, herbaceous lycophytes, such as *Lycopodium*. It is likely that as additional specimens of these plants are discovered in Devonian strata, there will be a rethinking of the current characterization of the role played by the Protolepidodendrales in the evolution of the Lycophyta.

One of the oldest plants that may be assigned to the Lycophyta is *Baragwanathia,* known from Lower Devonian rocks of Australia. *Baragwanathia longifolia* (Fig. 8-1A) was probably quite similar to a modern *Lycopodium* species in that it had dichotomous branches that bore closely spaced, helically arranged leaves. The plants were much more robust than those

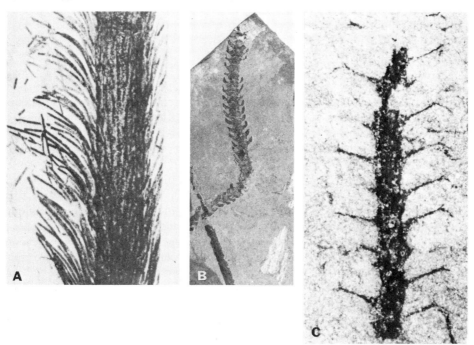

Figure 8-1 A. *Baragwanathia longifolia.* ×1. B. *Archaeosigillaria (Clwydia decussata).* ×1. C. *Protolepidodendron gilboense.* ×1.7. *(A from Lang and Cookson, 1935; C from Grierson and Banks, 1963.)*

of *Lycopodium,* however, with stems reaching 6.5 cm in diameter and leaves up to 4 cm long. Associated with some of the leaves were reniform sporangia that produced trilete spores 50 μm in diameter. The compressed nature of the fossil material makes it difficult to determine whether the sporangia were attached to the upper surfaces of the sporophylls or borne on short stalks in the axils of leaves. The stele is stellate in cross-sectional outline, and the exarch xylem had annular tracheids.

An interesting representative is *Asteroxylon mackiei,* one of the original plants described from the Rhynie chert beds in Scotland (Fig. 8-2C). In the original description of this Lower Devonian plant, Kidston and Lang described some distal branches with terminal sporangia that, although not actually attached, were thought to be the fertile portion of the plant. Although quite different from the other Rhynie vascular plants, the presumed terminal position of sporangia in *Asteroxylon* was regarded as evidence that it was closely related. Subsequent studies of Rhynie chert blocks containing *Asteroxylon* axes demonstrated that the sporangia were borne laterally on the stems near the axils of leaves instead of in a terminal position. This important discovery markedly changed the taxonomic position of the genus.

Asteroxylon was approximately 50.0 cm tall and consisted of upright, monopodial branches supported by a horizontal, presumably underground, rhizome (Fig. 8-2C). From the principal aerial branches arose secondary axes that were regularly dichotomous. In contrast with other Rhynie vascular plants, the aerial stems of *Asteroxylon* were densely covered by numerous leaflike flaps of tissue up to 5.0 mm long. These structures have been called "leaves," "scalelike leaves," "leaflike scales," or "enations." They lacked vascular tissue and stomata, and they were not produced in a definite phyllotactic sequence. For these reasons, many botanists hesitate to regard them as true leaves. There can be little doubt, however, that they represent the precursors of the microphylls that characterize the Lycophyta.

In the rhizomatous portion of the plant, the stele has a central core of tracheids. Sections of the aerial branches, however, indicate that the stele has a stellate cross-sectional configuration (Fig. 8-3), the feature from which the generic name is derived. The primary xylem is slightly mesarch, and the protoxylem elements are situated near the edges of the xylem ridges. Xylem elements have annular and helical secondary thickenings (Fig. 8-4B). Thin-walled cells in the furrows between the xylem ridges are thought to represent phloem. In a transverse section of an aerial axis of *Asteroxylon,* numerous small strands of vascular tissue can be seen in the cortex (Fig. 8-3). These traces originated at the outer edges of the xylem ridges and extended out through the cortex, ending abruptly near the periphery of the stem near the bases of the enations. Sporangia, which may have been axillary, were reniform or purse-shaped (Fig. 8-4A), and dehiscence was probably at the distal edge. The spores were 40 to 60 μm in diameter and ornamented by closely spaced spines covering the distal surface.

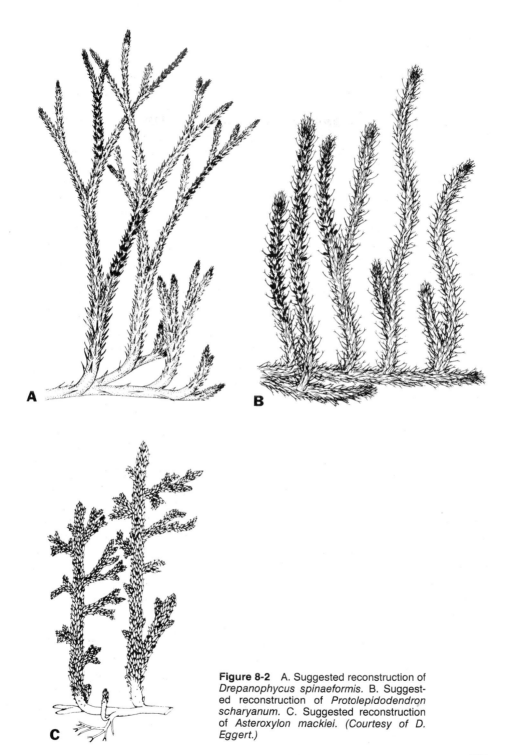

Figure 8-2 A. Suggested reconstruction of *Drepanophycus spinaeformis*. B. Suggested reconstruction of *Protolepidodendron scharyanum*. C. Suggested reconstruction of *Asteroxylon mackiei*. *(Courtesy of D. Eggert.)*

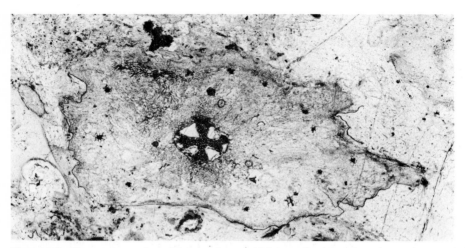

Figure 8-3   Transverse section of *Asteroxylon mackiei* stem showing stele and vascular strands in cortex. ×10.

The basic *Lycopodium* structure is also apparent in specimens of *Drepanophycus spinaeformis,* which is now known throughout the Devonian. At one time, the species was regarded as a good indicator for Lower Devonian strata, but in recent years, the discovery of material from Middle and Upper Devonian beds in New York State indicates a more extensive geologic range of these plants. Aerial axes were probably produced from horizontal rhizomes, which are said to have branched in an H or K configuration, possibly resulting when a branch departed from a stem at a right angle and then dichotomized at an angle of approximately 180° to produce two stems parallel to the primary axis. Known specimens of *Drepanophycus spinaeformis* (Fig. 8-2A) measure up to 27.0 cm long and 4.2 cm wide. The surface is covered with raised mounds (leaf cushions) that represent bases of leaves that were broken off. In a specimen preserved in such a way as to expose the inner surface of the outer part of the stem, with the leaves buried in the matrix under the specimen, instead of mounds, one sees depressed horizontal or circular areas that denote the position of leaves still in place in the matrix. Leaves up to 2.0 cm long were borne in a shallow helix, with approximately eight rows of leaves. Stomata have been described as occurring randomly among elongate and polygonal epidermal cells. The stomatal apparatus of *D. spinaeformis* is the type referred to as paracytic, consisting of two guard cells and two reniform subsidiary cells surrounded by a ring of epidermal cells that vary in number. Although precise details regarding the structure of the stele and the pattern of primary xylem maturation remain to be determined, the tracheids of the flattened vascular strand are known to have possessed annular secondary wall thickenings. Within the genus, sporangia are known to have been borne in either an axillary position or adaxially on leaves.

Figure 8-4 *Asteroxylon mackiei.* A. Longitudinal section of stem with enation (E) and sporangium (S). ×12. B. Tracheids with annular secondary wall thickenings. ×150. C. Suggested reconstruction of vegetative axis with enations and reniform sporangia. *(C reproduced with the permission of the Palaeontological Association; photograph courtesy of W. Chaloner.)*

Inadequate preservation of specimens has precluded a detailed description of spores, although it is believed that the genus was homosporous.

Another species, *D. gaspianus,* had more robust axes characterized by rhombic leaf bases that bore leaves with broad bases and recurved tips. Leaves were produced in a flat helix that contained 18 to 22 rows. Specimens are known from both Lower and Middle Devonian strata.

The generic name *Protolepidodendron* has been used for a variety of Middle Devonian dichotomously branched lycophytes. Their stems may have been up to 2.0 cm in diameter and covered with helically arranged microphylls that were typically bifurcated at the tip (Fig. 8-1C). Compression specimens generally exhibit a longitudinal series of elongate cushions on which the leaves were borne. The stems contain an exarch or mesarch strand of primary xylem that is toothed or triangular in cross section. The tracheids range from annular to bordered pitted, and the sporangia are globose to reniform and are borne on the adaxial surfaces of unmodified sporophylls (Fig. 8-3B).

One of the better-preserved members of the Protolepidodendrales known from Middle and Upper Devonian rocks in New York is *Colpodexylon deatsii.* Its dichotomously branched stems are up to 2.5 cm wide and reveal elliptical leaf bases arranged in a low helix or appearing whorled. The characteristic features of this fossil are the trifurcate leaves, which reached 3.0 cm in length (Fig. 8-5B).

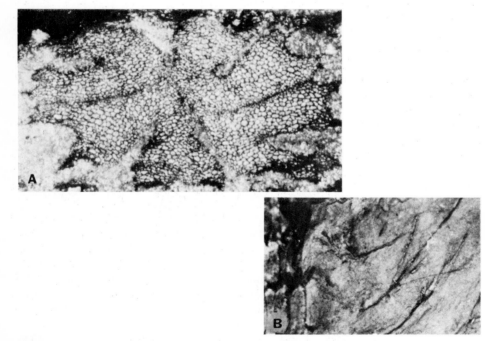

Figure 8-5 *Colpodexylon deatsii.* A. Transverse section of stele showing lobed xylem strand. ×14. B. Leaves showing trichotomous branching. ×3. *(A from Grierson and Banks, 1963.)*

The primary xylem strand is lobed in cross section, exhibiting exarch to mesarch annular elements (Fig. 8-5A). Sporangia are borne on the upper surfaces of unmodified leaves that are scattered along the stem surface.

Archaeosigillaria (= *Clwydia*) (Fig. 8-1B) is a small dichotomously branched herbaceous lycopod known from the Devonian and well into the Carboniferous. The leaf bases range from fusiform on smaller axes to hexagonal on larger stems. Despite the helical arrangement of the small leaves, they are decussate and organized into vertical ranks. Some specimens superficially resemble *Lycopodites,* differing only in the decussate, needlelike leaves. In other species such as *A. vanuxemii* the leaves are deltoid in outline and possess a toothed margin; extending from the apex of the leaf is an elongate hair. Although *Archaeosigillaria* and *Clwydia* are now regarded as the same plant, some authors have suggested that the poorly known leaves of *Archaeosigillaria* and the Devonian age may mean that the taxa are distinct.

Phytokneme is the generic name of a petrified lycopod axis about 3.0 cm in diameter discovered in an Upper Devonian phosphatic nodule zone (Chattanooga shale of Kentucky). The specimen is exquisitely preserved, with all cells and tissues systems in perfect order. In *P. rhodona,* the middle cortical zone, typically poorly preserved in fossil lycopods, is unique in containing a network of radially aligned raylike strands that appear similar to cells that characterize the cone axis of *Lepidostrobus kentuckiensis.*

Probably the most completely known member of the Protolepidodendrales is a slender, herbaceous plant known from Middle Devonian rocks of New York (Fig. 8-6A). Specimens of *Leclercqia complexa* measure up to 46.0 cm in length and vary from 3.5 to 7.0 mm in diameter. The dichotomously or pseudomonopodially branched axes are covered by microphylls that may have attained lengths of 6.5 mm (Fig. 8-6B). Leaves of *Leclercqia* are unusual in that a pair of lateral divisions appears at about the midpoint (Fig. 8-6C). Each division divides into two acuminate tips, whereas the remainder of the leaf tip gradually tapers and recurves abaxially. The closely spaced leaves, each with five slender tips, must have given the plant an unusual appearance (Fig. 8-6B). Stomata are present on the microphylls and stems, and a few have been observed on the wall of a sporangium. Delicate ligules have recently been reported on the microphylls of *Leclercqia* (Fig. 8-6B and E). Some specimens are known in which the vascular cylinder has been preserved as a pyrite petrifaction. In cross section, the stem stele is circular with up to 18 radiating protoxylem points. Metaxylem tracheids are scalariform or have oval pits on their walls. Outside the stele are a narrow zone of parenchyma and occasional fibers that represent the cortex. Each leaf is vascularized by a single trace that originates from the protoxylem ridge of the stele. Sporangia are attached to the adaxial surfaces of sporophylls by a small pad of tissue just proximal to the lateral segments of the leaf. The distribution of sporophylls is similar to that of many species of *Lycopodium,* where fertile and sterile leaves are interspersed and almost indistinguishable. Immature spores are preserved in tetrads. At maturity, the spores were trilete, ranged from 60 to 85 μm in diameter, and were ornamented with numerous

Figure 8-6 *Leclercqia complexa.* A. Several leafy axes. ×1. B. Distal portion of vegetative leaf with ligule (L). ×40. C. Isolated leaf. ×6.5. D. Proximal surface of spore with verrucate ornament. ×700. E. Portion of leaf showing position of ligule. ×40. *(B and E from Grierson and Bonamo, 1979; D from Banks, Bonamo, and Grierson, 1972.)*

closely spaced spines with expanded bases (Fig. 8-6D). The large number of fertile specimens bearing sporangia with morphologically identical spores has been regarded as evidence that *Leclercqia* was homosporous.

LEPIDODENDRALES

Members of the Lepidodendrales constitute the arborescent plants that must have been the most conspicuous elements of the Carboniferous landscape. This group is no doubt responsible, in large part, for the extensive quantities of vegetable matter that resulted in the formation of the Carboniferous coal seams of the world. Because of the tremendous number of specimens collected and the variety of ways in which they were preserved, members of the Lepidodendrales are easily the best-understood fossil lycophytes. The occurrence of structurally preserved members of the order, as well as the extensive stratigraphic distribution of the group, has provided paleobotanists with a group of fossil organisms that may help answer a host of geologic and biological questions. The great diversity of Lycophyta fossil material has helped provide a basic biological understanding of the developmental stages of the vegetative parts and an appreciation of the high degree of diversity in reproductive systems.

The best-known member of the order is *Lepidodendron,* a generic designation initially established for some structurally preserved stems. Today the generic name *Lepidodendron* not only represents stem segments exhibiting cellular preservation, but also signifies an entire plant of enormous proportions that includes leaves, underground parts, reproductive organs, and a variety of other component parts (Fig. 8-7). Even though each of these plant organs can be assigned both generic and specific names and relatively few of these "species" have been shown to belong to the same biological species, the generic name *Lepidodendron* is used by most students of fossil botany to describe an entire plant.

Specimens of *Lepidodendron* have been discovered that indicate that some trees attained heights in excess of 38.0 m and were at least 2.0 m in diameter at the base. The massive, erect, upright trunks of some *Lepidodendron* species branched profusely to produce large crowns of leafy twigs. Some leaves were at least 1.0 m long (most were much shorter), and when they dropped from the branches, conspicuous leaf bases were left on the stem surfaces. Strobili were borne at the tips of distal branches. The underground portions of *Lepidodendron* consisted of dichotomizing axes that bore helically arranged lateral appendages that undoubtedly functioned as roots.

Some of the more commonly encountered fossils assignable to the lepidodendrids are compressions of stem surfaces that are marked by persistent, somewhat asymmetric, diamond-shaped leaf cushions (Fig. 8-8A). The leaf cushion actually represents the expanded leaf base left behind after the leaf drops off. In other words, abscission of the leaf did not take place right at the stem surface. In general, the cushions, or bolsters, have slightly pointed upper and lower angles and rounded lateral sides. The actual scar left by the abscised leaf is slightly above the midpoint of the cushion and is generally elliptical or rhombic in outline (Fig. 8-8B). On the surface of the leaf scar are three small, dotlike impressions. The central one represents the single vascular-bundle trace that extended into the leaf. The two scars on either side represent two channels of loosely arranged parenchyma tissue, termed parichnos, that originated in the cortex and accompanied the vascular bundle into the mesophyll of the leaf. On some *Lepidodendron* stem surfaces, two additional parichnos channels can be identified a short distance beneath the leaf scar. The parichnos strands that characterize the arborescent lycophytes are thought to have represented an

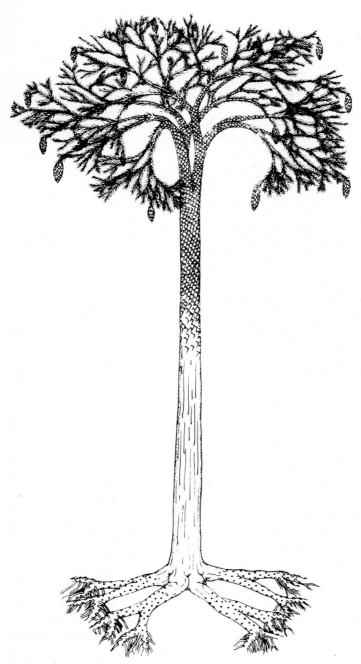

Figure 8-7 Suggested reconstruction of *Lepidodendron. (Courtesy of D. Eggert.)*

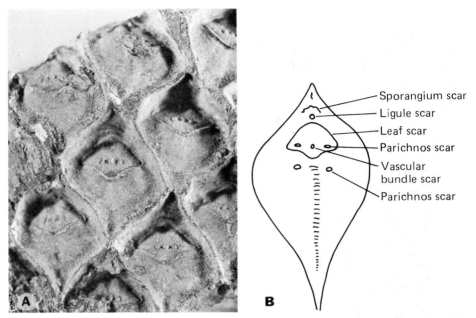

Figure 8-8 A. *Lepidodendron* leaf bolsters preserved in a Mazon Creek nodule. B. Idealized *Lepidodendron* leaf bolster.

aerating tissue system of the stem. A vertical line extends from the leaf scar (see Fig. 8-23C) to the lower pointed angle; this really represents an angle of the more or less pyramid-shaped base. In many specimens, lateral wrinkles cut across this line. Initially it was thought that these wrinkles were of systematic value, but it is now understood that they formed as a result of addition of secondary tissues in the stem. Just above the leaf scar is a mark that represents the position of a small flap of tissue, the ligule. Above the ligule scar is a triangular mark that has been interpreted as a vestigial sporangium scar. The rest of the markings on a leaf base consist of a line extending from the vestigial sporangium scar to the tip of the leaf base and two lines that extend laterally and downward from the same scar. Rarely is preservation so good that all these features can be observed in a single leaf base.

Compression specimens of arborescent lycophyte stems have provided information about the epidermis of these plants. A waxy cuticle covered the stem surface, including the leaf cushion, but not the leaf scar. The epidermis is simple and lacks such specialized cells as hairs and glands. Stomata are common and sunken in shallow pits, as in many gymnospermous plants.

Species of *Lepidodendron* have been delimited on the basis of internal stem organization. The configuration of the stele has been used as a taxonomic character, and it has also been used to suggest evolutionary changes that may have taken place within the arborescent forms. A knowledge of the stelar changes that took place at various levels of the stem has clearly demonstrated

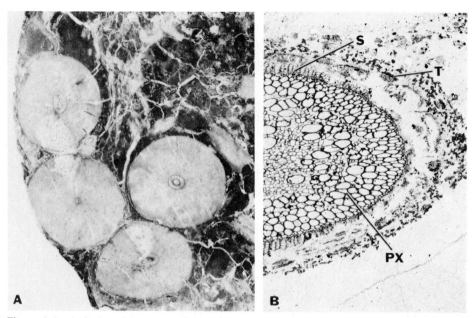

Figure 8-9   A. Steles of the Arran tree *(Lepidophloios wuenschianus).* ×3. B. Partial transverse section of *Lepidodendron selaginoides* stele. PX = primary xylem, S = secondary xylem, T = trace. ×12.

that many of the "species" of *Lepidodendron,* as well as the closely related genus *Lepidophloios,* merely represent different developmental stages of a single species. These studies have provided us with a basic understanding of just how these giant Carboniferous plants actually grew.

Before discussing the ontogenetic changes that occur during arborescent lycophyte growth, let us examine the internal structure of a typical *Lepidodendron* stem. The stem material of two common North American species, *L. scleroticum* and *L. schizostelicum,* is abundant in coal-ball deposits from the Eastern Interior Basin. These taxa will be used to present a composite picture of the internal organization of a *Lepidodendron* stem.

The central portion of the stem may be protostelic, or there may be a mixture of parenchyma cells interspersed with the tracheids in the very center; other stems may be siphonostelic (Fig. 8-9A). The tracheidlike cells in the second stele type are shaped more like short, squat parenchyma cells rather than long, slender cells (Fig. 8-9B). This condition is often cited as evidence that the pith in lycophytes originated when the cells in the center of stems failed to differentiate into tracheids. Surrounding the central zone is a narrow band of metaxylem tracheids with scalariform wall thickenings. Protoxylem is outermost. In a transverse section, the periphery of the primary xylem appears fluted because of the ridges of protoxylem. As in most members of this division, maturation of the primary xylem is exarch.

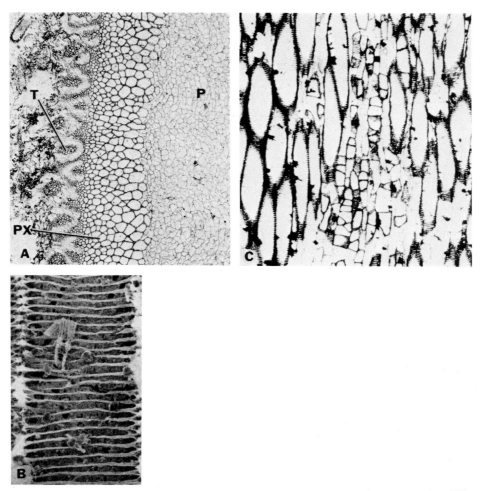

Figure 8-10 A. Partial transverse section of sigillarian stele with leaf trace (T), primary xylem (PX), and pith (P). ×12. B. Tracheid of *Lepidodendron* with scalariform secondary wall thickenings and Williamson striations. ×220. C. Longitudinal section of the primary xylem of *Lepidodendron selaginoides* showing tracheids of two sizes. ×40.

Surrounding the primary xylem may be a zone of secondary xylem, and this may reach a maximum thickness of several centimeters (Fig. 8-9A). Secondary xylem accounts for only a small proportion of the diameter of these trunks. Extensive development of periderm is responsible for their massive size. Tracheids of the secondary xylem are scalariform and, like those of the primary xylem, have delicate strands of secondary wall material extending between adjacent bars (Fig. 8-10B). These structures are called fimbrils, or Williamson striations, and they are characteristic of lepidodendrids. Numerous vascular rays radiate through the secondary xylem, and they are generally a single cell wide and up to several cells high. Scalariform thickenings on the walls of the radiating parenchyma cells (Fig. 8-10C) suggest to some that the phylogenetic origin of rays in this group is from tracheids.

Immediately outside the secondary xylem is what is assumed to be a vascular cambium. Recent studies suggest that this cambial zone was unifacial, with secondary tissues occurring only on the inner face. This organization is unlike the bifacial cambia of existing woody plants. The unusual manner in which this secondary vascular tissue was produced was determined by examination of stems with and without secondary vascular tissue, comparing the distribution of cell types within the stems. In *Lepidodendron,* the phloem zone is separated from the secondary xylem by a band of thin-walled cells termed the parenchyma sheath. Sieve cells with large, horizontally elliptical sieve areas are interspersed with strands of phloem parenchyma on the outer side of the parenchyma sheath. Cells of the phloem parenchyma tend to be axially oriented and lack sieve areas. In some specimens of *Lepidodendron,* a zone of radially seriate, thin-walled cells is in contact with the secondary xylem cylinder. Some workers believe that this tissue resulted from cambial activity. However, it appears that it was formed of living primary-sheath cells that were capable of reverting to a meristematic condition. Current evidence seems to suggest that no secondary phloem was produced within the arborescent lycophytes.

Cortical tissues of the lepidodendrids have been subdivided into three general zones termed the inner, middle, and outer cortex. These zones have been defined in terms of the nature of their cell types. The inner cortex is the narrowest of the cortical zones and is constructed of small, isodiametric parenchyma cells. Aggregations of cells presumed to be secretory cells, in addition to lacunae, fibers, and various types of sclerotic cells, also occur in this zone. The middle cortex is more extensive and is constructed of larger parenchyma cells. In young stems this zone is characterized by radially extending lacunae, and in older stems it is generally not preserved, except for a few parenchyma cells along the inner and outer edges. Cells of the outer cortex show no definite arrangement. They are slightly thicker-walled and superficially resemble collenchyma cells. In some species, this zone may be distinguished by longitudinally oriented, anastomosing bands of fibers.

What has been termed secondary cortical tissue, or periderm, was produced in the outer cortex, and judging from the extensive blocks of periderm that have been recovered in coal balls, it is this tissue that contributed to most of the trunk diameter in these plants. Periderm production is traditionally regarded as having originated from a single layer of meristematic parenchyma cells in the outer cortex just beneath the leaf bases. This meristematic layer, termed phellogen, produced some tissue toward the outside of the stem (phellem) and a greater amount toward the inner part. Cells of the periderm are radially aligned and often show a storied (horizontal) arrangement. In other lepidodendrids, the periderm is far more complex. For example, in *L. johnsonii,* three kinds of cells are described in the periderm. These include thick-walled, axially elongated fibers; radial rows of chambered cells, conspicuous because they are divided by transverse walls; and secretory cells aligned in sinuous bands that in transverse section give the appearance of growth rings.

Recent studies suggest that periderm may have formed within the arborescent lycophytes in several ways. One suggestion is that tangential bands of meristematic tissue were formed at varying depths within the cortex by a dedifferentiation of the primary cortical cells. The presence of short, radial files of secondarily derived cells supports this position. This pattern of periderm production is similar to that in some monocotyledons, in which cells of the outer cortical layers become meristematic and produce radially oriented files of cells. The meristematic cells lose their ability to divide, and successively deeper cortex cells repeat the process of periderm production. The presence of such short files of periderm cells in both stems and underground axes of *Lepidodendron* supports such a pattern of development.

In some plants, periderm does not result from production of secondary tissue, but rather is the result of differentiation of primary cortical cells. Although our understanding of growth in the arborescent lycophytes, including secondary tissue production, is extensive, it is still not clear how these plants produced extraxylary tissues.

One of the outstanding contributions to modern paleobotany involves detailed investigations of development in arborescent lycophytes. Studies of this type have not only contributed to an understanding of how these plants actually grew, but have also made it possible for paleobotanists to distinguish structural changes from one level to another in the same plant from those which are truly specific for individuals. The most comprehensive treatment involving the genera *Lepidodendron* and *Lepidophloios* is by Eggert (1961), who detailed the various growth phenomena in these plants. This study utilized a large number of structurally preserved axes that contain varying amounts of primary and secondary tissues in stems of varying diameters. It was possible, through these fossils, to reconstruct the pattern of growth in these plants. This was difficult because the pattern differs markedly in several basic features from that of most trees inhabiting the earth today.

In *Lepidodendron,* the upper portion of the main axis contains a large siphonostele that is characterized by a wide pith surrounded by a thick zone of primary xylem (Fig. 8-11B). When the plant was relatively immature, the cortex was extensive and the outer surface of the trunk was covered with numerous rows of raised leaf bases. As the tree continued to grow, secondary xylem and periderm were added to the stem. The resulting increase in stem diameter resulted in the sloughing off of the outer cortical tissues, including the leaf bases. Thus, in the older parts of the plant, the outer surface of the trunk was protected by periderm. Older reconstructions of *Lepidodendron* in museums and drawings often err in showing leaf bases present on old trunks all the way to the ground. Obviously, there must have been a change in stelar configuration from what was

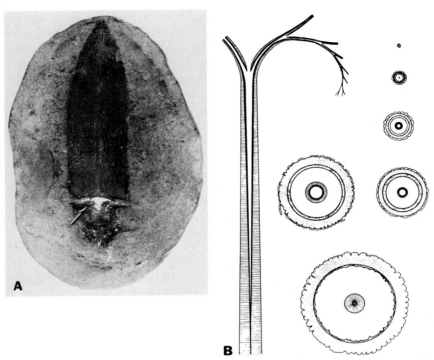

Figure 8-11 A. *Lepidostrobophyllum*. Arrow indicates position of sporangial attachment. ×1.5. B. Longitudinal and transverse sections showing the distribution of xylem in the aerial parts of an arborescent lycopod. Primary xylem is indicated by black, secondary xylem by solid horizontal lines. *(B from Eggert, 1961.)*

a protostelic sporeling stage to upper levels of the main trunk. This initial expansion of the primary body has been termed epidogenesis.

At more distal levels of the tree, the branches had smaller steles and, on the surface, fewer rows of smaller leaves. Sections of stems at these levels indicate that less secondary xylem and periderm were produced (Fig. 8-12C). Such a reduction in stele size and tissue production continued until the most distal branches contained a tiny protostele with only a few delicate tracheids, no secondary xylem or periderm, and just a few rows of leaves. This stage in development, in which the plant literally "grows itself out," has been termed apoxogenesis. Eggert's research has several important biological implications. We know that plants such as *Lepidodendron* and *Lepidophloios* demonstrated a determinate growth pattern that is unlike that of most living woody plants. It also demonstrates that the small distal twigs are not simply immature axes with the potential of developing into large branches in time.

The leaves of arborescent lycophytes are linear (Fig. 8-12A), and some reached lengths of up to a meter. Many of the species established for detached leaves no doubt represent forms that were produced by the same kind of plant but differed in size and shape because of their position on the plant. A single vascular bundle extends the entire length of the lamina and is flanked on either side by a shallow groove that extends the length of the leaf on the abaxial surface (Fig. 8-12B). Stomata are sunken in shallow pits and aligned in rows that paralleled the grooves. A well-developed hypodermal zone of fibers surrounds the mesophyll parenchyma and vascular bundle of the leaf; nothing resembling palisade parenchyma has been reported in these arborescent lycophyte leaves. The generic name *Lepidophyllum* was used for both structurally preserved and compressed lepidodendrid leaves, but because this name had been used earlier for a flowering plant, the name *Lepidophylloides* has been proposed in its place.

Underground axes are grouped under the generic name *Stigmaria*. These subaerial, dichotomizing structures represent one of the most common lycophyte fossils and constitute the principal organ found in the clay layer immediately beneath most Carboniferous coal deposits. This layer is believed to represent the soil in which these plants grew. Extensive specimens, some with

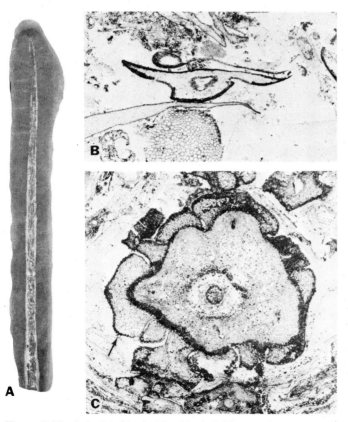

Figure 8-12   A. Isolated leaf of *Lepidophylloides* preserved in a Mazon Creek nodule. ×0.4. B. Transverse section of *Lepidophylloides*. ×12. C. Transverse section of arborescent lycopod twig with attached leaves *(arrow)*. ×14.

rootlike structures still attached, have been uncovered in a configuration that supports this contention. Although there are several named species, knowledge of the internal structure of underground systems of tree-sized lycophytes is based principally on *Stigmaria ficoides*.

The underground system of *Lepidodendron* arises from the base of the trunk as four primary axes, each of which radiates horizontally, allowing gradual penetration of the soil. These primary axes dichotomize repeatedly to form an extensive subterranean system that may have radiated up to 15.0 m from the trunk. Figure 8-13D is of an extensive specimen that was discovered near

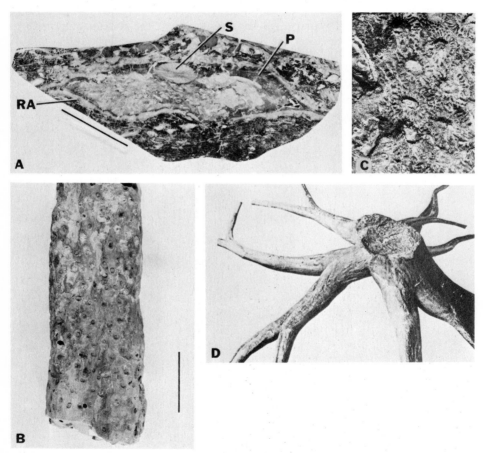

Figure 8-13 A. Transverse section of a large stigmarian axis. P = periderm, RA = rootlet attachment, S = stele. Scale represents 10 cm. B. Cast of *Stigmaria* showing helically arranged rootlet scars. Scale represents 4 cm. C. Surface pattern of *Stigmaria stellata*. ×1. D. Portion of an extensive *Stigmaria ficoides* system found near Bradford, England, and originally figured by Williamson in 1887. Distance across the system is 6 m. *(C courtesy of J. Jennings; D from Frankenberg and Eggert, 1969.)*

Bradford, Yorkshire, and measures 6.0 m across. Attached to each axis are helically arranged lateral appendages (Fig. 8-13B) that have been called rootlets. These rootlike structures were apparently abscised during the growth of the plant, leaving the circular scars seen on a variety of casts, compressions, and impressions of *Stigmaria* (Fig. 8-13B).

Primary axes have a parenchymatous pith that may have become interspersed with tracheids at more distal levels. Primary xylem is endarch and arranged in a series of dissected bands. These bands, in turn, are surrounded by a vascular cambium. Secondary xylem is distinctive because splitting along the wide vascular rays gives the wood a segmented appearance. Secondary xylem tracheids are aligned in radial files and possess scalariform wall thickenings with fimbrils identical with those of the aerial parts. Occasional imperfections in the secondary xylem apparently are the result of a temporary cessation of vascular-cambium activity, which caused an abrupt change in the diameter and distribution of the tracheids from the normal pattern of development. It has been suggested that the erratic cambial activity was a result of some abrupt change in the environment.

No secondary phloem has been identified in *Stigmaria,* and if it were indeed missing, translocation, as has been suggested for aerial stems, would have been carried on by the primary phloem.

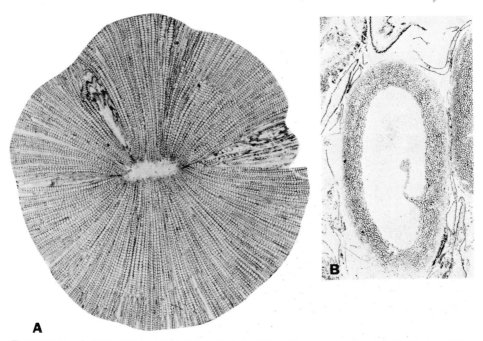

A

Figure 8-14   A. Transverse section of woody cylinder of *Stigmaria* produced by *Sigillaria.* ×8. B. Transverse section of lateral appendage (rootlet). ×6.

Both primary and secondary cortical tissues of *Stigmaria ficoides* are complex, having consisted of numerous cell and tissue systems, some of which are difficult to trace developmentally. In general, however, the production of secondary cortical tissues in the underground parts resulted in a narrow zone of periderm that is histologically similar to that of the aerial stem (Fig. 8-13A).

The lateral appendages ("rootlets") produced by the stigmarian axes are approximately a centimeter in diameter, gradually tapering distally. These appendages have a thin outer cortical zone, which is surrounded by a central, hollow, middle cortex, and a small monarch strand, which is surrounded by an inner cortex (Fig. 8-14B). At some levels, a connective extends from the outer cortex to the inner cortex. Recent work suggests, however, that the connective did not extend throughout the length of the appendage, but rather that the vascular bundle with its thin-walled cortical sheath was free in the hollow central region for most of its length.

Stigmaria stellata is the name applied to some Upper Mississippian lycophyte underground systems. Specimens exhibit radiating ridges around the lateral appendage scars in casts and impressions (Fig. 8-13C). Structurally preserved axes indicate a close relationship to *S. ficoides*, but *S. stellata* differs in several anatomic features, including the absence of a connective in the lateral appendages. Not all stigmarian underground parts are extensive dichotomously branched systems. Some, such as the Lower Mississippian genus *Protostigmaria*, consist of cormlike axes that bear helically arranged lateral appendages similar to those of *Stigmaria* (Fig. 8-15B). One specimen recently discovered from the Price Formation is believed to have been preserved in the growing position (Fig. 8-15A). The axes are preserved as impression-compression, mold-cast specimens, one up to 60.0 cm long and approximately 23.0 cm in diameter at the base. The maximum number of basal lobes reported appears to be 13. Leaf-scar patterns near the base of some specimens appear similar to those formed on

Figure 8-15 *Protostigmaria.* A. Cast of basal portion of stem. B. Base showing the position of lobes *(arrows). (Courtesy of J. Jennings, E. Karrfalt, and G. Rothwell.)*

decorticated portions of the stem *Lepidodendropsis,* and the presumed biological affinities of these two form genera are further strengthened by the constant association of both taxa at the same locality.

One feature of *Protostigmaria* that deserves additional comment is the ability of the plant to maintain an upright position despite the relatively small anchoring surface of the lobed base. Recent experimental studies suggest that during the development of *Isoetes,* the noncontractile roots in the furrows of the cormlike base move laterally as tissues are added, resulting in the plant being "pulled" farther into the substrate. It has been suggested that such a mechanism may have been operative in a system such as *Protostigmaria,* which appears to have lacked the extensively dichotomized anchoring system of some of the other arborescent lycopods.

Development of the underground parts of these plants was probably quite similar to the epidogenic and apoxogenic stages described for the aerial stems. Despite the large number of fossil specimens of *Stigmaria* that have been collected, there are still a number of features of these organs that remain to be determined and interpreted. For example, the helical arrangement of the lateral appendages is unlike the generally irregular arrangement of roots in most living plants. In addition, no root hairs have been identified, and it might be suggested that fungi in some of the cortical parenchyma cells functioned as mycorrhizae. Furthermore, the bilateral symmetry of the vascular bundle is different from the radial orientation of the vascular strand in the root. Finally, it appears as if the lateral appendages abscised from the parent axis in a manner similar to the process of foliar abscission in many existing plants. However, such a process is not seen in the roots of living plants. For this reason, it has been suggested that the "rootlets" of *Stigmaria* are actually homologous with leaves that have been adapted and modified for the functions of anchorage and absorption.

The reproductive units of the lepidodendrids consist of strobili or cones borne among the crown of distal branches (see Fig. 8-7). The basic organization of the cone is a central axis with helically arranged sporophylls (Fig. 8-16A). Sporangia are located on the upper surfaces (adaxial) of sporophylls (Fig. 8-11A) that are upturned at the distal ends and overlapped by sporophylls below. A portion of the lower surface of the sporophyll extends downward to form a heel. A ligule is present in a small pit just distal to the sporangium.

The generic name *Lepidostrobus* is the most common designation for lycophyte cones of this type. Taxonomic problems are considerable within the genus because it has been used not only for cones demonstrating all types of preservation (Fig. 7-16C), but also for cones that are both monosporangiate (having only one type of spore) and bisporangiate (having two types of spores). *Lepidostrobus oldhamius* is a cone known from Lower and Middle Pennsylvanian deposits in both North America and Great Britain. Specimens range from 2.0 to 6.0 cm in diameter and exceed 30.0 cm in length (Fig. 8-16A). Sporangia are massive (Fig. 8-16A and B) and, depending on stage of development, may have an irregularly shaped pad of sterile tissue extending from the sporophyll into the lumen of the sporangium. All the sporangia contain small (20 to 30 μm) spores

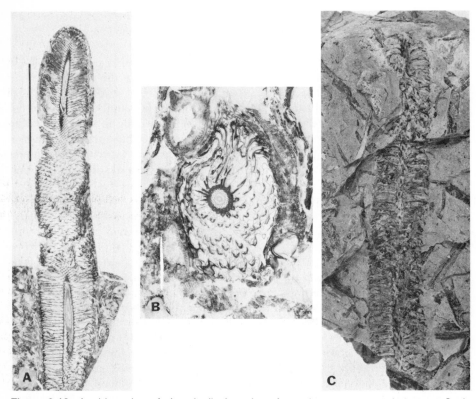

Figure 8-16 *Lepidostrobus.* A. Longitudinal section of massive monosporangiate cone. Scale represents 10 cm. B. Transverse section of cone showing axis and helically attached sporophylls. ×1. C. Compressed lepidostroboid cone from the Mississippian of Arkansas. ×0.8.

that are characterized by a trilete suture on the proximal surface and delicate spines on the distal face (see Fig. 8-19A). Many dispersed spores of *Lepidostrobus* are preserved in sediments, and one of the common generic names applied to these grains is *Lycospora.*

Lepidostrobus schopfii is a bisporangiate cone that in general organization resembles a massive *Selaginella* strobilus (Fig. 8-17A). Specimens are up to 8.0 cm long and 1.3 cm in diameter. The arrangement of parts and disposition of tissue systems are identical with those of *L. oldhamius*, except for the presence of two types of spores in *L. schopfii*. Distal sporangia contain a large number of *Lycospora*-like microspores, while more nearly basal sporangia contain 12 to 29 trilete megaspores. The megaspores range from 700 to 1250 μm in diameter and are marked by an elongation of the proximal surface into a structure termed the apical prominence. Dispersed megaspores of this type are called *Valvisisporites*. One of the interesting features of *L. schopfii* is the exquisite preservation of both the micro- and megagametophyte phases. Within some of the megaspores near the trilete suture is a parenchymatous cellular megagametophyte (Fig. 8-18A).

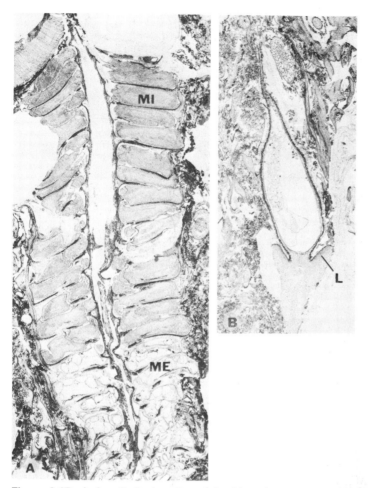

Figure 8-17 A. Longitudinal section of *Lepidostrobus schopfii,* a bisporangiate cone. Ml = microsporangia, ME = megasporangia. ×4.5. B. *Achlamydocarpon belgicum.* Note thickened sporangium wall and reduced lateral laminae (L). ×4. *(A from Brack, 1970.)*

Some of the surface cells bear elongate tufts of rhizoids that extend from the suture of the spore and actually penetrate the sporangium wall. Some mega-gametophytes possessed archegonia at the time of fossilization, and several archeogonial necks have been described as interspersed among the rhizoids (Fig. 8-18B). The archegonia have from one to three tiers of neck cells and, in a few specimens, an enlarged cell, suggestive of an archegonial venter, beneath the tier.

Some of the microspores in the distal sporangia are preserved in tetrad configurations (Fig. 8-19B). Other spores reveal stages in the development of the microgametophyte, including partitions suggestive of the antheridial initial and prothallial cells. Some of the microspores contain material that has been

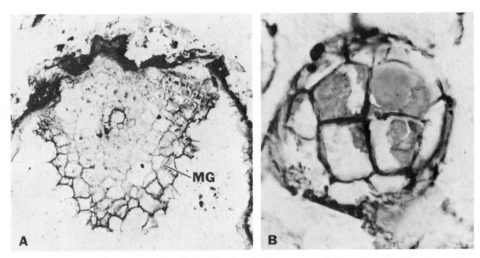

Figure 8-18 *Lepidostrobus schopfii.* A. Distal end of megaspore with cellularized megagameto-phyte (MG). ×200. B. Polar view of archegonium showing four neck cells. ×1200. *(From Brack, 1970.)*

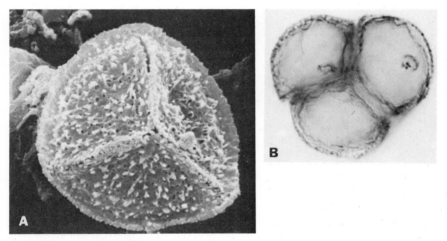

Figure 8-19 *Lepidostrobus schopfii.* A. *Lycospora* microspore showing proximal surface orna-ment. ×2400. B. Portion of a microspore tetrad. ×1200. *(B from Brack, 1970.)*

interpreted to be chromosomes, but the evidence is not completely convincing. When compared with the gametophytes of existing lycophytes, *L. schopfii* has microgametophytes that are more similar to those of *Selaginella*, whereas the structure of the megagametophytes more closely corresponds to that of *Isoetes*.

Both compressed (Fig. 8-16C) and structurally preserved lepidostroboid cones are known from the Upper Mississippian Fayetteville shale. These cones, which all appear to have been monosporangiate, may have attained lengths of

22.5 cm. Spores extracted from sporangia of both preservational types are excellent for comparing these reproductive units. In *L. fayettevillense* (see Fig. 1-1A), the small trilete miospores are characterized by a perforated flange that encircles the spore at the equator (see Fig. 8-25A).

Sporangiostrobus is the name used for large mono- and bisporangiate lycopod cones known from both compression and anatomically preserved specimens. One species from the Middle Pennsylvanian of Kansas, *S. kansanensis,* measures about 16.0 cm long and is nearly 12.0 cm in width. The basic organization of this cone is similar to that of other arborescent lycopod fructifications, but differs in having large megaspores of the *Zonalesporites* type and microspores that exhibit an extended range of morphologic variability that

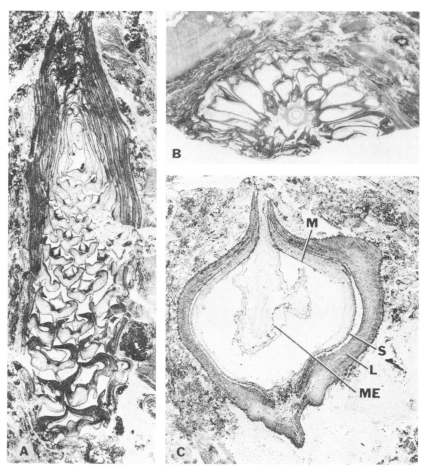

Figure 8-20 *Lepidocarpon.* A. Longitudinal section of cone apex. ×5.5. B. Transverse section of cone. ×1. C. Transverse section of lepidocarp showing position of lateral laminae (L), sporangium (S), megaspore (M), and cellular megagametophyte (ME). ×6.5.

includes such dispersed spore taxa as *Densosporites, Radiizonates, Cingulizonates,* and *Vallatisporites.*

Some cones of lepidodendrids were monosporangiate, but produced only megaspores. Possibly the most common of these is the genus *Lepidocarpon* (Fig. 8-20A), a cone type regarded as the most highly evolved because the organization of the sporophylls closely approximates the function of integuments in seed plants. In *Lepidocarpon,* sporangia are adaxial on a sporophyll (Fig. 8-20B) that is characterized by two lateral laminae or extensions of the sporophyll that partially envelop the sporangium (Fig. 8-20C). The sporophyll extends distally, as in *Lepidostrobus.* Within the sporangium is one large, functional, trilete megaspore and three aborted spores. The wall of the megaspore (called *Cystosporites* when found isolated) is unique in that it is constructed of loosely arranged strands of sporopollenin (Fig. 8-21B). Cellular megagametophytes containing archegonia are known, and recently, embryos have been described. Stages of the young sporophytes include nonvascularized embryos, vascularized axes up to 4.0 mm in diameter anchored in the gametophyte tissue, and some secondary tissues. The presence of septate hyphae in some of the young sporophytes suggests a mycorrhizal association.

Another megasporangiate cone has an unusually ornamented functional

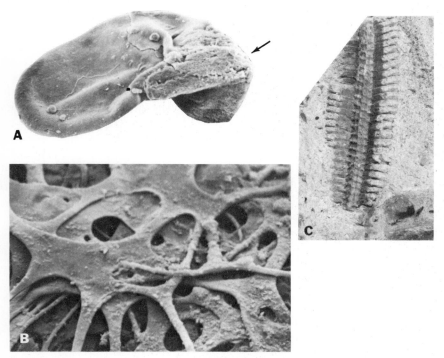

Figure 8-21   A. Abortive megaspore of *Achlamydocarpon varius* with proximal massa *(arrow).* ×50. B. Surface of *Lepidocarpon* functional megaspore. ×1000. C. Mold-cast preservation of a Mississippian *Lepidocarpon* cone. ×0.5. *(A from Taylor and Brack-Hanes, 1976.)*

megaspore. Fragments of apparently monosporangiate cones from eastern Kentucky show axes and helically arranged, unintegumented megasporophylls. The sporangium is large, and the wall is constructed of columnar cells. Each sporangium contains a tetrad of megaspores with one large, presumably functional spore (up to 4.0 mm long) and three smaller (200 to 500 μm) aborted spores. The sporoderm of the functional megaspore is approximately 10 μm thick and has two layers. The outer surface is covered with numerous spines about 50 μm long. The four spores are enclosed in a granulose spongy structure that is a distal winglike attachment to the large functional spore. This winglike extension on the distal end of the functional megaspore may have represented a form of perispore that was somehow involved in dispersal, or it may have functioned to orient the conspicuous apical prominence of the trilete suture so as to enhance the opportunity for fertilization.

It is probable that apparently monosporangiate cones such as *L. oldhamius* and *L. fayettevillense* represent the microsporangiate cones of heterosporous plants. In other instances, however, monosporangiate cones could have been produced by homosporous plants reproductively similar to *Lycopodium,* in which the spores germinate into free-living gametophytes. In this regard, the neutral term miospore might be more appropriate, because it is impossible to determine with certainty how the spores functioned in the life of the plant once they were released from the cone.

In another monosporangiate cone, *Achlamydocarpon,* lateral laminae are greatly reduced, and a single large, functional megaspore is present in each sporangium (Fig. 8-17B). In this cone type, the orientation of the trilete suture is toward the cone axis rather than away, as in *Lepidocarpon.* The suture of the functional spore in *Achlamydocarpon* is covered by a massa, or cap, of sporopollenin that may have functioned to protect the developing gametophyte and perhaps help retain moisture in the region of the suture (Fig. 8-21A). In the *Lepidocarpon* cone, this protection may have been provided by the conspicuous lateral laminae of the sporophyll, while in *Achlamydocarpon,* the developing megagametophyte may have been protected by a reverse orientation of the proximal suture and the sporopollenin cap on the megaspore. Microsporangiate cones have recently been discovered and assigned to *A. varius* on the basis of similarities in epidermal structure, pedicel alations, and other histologic details (Leisman and Phillips, 1979). The trilete spores average 64 μm in diameter and exhibit scattered papillae over their distal surfaces that may represent tapetal residues in the form of orbicules. If found dispersed, such grains would be included in the genus *Cappasporites.*

Another tree-sized lycophyte, *Lepidophloios,* occurred in the Carboniferous coal swamps along with *Lepidodendron* (Fig. 8-22). *Lepidophloios* was probably slightly smaller in stature, but in general features quite similar to *Lepidodendron.* One notable difference between the two is the arrangement and organization of leaf bases. In *Lepidophloios,* the leaves are also arranged in a shallow helix, as in *Lepidodendron,* but the leaf bases are flattened and wider than they are tall (Fig. 8-23B). The leaf bases are directed downward on the stem

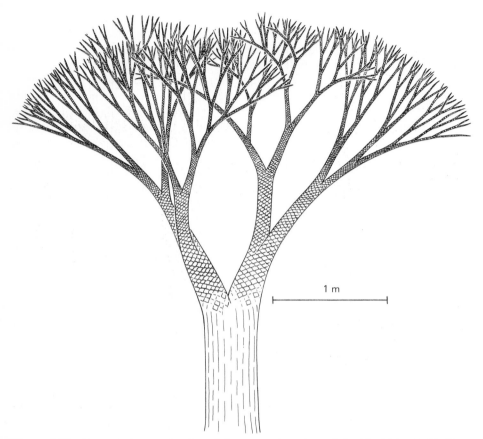

Figure 8-22 Suggested reconstruction of the crown branches of *Lepidophloios hallii. (From DiMichele, 1979a.)*

and overlap the bases below much like shingles on a roof (Fig. 8-23A). The leaf bends upward abruptly from the descending leaf base, and when a leaf abscised it left a scar at the bottom third of the base. Parichnos and vascular-bundle scars on the leaf scar are like those of *Lepidodendron,* but parichnos scars are not present on the base itself. *Lepidophloios* was ligulate, with the ligule attached just above the position of the leaf scar. Many *Lepidophloios* axes have circular to elliptical scars often as much as several centimeters in diameter. The origin of these scars has been debated for many years. Some workers regard them as former sites of vegetative branches (Fig. 8-24B) that abscised during the normal growth of the plants, while other workers suggest that they represent former positions of specialized branches that bore clusters of strobili. Stems with helically arranged scars of this type have been given the generic name *Halonia,* whereas those with oppositely arranged scars are called *Ulodendron* (Fig. 8-24A). Recent studies suggest that *Ulodendron* scars on the axes of *Lepidodendron, Lepidophloios,* and a related genus, *Bothrodendron,* represent

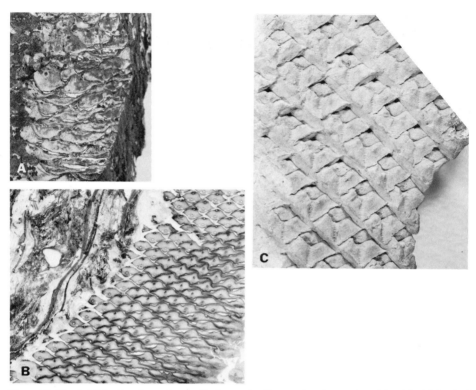

Figure 8-23 A. Etched surface of a coal ball showing the overlapping nature of *Lepidophloios* leaf bases. ×0.6. B. Tangential section of *Lepidophloios* leaf bases. ×1. C. Impression of *Lepidodendron volkmannianum* leaf bases. ×1.

the former positions of branches that abscised in a manner similar to that of some existing gymnosperms and angiosperms.

The outer surface of arborescent lycophyte stems is not the only surface to have been preserved in all instances. The loose construction of the cortex, the relatively thin-walled nature of the vascular elements, and the production of large amounts of periderm all contributed to the sloughing off of stem layers and tissues, either as a feature of normal development or as a result of mechanical separation during the fossilization process. As a result, a variety of "external" features unlike those of the zone of leaf bases are represented in fossils. A variety of generic names have been applied to these decorticated conditions, and the names do not really conform to the concepts of form or organ genera and are therefore of little value in systematic studies. These various fossil forms provide a great deal of information that can be used to reconstruct developmental changes in the component tissue systems of an axis. They actually represent manifestations of anatomic structures viewed from different perspectives.

One of the more common decortication stages is placed in the genus

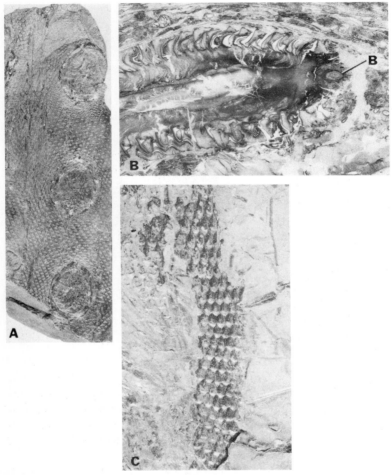

Figure 8-24 A. *Ulodendron* showing position of three branches. ×0.2. B. Transverse section of a *Lepidophloios* stem with branch (B) trace. ×1. C. Surface of *Lepidodendropsis* (Upper Mississippian of Virginia). ×1.

Knorria, which is used for stems in which all the tissues external to the xylem have been removed. The fluted nature of the columns results from numerous leaf traces that pass through the secondary xylem.

Decortication stages are sometimes difficult to distinguish from lycophyte stems in which the leaf bases are inconspicuous or lacking. For example, in *Bothrodendron,* an arborescent member of the group that was approximately 10.0 m tall, the leaf scars are flush with the surface of the stem and not on raised cushions. In some specimens, the leaf scars are arranged in an almost whorled pattern; in others, they are borne in a low helix. The ligulate microphylls are narrow and measure up to 25.0 cm in length. Cones, known from both

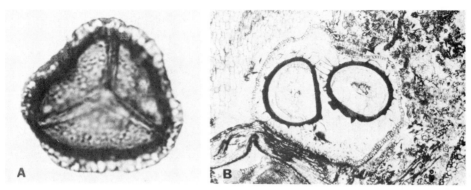

Figure 8-25 A. *Lycospora*-like spore macerated from *Lepidostrobus fayettevillense* (see Fig. 1-1A). ×1000. B. *Bothrodendron* sporangium containing two spiny megaspores. ×32. *(A from Taylor and Eggert, 1968.)*

compressions and petrifactions, consist of sporangia borne adaxially on sporophylls whose distal laminae are greatly elongated. The cones are bisporangiate, with trilete spores toward the apex and sporangia with up to 20 megaspores in each near the base. Megaspores of *Bothrodendron* have numerous spines that cover their surfaces (Fig. 8-25B). Megagametophytes similar to those of some *Lepidodendron* species have been described, including detailed stages in the development of the embryo.

Valmeyerodendron is a Mississippian lycophyte that appears to have been transitional between the Devonian members, which generally lacked leaf bases, and the Carboniferous genera, which were ligulate and possessed parichnos scars. Only compressed specimens are found, but they represent an arborescent plant with stems up to 3.1 cm in diameter (Fig. 8-26A). Helically arranged, quadrangular to hexagonal leaf cushions cover the stems. Each cushion bears a rhombic leaf scar at its apex, although ligule and parichnos scars are absent. Unlike the majority of arborescent lycophytes, which possess narrow, linear leaves, *Valmeyerodendron* has leaves that are nearly triangular in outline (Fig. 8-26B) with a constricted base and attenuated apex.

Duisbergia mirabilis has been described as a Middle Devonian lycophyte with wedge-shaped leaves. The plant is thought to have been about 2.0 m in height, with an upright, unbranched trunk arising from a club-shaped base (Fig. 8-27). The upper half of the plant produced a dense crown of leaves that were borne in a tight helix, but appeared to be in vertical rows. The fan-shaped leaves were approximately 5.0 cm long. Striations on the surface of the lamina suggest a venation pattern of numerous vascular bundles.

In the original description of *D. mirabilis,* the vascular system was characterized as polystelic (Kräusel and Weyland, 1929), and recently, well-preserved petrified specimens from Germany confirm the presence of up to 60 band-shaped strands of secondary xylem arranged in a ring. Although small, wedge-shaped leaves are known for at least one other member of the Lycophyta,

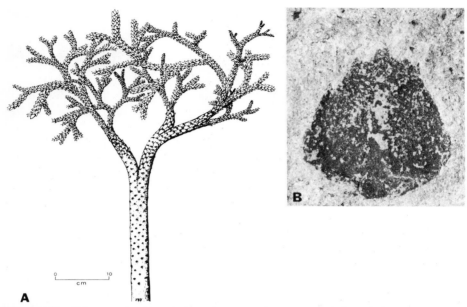

A

Figure 8-26 *Valmeyerodendron triangularifolium.* A. Suggested reconstruction of distal part of plant. B. Isolated leaf showing transverse groove. ×3. *(A from Jennings, 1972; B courtesy of J. Jennings.)*

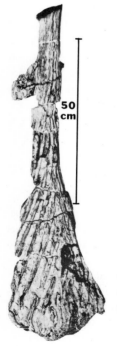

50 cm

Figure 8-27 *Duisbergia mirabilis* base. *(From Schweitzer, 1966.)*

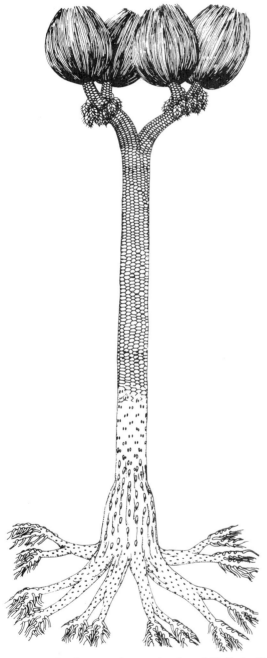

Figure 8-28 Suggested reconstruction of *Sigillaria. (Courtesy of D. Eggert.)*

the "polystelic" organization of the stele and heavily vascularized leaves of *D. mirabilis* are not lycophyte features. Although this plant superficially resembles *Sigillaria* and *Pleuromeia* and may eventually be classified as a lycophyte, the features ascribed to it up to the present suggest, instead, assignment to the Cladoxylopsida of the Pteridophyta.

Another Carboniferous lycophyte that did not branch profusely and was not so massive as the lepidodendrids is *Sigillaria* (Fig. 8-28). Although some specimens have been reported as close to 34.0 m tall, it is probable that most sigillarians were less than 20.0 m. The absence of repeated branching in the distal part of the plant and the structure of the leaf bases are the two principal features that distinguish *Sigillaria* from the other lepidodendrids. *Sigillaria* leaf bases are helically arranged, although they appear to have been aligned in vertical rows. Subgenera of *Sigillaria* have been established to include the various configurations and arrangements of the bases. *Eu-sigillaria* includes forms with ribbed stem surfaces, whereas *Sub-sigillaria* members lack ribs. In the section *Rhytidolepis* of the subgenus *Eu-sigillaria*, the leaf bases and ribs are separated and the furrows between adjacent ribs are straight or nearly so. In the section *Favularia*, the ribs and leaf bases are close together and the furrows have a zigzag configuration. The section *Leiodermaria* (subgenus *Sub-sigillaria*) has widely separated vertical rows of leaf scars with no raised cushions or ribs. *Clathraria*, another section of *Sub-sigillaria*, has closely arranged leaf bases that are not situated on elevated ribs.

Sigillarian leaf bases are typically hexagonal in outline, but they may have ranged to elliptical (Fig. 8-29C). Leaf scars are generally elliptical, with a central leaf-trace scar flanked by two large parichnos scars. A ligule scar is present above the leaf scar.

Most sigillarians must have been rather unusual looking plants with little distal branching and a large number of closely spaced, elongate leaves arising from the top of the trunk. *Sigillariophyllum* is the name applied to leaves that are similar to those of *Lepidodendron* except that some are vascularized occasionally by two laterally flattened strands instead of one. On the lower surface are two longitudinal grooves lined with conspicuous trichomes (Fig. 8-30B). Stomata are arranged in rows, and the guard cells are sunken.

Although compressed remains of sigillarians are rather common, structurally preserved stems are a rather rare fossil find. The central portion of the stem consists of a parenchymatous pith surrounded by a continuous narrow band of primary xylem (Fig. 8-30A). In sectional view, the primary xylem is sinuous, with leaf traces originating from the furrows of the exarch primary xylem (see Fig. 8-10A). Metaxylem tracheids possess fimbrils between the scalariform bars. Secondary xylem in *Sigillaria* is relatively narrow and consists of scalariform tracheids and narrow vascular rays. Distribution of cortical tissues is similar to that described for *Lepidondendron*, and tangentially banded periderm is common in these plants. In *Sigillaria*, the periderm often contains concentric bands of presumably secretory cells. In addition, tangentially expanded cells form distinct spindle-shaped clusters in transverse section. Extending radially through the periderm are cylindrical to laterally flattened strands of

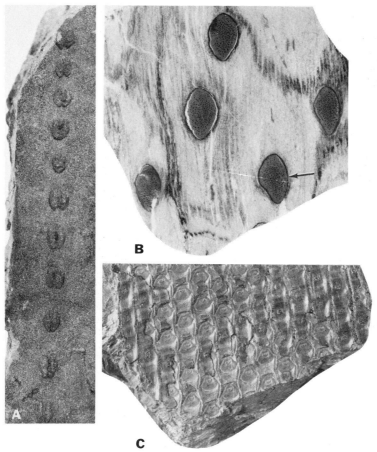

Figure 8-29 A. *Syringodendron.* ×0.5. B. Tangential section of sigillarian periderm showing parichnos tissue *(arrow).* ×1. C. Impression of *Sigillaria mamillaris.* ×1.

parichnos tissue (Fig. 8-29B) that can be related to the parichnos scars on the leaf bases.

Underground portions of *Sigillaria* are similar to the stigmarian root-bearing system of *Lepidodendron* and *Lepidophloios,* but there are a few anatomic differences (see Fig. 8-14A). In the stigmarian axes of *Sigillaria,* the pith is relatively narrow in proportion to the diameter of the stele, and it consists of an outer zone of mixed tracheids and parenchyma and a central zone of parenchyma. The cortex is also narrow and consists of two primary zones. Secondary cortical development involves concentric rings of meristematic cells in the outer, *Sigillaria*-like cortex, while in the underground parts of *Lepidodendron,* periderm was produced from a single, central meristematic layer. In the lateral appendages (rootlets), the connective is continuous, unlike the interrupted organization in *Lepidodendron.* The genus *Stigmariopsis* is known to have been the underground part of some sub-sigillarians and is

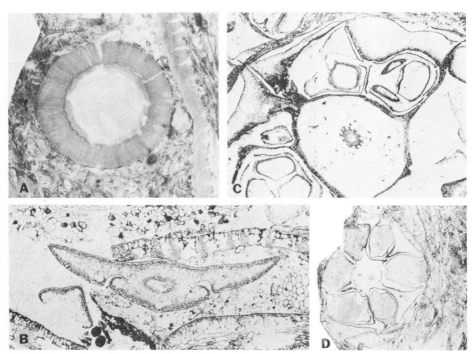

Figure 8-30 A. Transverse section of *Sigillaria approximata*. ×1. B. Transverse section of *Sigillariophyllum* showing central vascular strand and abaxial grooves. ×32. C. Transverse section of megasporangiate *Mazocarpon oedipternum* cone. ×15. D. Transverse section of *M. oedipternum* cone containing microspores. ×2.

distinguished from *Stigmaria* principally on the basis of unequal branching in which the smaller branch is directed downward. One might be inclined to view the subtle differences between the underground parts of the sigillarinas and *Stigmaria* as more apparent than real. If so, it might be impossible to determine which underground system is associated with a particular taxon in a locality in which several different types of lycophytes are present. This difficulty was minimized in one study by collecting in sites where certain lycophyte taxa were absent. For example, Frankenberg and Eggert (1969) were able to characterize *Stigmaria* from several of the Middle Pennsylvanian coal-ball localities where *Sigillaria* was absent. Eggert (1972), in turn, detailed the nature of the sigillarian underground system from an Upper Pennsylvanian site in which *Sigillaria* was present and *Lepidodendron* and *Lepidophloios* were absent. In these instances, a knowledge of the plants present at a given site has made it possible to distinguish which might be valid species from which represent only different stages of development.

Sometimes *Sigillaria* is found in a partially decorticated state. All that is visible on the surfaces of the compression fossils are vertical rows of large, often double, parichnos strands. Fossils such as these, which represent subsurface structural features of the stem, are given the generic name *Syringodendron* (Fig. 8-29A).

Sigillaria is known to have been heterosporous and to have produced cones of two types. It is thought that these cones were borne on elongate peduncles interspersed among the leaf bases just beneath the zone with leaves (Fig. 8-28). Evidence regarding cone position comes not only from compression specimens, but also from structurally preserved stems with persistent bases of sigillarian cone peduncles. Two cone genera thought to have been produced by species of *Sigillaria* are *Mazocarpon* and *Sigillariostrobus*. Specimens of *M. oedipternum*, the common North American form, are frequently in excess of 10.0 cm in length and 1.2 cm in diameter. The sporophylls are arranged in a low helix or are whorled, with the lamina forming conspicuous dorsal heels. The distal ends of sporophylls are relatively short. Megasporangia are roughly triangular in section view, with the cavity filled with a parenchymatous tissue (subarchesporial pad) surrounded by eight megaspores (Fig. 8-30C). Megaspores are large (2.0 mm) and trilete, and have been described with short archegonial necks extending from the proximal suture. Microsporangiate cones contain trilete spores that average 60 μm in diameter (Fig. 8-30D). No sterile tissue has been described in the microsporangia, although the appearance of this tissue may have been a reflection of ontogenetic changes, and possibly it was lost as sporangial contents matured.

Cones of *Sigillariostrobus* are known as compressions. Many no doubt represent different preservational states of the *Mazocarpon* cone type and have been correlated with the latter on the basis of their size, organization of sporophylls, and spore morphology. Specimens of *Sigillariostrobus* range from 15.0 to 30.0 cm long and may be up to 3.0 cm in diameter.

LYCOPODIALES

Lycopodiales include homosporous, eligulate, dichotomously branched herbaceous plants. Modern representatives include two genera, *Lycopodium* and *Phylloglossum*. The fossil members are among the most poorly understood within the Lycophyta. The generic name *Lycopodites* was first used to describe some Tertiary specimens consisting of axes bearing small scalelike leaves. The fossils were later determined to be fragments of conifer shoots. Today the genus includes axes with helically arranged or whorled scale leaves and, if present, sporangia on the adaxial surface, in the axil of foliage leaves, or in monosporangiate strobili. Specimens of *Lycopodites* (Fig. 8-31A) have been described from sediments ranging from Carboniferous to Recent, and they include forms that are both isophyllous (one type of leaf) and anisophyllous (two types of leaves).

One of the difficulties in dealing with fossils of the *Lycopodites* type is the inability to distinguish these remains from the distal twigs of members of Lepidodendrales (Fig. 8-31C). When sporangia are scattered along the stem in association with leaves resembling vegetative leaves, there is no problem, but

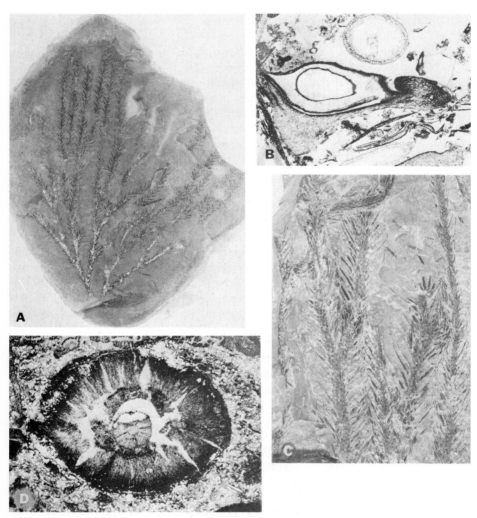

Figure 8-31 A. Compression of *Lycopodites.* ×1. B. Longitudinal section of *Miadesmia membranacea.* ×8. C. Transverse section of *Oxroadia gracilis.* ×3. D. Compressed *Lepidodendron* twigs with leaves. ×0.5. *(D from A. G. Long Collection No. 4627 in the Hancock Museum.)*

most known specimens of *Lycopodites* consist only of vegetative remains. The absence of ligules is another feature that can be used to distinguish the two, but even in exceptionally well-preserved specimens, these structures are often difficult to identify. Finally, some existing *Lycopodium* species have sporophylls that are aggregated into strobili, and it is conceivable that some of the small, apparently microsporangiate *Lepidostrobus* species that have been described may, in fact, represent a cone type such as that in *Lycopodium,* in which the isospores germinated into free-living gametophytes. The potential confusion in delimiting members of this group will no doubt continue until structurally preserved specimens can be correlated with compression fossils. Ultimately, epidermal features, including the distribution and type of stomatal pattern, may be useful in separating the fossilized twigs of the tree-sized lycophytes from the dichotomizing stems of the herbaceous forms.

Oxroadia gracilis is the binomial used for small, dichotomously branched lycophyte axes that lack distinct leaf cushions but possess decurrent leaf bases. The genus is based on structurally preserved specimens of the Lower Carboniferous (Calciferous Sandstone Series) and is thought to have represented an herbaceous lycophyte. The stem contains an exarch protostele with mesarch traces arranged in a helical manner. Microphylls are eligulate and vascularized by a single strand; parichnos is not present. Similar histology and association in the same block of material are used as the basis for assigning a small (4.0 cm long) cone to the stem remains. Sporangia are elongate and borne on sporophylls that have downward-projecting heels. A massive parenchymatous pad of tissue extends from the surface of the sporophyll and partially fills the sporangium cavity. Nothing is known about the spores. The genus is regarded as an herbaceous lycophyte rather than distal branches of an arborescent form because of the absence of secondary tissues in the vascular system and cortex. However, current ideas pertaining to the ontogeny of arborescent lycophytes make such a distinction less certain.

An interesting lycopod from the Mesozoic (late Jurassic to early Cretaceous) of Siberia has recently been described as possessing cones of an unusual morphology. *Synlycostrobus tyrmensis* is thought to have been a creeping plant, probably not too unlike the modern genus *Lycopodium*. The ligulate leaves are scalelike and anisophyllous. Cones are borne on what have been termed fertile shoots, each located in the axil of a scalelike leaf (Fig. 8-32D). The cones are small (5.0 mm long) and consist of approximately 20 helically arranged sporophylls (Fig. 8-32C). Each sporophyll has a conspicuous distal end and a downward-projecting heel that partially protects the adaxial sporangium of the sporophyll below. Only monosporangiate cones that contain radial, trilete spores in the 20 to 22 μm size range have been isolated from the cones, although a single megasporangium containing four spores was isolated from the same matrix. Superficially, the fertile branches of *Synlycostrobus* resemble the primary axis and dwarf shoots (cones) that characterize the Cordaitales. This represents an unusual situation among lycopods and suggests the existence of a totally unique group of lycopods during the Mesozoic.

Associated in the same sediments are well-preserved vegetative axes that are placed in the genus *Lycopodites*. Although morphologic and cuticular features suggest affinities with that taxon, the presence of a ligule associated with each leaf warrants inclusion with the Selaginellales.

SELAGINELLALES

Another herbaceous group that coexisted with the Carboniferous arborescent lycophytes is the order Selaginellales, today represented by a single genus that includes several hundred species. Plants assigned to this order are herbaceous,

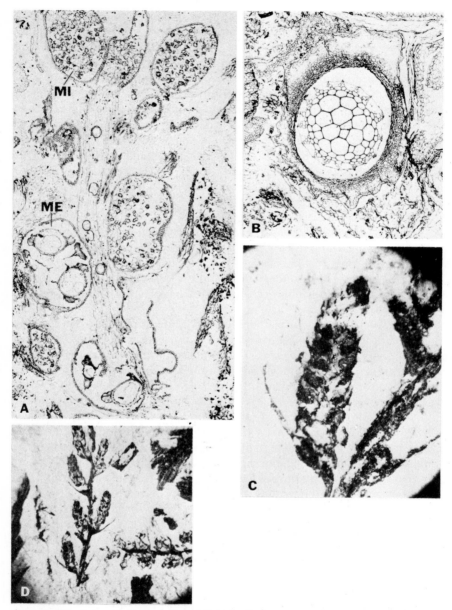

Figure 8-32 A. Longitudinal section of *Selaginellites* cone containing both microspores (MI) and megaspores (ME). ×20. B. Transverse section of *Paurodendron (Selaginella fraipontii)* aerial stem. ×22. C. Single strobilus of *Synlycostrobus tyremensis*. ×7. D. Several strobili of *Synlycostrobus tyremensis* attached to an axis. Note subtending "bracts" for each. ×3. *(C and D courtesy of V. Krassilov.)*

ligulate, and heterosporous. The best-known fossil member, *Selaginella fraipontii,* represents an excellent example of the piecing together of isolated organs of a fossil plant into a single entity. For many years the generic name *Paurodendron* was used for relatively commonly encountered stems bearing helically arranged, ligulate microphylls (Fig. 8-33B). Axes reached 4.0 mm in diameter and were characterized by protosteles that were exarch and stellate in cross section (Fig. 8-32B). Subsequently, the underground portion was discovered attached to a *Paurodendron* axis. It consisted of an unbranched, clavate, unlobed rhizophore (root-bearing organ) from which helically arranged, monarch roots arose (Fig. 8-33A). Despite the small size of the rhizophore stele, some secondary xylem was present. Reproductive parts of the plant were in the form of bisporangiate cones that were initially described under the binomial *Selaginellites crassicinctus* (Fig. 8-32A). Cones of this type were 1.2 cm long and approximately 5.0 mm in diameter. Sporophylls were ligulate and attached to

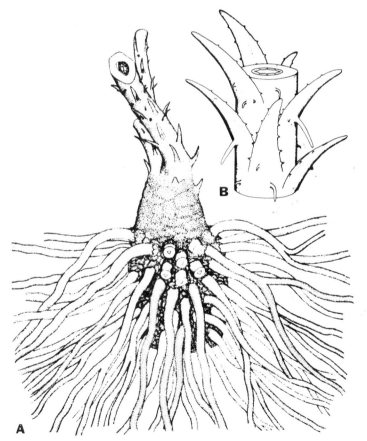

Figure 8-33 *Selaginella fraipontii.* A. Suggested reconstruction of basal portion of plant. B. Aerial stem with leaves. *(From Phillips and Leisman, 1966.)*

the axis in alternating verticils of four. Megasporangia were restricted to the basal region of the cone, with each sporangium containing four or occasionally, up to seven megaspores of the *Triletes* type (Fig. 8-32A). Microspores are assignable to the *sporae dispersae* genus *Cirratriradites.* Demonstration of organic attachment of *Selaginellites* cones to *Paurodendron* axes has made it possible to reconstruct this plant, and it is now referred to as *Selaginella fraipontii.* The plant is reconstructed as a sprawling, sparsely branched herb that produced cones terminally. There is some suggestion that the plant was determinate in growth, much like the arborescent lycophytes. It would appear that *S. fraipontii,* known throughout the Carboniferous, is almost morphologically identical with many of the existing *Selaginella* species that inhabit relatively moist environments. These plants differed, however, in their organization of underground parts. In living selaginellas, roots are not produced indiscriminately, but rather are formed between adjacent older roots, resulting in a configuration resembling that of the rhizomorph of *S. fraipontii.* This feature might suggest a closer affinity with the Lepidodendrales than had been formerly realized. Some workers have recently suggested that based on the helical arrangement of the appendages and monarch roots, *S. fraipontii* is more closely related to some members of the Lepidodendrales than to the Selaginellales.

   Selaginella amesiana is the name applied to a bisporangiate cone preserved in a Pennsylvanian nodule from Mazon Creek, Illinois. The cone measures approximately 2.7 cm in length and 3.5 mm in diameter at the widest point. What is most unusual about this *Selaginella*-like fossil is the exquisite preservation of some gametophytes within the megaspores; in fact, they reveal cellular details, including structures similar to nuclei and chromosomes. Specimens of *Selaginella* are also known from rocks of the Cretaceous. *Selaginella hallei* is based on dichotomously branched shoots bearing anisophyllous microphylls. The strobili have imbricate sporophylls that bear distal microsporangia with trilete spores 50 μm in diameter and proximal megasporangia with four megaspores each. The megaspores average 425 μm in diameter and are trilete.

   Recently, several small lycophyte cones have been discovered in Upper Famennian (Devonian) deposits from Belgium that exhibit an interesting collection of features unlike those of other known Devonian lycophyte cones. They are up to 14.0 cm long and bear helically arranged sporophylls and stalked sporangia. The sporophyll margins of *Barsostrobus* are evenly toothed, with the margins slightly enveloping the sporangium. The vascular system is that characteristic of lycophyte cones, and the traces to the sporophylls have centrifugal and centripetal metaxylem. The spores are 240 to 320 μm in diameter, and they are trilete and evenly ornamented. The cones are thought to have been heterosporous, although no microspores have been discovered. Features of this cone suggest affinities with members of the Lycopodiales or Selaginellales; preservation prevents recognition of ligules. The presence of a reticulate network of fimbrils between the scalariform bars of the metaxylem tracheids similar to those described for some species of *Drepanophycus* suggest that further affinities may be found within the Protolepidodendrales, a group that lacks heterospory and strobilar organization of sporangia.

Miadesmia membranacea (Fig. 8-31B) is the binomial given to megasporophylls known only from the Carboniferous of Europe. The cones contain only megasporophylls that are attached to the axis at right angles. Each megasporophyll is approximately 3.0 mm long and contains a megasporangium that attaches near the proximal end of the sporophyll. Outgrowths of the sporophyll (lateral laminae) completely envelope the sporangium, except in the distal region. The enveloping sporophyll is divided into elongate, tentaclelike extensions that project beyond the distal opening. The sporangium is somewhat flattened on the sporophyll, so that the opening is directed away from the cone axis. A large ligule is present just distal to each megasporangium. *Miadesmia* is interesting in that the sporangium contains one large, functional megaspore; some of these megaspores are known to have contained a cellular gametophyte. The precise affinities of *Miadesmia* remain in doubt. In the original description, it was noted that they occurred in the same coal balls as specimens of *Lepidodendron harcourtii.* The small size of the units has suggested to some workers that they may represent a ligulate cone type within the Selaginellales that parallels the development of heterospory (leading to a reduction in functional megaspore number to one megaspore per sporangium) in the Lepidodendrales.

PLEUROMEIALES

The Pleuromeiales represent an interesting group of Mesozoic lycophytes, and they may represent transitional forms related to some arborescent members, on the one hand, and existing lycophytes such as *Isoetes,* on the other. The order is known from so few species and specimens that is difficult to characterize. The Triassic genus *Pleuromeia* has an unbranched, erect truck 2.0 m tall (Fig. 8-34A). At the base are four lobes from which arise helically arranged roots (Fig. 8-34C). At the apex of *P. longicaulis* is a crown of elongate ligulate leaves, each with two vascular bundles. Slightly below the attached leaves is a zone of persistent leaf bases that grade into an area with widely separated leaf scars. Decortication stages that have been found suggest that there was some secondary tissue production in *Pleuromeia,* although the absence of petrified specimens currently makes it impossible to determine whether these tissues were vascular or cortical in origin.

At the apex of *Pleuromeia* is a large cone (Figs. 8-34B and 8-35A), although there is no compelling reason why some species could not have produced more than one cone. In fact, the large number of small cones of *Cylostrobus,* the name applied to detached cones thought to have been produced by *Pleuromeia,* found at the same stratigraphic level and geographic locality support such an idea. Earlier reports, based on fragments of cones, suggested that *Pleuromeia* was a dioecious plant in which microsporangiate and megasporangiate cones (Fig. 8-35C) were produced on different plants. Recently, however, it has been shown

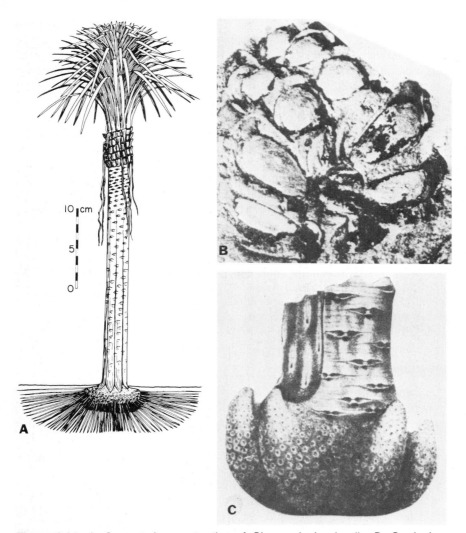

Figure 8-34 A. Suggested reconstruction of *Pleuromeia longicaulis*. B. Crushed cone of *Pleuromeia rossica*. ×2. C. Lobed base of *Pleuromeia sternbergii* showing root and leaf scars. ×3.5. *(A from Retallack, 1975; B and C reproduced from* Handbuch der Paläobotanik *with the permission of R. Oldenbourg.)*

that *Cylostrobus* was bisporangiate, with the megasporangia located in the basal portion. The sporophylls are circular (Fig. 8-35B) and imbricate, and they lack any downward extension in the form of a heel. The large (up to 700 μm) megaspores are trilete and ornamented with numerous elongate spines; the microspores are monolete and up to 30 μm in diameter.

Austrostrobus ornatum (Triassic of Argentina) is the name recently given a large, structurally preserved lycophyte cone that represents a petrified *Cylostrobus* (Morbelli and Petriella, 1973). The only difference between the two

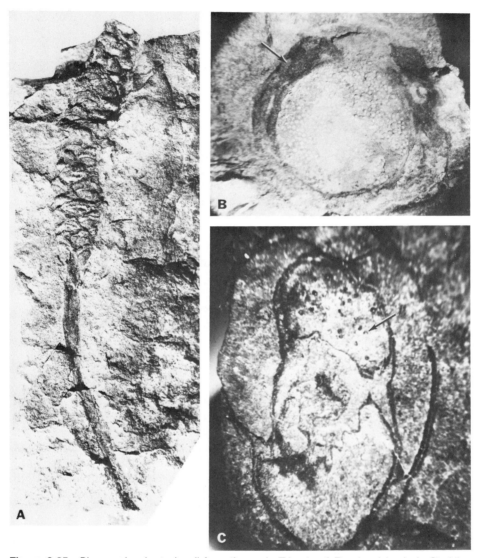

Figure 8-35 *Pleuromeia obrutschewii* from the early Triassic of Russian Island. A. Strobilus terminating an axis. ×1. B. Megasporophyll *(arrow)* with casts of megaspores. ×3. C. Transverse section of a megastrobilus. Arrow indicates one sporangium. ×5. *(From Krassilov and Zakharov, 1975.)*

appears to be size of the megaspores, and that may simply represent a combination of preservational phenomena and cone development.

Discovery of numerous specimens of *Pleuromeia* in Lower Triassic beds north of Sydney, Australia, and a detailed analysis of the lithology of the beds at the collecting sites have suggested to some that the genus grew in dense groves as a coastal halophyte. It is believed that the genus may have originated in Eurasia and migrated along the early Triassic shorelines.

Petrified Triassic stems known as *Chinlea* were initially thought to represent stems of osmundaceous ferns, but they are now regarded as lycophytes, possibly related to *Pleuromeia* and *Nathorstiana*. The stems contain an ectophloic siphonostele with a distinct perimedullary zone of thin-walled parenchyma. Leaf traces are numerous (up to 165 in one transverse section) and collateral.

Ferganodendron is a Triassic genus that resembles *Pleuromeia* and *Sigillaria* in many respects. The trunk of the plant varies from 20 to 30 cm in diameter and is ornamented by numerous helically arranged leaf bases that range from elliptical to rhombohedral in outline. The leaves are small and are found only on the more distal portions of the plant. Nothing is known about the internal structure or reproductive parts.

The genus name *Lycostrobus* is used for isolated cones common in Triassic deposits and thought to be associated with the Pleuromeiales. The basic construction of these cones is similar to that of a bisporangiate *Lepidostrobus* with helically arranged sporophylls and adaxial sporangia. In one species, *Lycostrobus chinleana,* from the Triassic of Arizona, the sporophylls are described as deciduous, with each consisting of a peltate scale attached to a four-angled stalk. In *L. scottii,* the microspores are described as occurring in groups, and it has been suggested that the grouping may have been the result of sporangial trabeculae (partitions) that were not preserved.

Nathorstiana is a Cretaceous genus often included in this order. The plants were probably less than 30.0 cm tall and consisted of a crown of elongate leaves attached by conspicuous bases to the stem. The underground parts consist of longitudinal ridges that bear helically arranged roots. Although nothing is known regarding the anatomy of the plant or the method of reproduction, the general growth habit of *Nathorstiana* has attracted the attention of paleobotanists as a possible intermediate in an evolutionary reduction series involving the arborescent members of the Lycophyta. Another probable lycophyte often assigned to this group is *Nathorstianella,* an incompletely known plant from the Lower Cretaceous. It differs in overall size, and it has an underground portion intermediate between those of *Pleuromeia* and *Nathorstiana*.

ISOETALES

There are two genera of living plants included in the Isoetales: *Isoetes,* which has an extensive distribution ranging from the tropics to the sub-Arctic, and *Stylites,* which is restricted to the high Andes of Peru. Some authorities now regard *Stylites* as simply another morphologic form of *Isoetes. Isoetes* is characterized by a short, squat stem (usually less than a few centimeters long) that bears helically arranged monarch roots from the lower surface and elongate, ligulate leaves in a dense rosette from the upper portion. Both micro- and megasporangia are produced on the same plant. Microspores are bilateral and monolete; megaspores are radial and trilete.

It has been suggested that the order may be traced back to the Cretaceous genus *Nathorstiana,* a plant included with the Pleuromeiales in this treatment. Regardless of the geologic distribution of the order, several examples of earlier *Isoetes*-like plants can be found in rocks as old as the Triassic, suggesting that by Mesozoic time the morphologic form had been well-established. The generic name *Isoetites* is applied to these early *Isoetes*-like plants.

Isoetites serratifolius is the name used for compression specimens of sporophylls from the Triassic of India. Sporophylls range up to 6.6 cm long and are characterized by a serrate margin. A single vascular bundle extends the length of the sporophyll. Sporangia are represented by an elongate impression near the leaf base. In another species, *I. indicus,* of the same age, sporophylls with megasporangia were preserved. The sporophylls are slightly smaller than those of *I. serratifolius,* but none is preserved with a visible tip. Megasporangia contain up to 1500 trilete spores that range from 285 to 430 μm in diameter.

Possibly the most convincing fossil specimen of the order is *Isoetites serratus,* known from Upper Cretaceous (Frontier Formation) sediments in Wyoming. The specimens show rosettes of narrow, strap-shaped leaves with spatulate ends and serrate margins. Leaves arise from the edge of a round corm that is 1.3 cm in diameter. The upper surface has two rows of rectangular cavities interpreted either as wrinkles of the sporophyll or as the remains of collapsed internal air sacs. At the base of each sporophyll are compressed elliptical sporangia that contain impressions of either megaspores or microspores. Dichotomously branched roots are attached to the corm beneath the outer rosette of sporophylls.

CONCLUSION

Many comparative morphologists and paleobotanists believe that the fossil record, although admittedly sketchy, provides sufficient evidence to suggest that *Isoetes* could have represented the end of an evolutionary series that had its beginning among the arborescent lycophytes during the Carboniferous. In this regard, it has been suggested that *Isoetes* represents a *Lepidostrobus* seated on a stunted stigmarian base. Proponents of this concept suggest that a sparsely branched heterosporous member of the Lepidodendrales represents the starting point of the series. The reduction of aerial branches, together with an overall decrease in the stature of the plant, might be represented in the fossil record by a plant such as the Triassic genus *Pleuromeia.* Further reduction of the main stem would suggest a *Nathorstiana*-like plant, which stratigraphically fits the sequence. A continued reduction in the plant body would culminate in an organization not too unlike that of *Isoetes* or *Stylites.* Features that arborescent members share with *Isoetes* include the helical arrangement of the microphylls, the presence of ligules, secondary tissue production, massive sporangia, heterospory, reduced gametophytes, and the arrangement and organization of the monarch roots. It is important to understand that such a series does not indicate direct relationships among the plants used as examples. Information regarding reproductive parts of *Nathorstiana* and the internal structure of both *Nathorstiana* and *Pleuromeia* is obviously needed. These plants should be regarded as forms that stratigraphically and morphologically indicate a plexus of organisms from which a plant similar to *Isoetes* could have evolved. Recent developmental studies of *I. tuckermanii* add further support to this concept. These studies indicate that the corm of *Isoetes* does, in fact, dichotomize and is therefore bipolar and identical with the fossil forms to which it may be related.

The occurrence of *Isoetites* in deposits as old as Triassic emphasizes that *Isoetes* probably is not directly derived from *Nathorstiana* or *Pleuromeia*. The diversity within the Lycophyta certainly suggests that more than one trend was involved. One such series might involve the Lower Mississippian cormlike taxon *Protostigmaria* leading to a Pennsylvanian underground system such as that of *Selaginella fraipontii*. From this form, the series may have led to the *Isoetites* plants of the Triassic and, subsequently, to *Isoetes* and *Stylites*. Recently, Pigg and Rothwell (1979) described a structurally preserved woody lycopod axis that demonstrates the transition between the stem and root. Although features of the axis are similar to those found in the arborescent members of the Leipidoden-drales, the base of this Pennsylvanian plant consists of a rounded cormlike structure (Fig. 8-36A and B). These authors suggest that *Isoetes* and *Stylites* may have had their origins in plants that possessed basal corms initially and are traceable from plants such as *Lepidosigillaria* (Devonian), *Protostigmaria* (Mississippian), and the unnamed Pennsylvanian taxon to the stratigraphically younger genera. Thus, within the lycopods, at least two basic types of underground rooting systems appear to have been well-developed by the Carboniferous. These apparently different underground systems may represent levels of evolutionary change, or they may be the result of habitat and the general habit of the plant. Some support for this latter suggestion can be found by comparing the sites where the plants actually grew. Most of the arborescent forms with the branching stigmarian underground systems are known to have been swamp inhabitants, while the lycopods with cormose bases at least superficially appear to have grown on coarser, possibly firmer, soils. Thus the apparent extinction of the arborescent taxa with extensive rooting systems may have come about through the loss of suitable environments at the end of the Paleozoic, while the smaller plants with cormose bases were able to successfully compete with representatives of other taxa that were emerging at that time. There can be little doubt that a better understanding of the reproductive strategies among all these Carboniferous plants will greatly assist us in properly interpreting which of these hypotheses is most accurate.

Within the arborescent members of the Lycophyta are a variety of stelar types that suggest the way in which the siphonostele evolved within the group. Stratigraphically early forms such as *Lepidodendron pettycurense* are character-ized by a solid core of tracheids. Intermediate forms possessed a mixed pith in which the central portion of the stele contained tracheids interspersed with parenchyma. *Lepidodendron vasculare* is an example of the intermediate stele type. Species that are entirely siphonostelic include *L. serratum* and *Lepidophloios kansanus*. Although interruptions in the stele, termed branch gaps, were formed at the point of a departing branch, no leaf gaps were

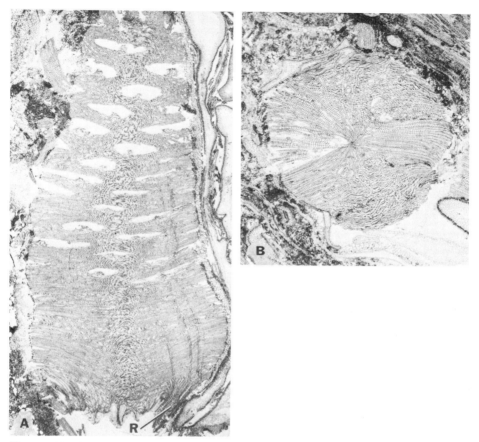

Figure 8-36 Stem-root transition of a Pennsylvanian lycopod. A. Longitudinal section of plant base with rooting region (R). ×3.5. B. Transverse section of base of transition region. ×8. *(From Pigg and Rothwell, 1979.)*

associated with the siphonostelic types. It should be noted, however, that within a lycopod stem, the organization of the stele, including the amount and distribution of tissues, is highly variable owing to the position of the axis on the plant and the level of development. In this regard, questions concerning the evolution of stelar patterns must take into account the ontogenetic stage of the stem being examined.

Both herbaceous and arborescent plants are included in the Lycophyta. The tree-sized forms demonstrate several unusual features associated with the production of secondary tissue. The massive diameter of the trunks is made up principally of secondary cortical tissues (periderm) rather than secondary xylem, which provides the supporting tissue of most living woody plants (see Fig. 8-11B). Secondary phloem was not produced in the arborescent forms, a feature that is interesting with respect to the apparent capacity of the primary phloem to conduct for a long time. Such a unifacial cambium is unknown in living plants. Finally, the determinate growth pattern in these plants is also unlike that of most extant woody trees.

Within the Devonian members of the group (Protolepidodendrales) are some species that are structurally preserved in such a way that features of the stele are known. Cross-sectional configurations of these steles indicate two principal types. In one form, the protostele is lobed, as in some species of *Drepanophycus* and the genera *Colpodexylon* and *Archaeosigillaria*. The other basic protostele type includes such forms as *Protolepidodendron, Leclercqia,* and *Drepanophycus colophyllus,* in which the external surface of the primary xylem cylinder is ridged. Such a configuration is more similar to that of the primary xylem of the arborescent members in the Carboniferous and may be the stelar pattern common to that group. Forms with the lobed arrangement have several features in common with the herbaceous members, including the existing forms, and may be the lineage that gave rise to that group. As more petrified Devonian specimens are uncovered, a clearer picture of the lines of evolution leading from the Protolepidodendrales should emerge.

The arborescent lycophytes constitute an interesting group with respect to evolution of their reproductive mechanisms. It seems that heterospory predominated, but it is conceivable that some of the smaller cones that produced only miospores were, in fact, the reproductive units of homosporous plants. In other instances, these seemingly monosporangiate cones were microsporangiate. The group includes heterosporous forms in which both megasporangia and microsporangia were produced in the same cone (bisporangiate). In others, heterospory may have advanced to the point at which the number of megaspores per sporangium was reduced to one, as in *Lepidocarpon* (see Fig. 8-21C). These spores, because of their size, would have been adapted toward storing greater amounts of food, which, in turn, might have been advantageous in extending the time during which sex organs were produced. By extending the time during which archegonia were produced, there would have been more time to permit fertilization from other genotypes in the population. Another advantage of large megaspores with greater amounts of stored food is related to developmental events of the embryo. The arborescent lycophytes had evolved at least one reproductive mechanism that closely parallels the seed habit, which was also rapidly evolving during the late Carboniferous. Obviously, this does not imply any relationship between seed plants and arborescent lycophytes. What is important is the parallel development of the two reproductive systems. The fossil lycophytes were still free-sporing plants; that is, at some stage the *Lepidocarpon* megaspore may have been released from the sporangium. Whether this occurred on the plant or, as is more likely, after the sporophylls abscised cannot be determined, but the sporophyll design strongly suggests that the megasporophylls were efficient floating structures (Phillips, 1979). One other fundamental difference between gymnosperm seeds and lycophyte reproductive structures such as *Lepidocarpon* is the origin of the structures that protect the megasporangium. In *Lepidocarpon* the lateral laminae were outgrowths of the sporophyll, while the integumentary system of seed plants had its origins from the reduction of a branching system.

The Lycophyta are an interesting group because they demonstrate a number of kinds of reproductive mechanisms, ranging from homospory to heterospory. So far as is known, the Protolepidodendrales were all homosporous. The Lepidodendrales possessed a number of systems that involved heterospory, including forms bearing cones of one type and some bearing two kinds. It is not known whether the two types of cones were borne on one plant or on different plants. It is also possibile that some of the small, presumably microsporangiate cones represented cones of homosporous arborescent plants. Cones such as *Achlamydocarpon, Leipidocarpon,* and *Miadesmia* represent heterosporous examples in which the megasporangium has only one functional megaspore. In an extremely interesting paper by Phillips (1979) detailing the reproductive biology of Carboniferous swamp-inhabiting lycopods, it is suggested that some of these plants failed to survive during times of major swamp fluctuation because their reproductive mechanisms were so well adapted to existence in an aquatic environment.

We probably know more about the fossil lycophytes than any other group of fossil plants. Yet, as structurally preserved specimens continue to be evaluated and new ones continue to be discovered, it is apparent that we are only beginning to understand this complex and extremely interesting group of organisms.

Chapter 9

Sphenophyta

The geologic history of the Sphenophyta closely parallels the evolution and diversification exhibited by the Lycophyta. Sphenophytes were first encountered in sediments of the Devonian and can be traced into the Carboniferous, where they attained their maximum diversification. From the Carboniferous to the Recent, the group experienced a gradual decline, until today the Sphenophyta is represented only by the genus *Equisetum,* comprising approximately 20 species.

Members of the Sphenophyta are characterized by axes with distinct nodes, from which were produced whorls of leaves or branches, and regularly spaced ribs and furrows that longitudinally ornament the internodal regions. Leaves are typically small and thought to represent the modification of a branching system. The vascular cylinder ranges from protostelic to siphonostelic, with the primary xylem either exarch or endarch. Secondary tissues are present in a few groups, most notably some Carboniferous members of the Equisetales and the Devonian genus *Pseudobornia*. The reproductive organs are loosely arranged strobili or cones that consist of a central axis bearing whorls of modified branches, termed sporangiophores, that produced recurved, thick-walled sporangia. Some of the spores in this group are characterized by an extraexinous layer that, in some genera, is organized into elaters. Most sphenophytes were homosporous, although a few heterosporous fossil members are known; heterospory was not developed in the Sphenophyta to the level exhibited in the Lycophyta.

In this book, the Sphenophyta include the following orders:

Pseudoborniales: Devonian
Sphenophyllales: Mississippian to Permian
Equisetales: Devonian to Recent

One group that has been traditionally included within the Sphenophyta is the Hyeniales. Recent studies, however, indicate that the anatomy of the Hyeniales is more similar to that of ferns and fernlike plants, and consequently, a discussion of the genera *Calamophyton* and *Hyenia* can be found in Chap. 10.

PSEUDOBORNIALES

The Pseudoborniales represent a unique order of plants that are known from relatively few localities and, to date, are represented by a single species, *Pseudobornia ursina*. In 1894, the noted paleobotanist A. G. Nathorst (Fig. 9-1B) collected a number of Upper Devonian fossils from Bear Island, south of Spitzbergen. Included in the collection were a number of interesting compression and impression remains that consisted of axes bearing whorled lateral appendages. The only other fossils that have been referred to this group were discovered in Devonian rocks in northeastern Alaska. Since the original description by Nathorst, additional specimens have been discovered at other Bear Island sites and have been useful in determining many previously unknown features of the genus.

Pseudobornia ursina was a monopodially branched plant that is believed to have been 15.0 to 20.0 m tall (Fig. 9-1A). The largest axis measures 60.0 cm in diameter and is thought to have represented a basal portion of the plant. It is not known what the underground parts looked like, but the basal region has been reconstructed as a rhizome bearing roots. The primary stem axis of *Pseudobornia* consisted of nodes separated by internodes about 80.0 cm long. In the basal regions of the plant, each node produced one or two first-order branches up to 3.0 m long and approximately 10.0 cm in diameter. Second-order branches were produced in a decussate arrangement; each of these laterals bore axes in a pseudodistichous arrangement.

Leaves that were less than 1.0 cm in diameter were produced only from the distal branches and were arranged in superimposed whorls of four leaves each. Each leaf consisted of an elongate, twice dichotomized petiole to which a "pinna" was attached. Pinnae were up to 6.0 cm long and about 1.0 cm wide and consisted of a lamina that was highly dissected along the margin (Fig. 9-1C). Nothing is known of the venation, but the configuration of the lamina suggests a dichotomous system of terete strands.

Figure 9-1 A. Suggested reconstruction of *Pseudobornia ursina*. B. Alfred Gabriel Nathorst. C. Several leaves of *Pseudobornia ursina*. ×0.8. *(A and C from Schweitzer, 1967; B reproduced from* Geschichte der Botanik *with permission of Gustav Fischer Verlag.)*

Fertile branches up to 30.0 cm long were produced at the distal ends of primary branches (Fig. 9-1A). Each fertile unit consisted of whorled bracts and sporangiophores, with the sporangiophore tip upturned and divided into two segments. Approximately 30 sporangia were produced by each sporangiophore.

Nothing is known about the anatomy of *Pseudobornia*, although Schweitzer (1967) has suggested that the axes were hollow, except at the nodes, where nodal diaphragms served to strengthen the stems. The affinities of the order continue to remain obscure. Some have suggested a relationship with the Sphenophyllales, and the present organization of the reproductive units would appear to support such affinities.

SPHENOPHYLLALES

Members of the Sphenophyllales are relatively small plants that were probably less than a meter tall and formed a portion of the understory in many Carboniferous forests. Sphenophyllaleans can be traced from the Devonian into the Triassic, but they are best known from petrified and compressed remains of the Carboniferous. As the name of the order suggests, the leaves in this group were wedge-shaped and borne many in a whorl (Fig. 9-2A). Stems were protostelic, and in some, secondary tissues in the form of wood and periderm were produced. Reproductive parts were aggregated into cones or loosely constructed strobili. All members were apparently homosporous.

The generic name *Sphenophyllum* was initially used for impression-compression specimens of wedge-shaped leaves occurring in whorls of six to nine per node (Fig. 9-2A). Today the generic name not only includes numerous species of leaves, but also impression-compression and structurally preserved stems, roots, and leaves.

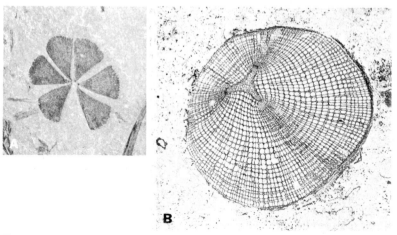

Figure 9-2 A. Whorl of *Sphenophyllum* leaves. ×1. B. Transverse section of *Sphenophyllum plurifoliatum* stem with abundant secondary xylem. ×6.5.

Impression-compression foliage assigned to *Sphenophyllum* includes fan-shaped leaves that range up to several centimeters in length. Many of the species have been determined on the basis of the configuration of the distal leaf margin, which can range from entire to deeply lobed or even filamentous. Each leaf was vascularized by a single bundle that entered the base and dichotomized several times before terminating at the margin. Stomata were confined to the abaxial surface and interspersed among elongate cells with sinuous walls. In some species, hairs up to 1.0 mm long occurred along the margins. The identification of *Sphenophyllum* foliage species has been based upon such features as the

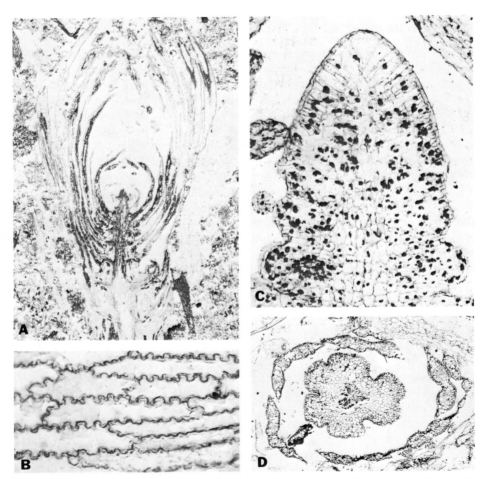

Figure 9-3   A. Longitudinal section through the apex of *Sphenophyllum lescurianum.* ×25. B. Leaf epidermal cells of *Sphenophyllum constrictum.* ×266. C. Median longitudinal section through the apex of a *Sphenophyllum* stem showing the apical cell and derivatives. Leaf primordia are visible farther down the apex. ×150. D. Transverse section of young *Sphenophyllum* stem with leaves. ×22. *(A and C from Good and Taylor, 1972; B from Good, 1973.)*

number of leaves per whorl, size of the leaf, number of marginal teeth, and degree of dissection of the lamina between the teeth. Many of the species exhibit foliar polymorphism, and consequently, many will continue to be reduced into synonymy as research continues with the genus.

One structurally preserved stem that has been found with leaves attached is *Sphenophyllum multirame* (Fig. 9-3A), from the Middle Pennsylvanian of Illinois. Two types of leaves were produced. The species reveals small, linear leaves, (1.0 to 4.0 mm long) containing a single vein, and they occur in whorls of five to twelve. Larger leaves are borne in whorls of six and are superimposed from whorl to whorl. The margin is blunt or deeply incised, with up to nine veins present at the distal margin. On the abaxial surface are longitudinal furrows that correspond to each leaf lobe in the highly dissected forms. In *S. multirame*, stomata are hypostomatic, and occur in two rows in the furrows. Stomata are slightly sunken and randomly oriented. Many species of *Sphenophyllum* had epidermal cells that were thin-walled and possessed sinuous margins (Fig. 9-3B). A distinct mesophyll was present, but no palisade layer was identified.

Structurally preserved stems of *Sphenophyllum* are common in coal ball petrifactions throughout the world (Fig. 9-2B). Specimens of *S. plurifoliatum*, the common Pennsylvanian form, are up to 2.0 cm in diameter and include several orders of branching. The primary xylem of the protostele is triangular to subtriangular in outline with three concave sides (Fig. 9-3D). Protoxylem is exarch, although in a few cases mesarch development has been described. Thin-walled cells that make up the primary phloem alternate with the arms of xylem. In young stems, the remainder of the axis consists of a parenchymatous cortex bounded by an epidermis in which the cells are filled with opaque materials. Older stems are characterized by abundant secondary xylem (Fig. 9-2B), with the tracheids opposite the protoxylem arms (fascicular wood) considerably smaller than the tracheids between the arms (interfascicular wood). The secondary xylem of *Sphenophyllum* consists of vertically elongated tracheids with tapering end walls and circular to elliptical bordered pits on the lateral walls. Some tracheids are up to 8.0 mm long and have been suggested as representing vessels. Between the tracheids are vertical strands of parenchyma that form a postmeristematic parenchyma sheath. External to the sheath is secondary phloem constructed of elongate elements with horizontal end walls and biseriate rays. In *Sphenophyllum*, secondary cortical tissues were produced by a single persistent phellogen. Cells of the periderm appear tabular in transverse section and arranged in distinct radial files.

Recent studies indicate that the meristematic region of a *Sphenophyllum* shoot consisted of an apical cell with the three-dimensional configuration of a tetrahedron (Fig. 9-3C), including a triangular upper surface and three triangular internal cutting faces. The production of derivative cells (segment and sextant cells) occurred in a dextrorse direction similar to apical-cell production in the genus *Equisetum*. These patterns appear to be consistent for a given species. In addition to apical growth, *Sphenophyllum* axes increased in length as a result of intercalary meristematic activity.

Although the exact habit of *Sphenophyllum* is not known, present evidence suggests a plant consisting of a horizontal rhizome bearing branched aerial stems. Aerial axes branched several times and bore whorls of leaves. Like certain lycophytes, *Sphenophyllum* had limited growth potential and was presumably determinate. Associated with this type of growth habit were a series of dimensional changes involving the progressively smaller size of the primary body distally and fewer, simpler leaves per node. *Sphenophyllum* is unique in representing the only nonseed plant that produced secondary xylem and phloem from a bifacial cambium.

The roots of *Sphenophyllum* were adventitious and rarely produced laterals. Anatomically they possessed the same complement of tissues as the stems, although the primary xylem in the roots was typically diarch. In some specimens, an extensive periderm was developed.

The reproductive organs of the Sphenophyllales consisted of aggregations of sporangiophores and bracts forming cones. Many types are known and include a variety of preservational modes. *Bowmanites dawsonii* is a form known in both European and North American floras and it will be used to characterize the basic strobilus organization. Specimens exceed several centimeters in length and consist of a central axis bearing a variable number of bracts (14 to 20) that alternated from whorl to whorl. The stele of the axis varies from triarch to hexarch, with the number of protoxylem points also variable. Metaxylem tracheids have reticulate pits.

In a *Bowmanites* cone, a variable number of bracts are inserted at right angles to the cone axis and laterally fuse to form a shallow saucer (Fig. 9-4A). Toward the margin of the disk, the individual bracts are separated and upturned to overlap bracts of several whorls above. Bracts are fusiform in outline and are vascularized by a single trace. In *B. dawsonii,* each bract subtends two sporangiophores of unequal length that arise from the adaxial surface of the bract close to the cone axis (Fig. 9-4A). At the distal end, each sporangiophore is reflexed and bears a large sporangium at the end. Sporangia are about 2.0 mm in diameter and reveal several layers of parenchyma cells (Fig. 9-4A). Spores are trilete and range from 95 to 162 μm in diameter. The spore surface is covered by an extraexinous membrane that often masks the suture (Fig. 9-4B).

Bowmanites moorei (Fig. 9-4C) is a relatively small cone with a maximum diameter of approximately 4.0 mm. Three bracts are produced at each node and laterally fuse to form a disk. Each bract consists of a median fertile lobe that is flanked by two sterile lobes. Bract tips do not overlap the whorl above. Each fertile lobe produces two recurved sporangia. In *B. fertilis* from the lower Coal Measures of Belgium, six adaxially oriented stalks are borne at each node, and they are branched at their tips to form 14 to 18 sporangiophores. In this taxon, each sporangiophore produced two recurved sporangia. Two sporangia per sporangiophore are also present in *B. römeri.* In this species, however, each bract subtends three concentric whorls of sporangiophores. Further morphologic variability is present in *B. trisporangiatus,* a cone 6.0 cm long. Eighteen bracts

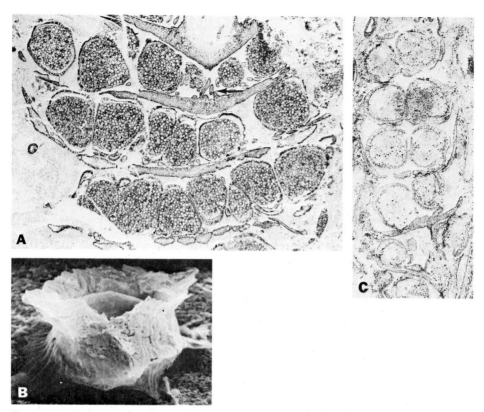

Figure 9-4 A. Tangential section through *Bowmanites dawsoni* cone showing bracts, stalks *(arrow)*, and sporangia. ×9. B. Lateral view of *Bowmanites dawsoni* spores. ×500. C. Longitudinal section of *Bowmanites moorei* cone. ×8. *(A from Taylor, 1969; B from Taylor, 1970.)*

are present in each whorl, and each produces three sporangiophores. The spores are large (100 to 150 μm) and trilete. Despite considerable variability in the size of some spores, which, in part, may reflect measurements that include the extraexinous portion of the sporoderm, all species of *Bowmanites* were monosporangiate, and the genus is regarded as homosporous. Not all species of *Bowmanites* had trilete spores. Some, such as *B. bifurcatus,* contained sporangia with monolete spores. The taxon is represented by a small cone 1.5 cm long and 3.0 mm in diameter. Each bract whorl contains six bracts with a single sporangiophore arising from the adaxial surface of the bract and bearing two sporangia.

    Litostrobus is a small sphenophyllalean cone described from several Pennsylvanian localities. Specimens range up to 1.3 cm long and consist of whorls of at least 12 bracts. Each bract whorl is associated with 8 to 11 sporangia, each of which is borne at the end of a short pedicel. This genus, which was originally included with the Sphenophyllales on the basis of arrangement of the bracts and sporangiophores, histology of the sporangia, and trilete spores (Fig. 9-5D) with extraexinous membranes, is now known from specimens organically attached to stems of *Sphenophyllum.*

Another cone type that is known to have produced monolete spores and is thought to be associated with the Sphenophyllales is *Peltastrobus* (see Fig. 1-7B). Specimens of *P. reedae* are known from Upper and Middle Pennsylvanian deposits and include cones approximately 4.0 mm in diameter (Fig. 9-5C). Whorls of six fertile and sterile bracts alternate with the fertile units, subtending axillary clusters of five sporangiophores. Two of the sporangiophores are directed up and two downward. The remaining sporangiophore extends 90° from the cone axis. Each sporangiophore bears an inner and outer whorl of up to eight sporangia. The epidermal cells on the sporangiophores are thin-walled with sinuous margins.

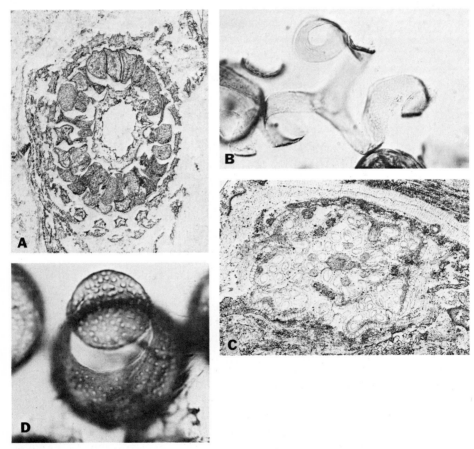

Figure 9-5   A. Transverse section of *Palaeostachya decacnema.* ×9.6. B. Detached elater from *Palaeostachya decacnema* spore. ×370. C. Transverse section of *Peltastrobus reedae* cone. ×9. D. *Litostrobus* spore showing operculate lid. ×670. *(A, B, and D from Good, 1975.)*

Another Pennsylvanian cone type that is often included within the Sphenophyllales is *Sphenostrobus thompsonii*. The cone is approximately 1.0 cm in diameter and consists of whorls of 16 bracts, each of which subtends an elongate, sessile, saclike sporangium that attaches to the bract along the inner surface. In transverse section, the cone stele is tetrarch, with metaxylem tracheids containing scalariform to multiseriate circular bordered pits. Spores are circular, trilete, and ornamented by a delicate reticulum of the exine.

Cheirostrobus is an unusual cone that is often included among the Sphenophyllales because of its occurrence in Lower Carboniferous deposits rich with *Sphenophyllum* stems. The cone exceeds 10.0 cm in length and includes crowded whorls of 12 bracts each that are superimposed between successive bract whorls. The bracts of *C. pettycurensis* are more complex, in that each is divided horizontally to form two lobes, each of which is subdivided into three segments. The upper segments produce elongate, flattened sporangia that extend inward to the cone axis. Spores are approximately 65 μm in diameter.

An unusual organization of sporangiophores is also present in specimens of *Tristachya*, a cone type extending from the Upper Pennsylvanian into the Lower Permian. In *T. crockensis*, each node bears three *Sphenophyllum*-like leaves. Above each leaf is a cluster of globose sporangia containing monolete spores. All the specimens are known only from compression remains.

Among the problematic cone types that are sometimes included in the Sphenophyllales is an Upper Devonian type that is known from both compression and structurally preserved specimens. *Eviostachys* has been regarded as occupying a position that is intermediate between the Sphenophyllales and the now defunct order Hyeniales. Specimens are known that measure 5.5 cm long and up to 0.8 cm in diameter. Morphologically, the cone consists of a basal whorl of six bracts and numerous whorls of sporangiophores. Each of the fertile whorls includes three pairs of sporangiophores, with each divided several times to form a total of 27 sporangia. The trilete spores are circular to subtriangular and measure 35 to 55 μm in diameter.

EQUISETALES

Historically, the Equisetales have been represented by a small number of taxa thought to be related on the basis of their presumed herbaceous habit and lack of secondary tissues. The order Calamitales was used for those genera which were arborescent and produced secondary tissues. Within recent years, comprehensive studies of several sphenophyte genera have suggested that herbaceous versus arborescent habit, morphology of the spores, bracteate versus nonbracteate cones, and the degree of fusion of the leaves can no longer be used to separate the two groups. Accordingly it now appears appropriate to include all the genera within a single order, the Equisetales. Combining the two orders into a single one is based on the apparent absence of anatomic and morphologic differences between the two groups, including the recognition of elaters on the spores in both and the similarity in primary vascular structure and meristematic organization of the vegetative axes. The establishment of a single order is not intended to imply that calamitean plants are part of the existing genus *Equisetum.* Rather, it has been suggested that the organ genera previously placed in the Calamitales may belong to a single natural genus that differs from *Equisetum* and from which *Equisetum* might have directly evolved (Good, 1975).

In general, the Equisetales may be characterized as plants with distinct nodes, internodes, and longitudinal internodal ridges on their stems. Branches and leaves were borne in distinct whorls, with the leaves univeined, connate, or free. The underground portion of the plant consisted of a rhizome bearing numerous adventitious roots. The vegetative meristems contained a single, large apical cell and intercalary meristems at the base of each internode. The vascular tissue was organized into bundles that alternated at successive internodes. At the internode, each bundle possessed a protoxylem canal. Sporangia were recurved and grouped into strobili with sterile bracts present or absent. Spores possessed superficially attached elaters. The geologic history of the Equisetales can be traced from the Devonian to the Recent, with the most conspicuous components of the flora present during the Carboniferous. As more information is accumulated about the plants of this order, it may be desirable to delineate several families. For example, Good (1975) has suggested that a basic distinction may involve the shape and derivatives of the vegetative apical cell and the number of elaters present on the spores.

One of the oldest members of the Equisetales is the genus *Archaeocalamites,* a genus that extended from the Upper Devonian into sediments of the Mississippian. Because of the siphonostelic nature of this group, many of the fossils were represented by pith casts. These were arborescent plants that had stems several centimeters in diameter. The principal feature that has been used to distinguish stems of *Archaeocalamites* from those of other genera includes the nonalternating ribs and furrows at the nodes. At the nodes the surface ribs are truncated, unlike the pointed ribs of other equisetalean stems. The generic name *Paracalamites* has been used for large stems lacking leaves in which the ribs do not alternate. Sandstone casts, with occasional molds still intact, have been described from the Mississippian (Chester Series) as *Archaeocalamites radiatus.* The stems vary from 0.5 to 1.2 cm in diameter, with nodes approximately 3.0 cm apart. Longitudinal ribs are about 1.0 mm wide and pass through the nodes without alternating. In one specimen, five circular scars are present, suggesting a highly branched axis. Near the base the axis rapidly tapers, and the ribs alternate from node to node.

Structurally preserved stems are known and consist of a central pith with inwardly projecting primary xylem strands that are responsible for the furrows on the pith casts. Protoxylem elements are identified as canals near the tip of each primary-xylem wedge. The remainder of the stem consists of secondary xylem composed of elongate tracheids with scalariform to multiseriate circular pits and narrow vascular rays. Cortical tissues are rarely preserved.

Leaves of *Archaeocalamites* are slender, dichotomizing foliar units borne in whorls on the distal branches; some are up to 10.0 cm long. Each dichotomy of the leaf is vascularized by a single terete strand; nothing is known about the stomata and tissues of the leaf.

Roots are borne on rhizomes in irregular whorls, and they are infrequently branched. Uniseriate rays are present in the first-order roots, but lacking in subsequent branching orders.

The reproductive parts of *Archaeocalamites* consist of cones that are borne in whorls on the leafy branches. *Pothocites grantonii* measures up to 9.0 mm in diameter and bears up to 12 nonalternating whorls of sporangiophores. The axis of the cone contains a ring of mesarch bundles; the number of bundles equals the number of sporangiophores. Each sporangiophore is cruciate at the end, with the tip bearing a single, recurved globose sporangium. Extending inwardly toward the sporangial cell lumen are delicate peglike processes. Spores range from 82 to 104 μm in diameter and are of the *Calamospora* type (see Fig. 9-12B). The trilete spores have a two-layered exine, suggesting that these spores may have contained an extraexinous layer homologous to elaters. *Pothocitopsis* is the generic name of a cone described from the Devonian of Spitzbergen that probably represents a poorly preserved specimen of *Pothocites*.

Another cone that is known to have been borne on *Archaeocalamites* and is regarded by some as identical to *Pothocites* is *Protocalamostachys*. Specimens are at least a centimeter long and contain three pairs of sporangiophores per whorl. The cone axis is vascularized by three mesarch strands that correspond to the position of the sporangiophores. Distally the sporangiophore is divided into four segments, and each bears an elongate sporangium. The spores are trilete and up to 44 μm in diameter. Although *Protocalamostachys* cones have not been found organically attached to *Archaeocalamites* twigs, the similarity of the vascular bundles of both and their occurrence in the same Mississippian Pettycur limestone have been used to suggest their biological relationship. Chaphekar (1963) has suggested that *P. pettycurensis* was attached to petrified stems of *A. goeppertii*. The primary difference between these Lower Carboniferous cones and the younger ones is the absence of sterile members alternating with the fertile whorls.

The generic name *Calamites* was initially used for pith casts (Fig. 9-6A), but it now encompasses a variety of preservational modes that may include impressions, compressions, and pith casts of the external surfaces of stems or of the central canals or pith. In addition, the generic name is used for structurally preserved stems (Fig. 9-6B). In the following discussion, the generic concept will encompass the entire plant, much as was followed in the description of the lycophyte *Lepidodendron*. *Calamites* is represented in the Carboniferous as an upright arborescent plant that grew to a height of approximately 20 m. They were slightly smaller plants than the arborescent lycopods *Lepidodendron* and *Lepidophloios*, and no doubt constituted the second story of the Carboniferous forests.

Several subgenera of *Calamites* have been established on the basis of size and regularity of the branches. In the subgenus *Calamitina,* for example, numerous branches were produced at each node, although branches were not present at every node. *Stylocalamites* had even fewer branches, and when they were produced, each was rather large. A more regular branching pattern occurred in species of *Diplocalamites,* where only two or three branches were produced per node. In this subgenus, however, the branches alternated from node to node in a distichous pattern. Moreover, the internodal distances were greatly telescoped. The most profusely branched arborescent calamite was *Crucicalamites.* Numerous large branches were borne at each node, and the diameter of the stems of this subgeneric type suggests that these trees were among the largest of the calamites.

Since relatively few calamite stem specimens have ever been found with branches attached, the establishment of the preceding subgenera has been based principally on the occurrence and number of branch scars present on stems, and

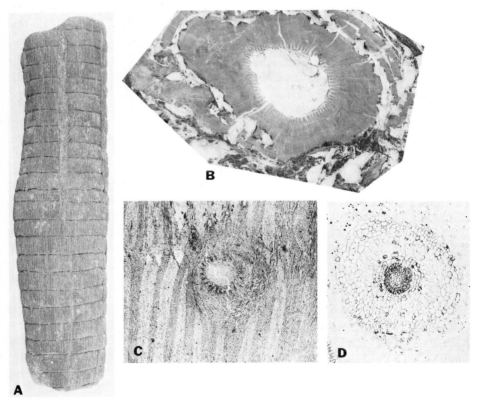

Figure 9-6 A. Calamitean pith cast. ×0.5. B. Transverse section of a large calamite stem *(Arthropitys).* ×0.5. C. Tangential section through secondary xylem of *Arthropitys communis* showing branch scar. ×4.6. D. Transverse section of young calamite root *(Myriophylloides).* ×12. *(C from Good, 1975.)*

it is highly probable that branches were shed as the plant continued to grow. The size of the scars were variable, but their general morphology was rather constant and consisted of a circular to slightly oval structure with a central area that marked the position of the pith (Fig. 9-7C). In well-preserved specimens the scars are ornamented by a series of wrinkles that extend out from the central scar like the spokes of a wheel. The presence of such features immediately distinguishes the external surface of the stem from a cast of the inside. Distinguishing the surface of the stem from a pith cast becomes more difficult in those instances where branches were not produced. Pith casts of calamites were formed by sediments invading the hollow central canal and solidifying as the more resistant tissues of the stem were broken down by various biological agents. The presence of additional sediment around the cast resulted in the

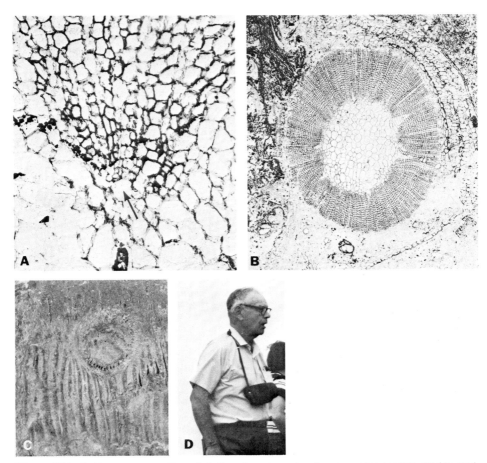

Figure 9-7 A. Transverse section of *Arthropitys* stem showing secondary xylem wedge and carinal canal *(arrow).* ×120. B. Transverse section of *Astromyelon.* ×6.5. C. Calamite branch scar. ×1. D. Chester A. Arnold. *(D courtesy Charles N. Miller, Jr.)*

common mold-cast preservation type. The structural organization of a calamite stem includes wedges of primary xylem (Fig. 9-7A) that extend into the central canal, with broad channels of parenchyma representing the vascular rays between. On the surface of a pith cast are a series of ribs and furrows that are also common on the external stem surface. In the pith casts, the furrows mark the former position of the primary xylem wedges, while the ribs correspond to the indentations between. In many pith casts it is possible to distinguish a small oval scar just below the node on the ribs. These scars mark the former position of the vascular rays and are termed infranodal canals. On some specimens preserved in very fine matrix, an additional scar may be seen on the lower end of the rib between two adjacent infranodal canals. This scar identifies the former position of the leaf trace. The presence of infranodal canals or leaf traces also can be of value in orienting the specimen, since pith casts of calamites characteristically exhibit a tapered end, which was initially thought to represent the growing point of the stem. The tapered end is now known to represent the basal portion of branches, where there was a rapid increase in the size of the pith. There are some internal fillings that are described as pith casts in which infranodal canals are not visible, even though the surfaces consist of a series of ribs and furrows that alternate at the nodes. These casts were formed by the decortication of extraxylarly tissue, which resulted in casts that lacked branch and infranodal canal scars. A number of years ago, Arnold (Fig. 9-7D) described a large *Calamites* trunk from the Pennsylvanian of Colorado. He was able to demonstrate that the vertical lines on the surface of the specimen he named *C. huerfanoenisii* were the result of sediment forming between the woody cylinder and outer surface of the trunk where the cortical tissues were once located. This was confirmed when it was shown that the reverse side of the specimen clearly showed features of the outer trunk surface. The impression of the outer surface of the xylem cylinder and the pith cast looked almost identical, even in the alternation of ribs and furrows at the node. Another way in which such pith casts were formed in the calamites was through the tangential splitting of some of the secondary xylem. A tangential section of the wood of a typical calamite reveals alternating wedges of tracheids and large parenchymatous rays (Fig. 9-6C), which, if preserved as a cast, would consist of a number of ridges and furrows.

Numerous structurally preserved calamitean stems have been found, and details regarding how the plants actually grew have been worked out. In transverse section, the stem consists of a large central canal (Fig. 9-6B) with a few parenchyma cells near the periphery. Surrounding the pith are a variable number of collateral vascular bundles, each with a conspicuous carinal or protoxylem canal (Fig. 9-7A). Carinal canals were formed in the aerial axes of calamites by the rupturing of the first-formed protoxylem tracheids. The maturation of the primary xylem is generally regarded as endarch, although in *Equisetum,* which has the same basic anatomy, mature stems are endarch while developmentally young stems are mesarch. In *Calamites,* the number of collateral bundles increased by the addition of new strands at each node, so that at higher levels of the stem there were a greater number of primary vascular bundles.

Surrounding the primary vascular bundles is a zone of secondary xylem known to have been at least 12.0 cm thick in one Upper Pennsylvanian specimen. Tracheids are thick-walled and elongate; pitting on the radial walls ranges from scalariform to circular bordered. Vascular rays extend out between the primary xylem wedges and give the secondary xylem a sectored appearance in transverse section (Fig. 9-6B). Tangential sections of the secondary xylem have provided a basis for distinguishing three basic structural types now recognized at the generic level. Possibly the most common petrified calamitean stem type, and the one that exhibits the simplest tissue organization, is *Arthropitys*. The genus includes approximately 20 species and several varieties. The secondary xylem in *Arthropitys* is segmented into distinct sectors of wood that radiate out from the carinal canals of the primary strands. Between the wedges of wood are large interfascicular rays (Fig. 9-6C) that may vary considerably in size and shape as they extend through the secondary xylem.

In *Arthroxylon,* the cells that make up the interfascicular rays are greatly elongate, some up to 3.0 mm long. The secondary xylem consists of two types of cells: elongate tracheids 0.5 mm long and secondary ray cells. Because of the length of the cells in the secondary xylem and rays, it is sometimes rather difficult to distinguish the rays from the wood in tangential section. The third petrifaction genus of calamite stems is *Calamodendron*. The secondary xylem of this type is the most complex of the three, consisting of bands of thick-walled fibers that separate interfascicular rays from zones of secondary xylem. There is some question as to the value of this artificial separation of taxa based on selected histologic features of the secondary xylem. Eggert (1962) has suggested that the organization of the wood rays and the type of pitting may be the only reliable features used to identify woody stems produced in different regions of the same plant. Good (1975) has suggested that the distinctions between the stem genera are partially developmental and further notes that several stem genera may have produced the same cone type. Moreover, it is now known that several different cone types were produced by the same stem type.

The extensive amount of secondary xylem produced by some calamites has been used as the principal criterion for suggesting that a bifacial cambium was present in this group. There is no other group of fossil cryptogams that is known to have produced more secondary xylem. Extraxylarly tissues have been reported from small branches and a few large stems. In *Arthropitys*, the tissues outside the secondary xylem are of two principal types based on the histology of the cells. Cells of the inner cortex include thin-walled parenchyma with some resinous materials. In older stems, this zone is often occupied by elongate resin canals. Cells of the outer cortex are also thin-walled, but appreciably smaller than the cells of the inner zone. Neither of these two zones has the appearance of secondary phloem. Although there have been several reports of calamite stems with radial files of cells in the cortex, there is no conclusive evidence that periderm was present at any stage of development.

Several calamitean apices have been found in coal-ball petrifactions. The apical cell consists of a five-sided pyramid with a roundly rectangular upper surface and four internal triangular surfaces that cut off apical-cell derivatives. This configuration is different from both *Sphenophyllum* and *Equisetum,* which are characterized by a tetrahedral apical cell with three internal cutting surfaces. Derivatives of the calamitean apical cell were produced in a dextrorse (counterclockwise) direction and apparently matured at a slower rate than those of *Sphenophyllum.* In addition, the cells produced toward the center of the apical cap in the calamites developed into the pith meristem, while the topographically identical cells in *Sphenophyllum* formed the procambium. In small twigs, the procambial vascular strands matured at approximately the third node, with metaxylem tracheids first observed between the third and fourth nodes. At the node, the vascular bundles fused in a ring. Surrounding the bundles was a cortex of elongated parenchyma and scattered areas of melasmatic tissue. Carinal canals were present at about the fifth node. In general tissue organization, the distal twigs of the calamites appear similar to twigs of *Equisetum,* except that vallecular or air canals are not present in the cortex of the calamites.

In general, the manner in which the calamites grew tends to parallel the epidogenetic and apoxogenetic development present in the arborescent lycopods. The underground rhizome system and major branches attached to it were characterized by a large pith surrounded by a large number of primary vascular strands. The maximum number of vascular bundles is believed to have occurred in the aerial stems that developed from the rhizome. At these levels, there was also abundant secondary xylem. Lateral branches were smaller and had fewer vascular bundles than the primary axes at the levels of their origin. The decrease in size of the primary body continued at each successive order of branching, resulting in minute branches with only a few vascular strands and no pith. The number and size of the leaves is also related to the size of the stem, with larger leaves produced on the larger stems. A similar pattern of development was present in the roots, but the branch roots did not greatly increase in size as they grew. In all instances, the stele of the lateral roots was smaller than that of the parent root and had fewer primary vascular strands.

Calamitean roots are described under a number of generic names, with *Astromyelon* the most common petrified form (Fig. 9-7B) and *Pinnularia* the generic name used for impression and compression specimens. The generic name *Myriophylloides* (Fig. 9-6D) has been used for petrified calamitean roots, but is now regarded as a synonym for small *Astromyelon* specimens. Morphologically, the roots differ from stems in lacking nodes and branching in a more irregular manner. Histologically, axes of *Astromyelon* appear superficially like aerial stems. In transverse section, the root consists of a parenchymatous pith surrounded by a variable number of bundles that do not anastomose. Maturation of the primary xylem is exarch, although mesarchy has been reported in one species. Carinal canals are not present in the roots, and the vascular rays are greatly reduced. Secondary xylem is present, but in far smaller amounts than in

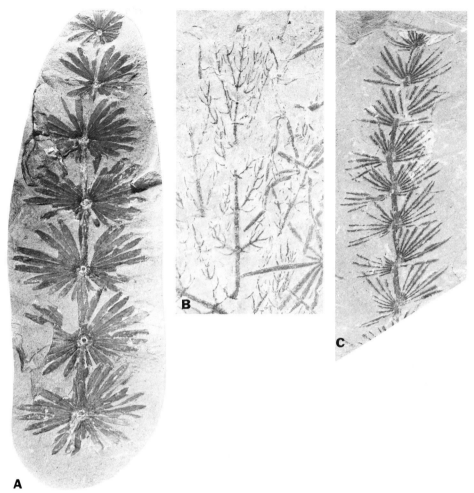

Figure 9-8 A. Several whorls of *Annularia stellata* leaves. ×0.6. B. Leaves of *Asterophyllites charaeformis.* ×1.5 C. Several whorls of *Asterophyllites* leaves. ×1. *(A from Good, 1976.)*

the stems. In very small roots, the cortex is three-parted. In more mature roots, two types of thin-walled tissue are present immediately outside the secondary xylem. Zones of phloem alternate with primary parenchyma that is opposite the primary xylem strands. Outside these areas are groups of cells with amorphous contents. Cells of the phloem are in radial files, suggesting that they represented sieve elements derived from fusiform cambial initials. Thus it appears that the vascular cambium of *Astromyelon* had both fusiform and ray initials. A large amount of secondary cortical parenchyma was produced by a proliferation of cortical cells, and there is some evidence to suggest that a small amount of periderm was developed in very old roots as well.

Some specimens suggest that branch roots were produced over a long period of time after a considerable amount of secondary xylem was present in the parent stele. It is not known whether they were produced from a pericycle or from the vascular cambium. In addition, branch roots appear to have maintained a relatively small primary body, unlike the aerial stems. Fungal remains have been identified in the peripheral cortical cells of *Astromyelon cauloides,* and it has been suggested that they represent a mycorrhizal association. Unfortunately, it remains an impossible task to demonstrate conclusively that such fungi were present in the cells while the plant was living.

Calamitean foliage is typically placed in the two morphologic form genera, *Annularia* and *Asterophyllites.* The leaves of *Asterophyllites* are needlelike and borne in whorls from 4 to 40 (Fig. 9-8C). They arch steeply upward from their position on the stem and overlap the leaves of several whorls above. *Asterophyllites charaeformis* (Fig. 9-8B) is an impression-compression species that includes forms with 4 to 10 leaves per whorl. Each leaf is approximately 3.0 mm long and is widest at the base. Petrified leaves apparently identical to *A. charaeformis* that provide histologic information about the taxon have been discovered in coal balls from Britain and eastern Kentucky. In transverse section, the leaf varies from three-sided to five-sided in outline, with a median ridge on the abaxial surface. Leaf shape appears to have been determined in part by the position on the plant and the degree of preservation. A single vascular bundle consisting of a small group of tracheids is surrounded by a sheath of thin-walled cells that may represent the phloem. Thick-walled fibers are present on the adaxial side of the vascular bundle; thin-walled parenchyma surrounds the vascular strand in other areas. This sheath has been suggested as a temporary storage site for assimilation products before they reached the phloem. Columnar mesophyll parenchyma makes up the remainder of the leaf. Cuticles of the Kentucky leaves possess stomata randomly arranged on all surfaces. The stomata are simple, consisting of two bean-shaped guard cells surrounded by two subsidiary cells. The long axis of the stoma parallels the long axis of the leaf. Multicellular hairs are present on some leaves.

Calamites rectangularis is the name used for leaves of the *Asterophyllites* type that are known from Upper Pennsylvanian coal balls. Complete leaves are approximately 4.0 mm long and rectangular in cross section. The stomata have conspicuous ridges that are associated with the common walls of the guard and subsidiary cells. It has been suggested that there was an increase in the size of *Asterophyllites* leaves moving up through Pennsylvanian strata, although such a trend has not been correlated with stem remains.

The leaves of *Annularia* are lanceolate to spatulate in shape, and they are fused in a shallow disk where they are attached to the stem (Fig. 9-8A). There are 10 recognized species in North America that range from 5 to 32 leaves per node. Unlike the organization of *Asterophyllites,* whorls of *Annularia* leaves do not overlap from node to node. Individual leaves are variable in length, with those of *A. stellata* almost 8.0 cm long. Until relatively recently, little has been known about the internal organization of *Annularia* leaves. *Annularia hoskinsii* is a Middle Pennsylvanian form that is common in coal-ball petrifactions from the Eastern Interior Basin of the United States. The leaves are borne on axes up to 4.0 mm in diameter that are characterized by carinal canals, a multilayered cortex, and no secondary xylem. Leaves are approximately 3.0 mm wide and 0.8 mm in thickness. The shape of the leaf is convex abaxially, with the lateral sides overhanging. The vascular bundle consists of numerous barrel-shaped tracheids that are surrounded by a bundle sheath that includes fibers on the adaxial surface. The remaining tissue consists of palisade parenchyma. Stomata are confined to the adaxial surface and aligned obliquely with the long axis of the leaf. Based on their common occurrence and similarity in tissue organization, *A. hoskinsii* has been suggested as the foliage type on the plant that produced *Calamocarpon* cones.

One of the primary characteristics of compression-impression specimens of *Annularia* involves the consistent orientation of the leaf whorls, which are typically in the same plane as the stem on which they were borne (Fig. 9-8A). In some specimens, nodal diaphragms are also present in the same plane. There has been much speculation as to whether such a morphologic configuration was the result of compression and deformation during the fossilization process, or whether the plants actually produced leaf whorls obliquely attached to the stems, possibly to maximize the exposed leaf surface. Strengthening such a hypothesis are the obliquely positioned nodal diaphragms observed in petrified calamitean twigs that were apparently not the result of preservation deformation. One unanswered problem regarding the plant that produced *Annularia* leaf whorls concerns the manner in which the leaf-bearing branches were borne on larger axes. Several orders of branching would result in some leafy twigs being positioned at a variety of angles, including some in which the twigs would be at right angles to the ground. To maximize the foliar surface on these twigs, the leaf whorls, it would seem, would be borne at right angles to the twigs. Such leaf-bearing shoots should also be encountered in the fossil record with some of the leaves in different planes. However, such *Annularia* specimens are very infrequently found.

Dicalamophyllum is another calamitean foliage type that in many features is intermediate between *Annularia* and *Asterophyllites*. Structurally preserved forms contain two small furrows on the abaxial surface, with stomata confined to the furrows. The genus *Lobatannularia* is a Permian form that consisted of whorls of up to 40 linearly oblanceolate leaves. Leaf whorls are divided symmetrically into two lateral lobes separated by gaps at both the upper and lower sides of the whorl. Leaves of this type are anisophyllous.

Calamitean cones exhibit a variety of morphologic types that have proved useful in establishing more naturally related groups of plants. These cones vary considerably in size and degree of morphologic complexity, especially in features associated with the sporangiophore. Compression and impression specimens suggest that cones were produced in a variety of ways, including some that were borne singly or in clusters at nodes or on specialized branches. All consist of alternating whorls of sporangiophores and bracts. Most are homosporous, apparently producing spores with elaters.

Paracalamostachys is the name of a Middle Pennsylvanian impression-compression cone that consists of alternating whorls of bracts and sporangio-phores. The cones are relatively small and bear trilete spores assigned to the *sporae dispersae* genus *Calamospora*. Specimens of *Paracalamostachys cartervillei* are about 1.7 cm long and are borne in clusters at each node. Approximately six sporangiophores were produced per whorl, with each bearing four sporangia; the number of bracts is approximately double the number of sporangiophores. Spores range from 40 to 100 μm in diameter and are smooth-walled. Despite the large size range demonstrated by the spores, the cones are regarded as homosporous. An unusual specimen of *Paracalamostachys* from the Westphalian A or B horizons of Britain is *P. spadiciformis*. This species is about 9.0 cm long and contains 16 bracts. Sporangiophore number is variable, although six appears to be the most common. The position of the sporangio-phores suggests that they arose from near the axil of the bract whorl. The individual cones are borne at the distal end of a leafy branch and are of different sizes, possibly reflecting different stages of cone development. In addition, the presence of *Calamospora* spores of two sizes (65 to 130 μm) suggests that the cones may have been bisporangiate. If *Paracalamostachys* was structurally preserved, it probably would be assigned to the genus *Calamostachys,* which currently includes considerable morphologic variability as well as forms that are both homosporous (monosporangiate) and heterosporous (bisporan-giate).

One of the largest species of *Calamostachys* is *C. americana,* from the Upper Pennsylvanian of North America. Specimens are known that are at least 12.0 cm long and include both mono- and bisporangiate forms. The peduncle of the cone contains 18 primary bundles that alternated from node to node and 30 bundles that did not alternate in the fertile region of the axis. Sterile whorls contain 30 to 45 bracts that are laterally fused to form a cup. Sporangiophores are inserted on the cone axis midway between the bract nodes in whorls of 30. Spores *(Calamospora)* are spherical, trilete, and possess a perispore. Bisporan-giate specimens contain microspores with elaters that ranged from 70 to 118 μm in diameter; megaspores vary from 140 to 275 μm and are enclosed by an unornamented perispore.

Probably the most commonly encountered and best-known *Calamostachys* species is *C. binneyana* (Fig. 9-9A and B). This taxon is common in European Coal Measures and is also known from the Lower Pennsylvanian of North America. Specimens from eastern Kentucky are approximately 1.6 cm long and 3.1 mm in diameter; some of the European specimens have been reported as up to 3.5 cm in length. The cone axis consists of a hollow pith surrounded by a ring of endarch vascular bundles and a narrow zone of secondary-xylem tracheids (Fig. 9-9C). Regularly spaced alternating whorls of 18 to 22 bracts and a variable number of sporangiophores are borne on the cone axis. The bracts are basally fused to form a shallow disk. Stomata are confined to the adaxial surface of the bract. Sporangiophore number appears to be dependent on the level of the section, but 12 appears to be the most common number. The distal portion of the sporangiophore is flattened into a cruciate-shaped structure, with each arm bearing a large, pyriform sporangium (Fig. 9-9B). The sporangium wall is a single cell layer thick, with the cell walls ornamented by inward-facing buttresses that appear to be a constant feature of many sphenophyte fructifications. Immature cones of *C. binneyana* indicate that during cone ontogeny, the shape of the sporangiophore was highly variable. In *C. binneyana*, the spores *(Calamospora)* are smooth-walled, trilete, and possess three coiled elaters.

Adaxially convex bracts with two furrows on the abaxial surface distinguish specimens of *C. inversibractis*. Transverse sections of the cone bracts appear similar to those of leaves of *Dicalamophyllum*. This association is further

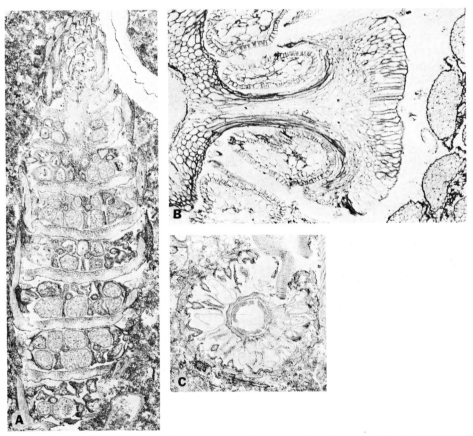

Figure 9-9   A. *Calamostachys binneyana*. Longitudinal section of cone. ×10. B. Transverse section of sporangiophore with attached sporangia. ×55. C. Transverse section of cone. ×8. *(A and B from Taylor, 1967.)*

strengthened by the consistent occurrence of these two genera in the same petrifactions.

A cone type that is quite similar to *Calamostachys*, but differs principally in the manner in which the sporangiophores are attached to the cone axis, is *Palaeostachya*. *Palaeostachya andrewsii* is a Middle Pennsylvanian taxon that includes both monosporangiate and bisporangiate types. Specimens exceed 15.0 cm in length and consist of 6 to 10 pairs of endarch vascular bundles that extend through the cone axis. Bracts are rectangular in transverse section and alternate from node to node. The sporangiophores of *Palaeostachya* are inserted obliquely, and in *P. andrewsii,* the number per whorl ranges from 12 to 20. Specimens of *P. decacnema* (Fig. 9-5A) are about 6.5 cm long and are characterized by a stele with four to five lobes. In *P. decacnema*, sporangiophores and bract traces originate from paired bundles that traversed the length of the cone axis, with the traces to the sporangiophores extending directly into the sporangium-bearing unit. In *P. andrewsii*, however, the sporangiophore traces originate just above the bract traces. From this level they extended through the cortex to approximately the middle of the internode above before recurving downward and extending into the base of the sporangiophore. *Palaeostachya vera* is a cone type known from the Lower Coal Measures of England and recently from the slightly younger Middle Pennsylvanian of North America. Currently, the species may be distinguished from others by the degree of lateral bract fusion, low ratio of bracts to sporangiophores, length of bracts,

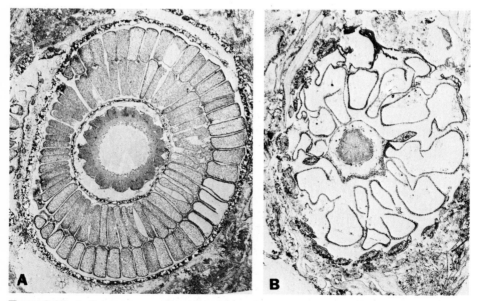

Figure 9-10   A. Transverse section of *Pendulostachys angulariformis* cone. ×4.5. B. Transverse section of *Weissistachys kentuckiensis.* ×14. *(A from Good, 1975; B from Rothwell and Taylor, 1971a.)*

and size of the spores. All species of *Palaeostachya* possess trilete spores with three distally attached elaters. The heterosporous species *P. andrewsii* has megaspores up to 345 μm in diameter with an encircling perispore.

Weissistachys is a structurally preserved cone known from a single locality of the Lower Pennsylvanian. The axis consists of a ring of endarch bundles that surround a parenchymatous pith (Fig. 9-10B). Specimens are approximately 5.0 cm long. Sporangiophores are diamond-shaped in transverse section, with the distal ends fused. The sporangia are attached along the upper and outer surface. Spores range up to 75 μm in diameter and possessed elaters. Another structurally preserved cone type that further expands the morphology of calamitean cones is *Pendulostachys* (Fig. 9-10A). These cones are large (14.0 cm long) and basically similar to other calamitean cones. The unusual feature of *P. cingulariformis* concerns the sporangiophores, which were fused to the lower surface of the bract disk and hung pendantly. Each sporangiophore bears four sporangia that are directed upward. The spores contain elaters.

One calamite cone that shows an interesting level of preservation is *Mazostachys pendulata*. The genus is known from an ironstone concretion collected from the famous Mazon Creek area that contains 15 cones attached at the nodes of a branching system. Foliage associated with, but not organically attached to, the specimen is *Annularia sphenophylloides*. Individual cones are approximately 2.6 cm long and contain half as many sporangiophores (six) as bracts. Sporangiophores are inserted just below a whorl of bracts and are characterized by parenchyma tissue near the distal end. In this feature *M. pendulata* is similar in organization of the sporangiophores to *Weissistachys*.

Sporangiophores borne immediately below bract whorls also identify specimens of *Metacalamostachys*. In this form, however, each sporangiophore bears only one sporangium. A similar relationship between bracts and sporangiophores also is present in the Upper Carboniferous compression genus *Cingularia*. In *Cingularia typica*, the sporangiophores are flattened and strap-shaped, with four large sporangia attached in a pendant manner to the lower surface. In *C. cantrillii*, all sterile appendages are absent, with the sporangiophores borne at intervals of approximately 8.0 mm.

An interesting example of heterospory within the Equisetales is found in the cone *Calamocarpon* (Fig. 9-11A). The genus has a wide geographic distribution and is known from throughout the Pennsylvanian. Currently the taxon is known only from North American sediments. Cones are both mono- and bisporangiate. In the bisporangiate cones, there is no transitional zone; megasporangia appear to have been produced in the more distal regions. Specimens range from 4.0 to 12.0 mm in diameter and are at least 8.0 cm long. Sterile bracts alternate with sporangiophores. Microsporangia are a single cell layer thick with pegs extending into the lumen of each cell. The spores are 30 to 40 μm in diameter and are characterized by three elaters attached to a pad on the distal surface. Spores of this type were initially described under the *sporae dispersae* binomial *Elaterites triferens*. Megasporangia are rectangular and up to 3.0 mm long. The wall is a single cell layer thick, but peglike processes are absent. In some

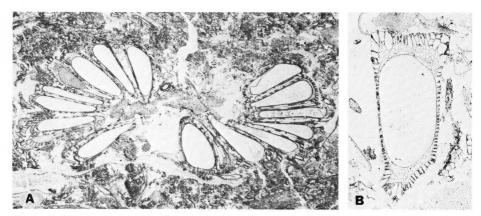

Figure 9-11 *Calamocarpon insignis.* A. Transverse section of cone. ×12. B. Single megasporangium. ×30.

specimens, sterile tissue, especially at the proximal and distal ends, separates the sporangium wall from the megaspore (Fig. 9-11B). In *C. insignis,* each megasporangium bears a single, large (2.7 by 0.7 mm) megaspore. Attempts to macerate the megaspore from the sporangium have been unsuccessful, with only small fragments released during acid treatment. Ultrathin sections of the megaspore indicate that it is constructed of several thin layers. Cellular megagametophytes have been observed, and in some instances, archegonia were present.

Good (1975) demonstrated that many of the *Calamospora*-like spores of the calamiteans possess distinctive elaters (Fig. 9-12A). In situ spore studies indicate that the elaters may assume a variety of configurations according to the ontogenetic stage of spore development. At least three different spore types are known to have been produced by calamitean cones. The most common of these is *Calamospora* (Fig. 9-12B). This type of spore is delimited by its thin, smooth wall and thickened areas between the arms of the trilete. Spores of this type have lost the elaters either through development or by mechanical separation. The second spore type commonly encountered in cone-spore macerates is *Vestispora.* In this grain type, the elaters tightly surround the spore body and are visible only as oblique striations on the surface of the grain. These spores represent an immature ontogenetic stage in which the elaters are not fully developed. The third stage in calamite spore ontogeny is characterized by *Elaterites* (Fig. 9-12A). The genus is delimited by three elaters that are attached to a triangular pad on the distal surface. The fragile nature of the elaters is the principal reason spores of this type do not constitute an important component of *sporae dispersae* assemblages.

It appears highly probable that all calamitean fructifications produced spores with elaters. The fact that elaters have not been reported to date may be reflected in the developmental level of the spores at the time of fossilization or the failure of investigators to describe those spores which appear wrinkled and folded. Such folds are now known to represent the elaters. One additional reason why elaters have not been described on spores may concern the ultimate function of these structures. Elaters in the living genus *Equisetum* remain attached to the sporoderm throughout the life of the spore, while the spores of the calamites may have possessed elaters that broke off during the dispersal phase (see Fig. 9-5B). In this context, they may have functioned in a manner similar to that of the sporangial elaters in certain bryophytes. Some support for this hypothesis is derived from the large number of calamitean sporangia that contain detached and broken elaters, but no spores.

The generic name *Equisetites* was established many years ago for casts, impressions, and compressions of stems that morphologically resemble the modern genus *Equisetum*. Specimens have been distinguished from distal branches of calamites partially by the fusion of small leaves in a sheath and the apparent absence of secondary xylem. Although the majority of specimens are known from rocks of the Triassic or younger, there have been several reports of the genus dating back to the Carboniferous. *Equisetites hemingwayi* is known from the Middle Coal Measures of Yorkshire and consists of jointed stems, some of which bear oval cones. The cones are constructed of groups of hexagonal plates that have been regarded as the sporangiophores; unfortunately no cuticular remains or spores were preserved. The fact that these cones are laterally borne is an interesting feature that has suggested to some that *E. hemingwayi* may not be related to *Equisetum,* which produces terminal cones.

Equisetites muensterii is known from numerous specimens from several Triassic localities in Europe. Possibly the most detailed account based in part on

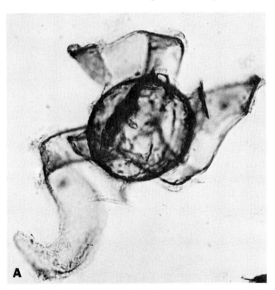
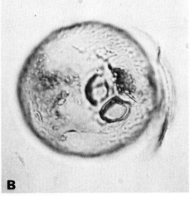

Figure 9-12 *Calamostachys binneyana* spores. A. Specimen with elaters intact. ×770. B. Spore with elaters detached showing three prominent contact areas characteristic of *Calamospora* spores. ×900. *(From Good, 1975.)*

cuticular remains is that of Harris (1931), who described the taxon from Scoresby Sound in eastern Greenland. Stems are approximately 1.0 cm in diameter, with variable internodal dimensions. Branching specimens are not known, although small scars that alternate with the leaves may indicate the former positions of branches or adventitious roots. Approximately 12 leaves are fused into a sheath at each node, with the number of leaves per node constant irrespective of the size of the stem. Cuticle preparations exhibit numerous stomata at the base of the leaf sheath, with stomata more scattered on the stems. Guard cells are characterized by a beaded border and two longitudinal rows of pits. Cones up to 4.0 cm long occur at the tip of the stem. Each cone is constructed of whorls of peltate, hexagonal sporangiophores. Spores in the 40 to 50 μm size range, but lacking elaters, have been recovered from the sporangia. In almost all features, *E. muensterii* is identical to species of *Equisetum,* with the exception of the spores. However, this may be a reflection of preservation or the developmental level at the time of fossilization.

Specimens that are so well preserved that they have been assigned to the genus *Equisetum* have been collected from the Eocene of Oregon. *Equisetum clarnoi* is the name used for petrified stems up to 0.8 cm in diameter. Externally the stems contain ridges and furrows, but leaves are absent from the nodes. Transverse sections show a central pith cavity surrounded by a ring of evenly spaced vascular bundles. A fibrous hypodermis with alternating long and short inwardly projecting bands forms a continuous layer around the stem. Stomata are sunken in the hypodermis and occur in a single row. Numerous roots were found intermixed in the matrix with the stems, but none were organically attached to a stem. Roots are typically 2.0 mm in diameter and frequently possess root hairs. There can be little doubt that *E. clarnoi* represents a fossil stem that is correctly assigned to the genus *Equisetum.* In fact, when compared with *Equisetum* species, *E. clarnoi* appears almost identical to existing specimens of *E. hyemale* var. *affine.*

Compression and impression specimens and pith casts thought to be stems of *Equisetum* also have been described from sediments as old as the Carboniferous. The only diagnostic features that can be used to distinguish *Equisetum* or *Equisetites* are the leaf sheaths borne at a node or the terminally positioned cones. Compression and impression specimens and pith casts lacking these features may represent distal branches of a calamitean plant. Even structurally preserved, small calamite branches may superficially resemble an *Equisetum* stem. If a large branch were fossilized while young, the absence of secondary xylem and the configuration of the primary body would closely resemble the herbaceous stem of *Equisetum.*

The genus *Phyllotheca* is an apparent sphenophyte that has an extensive geologic range traceable from the Pennsylvanian through the Permian, where remains are most abundant, and into the Cretaceous. It has been included with the old Calamitaceae, Equisetaceae, or transitional between plants with archaeocalamite and calamite features. Recent studies suggest that most of the features are equisetalean. *Phyllotheca indica* is used for monopodially branched axes with swollen nodes. First-order branches bear whorls of 20 to 24 leaves that are fused basally to form a narrow sheath. Branches are ornamented with conspicuous ridges and furrows that do not alternate from node to internode. Axial vascular bundles dichotomize and anastomose near the nodes to form nodal loops that supply the vascular bundles to the leaves. The diameter of the stems (2.0 cm) and abundant tracheids with bordered pits suggest that some secondary xylem was produced. In *P. australis,* the leaves are fused to form a pronounced cup that surrounds the sporangiophores. Other species, such as *P. equisetitoides,* have leaves that are fused in a narrow sheath with the individual leaf segments hanging down.

Information about the reproductive parts of *Phyllotheca* are known from compression specimens of *P. australis.* Sporangiophores are borne in whorls of six to eight and apparently are protected by the enveloping leaf whorl below. The sporangiophores are unusual in that each is dichotomized twice, with the ends bearing two slightly recurved sporangia. In *P. deliquescens* from the Lower Permian of Siberia, the sporangiophores are more numerous, and there are a larger number of sporangia attached to each peltate head. *Umbellaphyllites* is a Lower Permian foliage genus that combines vegetative features of *Phyllotheca* and *Annularia* and is regarded as being intermediate between the two.

CONCLUSION

Many workers believe that some of the arborescent calamites have evolved from a group of plants characterized by *Archaeocalamites.* It is for this reason, and because of the stratigraphic position of the group, that the *Pothocites* cone type is used as the starting point in discussions about calamitean cone phylogeny. Some workers believe that the near-axillary position of the sporangiophore trace in *Palaeostachya* represents the primitive condition, with the phylogenetic migration of the sporangiophore into an internodal position (*Calamostachys*) representing an intermediate evolutionary level. According to this series, cones such as *Mazostachys* and *Cingularia,* in which the sporangiophores are either fused to or immediately beneath the bract, constitute the most highly advanced forms. Unfortunately, the stratigraphic position of the cones does not support such a sequence. Others believe that the *Calamostachys* cone organization is basic, with forms in which the sporangiophores are in an axillary or abaxial position being derived. Proponents of this phylogeny view the *Pothocites* cone type as primitive, with forms in which the sterile bracts are intercalated between the whorls of sporangiophores being more highly evolved. Another view suggests that vegetative whorls have phylogenetically developed as a result of the failure of some sporangiophore verticles to ontogenetically develop sporangia. The stratigraphic position of many of the cone types in which sporangiophores are associated with the abaxial surface of the bracts suggests that this trend may have developed as a result of selective pressures for greater sporangial protection.

Most members of the Equisetales were apparently homosporous. Although a few heterosporous forms are known, the variability in cone organization and sporangial contents within this group does not approach the heterospory present in the Lycophyta. The most highly evolved heterosporous system within the Equisetales is *Calamocarpon.* It might be argued that the *Calamocarpon* cone type is more highly evolved because evidence to date suggests that the megaspore was not shed from the sporangium. In this regard, the reproductive strategy more closely approximates the seed habit than that of such lycopods as *Lepidocarpon, Miadesmia,* and *Achlamydocarpon,* which have been suggested as shedding their single functional megaspore. The eleaters now known to have been present on almost all equisetalean spores represent a modification of the sporoderm that is more highly evolved than the microspores present in the lycopods. It would appear that within the Lycophyta, much of the emphasis in the evolution of the reproductive system was directed toward the megaspore-producing cone and features of the megaspore and megagametophyte. In the Equisetales, however, there were apparent evolutionary modifications directed at both the microgametophyte and megagametophyte phases.

One additional comment must be made relative to the spores of the Equisetales. In many species, the size range of the spores is extensive, sometimes including a range of several hundred micrometers. In *Paracalamostachys spadiciformis,* for example, the known range of the *Calamospora* spores varies from 55 to 350 μm in diameter. In this species, the larger spores have been designated megaspores and the cone is considered bisporangiate. The possibility exists that some of the presumed homosporous calamitean cones were in fact bisporangiate (heterosporous), with the mega-spores and microspores lumped together in the descriptions. Because of the difficulty in identifying immature eleaters on spores, there is no way to distinguish megaspores from microspores. Another problem concerns the role that each spore type may have played in the reproductive process. Microspore and megaspore are in reality functional terms delimited by whether a microgameto-phyte or a megagametophyte finally develops from the spore. Generally the larger spores develop into the megagametophyte, although in some living plants, the megaspores are the smaller of the two types early in spore development. The Equisetales may have demonstrated such a heterosporous system in which the ultimate function of the spore cannot be determined by its size. This incipient form of heterospory is known in a number of living plants, including *Equisetum,* where the genome is responsible for gametophytes that may contain one or both types of sex organs.

Although not as large as the lycopods, some members of the Equisetales were arborescent plants that attained their tree-sized habit through a different method of producing supporting tissue. In the arborescent forms, the diameter of the stem was the result of a central pith and a large amount of secondary xylem produced by a bifacial cambium. In the lycopods, stem diameter came principally from the extensive development of secondary cortical tissues in the form of periderm. A reduced amount of secondary xylem appears to have developed from a unifacial cambium. Physiologic comparisons are sometimes misleading when based on histologic features alone. Nevertheless, the apparent absence of secondary phloem in the lycopods and the presence of this tissue in the woody calamites represent an important difference between these contempory arborescent plants. These two groups of tree-sized plants represent an excellent example of parallel evolution in which the arborescent habit and many of the features associated with the reproductive process have been achieved in different ways.

In addition to understanding the variability of fossil plant species, learning how the plants grew and reproduced, and tracing them through time, one of the primary aims in paleobotany has always been reconstruction of the whole organism. This process depends on accurate morphologic and anatomic descriptions based on many specimens. One of the intriguing aspects of such reconstructions concerns the assignment of reproductive parts to vegetative remains. Good's (1975) study of calamite cones is an excellent demonstration of how reproductive organs may be related to the probable parent plant. For example, the histology of the cone peduncle and anatomy of the sterile bracts of *Calamostachys americana* are almost identical to the leaves that have been described as *Calamites rectangularis* and stems of *Arthropitys communis* var. *septata*. Uniseriate, circular bordered pits known to be present on *Arthropitys* stems and foliage assigned to the genus *Dicalamophyllum* have been used to suggest the relationship of *Calamostachys inversibractis* with these vegetative organs. *Calamocarpon* cones are thought to have been produced on large vegetative stems assignable to the genus *Calamodendron,* which had smaller aerial branches of the *Arthroxylon* type. Relationships that are based on certain similarities in the anatomy and morphology of the detached parts are, of course, strengthened when the different taxa can be identified at the same geographic locality and stratigraphic position, and they are even more valuable when all parts are found in the same coal ball.

Chapter 10

Pteridophyta

The plants described in this chapter may be considered ferns, although some of the Devonian members are better regarded as fernlike. In general, these plants exhibited a type of leaf termed a megaphyll. Such leaves typically possess a branched vascular system, with gaps produced in the stele when petiole traces are given off. The croziers, or immature fronds, unroll in most members of this group. There are two basic types of sporangial development and structure within the Pteridophyta. The eusporangiate type is characterized by the Ophioglossales and Marattiales and includes sporangia developed from periclinal divisions of initials that are superficial in position. The wall of the eusporangium is several cell layers thick, and the number of spores produced per sporangium is large. In contrast, the leptosporangium is small and develops from the transverse division of a single superficial initial cell. Subsequent cell divisions result in a stalked sporangium that is usually one cell layer thick. Sporangial dehiscence is either transverse or longitudinal, and the spore output is typically small. Leptosporangia tend to characterize the filicalean ferns. It is important to point out that the terms eusporangium and leptosporangium do not indicate levels of phylogenetic specialization, nor are they especially valuable in systematic studies. Several recent studies have suggested abandonment of the terms because the critical examination of sporangial development in modern plants shows a high degree of variability in all sporangium-related features. For example, within the Ophioglossales, one to several cells may be involved in sporangial initiation. Because the eusporangium is produced by plants that are regarded as primitive on the basis of other features, for a long time this sporangium type has been considered the primitive form. In contrast, Bierhorst (1971) believes that a sporangium similar to the leptosporangium type was primitive among most vascular plants. He suggests that the ancestral filicalean sporangium was elongate, exhibited longitudinal dehiscence, and lacked an annulus. Although the fossil record provides little information about sporangial development, the two terms can be used in a descriptive sense, since systematic and evolutionary implications are not involved.

Many of the fernlike characters just noted cannot be applied to some of the fossil representatives that have been included in this group. For example, some of the Paleozoic taxa lack planated fronds, and the stelar systems do not conform to the set limits of trace and gap production. Nevertheless, there is general agreement that these plants probably gave rise to the more representative, geologically younger ferns that are familiar to all. In effect, many of the fossil representatives demonstrate stages in the evolution of fern characteristics and, by definition, have not phylogenetically acquired all the features that characterize the later-appearing ferns.

PTERIDOPHYTA

CLADOXYLOPSIDA: Devonian to Mississippian
RHACHOPHYTOPSIDA: Devonian
COENOPTERIDOPSIDA: Devonian to Permian

Stauropteridales
Zygopteridales

FILICOPSIDA

Marattiales: Carboniferous to Recent
Ophioglossales: Jurassic to Recent
Filicales

BOTRYOPTERIDACEAE: Carboniferous to Permian
ANACHOROPTERIDACEAE: Pennsylvanian to Permian
SERMAYACEAE: Pennsylvanian
TEDELEACEAE: Carboniferous to Permian
OSMUNDACEAE: Permian to Recent
SCHIZAEACEAE: Jurassic to Recent
GLEICHENIACEAE: Jurassic to Recent
DICKSONIACEAE: Jurassic to Recent
CYATHEACEAE: Jurassic to Recent
MATONIACEAE: Triassic to Recent
POLYPODIACEAE: Jurassic to Recent
TEMPSKYACEAE: Cretaceous

Marsileales: Tertiary to Recent
Salviniales: Cretaceous to Recent

CLADOXYLOPSIDA

The Cladoxylopsida represent an interesting group of plants that have had a varied taxonomic history. Some forms have been included with the later-appearing seed ferns; others have been regarded as the oldest members of the Sphenophyta. Today the subdivision is regarded as a group of fernlike plants that has its oldest representative in rocks of the Lower Devonian (Emsian). Most taxa are known from the Devonian, and several species extend into the Carboniferous. The group is thought to have evolved from the Trimerophyto-phyta, but was probably not directly involved in the origin of any later-appearing groups of plants.

Although a few genera are based on compression-impression specimens, the majority of taxa are based on transverse sections of structurally preserved stems. The stelar system consists of a series of radiating plates of mesarch xylem, some of which are longitudinally interconnected. The term polystele has been used to describe the vascular organization in these plants, but in light of some current concepts regarding the nature of the stele in the Carboniferous medullosans based on the position of the protoxylem bundles (Basinger, Rothwell, and Stewart, 1974), the term polystele for the Cladoxylopsida may not be appropriate. One of the characteristic features of the vascular tissue in the Cladoxylopsida is the presence of "peripheral loops" near the outer edge of each xylem segment. Peripheral loops are present in several other groups of early ferns and consist of thin-walled parenchyma cells surrounded by protoxylem elements. In some species, secondary xylem is present in the form of radially aligned tracheids that are uniformly distributed around the primary xylem or more extensively developed toward the center of the stem. Many of the species have been characterized by the number and position of the xylem strands and the presence or absence of secondary tissues. Since the vascular system is now known to be highly variable from level to level, subsequent studies of additional specimens will probably reduce the number of valid taxa.

In general, the plants included in this subdivision are thought to have been small, exhibiting irregular branching of the main axes and dichotomous branching at more distal levels. Ultimate stem segments consisted of forked, planated appendages that have been termed "leaves." Fertile units bore terminal sporangia. All species are thought to have been homosporous.

The genus *Cladoxylon* was delimited in 1856 by Unger for anatomically preserved axes. Unger initially assigned the specimens to the Lycophyta, but they were later transferred to the Cycadofilices. After the discovery of *C. scoparium* by Kräusel and Weyland (1926) (Fig. 10–1B), the group was elevated to the ordinal level, where they were regarded as intermediates between filicalean ferns and sphenophytes. Despite acceptance of these plants as fernlike, their taxonomic position with reference to other groups is still problematic. For example, Walton (1953) and other authors placed them with the coenopterid ferns, Andrews (1961) positioned them between coenopterids and marattialean ferns, and Gothan and Weyland (1964) included them within the order Filicales.

Today *Cladoxylon* is used as a form genus by most authors for petrified axes that exhibit a particular type of anatomy. Several authorities have suggested that species known in extensive morphologic detail should be removed from the genus and placed in a new taxon.

One of the better-known species is *C. radiatum* from the lower portion of the Carboniferous. Stems range up to 6.5 cm in diameter and contain

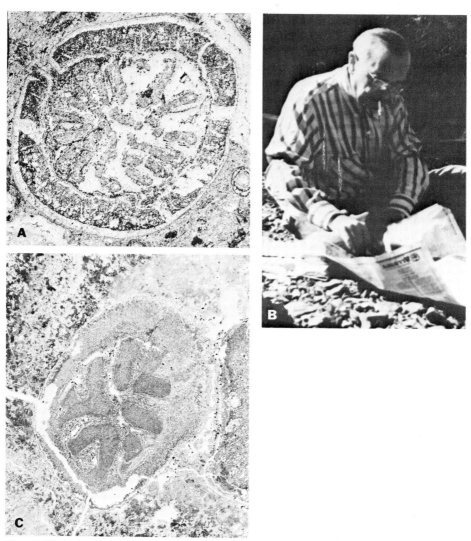

Figure 10-1 A. Transverse section of *Cladoxylon waltonii.* ×6.5. B. Richard Kräusel. C. Transverse section of *Cladoxylon taeniatum. (A from A. G. Long Collection No. 2708 in Hancock Museum; B courtesy of H. Banks; C courtesy of J. Galtier.)*

approximately 17 stelar segments (meristeles of some authors) that radiate out from the center of the stem. All the xylem is primary, with the tracheids exhibiting scalariform pitting. Thick-walled cells are present in the ground tissue of the stems. When laterals are apparent in *C. radiatum,* four to six arms of xylem extend into the petiole and subsequently divide to form a tangentially flattened ring of up to eight xylem strands. Smaller aphlebia traces were produced at right angles to the petiole. The arrangement of the xylem strands is different in the smaller (3.5 cm) species, *C. taeniatum.* In this species (Lower Carboniferous), there are two stelar zones. Around the periphery of the stem are numerous (up to 20) radially elongate xylem strands that, in turn, surround five centrally located cylindrical xylem strands. In *C. taeniatum* (Fig. 10-1C) and numerous other European species, the primary xylem is surrounded by a zone of uniformly developed secondary xylem that consists of scalariform tracheids and narrow parenchymatous rays.

Several specimens exhibiting cladoxylalean anatomy have been described under the binomial *C. valtonii* (Fig. 10-1A). Axes that come from the Lower Carboniferous Calciferous Sandstone Series include both stems and petioles of two distinct size classes. One group includes radially symmetrical stems up to 1.2 cm in diameter that produced helically arranged petioles containing a clepsydroid-shaped xylem strand. The second group includes smaller (2.0 to 7.0 mm diameter) stems with alternately borne petioles. The larger stems contain 9 to 15 arms of primary xylem, whereas the smaller axes reveal 4 to 9 strands of xylem arranged in a U-shaped configuration. Secondary xylem is not present. When petioles are apparent, a band of xylem is formed by the fusion of two adjacent xylem strands.

Cladoxylon hueberii is a form that was described from Middle and Upper Devonian rocks (Givetian) of eastern New York. The partial compression-petrifaction specimens range up to 5.5 cm long and 2.2 cm in diamter. The number of xylem strands is highly variable, ranging from approximately 15 to 34. Strands exhibit a variety of configurations, with those near the periphery radially elongate and those more centrally positioned, cylindrical in transverse section. Tracheids are all primary, and pitting is scalariform to bordered pitted. Secondary tissues are not present. Peripheral loops are not observed, although their absence may reflect preservational phenomena. Trace formation to laterals involves the fusion of portions of three contiguous xylem strands of the stem. *Cladoxylon dawsonii* is the name applied to a single specimen collected from western New York in the Upper Devonian Genesee shale. The size of the stem is estimated to have been between 6.0 and 8.0 mm in diameter. As is typical for the genus, the strands of xylem assume a variety of configurations, including U-, V-, and W-shaped structures. The exact number of xylem arms is not known, but judging from the partial stem, at least 20 were present. All those present are radially elongate, with conspicuous peripheral loops. Most of the tissue of each arm is composed of primary xylem, but some secondarily derived tracheids are present near the periphery of several arms. Poorly preserved cells thought to represent phloem are present in the embayments between the xylem arms and, to a lesser extent, around the xylem. The ground tissue consists of a broad zone of parenchyma with occasional lacunae.

The external morphology of *Cladoxylon* is best demonstrated by specimens from the Middle Devonian of Germany that have been described as *C. scoparium*. This species was reconstructed as a plant approximately 35.0 cm tall with a digitately branched main axis bearing helically arranged, segmented leaves and fan-shaped structures that possess terminal sporangia. In transverse section, the number of xylem arms is variable, ranging from 10 to 33. Strands of xylem are radially elongate, and secondary tissues are seen in a limited amount. Nothing is known about the vascularization of the presumably photosynthetic, highly dissected leaves. Successive transverse sections at more distal levels indicate that there were fewer groups of xylem arms. Clusters of fibers are present in the ground tissue of the stem.

The genus *Hierogramma* was established for small axes typically associated with *Cladoxylon* remains and characterized by two elongate xylem bands, one of which may be T-shaped, surrounding two smaller xylem strands. At higher levels, the distinctly bilaterally symmetrical vascular system assumes a more U-shaped configuration. In *H. mysticum*, leaf traces alternate left and right as small terete strands. Bertrand (1935) suggested that *H. mysticym* was the petiole of *C. taeniatum*. *Syncardia*, *Voelkelia*, and *Arctopodium* are petrifaction genera that anatomically resemble other cladoxylalean species.

The generic name *Pseudosporochnus* was established for some Middle Devonian fossils that were initially described as algae, but later were shown to contain vascular elements. The plant is now one of the best-known members of the Cladoxylopsida and is regarded as having been a small tree approximately 3.0 m tall (Fig. 10-2A) with a trunk that bore large roots and at least three orders of branches. The apex is unusual in that a crown of branches is apparent. These branches, in turn, give rise to second-order branches that dichotomize (Fig. 10-2B). Arising from these axes are bilaterally symmetrical fronds up to 4.0 cm long that are helically arranged. Each frond produced subopposite pinnae, and the pinnae dichotomized at least three times to form flattened segments. There is little distinction between the sterile and fertile fronds, except that the latter produce pairs of sessile, ellipsoidal sporangia in place of the ultimate vegetative frond segments (Fig. 10-2B). Sporangia are up to 3.0 mm long, but no spores have been isolated. One of the interesting features of this plant that has provided a basis for determining the biological affinities of detached parts is the presence of round to elongate structures on the compression fossils that represent nests of cortical fibers. These structures were distributed on all parts of the plant.

In transverse section, *P. nodosus* shows an outer ring of up to 24 radially elongate, straight or clepsydroid arms of xylem that surround an inner zone of up to 20 circular to oval xylem masses. The xylem in both zones is primary and, depending on the stage of development, has well-developed peripheral loops. Maturation of the primary xylem is mesarch, with pitting typically scalariform, although annular, helical, and reticulate tracheids have been reported. Ground tissues of the stem are organized into two zones: an outer parenchymatous zone and an inner region characterized by nests of sclereids. An interesting feature of *P. nodosus* is the apparent change in the vascular system at successively higher branching levels. Transverse sections of first- and second-order branches show that the xylem arms are separate and of unequal length. Third-order branches reveal masses of xylem that are laterally connected in groups, and these may have resulted from the fusion of the radial and central xylem strands. Thus, in *Pseudosporochnus,* the number of central xylem strands decreases at higher levels. Peripheral loops are present only in mature xylem strands, and this may account for the apparent absence of loops in some species of *Cladoxylon* and the inconsistent appearance in other species.

One species that appears to be anatomically similar to *Pseudosporochnus* is *Pietzschia.* The stems are about 2.5 cm in diameter and contain a cylinder of radially aligned xylem arms embedded in a parenchymatous ground tissue. The number of xylem arms is high (54) in *P. polyupsilon* (New Albany shale of Kentucky), and secondary xylem is absent. At some levels, sclerenchyma plates are apparent between adjacent xylem arms. Four bundles are involved in the development of a trace to the lateral appendages; each provides a small amount of xylem from the peripheral portion of the arm. At higher levels, these concentric strands form an inverted U shape through fusion. Peripheral loops are present in some *Pietzschia* specimens and absent in others, but when present,

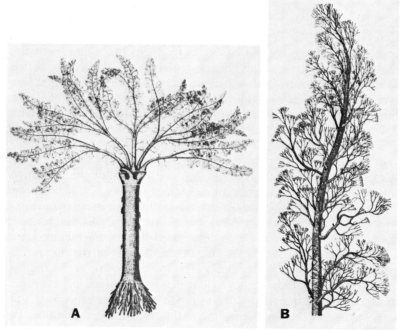

Figure 10-2 *Pseudosporochnus nodosus.* A. Suggested reconstruction of the plant. B. Suggested reconstruction of branch with both vegetative and fertile regions. *(From Leclercq and Banks, 1962.)*

each xylem arm exhibits one at each end. In *P. schullerii* known from Germany, the central portion of the stem contains numerous centrarch or mesarch xylem strands.

Central, terete, and radially aligned peripheral xylem arms also are present in the Middle and Upper Devonian genus *Xenocladia*. Specimens of *X. medullosina* measure approximately 10.0 cm in diameter and possess secondary xylem. Abundant secondary xylem and reduced primary xylem are features of another cladoxylalean stem genus, *Stenoxylon*. *Stenoxylon ludwigii* is known from deposits in Siberia, of which the precise age is not known. Some authorities suggest that the fossils are Permian. The genus is characterized by large stems that often exceed 15.0 cm in diameter and reveal both central and peripheral xylem strands. Peripheral loops are not present. In *S. ludwigii*, the xylem strands anastomose to form a complex network of vascular tissue with numerous small petioles arranged helically around the stem. Trace emission includes the fusion of two or more strands, with the resulting petiole strands composed almost entirely of secondary xylem. Tracheal pitting is multiseriate bordered with rays widest toward the center of the stem. In *S. irvingense* (New Albany shale), secondary xylem development is more pronounced on one side of the xylem arm. Irregular strands of thick-walled fibers in the parenchymatous ground tissue further distinguish this species.

Another plant exhibiting cladoxylalean anatomy is *Rhymokalon trichium*, and it is known from the Upper Devonian (Frasnian) of New York. The genus is based on three specimens preserved as pyritized compressions. Because the specimens possess overlapping features, it is possible to demonstrate three orders of branching. The largest axis measures approximately 3.0 cm in diameter and exhibits second- and third-order branches that are helically arranged. The smallest branches are approximately 1.0 mm in diameter. Longitudinal striations on the largest axes correspond to the positions of vascular strands. Numerous hairs up to 1.0 mm long are present on the surface of the more distal branches.

Transverse sections of the largest axes of *Rhymokalon* contain a multiribbed strand of primary xylem up to 1.8 cm in diameter (Fig. 10-3A). Histologically, the xylem consists of plates of tracheids interspersed with parenchyma. Metaxylem elements have scalariform to alternately arranged circular pits. Protoxylem tracheids are not identifiable in the first-order axes. Traces that supply second-order branches arose through division of the outer margins of the ribs of the stele. At higher levels, each xylem strand is mesarch with one to three protoxylem strands. As these strands extend in the axis, the peripheral loops divide so that the number of traces increases distally. The cortex consists of elongate parenchyma with abundant lacunae. Nothing is known about vegetative or fertile organs of the plant.

Two additional plants included in the Cladoxylopsida have a long and interesting taxonomic history. For a long time both were included in the Protoarticulatae (= Hyeniales), a group established by Kräusel and Weyland in 1926 for Devonian, presumably herbaceous, plants with features suggestive of affinities within the Sphenophyta. During this period of time, members of the

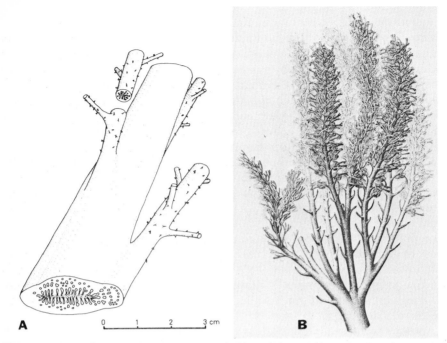

Figure 10-3 A. Suggested reconstruction of *Rhymokalon trichium* showing three orders of branching. B. Suggested reconstruction of a fertile branch of *Calamophyton primaevum. (A from Scheckler, 1975; B from Schweitzer, 1973.)*

Hyeniales were regarded as precursors of the articulates because of their Devonian age and certain morphologic features. In general, the order was characterized by dichotomous branches arising from a rhizome system. Ultimate branches bear sterile appendages termed leaves, and these, in turn, are thought to have been borne in a pseudowhorl or low helix. Sporangia are borne on modified branches and are sometimes recurved. All forms are thought to have been homosporous. In general, the Hyeniales were regarded as having occupied an evolutionary position that paralleled the Protolepidodendrales of the Lycophyta.

In recent years, however, our concept of this group of plants has radically changed, principally owing to the discovery of a petrified axis assignable to one of the two genera in the order, *Calamophyton.* This important discovery by Leclercq and Schweitzer (1965) and subsequent reports by Schweitzer (1972, 1973) have demonstrated that both *Calamophyton* and *Hyenia* are more fernlike in their anatomy (Fig. 10-4E), and therefore, both can no longer be included within the Sphenophyta.

The type genus of the order was *Hyenia,* known from both compressed and structurally preserved axes of the Middle Devonian. *Hyenia elegans* is represented by a large rhizome up to 5.0 cm in diameter that produced numerous closely spaced, upright branches, some of which may have extended to 15 cm in length.

Rarely did these axes branch. Extending from the upright branches were dichotomizing appendages; some represented fertile branches, while the others are thought to have been leaves. Both types of structures appear whorled, but recent anatomic studies suggest that they may have been borne in a low spiral. The leaves were three-dimensional structures that dichotomized several times, although features of the vascular system and information regarding the presence of stomata are lacking. The designation of these reduced branches as leaves was made initially on the assumption that their planation and filling in with laminar tissue would closely approximate leaves in the articulates.

The fertile branches of *Hyenia* are now known to have been relatively complex structures borne in pairs. Each member of the pair produced three lateral arms, each of which was terminated by a pair of elongate sporangia. Sporangia opened by a longitudinal slit, and the spores were large and trilete. Relatively little is known about the vascular system of *Hyenia,* with the exception of the original report in which a xylem strand was reported as being V-shaped. Schweitzer (1972) described a specimen of *H. elegans* (Fig. 10-4F) that consists of a rhizome almost 2.0 m long and 4.4 cm in diameter. This specimen possesses helically arranged aerial appendages that branch dichotomously, as opposed to the whorled pattern originally thought to characterize the genus.

Not all species of *Hyenia* branch as in *H. elegans.* In *H. vogtii,* which is placed by some in the subgenus *Hyeniopsis,* lateral branches occupy the place of leaves on some of the upright axes. The presence of leaves and branches in the same phyllotactic sequence is considered by some as additional evidence of the evolutionary history of the leaves in this group.

Calamophyton (Fig. 10-4A) was a larger plant than *Hyenia,* reaching a height of approximately 60.0 cm. Middle Devonian specimens of *C. bicephalum* consist of a central axis bearing subsequent branches in a digitate pattern from about the same point. Second-order branches reveal a dichotomous pattern. Some of the digitate branches are up to 1.0 cm in diameter. In earlier reports the presence of transverse striations was thought to indicate nodes, but now the striations are regarded as cracks caused during fossilization.

In *C. bicephalum* there is a gradation in the size of the sterile appendages (leaves), with those farther down the axis being larger and more fully developed. As in *Hyenia,* the leaves of *Calamophyton* were three-dimensional structures, each dichotomizing once in a horizontal plane and once in a vertical plane. Young leaves in the distal region forked only once, while those in the more basal regions of the axis may have dichotomized up to four times.

Some *Calamophyton* specimens suggest that there was a distinct separation between branches containing only leaves and those bearing sporangia. There is no suggestion, however, that the sporangia were aggregated into strobili or cones. The sporangium-bearing branches are borne oppositely along the fertile branches in a pseudowhorled arrangement. Occasionally, however, sporangium-bearing branches do occur between the sterile whorls. Each fertile branch consists of a basal stalk that is divided into an upper and lower segment.

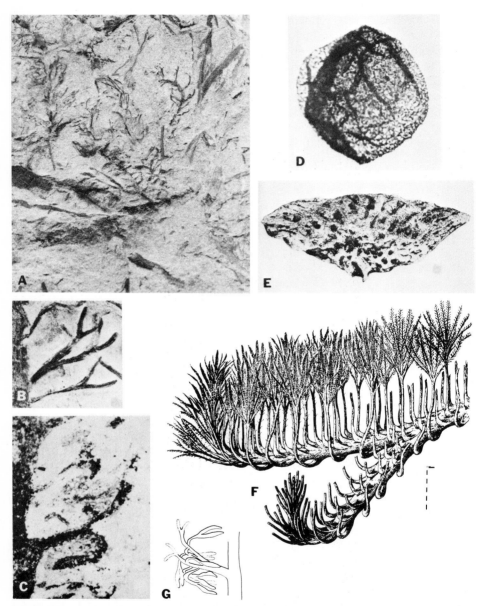

Figure 10-4 A. Specimen of *Calamophyton primaevum* from the Middle Devonian of Germany. ×1. B. Dichotomy of *Calamophyton primaevum* leaf. ×3. C. Reflexed sporangium of *Calamophyton primaevum*. ×5. D. *Calamophyton bicephalum* spore. ×300. E. Transverse section showing the scattered vascular strands in an axis of *Calamophyton primaevum*. ×4. F. Suggested reconstruction of *Hyenia elegans*. G. Sporangiophore of *Calamophyton primaevum*. (*B, C, E, and G from Schweitzer, 1973; D from Bonamo and Banks, 1966; F from Schweitzer, 1972.*)

The segment is further subdivided into three shortened side branches that terminate in a reduced bifurcation, each bearing a single sporangium. Thus, in *C. bicephalum,* each branch produced 12 sporangia.

Each sporangium is cylindrical and pointed at the distal end. Dehiscence is thought to have occurred on the ventral side. *Calamophyton bicephalum* spores exhibit a considerable variability in size, ranging from 86 to 166 μm in diameter. Each is circular to subcircular in outline, with a distinct trilete and ornament of delicate spinae (Fig. 10-4D).

In 1965, Leclercq and Schweitzer described a structurally preserved specimen of *C. bicephalum.* It consists of an unbranched axis approximately 9.5 cm long that is believed to represent a third or fourth order of branching. In cross section the axis shows 14 to 16 distinct vascular segments that are either oval or reveal four or five radially disposed arms. All the xylem segments are composed only of primary tissues, with the ones near the periphery of the stem containing peripheral loops of parenchyma surrounded by mesarch metaxylem.

Further evidence that *Calamophyton* should be regarded as more fernlike than sphenophyte is found in the recent discovery of both compressed and structurally preserved specimens of *C. primaevum* from Germany (Fig. 10-4E). The specimens suggest a plant that consisted of an upright trunk that arose from a bulbous base bearing numerous delicate roots. The entire plant may have been at least 3.0 m tall. In one specimen, the main stem is approximately 10.0 cm in diameter and bears helically arranged lateral branches. Larger, presumably older, stems lack branches near their bases, and it is suggested that they were deciduous. Lateral branches are up to 60.0 cm long with repeated dichotomies that provided a dense pattern to the plant. These lateral branches are thought to represent the typical *Calamophyton* axis system that has resulted in reconstructions such as that of Fig. 10-3B.

Lateral appendages up to 2.0 cm long are arranged helically on the more distal branches. These structures are similar to the "leaves" of *Hyenia* in that they consist of up to four dichotomies (Fig. 10-4B). Fertile branches are about 1.0 cm long and dichotomize once or twice. Each unit consists of three recurved stalks (Fig. 10-4G) with each stalk containing two elongate sporangia up to 3.0 mm long (Fig. 10-4C). Spores are trilete and assignable to the *sporae dispersae* genus *Diabolisporites.* Within the stem are numerous irregularly shaped masses of xylem. Tracheids are scalariform, and secondary tissues are absent.

There can be little doubt that the vascular system of *Calamophyton* is more like that of a fern than a sphenophyte. Specimens of *Hyenia* with comparable anatomic detail have not been discovered, but the V-shaped strand reported by Kräusel and Weyland strongly suggests a similarity with *Calamophyton* and a vascular system, even if partially understood, unlike that of any known sphenophyte. The similarity in lateral appendages (leaves) between the two genera further strengthens this comparison. The rhizomatous portion of *Hyenia* also suggests affinities with the ferns.

The Cladoxylopsida constitute an interesting and perplexing group of vascular plants that are united on the basis of their vascular system. It is doubtful that the taxa will still constitute a natural assemblage when sufficient fossil evidence is discovered for all the species. Nevertheless, the group does demonstrate several interesting features that show a degree of evolutionary specialization by the Middle Devonian. One of these is the highly dissected vascular system that appears to increase the number of xylem strands at higher levels of the plant. It has been suggested that the cladoxylalean vascular system may have evolved by the further dissection of an actinostele. It was noted in Chap. 7 that the modification of a simple protostele (characteristic of the Rhyniophyta) into the actinostele (e.g., *Asteroxylon*) may have resulted from the increased surface area and necessity for added conduction during the evolution of preleaves in the form of enations. Although important details regarding the anatomy of very distal branch segments is lacking in the Cladoxylopsida, the unique configuration of the vascular system may be a further modification of the actinostele that is consistent with the evolution of a frond system.

The term polystele has not been used to describe the vascular organization within the Cladoxylopsida for several reasons. First, it may be that the secondary xylem reported in some species does in fact represent radially aligned metaxylem; and second, the vascular system may have evolved from a simple dissection of an actinostele.

In light of recent anatomic evidence regarding the systematic position of some members of the group, the lateral appendages that have been termed preleaves in *Hyenia* and *Calamophyton* deserve further comment. Such structures constitute the basis for the suggested relationship with the sphenophytes via planation and webbing. This notion was especially appealing when these laterals were thought to have been borne in a whorled arrangement. An alternative view might be to regard the ultimate segments as pinnules of a fernlike vegetative frond. Such a view is strengthened by the bilateral symmetry of the fronds of *Pseudosporochnus* and the apparently identical morphology of both fertile and vegetative fronds.

The phylogenetic position of this group remains questionable. Some workers have suggested a relationship with the medullosan seed ferns based on the supposed similarity of the vascular system. Although true polystelely seems to have been absent in *Medullosa* (Basinger, Rothwell, and Stewart, 1974), the dissection of the vascular system in both groups does appear to be similar. Proponents of this relationship point to the production of secondary xylem in some cladoxylaleans as further evidence of such a relationship. Other authors regard the Cladoxylopsida as a plexus of vascular plants from which a number of groups may have evolved, including the Sphenophyta. Finally, the Cladoxylopsida are regarded by still other workers as the progenitors of such fernlike plants as the Coenopteridopsida. This relationship is based principally on the presence of parenchyma-filled peripheral loops in both groups. Scheckler (1975) has suggested that the peripheral loops within the group are of two distinct types. In one type, longitudinally oriented rods of parenchyma are surrounded by mesarch protoxylem tracheids. This type of organization is most common in the Cladoxylopsida, exemplified by *Cladoxylon taeniatum, C. radiatum,* and others. The other configuration is typified by *Rhymokalon,* in which the protoxylem strands disintegrate to form lacunae that resemble peripheral loops. These peripheral loops contain no parenchyma and only remnants of protoxylem tracheids. Scheckler has suggested that these two conditions may provide clues to relationships with other vascular plant groups: the type with parenchyma being related to certain coenopterid ferns, the type lacking parenchyma being more closely allied with other groups.

RHACOPHYTOPSIDA

The class Rhacophytopsida is suggested as a repository for two genera and several species of Devonian plants that comprise an interesting suite of anatomic and morphologic features, and it is further suggested that this class has affinities with both ferns and members of the Progymnospermophyta. Initially the genus *Rhacophyton* was placed in the Aneurophytales, an order established for primitive plants believed to be progenitors of the pteridosperms and true ferns. *Rhacophyton* also was included in the Protopteridales, an order of fernlike plants with clusters of terminally produced sporangia but no laminar pinnules. Other authors have suggested that *Rhacophyton* is closely related to certain coenopterid ferns.

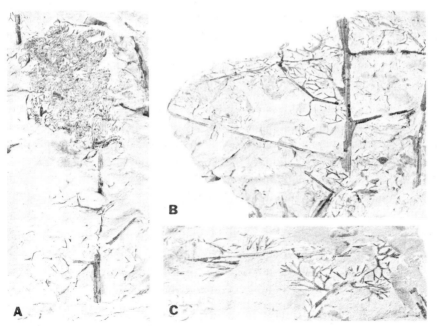

Figure 10-5 *Rhacophyton.* A. Portion of a fertile frond showing aggregation of sporangia. ×1. B. Several orders of branching. ×1. C. Ultimate leaflike segments. ×1.6.

The most completely known member of the class is *Rhacophyton*. The genus is known from the Upper Devonian (Famennian) from several localities in North America, Belgium, and western Siberia. *Rhacophyton ceratangium* (Andrews and Phillips, 1968), probably the best-known species, is an upright plant approximately 1.0 m tall. Fronds are borne on the stem in two vertical rows by alternately arranged pairs of rachides arising from a common base (Fig. 10-5B). This type of arrangement is quadriseriate or tetrastichous. Some frond segments are at least 50.0 cm long. In *R. ceratangium,* frond morphology is highly variable, including a gradational series between two- (Fig. 10-6C) and three-dimensional forms. Aphlebia-like appendages that superficially resembled pinnules are attached to the main stem in pairs. Numerous pinnulelike structures (Fig. 10-5C) are borne at the distal levels of the fronds (primary pinnae). Pinnules are of three basic types in *R. certangium,* all nonlaminate and differing in the degree of flattening and ultimate segment morphology (Cornet, Phillips, and Andrews, 1976).

Fertile fronds of *Rhacophyton* are common, but to date none have been found organically attached to the main axis (Fig. 10-5A). In general, the fertile frond is three-dimensional with two elongate, sterile pinnae and two branched, fertile pinnae (Fig. 10-6A). This four-parted branch has been described as a nodal unit. Each fertile pinna consists of a basal stalk that dichotomizes several times in a relatively short distance to produce a dense, three-dimensional structure about 2.5 cm in diameter. Penultimate branches of the cluster are slightly curved toward the center of the mass and bear smaller branches along their inner surfaces. These smaller branches in turn dichotomize, each terminating in a sporangium. In the reports describing *R. certangium* with fertile units, considerable variation has been noted in the number of parts present in each nodal unit. In some specimens, either one fertile or sterile pinna is lacking. Similar variation in frond morphology also is noted in a specimen from West Virginia, in which a sterile frond branches at about the midpoint to produce both a fertile and a sterile segment.

Sporangia of *R. ceratangium* are fusiform with an elongate, curved tip (Fig. 10-6A); they measure up to 2.4 mm long and 0.4 mm in maximum diameter. Dehiscence is longitudinal and apparently does not involve the tip. Spores are ovoid and about 50 μm in diameter, and their proximal surfaces are marked by a faint trilete suture. The sporoderm is often wrinkled and ornamented by delicate grana. *Rhacophyton ceratangium* spores have been compared with the dispersed grain *Perotriletes.*

In transverse section, *R. ceratangium* contains a central bar-shaped strand of primary xylem surrounded by radially aligned rows of secondary tracheids. At each end of the narrow primary xylem bar is an interruption or loop that is thought to contain parenchyma. Secondary tracheids are of the scalariform type.

Additional information about the anatomy of *Rhacophyton* is known from Leclercq's (1951) detailed study of *R. zygopteroides.* This species, known from the Upper Devonian of Belgium, is described as an upright axis bearing helically arranged fronds. Pinnae are produced in two rows and contain small (up to 1.0

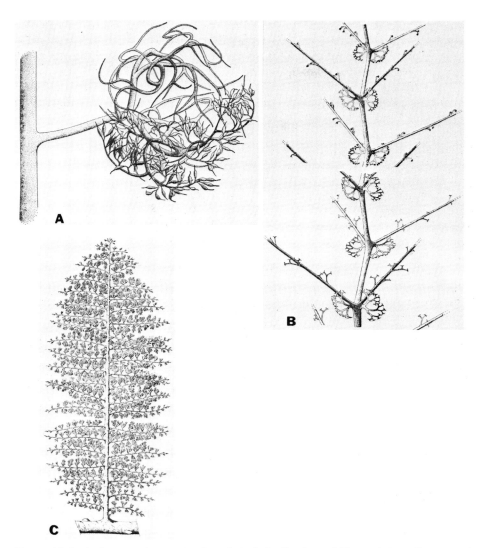

Figure 10-6 A. Suggested reconstruction of single fertile pinna of *Rhacophyton* with sporangia removed from upper portion. B. Suggested reconstruction of *Protocephalopteris praecox.* C. Suggested reconstruction of vegetative frond of *Rhacophyton. (A and C from Andrews and Phillips, 1968; B from Schweitzer, 1968.)*

cm long), dissected pinnules. In cross section, the stem contains a star-shaped xylem strand with an outer zone of scalariform tracheids and an inner zone of poorly preserved cells. Traces initiate from the arms of the stele as rectangular bars with two opposite peripheral loops. At higher levels the traces become clepsydroid in transverse configuration (see Fig. 10-12C). Pinna traces are crescent-shaped in cross section, with subsequent pinnule traces C-shaped in sectional view. Traces to the fertile pinnae are similar, except that two strands are apparent in the common bases of paired pinnae. There is a small amount of secondary xylem in *R. zygopteroides.* Another marked distinction between the two species is the apparent bilateral symmetry of *R. ceratangium;* the axis of *R. zygopteroides* is more stellate in outline.

Two specimens of *R. ceratangium* from the Givetian (Upper Middle Devonian) of New York exhibit bipolar primary xylem with well-developed mesarch protoxylem at each pole. Radially elongate gaps between the secondary xylem tracheids have been interpreted as vascular rays.

Rhacophyton condrusorum was a much larger plant, as suggested by the size of the axes and frond segments. Primary pinnae were approximately 35.0 cm long for this species, while in *R. zygopteroides* and *R. ceratangium* the pinna length was about 6.0 cm. In addition, *R. condrusorum* had vegetative fronds that were apparently tripinnate, as opposed to the bipinnate configuration of the other species. In a recently discovered specimen of *R. condrusorum* from the Upper Devonian of Germany (Schultka, 1978), the stele is described as being diarch with abundant secondary xylem and numerous vascular rays.

Another plant that has been compared with *Rhacophyton* is the Middle Devonian genus *Protocephalopteris* (Fig. 10-6B). Specimens are known from Spitsbergen and Siberia and consist of large, bipinnate fronds with alternately arranged pinnae (Schweitzer, 1968). Sterile pinnules, similar to those of *Rhacophyton,* are arranged alternately. The fertile unit consists of pairs of primary pinnae that are subtended by aphlebialike fertile structures bearing terminal sporangia. A major distinction between *Protocephalopteris* and *Rhacophyton* is the apparent quadriseriate branching of the ultimate fertile appendages.

The systematic position of *Rhacophyton* and *Protocephalopteris* is currently unsettled. Anatomically, *Rhacophyton* superficially appears similar to members of the Aneurophytales, but differs in several important features. These include the scalariform pitting of *Rhacophyton;* members of the Aneurophytales are characterized by circular bordered pits on the secondary xylem tracheids. Traces to branches are lobed and single in the Aneurophytales; terete and clepsydroid shapes delimit *Rhacophyton.* Clepsydroid traces with peripheral loops are not known among the Aneurophytales. Both groups exhibit dichotomizing, nonlaminate pinnules, but in the Aneurophytales there is nothing like the aphlebialike fertile pinnae of *Protocephalopteris.*

Features that have been used to suggest affinities with coenopterid ferns include the clepsydroid-shaped traces with peripheral loops, the presence of secondary xylem (*Zygopteris*), the morphology of the sporangia, the radially symmetrical stellate stele of the stem, the *Etapteris*-like trace emission, the scalariform tracheids, and the organization of the fertile parts. *Rhacophyton* also has been compared with the Upper Devonian (Frasnian) genus *Stenokoleos,* believed to be a Lower Carboniferous protostelic seed fern. Common features include pairs of distichous lateral appendages, a bilaterally symmetrical stele in transverse section with mesarch xylem and peripheral loops, and clepsydroid-shaped traces.

Recently, it was suggested that *Rhacophyton* be placed in the emended order Protopteridales, an order established for fernlike plants with minor differences between branches and fronds, nonlaminated pinnules, and terminal sporangia. Despite the inherent problems of attempting to properly assign such plants as *Rhacophyton* and *Protocephalopteris* to some higher taxonomic category, members of the class Rhacophytopsida do demonstrate several intermediate levels in the evolution of the frond. In this context, the alternately pinnate branch systems of *Rhacophyton* suggest an intermediate stage in the evolution of a planated, biseriate system from the three-dimensional quadriseriate organization. Ancestral to the *Rhacophyton* frond system might have been a complete quadriseriate arrangement such as that suggested by *Protocephalopteris*. The biseriate frond morphology of filicalean ferns may have evolved through the loss of one pinna pair. Variations in pinnule morphology also may represent selection toward increased planation.

COENOPTERIDOPSIDA

The Coenopteridopsida are represented by ferns and fernlike plants that can be traced from the Upper Devonian into the Permian. With relatively few exceptions, coenopterid ferns possess megaphylls, circinate vernation, adventitious roots, and foliar sporangia. Geologically older taxa are protostelic, with some later forms exhibiting siphonosteles. Secondary xylem is present in only one genus. Multicellular hairs, scales, and aphlebiae are present on the vegetative parts, and foliar units are characterized by bilateral symmetry. Unusual geometrically shaped xylem strands in transverse section also have been used to delimit coenopterid ferns. Pitting ranges from multiseriate scalariform to circular bordered. Most coenopterid specimens have vegetative structures considered to be homologous with the fronds of living ferns. In general, taxa are assigned to the coenopterid complex on the basis of such anatomic features as the symmetry and histology of the leaf traces and the morphology of the frond. This is in contrast to the manner in which living ferns are classified, which primarily is on the basis of the structure, arrangement, and position of the sporangia.

The Coenopteridopsida should be viewed as a heterogeneous group of Paleozoic ferns that demonstrate considerable morphologic and anatomic variation and represent an artificial class. Recent studies describing the fertile parts clearly indicate that several groups of coenopterids should be included with the true ferns. Where such features have been demonstrated, the taxa have been transferred to the Filicales. For the remaining coenopterid taxa, however, the class Coenopteridopsida has been retained, in part because diagnostic features of the sporangia are not known, and because our current understanding of the major lines of fern evolution remain uncertain. In this regard, the coenopterids occupy a position similar to that of the cladoxylaleans, in which the taxa are united on the basis of certain anatomic features. Few researchers believe that the specimens included in these two groups are all naturally related. With the discovery of more specimens that reveal features about the sporangia and the way they were produced on the plants, both classes will become reduced as the individual taxa are transferred to their proper groups.

The historical development of coenopterid classification is important in illustrating the preceding point. Through the years there have been several schemes of classification for coenopterid ferns. Such schemes have been more convenient than natural. A classification that has been widely adopted delimits four families:

STAUROPTERIDACEAE: Small, bushy plants with three-dimensional branches lacking lamina and producing terminal sporangia; four-ridged xylem strand repeated in branches of higher orders

BOTRYOPTERIDACEAE: Fronds ranging from two to three-dimensional with petiole trace omega-shaped in transverse section: sporangia borne in massive clusters or on abaxial pinnul surface

ANACHOROPTERIDACEAE: Abaxially curved petiole traces arising from protostelic stems

ZYGOPTERIDACEAE: Three-dimensional fronds bearing primary pinnae in four ranks; sporangia elongate and produced in clusters from abaxial surface of pinnules or from tips of frond branches

Recent discoveries of the fertile parts of several genera have resulted in a modification of the preceding classification of the coenopterids, with several taxa now transferred to the Filicales. The classification adopted here includes the Coenopteridopsida with the following orders: Stauropteridales and Zygopteridales. The Botryopteridaceae, Tedeleaceae, and Anachoropteridaceae are now included as extinct families within the order Filicales.

Stauropteridales

The Stauropteridales are represented by a single genus and three species. *Stauropteris* is known from both Lower and Upper Carboniferous deposits of Europe (one report from the Carboniferous of North America is probably in error). The plants were relatively small, and based on the branching patterns of the axes, apparently exhibited a bushy appearance (Fig. 10-7A). Specimens show axes that are stemlike and contain a slightly bilaterally symmetrical xylem strand that is four-lobed in transverse section (Fig. 10-7C). Subsequent branches are borne in pairs, with strands of xylem similar to that of the primary axis. Six orders of branches have been reported, with the xylem strands continuously smaller at higher levels and each branch terminating in a terete protostele. Protoxylem is mesarch, revealing only primary tissue; pitting is scalariform. Phloem is thought to occupy furrows between the xylem ridges. The three-dimensional branching pattern in *Stauropteris* has been interpreted by some

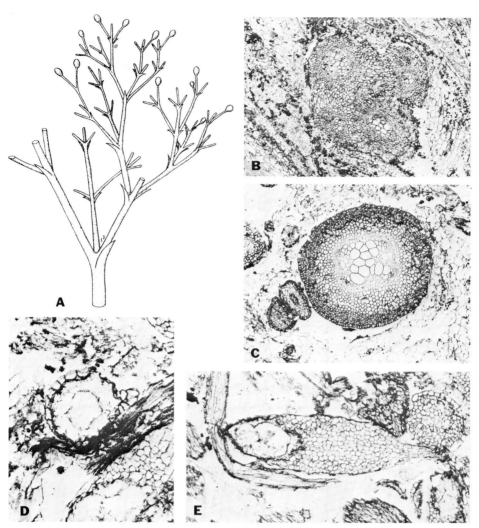

Figure 10-7 A. Suggested reconstruction of *Stauropteris oldhamia*. B. Transverse section of *Rowleya trifurcata* at level at which branches are given off. ×16. C. Transverse section of *Stauropteris burntislandica* axis. ×26. D. Transverse section through *Stauropteris burntislandica* sporangium. ×70. E. Longitudinal section of *Stauropteris burntislandica* sporangium. ×42. *(A from Eggert, 1964; B from Long, 1976.)*

researchers as demonstrating the initial stages in the evolution of a frond or megaphyll.

In the Upper Carboniferous (Pennsylvanian) species, *S. oldhamia*, pairs of highly dissected aphlebiae are present at each level of branching. Thick-walled cells and small vascular strands in the aphlebiae have suggested to some that they were nonphotosynthetic rigid structures similar to thorns or spines in some extant plants.

Sporangia are borne terminally on ultimate axes and have thick walls. The number of wall layers near the distal end of the sporangium is reduced, suggesting that the exannulate sporangium dehisced through an apical pore or stomium. The spores are spherical and range from 32 to 40 μm in diameter. Based upon the consistent occurrence of one type of spore, *S. oldhamia* is thought to have been homosporous.

Stauropteris burntislandica is known from Mississippian sediments. The axes are similar to those already described for *S. oldhamia,* although the aphlebiae demonstrate considerable morphologic variation. Each aphlebia is attached to the axis by an oblique ridge slightly below the insertion point of the branch. At other levels aphlebiae are attached by a small pad of tissue. In all cases, aphlebiae branch irregularly with some ultimate segments up to 4.0 mm long. One of the interesting features of this species is its heterosporous nature. This was initially recognized in 1952 by the noted Indian paleobotanist K. R. Surange, although the megasporangia had been described earlier under the binomial *Bensonites fusiformis* and were thought to represent glandlike structures. Each megasporangium is spindle-shaped and approximately 1.3 mm long. The lower half of the sporangium is parenchymatous and merely represents the tip of a branch. The upper (distal) half consists of a sporangial cavity (Fig. 10-7E) with a single-cell-layer-thick wall (Fig. 10-7D). At maturity, the contents were released from the distal tip. The number of megaspores contained in the *S. burntislandica* sporangium is typically two, but some specimens are known with three. One report suggested that up to eight megaspores per sporangium were present, but this may have been the result of folded spores viewed in section. An interesting paper by Chaloner (1958) described dispersed megaspores of the *S. burntislandica* type (= *Didymosporites*) in which two smaller (presumably abortive) spores are associated with the two larger, functional megaspores. Both large and small spores are embedded in what appears to have been a series of tapetal membranes. The large spores range up to 580 μm in diameter, while the smaller ones are generally in the 45 μm size class. Both types are trilete.

Microsporangia have been described in *S. burntislandica.* They are ovoid and approximately 0.6 mm long. They differ from the sporangia of *S. oldhamia* in having a one-cell-layer-thick wall. Microspores are approximately 30 μm in diameter and trilete. It is not known whether the sporangia were borne on the same or different branching systems or on different plants.

Rowleya trifurcata (Westphalian A of Lancashire, England) is a protostelic axis that bears lateral branches in threes (Fig. 10-7B). Anatomically, the axis contains a tetrarch protostele that compares closely with the stelar structure of *Stauropteris.* At more distal levels, terete branches, interpreted as leaves, are arranged in pairs. The genus has been compared with *Stauropteris, Psalixochlaena,* and some species of *Botryopteris.*

Zygopteridales

The Zygopteridales represent the largest of the coenopterid fern groups and have the longest geologic history (Devonian to Permian). Members are characterized by elaborate fronds, and because of a paucity of information about the stems of many taxa, the anatomy of the branching pattern of the foliar members has been used to subdivide the order. Zygopterid ferns exhibit an apparent radial symmetry of the rachis that is often referred to as a phyllophore. This term has been widely used in discussions of coenopterid ferns to emphasize an organization different from the typical C-shaped vascular strand of fern leaves. In transverse section, the phyllophore often exhibits lateral parenchymatous peripheral loops. Traces to pinnae depart the xylem strand as crescentshaped bundles that, in turn, produce lateral traces. Members of the Zygopteridales are often separated into two groups on the basis of frond morphology. The etapterid (Etapterideae) type reveals four ranks of primary pinnae, with the formation of temporary peripheral loops when pinna traces are produced. The clepsydroid (Clepsydroideae) branching pattern exhibits two ranks of primary pinnae, as in living ferns. In transverse section, the phyllophore is hourglassshaped (clepsydroid), and the peripheral loops remain closed when traces to the pinnae are given off.

Probably the best-known member of the etapterid group is *Zygopteris*, known from Carboniferous and Permian deposits. Dennis (1974) recently examined specimens from the Middle and Upper Pennsylvanian of North America, and the two common species, *Z. berryvillensis* and *Z. illinoiensis*, will serve to characterize the genus. The habit of the plant consisted of an elongate rhizome (Fig. 10-8) that produced dichotomous branches, from which were borne petioles in two ranks. The surface of the rhizome was covered by helically arranged pairs of vascularized aphlebiae. In transverse section, the exarch protostele is stellate in outline. In *Z. illinoiensis*, the ratio of parenchyma cells to tracheids is 1 to 5, whereas in *Z. berryvillensis*, the ratio of parenchyma to tracheids is 2 to 1. One of the unusual features of *Zygopteris* is the presence of secondary xylem, a feature of only one extant fern, *Botrychium* (Ophioglossales). Although several authors have regarded the tissue as primary, recent studies substantiate the contention that the tracheids of *Zygopteris* originated

Figure 10-8 Suggested reconstruction of *Zygopteris berryvillensis*. (From Dennis, 1974.)

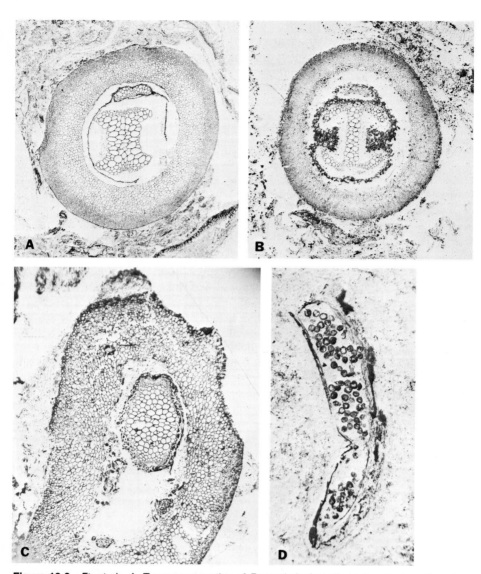

Figure 10-9 *Etapteris*. A. Transverse section of *Etapteris leclercqii* petiole with departing pinna trace. ×12. B. Transverse section of *Etapteris scottii* petiole. ×9. C. Transverse section of *Dineuron pteroides*. ×20. D. Longitudinal section of a *Musatea globata* sporangium. ×60. *(C and D courtesy of J. Galtier.)*

from a lateral meristem. Uniseriate and multiseriate vascular rays divide the secondary xylem into wedges. Tracheid pitting is variable, consisting of elongate to circular bordered pits. Primary phloem surrounds the xylem, but secondary phloem is not apparent. Clusters of sclereids are present within the parenchymatous cortex, and in older specimens, a weakly developed periderm zone can be distinguished. The epidermis is covered with multicellular peltate hairs. Numerous adventitious roots, each with a diarch stele, are randomly distrubuted along the rhizome.

The petiole traces of *Zygopteris* are H-shaped in transverse section (Fig. 10-9B), and because of the similarity of their shape to the Greek letter *eta,* isolated axes are called *Etapteris* (Fig. 10-9A). Prior to petiole trace formation, the rhizome stele becomes oval in cross section, with two conspicuous protoxylem points. At a slightly higher level, the trace is abaxially curved and bipolar; more distal sections show the development of sinuses between antennae and the characteristic tetrapolar structure of the *Etapteris* petiole. Pairs of aphlebiae are present at the lower levels of the petiole and may have served initially as protective structures for developing leaf primordia and later as photosynthetic structures on the mature leaf. In one Middle Pennsylvanian specimen, the *Etapteris* petiole bears pairs of primary pinnae that give rise to second-order pinnae with alternately arranged laminar pinnules. *Nemejcopteris feminaeformis* is a fossil plant from the Lower Permian of East Germany that is believed to have been a zygopterid fern with laminar pinnules. The species is known only from compression remains and includes a dichotomous rhizome that bears quadriseriate fronds in an erect manner. Each frond is subtended by a pair of aphlebiae, and the leaves exhibit circinate vernation. Sporangia are borne on modified pinnules, similar to those of *Corynepteris,* and contain trilete spores.

Etapteris leclercqii (Fig. 10-9A) is a Lower Pennsylvanian species discovered recently in coal balls collected in eastern Kentucky. The petioles measure approximately 5.0 mm in diameter and possess the characteristic H-shaped exarch xylem trace. In this species, the lateral arms (antennae) are attached broadly to the central bar of xylem (apolar) and taper to a point. Trace formation includes the development of a peripheral loop below the separation of pinna traces from the petiole. The surface of the petiole is covered with numerous multicellular hairs. Several authors have suggested that the thickened apolar, the reduced number of pinnae, and the lack of differentiation between apolar and lateral arms constitute primitive characters in the genus. The Lower Pennsylvanian age of *E. leclercqii* supports this idea.

Information about fossil phloem is relatively rare because the thin-walled nature of the cells allows them to be destroyed during preservation and because there are few suitable techniques with which to study the small sieve areas on the cell walls. In some cases, exceptionally well-preserved specimens provide information about fossil phloem (Smoot and Taylor, 1978). In *E. leclercqii,* a zone of phloem tissue approximately four cells wide surrounds the xylem core. This tissue is constructed entirely of sieve elements, each approximately 120 μm long and 40 $\mu\mu$m in diameter. End walls vary from horizontal to oblique and often exhibit swollen ends similar to those reported in extant ferns. When these cells are etched in acid and examined with the aid of a scanning electron microscope, distinct sieve areas are visible. They occur as regularly spaced, elongate depressions aligned perpendicular to the long axis of the cell.

Several examples of *Zygopteris* (*Etapteris*) have been described in which the sporangia are attached to distal branches of the petiole in clusters; others are described on the basis of the size and general histology of the sporangia. *Etapteris lacattei* bears small tufts of three to eight sporangia, and each sporangium is attached by a small stalk (Fig. 10-10A). The sporangia are

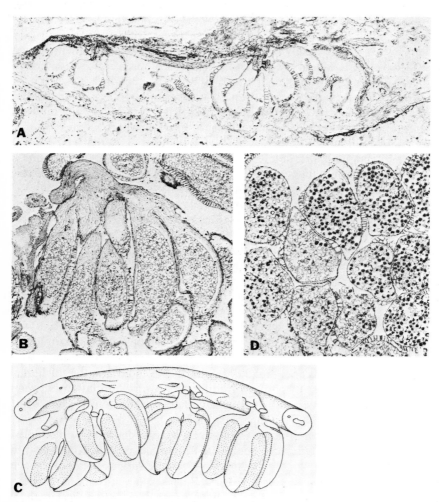

Figure 10-10 A. Portion of a fertile *Zygopteris* pinna. Note thick-walled cells of annulus. ×14. B. Cluster of *Biscalitheca* sp. sporangia. ×16. C. Suggested reconstruction of *Corynepteris scottii* fertile pinna. D. Sections of several *Biscalitheca musata* sporangia showing thickened cells of lateral annuli. ×16. *(C from Galtier and Holmes, 1976.)*

approximately 2.5 mm long and slightly curved. The wall of the sporangium exhibits two opposite rows of elongate cells that mark the position of an axial annulus. The spores are about 80 μm in diameter and trilete.

Biscalitheca musata is the name applied to elongate, slightly curved sporangia recovered from Upper Pennsylvanian petrifactions collected in southeastern Illinois. The sporangia are borne on bipinnate fertile fronds that consist of a nonlaminate rachis that reveal alternate penultimate pinnae and opposite to subopposite ultimate pinnae. The xylem strand is C-shaped in transverse section in both the rachis and the ultimate pinnae. Seven to nine sporangia are attached by a soral stalk (Fig. 10-10B) near the junction of the primary and ultimate pinnae. The sporangia are approximately 4.0 mm long and exhibit a pair of longitudinal, multiseriate annuli extending the length of the sporangium wall (Fig. 10-10D). Patches of small, thick-walled cells occur between the annuli near the distal end of the sporangium. The trilete spores of *B. musata* are spherical and range from 40 to 110 μm in diameter. Many spores contain preserved endosporal gametophytes that are composed of from 1 to 10 cells. At the ultrastructural level, the cytoplasmic contents of the spores vary from homogeneous to vesiculate and can be compared to stages in the development of the gametophyte of an extant fern.

A compression specimen exhibiting features of *Biscalitheca, B. kansana*, is known from the Lawrence shale (Upper Pennsylvanian) of Kansas. The specimen is described as a rachial lamina bearing subopposite fertile appendages. Sporangia are borne in groups on the abaxial surface and reveal paired, multiseriate annuli. The spores average 80 μm in diameter and are characterized by anastomosing ridges on the surface. They appear similar to the *sporae dispersae* genus *Convolutispora*.

Another fertile *Zygopteris* specimen reveals laminar pinnules of the *Alloiopteris* type and clusters of five to seven large, elongate sporangia. *Corynepteris sternbergii* bears sporangia approximately 2.0 mm long, each with multiseriate paired annuli. In *Corynepteris scottii* (Fig. 10-10C) from the Westphalian A of Britain, the pinnules are greatly reduced, and the trilete spores (46 to 52 μm) are similar to those described as *Apiculatisporis*.

Banana-shaped sporangia with an elongate zone of thick-walled epidermal cells are referred to as *Musatea globata* (Fig. 10-9D). Each sporangium contains trilete spores approximately 30 to 35 μm in diameter. Although not organically attached, the clusters of sporangia are observed in association with axes of *Diplolabis*. A similar case of association between axes of *Metaclepsydropsis duplex* and clusters of sporangia has recently been reported from a Pettycur limestone specimen (Lower Carboniferous) collected from Burntisland, Scotland. The sporangia are arranged in sori of three to four sporangia each and are attached to delicate laterals (fourth-order pinnae) by a common soral stalk containing a weakly developed vascular strand. Sporangial dehiscence occurs toward the center of a cluster along a line of smaller cells with unevenly thickened walls. Spores range to 52 μm in diameter and are trilete. *Musatea duplex* has been proposed as the name for this plant.

Unlike other species of *Zygopteris* with a rhizomatous habit, *Z. primaria* is thought to have been treelike, with a stem diameter up to 20.0 cm. Known from the Lower Permian of Saxony, this fossil plant contains a xylem core that is pentagonal in section and surrounded by abundant secondary tracheids. The bulk of the stem consists of clepsydroid-shaped leaf traces and adventitious roots. Pinna traces are of the *Etapteris* type, and the pinnae are covered with numerous multicellular scales. The roots are diarch and also contain abundant secondary xylem.

Another genus included in the etapterid group of the Zygopteridales is *Metaclepsydropsis* (Fig. 10-11A). *Metaclepsydropsis duplex* (Lower Carboniferous) has a horizontal rhizome that bears widely separated fronds. In transverse section, the stem stele is circular, with xylem consisting of an inner zone of long, narrow scalariform tracheids and an outer zone of elongate, reticulate xylem elements. During the formation of petiole traces, the two protoxylem points of the oval bipolar (Fig. 10-12E) originate in the outer xylem of the stem stele.

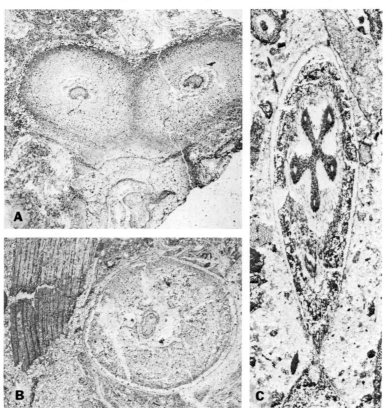

Figure 10-11　A. Transverse section through petiole and attached pinnae of *Metaclepsydropsis duplex.* ×4. B. Transverse section of *Clepsydropsis antiqua.* ×3.5. C. Transverse section of *Protoclepsydropsis kidstonii* with well-developed peripheral loops. ×6.5. *(B and C from A. G. Long Collection Nos. 11059 and 1072 in the Hancock Museum.)*

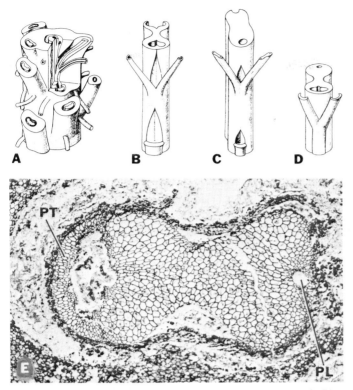

Figure 10-12 A. *Catenopteris simplex*. B. *Diplolabis roemeri*. C. *Rhacophyton zygopteroides*. D. *Metaclepsydropsis duplex*. E. *Metaclepsydropsis duplex* showing pinna trace (PT) and peripheral loop (PL). ×16. *(A–D from Phillips, 1974; E from Smoot and Taylor, 1978.)*

Pairs of pinna traces were subsequently given off, so the ultimate frond was quadriseriate in organization (Fig. 10-12D).

Both *Metadineuron* and *Dineuron* (Fig. 10-12B) are known only from petiole traces. In *Dineuron pteroides* (Lower Carboniferous of France), two types of pinna-trace emission are present on the same frond (Fig. 10-9C). In one, peripheral loops opened, closed, and then reopened to form C-shaped pinna traces that departed from the open loop. A second type produced a pair of small peripheral loops, and each individually produced a C-shaped pinna trace. Pinna traces in both genera are much smaller than the petiole axes. *Diplolabis roemerii* (Lower Carboniferous of Pettycur) has a solid protostele. Pinna traces are borne in pairs, and the configuration of the petiole stele is cruciate.

Some workers have suggested that the lateral expansion of the perpheral loops of the *Metaclepsydropsis* petiole configuration is represented in *Diplolabis*. The culmination in such a series could have produced the *Etapteris* petiole configuration, in which there is a radial extension of the trace arms without a corresponding increase in the size of the now open peripheral loop. Such a trend should not be interpreted as suggesting any relationships among the genera, but rather as a way in which frond morphology and the corresponding anatomy may have evolved.

One of the better-known clepsydroid zygopterids is *Clepsydropsis australis,* a species known from the Lower Carboniferous of Australia. The plant is apparently a tree fern that has a trunk approximately 30.0 cm in diameter, consisting of numerous leaf-bearing stems and intertwined roots. Each stem is radially symmetrical and bears petioles in a ⅖ phyllotaxy. Stem xylem is stellate in section with a central pith and scalariform tracheids. Petiole traces are initially triangular; they later assume the characteristic clepsydroid or hourglass configuration. Many dichotomized aphlebiae are borne in pairs along the rachis. Although spores have been found associated with the root mantle of the false stem, nothing is known about the reproductive parts of this plant.

Recently, Galtier (1966b) reveiwed the features of several species of *Clepsydropsis* (Fig. 10-11B) from petrified specimens collected in the Lower Carboniferous of France. In general, the peripheral loops of the hourglass-shaped petiole vascular strand seem to have remained closed when pinna traces were produced (with biseriate pinnae). In one species, *C. leclercqii,* from the Lower Visean of France, the clepsydroid anatomy is maintained, but the frond is quadriseriate, like members of the etapterid group.

Underscoring the unusual nature of *Clepsydropsis* is the fact that petioles of its type have been found attached to more than one type of stem. For example, *Asterochlaena* is a Permian genus characterized by a deeply lobed cylinder of primary xylem. The stem is approximately 8.0 cm in diameter and includes adventitious roots and numerous petioles of the *Clepsydropsis* type. The stem stele contains a mixed pith surrounded by scalariform tracheids. Traces arise from the blunt arms of the stele, becoming hourglass-shaped, but the peripheral loops are located toward the abaxial surface. At higher levels, the petioles are C-shaped and adaxially directed. *Asterochlaenopsis kirgisica* (Permian of Siberia) is a silicified stem approximately 15.0 cm in diameter that contains a cylindrical stele with a mixed pith. Leaf traces are clepsydroid, and pinnae are apparently biseriate and borne alternately. *Asteropteris* is an Upper Devonian genus that has a stellate protostele with conspicuous peripheral loops. Petiole traces are tetrapolar and arranged in a very shallow helix.

The name *Alloiopteris* has been used for impression-compression foliage of the Carboniferous and includes approximately 40 species (see Fig. 13-41Q). In general, the pinnae reveal alternate pinnules that are decurrent at the base and possess prominent apical lobes or teeth. Recently, specimens preserved as both compressions and petrifactions have been found in the Caseyville Formation (Lower Pennsylvanian) of southern Illinois, and they suggest that the affinities of the genus are with *Zygopteris* (Jennings, 1975). The vascular strand of the primary pinna is butterfly-shaped in transverse section, and the pinnule traces are terete. The demonstration that *A. sternbergii* represents the foliage of one Pennsylvanian *Zygopteris* frond system underscores the difficulty of attempting to characterize frond morphology in many of the early Paleozoic fernlike plants.

Conclusion

The genus *Stauropteris* has been regarded as a fernlike plant with appendages transitional between branches and fronds. Several authors have pointed to the similarity in structure of the stem and lateral branches as evidence of the intermediate evolutionary position of these appendages. The apparent heterosporous nature of at least one species of *Stauropteris* suggests that it possessed a highly advanced type of reproductive system that is not consistent with the level of frond evolution. Among living ferns, heterospory is present only in two families of reduced, aquatic forms. The unmodified stem tips represented by megasporangia in *Stauropteris* underscore the early occurrence of this type of reproductive system. If the suggestion that both microspores and megaspores were produced in the same sporangium and shed as a unit were true, this would represent a unique occurrence among plants—either living or fossil. It has generally been assumed that the megaphyllous habit arose through the planation and subsequent webbing of a branch system, not unlike that present in *Stauropteris*. It is not known whether planation preceded the quadriseriate arrangement of pinnae, during the evolution of megaphylls, although the Devonian fernlike plant *Rhacophyton* suggests that the flattening of the pinnae took place prior to any major change in pinna arrangement. Within the Zygopteridales there are several taxa that possessed clepsydroid anatomy and biseriate pinnae, and this suggests that they may have evolved from the quadriseriate type in the etapterid line. A few forms had quadriseriate fronds with clepsydroid anatomy, and this underscores their intermediate position.

Although the fertile parts of many etapterid forms have not yet been discovered, those which have been identified typically consist of large sporangia with well-defined annulus mechanisms in the form of one or two multiseriate bands of thick-walled cells. Sporangia are attached to flattened pinnae that have very reduced pinnule segments or none at all. From the evidence assembled to date, it appears that the fertile fronds were biseriate.

One interesting feature of a large number of Coenopteridopsida is the highly dichotomous aphlebiae that occur along the petioles or arise from the stem. In some taxa, the aphlebiae are three-dimensional, while in others, they are planated. Such structures could be interpreted as reduced branching systems that evolved in manner similar to that noted for the megaphylls. Another interpretation considers these aphlebiae as the end products of several fused and partially planated vascularized enations.

FILICOPSIDA

The ferns dealt with in the rest of this chapter can be referred to as true ferns in that both their vegatative features and the nature and organization of their sporangia provide a clue as to the relationship these fossil plants have with extant representatives. Four orders are recognized: Marattiales, Filicales, Marsileales, and Salviniales, with several of the filicalean families discussed in detail.

Marattiales

Various interpretations have been suggested relative to the taxonomy of this group. Some authors delimit two families, while most include the 6 living genera and the approximately 100 species in a single family, the Marattiaceae. Today marattialean ferns are tropical and confined to narrow geographic regions. Living marattiaceous ferns typically consist of a short, unbranched trunk that produces large, pinnately compound leaves. The leaves develop circinately and are characterized by a pair of fleshy stipules at the base of each frond rachis. The eusporangia are typically grouped into elongate sori or united into synangia on the abaxial surface of the pinnules. The roots are typically polyarch and contain abundant mucilage. The vascular tissue of the stem is arranged in a complex dictyostele. All the genera are homosporous.

The Marattiales may be traced back to the Carboniferous, where numerous fossil specimens attest to the diversity of the order. One of the most common fossil marattialean genera is *Psaronius,* a tree fern about 10 m tall, that is characterized by a crown of pinnate fronds (Fig. 10-13). Adventitious roots emerge some distance below the apex of the stem and project downward forming a dense root mantle toward the base of the stem. The generic name *Psaronius* was originally applied to structurally preserved stem sections (see Fig. 10-15B), but today the genus is used for the entire plant, including petrified stems. Specimens of *Psaronius* are known from the Carboniferous (Pennsylvanian) into the Permian (Fig. 10-14D).

Transverse sections of *Psaronius* stems reveal a complex stelar structure and, in several features, are like those of modern tree ferns. Near the base of the plant the stem is believed to have consisted of a small protostele and abundant adventitious roots; at higher levels the stem increases in diameter and the adventitious root mantle becomes reduced. Thus the trunk of *Psaronius* is a false stem consisting of an obconical stele surrounded by a zone of adventitious roots. In *Psaronius,* the stelar system consists of a series of concentric amphiphloic cauline strands separated by evenly spaced interruptions or gaps (Fig. 10-14C). Near the top of the plant there are at least 14 cycles present with as many as 14 orthostichies of leaves (Fig. 10-14A). Leaf traces initiate in the center of the stem and progress upward and outward, joining the free edges of the gaps in one cycle as they separate from an inner cycle and move toward the periphery of the stem. Although the apex of *Psaronius* has not been identified, it must have been massive, because the entire plant is composed only of primary tissues.

Features of stem histology will be presented for *P. blicklei* (Fig. 10-14A), probably the most completely known species of the genus. The primary component of the stem is a ground tissue constructed of thin-walled parenchyma cells. In a few species, the cortical tissue cells are loosely arranged with numerous intercellular spaces suggestive of aerenchyma tissue. Some cortical cells contain amorphous substances suggestive of tannin. Interspersed in the cortex are elongate, lysigenous lacunae, and they are scattered throughout the ground parenchyma and petiole bases and superficially resemble mucilage canals in living marattiaceous ferns. The periphery of the stem of *Psaronius* is

Figure 10-13   Suggested reconstruction of *Psaronius. (From Morgan, 1959.)*

constructed of thick-walled fibers that form a sclerenchyma sheath. At some levels, secondary parenchyma cell proliferation occurs, especially in the region of petiole attachment.

The dictyostelic vascular cylinder of *Psaronius* consists of primary xylem and xylem parenchyma intermixed among the tracheids. Protoxylem tracheids are clustered in groups along the inner surface of the strand. Metaxylem elements possess scalariform wall thickenings. Each vascular strand is surrounded by a phloem zone two to three layers deep. The elongate, thin-walled cells have been termed sieve cells, although sieve plates have not been identified.

Stems of *P. blicklei* are known from Upper Pennsylvanian deposits, and the specimens possess 3 to more than 14 orthostichies of leaves. Accompanying the increase in the number of rows of leaves is a change from a helical to a whorled arrangement at the distal end. Sclerenchyma occurs in patches in the basal

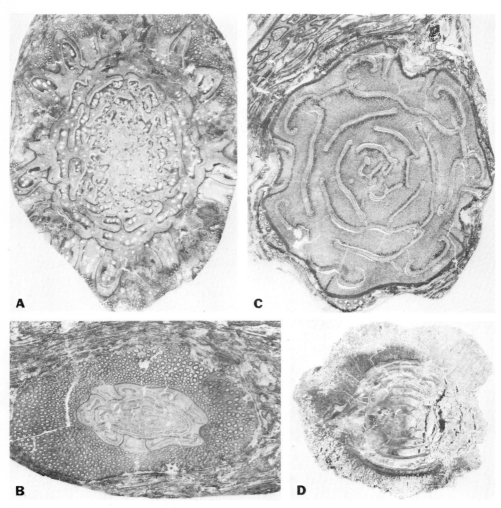

Figure 10-14 *Psaronius* stems. A. *Psaronius blicklei.* ×0.5. B. *Psaronius* sp. ×0.5. C. *Psaronius melanedrus.* ×1. D. *Psaronius simplex* (Lower Permian of Germany). ×0.5.

regions of the stem and is arranged in tangential bands at higher levels. Possibly the most characteristic features of the species are the numerous lacunae interspersed between the xylem strands (Fig. 10-14A).

Specimens of *P. chasei,* also from the Upper Pennsylvanian, are distinguished by the absence of ground tissue lacunae and the presence of bands of sclerenchyma between the second and third stelar cycles. The absence of lacunae is also a feature of the Middle Pennsylvanian species *P. melanedrus.* Stems of *P. melanedrus* are further delimited by a heavy band of fibers that occurs near the outer limit of the cortex (Fig. 10-14C). A smaller number of stelar cycles (five) has been reported in *P. pertusus.* This species reveals parenchyma cells of the ground tissue arranged in a netlike pattern.

All the foregoing species represent polycyclic dictyostelic stems in which the vascular strands are arranged in concentric cycles. Recently, a monocyclic stem was described from Lower Pennsylvanian deposits in northern Illinois. *Psaronius simplicicaulis* measures approximately 6.5 cm in diameter and contains a single monocyclic stele. Maturation of the primary xylem is endarch, and numerous longitudinally oriented secretory ducts are present in the ground tissue. Leaf traces are borne alternately in two opposite orthostichies in a distichous manner. The stratigraphic position of this species suggests that the larger polystelic psaronii were derived from the smaller monostelic ancestors as a result of an increase in size and a concomitant increase in anatomic complexity.

One of the unusual features of *Psaronius* is the massive adventitious root mantle (Fig. 10-14B), which in some specimens may have been nearly 1.0 m in diameter at the base of the stem. Roots originate from the stem, and after emerging, bend abruptly downward and parallel the stem surface. Lateral roots appear in no recognizable pattern at the base of mature plants. Outer roots are actinostelic in transverse section (Fig. 10-18C), with three to nine protoxylem points and scalariform, pitted metaxylem tracheids. The cortex is constructed of chains of parenchyma cells, suggesting that the tissue was aerenchymatous. This zone is bounded by a sclerenchyma sheath that is several cells thick. The epidermis of *Psaronius* roots apparently commonly proliferated to produce a dense mass of parenchyma tissue that held the outer root zone together. The apices of some *Psaronius* lateral roots have been identified. They consist of a multilayered root cap and up to four apical initials.

When fronds abscised naturally or otherwise from *Psaronius,* evidence of their former position is seen in the form of elliptical scars on the stem. Leaf traces originate from the innermost cycle and unite with successive cycles, closing gaps left by other traces as they moved toward the petiole base. The configuration of the leaf trace is variable in *Psaronius* depending on the position of the petiole on the stem, the variability of the vascular system of the stem, the root mantle development, and possible stem differences reflecting species.

Stipitopteris and *Stewartiopteris* are generic names applied to isolated structurally preserved *Psaronius* foliar members. *Stipitopteris gracilis,* a common species from the Pennsylvanian of North America, may have been several centimeters in diameter. The genus is characterized by a W-shaped vascular strand constructed of endarch primary xylem. Pinnae are borne in two rows along the adaxial surface. Traces to the pinnae are C-shaped, and interruptions occurred during their formation. The monocyclic rachis trace is embedded in a parenchymatous groud tissue that is surrounded by a zone of sclerenchyma. Surrounding this sclerenchymatous layer is a delicate cortex form which arise numerous epidermal borne scales. In *Stewartiopteris,* there is a thin zone of sclerenchyma beneath the epidermis. The rachis trace is horseshoe-shaped, and the edges enroll adaxially. Pinna traces are produced by the gap left by the separation of the inrolled edge of the xylem strand. Initially the pinna trace is cylindrical, but at higher levels it opens to form a C-shaped strand. Stems of *Psaronius chasei* and *P. melanedrus* typically possessed petiole trace configurations of the *Stewartiopteris* type, while *Stipitopteris* is the petiole configuration most commonly found on *P. blicklei* stems. One rachis specimen has been reported that displays a transition from the stewartiopterid to the stipitopterid type. It is probable that most fronds possess the stipitopterid vascular configuration at the base of the petiole, although the stipitopterid configuration may be derived from the stewartiopterid type toward the distal end of the rachis. Several well-preserved *Psaronius* crosiers have been found that suggest that at least some species produced tripinnate fronds. In some crosier specimens, separate tracheal groups make up the vascular strand, a feature typically associated with small axes in which subsequent differentiation between the tracheid groups forms the normal, solid strand. The crosiers are covered by numerous scales that are each approximately 2.0 mm long.

Casts, as well as impression-compression specimens of *Psaronius* trunks, have been delimited on the basis of size, shape, and arrangement of the leaf base. *Megaphyton* is the generic name applied to stem surfaces that exhibit leaf scars in two vertical rows on opposite sides of the stem. The scars are variable in shape, ranging from oval to almost rectangular. The configuration of the vascular strand may be of the stewartiopterid or stipitopterid type. *Hagiophyton* is similar to *Megaphyton,* but it is distinguished by a thick band of sclerenchyma

Figure 10-15 A. Surface of *Psaronius* stem showing typical *Caulopteris* petiole base configurations. ×0.5. B. Transverse section of *Psaronius brasiliensis.* ×0.4.

surrounding the vascular strand. Stem surfaces with petiole scars in more than two vertical rows, which indicate a helical or whorled pattern, are assigned to *Caulopteris* (Fig. 10-15A). Leaf scars are variable in shape and may be solitary, overlapping, or covering the entire stem. *Artisophyton* exhibits two vertical rows of leaf scars on opposite sides of the stem, but the vascular strand is closed, often with a deep indentation on the abaxial side. Each half of the outer xylem strand contains a smaller S-shape trace.

Marattialean sporangia of the Paleozoic are arranged in synangia borne on the lower surfaces of *Pecopteris* pinnules (see Fig. 13-17E and F). The most completely known petrified genera are from North American coal balls, and they include *Scolecopteris, Acaulangium, Cyathotrachus,* and *Eoangiopteris.* Millay (1979) recognized 18 species of *Scolecopteris* (Fig. 10-16A), the most widely represented and best understood genus of marattialean synangia. The genus is characterized by small, pedicellate synangia composed of rings of laterally appressed sporangia that separate on dehiscence. The genus is now delimited into three basic types on the basis of synangium anatomy and pinnule morphology. The *latifolia* type has thin-walled synangia composed of a small number of sporangia that are completely enclosed on the abaxial surface of pinnules with fibrous margins (Fig. 10-16C). The *minor* type (Fig. 10-16A) has

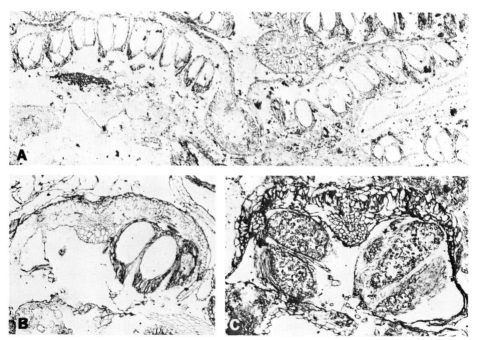

Figure 10-16 A. Transverse section through pinna of *Scolecopteris saharaensis.* ×24. B. Transverse section through a pinnule of *Acaulangium bulbaceus.* ×45. C. Transverse section of a *Scolecopteris vallumii* pinnule with attached sporangia. ×50. *(A and C from Millay, 1979; B courtesy of M. Millay.)*

pinnules that exhibit thin, lateral extensions of lamina (composed of hypodermal cells) that envelope the synangia, which have thin, outer-facing walls near the base. Members of the *oliverii* group exhibit uniformly thick-walled synangia (Fig. 10-17A) that are borne abaxially on unmodified foliage (Fig. 10-16B).

In *S. saharaensis* (*minor* group), the synangium consist of four to five sporangia arranged around a reduced vascularized pedicel. The synangia measure up to 1.0 mm long and display prominent sporangial tips that are curved toward the center of the unit. Longitudinal dehiscence takes place along a line of thin-walled cells directed toward the center of the cluster. The pinnules that produce *S. saharaensis* synangia exhibit incised margins with teeth alternating with synangia. The spores are oval, monolete, and ornamented with spines (Fig. 10-17D).

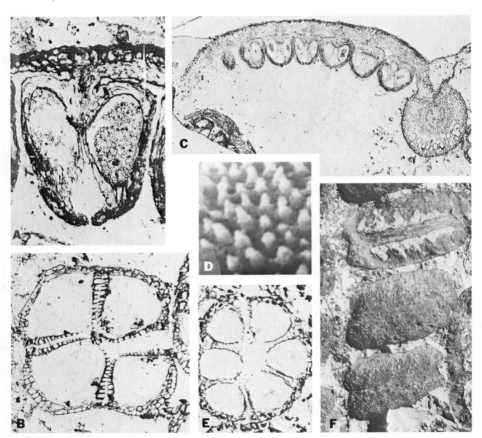

Figure 10-17   A. Longitudinal section of *Scolecopteris parvifolia* synangium. ×60. B. Transverse section through a synangium of *Scolecopteris major.* ×42. C. Ultimate pinna axis with attached pinnule of *Acaulangium bulbaceus.* ×15. D. Ornamentation on the spore of *Scolecopteris saharaensis.* ×10,000. E. Transverse section through a *Scolecopteris iowensis* synangium. ×42. F. Several pinnules of *Acaulangium bulbaceus* exposed on the surface of a coal ball. ×10. *(A, D, and E courtesy of M. Millay; B from Millay, 1979; C and F from Millay, 1977.)*

Scolecopteris illinoensis is a member of the *oliverii* group common in Upper Pennsylvanian coal balls. There are four to six sporangia basally attached to a short pedicel, and dehiscence occurs by rupture of one to two rows of narrow cells along the inner sporangial midline. Spores are monolete. In the Middle Pennsylvanian species *S. iowensis* (Fig. 10-17E), the spores are large (up to 83 μm) and trilete. Members of the *latifolia* group of scolecopterids have thin-walled sporangia and abaxially curved pinnule margins. In *S. calicifolia,* the synangia are borne in two rows and constructed of three to four exannulate sporangia each. This Middle Pennsylvanian species is characterized by its short synangium pedicel. Rather large pinnules delimit *S. incisifolia* specimens, some of which measure in excess of 6.5 mm long. The spores of *S. mamayi* are ornamented with delicate spines.

Ironstone nodules from southern Illinois (Middle Pennsylvanian) have provided both fertile and sterile foliage of a new species of *Scolecopteris*. The partially petrified specimens of *S. macrospora* (*minor* group) include pinnules up to 1.0 cm long with dissected margins. Synangia are borne in a single row of each side of the midrib and in sporangial features are identical with other species of the group. Although the pinnules could not be related to any known species of *Pecopteris,* the material is important in providing a method whereby compression taxa can be correlated with species that have been based solely on structurally preserved specimens. Although only three basic types of *Scolecopteris* are described, the genus is extensive, with many of the other species intermediate and demonstrating a continuum of forms.

A common marattialean fructification of the Upper Pennsylvanian that superficially resembles *Scolecopteris* is *Acaulangium* (Fig. 10-17C). Each synangium is oval in transverse section and is composed of four to six sporangia. Dehiscence occurs along the inner-facing walls toward the center of the unit. Specimens of *A. bulbaceus* (Fig. 10-16B) share several features in common with *S. illinoensis,* but they can be distinguished by the sessile attachment of the sporangia. The tendency toward bilateral symmetry and the sessile nature of the sporangia are features that suggest affinities with extant members of the order such as *Marattia.* Detracting from such a hypothesis is the pecopterid foliage type known to have produced *Acaulangium* synangia (Fig. 10-17F).

One Pennsylvanian taxon with distinctly bilateral synangia is *Eoangiopteris* (Fig. 10-18A and B). In this feature, specimens of *Eoangiopteris* appear more like the synangia of extant marattialeans than like the radial synangium organization present in the other Paleozoic forms. *Eoangiopteris goodii* is an Upper Pennsylvanian (Ohio) species that reveals a linear synangium (0.9 mm wide by 3.5 mm long) of 10 to 19 sporangia. The sporangia are partially embedded in an elongate pad attached to the abaxial surface of pecopterid pinnules. Pinnules are about 1.0 cm long and are vascularized by a small C-shaped trace. The edge is downturned and consists of hypodermal fibers. If found dispersed in Pennsylvanian sediments, the trilete, oval spores of *E. goodii* would be included in the genus *Verrucosisporites. Eoangiopteris* exhibits several features in common with extant species of *Angiopteris* that possess laterally free

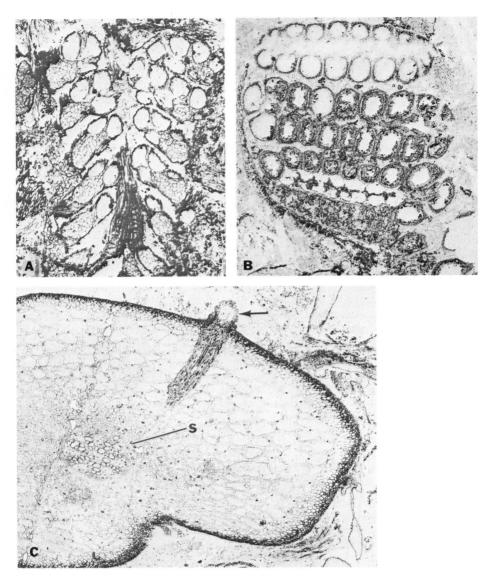

Figure 10-18   A. Paradermal section of *Eoangiopteris andrewsii.* ×16. B. Paradermal section of several *Eoangiopteris goodii* synangia. ×16. C. Transverse section of *Psaronius* root showing actimostele (S) and departing branch root (*arrow*). Note aerenchymatous cortex. ×6.5. *(Courtesy of M. Millay.)*

sporangia held together by a common pad of tissue. Both forms are also similar in spore morphology and mode of dehiscence.

A distinctive compression species is *Pecopteris unita* from the Francis Creek shale (Middle Pennsylvanian) of Illinois. Fertile pinnules bear abaxial synangia in two rows, one on each side of the pinnule midvein. Each synangium is constructed of five to seven radially arranged, laterally appressed sporangia that separate and became free at their tips on dehiscence. The spores are monolete and range from 14 to 20 μm in diameter. Synangia exhibiting a different morphology, as well as spores of a different type, have been identified on *P. unita* foliage. The presence of a different synangial organization and spore morphology from other *P. unita* pinnules underscores the fact that several different biological species are present among the compression forms. Historically, compressed or impressed pecopterid pinnules of this general type with abaxial sporangia have erroneously been assigned to *Ptychocarpus*. Synangia of this Pennsylvanian fossil are bipartite, bilaterally symmetrical, elliptical in outline, and grouped in three rows.

In addition to the numerous synangial types borne on *Pecopteris* foliage, there is one other marattialean foliage form that was present during the Carboniferous. *Radstockia kidstonii* (Fig. 10-19) is a Middle Pennsylvanian compression fossil collected from the famous Mazon Creek locality. The largest specimen is an antepenultimate axis approximately 9.5 cm long and bearing 15 alternately arranged, pinnatified pinnules. The pinnules are lanceolate and constricted at the point of attachment; the margins are deeply lobed and free from adjoining foliar members. Synangia are partially embedded in the abaxial surface of the foliar lobes. Each synangium is approximately 2.0 mm long and

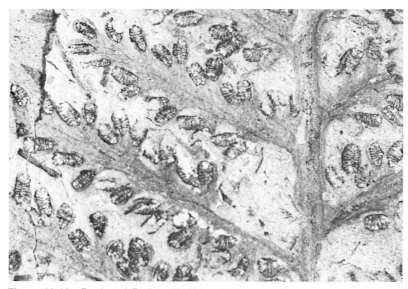

Figure 10-19   Portion of *Radstockia kidstonii* pinna. ×3.5.

1.0 mm wide. The fructification has a segmented appearance formed by a median furrow and secondary furrows that arise at right angles. Although histologic features of the unit could not be determined, smooth, trilete spores in the 40 to 60 μm size range were isolated from the fossil. Morphologically, the pinnules and fructification appear almost identical to those produced by the extant marattialean fern *Marattia alata.* In this species, the fructification consists of a partially embedded synangium, with the median furrow dividing the synangium into equal halves. The smaller subdivisions in *R. kidstonii* may represent the individual sporangia.

There are several geologically younger foliage types with sporangia that have been referred to the Marattiales on the basis of the apparent synangiate nature of the sporangia and, to a lesser degree, on the basis of pinnule morphology. *Marattiopsis macrocarpa* is known from the Jurassic Rajmahal Hills of India. Specimens consist of fertile pinnae bearing broadly linear, obtuse pinnules. Each synangium has a short central groove, with radial ridges representing individual sporangia. Nothing is known about the spores.

Harris (1961) adopted the generic name *Marattia* for Jurassic specimens collected from the famous Yorkshire locality. *Marattia anglica* includes fertile and sterile pinnae up to 50.0 cm long. Pinnae measure about 2.5 cm at the widest point, and the margin is entire. Synangia range from 4.0 to 7.0 mm long and are composed of about 30 pairs of sporangia. Spores are monolete and average 24 by 30 μm. Several specimens of *Marattia* have been described from the Rhaeto-Liassic flora in northern Iran. *Marattia intermedia* includes entire margined pinules up to 50.0 cm long. Synangia are elongate and up to 1.0 cm long; spores are monolete. Specimens of a similar age from Sweden are described as *Marattiopsis crenulatus.* The specimens are interesting in that a double set of veins is present similar to the false veins that have been figured in a number of extant marattialean taxa. Each synangium contains about 20 sporangia that produce oval to elongate, monolete spores.

Fertile pinnule segments similar to those of extant species of *Danaea* have been described under the generic name *Danaeopsis.* The Triassic species *D. fecunda* consists of pinnate fronds with lanceolate pinnules up to 10.0 cm long. The abaxial surface is covered with numerous synangia; each consists of a double row of ellipsoidal sporangia. At the apex of each sporangium is a small depression that probably represents the stomium. Spores are trilete and range to 70 μm in diameter. The spore output per sporangium is high, with more than 1000 spores counted from each of several sporangia on the pinnule. *Danaea coloradensis* is an Eocene impression species from the Green River Formation. Fertile pinnules measure 3.0 cm long and contain numerous closely packed synangia partially embedded on the abaxial surface.

Several authors have suggested that the bilateral synangium of extant marattialean members evolved by the lateral fusion of radial Paleozoic types, although probable intermediate stages are not known in the Carboniferous. *Acaulangium* synangia suggest elongation of radial forms as the origin of the bilateral synangia exhibited in extant members of the order. The unmodified pinnules and large spores, together with the absence of sporangial wall differentiation, have been regarded as primitive characters among the Paleozoic marattialean fructifications. Based on such features, Millay (1978) has proposed two basic lines of Paleozoic marattialean synangial evolution. One trend, characterized by *Acaulangium* and some species of *Scolecopteris,* may be related to such completely synangiate extant genera as *Marattia,* while the synangial organization of *Eoangiopteris* (Fig. 10-18B) is more like that of *Angiopteris,* in which sporangia are free, but held together by a common zone of tissue. The one obvious difference between the Paleozoic members and the post-Paleozoic fossils, including the modern genera, concerns the organization of the foliage. The Mesozoic members possess foliage that is once pinnate and modern in appearance. The Paleozoic foliage is at least four times pinnate with small pinnules. It is not known what triggered the abrupt change in folair morphology, although it has been demonstrated that when *Angiopteris lygodiifolia* is grown at cooler temperatures, the foliage becomes less complex. Thus climatic variability during the late Paleozoic may have been responsible for the apparent modification of psaroniaceous foliage.

Ophioglossales

This order of ferns is represented by 3 living genera (*Ophioglossum, Botrychium, Helminthostachys*) and approximately 70 species. The plants are relatively small and consist of a fleshy stem containing an ectophloic siphonostele embedded in a parenchymatous ground tissue. Prominent leaf gaps are produced. Xylem maturation is mesarch or endarch, with secondary xylem and cortical periderm produced only in *Botrychium.* Tracheal pitting ranges from scalariform to circular bordered. All species lack sclerenchyma tissues.

Each plant consists of a sterile and fertile frond. In *Botrychium* and *Helminthostachys,* the aerial portions are pinnate; in *Ophioglossum,* the frond may range from simple to dichotomously branched in some epiphytic species. The fertile spike is pinnate in *Botrychium,* dichotomously branched in *Ophioglossum,* and constructed of reduced branches radial in their symmetry around the spike axis in *Helminthostachys.* The eusporangia are massive and produce trilete, spherical to subtriangular spores that are morphologically similar in all species. All are homosporous.

To date there is no megafossil record of this group. A few spores have been described from deposits of early Jurassic and Cretaceous in the U.S.S.R., but the grains are so similar to those of several other groups of ferns that their importance is diminished.

In the absence of a megafossil record, comments regarding the origin of the group and subsequent evolutionary history are at best speculative. Historically, the Ophioglossales have been considered related to lycopods, bryophytes, rhyniophytes, and filicalean and coenopterid ferns. The association with the filicalean fern *Botryopteris* is supported by the thick-walled, globose sporangium that exhibits transverse and apical dehiscence. As a group, the extant representatives of the order are distinguished from all other ferns by the following features: collateral vascular bundles, fertile spike, absence of root hairs, endophytic fungi, absence of circinate vernation, absence of sclerenchyma, and subterranean gametophytes.

Filicales

The Filicales, or true ferns, are represented by approximately 300 genera and some 10,000 species. Today they are most widely developed in the tropics, where they are common as both epiphytes and tree ferns; many species are known from temperate regions as well. Although some ferns exhibit dichotomously branched fronds, the majority have pinnatifid, pinnate, or simple leaves. Frond size ranges from massive in some tree ferns to extremely small in water ferns. Generally, the leaf is dorsiventral and the epidermal cells contain chloroplasts. The arrangement of vascular tissue in the stems ranges from simple protosteles to complicated dictyosteles. Filicalean leptosporangia are arranged in clusters termed sori that may be marginal or attached to the abaxial surface of the leaf. The position of specialized cells (annulus) involved in the opening of the sporangium has been used as an important character in delimiting families of filicalean ferns. Spore output is typically small, with both monolete and trilete spores produced in the order. All members are homosporous.

It is important to underscore that the classification of filicalean ferns is not agreed on by all pteridologists and vascular plant morphologists. Opinions differ relative to the importance of certain features that have been used as the basis of systematic comparisons. These features include the developmental sequence of the sporangium, the position and type of annulus, the presence or absence of an indusium, and recently, the base chromosome number. The classification scheme used here combines features of several previously recognized systems, but differs in that it also incorporates three families of extinct ferns. The reader is referred to the systems suggested by Bower (1935), Copeland (1947), Holttum (1947), Pichi-Sermolli (1958), and Wagner (1969) for additional details on the taxonomy and phylogenetic positions of extant families. Not all recognized groups of living ferns are listed, only a few are described to demonstrate the diversity within the families.

Botryopteridaceae   The Botryopteridaceae constitute one of the old coenopterid fern families that has been transferred to the Filicales on the basis of recent studies. The family includes three structurally preserved genera, with *Botryopteris* being the most common member. *Botryopteris* is known from both vegetative and fertile specimens that range from the Lower Carboniferous into the Permian. The most distinguishing feature of the genus is the omega-shaped, adaxially directed xylem strand of the foliar axis (Fig. 10-20A and D). As occurs with many other intensely studied genera the name *Botryopteris* has been extended from stems and petioles exhibiting a particular anatomy to the concept of a whole plant. The genus is now regarded as a prostrate, rhizomatous fern with helically arranged bilateral fronds. At least one species (*B. mucilaginosa*) may have been an erect climbing plant. Branching was generally lateral and

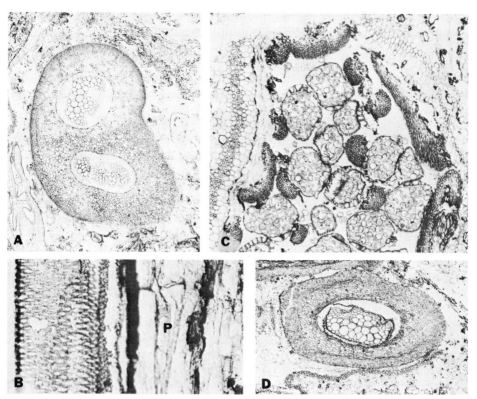

Figure 10-20 *Botryopteris.* A. Transverse section of *Botryopteris tridentata* foliar member with characteristic omega-shaped trace. ×12. B. Pitting on wall of *Botryopteris cratis* metaxylem tracheid. Phloem is to right (P). ×165. C. Transverse section of portion of sporangial cluster of *Botryopteris cratis.* ×27. D. *Botryopteris cratis* foliar member with well-developed protoxylem. ×13.5.

distichous. It has been suggested that the vegetative organs be termed "foliar members" because in most instances it is not possible to determine whether an axis represents a rachis or pinna (since some species have up to nine orders of lateral pinnae).

The oldest (Visean) member of the genus, *B. antiqua* (see Fig. 10-22B and D), exhibits several patterns of frond branching. The buds are supplied with a cauline trace from a foliar member; the first petiole is oriented with respect to the foliar member bearing the shoot as pinna. In addition, other specimens demonstrate a "common" trace from a foliar member (resulting in a stem) and a foliar member that may be regarded as either the first petiole of the stem or a pinna that produced the shoot. *Botryopteris antiqua* also exhibits the simplest xylem strand, which consists of a protostele of scalariform tracheids. The oval petioles have one or two protoxylem points. Modification of the foliar xylem configuration in the genus is thought to have involved a shift of the lateral protoxylem groups to form a median group and the elaboration of the strand into three adaxial xylem arms. Other suggested phylogenetic changes within the genus include a shift from scalariform to circular bordered pitting (Fig. 10-20B), an increase in the size of the stems and leaves, and the development of lamina (Phillips, 1974). Most stems are terete protosteles, but in *B. tridentata* (Fig. 10-20A), the trace is siphonostelic, formed by a progressive differentiation of tracheids along the lateral foliar arm that subsequently enclosed a sclerenchyma pith.

A recently discovered specimen of *B. hirsuta* from Lancashire (Westphalian A) not only attests to the varied branching in the genus, but also suggests that xylem-strand configuration may not be a very reliable systematic character. The specimen is unusual in that opposite, twin lateral shoots are apparent, and they bear numerous petioles. Although the axis is quite long, no other type of branching is present. Moreover, within the length of the axis, the anatomy changes from an ellipsoidal shape with barely detectable protoxylem points, which has been regarded as primitive, to the highly trident form, which has been regarded as more advanced.

In *B. forensis,* a common Upper Pennsylvanian species, the stem is protostelic, with parenchyma usually lacking; tracheal pitting ranges from uniseriate scalariform to multiseriate oval bordered. In *B. forensis,* the stem bears leaves in a helical ⅓ to ⅖ phyllotaxis. These petioles and their pinnately produced laterals sometimes bear pairs of small adventitious stems near their bases. The stems are oriented so that their first leaf occupies the same position as the lateral pinna of the frond member on which it was borne. What is unusual about this species is the large number of stems and leaves that were produced that formed a false stemlike morphology to the plant. In transverse section, the foliar members are circular and exhibit numerous equisetiform hairs ranging from 30 to 300 μm long. Hair bases are unimulticellular, with the tips sharply pointed. The cortex is two-parted, with the outer zone constructed of thick-walled cells that grade into fibers near the epidermis. The inner zone consists of thin-walled parenchyma. A zone of sieve cells 2 to 10 cells thick represents the phloem in *B. tridentata* (see Fig. 10-22E). Scattered among the small sieve elements are larger mucilage cells that typically reveal dark contents. Sieve areas consist of elliptical areas on the radial walls with irregular pores.

The morphology of the frond in *B. forensis* is pinnately compound with distal portions bearing laminar pinnules. Pinnules range from pecopteridlike with pinnatifid tips of the ultimate pinnae to others that are sphenopterid in outline. Stomata are apparently confined to the lower surfaces and are borne among multicellular equisetiform hairs. Crosiers are circinate. Diarch adventitious roots are borne along the axes.

Botryopteris globosa (Fig. 10-21A), common in North American sediments, is one type of reproductive structure borne on the foliar members of *Botryopteris.* It consists of a fertile pinna that repeatedly branches in a pinnate manner with the ultimate segments terminating in sporangia. Some specimens of *B. globosa* exceed 5.0 cm in diameter, with some of the axes in the unit displaying the omega-shaped botryopterid anatomy. This highly reduced

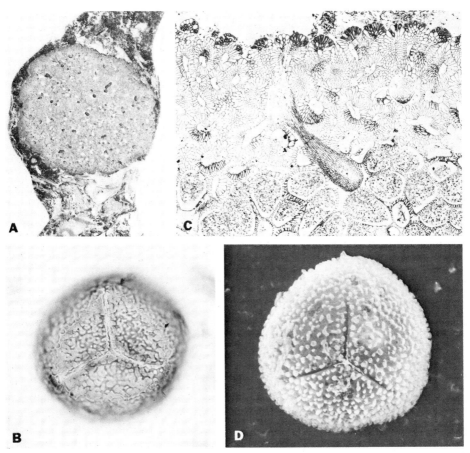

Figure 10-21 A. *Botryopteris globosa.* ×1. B. *Botryopteris cratis* spore. ×500. C. *Botryopteris globosa* showing outer sterile zone. ×12. D. Spore of *Botryopteris forensis.* ×1000.

branching system organized in a massive cluster of sporangia is estimated to have contained about 50,000 sporangia (Fig. 10-21A). In transverse section, the unit is circular with a centrally positioned, omega-shaped trace surrounded by smaller distichously arranged pinnae. Externally, the sporangial cluster has a median groove that marks the sporangial masses on each side of the central pinna. Two types of sporangia are apparent in the aggregation. Sterile sporangia are located around the periphery of the mass (Fig. 10-21C) and consist of radially elongated cells, often with parenchymatous contents. Sporangia that contain spores are usually teardrop-shaped (Fig. 10-22A and C) and constructed of a single, outer layer of thick-walled cells overlying a zone of cells with thin walls. The annulus consists of a equatorial patch of cells that extends to near the base of the sporangium on one face (Fig. 10-22A). Cells of the annulus are elongate and thick-walled. The globosoid type of fructification has been

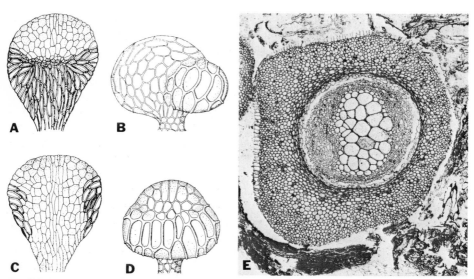

Figure 10-22 A. Sporangium of *Botryopteris globosa* showing sporangium face. ×30. B. Lateral view of *Botryopteris antiqua* sporangium. ×100. C. *Botryopteris globosa* sporangium showing region of dehiscence and lateral occurrence of annulus. ×30. D. Face view of *Botryopteris antiqua* sporangium. ×100. E. Transverse section of *Botryopteris tridentata* frond member showing continuity of tissues, including phloem, throughout axis. ×27. *(A and C from Phillips and Andrews, 1965; B and D from Galtier, 1967; E courtesy of E. Smoot.)*

separated into two species, *B. globosa* (Middle Pennsylvanian) and *B. forensis* (Upper Pennsylvanian), based on the type of spores present. Spores of both species are subtriangular to oval, trilete, and range from 23 to 59 μm in diameter (Fig. 10-21B and D). Those of *B. forensis* exhibit a verrucate to rugulate ornament, while *B. globosa* spores are vermiculate to densely rugulate. In other species of *Botryopteris* (e.g., *B. hirsuta*), annulate sporangia are attached superficially to laminar frond segments. All species of *Botryopteris* are homosporous.

Recently another species of *Botryopteris*, *B. cratis*, has been described that demonstrates still another organization of the reproductive parts (Fig. 10-20C). This Middle Pennsylvanian species consists of branched frond members that bear numerous spherical sporangia, each with a bandlike annulus that extends transversely across the lower half of the sporangium. This species is unlike the other fructifications of *Botryopteris* in that it possesses an outer ring of slightly larger sterile frond members that surround the sporangial cluster (Fig. 10-20C). Although the genus *Botryopteris* was initially delimited on the basis of a particular anatomy of the stem and foliar member, the time is rapidly approaching when the different types of reproductive structures will no doubt dictate a reevaluation of this filicalean genus on the basis of whole-plant systematics.

The genus *Rhabodoxylon* was initially described from specimens of the Lower Pennsylvanian coal fields of Britain. *Rhabodoxylon dichotomum* is a small dichotomously branched fern densely clothed by unbranched, multicellular hairs. The stem is about 2.0 mm in diameter and contains a small, circular, centrarch protostele. An Upper Pennsylvanian specimen, *R. americanum* is slightly larger and produces numerous, helically arranged foliar units. Adventitious roots are borne in no specific sequence from the petiole bases and stem. Petiole vascular strands depart from the stem stele through the initiation of a parenchymatous plate that separates the xylem into almost equal halves. Initially the leaf trace is flattened, but at higher levels it becomes more circular in transverse section. Throughout its course, the protoxylem remains in an adaxial position relative to the stem. Pitting on the metaxylem tracheids ranges from scalariform to reticulate. Additional specimens of *R. dichotomum* recently described by Holmes (1979) suggest a plant that was prostrate, whereas the closely spaced leaves that characterize *R. americanum* suggest a plant that was probably more errect. Holmes has noted, however, that such differences may simply represent ontogenetic variations.

Another protostelic fern that has been included in the Botryopteridaceae on the basis of the adaxial position of the protoxylem is *Catenopteris*. *Catenopteris simplex* (Fig. 10-12A) is a small, structurally preserved pteridophyte stem from the Upper Pennsylvanian of Illinois. It is approximately 6.0 mm in diameter and contains a small protostele constructed of tracheids with scalariform pits. Petioles are borne in an apparent ⅖ phyllotactic sequence and contain adaxially curved, C-shaped traces with smaller (protoxylem) tracheids present on the concave surface. Near the base of each petiole is a diarch adventitious root. Nothing is known about the foliar or fertile parts of this plant.

Anachoropteridaceae The Anachoropteridaceae constitute an entirely extinct family of filicalean ferns. Members of this family are characterized by protostelic stems, when known, and petioles with abaxially curved C-shaped traces (Fig. 10-23A). The petiole vascular strand configuration in this family is the reverse of that in other families where the C-shaped trace is directed toward the stem (adaxial curvature). Anatomically, the members of this group resembled living ferns more closely than other groups, but they are markedly different because of the reverse orientation of the leaf trace. Fronds are essentially planated, although in several genera the more distal levels are not known. Some stems are protostelic, including both centrarch and exarch forms, while others have mixed protosteles or siphonosteles. The family is known to have ranged from the Pennsylvanian into the Permian.

Anachoropteris is the type genus of the family and is represented by petioles with C-shaped xylem strands known to have belonged to stems of the *Tubicaulis* type. One of the common Pennsylvanian species that extended into the Permian is *A. involuta* (Fig. 10-23A). Specimens possess a C-shaped vascular strand with the edges inrolled or involute in shape. Two to four protoxylem points are present along the adaxial surface of the xylem strand. The Permian species, *A. pulchra,* exhibits conspicuously inrolled arms that are folded back on themselves.

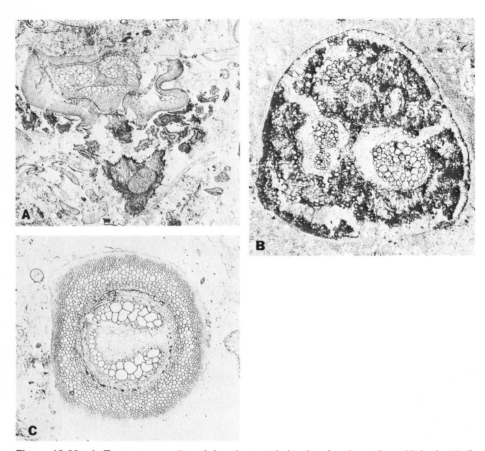

Figure 10-23 A. Transverse section of *Anachoropteris involuta* frond member with bud. ×7. B. Transverse section of *Psalixochlaena berwickense* at level of trifurcation. ×50. C. Transverse section of *Anachoropteris clavata.* ×15. *(B from A. G. Long Collection No. 6875 in the Hancock Museum.)*

Anachoropteris clavata (Fig. 10-23C) is an Upper Pennsylvanian species that was at one time thought to be the more distal region of *A. involuta.* One specimen from the famous Berryville locality in Illinois consists of an axis about 15.0 cm long that bears stems that in turn bear petioles like the parent one. In transverse section, the petiole is about 2.5 mm in diameter and contains a C-shaped xylem strand with the ends of the arms greatly expanded. Protoxylem tracheids in four to five groups are situated along the convex, adaxial surface of the trace. Some metaxylem tracheids are up to 200 μm in diameter and exhibit closely spaced, circular bordered pits. Surrounding the xylem strand are thin-walled cells topographically equivalent to phloem; the vascular bundle is embedded in parenchyma. The surface of the petiole is covered with numerous multicellular hairs. Traces to laterals are borne on the side of the C-shaped strand and, at higher levels, become terete. Petiole traces and adventitious roots are seen along the stem. Species of *Anachoropteris* that are known in sufficient detail demonstrate the same type of lateral production as that present in *Botryopteris*.

The relationship between *Anachoropteris* petioles and stems referred to as *Tubicaulis* was initially made by Hall (1961) from a specimen of the Middle Pennsylvanian. The stem is subelliptical in outline, the result of numerous closely spaced leaves arranged in a ⅗ phyllotaxy. Multicellular hairs cover the stem surface, together with regularly spaced adventitious roots. The xylem strand of the stem is exarch and constructed of metaxylem tracheids with scalariform pits and plates of radiating parenchyma. *Tubicaulis multiscalariformis* (Middle Pennsylvanian) lacks xylem parenchyma, but is anatomically distinct in that it has prominent strands of protoxylem that extend along the stem stele. These features contrast with *T. stewartii* (Upper Pennsylvanian), which lacks prominent protoxylem strands and contains abundant parenchyma associated with the primary xylem of the stem stele. Among the *Tubicaulis* species now known, there would appear to be two different stelar types that produced the same type of petiole. One group contained solid protosteles with circular bordered pits, while the second group contained mixed protosteles with metaxylem tracheids characterized by multiseriate scalariform pitting. Further attesting to the very artificial nature of the genus are the various sizes of the recognized species. Some, such as the Upper Pennsylvanian species *T. scandens,* are small and are regarded as epiphytic; others, such as the Permian from *T. solenites,* are estimated to have been at least a meter tall based on the large diameter of the stele (6.0 mm).

The genus *Grammatopteris* has been suggested as being closely related to *Tubicaulis,* although the petiole traces are typically bar-shaped and do not exhibit the distinct abaxial curvature. The genus is known from two species that occur in deposits of the Stephanian and Lower Permian. The stem contains clusters of small tracheids toward the center, and these are believed to represent a stage in the vitalization (mixture of tracheids and parenchyma cells) of a protostele. Protoxylem tracheids are present on the adaxial surface of the petiole strand near the margin. Metaxylem tracheids possess multiseriate pitting. In the Permian species *G. rigollatii,* the stele is protostelic, with an outer zone of radially aligned tracheids interpreted as secondary xylem. The genus has been suggested as closely related to members of the Osmundaceae on the basis of the bar-shaped petiole xylem strand in transverse section, the two-zoned protostele, histoloigic features of the cortex, and indentations of the stele suggestive of the vascular configuration in the Osmundaceae when leaf traces are produced.

The genus *Psalixochlaena* (Fig. 10-23B) was established by Holden in 1960 for fern axes that had earlier been referred to as *Rachiopteris cylindrica* and *Botryopteris cylindrica*. The genus is now known from numerous specimens collected from the Westphalian A of Britain, Belgium, and Holland, as well as from the Lower Carboniferous of Britain. *Psalixochlaena cylindrica* is a fern with long, slender stems suggesting a rhizomatous habit. Branching is of three general types and includes leaves produced by the stem, leaf and axillary branches produced by the stem, and equal dichotomies of the stem. In transverse section, the axes are circular and up to 2.5 mm in diameter. The protostele is composed of large, more or less radially aligned tracheids surrounding a zone of smaller central ones. The xylem strand is protostelic with one to four groups of protoxylem tracheids. Metaxylem tracheids have scalariform to reticulate pits. Holmes (1977a) recently described some beautifully preserved specimens in which phloem, endodermis, and a multilayered cortex are preserved.

Vegetative branching of the rhizome is monopodial, with all orders of branches producing leaves. Petiole xylem strands are initially circular, but in more distal regions of the leaf, they become abaxially C-shaped with three protoxylem points along the adaxial surface. Changes in stelar size and the number and position of the protoxylem tracheids at different levels of the axes suggest that *Psalixochlaena* had a determinate type of growth habit. In *P. berwickense* (Lower Carboniferous of Berwickshire), the stems bear trifurcating laterals that superficially suggest the branching of some members of the Trimerophytophyta. The trifurcate laterals of *P. berwickense* are interpreted as the culmination of three closely spaced, unequal dichotomies in which two alternate in a plane at right angles to the other one. The presence of axillary branching associated with a true frond in *Psalixochlaena* suggest that the two organs may have been derived from a lateral pair of branches in which only one of the members became planated. In this regard, the genus may demonstrate an intermediate condition between an early rhyniophyte branching pattern and that of some extant ferns (e.g., *Stromatopteris*) that have maintained a simple stelar structure and unmodified branching pattern.

In many features, the Upper Pennsylvanian fern *Apotropteris minuta* is similar to *Psalixochlaena*. In the original description, the stem stele is characterized as protostelic, but additional, larger specimens indicate a few centrally positioned cells forming a pith. Petioles are apparent in no specific sequence, and diarch adventitious roots are borne along the stem. Petiole traces are abaxially C-shaped and may or may not have produced a gap in the stem stele when they were formed. Like *Psalixochlaena,* when traces are evident, there are almost equal divisions of the stem stele. The genus is known from relatively few specimens, and nothing is known about the reproductive parts.

Sermayaceae The Sermayaceae constitute the most recently established family of extinct filicalean ferns of the Carboniferous (Eggert and Delevoryas, 1967). The family consists of two genera, *Sermaya,* which was discovered in petrifaction material collected at the Berryville site in southeastern Illinois, and *Doneggia,* also from the Upper Pennsylvanian (Ohio). Nothing is known about the habit or stems of these genera; both are based on detached petioles of the *Anachoropteris* type that produced alternately arranged pinnae and bluntly lobed *Sphenopteris*-like pinnules. The vascular strand of the pinnae also is slightly C-shaped in the abaxial plane. The pinnules are relatively delicate and lack differentiation between mesophyll and palisade layers.

One of the exciting features of *S. biseriata* is the presence of pinnules containing sporangia. The sporangia are arranged in radial sori, each consisting of about four sporangia. Sporangia are sessile and average about 0.3 mm in diameter. Each sporangium is a single cell layer thick and exhibits an annulus of two rows of thick-walled cells on the distal face. The annulus extends down the sides of the sporangium for about one half the circumference. The configuration of the annulus is horizontally oblique with reference to the long axis of the sporangium. Dehiscence is evident along a row of thin-walled cells extending medianly near the annulus to the area of attachment. Spores of *S. biseriata* are subtriangular and average 30 to 40 μm in diameter. They are trilete and

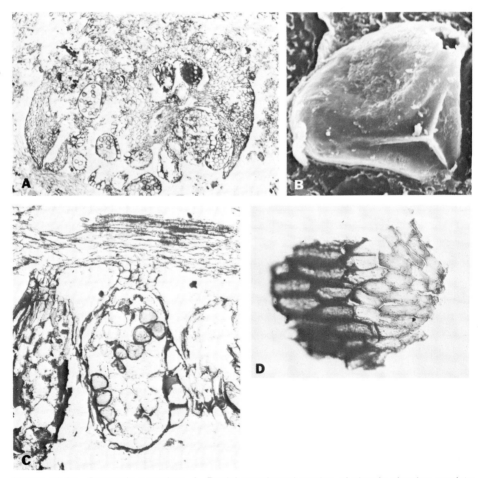

Figure 10-24 *Doneggia complura.* A. Partial paradermal section of pinnule showing revolute margins and sporangia. ×23. B. Trilete spore assignable to the *sporae dispersae* taxon *Leiotriletes.* ×1000. C. Sporangium attached to pinnule underside. ×87. D. Portion of a sporangium. ×110. *(From Rothwell, 1978.)*

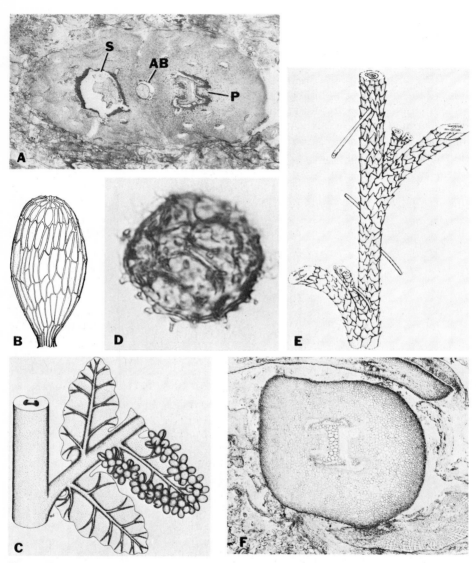

Figure 10-25 A. Transverse section of *Ankyropteris glabra* axis showing stem (S), axillary branch (AB), and petiole (P). ×2. B. Suggested reconstruction of *Tedelea glabra* sporangium. C. Suggested reconstruction of a portion of the fertile frond of *Tedelea glabra*. D. *Tedelea glabra* spore of the *Raistrickia* type. ×800. E. Suggested reconstruction of *Ankyropteris* with aphlebiae and adventitious roots. F. Transverse section of petiole showing characteristic H-shaped vascular strand. ×14. *(B and C from Eggert and Taylor, 1966; E from Eggert, 1959.)*

unevenly ornamented by delicate punctae. When compared with *sporae dispersae* taxa, they resemble forms placed in the genus *Leiotriletes* (Fig. 10-24B).

In *Doneggia complura,* the sori are much larger (Fig. 10-24A), containing 25 to 35 stalked sporangia (Fig. 10-24C) that are restricted to the pinnule lobes. The annulus is similar to that of *Sermaya,* consisting of a horizontally oblique structure of two rows of intergrading cells (Fig. 10-24D). On some pinnules are stalked-peltate structures that may have represented some type of gland, anomalous sporangium, or early stage of asexual plantlet.

The sporangia of *Sermaya* and *Doneggia* are more similar to those of some living fern families than they are to other extinct groups of ferns. In the Gleicheniaceae, for example, the sporangium is stalked and exhibits a single row of annulus cells. Although dehiscence and sporangial shape are similar in the two families, the anatomy of the frond is markedly different. At this time, *Sermaya* and *Doneggia* represent Carboniferous ferns that probably developed leptosporangia of the gleicheniaceous type; but on the basis of vegetative features, it appears that they are not directly related to the Gleicheniaceae.

Tedeleaceae The Tedeleaceae is also a family of entirely extinct ferns and can be traced from the Upper Mississippian into the Lower Permian. The taxa that make up this family were previously included in the Zygopteridales, but recent discoveries of the fertile parts of some members suggest that the plants are more correctly allied with true ferns. The type genus *Ankyropteris* is based on specimens known from petioles, as well as from both stems and petioles.

The best-known species, *Ankyropteris glabra,* is known from Middle and Upper Pennsylvanian deposits of North America. In transverse section, the stem is angular, usually with five lobes (Fig. 10-25A), consisting of an inner network of parenchyma cells and small scalariform tracheids; the remainder of the stem stele contains large metaxylem tracheids. The cortex consists of several layers; the inner cortex is constructed of thick-walled sclerotic cells with dark contents. Surrounding it is a zone of thin-walled parenchyma that represents the outer cortical zone. The outer surface of *A. glabra* is covered with numerous scalelike aphlebiae (Fig. 10-25E), some of which are 2.0 mm long. Each is vascularized by a mesarch trace that extends from a lobe of the pentarch stele. Multicellular hairs are also present on the surface of the stem.

Leaves are borne in a $\frac{2}{5}$ phyllotaxy, although there is evidence that petioles may have developed randomly. In transverse section, the trace to the petiole is at first tangentially flattened, but at a slightly higher level, it becomes H-shaped (Fig. 10-25F). Peripheral loops are seen at the four ends (antennae) of the xylem strand. Primary pinnae were produced from opposite sides of the petiole in two closely spaced, alternating series, with secondary pinnae appearing along the opposite sides of the primary member. The ultimate segments of the frond are laminar pinnules, with the basal pair slightly larger and characterized by undulating margins. Scalelike aphlebia occur on the adaxial side of the petiole at the base of each primary pinna. Thus the frond of *A. glabra* may be compared with the frond of a living fern in that it is biseriate, pinnately compound, and bears planated pinnae with small laminar pinnules.

One feature of *Ankyropteris* not present in modern ferns is the axillary branch. Figure 10-25A is a transverse section of a stem showing the position of the stem, axillary branch, and petiole. At low levels of the axis, the configuration of the branch is terete. In a short vertical distance, two distichous, di-upsilon-shaped petiole traces are produced from the axillary branch. The production of axillary branches resulted in several additional orders of stems and petioles that provided a rather bushy appearance to the plant.

The fertile frond of *Ankyropteris glabra* is now known in some detail and given the generic name *Tedelea*.[1] Fertile pinnules are about 3.6 mm long and 2.2 mm at the widest point. They are shallowly lobed and morphologically similar to some forms of *Pecopteris* or *Sphenopteris*. Sporangia are attached in a submarginal position to the lower surface of the pinnule near the end of a lateral vein (Fig. 10-25C). The number of sporangia per cluster is variable (two to seven), and on the basis of sporangial features, soral maturation is thought to have been of the simple type. Mature sporangia are stalked and contain a conspicuous annulus on the distal one-third (Fig. 10-25B). Spores of different developmental stages are known, with mature ones included in the genus *Raistrickia* (Fig. 10-25D). Mature grains are trilete and up to 70 μm in diameter. Spore masses extracted from sporangia suggest that approximately 140 spores were produced per sporangium. Based on sporangium position and histology, *T. glabra* compares most closely to certain primitive filicalean ferns such as the Osmundaceae and Schizaeaceae, although vegetative features of the frond are rather different. For now it is best to regard *T. glabra* as a member of an extinct filicalean fern family that cannot be related to any extant taxa.

A specimen that had earlier been described as a massive anachoropterid fructification is now thought to be more closely related to *Ankyropteris* on the basis of the anatomy of the petiole strand. Features of the sporangia, including the nature and position of the annulus, and spores of the *Raistrickia* type support the ankyropterid affinities of this fertile specimen. It is not known whether the sporangia were attached to pinnule frond members in a manner similar to those of *Botryopteris globosa* and *B. forensis* or were borne on laminate foliage that was simply poorly preserved.

Ankyropteris hendricksii is an interesting species that consists of a false stem constructed of numerous petioles tightly associated with a dense ramentum of adventitious roots (Fig. 10-26). The taxon is known from a single specimen about 30.0 mm in diameter that was contained in a silicified boulder. The stratigraphic position is believed to be Lower Pennsylvanian, although Mississippian may be equally possible because the exact source of this fossil is unknown.

---

[1]When the diagnosis of *Tedelea glabra* was published (Eggert and Taylor, 1966), the holotype was designated as the fertile specimen upon which the new description was based. Baxter's holotype for *Ankyropteris glabra* (slides 150 and 151 in the University of Kansas Paleobotanical Collection) should have been retained as the holotype for the new taxon.

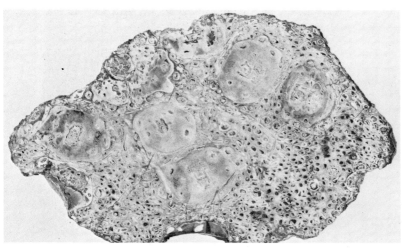

Figure 10-26 Transverse section of *Ankyropteris hendricksii* showing several petioles and adventitious root mantle. ×0.8. *(Courtesy of F. Hueber.)*

Laminated foliage has not been found associated with the frond system of *A. westphaliensis,* a species known from the Lower Carboniferous of Europe. The frond is at least bipinnate and three-dimensional, like members of the Zygopteridales. Possibly the simplest species of the genus is *A. corrugata.* This Lower Pennsylvanian plant was relatively small and exhibited a prostrate habit. Petioles are distichously arranged and at higher levels occasionally dichotomized. Aphlebiae are borne in two alternating series and cover the petioles. Radiating files of tracheids near the base of the adventitious roots and in the stem have been suggested as secondary in origin.

The origin of the axillary branch system in ferns has been speculated on for some time. Opinions differ as to whether the branch represents a reduced member of a cauline dichotomy with an associated leaf or one member of a lateral pair of petioles. Most evidence tends to support the concept that the axillary branch was initiated on the stem and that the leaf later became associated with the branch. *Ankyropteris corrugata* apparently did not produce axillary branches, a condition that has been suggested because of the appearance of a protoxylem strand in the base of the leaf trace. This trace may represent evidence of an old axis. It cannot be determined whether the basal strand represents a reduced axis or, as Eggert (1959) has suggested, has no phylogenetic significance whatsoever.

Osmundaceae The Osmundaceae represent primitive filicalean ferns that are often regarded as intermediate between eusporangiate and leptosporangiate ferns. Initially, the group was regarded as the possible ancestral stock to other fern families, although current theories suggest that they are an early offshoot from filicalean ancestors that had little or nothing to do with the evolution of other families. The family can be traced back to the Upper Permian, where there

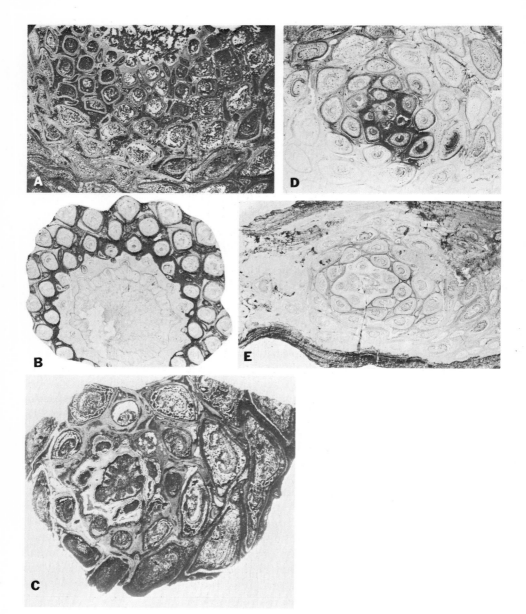

Figure 10-27   A. Transverse section of *Palaeosmunda williamsii* (Permian). ×1. B. Transverse section of *Osmundacaulis skidegatensis* (Lower Cretaceous). ×1.5. C. Transverse section of *Palaeosmunda playfordii* (Permian). ×1. D. Transverse section of *Osmunda arnoldii* (Paleocene). ×2. E. Transverse section of *Osmunda pluma* (Paleocene). ×2. *(A and C courtesy of R. Gould; B, D, and E courtesy of C. Miller.)*

are a number of structurally preserved genera that possess osmundaceous features. Today the family is represented by 3 genera [*Osmunda* (Fig. 10-27D), *Todea, Leptopteris*] comprising 16 species. They vary from arborescent forms to rhizomatous stems surrounded by tightly packed petiole bases. In some species, dimorphic fronds are produced with sporangia attached along narrow foliar segments; in others, sporangia occur on the abaxial surfaces of fertile lamina. Stem transverse sections exhibit a variety of stelar configurations ranging from protosteles to highly dissected ectophloic or amphiphloic siphonosteles. Secondary xylem is not produced, but sclerenchyma is common in the ground tissue.

Most information about the fossil history of the family comes from structurally preserved stem segments, many of which have been reassigned to extant genera. In some instances, foliage has been described from the same stratigraphic level as the stem, but organic attachment has not been demonstrated in most cases. Isolated osmundaceous sporangia and spores are common in Mesozoic rocks and are typically identical with extant forms.

Osmundacaulis (Fig. 10-27B) is the generic name applied to structurally preserved osmundaceous stem, root, and petiole remains that cannot be assigned to extant taxa. The oldest osmundaceous stem that produced cataphylls is *O. herbstii,* a silicified specimen from the Upper Triassic of Argentina. This species, which was found in association with *Cladophlebis* foliage, consists of a small stem (9.0 mm diameter) surrounded by a zone of persistent petiole bases and roots. The stele is dictyostelic and ectophloic. A slightly larger rhizomatous stem typifies *O. dunlopii* (Jurassic, New Zealand). The xylem cylinder is approximately 0.5 mm thick and possesses narrow to incomplete leaf gaps. It has been suggested that *O. kolbei* was arborescent. It had a stem about 3.6 cm in diameter and several features regarded as primitive, including a mixed pith and the bifurcation of the leaf trace protoxylem in the petiole base. The presence of sclerenchyma in the pith has been regarded as an advanced feature of this Lower Cretaceous species.

A late Permian species, *O. carnierii* (= *O. braziliensis*) is distinct from other taxa in having a large stem suggesting an arborescent habit and several anatomic features including the abaxial orientation of leaf traces, discontinuous phloem and endodermis, and lack of sclerenchyma in the cortex. This suite of characteristics was once thought to represent a link between the two subfamilies (Thamnopteroideae and Osmundoideae). Now many believe that *O. carnierii* shows greater anatomic diversity within the osmundaceous line, possible representing a dead end in the evolution of certain features.

Arborescent protostelic stems that consist of a mantle of petiole bases and adventitious roots are included in the form genus *Thamnopteris.* Many believe that there is sufficient evidence to suggest that the stele of the Osmundaceae evolved from the conversion of tracheids to parenchyma in a partially protostelic axis such as *Thamnopteris.* The Permian age of this plant, coupled with the relatively simple stem anatomy, has led some to regard members of this genus as potential progenitors for other osmundaceous taxa. In several species of *Thamnopteris,* parenchyma cells are associated with the inner xylem tracheids.

Thamnopteris schlechtendalii consists of a massive trunk approximately 12.0 cm in diameter with a stele (5.0 cm diameter) constructed of two zones of tracheids. The inner core contains thin-walled tracheids that are surrounded by an outer zone of thicker-walled scalariform elements. In transverse section, the petiole trace is C-shaped. *Zalesskya* is another Permian stem genus whose xylem is organized into distinct zones. The cortex of this genus contains numerous (100 to 150) leaf traces.

The next level of stelar evolution may have involved a form such as *Chasmatopteris principalis* (Upper Permian), which is characterized by rudimentary invaginations of the stele, but still lacks distinct leaf gaps. Continued indentation of the xylem cylinder above the point of leaf-trace departure would result in the formation of the dictyoxylic siphonostele, which is characteristic of geologically later-appearing osmundaceous taxa. Such a sequence has been termed the intrastelar origin of a siphonostele and, within the Osmundaceae, is supported by the shortening of central xylem tracheids in the Permian thamnopterids. Thus, within the Osmundaceae, there is substantial evidence that the siphonostele evolved through the phlogenetic conversion of central xylem tracheids to pith parenchyma and subsequent dissection of the xylem cylinder by leaf gaps rather than from the intrusion of cortical parenchyma (extrastelar origin).

The Upper Permian Coal Measure of Queensland have provided exceptionally well-preserved stem remains of osmundaceous ferns that fill several gaps in our knowledge regarding the evolution of the stele. *Palaeosmunda* differs from all other reported Permian stem genera (*Bathypteris*, *Chasmatopteris*, *Iegosigopteris*, *Petcheropteris*, *Thamnopteris*, and *Zalesskya*) in that it possesses an ectophloic, dictyoxylic siphonostele with uniform metaxylem tracheids and parenchymatous pith (Fig. 10-27 A and C). Leaf traces are typically endarch, and leaf bases are rhomboidal in transverse section with an adaxially curved, C-shaped strand (Fig. 10-28B). In *P. williamsii*, the cortex is differentiated into

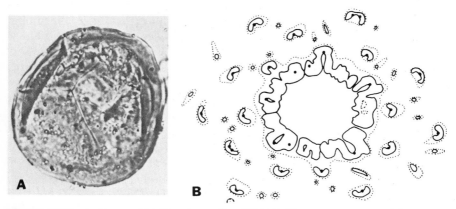

Figure 10-28 A. Spore of *Todites thomasii*. ×1075. B. Transverse section of *Palaeosmunda playfordii* with protoxylem represented by black dots, endodermis by dotted lines. *(A from Van Konijnenburg-Van Cittert, 1978; B from Gould, 1970.)*

two zones and contains as many as 43 traces in transverse section. Preservation is so perfect that in *P. playfordii* a zone of metaphloem elements could be identified around the xylem strands. The modern-appearing stele of *Palaeosmunda* suggests a far earlier geologic origin for the family and a separation of distinct lines in stelar evolution earlier than previously thought.

The Triassic genus *Itopsidema* has been suggested by some authors as representing an early member of the family. Other workers, however, regard the presence of a mixture of parenchyma and tracheids in the xylem, different petiole trace configuration near the base, and a homogenous parenchymatous cortex lacking the characteristic outer sclerotic zone as nonosmundaceous features. Although the affinities of *Itopsidema* are not known, the Triassic age and anatomic features make it a tempting evolutionary link. *Itopsidema* may represent an offshoot of the Paleozoic group that was directly involved in the evolution of the Osmundaceae.

Several examples of osmundaceous foliage have been described from sediments ranging from Triassic to Recent. *Osmundopsis* is the form genus used for dimorphic foliage of the Jurassic. *Osmundopsis sturii* (Yorkshire) consists of delicate branches covered by obovate sporangia each with a thickened distal cap. Dehiscence was longitudinal, and spores are subtriangular and trilete. Sterile, bipinnate frond material of Mesozoic age similar to leaves of extant *Todea* is referred to as *Cladophlebis*. Specimens that contain large sessile sporangia are generally included in the genus *Todites*. The Yorkshire Jurassic species *T. thomasii* includes widely spaced pinnules 2.0 cm long and 4.0 mm wide. The pinnule midrib is pronounced, and the margin is dentate. Fertile pinnules are slightly shorter with a blunt apex. Sporangial clusters are oval and are attached over a lateral vein. The apical portion of the sporangium consists of a thickened patch of cells. The trilete spores are smooth and up to 50 μm in diameter (Fig. 10-28A). *Todites princeps* is a widely distributed Jurassic species that includes fronds up to 100.0 cm long. Pinnae are almost opposite, and pinnules vary from those with smooth margins to others that are deeply lobed. The sporangia are oval (250 μm in diameter) and tightly packed on the pinnule underside.

The spores of all Middle Jurassic Yorkshire osmundaceous ferns have recently been compared with other Jurassic spores and with those of living taxa. In general, the fossil Osmundaceae have rather uniform spores differing only slightly in size, sporoderm thickness, and ornamentation.

Although the fossil record of the Osmundaceae appears extensive, there are numerous gaps in our knowledge about the origin of the family and relationships among the taxa. The most comprehensive treatment of the family is that of Miller (1971), who examined 29 fossil and 14 extant species using multiple-character correlation. Using this technique, he distinguished 9 groups of phylogenetically related species and suggested that the group originated from a grammatopteridlike (*Grammatopteris*) Paleozoic ancestor, rapidly radiating during the Permian. Since the Permian, the family has evolved slowly, with some specialized forms dying out near the end of the Mesozoic. Two subfamilies are recognized, the Permian Thamnopteroideae and the Osmundoideae, which are represented by the Mesozoic, Tertiary, and Recent species. There is presently insufficient fossil evidence to suggest what the origins of *Todea* and *Leptopteris* might be, but it appears that the family is not directly related to any other filicalean group. The reader is referred to the excellent treatment by Miller detailing character-analysis data and the relationships suggested among the extant species.

Schizaeaceae   Today the Schizaeaceae is for the most part a tropical and subtropical family consisting of *Mohria, Lygodium, Anemia,* and *Schizaea.* Some authors have recently treated the preceding extant genera as members of three different families. Leaves vary from simple to pinnately compound and, in *Lygodium,* may be up to 30 m long. Sporangia are protected by a slight inrolling of the pinnule margin and are arranged singly. Sporangia are typically large and possess short stalks; the annulus is apical, and dehiscence is longitudinal.

For a long time the Schizaeaceae have been regarded as an ancient family traceable to the Carboniferous genus *Senftenbergia.* The principal feature used to identify the relationship of *Senftenbergia* with the family is the presence of an apical annulus. In addition, the sporangia are arranged in a double row, dehisce longitudinally, and are borne on pecopterid foliage. Recently, Jennings and Eggert (1977) reported on a partially petrified specimen of *Senftenbergia* that substantiated that the genus was not schizaeaceous. Rather, the biseriate frond, features of the petiole trace, and sporangial organization indicate a much closer association with the fossil filicalean fern *Tedelea.* Interestingly, the clepsydroid-shaped vascular trace of *Senftenbergia* is not ankyropterid, but rather is similar anatomically to *Clepsydropsis.*

Several species of schizaeaceous ferns are known from compression-impression remains of the Jurassic. *Klukia* is a relatively common foliage type consisting of pecopteridlike pinnules borne on bipinnate fronds of unknown length. Sterile pinnules are slightly convex, with the lower surface densely covered with delicate hairs. In *K. exilis,* the fertile pinnules contain 6 to 14 sporangia, each with a uniseriate annulus extending over the distal tip. Spore counts range from 150 to 400 per sporangium and include radial, trilete grains with large sutures. The Mesozoic species from Japan, *K. yokoyamae,* differs in having larger pinnules and smaller spores. Other species have been reported from the Cretaceous of Canada.

The fertile spikes of *Stachypteris* consist of small axes bearing alternately arranged, reduced pinnule segments. The sporangia of this Jurassic (Yorkshire) fossil are borne in two rows on the abaxial surfaces of the pinnules. Features of the annulus remain in doubt, but the general morphology of the spores and organization of the fertile spike are characteristics that have led some to regard the genus as closely related to *Lygodium.* Cretaceous rocks from Wyoming have yielded several excellent foliage specimens that are described as *L. pumilum.* All the specimens consist of sterile pinnules that are palmately lobed. Venation results from two dichotomies; lateral veins dichotomize once. Tertiary specimens of *Lygodium* include both fertile and sterile foliage. The fertile pinnules of *L. kaulfussii* (Great Britain) consist of axes bearing sporangia in clusters of three. Sporangia are embedded in the pinnule surface and are partially covered by what has been termed a bract or indusium. Spores are smooth and trilete. They range from 75 to 112 μm in diameter and have thin walls. *Lygodium poolensis*, another species from the same locality, is delimited only on the basis of spore morphology.

Anemia poolensis is the binomial established for numerous, fertile Tertiary specimens. The fertile pinnules are divided in four to seven segments that are recurved into a compact sporangial mass. Sporangia are globular and about 0.5 mm long. The annulus is terminal and occupies the upper third of the sporangium. Spores are trilete and up to 60 μm in diameter.

Schizaeaceous spores are common in rocks of Cretaceous and younger age, and they are included in the genera *Cicatricosisporites*, *Lygodioisporites*, and *Trilobosporites*.

Gleicheniaceae Extant members of this family are tropical in both hemispheres, with the single extant genus *Gleichenia* including approximately 130 species. The plant body consists of a long creeping rhizome bearing large, several times pinnate fronds. Stems are typically protostelic, with some containing various amounts of parenchyma. Petiole vascular strands may be solid or C-shaped with inrolled ends. Sporangia occur in a ring on the abaxial surface of the pinnule; the number is usually small, but in some species up to 15 sporangia are seen in each sorus. In some species the pinnule segments are greatly reduced and cup-shaped. The annulus is transverse or oblique with reference to the major plane of the sporangium.

Historically, the family occupies a position parallel to that of the Schizaeaceae, with representatives reported from the Carboniferous. However, the one Carboniferous representative, *Oligocarpia* (see Fig. 1-1E), has been suggested as representing a compressed specimen of *Sermaya*. This comparison is based on similarities in foliar morphology and the size, shape, and structure of the sporangium. *Chansitheca* is a Paleozoic form that has been included in the Gleicheniaceae by some authors. Clusters of large sporangia are attached to pinnules of both *Pecopteris* and *Sphenopteris* in *C. palaeosilvana* (Pennsylvanian of central China). The annulus is described as being equatorial, but preservation makes the determination of this characteristic doubtful. Another species, *C. kidstonii*, is distinguished by a large number (16) of sporangia per sorus.

Despite the paucity of gleicheniaceous remains in rocks of the Paleozoic, the family appears to have been well represented in the Mesozoic. Fertile and sterile frond members bearing lobed and pecopterid foliage have been included in the genus *Gleichenites*. Specimens of *G. coloradensis* (Fig. 10-29A) were discovered in the Frontier Formation (upper Cretaceous) of Wyoming as almost a pure stand. Although fertile remains were not encountered, the trichotomous branching pattern and pinnule morphology are almost identical to certain species of *Gleichenia*.

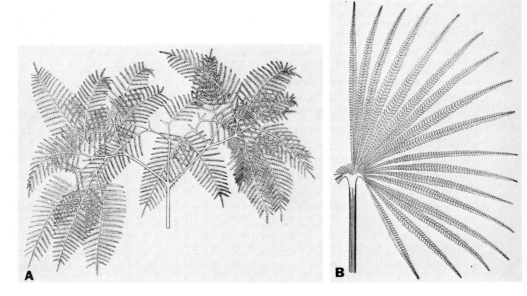

Figure 10-29 A. Suggested reconstruction of *Gleichenites coloradensis*. B. Suggested reconstruction of *Matonidium americanum*. *(A from Andrews and Pearsall, 1941; B from Berry, 1919.)*

Numerous spores have been referred to the family from as early as the Jurassic. In general, the fossil spores (*Plicifera* and *Gleicheniidites*) are similar to extant forms in that they exhibit a pronounced triangular morphology and conspicuous trilete suture.

Dicksoniaceae Most members of this group exhibit large pinnate fronds, but a few have simple leaves. Stems vary from simple siphonosteles to dictyosteles. Hairs or paleae are common on fronds and rhizomes. The position of the sorus may be variable, ranging from marginal to covering the entire abaxial surface of the fertile segment. The annulus may vary from oblique to longitudinal. Spores are typically trilete.

The family was widespread during the Jurassic, especially in the Yorkshire flora, where specimens of *Coniopteris* represent one of the dominant elements. In *C. hymenophylloides,* the leaves are lanceolate and usually about 12.0 cm wide. Pinnae are alternate, with the pinnules multilobed. The fertile leaf is about the same size as the vegetative segment, but differs markedly in that it bears fertile pinnules constructed of a midrib with pairs of sori at the ends of pinnule lobes. In some fertile pinnae, the basal pinnules are vegetative. Sporangia are borne in a cup-shaped structure formed by the indusium. The annulus is vertical and extends about two-thirds of the way around the sporangium. A slightly different soral arrangement is present in *C. bella,* where the indusium is divided into upper and lower lobes. The number of spores per sporangium is relatively low (up to 72), and all are trilete.

Kylikipteris is another Yorkshire flora member assigned to the Dickson-iaceae by Harris (1961). The fronds are large and pinnate. Some frond specimens of *K. arguta* are at least 50.0 cm wide. The pecopteridlike pinnules are relatively small, and both vegetative and fertile pinnules are borne on the same pinna. Fertile pinnules are reduced to a midrib bearing a single-stalked apical sorus surrounded by a cup-shaped indusium.

Cup-shaped sori also are borne marginally along the strongly recurved pinnules of *Eboracia* (Yorkshire, Jurassic). In *E. lobifolia,* the sorus is strongly curved along the pinnule margin. *Dicksonia* (Jurassic) specimens have marginal sori with bivalve indusia.

Cyatheaceae   Included in this family are the tree ferns, some of which are up to 30 m tall. Extending from the apex is a crown of massive, pinnately compound leaves. The trunk is represented by a false stem consisting of a tangled mass of adventitious roots and a small dissected dictyostele. Although the number of cycles is smaller, the stelar organization in *Cyathea* parallels the structure in the stem of *Psaronius*. In the Cyatheaceae, the abaxial sori are round; a cup-shaped indusium may be absent in some taxa. Sporangial development occurs in a specific sequence (gradate), and the annulus is oblique.

Unlike several other filicalean families, the fossil record of the Cyatheaceae is evident in a number of structurally preserved stem remains. *Cyathodendron texanum* is the binomial for silicified stems discovered in the Upper Eocene of Texas. The stem surfaces consist of helically arranged leaf bases and flattened multicellular hairs. In transverse section, the stems contain a siphonostele that at some levels is deeply fluted and not interrupted by leaf gaps. The xylem band is flanked on both sides by a narrow zone of sclerenchyma. Tracheids are pitted by scalariform bars, and numerous medullary xylem bundles occur intermixed with the ground parenchyma of the pith. Each petiole contains numerous vascular strands that are derived from the xylem of the siphonostele and associated medullary bundles. *Cyathodendron* is similar to the stems of some extant members of the family in certain morphologic features, but it differs in that it lacks interruptions in the stele when traces were produced.

Cibotiocaulis is an early Cretaceous silicified stem from Japan. *Cibotiocaulis* has large leaf gaps in the stele, and the petiole trace is initially continuous, but at higher levels divides into numerous bundles. *Protopteris* is a form genus that includes casts of stem remains on which the petiole trace scar appears horseshoe-shaped in outline.

Alsophilocaulis is a silicified Tertiary specimen from Argentina. The stem is about 6.0 cm in diameter and includes abundant sclerenchyma associated with the xylem. In *A. calveloi,* the xylem is dissected into V- and W-shaped strands; the pith region contains numerous clusters of tracheids and fibers.

Alsophilites is a foliage genus that includes clusters of sporangia with thickened, oblique, annuluslike cells. The specimens were poorly preserved, and consequently, details of the sorus make the assignment of the genus questionable. Tertiary foliage specimens have been described as several species of *Cyathea* and *Alsophila*, although in most instances features of the sporangia were not present.

Matoniaceae   This family is represented by two extant genera, *Matonia* and *Phanerosorus*, that are geographically confined to Indonesia, Borneo, and New Guinea. The frond is divided into two major segments, each of which undergoes a series of unequal dichotomies. The rhizome consists of two or three concentric amphiphloic siphonosteles, with leaf traces produced from the outer cycle. Sporangia are arranged in a ring around a receptacle that continues as the stalk of a peltate indusium. The position of the annulus is oblique, and spores are trilete.

The family was widespread throughout the Mesozoic and, like today, is represented by a very small number of species. *Phlebopteris* (*Laccopteris*) is a foliage genus that extends from the Upper Triassic into the Cretaceous. *Phlebopteris utensis* is the binomial used for specimens collected from the Chinle Formation of Utah. Fronds consist of mature pinnae up to 20.0 cm long that bear pinnules with tapered apices and slightly crenate margins. Features of the sori are determined by making cellulose transfers of the carbonaceous films of the fossils. Each sorus is circular and consists of seven to nine sporangia each with an incomplete marginal annulus. Spores are triangular and 45 μm in diameter. In *P. hirsuta,* a Jurassic species, the pinnules are narrow but broadly attached to the rachis. The sorus is ringlike and contains up to 12 sporangia; spores are in the 50 to 60 μm size range. *Phlebopteris polypodioides* is known from a number of localities in Europe, as well as from Greenland and Korea. The taxon extended from the Upper Triassic well into the Jurassic. Specimens from Yorkshire consist of fronds with fused pinnule veins. Sporangia are crowded in a ring of approximately 14. *Selenocarpus* is a Lower Jurassic genus that differs from *Phlebopteris* in that it has semicircular sori.

Another Jurassic-Cretaceous genus included in the Matoniaceae is *Matonidium* (Fig. 10-29B). Specimens of *M. americanum* consist of digitate fronds with stipes up to 1.0 cm in diameter. The distal end of the stipe is flared into a collar from which arises numerous pinnae. Pinnules are subopposite and obtusely rounded at the tip. The sori are arranged in two rows and decrease in size toward the distal end of the pinnule. The peltate indusium makes it impossible to determine the number of sporangia per sorus.

Weichselia reticulata (Fig. 10-30) is a fern with a massive stem that bears large petioles (5.0 cm in diameter) in a helical pattern. Primary pinnae are at least 1.0 m long and bipinnately compound. Pinnules are about 5.0 mm long and broadly attached to the pinna midrib. Stomata are confined to the lower surfaces in the intervein areas and have large guard cells. Soral clusters are borne in a conelike unit on separate fertile fronds. The ultimate fertile units are nearly peltate and bear approximately 12 sporangia. Spores range up to 80 μm in diameter and show distinct contact areas on their proximal surfaces. Extending from near the base of each petiole is a downwardly projecting axis believed to represent an adventitious root. Transverse sections of partially petrified

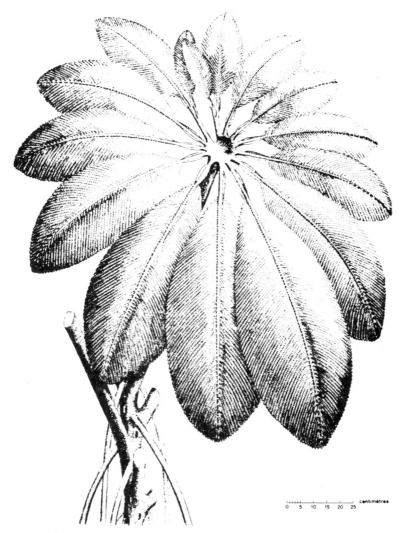

centimètres
0 5 10 15 20 25

Figure 10-30 Suggested reconstruction of *Weichselia reticulata. (From Alvin, 1971.)*

specimens from the Cretaceous of Belgium indicate that the petioles contain approximately 12 rings of vascular tissue termed meristeles.

Weichselia exhibits several features that appear to be matoniaceous, including the sori, indusia, and spores. In other characteristics, such as the bipinnate nature of the frond, the stem with presumed rhizophores, the polycyclic dictyostele, the nonlaminar fertile pinnules, and certain histologic characters, the genus does not resemble living members of the Matoniaceae. This has suggested to some that *Weichselia* represents an early offshoot from the group that ultimately gave rise to the family. Others have argued that despite the similarities, the genus should be treated as a member of a separate family.

Polypodiaceae   It is difficult to define the characteristics of fossil polypodiaceous ferns because pteridologists working with living members of this family
are not in agreement regarding the systematics of the group. The common genus
Polypodium includes once pinnate leaves with anastomosing veins. The vascular
system of the rhizome is a dictyostele. Soral position may be variable on the
underside of the lamina, and an indusium is absent. The sporangium contains a
stalk, usually of three cells, and the position of the annulus is longitudinal.
Spores are monolete.

Fossil polypodiaceous ferns include both compression remains and structurally preserved rhizomes. These fossils are restricted to sediments beginning in
the Upper Cretaceous. From the Clarno Formation (Eocene) of Orgeon have
come numerous silicified rhizomes of at least two distinct polypodiaceous
genera. *Dennstaedtiopsis aerenchymata* consists of horizontally oriented rhizomes that bear alternately arranged, distantly spaced pinnae. The rhizome is
about 1.0 cm in diameter and contains a siphonostele with internal and external
endodermis, pericycle, and phloem (Fig. 10-31B). Tracheal pitting is scalariform. The most diagnostic features of the species are the aerenchyma tissues of
the pith and cortex that are arranged in a series of tangentially oriented

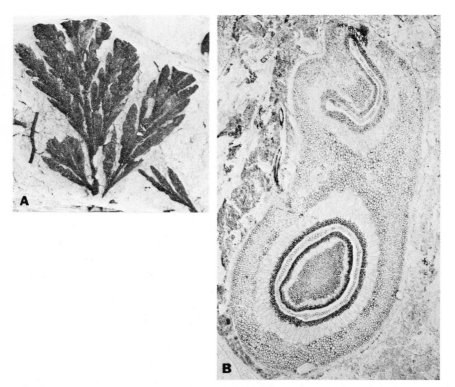

Figure 10-31 A. *Anemia fremontii.* ×0.8. B. Transverse section of *Dennstaedtiopsis
aerenchymata* just after U-shaped petiole has departed from stem. ×10. *(B courtesy of R.
Stockey.)*

partitions. Multicellular epidermal hairs are scattered over the surface of the rhizome. The vascular trace to the petiole is initiated adjacent to the formation of a gap in the rhizome stele and is U-shaped near the base. At higher levels, the sides are indented and appear almost identical to the petiole traces of the extant fern *Dennstaedtia*. The distal portions of the frond are not known, nor were any sporangia found associated with the specimens.

Another member of the family that is common in the Clarno chert beds is *Acrostichum*. *Acrostichum preaureum* consists of erect rhizomes bearing large petioles. In transverse section, the stele consists of a narrow band of closely packed tracheids. The cortex is three-parted, consisting of an inner and outer sclerotic zone and a middle region of parenchyma. A conspicuous ramentum of compact scales covers the stem. The petioles display a distinct adaxial groove, with the vascular bundles arranged in an omega-shaped configuration when viewed in transverse section. In large petioles, the number of bundles in any one transverse section approaches 1000. The orientation of the protoxylem elements is of two general types. Those bundles located near the sloping sides of the adaxial groove have protoxylem directed toward the outside, while the remaining peripheral bundles demonstrate a reverse orientation of the protoxylem tracheids. At the distal level of the frond are laminar pinnules with abaxially positioned sporangia in no definite soral arrangement. The annulus is vertical and extends about two-thirds of the length of the sporangium. Spores are trilete and smooth.

The Clarno chert represents an excellent example of a fossil site from which ecological information can be determined on the basis of the kinds of plants present and the features of the depositional environment. It has been suggested that the plant-bearing chert was an indurated soil of a marsh in which the primary inorganic portion of the soil was reworked volcanic ash. Hot springs in the area are believed responsible for transporting quantities of dissolved silica to the site and, also, possibly, for elevating the temperature in the area so that subtropical conditions could prevail on a local scale. It has been suggested that the cooler post-Eocene climates were responsible for the elimination of a number of plants, such as *Acrostichum,* from the area.

The Cretaceous Dakota sandstone of east central Utah and southwestern Colorado contained a polypodiaceous fern that is similar to the extant genus *Drynaria* of southeastern Asia. *Astralopteris coloradica* bears large fronds with alternate to opposite coriaceous pinnules. Sori are round and are arranged in a linear row on both sides of the midvein. Nothing is known about the spores.

Brown (1962) described a number of polypodiaceous ferns from the Paleocene of the Rocky Mountains and Great Plains. *Onoclea hesperia* has sterile pinnae with entire margins, whereas another common member of the family, *Woodwardia,* has serrated margins and a slightly different pattern of venation.

Tempskyaceae   The Tempskyaceae are an entirely extinct family of Mesozoic ferns known principally on the basis of silicified trunks common in Middle and Upper Cretaceous deposits in the West. Trunks range up to 50.0 cm in diameter and are composed of numerous intertwined stems, petioles, and adventitious roots that provide a false trunk morphology to the primary axis. Trunk diameters suggest that *Tempskya* may have attained heights of approximately 6.0 m (Fig. 10-32A). The stems of *Tempskya* are dichotomously branched, amphiphloic siphonosteles that produced traces to small petioles. More than 200 stems have been recorded in a single transverse section of some specimens (Fig. 10-32B). Individual stems are variable in size, with the largest stem only about 1.0 cm in diameter. The stem stele is exarch and is constructed of scalariform tracheids and parenchyma (Fig. 10-32C). The cortex is typically multilayered, and it is distinguished by the presence of sclerenchyma in the outer zone.

The roots are profusely branched and diarch; numerous root hairs extend from the epidermis, even in areas that are quite mature. Such persistent root hairs probably functioned for a considerable period of time in drawing water from the aerial adventitious root zone of the false trunk. This suggestion appears to be consistent with theories about how *Tempskya* actually grew.

A comparison of numerous transverse sections of *Tempskya* indicates that the largest-diameter axes contain the smallest number of stems, while the

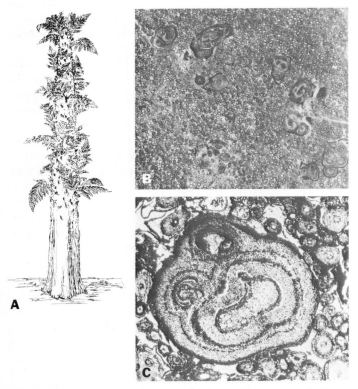

Figure 10-32 A. Suggested reconstruction of *Tempskya* plant. B. Transverse section of *Tempskya* false stem. ×1. C. Transverse section of *Tempskya* stem and petioles embedded among adventitious roots. ×6.5. *(A from Andrews and Kern, 1947.)*

small-diameter trunks contain a large number of stems. Such information has been used to suggest that the sporeling stage of a *Tempskya* plant consisted of a single stem that continued to branch at more distal levels. Numerous adventitious roots were produced that held the stem system together. As the plant continued to grow, the basal stems began to decay; continuity with the soil was provided by the adventitious roots. One additional unusual feature about *Tempskya* is the manner in which leaves were produced. Although no foliage has ever been found attached to the trunks, the size of the petioles and the position of petiole traces never more than a few millimeters from the stem stele suggest that the leaves were small (Fig. 10-31A) and did not persist for any appreciable period of time. Petiole and stem relationships suggest that the leaves were borne in two rows over the upper two-thirds of the trunk instead of as a crown of fronds.

Based on anatomic details, the American species of *Tempskya* have been subdivided into two general groups. One group is characterized by large stems with short internodes; parenchyma is abundant in the xylem. Contrasting features delimit the second group. It is highly probable that many of the species named merely represent different levels and stages of development of the same plant. Such features as internode length and tissue distribution are highly variable and are probably not reliable taxonomic characteristics.

Although a few isolated spores and several sporangial remains have been found associated with *Tempskya* stems, none has ever been recorded in a position that might indicate attachment. Thus the fossil record still retains many important pieces of information about this very unusual Cretaceous plant. In light of the quality of the preservation and nearly ubiquitous occurrence of stems, it would appear to be a potentially rewarding area for subsequent collection and research.

Marsileales

The Marsileales represent one of two orders of heterosporous water ferns that include about 67 species of extant plants distributed within the genera *Marsilea, Pilularia,* and *Regnellidium.* The plants are rhizomatous, often growing in dense mats that extend out over deeper water. Leaves are small and range from two opposite pinnae in *Regnellidium* to three pairs of pinnae in some species of *Marsilea.* In *Pilularia,* the leaves are filiform and lack lamina. The stem has a siphonostele with internal and external endodermis; xylem maturation is mesarch. The reproductive structures of the Marsileales are modified into hard, bean-shaped structures termed sporocarps. They represent specialized units of a foliar nature that contain both mega- and microsporangia. Sporocarps are well-adapted to prevent dessication, and some are known to have "germinated" 40 years after they were collected. The megaspores of this group are large and characterized by a cone-shaped gelatinous mass. A few megaspores and vegetative remains from the Cretaceous have been attributed to this group, but in general, the fossil record is rather poor.

Rodeites is the generic name applied to megaspores, microspores, and sporocarps from the silicified Deccan Intertrappean cherts of India. The bilateral sporocarps measure approximately 1.3 cm long and contain seven sori. Megaspores are about 600 μm in diameter, whereas the trilete microspores measure 45 μm. *Rodeites dakshinii* compares most closely with *Regnellidium*.

Salviniales

Some authors include the Marsileales and Salviniales in a single order of heterosporous aquatic ferns. However, the two groups do display distinct structural differences and therefore are treated here as separate orders. The Salviniales are represented by two extant genera (*Azolla* and *Salvinia*) consisting of approximately 16 species. The plants are generally small and free-floating in lakes and ponds. In *Salvinia,* the leaves are whorled in threes on a rootless rhizome, with one leaf highly dissected and submerged. Leaves of *Azolla* are borne clustered from a root-bearing rhizome. Sporocarps are borne on submerged leaves and differ from those of the Marsileales in that they have a highly modified sorus. Microsporangia and megasporangia are borne in separate sporocarps on the same leaf. The vascular system of the stem consists of a few tracheids embedded in a parenchymatous ground tissue.

Unlike the Marsileales, the fossil record of the Salviniales is rather extensive, consisting of some vegetative remains, but mostly of dispersed megaspores and microspores. The megaspores have large massulae, or floats, above the spore (Fig. 10-33B) that provide a diagnostic feature for their identity in fossil sediments. The proximal region consists of a tripartite prolongation of the perispore termed the acrolamella. The stratigraphic distribution of the group back to the Cretaceous is based principally on identification of the megaspores. The Cretaceous members of this group have been extensively studied by several authors and, according to Hall (1974), include the following genera: *Azolla, Azollopsis, Ariadnaesporites, Salvinia, Parazolla,* and *Glomerisporites.*

Glomerisporites is an oval megaspore covered with a hairy perispore. Small floats (19 to 30 μm in diameter) are enmeshed in the perispore hairs. The wall of the megaspore is two-layered, and ultrastructural studies indicate that the structure of the wall is an important systematic character. Microspores consist of a perispore with numerous hairs, especially prominent at the distal end. Based on the large number of small, simply constructed floats, *Glomerisporites* is regarded as the most primitive member of the order. In *Azollopsis* (Upper Cretaceous), there are a large number of floats arranged around the megaspore. Massulae are attached to the megaspores by multibarbed glochidia. The genus *Parazolla* includes large megaspores in which the floats are confined to the proximal region in one or two tiers. These megaspores have been compared with *Azolla,* but the massulae are distinct. They are banana-shaped and bear glochidia with terminal knobs.

In *Ariadnaesporites varius,* from the Cenomanian (Upper Cretaceous) of Minnesota, the megaspores are up to 1.5 mm long and are characterized by several proximal floats associated with hairs. Microspores possess a few long hairs that extend from the perispore. Based on the stratigraphy and morphology of the spores, Hall (1974) has suggested that there were two evolutionary trends within the family. The first trend involved the reduction in the number of floats

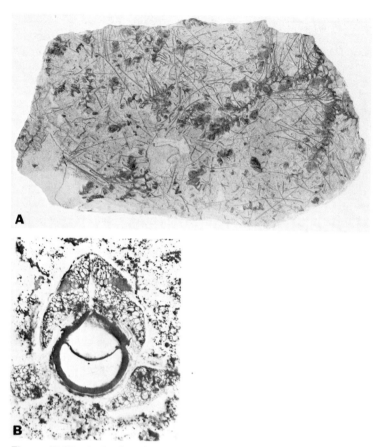

Figure 10-33 A. *Azolla primaeva*. ×1. B. Longitudinal section of *Azolla intertrappea* (Tertiary) showing the megaspore and two distal massulae. ×80. *(B from Sahni, 1941.)*

per megaspore in successively younger taxa. The second evolutionary trend involves the microspores that were initially produced singly and later appeared in massulae. Intermediate stages in the evolution of the massula involved coiled hairs that may have functioned as glochidia and the clustered appearance of some microspores that superficially resemble a massula.

Vegetative remains of the family were initially included in the genus *Azollophyllum* and later transferred to *Azolla*. *Azolla primaeva* (Fig. 10-33A) is described from Eocene sediments in southern British Columbia. The rhizomes are about 30.0 cm long and bear bilobed ovate leaves and unbranched roots. Associated with these fossils are abundant massulae up to 500 μm long, some containing recognizable anchor-shaped glochidia. In the genus *Salvinia*, which extends back to the Cretaceous, the megaspores lack floats. *Salvinia stewartii* is an Upper Cretaceous (Maestrichtian) species recovered from sediments near Edmonton, Alberta, Canada. The taxon is delimited for megaspores lacking hairs and large, trilete microspores not associated with massulae or glochidia.

Much smaller megaspores (240 to 320 μm in diameter) and distinct massulae containing about 32 microspores have been described under the epithet *S. aureovallis* (Eocene). Glochidia are not evident. The specimens are similar to extant species of *Salvinai,* differing only in their slightly smaller size. Leaf characteristics used to distinguish several species of *Salvinia* have been reviewed by Florin (1940) on a worldwide basis.

Conclusion

Despite a rather extensive fossil record of many extant fern families, the fossils provide relatively little information about the evolutionary relationships or origins of the families. At least four families (Botryopteridaceae, Anachoropteridaceae, Sermayaceae, and Tedeleaceae) were present in the Carboniferous, and most certainly were involved in the evolution of other filicalean families. With the exception of the Osmundaceae, which has an extensive fossil record in the late Paleozoic, all the other modern families of ferns are geologically separated from the first occurrences by a considerable time span. At first glance it would appear that all these families have their first appearance in the Jurassic, but this may simply reflect the well-preserved nature of some Jurassic floras, especially the Yorkshire material.

At least three families of Paleozoic representatives contain taxa that produced biseriate fronds with foliar-borne sporangia. In all these families, however, stem and petiole anatomy is markedly different from that of extant ferns. Variations in leaf organization are also apparent among these Paleozoic families. In many of the earliest fernlike plants, the annulus was terminal or subterminal in organization. With the exception of the unique situation presented in some species of *Botryopteris,* all the other Paleozoic families exhibit sporangia with laminar infolding for protection or some modification that might be homologized with an indusium. All produced ornamented, trilete spores.

In spite of the elimination of the Paleozoic members of the Schizaeaceae and Gleicheniaceae, these two families probably represent the two basic filicalean evolutionary lines. Families such as the Matoniaceae, Cyatheaceae, and Polypodiaceae have certain features that are more gleicheniaceous than any other group of ferns. The Osmundaceae do show some structural similarities to the *B. globosa* and *B. forensis* sporangial masses.

The fossil record is continuing to provide information about early fern evolution, and this information is being incorporated into current thinking regarding primitive versus advanced features. Many of these characteristics (see, for example, the 32 listed by Bierhorst, 1971) have been assembled for extant ferns and will never be demonstrated in the fossil record. It may be impossible to ever fully appreciate the total scope of the evolutionary relationships that exist among such a large and complex group as the ferns. In many instances, the first members that occur are similar to modern representatives, and it is quite possible that many of the genetic complexities common among living ferns were operative early in their geologic history, thus further obscuring the evolutionary relationships.

Progymnospermophyta

One of the most significant contributions to the study of fossil plants was made by Beck, who in 1960 recognized the existence of a group of vascular plants that possessed gymnospermous anatomy but reproduced by pteridophytic methods. Today the Progymnospermophyta consist of three orders that extend from the Devonian into the Lower Carboniferous. The Aneurophytales, considered to include the most primitive members of the division, had three-dimensional branches that were arranged in a helical or decussate manner. The ultimate appendages, or "preleaves," were not webbed or planated. The axis contained a lobed protostele, with primary xylem consisting largely of tracheids. The order of maturation of primary xylem was mesarch. Sporangia were produced on elongate stalks and were pinnately arranged. All specimens are thought to have been homosporous, although the extensive size range of the spores suggests that some may have been heterosporous.

In the Archaeopteridales, the branching systems were produced in a single plane, with the ultimate segments (leaves) ranging from highly dissected to laminar, but always flattened. Anatomically, the axes contained a eustele with mesarch bundles of primary xylem surrounding a pith. Sporangia were borne in two or more rows on the adaxial surfaces of modified leaves. Both homosporous and heterosporous forms are included in this order.

The third order, the Protopityales, is known from a limited number of specimens of the Lower Carboniferous. Endarch primary xylem strands arose from opposite sides of the pith, suggesting that the lateral organs were probably distichous in arrangement. Pitting in the secondary xylem of this group was predominately circular bordered, but with elliptical-shaped pits in the first-formed wood simulating scalariform pits. Stalked sporangia were produced on recurved ultimate appendages. Limited information suggests that the Proto-pityales were homosporous.

ARCHAEOPTERIDALES

The importance of Beck's research is significant not only in demonstrating the existence of a group of plants intermediate in certain features, but also in demonstrating the careful research methodology often necessary in paleobota-ny. The establishment of the Progymnospermophyta involved the demonstration that two different organ genera represented different parts of the same plant. One of these was *Archaeopteris,* a genus established in 1871 for the vegetative and reproductive structures of a free-sporing plant classified with the Pterido-phyta. Initially, the vegetative parts of the plant were thought to be fernlike, and consequently, early literature dealing with *Archaeopteris* referred to rachides bearing pinnae with ultimate pinnules. Continued research, especially with specimens showing anatomic detail, indicated that what had been termed the rachis of a frond was the main axis of a lateral branch system that produced both leaves and ultimate branches. Both the leaves and ultimate branches borne by the penultimate axes were helically arranged; leaves arising from the ultimate branches were opposite and decussate (Fig. 11-1B). Leaves of *Archaeopteris* exhibited extensive variability ranging from highly dissected forms (*A. fissilis*) to those with nearly entire margins (such as *A. obtusa*). Leaf shape varied from obovate to spatulate; some were sessile, while others were attached by a short stalk.

The anatomy of an *Archaeopteris* axis consisted of a central pith surrounded by a variable number of primary xylem strands. Secondary xylem consisted of files of angular tracheids and narrow vascular rays. Scheckler (1978) demonstrat-ed that a considerable amount of anatomic variability is present among the taxa assigned to the genus *Archaeopteris,* but that, in general, the branches and leaves are determinate. One of the unusual features of *Archaeopteris* was the production of both leaves and branches in the same organotactic spiral. Schlecker demonstrated that sections at many branch nodes reveal a continuity between the xylem of the branches and the parental axes, suggesting that the branches of *Archaeopteris* were not produced by lateral buds, but rather were developed from primordia like those which produced the leaves.

In *Archaeopteris,* the fertile branches contain several basal and terminal leaves (Fig. 11-2C). The remainder of the branch bears greatly reduced fertile leaves that contain sporangia on the adaxial surfaces (Fig. 11-1C). In *A. halliana* (Upper Devonian), the fertile units are broadly laminate and morphologically

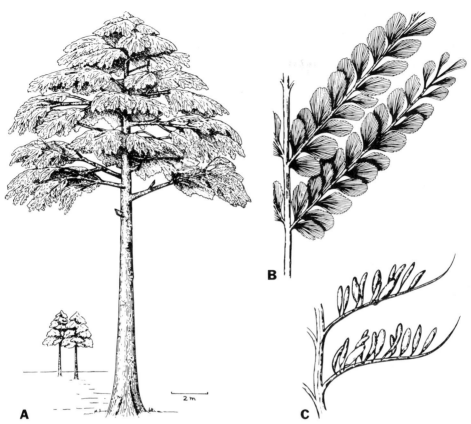

Figure 11-1 A. Suggested reconstruction of *Archaeopteris*. B. *Archaeopteris* branch with helically arranged leaves. C. Fertile appendages of *Archaeopteris* bearing adaxial sporangia. *(A from Beck, 1962; B and C reproduced from* Studies in Paleobotany *with permission of John Wiley, Inc., 1961.)*

similar to the vegetative leaves. Fertile leaves of this type generally occurred in transition regions between fertile and vegetative parts of the branch system. It is difficult to determine whether the sporangia were arranged in two rows (Fig. 11-2A) or if each pair possessed a common, reduced stalk. The distal end of the fertile leaf dichotomizes once or, in a few cases, twice. In *A. fissilis*, the sporangia are about 2.0 mm long; those of *A. macilenta* are up to 3.4 mm long. Sporangia are thick-walled, with dehiscence logitudinal. No specialized cells in the form of an annulus are present. Stomata, such as those present on the vegetative leaves, have been identified among the epidermal cells of the sporangia.

Heterospory (Fig. 11-2D and E) has been demonstrated in at least four species of *Archaeopteris* (*A. latifolia*, *A. jacksonii*, *A. halliana*, and *A. macilenta*). The microspores are circular to subcircular and range from 30 to 70 μm in diameter. The laesurae of the trilete scar are long, extending approxi-

Figure 11-2 A. Portion of a fertile region of an *Archaeopteris* branch showing adaxial position of sporangia. B. Suggested reconstruction of *Eddya sullivanensis.* C. Branch of *Archaeopteris* containing both fertile and vegetative leaves. D. Elongate mass of small spores obtained from *Archaeopteris* sporangium. E. Sporangial contents consisting of large spores. *(B from Beck, 1967; C–E reproduced from* Studies in Paleobotany *with permission of John Wiley, Inc., 1961.)*

mately three-quarters of the spore radius. The proximal surface, especially in the contact area, is psilate, while the distal surface is ornamented with closely spaced grana up to 1.0 μm tall. Although no comprehensive study of *Archaeopteris* microspores has been undertaken, sections of one species indicate that the exine was thin and homogeneous. Megaspores range from 150 to nearly 500 μm in diameter. The trilete scar is typically elevated and strongly developed. On the distal surface are closely spaced rods or coni; the proximal surface is smooth, occasionally ornamented with folds. A few small spores have been described as aborted megaspores. If found in the dispersed state, the megaspores of *Archaeopteris* are included in the genus *Biharisporites;* the microspores are assigned to the form genus *Cyclogranisporites.*

The main axes of *Archaeopteris* that bore lateral branch systems have the structure of the organ genus *Callixylon.* Specimens of *Callixylon* have been known since 1911 and include large, woody stems up to 150 cm in diameter. Some logs have been reported up to 10 m long. The genus was widespread during the Upper Devonian, typically found in marine sediments as driftwood. In transverse section, *Callixylon* reveals a central pith that is surrounded by a ring of mesarch primary xylem strands. In some specimens, these strands appear to be embedded in the parenchyma of the pith; in others, the strands are in contact with the secondary xylem. Secondary xylem of *Callixylon* consists of thick-walled tracheids and narrow to relatively broad vascular rays. In a few specimens, there is evidence of growth rings. The dense, compact (pycnoxylic) wood is similar to the secondary xylem of most coniferophytes as opposed to the loose, highly parenchymatous organization of the manoxylic wood of seed ferns and cycads. Wood rays of most species are typically narrow, but broader in the region of the pith. They are variable in height and are constructed of ray tracheids and ray parenchyma. Trabeculae similar to those in living conifers are present in the tracheids of *Callixylon.* Pitting occurs on the radial walls of the

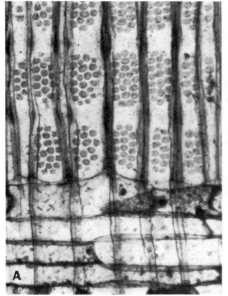

Figure 11-3 A. Radial view of secondary xylem of *Callixylon newberryi* illustrating radial arrangement of groups of multiseriate pits. ×200. B. Slitlike pit apertures on tracheid of *C. newberryi.* ×350. *(A from Beck, 1970.)*

tracheids (Fig. 11-3A), except in regions of later wood, in which they occur on the tangential walls instead. The circular bordered pits are arranged in groups in radially aligned rows and are multiseriate in most species; uniseriate pits characterize *C. arnoldii.* Pit borders range from circular to angular, with the apertures elliptical and lacking a torus (Fig. 11-3B). Between groups of pits are slightly thickened areas of the primary wall that have been likened to crassulae of extant conifers. Features of the secondary xylem have been used to distinguish species of *Callixylon,* although some of these characteristics may merely reflect different levels in the branching system.

The discovery of an *Archaeopteris* specimen attached to a *Callixylon* stem was the evidence used by Beck to establish the concept of the Progymnospermophyta. The rules of botanical nomenclature indicate that in a case where two organ genera are demonstrated as different parts of the same biological species, the generic name that was validly published first, in this case, *Archaeopteris,* should serve as the legitimate name of the plant. *Archaeopteris* was a tall forest tree (Fig. 11-1A) that in general habit looked much like any one of a number of modern coniferophytes. What is possibly the most interesting feature of these plants is the coniferlike secondary xylem coupled with a pteridophytic reproductive system. Several authors have commented on the morphologic and anatomic variability in *Archaeopteris* as possibly representing more than a single biological species. In addition to anatomic features and foliar morphology, the presence of heterosporous and possibly homosporous taxa lends support to this suggestion. One possibility that cannot be overlooked is that the species described as homosporous may represent one region of a branch system that included only small spores, megasporangia being confined to another region of the plant or produced in far less frequency than the microspores. Still another idea suggests that the microsporangia function to produce pollen in a plant that also produced seeds. Strengthening this hypothesis is the morphologic organization of the fertile leaves of *Archaeopteris* (e.g., *A. halliana*); the stalked sporangia are not too far removed from a primitive telomic system with enclosing sterile structures (cupule) similiar to those of the multiovulate cupule *Archaeosperma.*

Two other genera that are similar to *Archaeopteris* are *Siderella* and *Actinopodium. Siderella* is known from the New Albany shale, the stratigraphic position of which is believed to be intermediate between the Upper Devonian and Lower Mississippian. The petrified siphonostelic axes of *Siderella* contain 7 to 10 lobes of primary xylem with small patches of parenchyma superficially resembling peripheral loops near the end of each lobe. In *Actinopodium,* a central pith is surrounded by seven to nine lobes of mesarch primary xylem. In both genera, traces to laterals are produced like those in *Archaeopteris,* and the structure of the secondary xylem is similar as well. Another genus that may represent a species of *Archaeopteris* is *Svalbardia.* Described from the Upper Devonian, the genus is distinguished by its apparent irregular helical arrangement of lateral branches. With a more complete understanding of the relationship between the pattern of branching and the size of the axis in *Archaeopteris,* it now appears likely that *Svalbardia* and *Archaeopteris* are identical. Variability within *Archaeopteris* branching also suggests that *Actinoxylon,* initially distinguished by the production of helical branches with three and four xylem ridges and apparent absence of pith, also may represent a species of *Archaeopteris.*

Rarely does the fossil record provide specimens of immature stages of sporophytes so that morphologic and ontogenetic levels of development can be adequately traced to mature plants. *Eddya sullivanensis* (Fig. 11-2B) is an Upper Devonian plant that may have had a maxiumum height of approximately 30.0 cm. It consists of a slender axis that produced helically arranged, flabelliform leaves (6.0 cm long) with slightly undulating margins and dichotomous venation. The underground root system of the plant is extensive, with a main axis and numerous lateral roots. The vascular system of the tiny stem consists of a eustele with mesarch primary xylem surrounded by a small amount of secondary xylem with narrow rays, and tracheids with circular bordered pits. The evidence thus far assembled supports the view that *Eddya* may represent a juvenile *Archaeopteris,* and the ontogenetic data on progymnosperms recently assembled by Scheckler (1978) for mature plants further supports this conclusion.

ANEUROPHYTALES

There are several additional Devonian plants that are known in sufficient detail to be included within the Progymnospermophyta as the division was initially defined (gymnospermous anatomy combined with pteridophytic reproduction). One of these is *Aneurophyton,* known from Middle and Upper Devonian sediments from several sites (Europe, U.S.S.R., United States). The plant has at least three orders of helically arranged branches. The three-dimensional ultimate appendages (leaves) are one to three times dichotomized and unwebbed. The fertile branch systems of *A. germanicum* consist of three orders of branches that are helically arranged (Fig. 11-4A). The fertile units (fructifications) are represented by a central stalk about 6.0 mm long that dichotomizes with each end inwardly curved and terminating in a blunt, lyre-shaped structure (Fig. 11-4B). Arising from each arm of the unit are two rows of stalked, elliptical

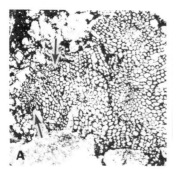

Figure 11-4 *Aneurophyton germanicum.* A. Triangular-shaped xylem strand with departing branch trace *(arrows).* ×45. B. Lyre-shaped fructification with elongate sporangia. *(From Serlin and Banks, 1978.)*

sporangia, each about 2.5 mm long. The number of sporangia per fructification is about 18 in *A. germanicum*. In other fructifications of *A. germanicum,* the ultimate arms are slightly recurved away from one another, with the sporangia borne on the concave side. Fructifications of this type are suggested as atypical, the result of preservation. Spores have been macerated from only a few specimens of *Aneurophyton*. They are trilete, about 40 μm in diameter, and included in the *sporae dispersae* genus *Aneurospora*.

The vascular system of *Aneurophyton* consists of a traingular-shaped strand of primary xylem when viewed in transverse section. Maturation of the protoxylem is mesarch and includes four strands, one near the tip of each lobe of the stele and one protoxylem strand in the center. Secondary xylem occurs between the lobes of the stele and completely surrounds the primary body in older stems. Secondary xylem tracheids have multiseriate pits with elliptical borders; vascular rays are unseriate.

In 1924, Goldring described some Middle Devonian trunk casts from Gilboa, New York, under the generic name *Eospermatopteris*. The plant was believed to be approximately 9 to 12 m tall, bearing massive fernlike fronds with seeds attached to the ultimate branch tips. The base of each trunk is cormlike, with numerous radiating roots. For some time, *Eospermatopteris* was regarded as the oldest seed fern, although an examination of the "seeds" showed them to contain spores (Kräusel and Weyland, 1935), thus removing the taxon from association with seed plants. Today, most workers believe that *Eospermatopteris* trunk casts represent the axis that produced branching systems of the *Aneurophyton* type. This supposition is based on the common stratigraphic association of the plant parts. It is probable that the original material upon which the generic name *Eospermatopteris* was instituted included several different plants now included within the Progymnospermophyta.

Another progymnospermous plant placed in the Aneurophytales is *Tetraxylopteris*. The genus is known from specimens that all demonstrate decussate branching that terminates in ultimate appendages interpreted as leaves. The leaves of *Tetraxylopteris schmidtii* are highly variable, exhibiting several levels of branching. In transverse section, the primary xylem consists of a cruciform-shaped mesarch strand that is maintained in successive orders of branches; in the leaves the xylem strand is terete. With a corresponding decrease in the size of the branches distally, there is a concomitant decrease in the number of protoxylem strands from as many as 18 in the larger branches to 15 in fourth-order branches, and 2 to 4 in the leaves (ultimate appendages). Some of the secondary-xylem tracheids have been described as branched and over 3.0 mm long. Pitting is of the circular bordered type. Parenchyma, and some ray tracheids, form uniseriate rays, some up to 100 cells high. The cortex contains parenchyma and bands of fibers near the periphery that form a "dictyoxylon" type of cortex. In some older stems, the formation of periderm results in the sloughing off of the cortex and the distinct tapering of the branches, suggesting that *Tetraxylopteris* was a relatively shrubby plant.

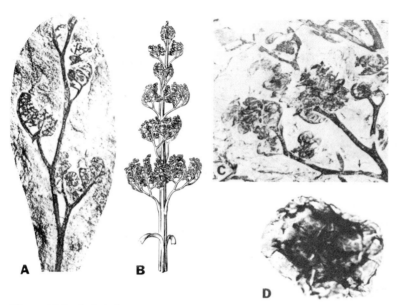

Figure 11-5 A. Spirally arranged fertile organs of *Milleria thomsonii (Protopteridium hostimense)*. ×0.6. B. Suggested reconstruction of the fertile branching system of *Tetraxylopteris*. ×250. C. Habit view of *Milleria thomsonii* showing two fertile organs. ×0.5. D. Proximal view of spore recovered from *Tetraxylopteris* sporangium. ×250. *(A and C from Leclercq and Bonamo, 1971; B and D from Bonamo and Banks, 1967.)*

The fertile regions of *Tetraxylopteris* are complex, consisting of opposite, decussately arranged sporangial complexes (Fig. 11-5B). Each complex consists of an axis that dichotomizes twice, with each of the four resulting branches three times pinnate. Each ultimate unit terminates in an elongate sporangium approximately 5.0 mm long. Dehiscence is longitudinal, with a dark line suggestive of an annulus extending along the opposite face of the sporangium. Spores are radial, and trilete, and range from 73 to 176 μm in diameter (Fig. 11-5D). The exine separates to form an equatorial pseudosaccus that is ornamented by minute grana.

Sporae dispersae grains such as those macerated from *Tetraxylopteris* sporangia fall within the generic circumscription of *Rhabdosporites*. It has been suggested that the large size range of the spores reflects stages in spore development rather than the condition of heterospory. The genus *Sphenoxylon* has recently been demonstrated as a poorly preserved *Tetraxylopteris* axis.

Some authorities include *Triloboxylon* within the Aneurophytale, because of the similarity in branching pattern and anatomy to *Tetraxylopteris*. In *Triloboxylon ashlandicum*, branch diameters range from 1.0 to 4.0 mm, with the primary xylem consisting of a three-armed mesarch protostele (Fig. 11-6A); ultimate appendages contain a terete trace. The formation of traces includes a small amount of parenchyma in the form of looplike areas at the ends of the

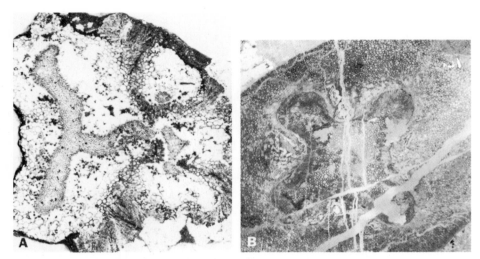

Figure 11-6 A. Transverse section of a vegetative axis of *Triloboxylon ashlandicum.* ×17. B. Transverse section of *Stauroxylon beckii.* ×7. *(A from Scheckler, 1975; B from Galtier, 1970.)*

lobes. Secondary xylem and extraxylary tissues are similar to those of *Tetraxylopteris,* except that the arrangement of the cortical fibers is of the "sparganum" type. The fertile organs are twice dichotomized and are borne in the place of second-order vegetative branches along the main axis. Each of the fertile units is about 2.0 cm long, with the sporangia borne singly or in pairs on the distal segments of the fertile organs. The xylem strand of the penultimate branch of the fertile axis is three-armed, with the trace to the fertile organ dividing into two strands above the level of separation. The sporangia of *T. ashlandicum* possess apiculate tips and are about 3.5 mm long. Nothing is known about the spores. Dehiscence is longitudinal and may have involved a patch of cells functioning like an annulus. Although the branches and leaflike ultimate appendages of the Aneurophytales bear a distinct relationship to each other in that they are borne by the last order of vegetative branches, the fertile organs of *Triloboxylon* are unique in that they are borne in the place of the penultimate vegetative branches. In addition, they are divided in one place and appear to be interspersed among vegetative branches.

Another genus included in the Aneurophytales is *Rellimia,* known previously as *Protopteridium* (Fig. 11-5A) and *Milleria* (Fig. 11-5C). Specimens of *R. thomsonii* are known from Middle Devonian (Givetian) sediments from several geographic regions (United States, Europe, U.S.S.R.). The genus has a long and complex history dating from 1871, when the first specimen was described. The reader is referred to the excellent summary of the nomenclature of the genus provided by Leclercq and Bonamo (1971, 1973). Recently discovered specimens, including impressions, compressions, and partial petrifactions, reveal a plant that was shrubby, consisting of helically arranged branches of four orders. Terminating these branches are ultimate appendages, the leaves or fertile organs. Some of the largest branches are about 2.5 cm in diameter and contain lobed mesarch primary xylem surrounded by pycnoxylic secondary xylem with bordered-pitted tracheids and high, narrow vascular rays. Surrounding the secondary xylem is a well-developed cortex with the "sparganum" arrangment of sclerenchyma bands.

The fertile branch of *Rellimia* contains vegetative segments below and fertile structures distally. The axis of the fertile unit branches once into two first-order pinnae, each with three or four pinnate subdivisions that contain sporangia. Sporangia are attached at three or four levels of the pinna, forming an overlapping massive structure. Sporangia are about the same size as those of *Tetraxylopteris* and produce spores of the *Rhabdosporites* type. Although the taxon was originally thought to be heterosporous, recent studies confirm the homosporous nature of the plant. At present, *Rellimia* and *Tetraxylopteris* may be distinguished by the once dichotomized fertile organ and helical branching in the former.

There are several additional taxa included within the Aneurophytales because of the anatomic similarities they share with *Aneurophyton, Tetraxylopteris,* and *Rellimia.* In none, however, have the fertile parts been identified. One of these is the genus *Proteokalon.* This Upper Devonian plant is known from petrified axes displaying two orders of branching, the second of which reveals planated ultimate appendages. The stele of *P. petryi* is four-armed in cross section, with the number of mesarch protoxylem strands as high as 36 in first-order branches. In second order branches, the primary xylem is three-lobed. Secondary xylem tracheids are typically four-angled, with crowded pits on the radial walls. Like most members of the Progymnospermophyta, *Proteokalon* contains secondary phloem fibers, tanniniferous cells, rays, and phloem parenchyma.

Another plant tentatively placed with the aneurophytes is *Cairoa.* The genus is known from a petrified axis approximately 1.0 cm in diameter containing a three-lobed mesarch protostele. The morphology of the ultimate appendages is not known, but the dichotomizing terete traces in the cortex suggest that the appendages were forked close to the insertion point with the branch that produced them.

An interesting axis that also contains a four-lobed protostele (Fig. 11-6B) is *Stauroxylon* (Lower Carboniferous of France). Branching is decussate, with some parenchyma associated with the mesarch bundles. Tracheal pitting is scalariform, an unusual feature among the Progymnospermophyta, but possibly the result of preservation. Nothing is known about the fertile parts, but the basic organization of the stele and stratigraphy make it a tempting plant to link with Mississippian seed plants.

Another Lower Carboniferous plant that appears to occupy an intermediate position is *Triradioxylon.* This genus is similar to members of the Progymnospermophyta in many features, including the trilobed protostele with the primary bundles near the ends of the lobes and anatomy of the secondary xylem. Other histologic features (sparganum cortex, sclerotic nests, and secretory canals) and the morphology and anatomy of the petioles in *T. primaevum* suggest affinities with early seed plants. On the basis of information now available, the taxon may be only slightly removed evolutionarily from the Aneurophytales.

PROTOPITYALES

The Protopityales were initially described by Walton (Fig. 11-7A) and are represented by a single Lower Carboniferous genus, *Protopitys*. The stem of *P. scotica* is about 6.0 mm in diameter and probably gave rise to distichously attached laterals. In cross section, the central region contains an elliptical parenchymatous pith with two endarch primary xylem strands located at each end of the pith. The pits on the radial walls of the secondary xylem tracheids are elliptical. The sporangia are terminal on recurved ultimate axes and are produced in relatively small clusters (Fig. 11-7B). Invidivual sporangia are about 3.0 mm long and contain spherical, smooth-walled trilete spores that range from 82 to 163 μm in diameter. It is probable that the taxon was homosporous, although so few specimens are known that heterospory cannot be ruled out.

CONCLUSION

Despite important gaps in our knowledge regarding several members of the Progymnospermophyta, there are some evolutionary trends that appear to be evident. These include a shift from three-dimensional branching systems to those which are planated, from helical to decussate branching, from consistent outline of the stele throughout the branching orders to changes in stele configuration at higher levels of branching, from protosteles to siphonostele, from uniform tracheal pitting on all walls to restricted pits on radial walls, from highly dissected and dichotomous ultimate appendages to those which are

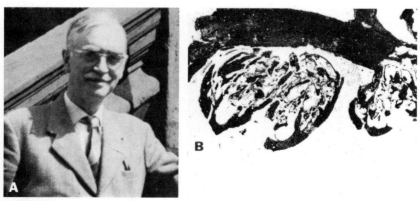

Figure 11-7 A. John Walton. B. Portion of the fertile organ of *Protopitys scotica*. ×1.6. *(A courtesy of H. Banks; B from Walton, 1957.)*

laminar, from azonate spores to zonate spores with sporoderm differentiation in the form of a pseudosaccus, and from homospory to heterospory. In addition, there appears to be some relationship between the known geologic occurrence of the various taxa within the Aneurophytales and the size, number of xylem arms and protoxylem strands, and the amount of parenchyma increasing in younger taxa.

Many authors have commented on the relationship between the Progymnospermophyta and the gymnosperms. There can be little doubt that the lateral branch systems of the Archaeopteridales exhibit the major features of conifer lateral-branching systems. Similarily, recent studies have shown the basic relationship between the stelar organizations of the progymnosperms and the primitive and extant gymnosperms (Namboodiri and Beck, 1968a, b, and c). Other features that strengthen the idea of an evolutionary relationship between these plants include the presence of secondary phloem, periderm, and the morphologically similar spores that are only slightly removed from some Carboniferous pollen types.

As progymnosperms become more completely known, it may be possible to identify the major groups of geologically younger plants with which they are most closely related. The Aneurophytales have been suggested as the potential progenitors of such Lower Carboniferous seed ferns as the Lyginopteridales, possible through the calamopityeans. The structural similarities in the wood of *Archaeopteris* (*Callixylon*) and the Coniferales has been used to suggest the close phylogenetic relationship between these two groups. However, as the genus *Archaeopteris* becomes more completely known, the time may be not too far off when it will be necessary to recognize several distinct genera within *Archaeopteris*. Some archaeopterids may be related to Carboniferous coniferophytes, while others may be associated with certain seed ferns.

Still another idea that is gaining popularity suggests that the Archaeopteridales may be closely related to an enigmatic group of plants referred to as the Noeggerathiales in some treatments. This is an interesting assemblage of plants that can be traced from the Upper Carboniferous into the Triassic. These plants represent a highly artificial group that has been regarded as closely allied to the sphenophytes by some and associated with ferns by others. Bierhorst (1971) has suggested that these fossils demonstrate tmesipteroid features and includes them at the familial level with the Psilotaceae.

Noeggerathia is the generic name used for leafy shoots bearing two opposite rows of leaves. Leaves are obovate and characteristically obliquely attached to the stems. The foliar organs may be several centimeters in length and are vascularized by numerous dichotomizing veins that terminate near the margin. In *N. chalardii*, the margin consists of delicate, elongate segments, while in others, the leaf margin appears entire. Reproductive organs are produced at the ends of vegetative branches in the form of a single cone (Fig. 11-8A). The basic cone organization consists of bractlike units arranged in semicircular disks around an axis. Sporangia are located on the upper surfaces of the disks in rows, but it is not known whether the sporangia are borne at the ends of sporangiopho-

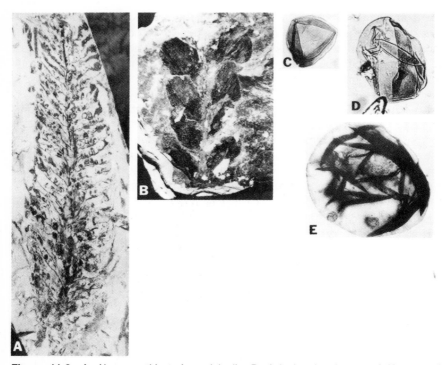

Figure 11-8 A. *Noeggerathiostrobus vicinalis*. B. Axis bearing leaves of *Noeggerathia*. C. Microspore of *Discinites*. D. Microspore of *Noeggerathiostrobus vicinalis*. E. Megaspore of *Discinites*. *(From Remy and Remy, 1956.)*

res attached to the bract surface or attached to the axis of the cone. Two types of spores are known. The smaller microspores are triangular in outline and trilete (Fig. 11-8D). Megaspores are larger (approximately 125 μm) and also trilete. Although the cones are presumed to be bisporangiate, the arrangement of the two sporangial types is not known.

Another bisporangiate cone often included in this group because of the arrangement of the bractlike units is *Discinites*. Specimens are Paleozoic and are organized in whorls of disks borne at closely spaced intervals along the axis. The upper surface of each disk is covered with several rows of apparently sessile sporangia. In one specimen collected from the Permian of Texas, the cone is approximately 4.5 cm long and contains 11 disk whorls. Each disk is approximately 2.5 cm in diameter; the distal margin is dissected into sharply tapered teeth. Sporangia are approximately 2.0 mm in diameter and are crowded on the adaxial surfaces of the disks. Spores have been recovered from *D. hlizae* and include microspores in the 60 to 100 μm range (Fig. 11-8C), while the megaspores are about 770 μm in diameter (Fig. 11-8E).

A similar cone organization is present in *Lacoea*. *Lacoea seriata* is a Lower Pennsylvanian taxon that consists of disks arranged around a central axis. The margin of each disk is dissected into elongate, tapering segments. Numerous diamond- to pyriform-shaped areas identify the position of sporangia in the compressed specimens. Nothing is known about the spores of this genus.

A foliage type that is similar to *Noeggerathia* but has longer leaves that are anisophyllous and borne in four vertical rows is *Tingia*. Leaves on the upper surface of the rachis are large and decurrent at the base, while those on the lower surface of the rachis are narrow and less variable in morphology. Venation consists of a single bundle that enters the leaf base and then dichotomizes several times in a short distance to produce numerous parallel veins. Reproductive organs attached to foliage of the *Tingia* type are given the generic name *Tingiostachys*. Cones may be up to 6.0 cm long and are constructed of four sporophylls per whorl. The distal ends of the sporophylls are sharply upturned. On the adaxial surface of each is a large, tetralocular sporangium that is rectangular in outline. It is not known whether the sporangia were attached to the sporophyll by a small stalk or were sessile on the surface. The spores are elongate and up to 150 μm in the long axis. Nothing is known about the suture configuration of the spores of these presumably monosporangiate cones.

The apparent adaxial position of the sporangia has suggested to some that *Tingiostachys* should be associated with the Lycophyta. Others have pointed to the loculate organization of the sporangium as synangiate and have argued in favor of affinities with *Tmesipteris* of the Psilotaceae. At the present time, Boureau (1964) treats the group at the ordinal level within the Noeggerathiophyta. One potential new source of information that may have some bearing on the systematic position of these plants is the spores. Ultrastructural studies of the sporoderm may demonstrate some features that can be used to identify the natural affinities of these plants. An examination of spores recovered from some cones in the group may prove rewarding. Finally, it will be interesting to see what the anatomy of the reproductive organs of these plants looks like because morphologically there is a potentially close homology to a fertile branch of *Archaeopteris*.

Chapter 12

The Origin and Evolution of the Seed Habit

The origin and evolution of the seed habit is a fascinating subject that is well-documented by the fossil record. There are several basic aspects to the way seeds evolved, including the establishment of the integumentary system (seed coats), formation of the pollen-receiving mechanism, and reduction in the number, size, and function of the spores.

HOMOSPORY AND HETEROSPORY

Thus far, only vascular plants possessing a pteridophytic method of reproduction have been discussed. In homosporous plants, all the spores produced were morphologically alike (isopores) and are believed to have germinated to form free-living gametophytes (exosporic). With the exception of the spore, almost nothing is known about the gametophytic phase of fossil homosporous plants. In heterosporous plants, the megagametophyte developed inside the spore wall (endosporic), a feature that certainly provided a greater opportunity for the delicate cells of the gametophyte to be preserved. Although details about the microgametophytes of most heterosporous plants are not known, there have been numerous reports of exceptionally well-preserved megagametophytes in most of the major groups of fossilized vascular plants. Some of the details have been discussed in earlier sections, especially those dealing with the arborescent lycopods.

Most regard the origin of the seed habit as a logical progression that began with homospory, was followed by stages of heterospory, and culminated in the structure termed a seed. Less agreement may be found regarding when these various events took place, and still less concerning what structural modifications were necessary for seeds to evolve. Although there is little doubt that the first vascular plants were homosporous, precisely when they first appeared is a matter of continuing debate. Some workers have suggested that pre-Devonian trilete spores demonstrate the existence of vascular plants, even though associated megafossils have not been identified. Others believe that to be a bona fide vascular plant, there must be evidence of vascular tissue and cuticle. It was already mentioned in Chap. 2 that caution must be exercised in interpreting the trilete mark present on the face of some Precambrian spores, and the same comments suffice here relative to whether a spore was produced by a bryophyte, some alga, or a vascular plant. It is also important to underscore that many of the earliest plants cannot be classified easily because they possess features shared by several groups.

A review of the literature dealing with isolated spores (*sporae dispersae*) recovered from the maceration of Devonian sediments indicates that not only were there spores of differing sizes, but also spores with different morphological shapes and patterns of ornamentation. Chaloner (1967) plotted the stratigraphic range of 74 genera of spores as they occurred in stages of the Devonian and Silurian. The histograms he developed (Fig. 12-1) indicate that there was an increase in the number of taxa moving progressively from the Silurian through the Devonian. In addition, these data show an increase in the size of the spores

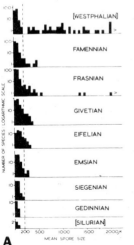 

Figure 12-1 A. Histogram showing the frequency in numbers of spore species and diameter suggestive of evolution of heterospory. B. Albert Charles Seward. *(A from Chaloner, 1967; B courtesy of A. Scott.)*

from the Lower to Middle Devonian and a segregation into small spores and megaspores by the Emsian. The presence of these two spore sizes is indicative of the first appearance of heterospory. The 200 μm size established for separating small spores from megaspores was initially arbitrary, but this size distinction appears to be supported by Chaloner's findings. It must be emphasized that the shift from small spore to megaspore was not an abrupt event, but one that was gradual, and involved a reduction, possibly predicated on nutritional require-ments, such that a smaller number of larger spores could be produced. In interpreting Devonian spores, it is also quite probable that some of the taxa reflect both microspores and megaspores that, although morphologically identi-cal, functioned in quite different ways. Unfortunately, the fossil record does not tell us whether the changes in spore size preceded or followed the shift from exosporic to endosporic gametophytes, but it appears almost certain that the protection afforded by the spore wall was associated with nutritional aspects of the newly encapsulated megagametophyte.

One interesting plant that provides some indirect evidence regarding the shift from the isospores of homosporous plants to the microspores and megaspores of a free-sporing heterosporous plant is *Barinophyton* (Fig. 12-2A). This Devonian to Lower Carboniferous genus consists of naked branches that are alternately arranged, with sporangia organized in two rows on laterally born spikelike fructifications. The unusual feature of *Barinophyton* is that both microspores and megaspores have been extracted from the same sporangium. In *B. richardsonii,* a thin, wrinkled membrane, possible a perine, is present on some grains. The megaspores are also trilete and range from 200 to 250 μm in diameter. They are ornamented with delicate punctae. Recently, Brauer (1979) described some structurally preserved specimens of *B. citrulliforme* from the Devonian of New York. The vascular system consists of an exarch protostele (Fig. 12-2E) with tracheids that possess a continuous secondary wall plicated into the cell lumen that simulates annular secondary wall thickenings. Between the plications, the wall contains numerous delicate pits, each with a recognizable border. The sporangiferous appendages are alternate and two-ranked; below the axis each appendage is recurved and bears one large sporangium inside the curve on the concave surface (Fig. 12-2C). In each oval bisexual sporangium are several thousand trilete microspores up to 50 μm in diameter and approximately 30 trilete megaspores ranging up to 900 μm in diameter (Fig. 12-2D).

There are some heterosporous species of *Archaeopteris* (*A. jacksonii* and *A. latifolia*) that also appear to have lacked sex-determined sporangia and possibly were not far removed from their homosporous ancestors. In these species, the sporangia are about the same size and contain either a large number of microspores in the 35 to 70 μm size range or a smaller number of larger megaspores (110 to 137 μm). The number of megaspores per sporangium is variable (9 to 16 in *A. latifolia* and 9 to 48 in *A. jacksonii*), and although they were morphologically identical to the microspores, there was some correlation between the number of spores and their size. Another Devonian plant that appears to represent an early stage in the evolution of heterospory is *Chaleuria*.

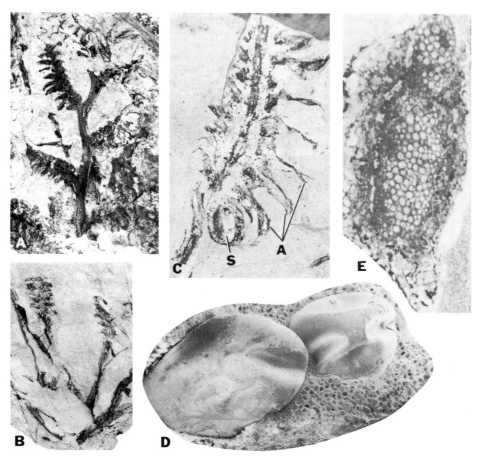

Figure 12-2 A. *Barinophyton obscurum*. B. Portion of a fertile axis of *Protobarinophyton* from the Price Formation of Virginia. C. Portion of a strobilar axis of *Barinophyton citulliforme* showing sporangiferous appendages (A) and sporangium (S). ×1. D. Two *Barinophyton citulliforme* megaspores embedded in microspores. ×40. E. Transverse section through the main axis of *Barinophyton citulliforme*. ×30. *(A courtesy of F. Hueber; B courtesy of S. Scheckler; C–E courtesy of D. Brauer.)*

In this plant, the main axis bears helically arranged branches that in turn bear branchlets that terminate in pairs of elongate sporangia (see Fig. 12-4B). The sporangia contain either small (30 to 48 μm) or large (60 to 156 μm) spores or, in some, both types. Both the microspores and megaspores are trilete, but they differ slightly in the nature of the exine ornamentation.

By the Upper Devonian, some plants produced megaspores that exceeded a millimeter in diameter. One of these was *Cystosporites devonicus*, the binomial assigned to a tetrad of spores from the Escuminac Formation of Canada. The tetrad consists of a large (2.2 mm long), saclike spore with a trilete mark on the proximal surface. In some specimens, the trilete suture is obscured by three smaller (approximately 100 μm diameter), presumably abortive spores. The sporoderm (exine) of the functional spore is about 15 μm thick and relatively smooth; extending from the distal pole is a stalklike process. Ornamentation of the abortive spores consists of conical projections. The size of the *C. devonicus* tetrad and the presence of a delicate membrane (tapetal membrane) surrounding the four spores suggest that each tetrad represents the contents of a single sporangium. Nothing is known about the nature of the sporangium that produced *C. devonicus*, although the single functional megaspore and three smaller abortive spores parallel the organization present in certain Carboniferous members of the Lycophyta. For example, the megasporangia of *Lepidocarpon*, and *Achlamydocarpon* all contained a single, large (approximately 1.0 cm long) functional megaspore and three smaller abortive spores attached to the proximal surface. When found dispersed, these megaspores are assigned to the genus *Cystosporites*. The exine is unusual in that it consists of anastomosing rods of sporopollenin that provide a very porous and presumably elastic matrix for the sporoderm. Surrounding the megasporangium in these forms are various outgrowths of the megasporophyll that some have likened to integuments. It has been suggested that in these lycopods the megaspores were shed from the sporangium in the typical free-sporing manner. This assumption has been based on the occurrence of numerous isolated *Cystosporites* megaspores in such sediments as coal. However, there are several reasons why it appears that these spores were not released from the sporangium at maturity. One concerns the very resistant nature of the megaspore, which may have prevented alteration during diagenesis and the formation of coal. The enormous size of the spore also detracts from it being shed from the sporangium at maturity, as does the fact that as far as this author is aware, no lepidocarps have ever been found lacking evidence of a megaspore. Thus, in the case of at least one group of nonseed plants, retention of a single, large functional megaspore was accomplished by the beginning of the Carboniferous and probably much earlier, during the Devonian. It is worth noting that although the functional and abortive megaspores of these lycopds possess trilete sutures, which indicates tetrad production of the tetrahedral type, the sutures are quite small and unlike those of the Devonian heterosporous spores previously described. This fact is of interest because, with only a few exceptions, there appears to have been a distinct shift from tetrahedral to linear tetrads with the establishment of the seed habit. One of these exceptions involves the lagenostomalean ovule *Conostoma anglo-germanicum*, which has been described recently with three aborted spores situated between the trilete arms of the functional megaspore (see Fig. 13-29B).

The fossil record provides no evidence as to whether megaspore retention preceded or followed the reduction to a single, functional megaspore per sporangium, nor is it possible to determine at what stage in the evolution of the reproductive system the distal end of the nucellus became modified for pollen reception or precisely when the forerunners to the integuments were established.

DEVONIAN SEEDS

Morphologically, a seed consists of a central body, the nucellus, surrounded by one or two sheathing integuments or seed coats. In the case of gymnospermous ovules, a cellularized megagametophyte develops inside the megaspore. In discussions of fossil plants, the terms seed and ovule are often used interchangeably, even though the term ovule may be more appropriate because evidence of embryo formation is very rare in Paleozoic seeds.

The oldest known structure that is definitely a seed is *Archaeosperma arnoldii,* a specimen collected from the Upper Devonian (Famennian) of Pennsylvania. It consists of two-seeded cupules that were apparently produced in pairs on dichotomously branched axes (Fig. 12-3A). Each cupule is about 1.5 cm long and contains two short pedicels, each bearing a small seed. The seeds of *A. arnoldii* are flask-shaped and about 4.2 mm long. At the apex of each seed the integument is serrated into a number of lobes that form a rudimentary micropyle (Fig. 12-3B). Because the specimens are compressed, it is not possible to determine any histologic features of the integument, nor is preservation sufficient that details of the distal end of the nucellus could be determined. Thus nothing is known about the pollen-receiving mechanism of *Archaeosperma.* Because of the resistant nature of the exine, it was possible to macerate megaspore tetrads from the seeds; others were obtained by bulk maceration of the sediments. The largest tetrad is about 3.8 mm long and 1.7 mm wide. A

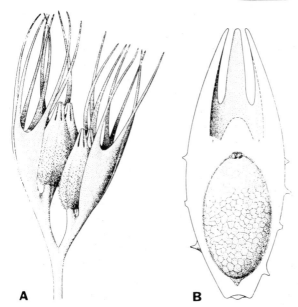

A   **B**

Figure 12-3 *Archaeosperma arnoldii.* A. Suggested reconstruction of a cupule containing four seeds. B. Isolated seed showing functional megaspore and integumentary lobes. *(From Pettitt and Beck, 1968.)*

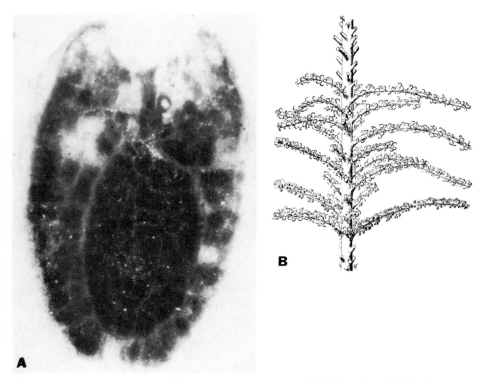

Figure 12-4 A. Compression of *Spermolithus devonicus.* ×32. B. Portion of *Chaleuria cirrosa* showing general habit. *(A courtesy of W. Chaloner; B from Andrews, Gensel, and Forbes, 1974.)*

complete tetrad consists of one large functional megaspore and three smaller, tetrahedrally arranged megaspores attached to the proximal surface. On the proximal surface of the functional spore is a small trilete suture; the entire tetrad is covered with a delicate nucellar membrane. Although certain structural features of *Archaeosperma* remain to be determined, the seeds do substantiate the existence of gymnosperms by the Upper Devonian. The parent plant that produced *Archaeosperma* is not known, but it is almost certain that the cupulate seeds were produced by some plant now included in the Progymnospermophyta. For example, some species of *Archaeopteris* existed that were heterosporous, while others (e.g., *A. fissilis* and *A. macilenta*) were clearly homosporous. Some of these presumably homosporous forms may have functioned as the pollen-producing phase of a seed plant such as *Archaeosperma arnoldii.* Recent ultrastructural evidence of the sutures of these grains shows a close correspondence to the trilete pollen produced by the slightly younger seed plants of some Lyginopteridales. Morphologically similar branching axes, apparently producing cupulelike structures, have been described from Upper Devonian sediments (Belgium) under the generic names *Moresnetia* and *Rancaria.* Unlike *Archaeosperma,* no seeds have been identified in these fossils.

One interesting seed recently reported from the Upper Devonian of southern Ireland is *Spermolithus devonicus* (Fig. 12-4A). It was preserved as a compression, and it is interesting because it appears to have been bilaterally symmetrical. Since the oldest known seeds include both platyspermic and radial types, it appears that the two groups either diverged from a basic seed type earlier than the Upper Devonian or the integuments evolved in more than one way.

CARBONIFEROUS SEEDS

The fossil record indicates that by the Lower Mississippian the seed habit was well established in several groups. Numerous ovules, some contained in cupules, are known from a variety of preservational states. In the absence of information bearing on the question of what plants produced these seeds, some authors have attempted to systematically treat the detached ovules by assigning them to one of three groups (orders) on the basis of symmetry and organization of certain tissue systems. These include the Trigonocarpales, which are characterized by large, radially symmetrical seeds that have a nucellus attached to the integument only at the base. Some members of this group contain vascular tissue in both the integument and nucellus. Some of these seeds [e.g., *Pachytests* (see Fig. 13-20A), *Stephanospermum,* and *Hexapterospermum* (see Fig. 13-10E)] were produced by members of the Medullosales. Bilaterally flattened seeds with simple pollen chambers and vascular tissue only in the integument are often included in the Cardiocarpales. Some of these seeds (e.g., *Cardiocarpus* and *Mitrospermum*) were borne on stems assigned to the Cordaitales and other coniferlike Paleozoic plants. Seeds of the third group, the Lagenostomales, are typically small and possess an integument that is adnate with the nucellus except at the seed apex. Vascular tissue is confined to the inner portion of the integument, and in many species, the pollen-receiving device is complex. A large number of the seeds of this order were produced in cupules, with most of the Lower Carboniferous forms assigned here. These seeds are of particular importance because they demonstrate a number of morphologic features that have been helpful in interpreting not only stages in the origin of the seed habit, but subsequent evolutionary trends as well. Space does not permit a detailed treatment of all the Mississippian seeds; only a few of the more important ones will be considered here, and others will be treated in the first section of Chap. 13 (Lyginopteridales).

One seed that combines features of all these groups is *Menaisperma,* a compression specimen discovered in Lower Carboniferous deposits in North Wales. The seed is about 7.0 mm long and is characterized by an entire integument, much like seeds typically assigned to the Trigonocarpales and Cardiocarpales. The attachment of the nucellus only at the base of the seed is another feature that suggests affinities with these groups. As in modern cycads, stomata are present on the nucellus of *M. greenlyii,* a feature not previously reported in Paleozoic seeds.

One of the simplest Lower Carboniferous seeds is *Genomosperma kidstonii* (Fig. 12-5A). The petrified specimens are known from several localities in Scotland, all stratigraphically within the famous Cementstone Group. The seeds

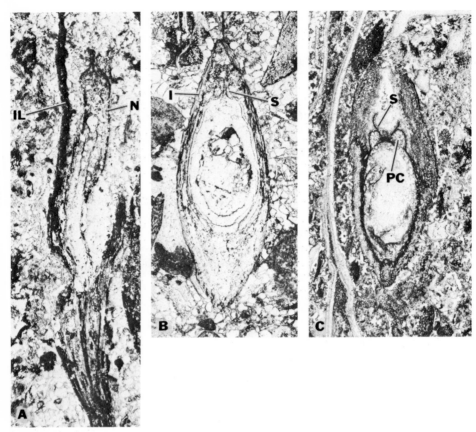

Figure 12-5 A. Longitudinal section of *Genomosperma kidstonii* showing integumentary lobes (IL) and nucellus (N). ×11.5. B. Longitudinal section of *Genomosperma latens* with investing integument (I) and salpinx (S). ×6.5. C. Longitudinal section of *Eurystoma angulare* showing pollen chamber (PC) and salpinx (S). ×9. *(From A. G. Long Collection Nos. 918, 1605, and 10316 in the Hancock Museum.)*

are radially symmetrical (about 1.5 cm long) and are borne on a small pedicel. The integument consists of 8 to 11 free lobes that surround the megasporangium or nucellus (Fig. 12-6A). Each of the lobes contains a single, terete vascular strand. There is no micropyle in this seed. The nucellus and integument are fused only at the base; distally the nucellus forms a ring-shaped pollen chamber with a central parenchymatous core. Small (31 × 38 μm) trilete pollen grains are present in the pollen chambers of some specimens. In another species, *G. latens* (Fig. 12-6C), the integumentary lobes are fused to a greater extent at the distal end (Fig. 12-5B). Although no cupulelike structures have been found associated with these seeds, the large number of specimens and their size suggest that they may have been borne in some form of enclosing structure or cupule.

There are numerous examples of other Lower Carboniferous seeds that demonstrate various stages in the evolution of the integument. In some of these, such as *Conostoma* (Fig. 12-10A) and *Lagenostoma* (see Fig. 13-2B), the

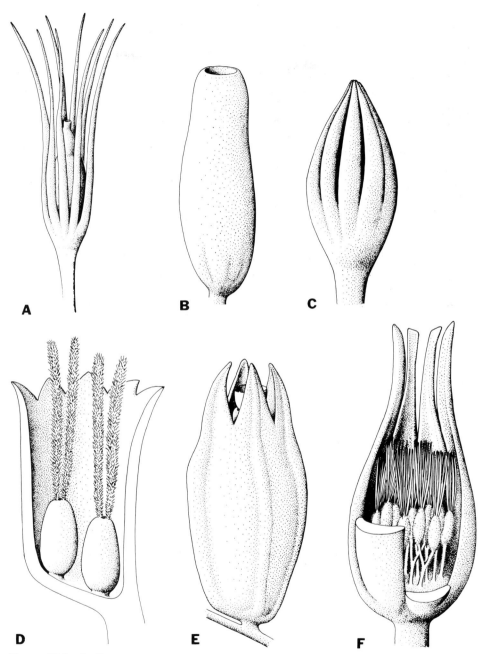

Figure 12-6   A. *Genomosperma kidstonii*. B. *Stamnostoma huttonense*. C. *Genomosperma latens*. D. *Gnetopsis* cupule with two seeds. E. *Eurystoma angulare*. F. *Calathospermum* cupule containing several stalked seeds. *(From Taylor and Millay, 1979.)*

micropyle is well-defined by the fusion of the integumentary lobes. An examination of the distal end of the nucellus in many of these seeds shows an interesting relationship between the evolution of the pollen-receiving mechanism and the micropyle. In seeds with widely separated and free integumentary lobes, the distal end of the nucellus is organized into a large, funnel-shaped device (Fig. 12-6E). This structure, which has been termed a salpinx (Fig. 12-7A), obviously functioned in the absence of a micropyle to direct pollen grains into the pollen chamber. In a seed such as *Eurystoma,* the salpinx is conspicuous (Fig. 12-5C) and up to 1.0 mm in diameter. With evolutionary fusion of integumental lobes, the micropylar orifice was formed, eliminating the

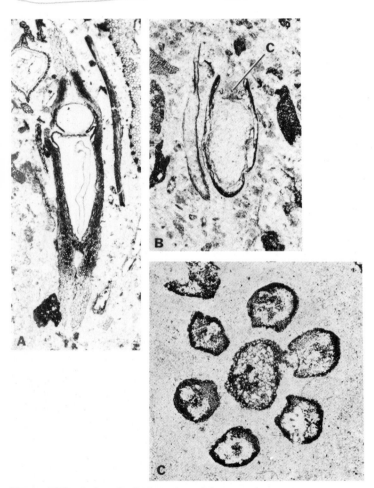

Figure 12-7 A. Longitudinal section of *Lyrasperma scotica.* ×6.5. B. Longitudinal section of *Stamnostoma huttonense* with central column (C). ×9.5. C. Transverse section of *Salpingostoma dasu* showing six free apical integumentary lobes surrounding the pollen chamber. ×9. *(From A. G. Long Collection Nos. 2015, 805, and 10272 in the Hancock Museum.)*

necessity for ornate pollen-catching structures. In geologically younger seeds, the distal end of the nucellus is differentiated into a simple pollen chamber with a nucellar beak that directly communicates with the micropylar canal, and it is interesting that by Pennsylvanian time, almost all the seeds with simple pollen chambers also had well-developed micropyles. Thus, it appears that in the early stages of the evolution of the seed habit the nucellus initially functioned to capture wind-borne pollen. Later, as evolutionary modifications of the seed habit continued, this function was taken over by the integument through evolution of the micropyle.

Not all the early seeds had elaborate pollen-receiving structures. Some seeds, such as *Genomosperma*, lack a highly differentiated nucellus. In some of these early seeds that lack micropyles, pollen grains may have been trapped by other methods, such as pollination droplets or hairs and other processes that may have aided in directing pollen flow. In *Salpingostoma* (Fig. 12-7C), for example, hairs lined both the inner and outer surfaces of the integument lobes (see Fig. 12-10C), while in the seed *Tantallosperma*, thought to have been produced on stems of *Buteoxylon*, pollen grains have been found associated with the bristlelike processes that extend from the integument. A slightly different method of pollen capture has been suggested for seeds of *Physostoma* (Fig. 12-8B). Here the outer surface of the integument is covered with tentaclelike projections (see Fig. 12-10A) that are thought to have produced a sticky material that aided in pollen capture. Once pollen made its way into the pollen chamber in these Lower Carboniferous seeds, the pollen chamber was sealed off by the

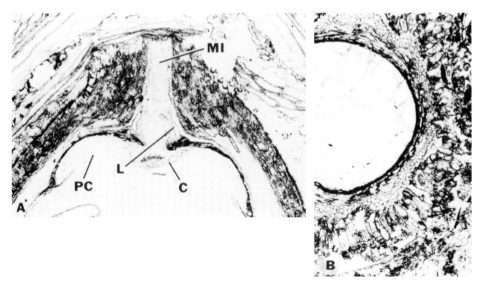

Figure 12-8   A. Median longitudinal section of *Conostoma oblongum* showing the micropyle (MI), pollen chamber (PC), lagenostome (L), and central column (C). ×50. B. Partial transverse section of *Physostoma elegans* with elongate integumentary cells. ×13.

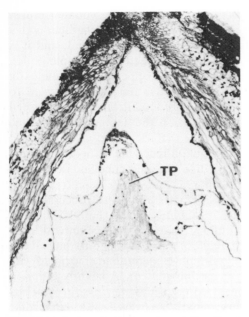

Figure 12-9 Longitudinal section of *Nucellangium glabrum* with well-developed tent pole (TP). ×24. *(From Taylor and Millay, 1979.)*

development of a small cellular pad of tissue in the distal end of the megagametophyte termed a "tent pole" (Fig. 12-9). It has been suggested that in many of these seeds the trapped pollen grains continued to develop and, upon germination, released flagellated gametes.

Not all Lower Carboniferous seeds exhibit all the preceding features, which suggests that there were several concomitant trends in the evolution of the seed during the Lower Carboniferous. In some, integumentary closure appears to have preceded the nucellar differentiation in pollen capture, while in others, just the reverse appears to have taken place. All the earliest seeds were relatively small (see Fig. 12-10B), and many were probably borne in multiovulate cupules. The pollen, when found in the pollen chamber or micropyle, was trilete, germinated from the proximal surface, and was almost identical to the isospores of homosporous plants. There was also a transition in progress regarding the manner in which megaspores were produced. In some compressed seeds, such as *Samaropsis bicaudata,* the large, functional megaspore reveals a trilete suture, while in the majority of others, the absence of a trilete on the proximal pole suggests that they were probably produced in a linear tetrad like extant gymnosperms (see Fig. 12-10A).

EVOLUTION OF THE INTEGUMENT

In discussions regarding the evolution of the seed, the morphologic unit that has received the most attention is the integument. Several of the ideas about the

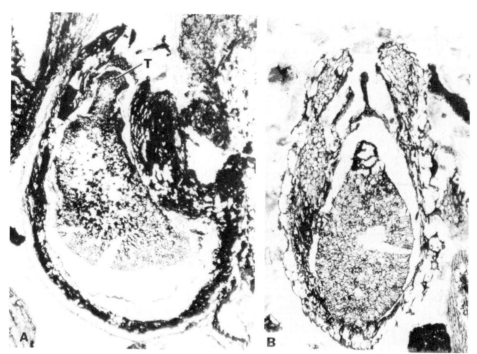

Figure 12-10 A. Cellularized megagametophyte and well-developed tent pole (T) in the Lower Carboniferous (Calciferous sandstone) seed *Camptosperma berniciense*. ×24. B. Longitudinal section of *Deltasperma fouldenense* (Calciferous sandstone). ×24. *(From Taylor and Millay, 1979.)*

origin of the seed integument are of historical interest and worthy of note in light of current paleobotanical evidence. In many cases, these ideas were advanced prior to any fossil evidence that either supported or refuted their credibility. One theory based on fossil evidence has been referred to as the synangial hypothesis. It was suggested by Benson (1904), who believed that the integument evolved from the sterilization of the outer sporangial ring in a radial synangium. During the evolution of the integument from the outer ring of sporangia, the number of spores in the central sporangium was reduced to one functional megaspore. Another early idea hypothesized the evolution of the seed integument from a cuplike indusium. In two other theories, leaves are suggested as the precursors of seed integuments. In one of these, termed the enation theory, a foliar-borne appendage in the form of an enation is believed to have evolved into a megasporangium, with the leaves phylogenetically serving as seed coats. According to the proponents of the axial-bud theory, the megasporangium evolved from a bud, with the associated leaves becoming the integuments. None of these ideas is strongly supported today, and most important, none can be substantiated with fossil evidence.

The coenopterid fern megasporangium *Stauropteris burntislandica* has been used to support a theory termed the nucellar modification concept (Andrews, 1961). According to this idea, a further reduction in the number of megaspores from two to one took place, with the surviving megaspore "sinking" toward the base of the sporangium. All that would be required to evolve a simple seed from the *S. burntislandica* megasporangium would be a further proliferation of the sporangial wall (increase in cellularization) and the subsequent division of the basal vascular bundle to extend into the newly formed integument. The existence of many Paleozoic seeds in which the integument and nucellus are adnate (e.g., *Lagenostoma* and *Conostoma*) lends some support to this idea.

By far the most attractive hypothesis concerning the evolution of the integumentary system is the telome concept, which was developed by Zimmermann (1952). According to this idea, the rhyniophyte dichotomous branching system with some terminal sporangia represents the primitive condition. Through the gradual reduction of some of the axes (telomes and mesomes), a terminal sporangium became enclosed by a ring of sterile branches. At some stage, the distal end of the sporangium became modified for pollen reception, with a possible transitional stage similar to that present in *S. burntislandica*. The "newly" evolved seed would then consist of a naked sporangium surrounded by a ring of vascularized "preintegumentary" lobes. Associated with this modification also would be a change in the contents of the sporangium from several megaspores to one. This is exactly the type of morphologic organization demonstrated by the Lower Carboniferous seed *Genomosperma kidstonii* (Fig. 12-6A). The lateral fusion of the enclosing telomes, with or without nucellar adnation, would result in a vascularized integument surrounding a megasporangium.

Both the telomic and nucellar modification theories appear, in light of available fossil evidence, to provide the best explanations of how the seed integument may have evolved. The most obvious adaptive feature of an integument appears to be one of protection, associated with the shift from free sporing to the retention of a single, large megaspore. Initially, such protection may have been in response to harsh environmental conditions, but later the seed coat may have functioned to protect the megaspores from various insects and other invertebrates that may have used them as an easily accessible nutritional source.

EVOLUTION OF THE CUPULE

The cupule is another structure that morphologically appears to represent an accessory ring of sterile processes. Although stages in the evolution of the cupule are less well defined in the fossil record, there appears to be sufficient evidence to suggest that the cupule was initially a three-dimensional branching system not too unlike the early evolutionary stages of the integument. Some cupules were organized in the form of a loose ring of sterile branches, while others consisted of fused units that formed a more closed structure. A variety of morphologic types are known among the seed ferns and include both uniovulate and multiovulate types.

One seed that is distinctly cupulate is *Eurystoma angulare* (Fig. 12-5C) (from the Calciferous Sandstone Series). The seed measures about 8.0 mm long

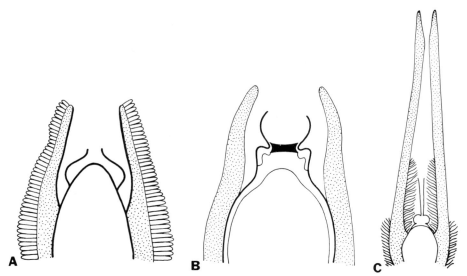

Figure 12-11 A. Distal end of *Physostoma elegans* showing pollen receiving mechanism. B. Distal end of *Eurystoma angulare*. C. Distal end of *Salpingstoma dasu* showing elongate salpinx and inwardly directed integumentary hairs. *(From Taylor and Millay, 1979.)*

and is square in transverse section. At the apex are four vascularized integumentary lobes, each corresponding to an angle of the seed. The nucellus and integument are adnate, except at the distal end, where the nucellar beak (= salpinx) of the pollen chamber flares into a bell-shaped structure (Fig. 12-11B). The cupule consists of a dichotomizing system of branches, with the largest number of sterile lobes about 15. The maximum size of a single cupule system is about 1.5 cm long by 1.1 cm in width. A variable number of ovules were produced (2 to 10), each associated with a sterile member at the end of a dichotomy.

Another species of *Eurystoma, E. trigona,* is characterized by triangular-shaped ovules, each about 4.5 mm long. In one specimen, approximately 330 ovules are attached to a petrified axis that is termed a megasporophyll. The megasporophyll is about 6.0 cm long and morphologically consists of an outer ring of sterile, flattened branches surrounding an inner set of highly dichotomous axes that bear the seeds. The anatomy and branching pattern of this structure has been described as approximating a young, unrolled *Alcicornopteris* frond segment, a genus commonly found associated with the seed fern stem *Stenomyelon.* A similar association has been made between the Lower Carboniferous stem *Tristichia* and seeds and cupules of *Stamnostoma huttonense* (Figs. 12-6B and 12-7B). These cupules consist of dichotomizing axes, each producing four seeds. Long (1966) has suggested that Lower Carboniferous cupules may be divided into three principal groups on the basis of their symmetry and organization. One type contains numerous ovules borne on an entire frond segment. In a second type (also multiovulate), the cupule is regarded as homologous to part of a frond system. The third type is uniovulate and radial in symmetry.

Some authors have suggested that the seed fern cupule is homologous with the second, or outer, integument of an angiosperm ovule. According to this theory, the uniovulate cupule became adnate to the integument of the seed. Others have suggested that Carboniferous multiovulate cupules represent a stage in the evolution of an angiosperm carpel in which one end has become closed through the fusion of the distal lobes. A slightly different morphologic arrangement is present in the cupules that bore seeds of *Hydrasperma* (see Fig. 13-11B) (Lower Carboniferous of East Lothian). These paired cupules are about 6.0 mm wide and are inverted (see Fig. 13-11). Morphologically they consist of two valves, each with 7 to 18 free lobes. Each cupule is multiovulate (up to 16), with the ovules sessile, and attached to the underside of the lobes. In one cupule there is a further subdivision that contains eight microsporangia, but preservation has precluded specific details about the sporangial wall or the contents. If additional specimens indicate that these sporangia were present in the cupule, it will represent the first report of a seed fern cupule containing both seeds and pollen in the same structure. Even their close association on a fertile branch is unusual in light of current ideas regarding how pollen organs and seeds may have evolved.

Long (1977*b*) has used the cupular organizations of *Hydrasperma* to support the hypothesis that the angiosperm carpel evolved from paired seed fern cupules. Other authors have suggested that the anatropous position of some Lower Carboniferous seeds (e.g., *Anasperma*) lends support to the idea that some seed ferns were only slightly removed from some primitive angiosperms. Obviously, more features are needed before an organism can be classified as an angiosperm, and many of these (e.g., double fertilization, stages in embryo development, the presence of endosperm) may never be fully demonstrated by the fossil record. Yet within some Paleozoic and Mesozoic seed ferns, there are morphologic structures that may provide a more complete picture of how a structure such as the carpel may have evolved.

The most obvious explanation for the function of a cupule is one of protection. Other ideas suggest that the cupule was an attractant structure associated with an early entomophilous pollination syndrome or a structure that assisted in directing pollen flow. Proponents of the first idea have suggested that the various glandlike structures that often ornament the cupule surface may have functioned to attract insects.

PALEOZOIC SEED EMBRYOS

Although there are numerous examples of exquisitely preserved embryos in the seeds of many Mesozoic gymnosperms, almost no Paleozoic embryos (Fig. 12-12B) have been reported. One idea used to explain the absence of recognizable embryos in Paleozoic seeds is the suggestion that delayed development occurred after dispersal, such as the condition in modern *Ginkgo* seeds.

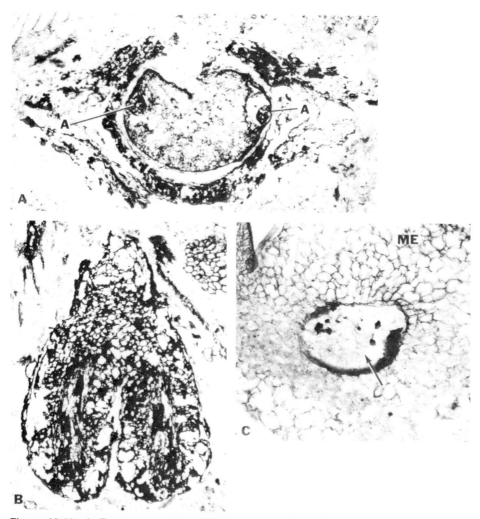

Figure 12-12 A. Transverse section of *Lyrasperma scotica* with two archegonia (A). ×40. B. Possible Lower Carboniferous embryo with two cotyledons. ×40. C. Archegonial chamber in megagametophyte (ME) of *Nucellangium glabrum* with remains of possible proembryo *(arrow)*. ×67. *(From Taylor and Millay, 1979.)*

Other workers have suggested that embryos were quickly formed and escaped the protective seed coats, or that they simply have not been properly identified or discovered to date. Two recent reports suggest that stages in the development of the embryo are preserved in Paleozoic sediments. Ovules of *Nucellangium* have been reported with well-developed archegonia in the distal end of the megagametophyte (Stidd and Cosentino, 1976). Contained in one archegonium was a small cellular mass that has been described as a proembryo (Fig. 12-12C). A more highly differentiated embryo has been described from Lower Permian conifer seeds collected in west Texas (Miller and Brown, 1973). The slightly flattened seeds are about 1.2 cm long and contain parenchyma tissue and several tracheids within the megagametophyte. The parenchymatous structure is elongate, with the cells histologically distinguishable from the surrounding parenchyma of the megagametophyte.

Pteridospermophyta

The historical development of the Pteridospermophyta is interesting in that it demonstrates how a number of isolated plant parts were recognized as belonging to a previously unknown group of vascular plants. In the late 1800s, the famous French paleobotanist Grand'Eury suggested that various Paleozoic foliage types [e.g., *Alethopteris* (see Fig. 13-17D), *Neuropteris,* and *Odontopteris* (see Fig. 13-17A)] may have been produced on petioles that are now known as *Myeloxylon.* Somewhat later, *Myeloxylon* was demonstrated as the petiole of *Medullosa.* At about the same time, it was suggested that certain foliage types that were regarded as the leaves of ferns may have represented the leaves of some other unknown group of plants. This suggestion was advanced by Stur on the basis of the consistent absence of sporangia on pinnules. In 1887, Williamson (Fig. 13-1A) recognized that the anatomic features of several stems combined structural characters from both cycads and ferns. The studies by these workers were incorporated into the concept of the Cycadofilices by R. Potonié (1899), who, on the basis of strictly anatomic evidence, suggested a group of vascular plants that was transitional between ferns and seed plants. In 1904, two British paleobotanists, F. W. Oliver and D. H. Scott (Fig. 13-1B), established the existence of seed ferns (Pteridospermae) by a remarkable piece of detective work that united stem, petiole, foliage, and most important, seeds of the same plant. It is important to underscore that the initial identification of the group was not based on organic attachment of the parts, but rather on the common occurrence of a peculiar epidermal appendage in the form of a gland on all the plant parts, and the frequent association of the vegetative remains and seeds at the same fossil-bearing localities. Today the group is known in some detail, and it includes three well-defined Carboniferous orders and one of the same age that is based only on anatomically preserved stems and petioles. In the Mesozoic, there were several orders that are believed to have been related to the Paleozoic forms, although the fossil record of some of these is scanty and their identity as seed ferns is sometimes argued.

Some members of the Pteridospermophyta looked much like modern tree ferns, with upright trunks bearing massive fernlike fronds. Other forms were more scrambling in habit and may have resembled lianas. Both pollen-producing organs and seeds were borne on leaves. The microsporangia were aggregated into clusters and, in many instances, formed synangia. Seeds were solitary or grouped in protective structures termed cupules. Manoxylic secondary xylem, which contained thin-walled tracheids and parenchyma, and cortical bands of sclerenchyma characterized most of the stems of these plants; a few stems are known that would be classified as having pycnoxylic wood. Eight distinct orders are recognized.

Lyginopteridales: Carboniferous
Medullosales: Carboniferous-Permian
Callistophytales: Pennsylvanian
Calamopityales: Upper Devonian to Lower Mississippian
Caytoniales: Triassic to Cretaceous
Corystospermales: Triassic
Peltaspermales: Triassic
Glossopteridales: Permian to Triassic

LYGINOPTERIDALES

Despite the historical importance of this group in the recognition of the pteridosperms, it today probably represents the least-understood order of Carboniferous seed ferns. *Lyginopteris*, like many fossil plants, was initially designated as the generic name of a particular organ (stem), but today is regarded as the name for an entire plant. Despite several reports, there is no conclusive evidence that the genus was present in North America during the Carboniferous. Information about the type species *L. oldhamia* comes principally from specimens collected from the Coal Measures of Britain. In transverse section (Fig. 13-2D), the largest eustelic stem is about 4.0 cm in diameter, with a central parenchymatous pith that contains scattered clusters of sclerotic cells. Around the pith region are 5 to 10 mesarch primary xylem strands, with metaxylem tracheids exhibiting multiseriate pits. The amount of secondary

Figure 13-1 A. William Crawford Williamson. B. Dukinfield Henry Scott. *(Reproduced from* Geschichte der Botanik *with the permission of Gustav Fischer Verlag.)*

xylem produced by *Lyginopteris* is relatively small in proportion to the total size of the stem. Secondary xylem consists of large tracheids with angular bordered pits on the radial walls (Fig. 13-3F). In some specimens, a small amount of secondary xylem is apparent toward the pith. This anomalous wood is the apparent result of a vascular cambium that formed secondary xylem toward the inside between the primary bundles. Vascular rays, one to several cells wide, extend through the secondary xylem; some rays are up to 2.0 cm in height.

In well-preserved stems, some thin-walled cells that topographically occupy the position of the phloem have been observed, although sieve areas have not been reported. Outside the phloem is a zone of cells suggestive of a pericycle, and it contains sclerotic nests like those of the pith. Near the outer limits of this zone is a narrow band of periderm. The cortex is divided into two zones; the inner zone is rarely preserved and consists primarily of parenchyma. The outer cortex is relatively extensive and includes parenchyma and, near the periphery of the tissue, bands of fibers that are radially aligned and extend longitudinally in the cortex (Fig. 13-2D). These bands anastomose from level to level, exhibiting a netlike structure when viewed tangentially (Fig. 13-3D). In transverse section, the bands appear similar to the roman numerals of a clock. Partially decorticated stems in which the fibrous bands represent the outer surface and compression fossils of stem surfaces have been said to have a "dictyoxylon cortex."

The epidermis of young stems of *Lyginopteris* is covered with numerous multicellular glands (Fig. 13-2F) that are also present on all other parts of the plant except the roots. They are about 3.0 mm long and consist of a flared base and glandular head; stomata are present on the stalk. The epidermis of the distal

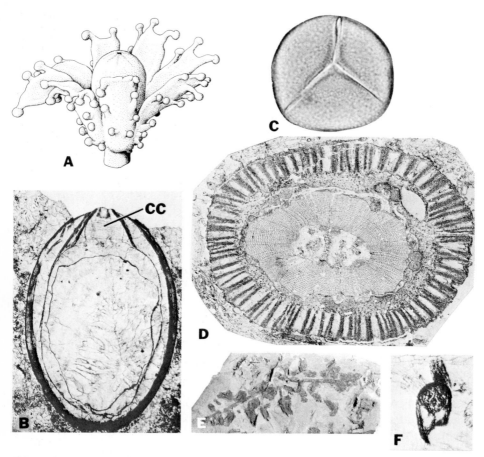

Figure 13-2 A. Suggested reconstruction of *Lagenostoma lomaxi*. B. Longitudinal section of *Lagenostoma lomaxi* showing central column (CC). ×20. C. Proximal surface of *Crossotheca* spore. ×1000. D. Transverse section of *Lyginopteris oldhamia* stem showing secondary xylem and broad cortex with radial fiber bands. ×7. E. *Crossotheca*. ×1. F. Stalked gland from *Lyginopteris* stem. ×40. *(A from Taylor and Millay, 1980.)*

end contains small tubular cells that surround a secretory tissue. Small multicellular hairs are also a common feature of the *Lyginopteris* epidermis.

Traces to the leaves are formed by a tangential division of a primary xylem strand. In the cortex, the trace separates into a pair of strands that fuse in the base of the petiole to form a V- or W-shaped bundle. Petioles with this type of anatomy have been referred to as *Lyginorachis* (Fig. 13-3G). They are produced in a ²⁄₅ phyllotaxy and dichotomize above the lowest pinna (Fig. 13-4C). Pinnae are oppositely to suboppositely arranged, and the large frond is conspicuously planated (Fig. 13-4A and B). Pinnules are lobed and conform to the form genus *Sphenopteris*. They are borne alternately on the small subdivisions of the rachis.

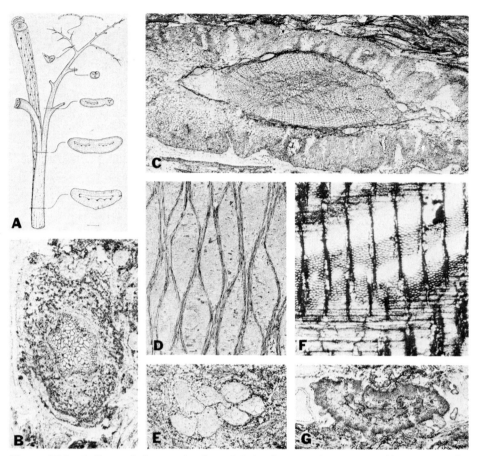

Figure 13-3 A. Suggested reconstruction of *Schopfiastrum decussatum* with representative transverse sections of the frond. B. Transverse section of *Lyginopteris (Kaloxylon)* root. ×200. C. Transverse section of *Schopfiastrum decussatum* stem. ×9. D. Tangential section of *Lyginopteris* outer cortex. ×6.5. E. Transverse section of *Telangium scottii* synangium. ×14. F. Radial section of *Lyginopteris* secondary xylem. ×70. G. Transverse section of *Lyginorachis (Rachiopteris)* petiole. ×10. *(A from Rothwell and Taylor, 1972.)*

Roots of *Lyginopteris* are adventitious, and they are borne on all sides of the stem, occasionally in vertical rows. Some are about 7.0 mm in diameter and contain secretory cells in the cortex. The stele varies from triarch to polyarch (Fig. 13-3B), and some secondary xylem is apparent. The generic name *Kaloxylon* is often used for the roots of *Lyginopteris*.

The best-known seed of *Lyginopteris* has been given the binomial *Lagenostoma lomaxii*. It is ellipsoidal and measures approximately 5.5 mm long and up to 4.2 mm in diameter (Fig. 13-2B). The integument is composed of thick-walled cells in two different zones; those of the inner zone parallel the long

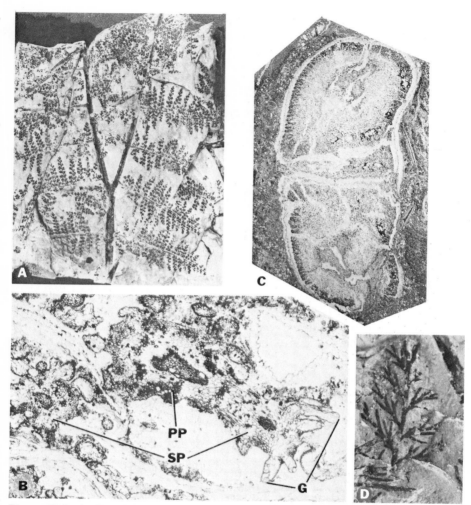

Figure 13-4 A. *Sphenopteris larischi* showing major frond dichotomy. ×0.2. B. *Rachiopteris aspera* at point of dichotomy showing position of primary pinna (PP), secondary pinnae (SP), and glands (G). ×20. C. Transverse section of *Lyginopteris arberi*. ×3. D. Compressed *Rhodea*-like foliage. ×2. *(A from an original photograph by K. H. Haupt, courtesy of R. Daber; C from A. G. Long Collection No. 7179 in the Hancock Museum.)*

axis of the seed, while those of the outer layer are oriented in a radial direction. At the micropylar end of the seed, the integument forms a "canopy" that is dissected into nine locules, each supplied by a vascular strand. Covering the sclerified portion of the integument is a relatively thin zone of parenchyma that is rarely preserved. In *Lagenostoma*, the inner portion of the integument is fused to the nucellus except in the distal region of the seed. Apically, the nucellus consists of an elongate collar or flask-shaped structure (lagenostome) that loosely surrounds a parenchymatous central column (Fig. 13-2B). The distal end of the lagenostome probably projected a short distance above the integument lobes. How the central column functioned in pollen reception is not known. It may have served as a source of the pollination droplet that trapped the wind-borne grains, or it may have somehow directed the grains to the peripherally located archegonia of the megagametophyte. Well-preserved specimens of *L. lomaxii* contain a cellularized megagametophyte within a delicate megaspore membrane. The megagametophyte is differentiated into an outer zone of radially elongate cells and an inner area of isodiametric cells. Up to three ovoid archegonia, lacking neck cells, are present in the distal end of the megagametophyte (see Fig. 13-27A). A triangular-shaped pad of tissue just below the central column in the megagametophyte is present in specimens judged to be mature on the basis of the cellular nature of the megagametophyte and the presence of archegonia. This structure, which has been termed the tent pole, is a common feature of the megagametophyte in several Paleozoic seeds. It may have functioned to seal the pollen chamber, elevate the necks of the archegonia, or rupture the megaspore membrane to allow gamete entrance into the archegonia.

Surrounding each seed is an enclosing structure termed a cupule (Fig. 13-2A). It consists of a series of husks that are fused at the base and longitudinally striated. The upper portion of the cupule consists of free lobes, each with a single, terete vascular strand. The outer surface of the cupule bears the same capitate glands (Fig. 13-2A) that are present on the vegetative parts of *Lyginopteris*. The large number of detached *Lagenostoma* seeds in the fossil record has led some to suggest that they were shed from the cupules at the same stage of development. The tulip-shaped cupules of *Lyginopteris* are often referred to by the generic name *Calymmatotheca*. Cupules are relatively common among many of the earliest seed plants and may have functioned initially as protective structures for the developing ovules. From time to time the cupules of *Lyginopteris* have been suggested as precursor of the angiosperm carpel. *Lagenospermum* is the name applied to compressed seeds that correspond morphologically to *Lagenostoma*. Several dichotomizing branching systems terminating in cupules, each with a single seed, have been described from Lower Mississippian sediments (Price Formation) of Virginia. The cupule ranges up to 3.0 cm long and consists of six apical lobes. The seeds, preserved as casts, measure about 6.0 mm long and 2.0 mm in diameter.

Despite a considerable amount of information about the seeds of *Lyginopteris,* the exact pollen-producing organs have not been demonstrated conclusively. The genus *Crossotheca* (Fig. 13-2E) is often regarded as the microsporangiate unit of *Lyginopteris,* but this relationship has been suggested only because of the association of the organ with *Sphenopteris* foliage and their occurrence at the same stratigraphic level. *Crossotheca mcluckiei* is a common North American species known from Mazon Creek nodules. It consists of a fertile pinna approximately 6.5 cm long that bears opposite, reduced fertile pinnules. Extending from the lower surface are approximately 20 sporangia, each about 1.5 mm long. The spores are about 70 μm in diameter and trilete

(Fig. 13-2C). In *C. sagittata,* possibly the most common North American species, the fertile unit is shaped like an arrowhead, with three basally attached pointed segments or one folded unit. Numerous (30) sporangia up to 4.0 mm long are attached to the lower surface of the slightly flattened pinna. It is suggested that the unusual shape of the synangial unit may have resulted from the fusion of three oval synangia on a small, pinnate frond segment. Basal pinnules of *Pecopteris* or *Sphenopteris* are attached to *Crossotheca* fertile units. If *Crossotheca* was the pollen organ of *Lyginopteris,* the absence of *Lyginopteris* in the North American Carboniferous suggests that *Crossotheca* may in fact represent a basic pollen organ type of several distinct seed fern genera.

The recently described lyginopterid pollen organ *Feraxotheca* (Millay and Taylor, 1977) may represent a different preservational stage of *Crossotheca.* Both fertile and sterile frond segments have been described from Lower Pennsylvanian deposits in Kentucky. The fertile axis includes three orders of branching, with ultimate pinnae alternately arranged (Fig. 13-5). Each fertile unit consists of a basal parenchymatous cushion (see Fig. 13-24D) that supports a variable number (6 to 10) of closely appressed, elongate, exannulate sporangia (Fig. 13-6D). The upper surface of the parenchymatous pad is vascularized, but no vascular tissue extends into the individual sporangia. The central region of the synangium is hollow and dehiscence takes place along the inner-facing sporangial walls. Pollen grains are small (40 to 60 μm), trilete, and ornamented with delicate coni (see Fig. 13-30H). Hypostomatic laminar pinnules are lobed

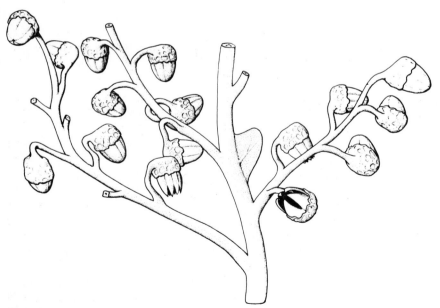

Figure 13-5   Suggested reconstruction of *Feraxotheca culcitaus* fertile frond. *(From Millay and Taylor, 1978.)*

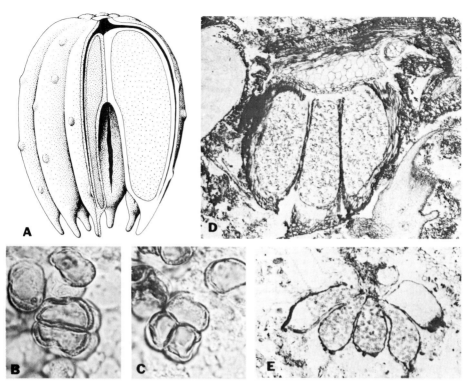

Figure 13-6 A. Suggested reconstruction of *Idanothekion glandulosum* synangium. B. Isobilateral tetrad of *Vesicaspora* pollen. ×1000. C. Decussate tetrad of *Vesicaspora* pollen. ×1000. D. Oblique longitudinal section of *Feraxotheca culcitaus* synangium showing parenchymatous cushion and sporangia. ×25. E. Longitudinal section of *Callandrium callistophytoides* synangium. ×36. *(B, C, and E from Hall and Stidd, 1971; D from Millay and Taylor, 1977.)*

and possess a dichotomous venation pattern. Associated with both vegetative and fertile frond segments of *F. culcitaus* are canals containing a yellow, apparently frothy material. These structures ultimately may provide a clue concerning the other portions of this plant, similar to the association of parts demonstrated in *Lyginopteris.*

Heterangium is a stem somewhat similar to *Lyginopteris,* but known from Carboniferous deposits in both North America and Europe. Stems typically measure about 2.0 cm in diameter, and they are rarely branched. The stem consists of a vitalized or mixed protostele consisting of clusters of tracheids and parenchyma (Fig. 13-7B). At some levels, the parenchyma is arranged in longitudinally oriented plates. The large metaxylem tracheids reveal multiseriate pitting; these grade into smaller tracheary elements near the periphery of the zone that are arranged into about 20 mesarch strands in *H. grievii* (Lower Carboniferous of Pettycur). Surrounding the primary xylem may have been a narrow band of secondary xylem only a few millimeters thick, with pitting on the radial walls. Surprisingly, phloem is preserved in a large number of *Heterangium*

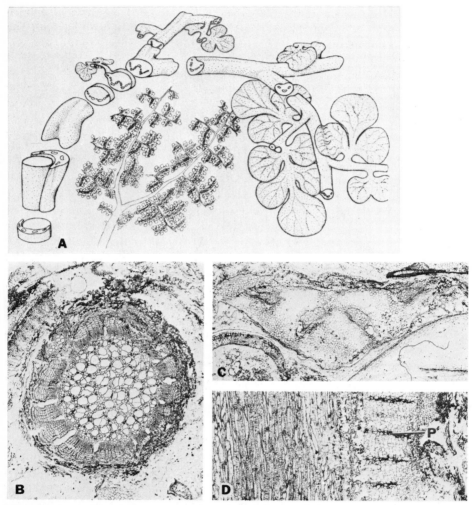

Figure 13-7 A. Suggested reconstruction of a frond of *Heterangium*. B. Transverse section of *Heterangium americanum* stem. ×9. C. Transverse section of *Heterangium* petiole. ×9. D. Longitudinal section through cortex of *Heterangium* stem showing sclerenchyma plates (P). ×12. *(A from Shadle and Stidd, 1975.)*

stems. In *H. americanum* (Upper Pennsylvanian), both primary and secondary phloem are preserved. The primary phloem consists of a small cluster of cells near the periphery of each secondary phloem zone. The secondary phloem is extensively developed and may have exceeded the amount of secondary xylem in width. It consists of elongate sieve cells, phloem parenchyma, and vascular rays that extend out from the secondary xylem. Roots are triarch and may have produced some secondary xylem.

The cortex of *Heterangium* consists of two zones: an inner zone of parenchyma and evenly spaced horizontal plates of thick-walled cells and an outer zone of longitudinally oriented fibers embedded in a parenchyma ground tissue (Fig. 13-7D) that divide as they passed through the cortex, entering the base as four distinct strands. In *H. grievii,* the petiole is supplied by a single trace. Fronds of *H. grievii* have laminar foliage of the *Sphenopteris elegans* type; other species also were associated with *Sphenopteris* foliage. The petiole of an Upper Pennsylvanian *Heterangium* contains 7 to 10 vascular bundles depending on the level. The frond of this species is dichotomized, with small pinnae above (Fig. 13-7A). The vascular bundles in the region of the dichotomy are W-shaped in transverse section. Laminar pinnules of *Sphenopteris obtusiloba* are borne alternately along the secondary pinna axis. Pinnules contain a prominent palisade layer and trichomes on the outer surface. This is similar to the frond morphology of *Lyginopteris.*

Several *Heterangium* stems and petioles have been found in Upper Mississippian sediments, and these are of interest because they demonstrate another type of foliage produced by this plant. The petioles are forked and bear foliage of the *Rhodea* type (Fig. 13-4D). This foliage lacks laminar pinnules, and the distal ends of the pinnae are composed of dichotomous sterile segments. The presence of this frond morphology during the Mississippian supports the concept that the geologically younger *Heterangium* frond evolved through the planation and webbing of a leaf such as that of *Rhodea.* The sporangium-bearing fronds of the Mississippian *Heterangium* species reveal the same anatomy as the sterile axes, but they are terminated by clusters of *Telangiopsis-Telangium* sporangia (Fig. 13-3E).

Another stem that has been included within the Lyginopteridales is *Schopfiastrum* (Fig. 13-3C). This genus was initially described by Andrews in 1954 from two fragments collected in Iowa, and today it is known from a number of Middle Pennsylvanian localities. In general, the stems are slightly larger than those of *Heterangium.* The primary xylem consists of two to four protoxylem strands that surround metaxylem of large, angular tracheids and a few scattered parenchyma cells. In transverse section, the protostele is oval in outline. Surrounding the primary body is a large zone of secondary xylem and wood rays. Tracheids exhibit multiseriate bordered pits with crossed slitlike apertures on the radial walls. Extending longitudinally through the inner cortex and phloem are large (1.0 mm diameter) canals (Fig. 13-3C) typically filled with an amber-colored material regarded as resinous by some authors. In the outer portion of the cortex are longitudinally oriented sclerenchyma strands.

Leaves are borne in *S. decussatum* in a two-ranked, alternate arrangement (Fig. 13-3A). Leaf traces divide repeatedly to produce six or seven protoxylem strands on the abaxial face of a lobed metaxylem band. At higher levels of the frond, the primary pinnae possess a Y-shaped vascular trace from which pinnule traces depart. Laminar pinnules that are morphologically similar to *Sphenopteris* and *Mariopteris* contain mesophyll plates that extend between the adaxial and abaxial surfaces.

The Lower and Middle Pennsylvanian seed fern *Microspermopteris* is known only from North American coal balls. The exarch protostele consists of metaxylem wedges separated by radially oriented plates of parenchyma (Fig.

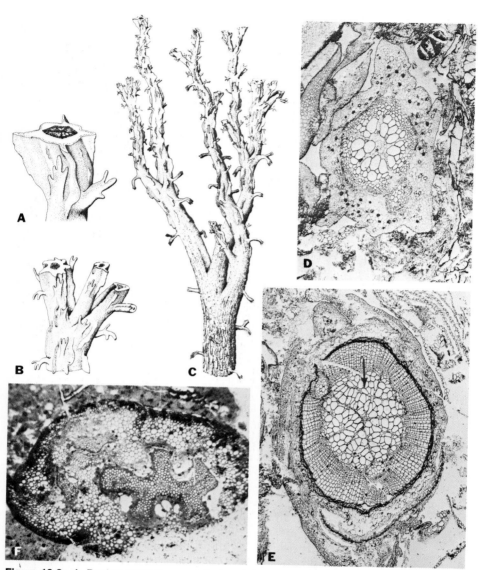

Figure 13-8 A. Portion of *Microspermopteris aphyllum* stem with irregular epidermal trichomes. B. *Microspermopteris aphyllum* stem, axillary branch, and petiole. C. Suggested reconstruction of *Microspermopteris aphyllum*. D. Young *Microspermopteris aphyllum* stem with small amount of secondary xylem. ×24. E. Older stem with secondary xylem and parenchymatous plates within metaxylem *(arrow)*. ×16. F. Transverse section of *Stenokoleos simplex*. ×18. *(A – E from Taylor and Stockey, 1976; F from Beck, 1960.)*

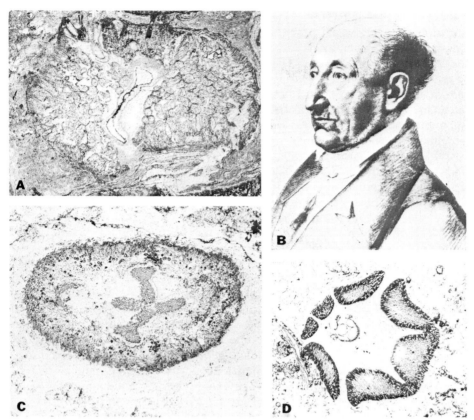

Figure 13-9 A. Transverse section of *Rhetinangium arberi.* ×3. B. Kaspar Graf Sternberg. C. Transverse section of *Tetrastichia bupatides.* ×8. D. Transverse section through apex of *Tyliosperma orbiculatum* ovule showing seven integumentary lobes surrounding the distal end of the nucellus. ×20. *(A from A. G. Long Collection No. 2636 in the Hancock Museum; B reproduced from* Geschichte der Botanik *with permission of Gustav Fischer Verlag.)*

13-8E). In some specimens in which a small amount of secondary xylem is present, the primary xylem consists of large metaxylem tracheids (Fig. 13-8D) in the center of the axis, with smaller tracheids toward the periphery. Stems with secondary xylem reveal a pentagonal primary body in transverse section. Protoxylem strands are positioned on either side of the parenchyma plates near the periphery of the stem. Metaxylem tracheids are long (up to 1.0 mm) and contain multiseriate, simple-reticulate pits. In some of the larger stems (1.1 cm in diameter) with abundant secondary xylem, the symmetry of the stem is apparently altered as a result of gaps in the wood where branches were formed. In *M. aphyllum*, short axillary branches with secondary xylem are present (Fig. 13-8B).

Petioles are produced in a ⅖ phyllotaxy and are attached to the stem by massive clasping bases (Fig. 13-8B). The petiole trace ranges from flattened to

V-shaped in section and reveals protoxylem on the abaxial side. Primary pinnae are alternately arranged. The cortex of *Microspermopteris* is composed of thin-walled parenchyma cells, a small amount of periderm in mature stems, and axially aligned mucilage cells. The presence of cortical fibers depends on the age of the stem, the degree of preservation, and the level of the section. Extending out from the stem as lateral extensions of the cortex in some specimens are irregular, winglike structures (Fig. 13-8A). Some of these extend several millimeters and are highly irregular in form. In addition to the cortical flaps, irregularly shaped multicellular trichomes (Fig. 13-8A) are most common at the nodes and distal parts of axes. Adventitious roots with well-developed secondary tissues are borne at various levels along the stems (Fig. 13-8C). They range from triarch to polyarch and contain abundant mucilage ducts.

Although much of the evidence for the existence of Lower Carboniferous pteridosperms has been based on the presence of seeds, there are several stem genera known from deposits of this age that demonstrate a unique set of characteristics. *Rhetinangium* is a Lower Carboniferous stem known only from Scotland (Fig. 13-9A). The stem has a mixed protostele with clusters of tracheids surrounded by thin-walled parenchyma and associated secretory cells. Primary xylem is exarch, and it is arranged in a series of axial bundles. The secondary xylem is narrow; pitting is reticulate. The inner cortex consists of parenchyma and numerous secretory canals; the outer cortex contains thick-walled fibers aggregated into radial bands. Leaves are helically arranged on *R. arberii* and, when found isolated, are referred to as *Lyginorachis arberii*. They are about 1.5 cm in diameter, and they dichotomize to form alternate pinnae bearing cylindrical pinnules. The petiole vascular bundle consists of numerous U-shaped leaf traces when viewed in transverse section. At higher level, these traces fuse to form a bandlike strand.

Another Lower Carboniferous stem that has been included with the seed ferns is *Tetrastichia*. The stems of *T. bupatides* are about 1.0 cm in diameter and contain a protostele that is cruciform in transverse section (Fig. 13-9C). Secondary xylem contains numerous vascular rays. Reticulate pits are present on both radial and tangential tracheid walls. The cortex is three-parted; the outer zone consists of plates of hypodermal fibers and mucilage cells that surround a middle region of parenchyma and nests of fibers. The inner region contains thin-walled parenchyma. Petioles are borne in a four-ranked arrangement, with opposite pairs alternating (decussate). Each petiole dichotomizes a short distance from the stem; subsequent levels of frond morphology are not known.

Calathopteris heterophylla is the name of a Lower Carboniferous protostelic seed-fern stem that contains some parenchyma interspersed with tracheids of the primary xylem. The primary xylem is surrounded by manoxylic secondary xylem and cortical sclerenchyma. Attached to the stem in a ⅖ phyllotaxy are numerous, closely spaced petioles, each with a large pulvinus. The pattern of trace emission suggests that two types of petioles were produced, one with bundles in a U-shaped arrangement thought to represent the vegetative frond, and one, the less common trichotomous petiole trace, thought to represent the fertile frond of the *Diplopteridium teilianum* type.

Another interesting Lower Carboniferous stem that has been correlated with both vegetative remains and cupulate seeds is *Tristichia,* which has a triangular protostele when viewed in transverse section. Protoxylem is mesarch, and secondary xylem with multiseriate bordered pits is present on some axes. Petioles of *T. ovensii* are large and borne in a ⅓ phyllotaxy; they bifurcate and at higher levels dichotomize several times. The petioles contain butterfly-shaped (tetrarch) traces and nests of cortical fibers. Numerous compression remains of small (1.5 mm long), delicate pinnules and bifurcating axes are associated with petrifactions. They are similar to those of the vegetative branches and bear cupules containing seeds. The cupules are borne in pairs at the ends of a dichotomized stalk, and each cupule is multiovulate. Morphologically, the cupules and macerated megaspore membranes appear identical with those of the seed *Stamnostoma huttonense.*

A number of petrified axes from the Upper Devonian and Lower Mississippian have been described as *Incertae sedis* because their affinities cannot be accurately determined. Some of these have been associated with progymnosperms, others with pteridosperms and coenopterid ferns. *Stenokoleos* (Fig. 13-8F) is a genus that consists of axes that bear alternately arranged pinnae with elliptical to celpsydroid-shaped traces. The primary xylem of the stem consists of a two- to five-lobed stele with mesarch protoxylem and weakly developed peripheral loops; tracheids are scalariform or have uni- or biseriate circular bordered pits. *Stenokoleos simplex* (Upper Devonian) reveals triangular traces in the rachis. Another species, *S. bifidus,* is distinguished by the variability in the configuration of its xylem strand. In many features, *Stenokoleos* is similar to *Tristichia* and *Tetrastichia,* both believed by some workers to be members of the lyginopterid seed fern complex. The discovery of reproductive parts associated with these stems will conclusively demonstrate whether this assignment is correct or whether they were produced by some progymnosperm ancestor.

Two Lower Mississippian (New Albany shale) taxa that may ultimately turn out to be the petioles of seed ferns are *Periastron* (see Fig. 13-12C) and *Aerocortex.* Specimens of *P. reticulatum* vary from circular to elliptical in transverse section and contain a nearly median row of 5 to 10 slightly curved amphicribral vascular bundles with helical-reticulate secondary wall thickenings. The cortex is aerenchymatous with longitudinal lacunae (air canals) and peripheral sclerenchyma associated with secretory canals or ducts. *Aerocortex kentuckiensis* has many of the same features as *Periastron,* but with fewer vascular bundles (two to four) and centrally located secretory ducts (see Fig. 13-12B).

Numerous seeds, in fact many more kinds than there are stems, have been referred to the Lyginopteridales because of their relatively small size. Several of these were discussed in Chap. 12; several additional ones will be considered here. Although *Lagenostoma* is the only anatomically preserved seed found attached in this order, several taxa have been suggested as the seeds of certain stem genera. The assignment of seeds and stems has been made principally on their association at the same locality. One of these is *Sphaerostoma ovale,* a

Lower Carboniferous seed from Pettycur, Scotland, that has been associated with stems of *Heterangium grievii*. The seed is approximately 3.5 mm long and up to 2.2 mm in maximum diameter. The integument and nucellus are fused to near the micropyle, where the tip of the nucellus is modified to form a low pollen chamber and cellular central column. The integument of *S. ovale* is three-parted with the middle zone (sclerotesta) constructed of elongate fibers. The outer layer, or sarcotesta, is conspicuous at the apex, where a crest of large axially oriented cells formed a frill around the micropyle. The cells of this structure may have broken down to form the pollination droplet. One of the interesting features of *S. ovale* is the presence of a delicate, vascularized cupule that tightly encloses the seed. Although this structure has been termed an outer integument, it is completely free from the integument except at the chalazal end of the seed.

Another Lower Carboniferous seed with a lagenostome is *Salpingostoma dasu*, known from the volcanic ashes of Oxroad Bay, Scotland. It is elongate (5.0 cm long by 6.0 mm in diameter), and its greatest diameter is near the distal end. In transverse section, the integument shows six prominent ribs that are organized into free lobes near the apex. The pollen chamber and the lageno-stome are similar to those of *Lagenostoma*, except that the distal end is elongated into a conspicuous funnel (salpinx) that extends between the integumentary lobes. Numerous multicellular hairs extend from the inner surface of the integument and may have functioned to maintain the position of the pollen-receiving device. The pollen in this seed is large (104 μm) and trilete.

The genus *Conostoma* (Fig. 13-10A) contains the largest number of species and is also known throughout the Pennsylvanian in both North America and Europe. The seeds are radially symmetrical and less than a centimeter in maximum length. In *C. anglo-germanicum,* a species known from Great Britain, Germany, and Kentucky, the outer surface of the integument is ornamented with four (Fig. 13-10D) longitudinally oriented ribs that extend to the distal end of the seed. Between these ribs are smaller secondary extensions of the sclerotesta. Four vascular bundles extend through the endotesta (inner integu-mentary layer) to near the apex of the seed. The lagenostome in *Conostoma* is a small, doughnut-shaped extension at the distal end of the nucellus (Fig. 12-8A); the remaining portion of the pollen chamber lacks a central column. The central column is thought to have formed during the development of the pollen-receiving mechanism. According to this idea, as the pollen chamber differentiat-ed, the central column was withdrawn, but later pushed into the base of the lagenostome to seal pollen grains in the pollen chamber. Such a force could have been exerted by the development of the tent pole (Fig. 13-10B) during the later stages of megagametophyte ontogeny. Evidence that the lagenostome and central column were at one time organically attached may be seen in the unusual scalariform thickenings on the cell walls of these structures.

A rather unusual integument morphology is present in *C. kestospermum,* a species known only from the Middle Pennsylvanian of Illinois. In this seed, approximately 4.0 mm long, the sclerotesta is composed of two distinct zones. Cells of the outer zone are aligned at right angles to the long axis of the seed and

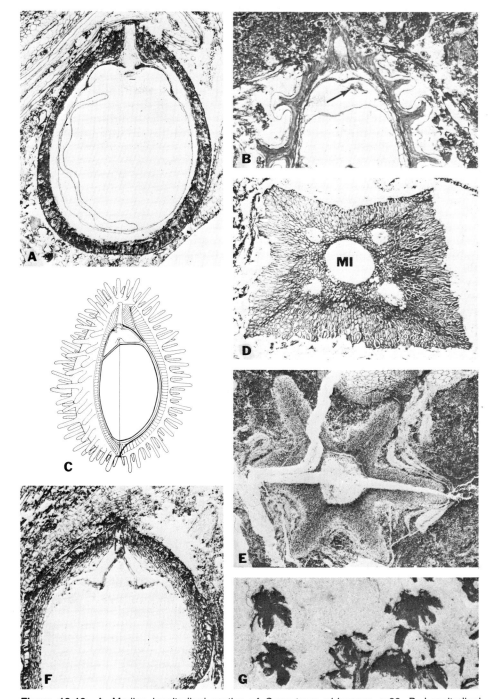

Figure 13-10 A. Median longitudinal section of *Conostoma oblongum.* ×26. B. Longitudinal section through the micropylar end of *Conostoma kestospermum.* Arrow indicates the position of the displaced central column. ×35. C. Cutaway reconstruction of *Conostoma villosum.* D. Transverse section through the apex of *Conostoma oblongum* showing the micropyle (MI) and four vascular bundle locules. ×60. E. Transverse section through the apex of *Hexapterospermum delevoryii* showing the six prominent ribs. ×7. F. Longitudinal section through the apex of *Coronostoma quadrivasatum.* ×25. G. Several *Telangiopsis* synangia. ×1. *(B from Taylor and Leisman, 1963; C from Rothwell and Eggert, 1970; D from Rothwell, 1971; E from Taylor, 1966.)*

form prominent irregular bands that girdle the seed (Fig. 13-10B). A slightly different integumentary morphology is present in *C. villosum* (Upper Pennsylvanian), where the outer layer of the integument (sarcotesta) consists of numerous radially elongate multicellular processes (Fig. 13-10C). Despite the large number of specimens known, it is surprising that no cellular megagametophytes have ever been reported in this genus. Pollen grains have been found in the pollen chamber of several species, and they are typically in the 50 to 80 μm size range and reveal reticulate markings on their walls. Many authors have suggested that *Conostoma* is the seed produced by *Heterangium,* although this speculation is based only on the common association of the seeds and stems at some collecting sites.

Coronostoma quadrivasatum (Fig. 13-10F) is the binomial for a small (4.5 mm long) Upper Pennsylvanian seed that superficially resembles *Conostoma.* The integument is constructed of an outer uniseriate layer of radially elongate cells and an inner region of axially aligned fibers. Four vascular bundles traverse the inner layer of the integument. The most distinctive feature of this species is the tubular elongation of the lagenostome that extends to the base of the micropylar orifice.

The genus *Physostoma* reveals an integument constructed of relatively thin-walled cells, vascularized integument segments that are free above the level of the pollen chamber, and a bell-shaped pollen chamber. In *P. elegans,* known only from the Upper Carboniferous of England, the surface of the seed is covered with large, quill-like unicellular hairs that are believed to have been mucilaginous (Fig. 12-8B). *Physostoma calcaratum* (Middle Pennsylvanian of Kansas) exhibits 6 to 10 integumentary lobes that are fused in the lower half of the seed. Each of the lobes is vascularized by a single, terete strand. The extension of the lagenostome (salpinx) is relatively short, and a central column is apparent near the top of the pollen-receiving structure.

A cupule of unusual structure characterizes the Middle Pennsylvanian seed *Tyliosperma* (Fig. 13-9D). The seed is about 3.7 mm in maximum length and has almost the same diameter. At the distal end, the integument is divided into seven apical lobes that form a canopy over the pollen-receiving mechanism. The nucellus and integument are fused to near the apex, where a simple extension of the nucellar tip extends to the base of the micropyle. A central column is present in the pollen chamber of *T. orbiculatum.* The seed developed in a fleshy cupule that consists of several (seven to eight) vascularized segments fused only at the base. The cupule segments are irregularly thickened.

Calathospermum is the name of a Lower Carboniferous (Scotland) cupule about 4.5 cm long and composed of six apically free segments (Fig. 13-11A). It has been estimated that the cupule of *C. scoticum* produced about 70 stalked ovules (see Fig. 12-6F). The ovule-bearing stalks are attached to the base of each of the cupule segments and contain numerous unicellular hairs. Each ovule is about 3.0 mm long and has been regarded as developmentally younger specimens of *Salpingostoma dasu.* Extending from the apex of the integument are several elongate processes. The position of the ovule stalks suggests that the

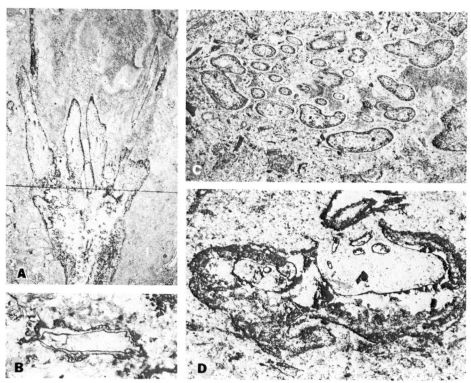

Figure 13-11 A. Longitudinal section of *Calathospermum fimbriatum*. ×2. B. Transverse section of *Hydrasperma* cf. *tenuis*. ×27. C. Transverse section of cupulate lobes of *Calathospermum fimbriatum*. ×3.5. D. Transverse section of cupulate structure of *Sphenopteris bifidum*. ×7. *(From A. G. Long Collection Nos. 10135, 11758, and 9018 in the Hancock Museum.)*

organ was bilateral, and this feature, together with the C-shaped vascular strand of the cupule pedicel, has been used to support the concept that the *Calathospermum* cupule is homologous with a frond or part of a frond. Such a structure may have evolved by the inrolling or folding of a frond segment, rather than the fusion of a whorl of foliar segments suggested by other cupule types.

Multiovulate cupules characterize *Gnetopsis*, but these are appreciably smaller (6.4 mm long) than *Calathospermum*. The Upper Carboniferous (France) specimen *G. elliptica* consists of a cupule that is almost entire at the distal end; cupule segments are identified by very shallow identations. Each cupule bears two to four seeds, each about 2.5 mm long (Fig. 12-6D). The integument and nucellar beak are similar to those of *Conostoma*, except that three to four elongate, hair-covered plumes extend from near the margin of the micropyle distally to the end of the cupule. *Gnetopsis hispida* is a small (8.0 mm long), compressed seed of the Lower Mississippian that possesses four to six elongate extensions from the micropylar region of the integument. Along the surface of these structures are numerous hairs. The specimens differ from the anatomically preserved *Gnetopsis* seeds in that they possess two winglike extensions of the seed coat. The hairlike structures may have served to trap wind-borne pollen, directing the grains to the region of the micropyle.

In addition to seed-bearing cupules, several cupules lacking seeds have been described from Carboniferous rocks, suggesting that at some stage in their development the seeds were shed. *Megatheca thomasii* is a cupule from the oil shales of Scotland (Lower Carboniferous). It is large, measuring up to 6.2 cm in length. The distal end of this compression consists of six free lobes composed of fibers that are much like the sclerotesta of most Paleozoic seeds. Nothing is known about the contents of *Megatheca*, but the size of the unit suggests that it might have been multiovulate.

The pollen organs of the lyginopterid seed ferns are less well known than the seeds. Based on the branching pattern and arrangement of the sporangia, two distinct groups are identified. The *Crossotheca* and *Feraxotheca* types are characterized by synangia borne near the ends of ultimate pinnae on a planated frond segment. The petrifaction genus *Telangium* (Fig. 13-3E) and the compression genus *Telangiopsis* (Fig. 13-10G) are borne on monopodial branching systems that may have replaced a portion of a vegetative frond or an entire leaf. *Telangium scottii* is a rarely encountered species in Westphalian A rocks of Great Britain. The synangia are about 1.7 mm long, and they are composed of eight thick-walled, basally fused sporangia. In transverse section, there is a distinct difference in thickness between the outwardly facing sporangial walls and the thinner, inwardly facing walls. This suggests that dehiscence took place toward the center of the unit. Several different preservational states of *Telangium* fertile structures have been found in rocks of upper Chester (Mississippian) age in Illinois. *Telangium* sp. is a small cup-shaped synangium composed of eight sporangia arranged in a radial plan. Individual sporangia are basally attached to a vascularized parenchymatous core. Dehiscence is similar to that of *T. scottii*. The pollen grains are unusual in that grains with both trilete and monolete marks are found among the sporangial contents.

The form genus *Telangiopsis* was instituted as a repository for synangiate clusters that appear morphologically similar to *Telangium*, but were preserved as compressions (Fig. 13-10G). *Telangiopsis arkansanum* (Chester Series) consists of radial clusters (five to six) of sporangia that are borne terminally on either dichotomously or monopodially branched axes lacking planated foliar structures. Some of the compressed synangia suggest that during dehiscence, the sporangia spread apart. The pollen grains range to 54 μm in diameter and are trilete. Like those of Upper Mississippian petrifaction specimens, they conform to the generic circumscription of the *sporae dispersae* genus *Punctatisporites*.

The few pollen organs that can be assigned to this order with certainty provide little evidence regarding the evolution of the pollen organs. The specimens available suggest that the planation of the Mississippian *Telangiopsis* frond may have resulted in the biseriate type present in *Telangium*. Such a trend may have been extended to the Middle Pennsylvanian genus *Canipa*, which is characterized by pinnate fertile fronds. *Canipa quadrifida* (Fig. 13-12) bears

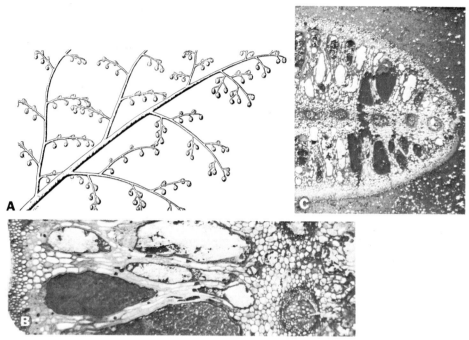

Figure 13-12   A. Suggested reconstruction of *Canipa quadrifida*. B. Transverse section illustrating the aerenchymatous cortex of *Periastron reticulatum.* ×18. C. Transverse section through *Periastron reticulatum.* ×5.5. *(A from Skog, Andrews, and Mamay, 1969; B and C from Beck, 1978.)*

Figure 13-13   *Eremopteris zamioides.* A. Portion of a leaf. Arrow indicates flattened bicornate seed. ×0.7. B. Fertile leaf. ×0.7.

terminal synangia on delicate, curved branches. Each synangium consists of four sporangia that are oppositely arranged. A second trend may have involved *Crossotheca* and *Feraxotheca,* with the sporangia becoming more closely appressed and altered to occupy the side of the pinna apex. Pollen of this group includes grains that are almost identical morphologically and ultrastructurally with the spores of certain homosporous ferns. This may truly reflect the level of pollen evolution for the order, or it may be merely a reflection of the few pollen organ types that have been discovered to date.

An interesting Paleozoic foliage type thought to have represented the leaves of a seed fern, principally because of the association of seeds and pollen producing structures, is *Eremopteris zamioides* (Fig. 13-13A). The leaves of this plant are about 20.0 cm long and consist of alternate to oppositely arranged pinnae. Pinnules are narrow and lack a midvein. The base of the rachis is sharply truncated, suggesting that the leaves abscised. Associated with the leaves are numerous flattened, bilateral seeds with two prominent distal spines (Fig. 13-13A). The seeds range up to 1.5 cm long and 6.0 mm wide in the primary plane. On some specimens, the integument is split, revealing a granulose megaspore membrane. Morphologically, the seeds appear similar to the structurally preserved Lower Carboniferous seed *Lyrasperma.* Numerous star-shaped structures are associated with the foliar and seed remains, and these represent either clusters of whole sporangia or portions of longitudinally dehisced synangia that may have been the pollen organ of *E. zamioides.* These structures may have been produced on modified foliar structures that have the same basic pinnate arrangement as the leaves (Fig. 13-13B) but differ in exhibiting short projections on the laterals (pinnae) to which might have been attached either seeds or sporangia.

In many features, the lyginopterid seed ferns represent a highly artificial and heterogeneous group of plants. The information gathered to date indicates that they were plants that produced cupulate seeds, often with elaborate pollen-receiving structures and systems that sealed pollen in the pollen chamber. The pollen organs consist of clusters of sporangia that dehisce centrally; pollen is small, uniformly ornamented, and probably wind-borne. Petiole morphology is rather constant, but species vary from having laminar pinnules to having unmodified branches. One feature that appears to have been relatively constant for the order is the organization of the stele and presence of cortical sclerenchyma. The steles of the various taxa are of interest in that they demonstrate stages in the evolution of the eustele from such seed-fern progenitors as the Calamopityales. Such a sequence may have involved the longitudinal dissection of a protostele, followed by the modification of columns of vascular tissue into discrete sympodial systems arranged in a cylinder. In addition, there appears to have been a concomitant increase in the amount of parenchyma present in geologically younger seed-fern stems. In this regard, *Microspermopteris* and *Heterangium* may demonstrate increasing amounts of parenchyma intermediate between the protostelic Devonian calamopityeans and the Pennsylvanian eustelic forms.

Figure 13-14 Suggested reconstruction of *Medullosa noei. (From Stewart and Delevoryas, 1956.)*

MEDULLOSALES

The medullosan seed ferns are an interesting group that extend from the Mississippian into the Permian. Judging from the size of the stems and petioles, they were probably the largest of the Paleozoic seed ferns, with some at least 10.0 m tall (Fig. 13-14). Like other fossil plants, the generic name of the stem has been adopted in discussions of the entire plant. This is true of the genus *Medullosa*, which was initially established by Cotta (see Fig. 13-16C) in 1832 for Lower Permian stem remains. In transverse section, medullosan stems are characterized by one to many segments of vascular tissue (Fig. 13-15A), and in earlier treatments they were considered to be polystelic. Recent studies suggest that the "individual steles" represent vascular segments of a single, highly dissected stele. *Medullosa noei* is one of the most common Pennsylvanian species and will be used here to describe the basic histology of the stem. In transverse section, the stem contains two to four segments of vascular tissue (Fig. 13-15A)

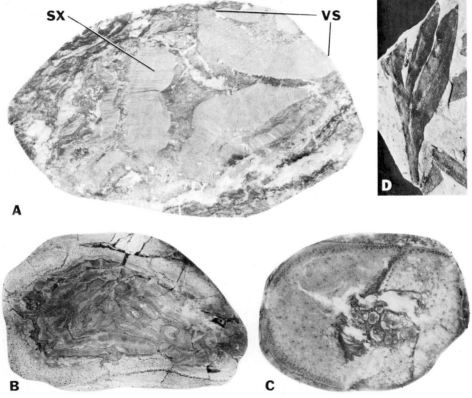

Figure 13-15   A. Transverse section of *Medullosa noei*. VS = vascular segment, SX = secondary xylem. ×1. B. Transverse section of *Medullosa leuckartii*. ×0.5. C. Transverse section of *Medullosa primaeva*. Note large *Myeloxylon* petioles. ×1. D. *Megalopteris* sp. ×0.5. *(B courtesy of G. Rothwell; D from Leary, 1975.)*

and, in older specimens, a ring of secondary parenchyma that superficially resembles another vascular segment. This variation from level to level is the result of the branching and fusion of the vascular tissue and, within the genus, has resulted in the naming of over 40 species and a number of varieties. Many of these "taxa" have been reported from relatively small stem sections, and no doubt they represent configurations of the stele of the same biological species. Each vascular segment is elliptical to band-shaped in cross section, with the primary xylem containing abundant parenchyma. Protoxylem is oriented toward the outer margin of the stele. Surrounding each primary vascular segment is a cylinder of secondary xylem of variable thickness that is characteristically more extensively developed toward the center of the stem. Secondary xylem tracheids are the largest known (up to 250 μm in the radial plane) and contain up to 12 rows of bordered pits on the radial walls. Multiseriate rays that are two to eight cells wide extend through the wood about every three rows of tracheids. Surrounding the xylem is a cambium and a zone of secondary pholem.

Periderm is common in many stems of *Medullosa*. It is seen in the inner cortical zone and may be up to a centimeter or more in thickness. The cells are isodiametric, thick-walled, and arranged in radial files. The disposition of the periderm in *Medullosa* suggests that the phellogen produced a phelloderm principally toward the inside of the stem, which differs from the typical method of periderm formation. The remaining tissues of *M. noei* are composed of cortical parenchyma and abundant elongate secretory canals filled with amorphous contents. These are several millimeters long and common in many of the plant parts of this genus. Surrounding each canal is a layer of small epithelial cells. Patches of sclerenchyma fibers form interrupted bands around the periphery of the stem.

Medullosa thompsonii is a smaller stem (4.0 cm in diameter) that contains three vascular segments surrounded by a narrow band of periderm. Like *M. noei*, the species is known from Middle and Upper Pennsylvanian deposits. *Medullosa endocentrica* is a smaller species believed to represent a stem section near the apex. This Upper Pennsylvanian (Berryville) species is known from a stem about 12.0 cm long. Three steles are present; the maximum diameter of each, including the secondary xylem, is only about 5.0 mm. As the specific epithet implies, the arrangement of secondary xylem is quite endocentric. Although *M. endocentrica* has been retained as a species, it is probable that it represents a more distal portion of the common *M. noei*.

A medullosan that contains quite a variable number of vascular segments that change from level to level in a relatively short distance is the Middle Pennsylvanian species *M. primaeva* (Fig. 13-15C). The stems are about 8.0 cm in diameter, with the individual vascular segments averaging 7.0 × 2.5 mm. A sequence has been demonstrated for this species in which the number of vascular segments changes from 2 to more than 20. This species is also important in demonstrating the presence or absence of secondary xylem associated with the leaf traces, a feature previously considered taxonomically important.

The first Carboniferous species described is *M. anglica* from the Lower Coal Measures of Lancashire. The stems are about 7.5 cm in diameter, and the leaves are borne in a ⅖ phyllotaxy. The number of vascular segments is typically three, with the basic anatomic features similar to those already discussed. Some specimens exhibit accessory vascular strands in the cortex. These strands are smaller than the main segments of the stele and are secondary in origin. Some secondary xylem is present with each leaf trace.

The majority of the geologically younger (Permian) medullosans differ markedly from the Carboniferous forms, principally in the arrangement and number of vascular segments. *Medullosa stellata* is one of the largest stems known. It is partially decorticated and up to 50.0 cm in diameter. In some specimens, the stems contain 43 separate central vascular segments, sometimes referred to as star rings. Surrounding these is a continuous zone of secondary xylem. In this cylinder, the outer secondary xylem is more developed than the inner portion. *Medullosa porosa* is similar to *M. stellata,* but differs in that it contains two zones of small central strands. Vascular segments of the outer zone are tangentially flattened and possess secondary xylem principally on the inner surface. A slightly different xylem configuration is present in *M. solmsii.* The segments near the periphery are numerous and arranged in two rings. The central ground tissue contains several very small star rings that are poorly developed. The peripheral strands of *M. leukartii* (Fig. 13-15B) are tangentially elongated and sinuously arranged. In the center of this stem are a variable number of small vascular segments with uniformly developed tissues.

The ontogeny of medullosan stems has been studied by several authors, each utilizing a large number of anatomically preserved specimens. A composite from these studies suggests that in young regions of the plant the amount of primary and secondary xylem was small and the stem was surrounded by leaf bases. As the stems increased in age, the amount of secondary xylem and phloem was increased, together with the production of cortical periderm. In the more mature regions of the stem, the outer surface lacked leaf bases, which were sloughed off owing to increased activity of the vascular cambium. At this level of development, the outer limits of the periderm marked the periphery of the stem. Delevoryas (1955) suggested that there was a consistent relationship between the size of the primary xylem and the amount of secondary wood. This relationship existed regardless of the age of the stem, suggesting that the primary xylem retained some meristematic potential in the form of a persistent procambium. The presence of so-called periderm rings within the primary xylem lends some support to continuous meristematic potential of the primary xylem of *Medullosa.*

An alternative view regarding the organization of the vascular tissue in a typical *Medullosa* stem has already been alluded to earlier in this section, and this view questions the use of the term polystele in referring to the vascular system. According to this view, an analysis of the primary structure of the vascular segments, including the position of the protoxylem strands and method of leaf trace production, suggests a pattern similar to those of other Carboniferous seed fern orders (monostelic forms). The number of protoxylem strands is not correlated with the number of vascular segments (steles), nor do the traces to a leaf arise from the protoxylem of a single vascular segment, as would be expected if the stem were polystelic in origin. This interpretation views the primary vasculature of *Medullosa* as a monostele constructed of axially interconnected bundles. The star rings containing secondary xylem are viewed as accessory vascular structures analogous to medullary bundles in some extant cycads.

Another stem genus included in the Medullosales is *Sutcliffia*. Until recently, specimens were known only from the Lower Coal Measures of Lancashire, England, but a variety, *S. insignis,* is now known from the Middle Pennsylvanian of Illinois. *Sutcliffia insignis* is a stem approximately 15.0 cm in diameter that contains a large central stele (vascular segment) from which arises other vascular segments. *Sutcliffia* stems may be further distinguished from *Medullosa* by the presence of leaf traces that appear as miniature vascular segments lacking secondary xylem, the concentric nature of the petiole bundles, and the distribution of sclerenchyma that surrounds the peripheral vascular traces in the petiole. Histologic features of the vascular segments, cortex, and periderm are similar to those discussed for *Medullosa*. The presence of conspicuous moundlike emergences on the surface of the stem and petiole bases has been used to identify *S. insignis* var. *tuberculata*. While the preceding features have been used to separate *Medullosa* and *Sutcliffia,* the variation known among medullosan species may ultimately demonstrate *Sutcliffia* as a species of *Medullosa* or a developmental stage of a currently recognized taxon.

The frond of *Stucliffia* is thought to have been 3 to 4 m long and four to five times pinnate. In transverse section, the bundles radiate in curved rows from the center of the axis, with those of the outer ring embedded in the outer sclerenchyma cortex. Pinnules assignable to the form genus *Linopteris* (Fig. 13-16C) are thought to have been produced by *S. insignis* var. *tuberculata* because of their consistent association in coal balls containing *Sutcliffia* petioles. Morphologically they appear similar to pinnules of *Neuropteris,* but they can be distinguished by their reticulate venation.

Roots of *Medullosa* are adventitious and represent a common component of many petrified Carboniferous remains. Specimens attached to stems of *M. anglica* are typically triarch and appear in vertical series on the stem. Older roots contain a wide band of periderm. Some Middle Pennsylvanian roots of *Medullosa* are known in detail and have provided a basis not only for determining stages in tissue differentiation, but also in suggesting characteristics of potential taxonomic significance. Some of the larger specimens are about 2.5 cm in diameter and exhibit abundant secondary tissues. In these roots, the center of the axis consists of an exarch actinostele with up to five protoxylem points. The secondary xylem is continuous around the primary body, a situation that is different form that in other *Medullosa* roots, which have wedges of secondary xylem opposite the metaxylem. Secondary xylem tracheids are angular in transverse section and exhibit 4 to 12 rows of crowded pits on the radial and oblique tangential walls. Secondary phloem is well developed in larger roots and consists of sieve cells and rays. Lateral roots originate from a thin-walled pericycle opposite the protoxylem strands. Surrounding the pericycle is a narrow endodermis and parenchymatous cortex. Histologic variations, including the number of protoxylem strands and the presence or absence of such tissues as endodermis, may reflect species differences or constitute stages of development. As more roots are found attached to stems of *Medullosa* and *Sutcliffia,* the significance of these apparent differences will be determined.

Leaves of *Medullosa* were massive structures, as determined by the size of anatomically preserved petioles and compression remains of the more distal frond segments. They branched dichotomously, or slightly unequally in the lower portions, and were regularly pinnate at more distal levels (Fig. 13-16A).

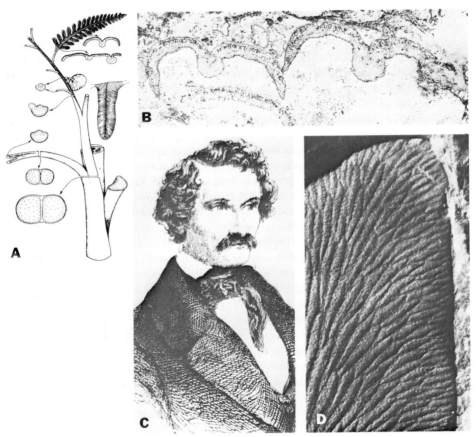

Figure 13-16   A. Suggested reconstruction of *Myeloxylon-Alethopteris* type medullosan frond. B. Transverse section of *Alethopteris* pinnules. ×12. C. Bernhard Von Cotta. D. Portion of *Linopteris neuropteroides* pinnule showing nature of the venation. ×7. *(A from Ramanujam, Rothwell, and Stewart, 1974; C reproduced from* Geschichte der Botanik *with permission of Gustav Fischer Verlag; D courtesy of R. Daber.)*

Numerous stem specimens with petioles attached suggest that a ⅖ or ⅓ phyllotaxy was common. The detached petioles of *Medullosa* are called *Myeloxylon* (Fig. 13-15C). In transverse section (some up to 20.0 cm in diameter), the petioles are circular or elliptical and consist of a parenchymatous ground tissue with a ring of peripheral strands and scattered, centrally located vascular bundles. They are abundant near the periphery of the rachis, decreasing toward the center. Surrounding the axis is a zone of hypodermal fibers similar to those of the stem. Scattered throughout the ground tissue are numerous secretory canals.

A leaf base on the stem is first recognizable as a small triangular, unvascularized area of cortex delimited by sclerenchyma strands. Numerous divisions of two or more protoxylem sympodia produce traces that pass out through the secondary xylem as primary monarch bundles. Continued dichotomies produced the large number of bundles apparent in the *Myeloxylon* petiole. The tertiary rachis of *Myeloxylon* is slightly flattened, with the vascular bundles fewer in number and more abundant on the adaxial side; hypodermal fibers are reduced in number, and a median ridge separates two longitudinal grooves from which the penultimate pinnae emerge. Penultimate pinnae lack sclerenchyma fibers around the periphery of the axis. At this level, the vascular bundles are arranged in a C-shaped configuration.

Paleozoic foliage form genera thought to have been produced by the medullosans include *Neuropteris* and *Alethopteris* (Fig. 13-17D). Anatomically preserved pinnules of *Alethopteris* are known that were organically attached to penultimate pinnae exhibiting *Myeloxylon* anatomy. Individual pinnules reveal a prominent midvein from which secondary veins emerge at sharp angles. In transverse section, the pinnule is revolute (turned under along the margin), and the midrib contains one to four vascular strands. Beneath the upper epidermis are one to two layers of palisade parenchyma that grade into the loosely arranged cells of the mesophyll. Stomata are hypostomatic, and they are associated with large, multicellular hairs that also occur along the rachis. *Alethopteris sullivantii* (Fig. 13-16B) pinnules are obliquely attached to the pinna rachis and broadly rounded at the apex. They range from 1.2 to 2.4 cm long and up to 1.2 cm wide. The upper epidermis is smooth and lacks papillae and stomata. Stomata are present in rows between the veins, with each stomatal apparatus surrounded by six to eight papillate subsidiary cells. In *A. lesquereuxi*, the margin of the pinnule is strongly inrolled, and the stomata occur between the secondary vein ridges.

Pinnules of *Neuropteris* possess a cordate base and a prominent midvein with widely spaced secondary veins that dichotomize several times before they reach the pinnule margin. In section view, *Neuropteris rarinervis* pinnules (Middle Pennsylvanian) reveal parenchymatous bundle sheaths. Cells of the upper epidermis possess undulating margins; stomata in tightly packed rows are confined to the lower pinnule surface. Each pair of guard cells is surrounded by four to six polygonal cells. Pinnules of *Reticulopteris* are similar to those of *Neuropteris*, differing only in the pattern of venation. In *R. muensterii*, porelike

Figure 13-17 A. *Odontopteris.* ×1.3. B. *Mariopteris.* ×0.8. C. *Sphenopteris.* ×0.5. D. *Alethopteris.* ×1.5. E. *Pecopteris.* ×1.6. F. Aphlebia. ×1. G. *Cyclopteris.* ×1.2.

openings are present near the vein endings, and they have been compared with hydathodes.

To date, information about the attachment of seeds to the fronds of *Medullosa* has been determined principally from compression fossils. In 1905, Kidston described large (3.0 cm long) seeds of the *Trigonocarpus* type from the Middle Coal Measures of Britain. The seeds are longitudinally striated and radial. Two pinnules of *Neuropteris heterophylla* are present at the base of the seed, suggesting that the ovule may have occupied the position of a terminal pinnule on the rachis. Several examples of seeds attached to foliage were described by Halle (1929) from the Permian of China. *Alethopteris norinii* is a tripinnate frond that produced large (4.0 cm long and 1.2 cm diameter) seeds attached to the midrib of the pinna, with typical alethopterid pinnules both above and below the point of seed attachment. Smaller seeds (7.5 mm long) that are probably bilaterally symmetrical are attached in the same position to pinnules of the *Lonchopteris* type. The specimens of *Emplectopteris triangularis*, also from the Permian of China, were preserved as impressions so that nothing is known about the internal organization of the ovules. Seeds with conspicuous micropylar beaks were preserved on foliage of *Sphenopteris* (*S. tenuis*) from the same locality. Bilateral seeds also have been described attached to the pinna rachis of species of *Pecopteris* (*P. pluckenetii*).

Spermopteris is the name applied to *Taeniopteris* foliage that contains seeds on the abaxial surface of the lamina. Fertile leaves of *S. coriacea* (Middle Pennsylvanian of Kansas) range up to 20.0 cm long and reveal a wide midvein that extends the length of the leaf. The seeds are borne in a row on either side of the midvein, each supplied by a lateral vein. They are ovoid, slightly flattened, and about 5.0 mm long. Distally they are notched in the region of the micropyle, suggesting that there may have been apical lobes in the integument. Presumed immature specimens are covered by the marginal lamina of the leaf. Because the seeds were preserved as impressions, nothing is known about the tissues. Seed fern seeds also have been described from penultimate frond segments of *Callipteris* foliage. The specimens were recovered from the Hermit shale (Lower Permian) of Arizona and consist of impressions of oval seeds, one at the tip of each pinnule. The abaxial attachment along the midrib (Fig. 13-18B) of the pinna is also the method of seed attachment in a recently discovered specimen of *Alethopteris* (Fig. 13-18A) collected from the Pennsylvanian of Indiana. Not all the previously mentioned seeds can be assigned to the medullosan seed ferns; some no doubt represent the ovules of several different groups of Carboniferous pteridosperms. They do suggest that the attachment of seeds was associated with vegetative fronds and that most were probably borne on the abaxial surface of the pinna rachis.

Seeds assignable to the medullosan pteridosperms represent a relatively common organ and are known from a variety of preservation states. The seeds are the largest of any seed fern group and are structurally almost identical with the seeds of extant members of the Cycadophyta. The basis of classifying the structureless forms with the medullosan seed ferns has been their relatively large size and the presence of three longitudinal ribs that divide the integument into three equal valves. Seeds of this type are common as sandstone casts that may represent several morphologic shapes determined by their method of formation. The genus *Trigonocarpus* (see Fig. 13-21D) was originally instituted by Brongniart (Fig. 13-19A) in 1828 for such casts, but it also has been applied to compression forms. Some specimens of *Trigonocarpus*, such as *T. leeanus*, a Middle Pennsylvanian form, are approximately 10.0 cm long. *Trigonocarpus leeanus* is interesting not only because it demonstrates features of the integu-

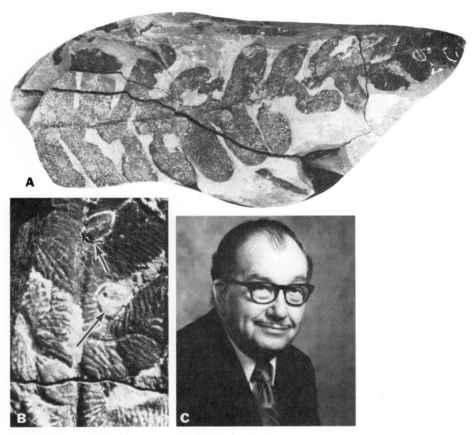

Figure 13-18 A. *Alethopteris* pinna with abaxially attached seeds. ×1. B. Close-up of pinnules and position of seeds *(arrows).* ×3. C. James Morton Schopf. *(A and B courtesy of R. Pheifer and D. Dilcher.)*

ment, including the extent of the ribs, but also because it contains a cast of the nucellar region. *Trigonocarpus* casts typically represent a morphologic expression of the ovule, but with *T. leeanius,* it was possible to make a latex transfer of the nucellar cast that reveals features of the inner surface of the integument. This technique, especially with very fine grained casts, may hold promise in defining more accurately the estimated 125 species of seeds preserved as compressions and casts. In some instances, it is difficult to determine whether the seed cast was formed from the outer surface of the integument (sarcotesta) or the inner surface. Similarly, it remains a difficult task to determine whether the longitudinal striations represent the ribs of the integument or the positions of vascular strands that extend through the nucellus. In another type of seed cast, fine-grained sediment filled the inside of the nucellus forming what have been termed nucule casts. Fossils of this type rarely show any longitudinal striations that mark the former position of the integumentary ribs.

Figure 13-19 A. Adolphe Brongniart. B. Charles Rene Zeiller. C. Ernst Friedrich von Schlotheim. D. Bernard Renault. *(A and C reproduced from* Geschichte der Botanik *with permission of Gustav Fischer Verlag; B reproduced from* Fossil Plants *with permission of Cambridge Univ. Press; D courtesy of A. Scott.)*

There are a number of radial, structurally preserved seeds thought to belong to the medullosan seed ferns. These are generally large (greater than 1.0 cm long), with a ribbed sclerotesta, and contain a nucellus that is attached to the integument only at the chalaza. The pollen chamber is simple, and both the integument (see Fig. 13-21E) and the nucellus contain vascular tissue (see Fig. 13-27C). The most commonly encountered, and largest, genus of the anatomically preserved medullosan seeds is *Pachytesta* (Fig. 13-20A). No doubt many of the species of *Trigonocarpus* represent different preservational states of *Pachytesta*. The genus currently consists of 14 species that range from the Lower Coal Measures of Britain to the Upper Carboniferous of France. Specimens range from slightly less than a centimeter (*P. pusilla*) to approximately 11.0 cm in length. *Pachytesta illinoensis,* a common species in North American petrifactions, is ovoid and about 2.5 cm in diameter. Some specimens range up to 4.5 cm long and consist of a three-parted integument that includes a parenchymatous outer layer (sarcotesta), a middle zone of fibers (sclerotesta), and a uniseriate innermost endotesta. Secretory canals identical with those of *Myeloxylon* and *Medullosa* are common in the seed coats of *Pachytesta*. The sclerotesta is ornamented with three prominent ribs that extend from the base to near the micropylar opening. Equidistantly arranged between these primary ribs are smaller, secondary and tertiary extensions of the sclerotesta. Although the

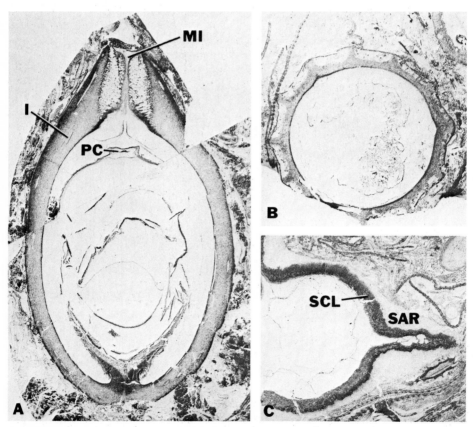

Figure 13-20 *Pachytesta.* A. Median longitudinal section of *Pachytesta gigantea* showing micropyle (MI), integument (I), and pollen chamber (PC). ×17. B. Midlevel transverse section of *Pachytesta composita.* ×3. C. Transverse section through rib of *Pachytesta vera* showing thick sarcotesta (SAR) and inner sclerotic portion of integument (SCL). ×3. *(A and C from Taylor, 1965; B from Stewart, 1958.)*

nucellus is attached to the integument only at the base of the seed, it was tightly appressed to the inner surface of the integument when the seed was alive. At the distal end, the nucellus forms a simple, bell-shaped pollen chamber with a small nucellar beak that communicates directly with the micropylar orifice. The vascular system of the integument consists of up to 42 distinct strands; the nucellus contains about 25 bundles, some of which are laterally fused. A reduced number of secondary and tertiary ribs (Fig. 13-20B) distinguish *P. composita* (Middle Pennsylvanian).

One of the largest anatomically preserved members of the genus is *P. gigantea* (Fig. 13-20A), initially described from the Stephanian (Upper Pennsylvanian) of France and now known from Middle and Upper Pennsylvanian sediments of North America. Some specimens exceed 7.0 cm in length, but unlike other species, the sclerotesta of the seed is not ornamented with ribs. A transverse section at the midlevel of this seed shows that the seed coat consists of three valves marked by indentations on the inner surface of the integument. A small number of secondary ribs are present only in the apex. Fibers of the sclerotesta contain simple pits on their walls. Fifty-one peripherally located vascular strands are present in the integument, while the nucellus contains about 40 tangentially flattened bundles that are comprised of scalariform tracheids. *Pachytesta vera* (Middle Pennsylvanian) is about the same size as *P. gigantea*, but it differs in having three prominent ribs (Fig. 13-20C). A slightly different sculpturing of the integument is present in *P. berryvillensis*, a species described from a large number of specimens differing in stages of pollen chamber development. The ovoid seeds are about 7.0 mm long and contain a short micropylar tube. The positions of the three primary ribs are marked by slight indentations on the inner integument surface. Three principal integument components are present, but the inner surface of the sclerotesta contain fibers that extend into the seed cavity (Fig. 13-21A) a short distance to form a reticulum of lacunae. In one species, *P. stewartii*, there is a chamber in the chalaza of the seed (Fig. 13-21F). In the pollen chamber of *P. berryvillensis*, numerous saccate grains of the *Florinites* type are seen, and they may represent anemophilous contaminants. In most of the other species, pollen grains of the *Monoletes* type have been identified and are thought to represent the pollen biologically associated with *Pachytesta*.

Patterns of the sclerotesta [whether the fibers of the outer zone are oriented tangentially, radially (Fig. 13-21G), or intermediate], together with the size of the seed, and numbers and extent of the ribs, have been used to position the species of *Pachytesta* phylogenetically (Taylor, 1965). Such a series shows three general trends. These include the large species with numerous vascular bundles, those with an increasing number of secondary and tertiary ribs, and those demonstrating a reduction in seed size and number of ribs.

Structurally preserved megagametophytes have been identified in only three *Pachytesta* species (see Fig. 13-27B). In these, the megaspore membrane contains two cell patterns interpreted as stages in cellularization. Cells near the periphery of the megaspore are arranged in radial files, while those more deeply

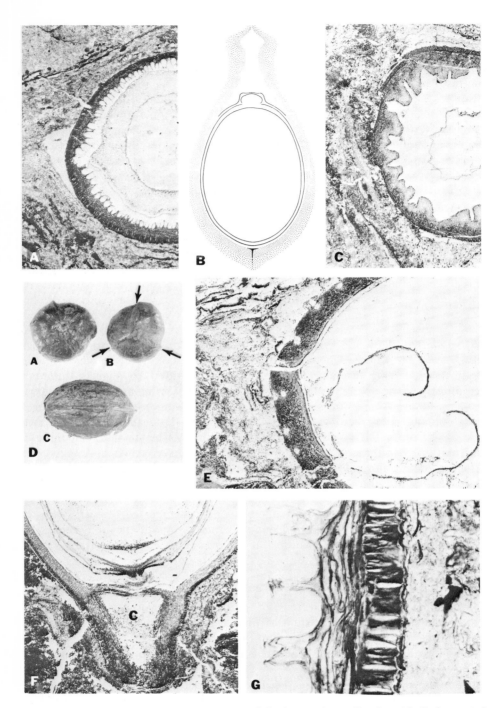

Figure 13-21   A. Midlevel transverse section of *Pachytesta berryvillensis*. ×16. B. Suggested reconstruction of *Rhynchosperma quinnii*. C. Midlevel transverse section of *Albertlongia incostata*. ×7. D. *Trigonocarpus* casts: (A) base, (B) apex with ribs *(arrows)*, (C) side. ×1. E. Midlevel transverse section of *Pachytesta noei*. Holes in sclerotesta mark position of integumentary vascular strands. ×2.5. F. Longitudinal section through the chambered base (C) of *Pachytesta stewartii*. ×5. G. Section of *Pachytesta berryvillensis* integument. ×150. *(A from Taylor and Eggert, 1969; B from Taylor and Eggert, 1967; E from Taylor, 1965; F from Taylor and Delevoryas, 1964.)*

positioned within the megagametophyte are polygonal in outline. The only report of clearly distinguishable archegonia in the genus is from *P. hexangulata.* At the distal end of the megagametophte are three oval archegonia, each about 1.0 mm in diameter. Histologic features of the archegonia were not preserved, but in one, a large, fimbriate mass of material has been suggested as representing the coalified remains of the egg cytoplasm. This seed is even more remarkable in that the pollen chamber contains a number of *Monoletes* pollen grains in close proximity to the archegonia. In one grain, two amorphous ovoid structures are preserved (see Fig. 13-30A), and these appear morphologically similar to the flagellated sperm of certain extant cycads.

Another common Carboniferous seed that may have been associated with the medullosan seed ferns is *Stephanospermum.* Specimens are about 1.0 cm long and possess an integumentary crown that encircles an elongate micropylar canal. Three primary ribs are present, but the sclerotesta is not ornamented externally. In *S. elongatum* (Middle to Upper Pennsylvanian), the apical crown is toothed, with each segment corresponding to a rib. Vascular tissue is present in both the integument and the nucellus; in the nucellus, the bundles are tangentially flattened and fuse to form a continuous ring (tracheal sheath). As in *Pachytesta,* the nucellus is free from the integument except at the base, and the pollen chamber is simple. *Albertlongia incostata* (Fig. 13-21C) is a Middle Pennsylvanian seed that is similar to *Pachytesta* in the arrangement of integumentary tissues, pollen chamber morphology, and vascularized integument and nucellus. The seeds are about 2.2 cm long and ovoid in outline. The outer surface of the seed is smooth; no ribs or sutures are present that divide the integument. The internal surface of the integument (sclerotesta) is convoluted into numerous irregular ridges and furrows.

The presence of six longitudinal ribs in the sclerotesta is a feature used by Brongniart to delimit the genus *Hexapterospermum* (Fig. 13-10E). The seed has a flattened base and a tapered apex when viewed in longitudinal section. Ribs are most conspicuous at the distal end, gradually reduced toward the base and extending into keellike structures that project below the base. The seed coat consists of a sarcotesta, sclerotesta, and endotesta, with the cells of each layer grading into those of the next zone. The six sclerotestal ribs are equidistantly spaced around the seed and, in transverse section, may be identified by a thin plate of cells that divides the integument radially (Fig. 13-10E). One of the interesting aspects of *H. delevoryii* (Middle Pennsylvanian of Illinois) is the presence of a small parenchymatous cone of tissue projecting through the nucellus toward the micropylar orifice. Topographically this structure resembles the persistent central column often present in some lagenostomalean seeds. Such a structure also may represent a portion of the cellularized megagametophyte projecting through the distal end of the pollen chamber, or it may represent some form of prepollination remnant. Whatever the function, seeds such as *Hexapterospermum* typically possess simple pollen chambers that lack the morphologically more complex forms of the smaller, geologically older lagenostomalean pteridosperm seeds.

Rhynchospermum is a Mississippian (Chester Series) seed with radial symmetry, and it is characterized by a two-layered integument. The seed apex is attenuated (Fig. 13-21B) and sculptured by 8 to 10 sclerotestal ribs; below the midlevel the seed is smooth. Some specimens are at least 2.2 cm long. The integument and nucellus are fused, as in seeds of the Lagenostomales, but the pollen chamber is relatively simple, consisting of a small dome. In *R. quinnii,* vascular tissue is identified only in the outer portion of the integument. Nucule and integumentary casts displaying similar morphologic features have been referred to the form genera *Boroviczia* and *Rhynchogonium.* One species, *Rhynchogonium fayettevillense,* is a fairly common seed cast of Chester age in southern Illinois, and no doubt it represents *Rhynchosperma* in a different state of preservation.

Like the seeds, medullosan pollen organs are rather large, with some up to several centimeters in diameter. The number of structureless forms is large, and their assignment to the Medullosales is based principally on the recognition of a particular pollen grain type. There are seven genera of petrified organs and numerous compression-impression forms. The structureless types have provided information about the position of the pollen organs on the plant. The petrified forms are small and solitary, large and aggregated, or fused into a compound unit. All consist of a system of elongate, tubelike sporangia embedded in a ground tissue. The pollen grains are typically large (100 to 600 μm long) and monolete.

Possibly the simplest of the anatomically preserved medullosan pollen organs is the Upper Pennsylvanian species *Halletheca reticulatus* (Fig. 13-22C). It was a pyriform synangium about 1.5 cm long. Each pollen organ is composed of five sporangia that are arranged around a central zone of fibers. In the distal region of the organ, the central area is hollow. A vascular bundle is associated with the outer wall of each sporangium, and sporangial dehiscence took place toward the center of the organ. Although the manner of attachment for *Halletheca* is not known, the gradually tapered end of the unit suggests that this pollen organ may have been borne singly at the end of a small branch. *Schopfitheca* (Fig. 13-22E) is a small medullosan pollen organ that may be a different preservation stage of a *Halletheca* synangium. The taxon is known from a single Maxon Creek nodule and has been placed with the medullosan seed ferns because of the *Monoletes* pollen grains that were macerated from the sporangia. Another simple synangium that is structurally homologous with *Halletheca* is *Sullitheca.* This pollen organ is slightly larger (2.5 cm long) and contains about 40 elongate sporangia embedded in a parenchymatous ground tissue. In the center of the organ in transverse section is an H-shaped zone of fibers (Fig. 13-22A) similar to the central sclerenchyma zone of *Halletheca.* Morphologically, the *Sullitheca dactylifera* unit has been convoluted symmetrically, thereby providing room for an increased number of sporangia, while at the same time providing a structural organization that allows internal sporangial dehiscence. Each sporangium is associated with a vascular bundle, and another ring of bundles present near the outer margin of the organ. On the surface of *Sullitheca* are numerous multicellular hairs.

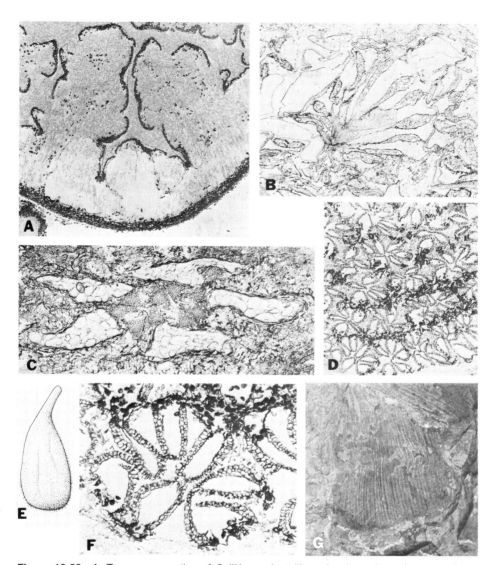

Figure 13-22 A. Transverse section of *Sullitheca dactylifera* showing sclerenchymatous inner plates. ×14. B. Several *Parasporotheca leismanii* sporangia. ×8. C. Transverse section of *Halletheca reticulatus*. ×19. D. Transverse section of *Potoniea illinoiensis* showing concentric rings of synangia. ×12. E. Suggested reconstruction of *Schopfitheca boulayoides*. F. Single synangium of *Potoniea illinoiensis*. ×44. G. Single synangium of *Whittleseya elegans*. ×3. *(A from Stidd, Leisman, and Phillips, 1977; B from Dennis and Eggert, 1978; C from Taylor, 1971; D from Stidd, 1978b; E from Millay and Taylor, 1979; F courtesy of B. Stidd.)*

Rhetinotheca tetrasolenata is a Middle Pennsylvanian pollen organ that consists of a central fibrous area surrounded by four sporangia; the distal end of the central area is apparently hollow. Each synangium is small (2.0 mm long) and is borne at the end of a greatly telescoped branching system, resulting in a complex mass of simple synangia. The surface of each synangium is covered with numerous peglike processes that probably provided the mechanical support that held the compound unit together. The pollen grains that were produced by *Halletheca, Sullitheca,* and *Rhetinotheca* are large, thick-walled grains that have been included in the genus *Monoletes*.

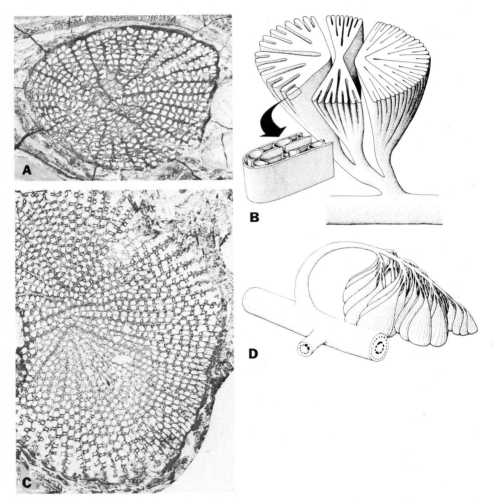

Figure 13-23 A. Transverse section of *Dolerotheca schopfii.* ×2.1. B. Suggested origin of *Dolerotheca formosa* from four simple, symmetrically folded synangia. C. Transverse section of *Dolerotheca formosa.* ×2.1. D. Suggested reconstruction of *Parasporotheca leismanii,* an aggregation of synangia. *(A and C courtesy of G. Rothwell; B and D from Millay and Taylor, 1979.)*

One of the most interesting and complex medullosan seed fern pollen organs is *Dolerotheca* (see Fig. 13-24A), the American species of which were critically examined by J. M. Schopf (Fig. 13-18C). Some specimens are 4.0 cm in diameter and are constructed of radiating pairs of elongate sporangia. In *D. formosa* (Fig. 13-23C), the common Pennsylvanian species, the campanulum is constructed of four radial synangia that are symmetrically folded. Figure 13-23B shows an idealized reconstruction of the entire unit that exhibits the folded configuration of the component synangia. Like the other medullosan pollen organs, dehiscence of each sporangial pair is directed inwardly through the breakdown of specialized cells (Fig. 13-23B). *Stewartiotheca* is an Upper Pennsylvanian campanulate synangium approximately 1.0 cm in diameter that superficially resembles a small *Dolerotheca* (Fig. 13-23A). In *S. warrenae* there are about 80 elongate pollen sacs that are vascularized in pairs. The central portion of the organ contains a cone-shaped hollow area that is surrounded by a narrow zone of sclerenchyma. A narrow pedicel is attached eccentrically. Morphologically, the unit is highly plicated and similar to a single unit of the compound *Dolerotheca* fructification. Pollen of both is of the *Monoletes* type.

Potoniea is a pollen organ initially described from European compression specimens, but now known from petrified remains as well. The unit is bell-shaped and about 1.0 cm in diameter. It is composed of numerous elongate sporangia embedded in a common ground tissue. The distal surface is unusual because the sporangial tubes protrude for about 1.0 mm. The entire structure has been interpreted as several (five) concentric rings (Fig. 13-22D) constructed of clusters of four to six radial synangia (Fig. 13-22F). Each sporangial group is vascularized like *Halletheca*. The pollen of this organ is radial and trilete (see Fig. 13-30C), and because it is so unlike other medullosan forms, the assignment of *Potoniea* to the group remains tentative.

A very different pollen type is also present in the fructification *Parasporotheca* (Fig. 13-23D). These grains are up to 275 μm long and are characterized by two vestigial sacci, one at either end. The suture is monolete and slightly bent at the midlevel (see Fig. 13-30G). The pollen organ is unusual in that it lacks the radial symmetry that apparently characterizes other medullosan types. In *P. leismanii* (Upper Pennsylvanian), the synangium is constructed of several scooplike synangia (Fig. 13-22B), each of which consists of alternating sporangial lacunae in the ground tissue. The whole sporangial aggregation measures about 20.0 cm in length and 3.0 cm in width. Each of the scooplike synangia is covered with peglike hairs that may have held the individual units together. Such a unit may have evolved from a laminar fertile telome system that underwent lateral fusion, or it may have been basically radial, becoming bilateral because a small area of the enlarging cone-shaped synangium failed to develop.

There are several compressed pollen organs that are referred to the medullosan seed ferns on the basis of their pollen. One of these is *Whittleseya* (Fig. 13-22G), a form that had been interpreted as a ring of fused, elongate sporangia surrounding a central hollow (Fig. 13-24G). Each synangium is

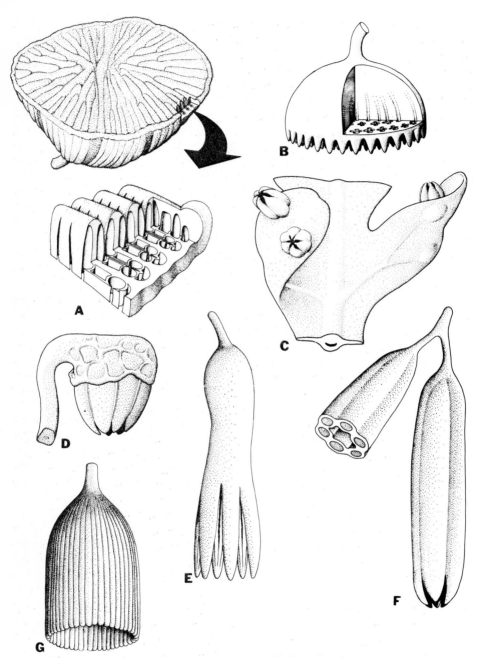

Figure 13-24 A. Lower surface of *Dolerotheca formosa* campanulum showing cutaway of sporangial tubes. B. Suggested reconstruction of *Potoniea illinoiensis*. C. *Callandrium callistophytoides*. D. Synangium of *Feraxotheca culcitaus*. E. *Codonotheca caduca*. F. *Aulacotheca hemingwayi*. G. *Whittleseya elegans*. *(A and D–G from Millay and Taylor, 1979.)*

approximately 5.0 cm long and 3.0 cm in maximum width. At the apex, the unit bears small teeth that correspond to the position of longitudinal grooves on the surface. In a recent review of Paleozoic pollen organs, Millay and Taylor (1979) offered the alternative view that each synangial unit was flattened and aggregated together. Another compressed pollen organ that has been interpreted as a ring of fused sporangial tubes is *Codonotheca* (Fig. 13-24E). Specimens are smaller than the synangia of *Whittleseya* and have individual sporangia (usually six) that are basally fused and free at the apex.

Some information regarding the manner in which certain medullosan pollen organs were borne on the plant has been determined from an excellent specimen of *Aulacotheca* (Fig. 13-24F), a Pennsylvanian form. *Aulacotheca iowensis* consists of a frond segment organized as a primary axis that bears six alternately arranged laterals. Planated foliar structures are absent, and the stalked synangia are borne in groups at the tips of small dichotomizing axes along laterals. A synangium consists of three or four pollen sacs, each about 5.0 mm long.

The attachment of *Dolerotheca* to a *Myeloxylon* frond bearing *Alethopteris* pinnules has been based on the arrangement and number of vascular bundles and common histologic features in the petiole and pedicel of the fructification. As interpreted by this study (Ramanujam, Rothwell, and Stewart, 1974), the *Dolerotheca* campanulum was borne in the position of a penultimate pinna on the frond (see Fig. 13-16A). Other medullosan pollen organs were apparently borne as paired synangia, possibly along the side of a common axis (e.g., *Codonotheca,* or *Paracalathiops*), or alternately along a fertile pinna (e.g., the Permian genera *Schuetzia* and *Dictyothalamus*).

All the medullosan pollen organs except *Potoniea* and *Parasporotheca* contain bilateral, monolete pollen assignable to the genus *Monoletes*. The grains of this genus range between 100 and 600 μm in length and possess a bent monolete suture on the proximal surface. On the distal surface are two longitudinal grooves that extend almost the entire length of the grain (see Fig. 13-30F). The sporoderm (wall) is thick (10 μm), and it is constructed of two layers: an inner homogeneous layer and an outer zone of sporopollenin units that are fused to form a meshlike layer (see Fig. 13-30I). Some grains of *Monoletes* that were extracted from sporangia contain small (0.3 to 0.8 μm), hollow, spherical units termed orbicules or ubisch bodies (see Fig. 13-30B). These structures are associated with a series of membranes (tapetal membranes) and are tapetal products. Unlike the other seed fern families whose pollen was easily transported and adapted for wind dispersal, *Monoletes* grains may have been carried by insects. According to one suggestion (Taylor, 1978), the luminate wall of the grain may have been adapted to contain certain recognition substances associated with insect pollination (entomophily).

There can be little doubt that the Medullosales provide some evidence for the evolution of the partially dissected eustele from a protostele. Within the order, some taxa, such as *Sutcliffia,* contain a single protostele; others of a younger geologic age contain a larger number of vascular segments. Variation also exists within stems of comparable age, in part reflecting that many of the "species" merely represent different levels of the same biologic species. Since stems with a small number of vascular segments are known from both the oldest and youngest geologic strata, the fossil record of the medullosans is difficult to interpret. One theory suggests that evolution among the medullosans was directed toward increased complexity of the stem, with the more primitive forms similar to a *Heterangium*. Another view interprets the multisegmented forms as primitive, suggesting that they lead to fewer vascular segments through phylogenetic fusion. Forms evidencing a peripheral ring of secondary xylem evolved through the tangential fusion of peripheral vascular segments. Proponents of this latter theory point to older Devonian plants included in the Cladoxylopsida as potential progenitors because of their similar stelar (symodial) organization. Others view the multisegmented Permian forms as having stelar arrangements similar to those found among the extant Cycadophyta, the group most workers believe is phylogenetically related to the Medullosales. Both the cycads and medullosans produced similar ovules, and a case can be made for the fact that at least some medullosans bore their seeds in a manner similar to the Cycadophyta. The pollen organs present possibly the biggest problem in relating the two groups. In the cycads, numerous sporangia are borne on the abaxial surfaces of microsporophylls that are aggregated into small strobili. Another conspicuous disparity between the two groups involves the marked differences in pollen size; the pollen of *Medullosa* may reach one-half a millimeter in some forms, while the distally germinating cycad pollen grains may be 30 μm in diameter. The occurrence of relatively modern cycad reproductive structures in late Paleozoic sediments that are contemporary with medullosan remains indicates that the two groups may have become separated by the Mississippian, and that the Permian medullosans played no part in the subsequent radiation of the Cycadophyta.

CALLISTOPHYTALES

Despite the relatively recent recognition of this group of seed ferns and the small number of taxa, the Callistophytales probably represent the best-known group of Paleozoic pteridosperms. The order includes plants with eustelic stems that produced pinnately compound fronds with axillary buds or branches at each node. Pollen organs were synangiate and borne superficially on pinnules of the frond; pollen was small and saccate. The seeds were slightly flattened, noncupulate, and contained a nucellus and integument that were free except at the base. Specimens are known principally from the Middle and Upper Pennsylvanian of the United States and Upper Carboniferous of France.

Although the name *Callistophyton* was initially intended for anatomically preserved axes, the generic name also refers to an entire plant. *Callistophyton* was a small scrambling plant (Fig. 13-25) that probably represented one of the understory elements of the Carboniferous forest. The plant consisted of an axis that produced branching stems about 50.0 cm long with large, widely separated fronds. Pinnules were laminar and highly dissected. Numerous adventitous roots were borne at many of the nodes.

The largest stem sections known for *Callistophyton* measure approximately 3.0 cm in diameter. The stem has a parenchymatous pith that is slightly angular and surrounded by up to 13 axial bundles of the primary xylem (see Fig. 13-26C). Bundle number is variable depending on the level of the stem and whether leaf traces are departing. The primary bundles of *C. poroxyloides,* the Upper Pennsylvanian species, are mesarch, while those of the Middle Pennsylvanian taxon are exarch. Pitting on the metaxylem tracheids varies from reticulate to bordered. Surrounding the primary body is an extensive zone of secondary xylem (see Fig. 13-26D) up to 70 cells in radial thickness. The secondary tracheids are arranged in files one to five cells wide that are separated by biseriate rays. Tracheal pitting is confined to the radial walls and shows crossed, slitlike apertures. A zone of fusiform and ray initials two to four cells in thickness is situated along the outer edge of the wood. The vascular cambium initially produced only secondary xylem, later producing about equal amounts of wood and secondary phloem. The position and extent of the primary phloem is not known with certainty, but secondary phloem consists of sieve cells and phloem parenchyma and associated phloem rays. Amber inclusions along the longitudinal walls of the sieve cells have been suggested as callose plugs. The cortex is composed of an inner parenchymatous zone and an outer area of longitudinally oriented fibers interspersed with parenchyma. The degree of fusions among the fibrous bundles of the cortex varies from level to level in the plant and also among stem specimens. Scattered throughout the cortex are enlarged cavities, some with an epithelial lining, that contain an amber-colored substance. Histologically identical secretory cavities are known to have occurred in the primary ground tissues of all plant organs of the genus. Periderm is apparent in the inner cortex, and in older stems, it became the outer limiting tissue of the stem.

The vascular system of *Callistophyton* has been interpreted as independent sympodia (axial bundles) that extended through the stem and produced leaf traces that were double at the petiole base and single at higher levels. Small axillary buds or branches are present at each node in *Callistophyton.* Buds made up of undifferentiated parenchyma are enclosed by two oppositely placed leaves or cataphylls that extend beyond the apex of the bud. Axillary branches have the same histologic features as the stems already described. The roots of *Callistophyton* are diarch, and older specimens contain abundant secondary tissues, including periderm. They are adventitious and attached to the stems in the axils of buds or branches.

The leaves of *Callistophyton* are borne in a ⅖ phyllotactic helix, with the larger leaves about 30.0 cm long. Fronds range from bi- to quadrapinnately compound and bear laminar pinnules (Fig. 13-25). The pinnules are deeply lobed with a constructed base. Multicellular hairs are present on the abaxial surfaces of some pinnules. Morphologically, the pinnules of *Callistophyton* correspond most closely to the form genus *Sphenopteris.*

Callospermarion (Fig. 13-26B) is the name of a bilaterally symmetrical seed that was produced by *Callistophyton.* Where the seeds were produced on the plant is not known for sure, but the occurrence of pollen organs attached to the

Figure 13-25 Suggested reconstruction of *Callistophyton. (From Rothwell, 1975.)*

lower surfaces of laminar pinnules suggests a similar mode of attachment for the ovules. In one report, a *Callospermarion* seed was described as attached to a long vascularized stalk, although the axis may represent a root that was compressed on the base of the seed and thus superficially appears organically attached. Specimens of *Callospermarion* range from 0.8 to 5.0 mm long, up to 3.8 mm wide in the primary plane, and 2.0 mm in the secondary plane. When sectioned transversely, lateral extensions of the integument show blunt wings in the primary plane. The integument is three-parted, with the majority of the seed coat composed of cells of the outer sarcotesta, including large secretory canals (Fig. 1326B). Utilizing a large number of specimens (125) of *Callospermarion pusillum* (Upper Pennsylvanian), Rothwell (1971) was able to demonstrate several ontogenetic stages of the ovule. Vascular tissue is present as two prominent strands in the "wings" of the integument and a small pad of tracheids at the base of the nucellus. The nucellus in *C. pusillum* is fused with the integument only in the chalaza; the distal end is modified into a flask-shaped pollen chamber. In many ovules judged immature on the basis of the

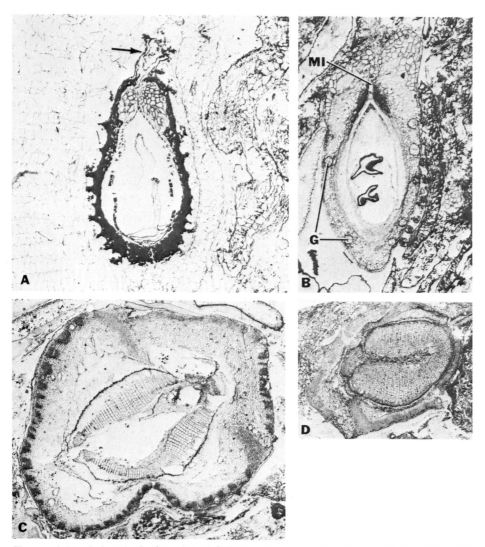

Figure 13-26 A. Longitudinal section of *Callospermarion* ovule with pollination droplet *(arrow)*. ×27. B. Immature *Callospermarion* ovule with weakly developed micropyle (MI) and integumentary glands (G). ×23. C. Transverse section of young *Callistophyton poroxyloides* stem. ×8. D. Transverse section of *Callistophyton boyssetii* stem with well-developed secondary xylem. ×6. *(A, C, and D courtesy of G. Rothwell; B from Rothwell, 1971.)*

differentiation of the integument, the pollen chamber contains numerous pollen grains of the *Vesicaspora* type. The ovules apparently were aided in trapping pollen by the production of a resinous pollination droplet (Fig. 13-26A) that extended from the micropylar orifice in a manner similar to those produced in many extant gymnosperms. In one specimen of *C. pusillum*, the fossilized droplet actually contained several pollen grains (Fig. 13-27D). Another species,

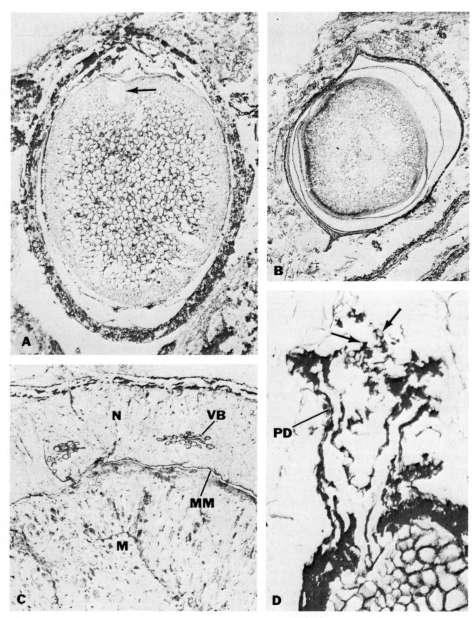

Figure 13-27   A. Longitudinal section of *Lagenostoma ovoides* with archegonium *(arrow)* and cellularized megagametophyte. ×24. B. Transverse section of *Pachytesta* sp. with cellular megagametophyte. ×13. C. Transverse section of *Pachytesta* sp. showing vascularized (VB) nucellus (N), megaspore (MM), and magagametophyte (M). ×32. D. Pollination droplet (PD) extending from the micropyle of a Pennsylvanian ovule. Arrows indicate pollen grains. ×110. *(A from Taylor and Millay, 1979; D courtesy of G. Rothwell.)*

C. undulatum, is slightly larger than *C. pusillum* and is known from sediments of the Middle Pennsylvanian.

Two pollen organs that differ only in minor features have been described for *Callistophyton.* Both are now known to have been borne on the abaxial surface of small laminar pinnules (Fig. 13-24C) of a tripinnate frond. *Idanothekion glandulosum* (Middle Pennsylvanian) consists of a ring of six to nine exannulate sporangia that are proximally fused around a vascularized central column (see Fig. 13-6A). Each synangium is about 1.0 mm long and radial. The wall of the sporangium is thick, except on the side facing the interior of the synangium, where dehiscence took place. Vascular tissue is present as a broad band in the outer layer of each sporangium. The structural features of *Callandrium callistophytoides* (see Fig. 13-6E) (Upper Pennsylvanian) are almost identical with those of *Idanothekion,* differing only in the absence of vascular tissues in the sporangial wall of *Callandrium.* It has recently been proposed that the two should be synonymized, with the genus *Idanothekion* being retained because it has priority. Both pollen organs bear small (40 μm) monosaccate grains of the

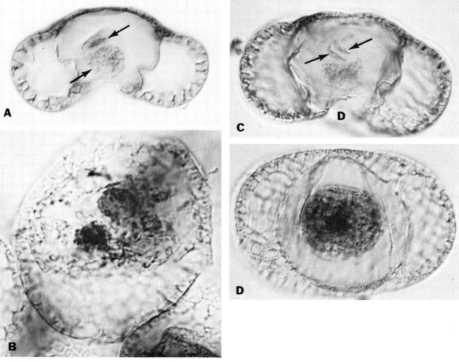

Figure 13-28 Microgametophyte development in the Callistophytales. A. Lateral view of pollen grain showing the embryonal cell *(lower arrow)* and prothallial cell *(upper arrow).* ×1500. B. Polar view of grain showing spherical structures that may represent the remains of the generative and tube cells. ×1500. C. Lateral view of grain with two prothallial cells *(arrows).* ×1500. D. Polar view of grain with well-preserved nucleus. ×2000. *(B–D from Millay and Eggert, 1974; A courtesy of M. Millay.)*

morphologic type generally associated with coniferophytes. If found in the dispersed state, these grains would be included in the genus *Vesicaspora* (Fig. 13-28A). Immature sporangia have provided evidence that both tetrahedral (Fig. 13-6B) and isobilateral (Fig. 13-6C) tetrads were formed in the Callistophy- tales. The grains are bilateral and elliptical in equatorial outline. The central body (corpus) is surrounded by an equatorial air sac (saccus) that is lined with a delicate ornamentation (Fig. 13-28D). On the proximal surface is a thickened cap (cappus); distally between the two lobes of the saccus is an elliptical sulcus (Fig. 13-28C).

A series of stages in the development of the microgametophyte are known for *Vesicaspora*. Grains have been found in *Idanothekion* and *Callandrium* sporangia that contain two-, three-, and four-cell stages of the microgameto- phyte, with the cells arranged in an axial stack within the corpus (Fig. 13-28C). Those closest to the proximal face of the grain represent prothallial cells, the largest cell representing either the embryonal cell (if further prothallial cells were produced) or an antheridial cell (if prothallial cell production was concluded). In one grain observed in polar view, two ovoid bodies may have represented the generative cell and protoplast of the tube cell (Fig. 13-28B). In this group of seed plants, pollen was not shed until the microgametophyte had at least developed to the four-cell stage, and judging from the immature nature of the pollen exine, the microgametophyte may have remained in the sporangium for a considerable amount of time.

The morphologic nature of *Vesicaspora* pollen was well suited for dispersal by wind, and, as already noted, the grains were trapped by the resinous pollination droplet extruded from the micropyle of the *Callospermarion* ovule. It is not known whether the trapped pollen grains floated into the pollen chamber of the ovule or were pulled in by the shrinking of the droplet. *Vesicaspora* pollen germinated from the distal sulcus. A *Vesicaspora* grain with a branched pollen tube (Fig. 13-29A) has been found in the nucellus of a *C. undulatum* ovule, further strengthening the biological relationship of the seeds and pollen organs of this family. Branched pollen tubes are typically haustorial in function (Cycadophyta), and within the Callistophytales, there may be evidence that the haustorial function of the pollen tube preceded siphonogamy.

As indicated earlier, more is known about the Callistophytales than about any other group of pteridosperms. This is particularly true when one considers the total biology of the plant. Available information details not only the structure and development of the vegetative parts of the plant, but also the ontogeny of the seeds and microgametophytes. All that is really missing from our understanding of this taxon is the manner in which the seeds were borne and stages in the development of the embryo. What is most surprising about these seed plants is their relatively modern, saccate pollen type and the equally modern appearance of the microgametophyte. The number of primary prothalli- al cells (three) present in the Callistophytales is greater than that in extant cycadophytes and closely approximates the upper number found in living

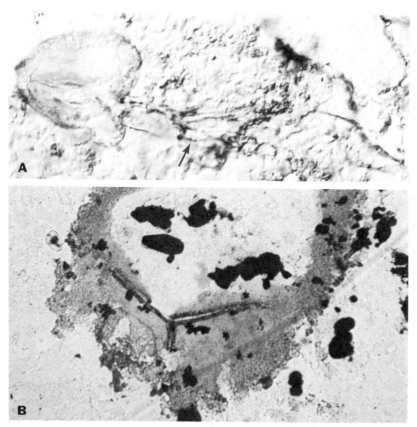

Figure 13-29 A. *Vesicaspora* pollen grain with branched pollen tube extending from distal surface. ×1100. B. Polar view of trilete suture on the distal end of the megaspore in a *Conostoma* ovule. ×200. *(A courtesy of G. Rothwell; B from Schabilion and Brotzman, 1979.)*

coniferophytes. These fossil microgametophytes do not support the long-held view that the microgametophyte of seed plants represents the reduced sexual phase that has arisen through loss of almost all the vegetative and sterile cells of an antheridium.

Within the Medullosales, the microgametophyte is morphologically similar to that found in certain members of the Cycadophyta. To date there is nothing that suggests pollen tubes were present, a structural feature that may not have been necessary because of the large size of the pollen grains and their inherent ability to contain a considerable amount of stored metabolites. The pollen grains of this group may have been some of the initial ones transported by means other than wind and gravity (e.g., insects). The pollen of the Lyginopteridales was probably anemophilous, judging from the size of the grains, the structural organization of the sporoderm, and the generally elaborate pollen receiving

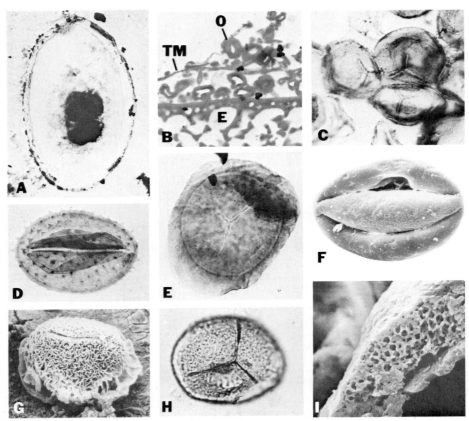

Figure 13-30   A. *Monoletes* pollen grain with spermlike contents. ×154. B. *Monoletes* pollen grain (E) with tapetal membranes (TM), and orbicules (O) on surface. ×13,000. C. *Potoniea* pollen grains. ×800. D. *Nanoxanthiopollenites* pollen grain. ×375. E. *Schulzospora* pollen grain. ×800. F. Distal surface of *Monoletes* pollen grain. ×200. G. Proximal surface of *Parasporites* pollen grain. ×225. H. Proximal surface of *Feraxotheca* pollen grain. ×1000. I. Fractured surface of *Monoletes* pollen grain wall showing alveolate infrastructure. ×2000. *(A from Stewart, 1951; B from Taylor, 1976; C and E from Millay and Taylor, 1979; D from Taylor, 1979; H from Millay and Taylor, 1977b; I from Taylor, 1976.)*

mechanism of the nucellus. How gametes eventually reached the archegonia is not known for any of the groups, but within the Medullosales it would appear that they were flagellated (Fig. 13-30A).

CALAMOPITYALES

The assignment of the Calamopityales within the Pteridospermophyta must be regarded as tentative, since no seeds, pollen-producing organs, or foliage have ever been found attached to the stems and petioles. The assignment of this group within the seed ferns has been made principally on the basic monostelic organization of the stem (Fig. 13-34C) and features of the secondary xylem that closely approximate the wood of most Paleozoic seed ferns. At the present time, the order represents a repository for stem and petiole remains that are known from deposits of the Upper Devonian and Lower Mississippian. The group was initially subdivided on the basis of the stelar organization and type of secondary xylem (manoxylic or pycnoxylic); however, as additional taxa have been added, this classification has broken down.

In the United States, numerous specimens of the Calamopityales have been found as nodular petrifactions in the New Albany shale, a stratum that bridges the Upper Devonian and Lower Mississippian. *Calamopitys americana* is a relatively common element and will be used to characterize the type of plant commonly encountered in this order. Some specimens have been found that exceed 4.0 cm in diameter; no appreciable stem lengths have been discovered. The central portion of the stem consists of a mixed pith, with many more parenchyma cells than tracheids. In transverse section, the stele is roughly triangular and contains five mesarch primary strands. Surrounding the primary body is a relatively broad zone of radially aligned secondary xylem tracheids and numerous multiseriate parenchymatous rays. Rays are from 1 to about 12 cells wide and variable in height. The cortex is parenchymatous and contains radial plates of sclerenchyma near the periphery. Petioles are apparent in a ⅖ arrangement. Leaf traces appear singly and then divide to produce four bundles that lack secondary wood in the base of the petiole. Another species, *C. foerstei*, differs in that it possesses widely separated primary xylem sympodia and axile vascular strands of unequal size.

Another genus included with the Calamopityales is *Stenomyelon*, considered by many to be the most primitive member of the order. *Stenomyelon tuedianum* (Fig. 13-31A), the type species of the genus, is known from the Calciferous Sandstone Series (Mississippian) of Britain. The stem was beautifully preserved and consists of a solid protostele dissected into nearly equal thirds by thin plates of parenchyma. Metaxylem tracheids contain multiseriate bordered pits. Secondary xylem is similar to that of other taxa in the order, differing only in the width of the vascular rays. Petioles are attached in a ⅖ arrangement, with traces containing two exarch primary groups. The surface of the stem is covered with multicellular projections that must have appeared similar to those described on the surface of *Microspermopteris*.

A slightly different stelar organization is present in *S. heterangioides*, in which clusters of parenchyma cells, in addition to parenchyma plates, divide the protostele. Possibly the simplest vascular arrangement occurs in *S. primaevum* (Fig. 13-31B), a Lower Carboniferous species from Britain. The stele is a trilobed protostele that lacks parenchyma; traces to the petioles divide repeatedly to form about eight mesarch bundles. The cortex in all *Stenomyelon* species contains radial plates of sclerenchyma.

One of the most common genera in the Calamopityales is *Kalymma*, a petiole genus. Anatomic features used to separate the numerous species include the distribution and shape of the vascular bundles, the level of tangential fusion between adjacent bundles, and the presence or absence of secretory canals.

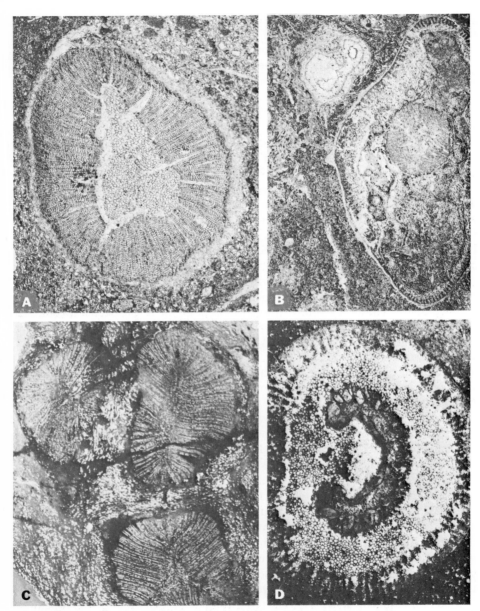

Figure 13-31 A. Transverse section of *Stenomyelon tuedianum.* ×6.5. B. Transverse section of *Stenomyelon primaevum.* ×3. C. Transverse section of *Bostonia perplexa.* ×5. D. Transverse section of *Kalymma minuta.* ×4.5. *(A and B from A. G. Long Collection Nos. 2164 and 4187 in the Hancock Museum; C from Stein and Beck, 1978; D courtesy of L. Matten.)*

Numerous specimens representing several species, from the New Albany shale have been shown to be fronds with few bundles near their petiole bases and an increased number at higher levels. Above the division in the frond, the petiole vascular bundles are arranged in a C-shaped ring; at higher levels, the number of bundles decreases. Petioles of *K. tuediana* have been suggested by Long (1964) as representing the base of the *S. tuedianum* frond. This suggestion is based on the position and number of vascular bundles and the common occurrence of both taxa in the same petrifactions. The petiole is about 1.0 cm in diameter and contains about nine vascular bundles; one side is slightly flattened. In one specimen, 20 vascular bundles are apparent in transverse section, many in the process of splitting. Foliage of the *Diplothmema* and *Sphenopteridium* types has been suggested as the laminar pinnules of *Stenomyelon* on the basis of its occurrence at the same stratigraphic level as *K. tuediana*. Another species initially described as *Arnoldella minuta* is now regarded as displaying features of *Kalymma*. *Kalymma minuta* consists of terete axes with a C-shaped xylem strand in transverse section (Fig. 13-31D). The abaxial surface of the trace contains several lobes of xylem, each containing a mesarch protoxylem strand. Tracheids are scalariform, and the cortex contains sclerenchyma plates that anastomose from level to level.

Chapelia is another genus that combines both stem and leaf features. In transverse section, the vascular system consists of a four-lobed protostele with mesarch xylem surrounded by a core of secondary xylem of the manoxylic type. The cortex contains both secretory cells and clusters of presumed fibers. Branching results in the production of two outer, papilionoid (butterfly-shaped in transverse section) strands of distinct bilateral organization and two inner, clepsydroid-shaped strands that are oriented with their long axes 90° to the major plane of the frond. The flattened nature of the frond and the presumed pattern of branching are similar to the configuration of the compression foliage genus *Diplopteridium*.

Diichnia kentuckiensis is the name of a New Albany shale stem that has a five-angled mixed pith with primary xylem strands opposite the lobes when viewed in transverse section. Features of the secondary xylem and cortex are similar to those of other calamopityean genera. The distinguishing feature of *D. kentuckiensis* is the double leaf trace that originates from adjacent primary xylem strands opposite the arms of the protostele.

Triphyllopteris (Fig. 13-32A) is the generic name applied to Lower Mississippian sphenopteridlike foliage that may represent a member of the calamopityeans. Individual pinnules are highly variable in outline, ranging from unlobed to fan-shaped (Fig. 13-32B) and occasionally dentate or pointed. Pinnules or pinnae are obliquely inserted on the rachis and abaxially concave. Fertile specimens have recently been discovered from the Price Formation of Virginia, and these consist of massive aggregations of elongate sporangia (Fig. 13-32C) that contain trilete spores (Skog and Gensel, 1980).

One stem recently described from the New Albany shale of Kentucky appears to have been polystelic. *Bostonia* was described from a single specimen

Figure 13-32 A. Leaf of *Triphyllopteris*. ×0.6. B. Several leaves of *Triphyllopteris uberis*. ×1.5. C. Sporangial cluster of *Triphyllopteris uberis*. ×10. D. *Kalymma grandis* (New Albany shale). *(A–C courtesy of J. Skog; D courtesy of L. Matten.)*

consisting of a stem about 3.0 cm long and 2.1 cm in diameter. In transverse section, the axis is composed of a parenchymatous ground tissue with nests of sclerotic cells and three longitudinally oriented columns of secondary xylem. The outer limits of the cortex were not preserved; consequently, it is not known whether sclerenchyma bands were present. The vascular tissue organization of *B. perplexa* is similar to that of a typical *Medullosa* stem, which contains three vascular columns, each with its own primary and secondary xylem (Fig. 13-31C). The mesarch primary xylem consists entirely of tracheids. Primary xylem strands (three in one column) are located toward the center of one column. Surrounding the primary body is a zone of secondary xylem up to 3.0 mm thick. Tracheids reveal bordered pit pairs with crossed, elliptical apertures. Multiseriate rays divide the manoxylic wood. Traces contain secondary xylem and divide at least once as they pass out to laterals. The incomplete stem fragment has been regarded as a seed fern of the calamopityean type on the basis of the presence of sclerotic cells, the nature of the secondary xylem with radial pits, and the association of secondary xylem with the traces.

Despite the uncertainty regarding the systematic position of the group, the Calamopityales are important in demonstrating significant intermediate stages in the evolution of the seed fern eustele. Beck (1970) presented convincing evidence that several calamopityean taxa represented a series leading to the eustele in a seed fern such as *Lyginopteris* and *Callistophyton*. Beginning with a species of *Stenomyelon* (*S. tuedianum*), there was a gradual dissection of the solid protostele through the addition of parenchyma in the form of both plates and clusters in *S. heterangioides*. The subsequent evolution of the stele involved the tangential separation of the primary xylem into distinct sympodia through the phylogenetic development of parenchyma in the pith region (e.g., *Calamopitys americana* and *C. foerstei*). Such a vascular system containing five sympodia surrounded by secondary xylem would be identical with the eustele of both early and late Carboniferous seed ferns such as *Microspermopteris* and *Heterangium*, and a second possible series in stelar evolution leading from *Bostonia* to the medullosans. Of particular interest will be the relationship of the fertile parts of the calamopityeans to those of the later seed ferns when the former are finally discovered and/or recognized.

There were a number of Triassic and Jurassic plants that appear to have retained features of the more widespread Carboniferous pteridosperms. These plants, which have been referred to as Mesozoic seed ferns in some treatments, are not known in as much detail as the Carboniferous pteridosperms and, in some instances, may be more closely related to other major plant groups. They are, however, of importance in that several structures (e.g., nearly closed cupules approximating carpels) present within the group demonstrate morphologic units that have been linked with the angiosperm level of evolution.

CAYTONIALES

The Caytoniales represent by far the best-known group of Mesozoic seed ferns. The group was initially described in 1925 by the distinguished British paleobotanist H. H. Thomas from specimens collected from Middle Jurassic plant-bearing beds along the coast of Cayton Bay, Yorkshire. Specimens have been described from Triassic and Cretaceous sediments as well. So striking and unusual are some of the features of this group of plants that Thomas in his initial treatment regarded them as a new group of angiospermous plants.

The most common element of the Cayton Bay flora is a palmately compound leaf type that consists of three to six leaflets. The lanceolate leaflets of *Sagenopteris serrata* are up to 7.0 cm long; each contains a prominent midvein and anastomosing laterals that form a reticulate venation pattern. In *S. nilssoniana,* the cuticle is thin, and epidermal cell walls are straight; stomata are present on the lower surface along with conspicuous hairs. Specimens of *Sagenopteris* were known long before their reproductive parts were discovered and include reports ranging from the Upper Triassic into the Cretaceous from a number of widely separated geographic localities (United States, Greenland, England, and Canada).

   Caytonanthus is a pollen-bearing structure that consists of a slender axis that bears flattened lateral branches; each of the branches bear from one to three elongate pollen sacs (Fig. 13-33D). Each synangium is about 1.0 cm long and is pointed at the distal end. In transverse section, each synangium contains three or

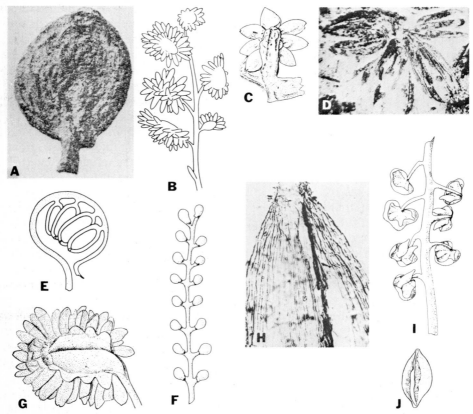

Figure 13-33 A. Cupule of *Caytonia harrisii.* ×12. B. Synangiate fertile branch of *Pteruchus johnstonii.* C. *Antevsia,* a Mesozoic pollen organ. D. Several pollen sacs of *Caytonanthus tyrmensis.* ×8. E. Suggested reconstruction of the cupulate head of *Caytonia sewardii.* F. *Caytonia nathorstii* showing distribution of cupules. G. Microsporangiate head of *Pteruchus africanus.* H. Inner cuticle membrane from a seed of *Caytonia sewardii.* ×150. I. Cupulate ovule-bearing structures of *Peltaspermum thomasii.* J. Pollen grain macerated from *Antevsia zeilleri.* (*A from Reymanówna, 1973; B, E, F, and I from Dilcher, 1979; C and J from Townrow, 1960; D and H from Krassilov, 1977; G from Townrow, 1962.*)

four sporangia or locules that are arranged around a central zone of tissue. The pollen-containing structures, which have been termed anthers in some treatments, are radially symmetrical, but exactly how dehiscence occurred is not known. The epidermis is composed of delicate fusiform cells, with some indication that thicker-walled fibrous elements are beneath.

The pollen grains are small and bisaccate; they are referred to the genus *Vitreisporites.* In *C. arberii,* the grains are about 30 μm long and contain distinct endoreticulations lining the interior of the sacci. The distal surface is marked by a conspicuous sulcus. Pollen from *C. kochii* is about the same size, but lacks endoreticulations on the inner surfaces of the sacci.

The ovule-bearing structure, *Caytonia,* consists of an axis about 5.0 cm long that bears stalked, multiovulate cupules in subopposite pairs (Fig. 13-33F). Scars along the megasporophyll suggest that the cupules were shed. Each cupule is nearly circular in outline and up to 4.5 mm in diameter (Fig. 13-33A). They are borne along the axis in such a way that the cupule is recurved, with a liplike projection near the point of attachment. Each cupule contains 8 to 30 seeds depending on the species; each is borne on a delicate stalk in an orthotropous position along the midvein of the cupule (Fig. 13-33E). The seeds are approximately 2.0 mm long and radially symmetrical. The integument consists of an outer uniseriate epidermis that covers a row of radially aligned, thick-walled cells. Beneath this zone are several rows of longitudinally directed fibers; the nucellus is attached only at the base. Macerations (Fig. 13-33H) suggest that the seed integuments are not vascularized. Dispersed seeds of this type are sometimes placed in the form genus *Amphorispermum.*

In the initial paper, pollen grains were noted in association with the lipped portion of the cupule, a structure termed the "stigmatic surface." Based on this information, the cupule was interpreted as a fruit that contains numerous seeds, with fertilization taking place through a pollen tube that developed from the stigmatic surface to the pollen chamber of the ovules. The fine strands of cuticle observed extending from the cupule to the seeds were interpreted as the remnants of pollen tubes or an extension of the seed micropyle. Subsequent studies indicated that pollen was present inside the cupule, probably drawn in by pollination drops that originated at the micropylar end of the seed. Transverse bars that formed long canals and appeared to be consistent with the number of seeds produced in each cupule (*C. sewardii,* 8; *C. nathorstii,* 15; and *C. thomasii,* 30) were extensions of the integument that may have faciliatated pollination. Thus, although *Caytonia* morphologically represented a multiovulate cupule and not a fruit, as originally thought, the structure does, in fact, represent at least one method whereby seeds may have become enclosed; therefore, it does approach the morphology of an angiosperm carpel.

Recently, Reymanówna (1973) has provided additional information about the histology of *Caytonia* from specimens collected in the Grojec area of Poland (Jurassic). In *C. harrisii,* the cupule is vascularized by a flattened plate of tracheids with bordered pits that extend up the middle of the cupule and give off laterals to the seeds. In addition, this species produced a cluster of seeds in the center of the cupule, and the seed cluster was covered by a cutinized membrane rather than being separated by cupule tissue, as in other species. The large number of isolated seeds found in the matrix when *Caytonia* specimens are uncovered suggests that seeds were dispersed from the *Caytonia* cupules.

CORYSTOSPERMALES

The Corystospermales constitute a relatively small group of plants known from Triassic beds of South Africa, Australia, Argentina, and India. In general, the plants were probably small and bore pinnate leaves with open dichotomous venation. Although the various plant parts have not been found attached, their consistent occurrence in the same beds, their similar cuticle, and the identical pollen found in both pollen sacs and seed cupules have been used to indirectly associate the various organs.

The family was instituted by Thomas (1933) for seed-bearing organs that revealed helmet-shaped structures. *Umkomasia* consists of a fertile branch about 3.5 cm long that dichotomizes and bears recurved cupules; a pair of pinnules is apparent at the point of each branch dichotomy. The entire fertile structure has been termed an inflorescence, but cuticle preparations suggest that the entire unit was flattened and represents a pinna. Although the cupules were preserved as compressions, their shape suggests an urnlike configuration with two prominent lobes. The wrinkled nature of the cupule surface has suggested to some that these were fleshy structures. Both surfaces of the cupule contain numerous stomata, each formed by a ring of simple subsidiary cells (four to six) around the guard cells. The seeds of *U. macleanii* are small (5.0 mm long) and appear either singly or in pairs in each cupule. The seeds are ellipsoidal and elongate, with a curved micropylar tube. In *U. verrucosa,* the cupule-bearing axis is larger, and there are distinct differences between the inner and outer cupule epidermis.

Based on the number of species described, *Pilophorosperma* was the most common seed-producing member of this group. In *Pilophorosperma,* the cupules are less pronounced and hemispherical in outline. Specimens of *P. granulatum* bear three cupules at the end of each branch, while in *P. gracile,* two are common. On the outer surface of the cupule are short papillae, and the inner surface is covered with long pointed hairs. In another species (*P. crassum*), the cupules are borne in an overlapping fashion along the axis so that the fertile structure is compact. Subtending pinnules are absent in some species. In *Spermatocodon,* another seed-producing form, the cupule-bearing branches are helically arranged. All the seeds of this group appear to have possessed a slightly curved, bifid micropylar canal. Macerations suggest that the integument contained no fibrous cells and the seed epidermis was covered with a thick cuticle. Embedded in the pollen chambers of several specimens are numerous saccate pollen grains similar to those found in the microsporophyll *Pteruchus.*

The pollen-producing organ *Pteruchus* consists of alternately arranged microsporophylls that are attached to an axis about 4.0 cm long; in one species, they may have been helically arranged (Fig. 13-33B). Each microsporophyll terminates in a flattened head that bears numerous elongate sporangia that are partially protected by the tissue of the head (Fig. 13-33G). The number of pollen sacs per head is variable (20 in *P. simmondsii* to over 100 in *P. dubius*); each is elongate, and dehiscence is longitudinal. The cuticle on all parts shows epidermal cells with slightly wavy margins and few stomata. The pollen grains are bisaccate, with the sacci slightly inclined and partially covering the distal sulcus. The sacci contain endoreticulations on their inner surfaces; the outer surfaces are smooth.

Except for the larger number of pollen sacs, *Pteruchus* morphologically appears similar to both *Crossotheca* and *Feraxotheca* of the Paleozoic lyginopterid group. Both appear to have been constructed of a planated pinna. They differ chiefly in the type of pollen produced: saccate grains in *Pteruchus* and trilete miospores in the lyginopterids. This difference is not too surprising now that at least one other group of seed ferns (Callistophytales) is known that possessed saccate pollen by the Middle Pennsylvanian. Although structural features are not known for *Pteruchus* microsporophylls, they do possess many more pollen sacs than the callistophytalean seed fern synangium *Idanothekion*.

One of the foliage types that was stratigraphically associated with the seed and pollen organs of the Corystospermales is *Dicroidium* (Fig. 13-34B). Specimens are characterized by the forking of the main rachis. Pinnules vary from almost square to elongate, and in some species they overlap. Venation consists of several veins entering the pinnule base and dichotomizing. Stomata are present on both surfaces, and in some species, small papillae are associated with the epidermal cells. *Dicroidiopsis*, *Diplasiophyllum*, and *Xylopteris*, other foliage types thought to have been related to the corystosperms, are now regarded as species of *Dicroidium*. The consistent association of *Dicroidium* with stems of *Rhexoxylon* has been suggested as representing foliage and stem remains of the plant that produced *Pteruchus* and *Umkomasia* fertile parts.

Rhexoxylon was a Triassic plant that was tree-sized; some specimens consist of trunks up to 50.0 cm across. In transverse section, the stem contains sectors of secondary xylem separated by wide vascular rays (Fig. 13-34A). In *R. piatnitzkyi* (Argentina), the young stem has about 15 primary bundles separated by a narrow zone of parenchyma. The central region of the stem contains a parenchymatous pith. Sclerotic nests are present in both the pith and the stem cortex. In the center of the stem is abundant secondary parenchyma that is organized into irregular masses. Tracheal pitting consists of one to two rows of circular bordered pits on the radial walls, and growth rings are regular in the wood. The outer surfaces of young stems contain rhombic leaf bases and branch scars or buds surrounded by small-scale leaves.

PELTASPERMALES

The Peltaspermales are known from Upper Triassic (Greenland and South Africa) foliar remains, as well as pollen and seed-bearing parts. The bipinnate

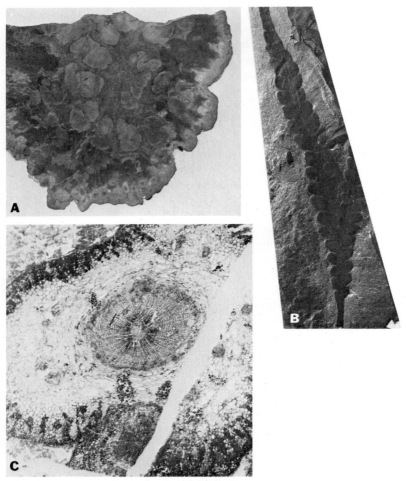

Figure 13-34 A. Transverse section of *Rhexoxylon africanum*. ×0.4. B. *Dicroidium odontopteroides*. ×0.5. C. Transverse section of *Calamopitys embergeri*. ×5. *(C courtesy of J. Galtier.)*

leaves are about 30.0 cm long and contain lanceolate pinnules with the margin of the larger ones broadly serrate; some pinnules are present on the rachis between pinnae. Pinnules of *Lepidopteris* are broadly attached and have a prominent midrib with forking lateral veins. The surface of the rachis of *L. ottonis* contains numerous irregular swellings suggestive of scalelike emergences. Stomata are present on both surfaces (amphistomatic) and consist of sunken guard cells surrounded by overarching papillae that originate from the subsidiary cells.

The seed-bearing axis *Peltaspermum* consists of shallow cuplike units that are helically arranged (Fig. 13-34I). In *P. rotula,* the seed-bearing disk is about 1.0 cm in diameter and contains about 20 seeds arranged in a ring around the periphery. In *P. thomasii,* another species from Greenland, the number of seeds

Figure 13-35 Suggested reconstructions of *Glossopteris* tree and component organs. *(From Gould and Delevoryas, 1977.)*

is about 10. The seeds of both species contain an elongate micropylar canal and, judging from the variation in size, developed at different times.

Like the corystosperms, the pollen organ of this group consists of pinnately arranged laterals that dichotomized and bear one to two rows of pollen sacs. The individual sacs are about 2.0 mm long and appear on one side of the reduced pinnule. The pollen sacs of *Antevsia* (Fig. 13-33C) apparently dehisce longitudinally to produce small (36 μm) monosulcate grains (Fig. 13-33J). Features of the cuticle, including the blisterlike swellings, on *Lepidopteris, Peltaspermum,* and *Antevsia* are similar and have been used to unite these taxa.

GLOSSOPTERIDALES

The plants included in the Glossopteridales are all extinct representatives of a flora that once dominated the continent of Gondwanaland (Australia, South Africa, South America, Antarctica, and the Indian peninsula) during the Permian. A few specimens are known from the Triassic. The glossopterids were arborescent (Fig. 13-35) specialized gymnospermous plants that have historically been assigned to the cycads, seed ferns, ferns, gnetophytes, cordaites, and angiosperms. The recent discovery of structurally preserved seed-bearing megasporophylls substantiates beyond any doubt their inclusion with the pteridosperms.

Figure 13-36 A. Specimen of *Mexiglossa varia*. ×1. B. *Belemnopteris elongata*. ×1. C. Scale leaf of *Glossopteris*. ×2. D. Venation pattern of *Mexiglossa varia*. ×2.5. E. *Dictyopteridium feistmantelii* (*Glossopteris tenuinervis*). (A and D from Delevoryas and Person, 1975; B and C from Lacey, Van Dijk, and Gordon-Gray, 1975; E from Chandra and Surange, 1976.)

By far the most common element of the flora is *Glossopteris,* a lanceolate-shaped leaf with a distinct midrib and reticulate venation (Fig. 13-36E). Since the original description of the leaf by Brongniart in 1828, there have been numerous species proposed. Lacey, Van Dijk, and Gordon-Gray (1975) have estimated that at least 80 species have been described, but this is probably a conservative number. Despite several attempts to develop a standardized classification for glossopterid leaves, little progress has been made in defining species on the basis of morphology, secondary venation, cuticular structure, or even associated reproductive organs. For the time being, the interpretation of *Glossopteris* in a broad sense appears to be the best approach until a sufficient number of leaf types with attached reproductive organs can be found to more accurately define the species. One of the most widely encountered species is *G. browniana.* Some specimens exceed 30.0 cm in length and are characterized by a rounded apex. Secondary veins form oblong-polygonal meshes that assume an oblique course to the entire margin. *Glossopteris fibrosa* is a slightly smaller species collected from the "Upper Coal Measures" of Tanganyika. It has an obtuse apex, and features of the petiole are unknown. The cuticle of the upper epidermis is typically devoid of stomata; stomata on the lower surface are haplocheilic with four to eight subsidiary cells arranged in an irregular ring. In *G. hispida,* the lower epidermis is covered with numerous multicellular hairs.

Gangamopteris is another common element of the Gondwana flora that closely approximates the general morphology of *Glossopteris.* The most distinct difference between the two taxa is the larger size and the absence of a well-defined midrib in specimens of *Gangamopteris.* Some species of *Glossopteris* exhibit a relatively inconspicuous midrib, but according to Pant and K. B. Singh (1968), the two taxa may be distinguished by cuticular features of the midrib area. Leaves with stomatiferous areas bounded by nonstomatiferous areas similar to those of the remainder of the lamina warrant assignment to the genus *Gangamopteris.* Other cuticular features show the same variability exhibited by leaves of *Glossopteris.*

Another common leaf type is *Belemnopteris* (Fig. 13-36B). In this form, the secondary veins are similar to those of *Glossopteris* and *Gangamopteris,* but the taxon can be identified by the sagittate base and trichotomous midrib.

Rhabdotaenia is another tongue-shaped leaf that is common in *Glossopteris* floras. In *R. fibrosa,* the midrib is distinct, with the lateral veins extending almost at right angles; a few branch before reaching the margin. Haplocheilic stomata are confined to the lower surface and consist of unspecialized subsidiary cells. A few vascular elements macerated from the midrib contain helical secondary wall thickenings.

Scale leaves (Fig. 13-36C) of many sizes and shapes are also common in the Gondwana facies associated with *Glossopteris* and *Gangamopteris,* with the rhomboidal-shaped ones possibly the most common. They have been regarded as bud scales, sterile scales from the reproductive organs, and organs that are intermediate between photosynthetic leaves and the foliar parts of the reproductive organs.

Glossopteris is believed to have been an arborescent plant with alternately arranged leaves or leaves arranged in tight helices that simulate whorls (Fig. 13-35). There is some evidence that the leaves were borne on long and short shoots like *Ginkgo. Glossopteris* is now considered a deciduous plant because of the numerous leaves that have been found in autumn-winter varved sediments as opposed to no leaves in the spring-summer layers. The main trunk of *Glossopteris* has pycnoxylic wood with conspicuous growth rings. Multiseriate

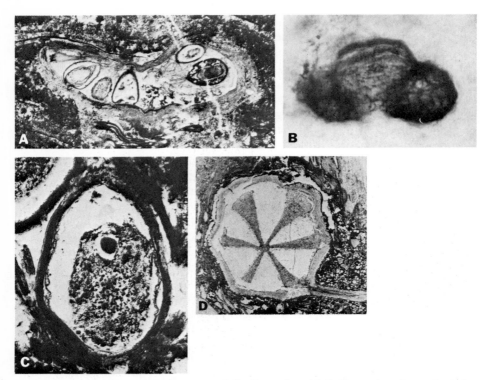

Figure 13-37 A. *Glossopteris* megasporophyll with seeds. ×12. B. Bisaccate pollen grain similar to those found in the micropyles of several seeds. ×485. C. Longitudinal section of seed with archegonial chamber. ×47. D. Transverse section of *Vertebraria*. ×2. *(A–C from Gould and Delevoryas, 1977; D from Gould, 1975.)*

pits are present on the radial walls of the tracheids; some are hexagonal in outline. The cross-field pits are of the cupressoid type; xylem rays are uniseriate. Secondary xylem of this type has been included in the genus *Araucarioxylon*.

The underground portions of *Glossopteris* are included in the genus *Vertebraria*. Initially illustrated in 1833 by Royle, the genus has been the subject of several studies, but is known from anatomically preserved specimens at only a few localities (e.g., Antarctica and Queensland). In transverse section, the axes consist of a central zone of exarch primary xylem surrounded by four to seven radiating arms of secondary wood (Fig. 13-37D). The secondary xylem is continuous near the periphery of the axis and typically contains distinct growth rings. Surrounding the zone of secondary xylem is a narrow band of periderm with well-developed cork. In longitudinal section, the secondary xylem wedges are connected at varying intervals by transverse segments of wood, termed platforms, that generally contained a root trace. A few crushed parenchyma cells have been identified in the hollow areas between the xylem arms and platforms, but it is believed that these areas were probably devoid of cells during the life of the plant. Protoxylem tracheids have annular pits, with up to six vertical rows of opposite or alternate bordered pits on the radial walls of the secondary xylem tracheids. Extending through the pycnoxylic wood of *Vertebraria* are uniseriate vascular rays with cross-field pits.

The reproductive organs of the glossopterids have been a constant source of controversy since the first report of "linear sori" on a *Glossopteris* leaf. Since that time numerous pollen- and ovule-bearing structures have been described from *Glossopteris* leaf-rich sediments around the world. Because almost all are known from compression-impression specimens, their morphology and anatomy, in most instances, remains speculative.

Several types of pollen-bearing structures have been identified associated with *Glossopteris*. One of the most commonly encountered forms is *Glossotheca*. It consists of a branched pedicel that extends from the petiole of the leaf. At the ends of the lateral branches are clusters of six to eight elongate pollen sacs. It has been estimated that each cluster contained approximately 100 pollen sacs. On the surface of the pollen sacs are longitudinal wrinkles. Nothing is known about the pollen of this fructification.

Another common pollen-producing glossopterid fructification is *Eretmonia* (Fig. 13-38D). The pollen sacs of this form also consist of pedicellate clusters of pollen sacs borne on a stalked fertile leaf. Individual pollen sacs are about 1.0 mm long and variable in overall morphology. The fertile leaves of *Eretmonia* are also highly variable in size, shape, and numbers of sporangia. In general, the leaf is rather small and characteristically rhombohedral in outline. Lacey, Van Dijk,

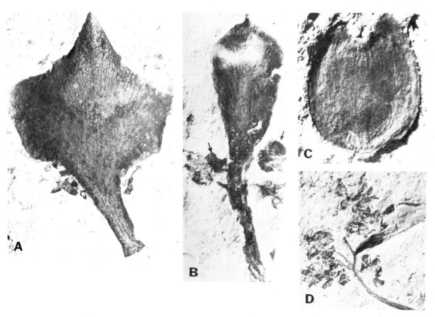

Figure 13-38 A. *Eretmonia natalensis.* ×2. B. *Lidgettonia africana.* ×2. C. Seed of *Mooia lidgettonioides.* ×10. D. *Eretmonia natalensis.* ×2. *(From Lacey, Van Dijk, and Gordon-Gray, 1975.)*

and Gordon-Gray, (1975) have demonstrated that several morphologic forms defined as species merely represent a gradational stage of a single species, *E. natalensis* (Fig. 13-38A).

Kendostrobus is another pollen-producing cone that has been suggested as having glossopterid affinities (Fig. 13-39A). It consists of a central axis with helically arranged, naked, exannulate sporangia arranged in groups. The surfaces of the sporangia are covered with minute pits; the spores of *K. cylindricus* are elliptical to subcircular and up to 100 μm long. Extending over the surface is a series of parallel ridges, and on one face, there is a suture described as monolete. Although the organization of *Kendostrobus* is unlike the other presumed *Glossopteris* pollen-producing structures, the monolete grains are like those macerated from the *Lithangium* sporangium type.

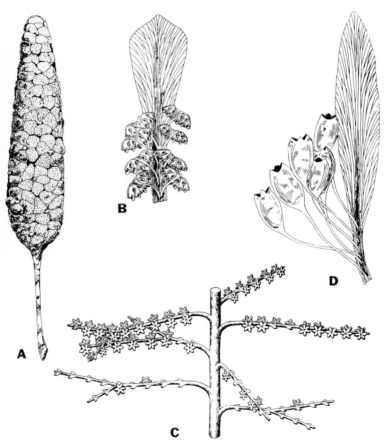

Figure 13-39 A. Suggested reconstruction of *Kendostrobus cylindricus*. B. Cupulate disks of *Lidgettonia mucronata*. C. Suggested reconstruction of *Perezlaria oaxacensis*. D. Cupulate fructification of *Denkania indica*. *(A, B, and D from Surange and Chandra, 1975; C from Delevoryas and Gould, 1971.)*

Arberiella, Lithangium, and *Polytheca* are the generic names used for isolated pollen sacs that are believed to have been produced by the glossopterids. In *A. africana,* the uniloculate sporangia are occasionally attached by slender stalks that closely approximate the arrangement of *Glossotheca.* The sporangia are about 3.0 mm long and exhibit twisted cells at the apex that may have served as a dehiscence mechanism. The pollen grains are bisaccate and appear to have had endoreticulations extending from the inner surfaces of their saccus walls. Folds or striations extend across the cappus of the central body. In one species, *A. vulgaris,* the grains measure up to 85 μm long and 55 μm wide. *Lithangium* and *Polytheca* are also uniloculate sporangia, but they have been described as containing monolete and trilete spores, as well as monocolpate pollen.

Despite the rather large number of ovulate structures described for the glossopterids, all are morphologically similar in general appearance. Each consists of a dorsiventral structure that has been variously termed capitulum, cupule, and fertiliger. *Scutum* is the generic name adopted by Plumstead (1952) for one type of reproductive structure attached to *Glossopteris* leaves. As the generic name suggests, this ovule-bearing structure is shield-shaped. In *S. conspicum,* there are approximately 75 centrally clustered scars that are surrounded by a striate margin or "wing." Each of the scars is believed to have represented the position of an ovule. In the initial description of *Scutum,* the structure was described as a bilaterally symmetrical, two-sided cupule borne on a pedicel attached to the midrib of a leaf. Specimens that were split open revealed ovules on one half of the cupule and bracts that were interpreted as microsporophylls on the other. Based on this interpretation, *Scutum* was considered to be a bisporangiate or bisexual reproductive sturcture. Subsequent studies have indicated that one half the unit was a receptacle that contained a large number of ovules borne on elevated projections; the other half of the structure was a fertile scale that protected the ovules when they were young, detaching later to expose the micropyles to presumably wide-borne saccate pollen. The ribbed or lobed edge of several ovule-bearing structures has been interpreted as ovule displacement during fossilization.

Isolated seeds of several types are common in sediments containing *Glossopteris* leaves. Two of the more commonly encountered types are *Pterygospermum* and *Stephanostoma.* Nucellar cuticle macerations of both types of seeds have yielded bisaccate pollen, further strengthening the relationship of the seeds to an ovulate structure such as *Scutum.*

Lidgettonia is a compound ovulate structure consisting of four to eight seed-bearing units per leaf (Fig. 13-38B): some specimens have been reported with up to 14. Each of the seed-bearing structures (megasporophylls) is disklike and about 7.0 mm in diameter (Fig. 13-39B). The margin is variously lobed and exhibits distinct crenulations or teeth. Numerous fine striations that radiate out from the center of the disk probably represent the vascular bundles or fiber bands of the leaf tissue. In *L. africana,* the seeds are described as being of the *Samaropsis* type. They are almost circular in outline and approximately 2.0 mm in diameter. The integument extends into a wing in the primary plane, which is uniform in width except at the micropyle, where it is notched.

As the specific epithet implies, *Mooia lidgettonioides* is closely comparable to *Lidgettonia,* differing only in the smaller number of seed-bearing units and the radial morphology of the seeds. The seed-bearing capsules are borne on unbranched pedicels from the adaxial surface of the fertile leaf. The seeds (Fig. 13-38C) are about 4.2 mm long and nearly radial in symmetry. It has been suggested that each unit produced only a single seed.

Rusangea (South Africa) is another seed-bearing structure known to have been produced on a *Glossopteris*-type leaf. Attached to each leaf are two scales, each bearing a single sessile seed. The leaves are rather uniform in size, with the largest specimen only 2.8 cm long. The unwinged seeds are oval and only 3.5 mm in diameter.

Another interesting ovulate structure that has been described from the Raniganj Stage of India is *Denkania* (Fig. 13-39D). In this ovulate structure, about six seed-bearing cupules are attached to long pedicels borne on the midrib of a fertile *Glossopteris* scale. Each unit is about 1.0 cm long. Apparently, only one seed was produced per cupule.

One ovulate glossopterid structure apparently produced platyspermic seeds that were attached to a narrow pedicel, but not covered by any leaflike or cupular structure. *Austroglossa walkomii* (Upper Permian of New South Wales) was attached to the petiole of a *G. conspicus* leaf.

There are numerous examples in paleobotany of a single fossil discovery that greatly alters the interpretation of previously described specimens and, in a few instances, influences the interpretation of the affinities of a particular group of plants. One such an example would be Beck's discovery of the attachment of *Callixylon* and *Archaeopteris* and the establishment of the Progymnospermophyta. Another is the recent report of anatomically preserved *Glossopteris* remains from the late Permian of Queensland (Gould and Delevoryas, 1977). Associated with these sediments were silicified layers of plant material that contained not only *Glossopteris* vegetative leaves, but also foliar structures with attached ovules. Although the ovule-bearing specimens were not found organically attached to the leaves, structural similarities and the overall morphology of the compressed reproductive structures clearly indicate that they were borne on the *Glossopteris* leaves. Attached to one side of a fleshy megasporophyll were numerous ovoid seeds (Fig. 13-37A). In transverse section, the edges of the megasporophyll are partially inrolled to surround the seeds. Histologically, the megasporophyll is similar to a *Glossopteris* leaf, but lacks the sclerenchyma hypodermal fibers. The seeds are sessile, each about 1.5 mm long, with the micropyles directed toward the center of the megasporophyll. The integument is thickened in the micropylar region; bisaccate pollen (Fig. 13-37B) and seeds with archegonia have been identified in some specimens (Fig. 13-37C). Between the seeds and arising from the outer portion of the integument are numerous cellular filaments or plate of cells that form a meshwork on the inside of the megasporophyll. Similar filaments also extend from near the micropyle, suggesting a mechanism that assisted in directing pollen flow, possible aided by a pollination droplet.

Other ovulate glossopterid reproductive structures such as *Dictyopteridium* are more difficult to interpret. This genus was established for a pedicellate ovule-bearing receptacle (probably a megasporophyll) that contained numerous small seeds. Covering the side containing the ovules is a scalelike leaf. Cuticular studies of *D. feistmantelii* indicate that the scale leaf and ovule-bearing megasporophyll are not parts of the same structure, but rather represent different organs. On the receptacle, the epidermal cells are small and papillate, with a network of cuticular thickenings. On the outside of the scale are prominent hairs; no hairs are seen on the inside. Based on the different cuticular patterns, it would appear that the reproductive unit of *Dictyopteridium* does not represent a single, partially inrolled megasporophyll that split along its edges. *Dictyopteridium* is known from India, Australia, and South Africa and has been found attached to specimens of *G. tenuinervis*.

Although the study by Gould and Delevoryas (1975) clearly indicates that at least one ovule-bearing structure was a leaf, this organization may not have been consistent for all the ovulate structures included within the glossopterids. The variety of morphologic forms, including both uniovulate and multiovulate types produced in solitary and compound structures, further suggests that there were several different types of plants within the *Glossopteris* group. The situation may in part parallel the great variety demonstrated among the seeds of Paleozoic seed ferns, which were produced on leaves, in cupules, and on naked branching systems. In the glossopterid *Denkania* (Fig. 13-39D), for example, the ovule-enclosing structure appears to show a close correspondence with the uniovulate cupules of some Carboniferous seed ferns. Among the glossopterids, seed morphology is also highly variable, with both radially and bilaterally symmetrical forms being produced. The presence or absence of wings may be related to how the seeds were ultimately shed. Thus it would appear that the glossopterids, despite the apparent uniformity of their vegetative organs, represent a rather diverse group fo Upper Paleozoic seed ferns that may ultimately rival the Carboniferous taxa in variability of reproductive structures.

The glossopterids have been suggested as closely related to several groups, including pteridosperms, cycads, cordaites, gnetophytes, and angiosperms. Possibly the earliest advocate of an angiosperm alliance was Plumstead (1956), who considered the "bisexual flower," the pollen, the enclosing of seeds within a fruit, and the dichotomous reticulate venation of the leaves as features indicating possible affinities with angiosperms. As several authors have pointed out, the reproductive organs of the glossopterids were not bisexual, and the bisaccate pollen and seeds are gymnospermous in organization. Although reticulate venation is characteristic of angiosperms, such a pattern appears to have evolved in several gymnospermous groups. Schopf (1976) has suggested the possibility that the glossopterids are more closely related to *Gnetum*. At the same time, however, he points out that in the gnetophytes the reproductive organs are arranged in loose cones or strobili, while in the glossopterids such an arrangement does not appear to have been present, with the exception of *Kendostrobus*. Others have suggested a morphologic similarity between certain glossopterid ovulate structures and the seed-bearing structure *Carnoconites* (Jurassic) of the Pentoxylales.

Before concluding the discussion of this interesting group of Permian seed ferns, mention should be made of *Glossopteris*-like foliage collected from the Middle Jurassic of Oaxaca, Mexico (Delevoryas and Person, 1975). Associated with the leaves and an interesting fructification were typical Jurassic foliage taxa, including *Zamites, Otozamites, Pterophyllum, Ptilophyllum,* several ferns, and some cones assignable to the genus *Williamsonia.* The leaves demonstrate the same range of morphologic characters that exist among species of *Glossopteris,* including forms that may be up to 26.0 cm long. Based on the geographic location and age of these leaves, the other floral elements, and the rapidly mounting evidence that the *Glossopteris* leaf type was probably produced by many biologically unrelated plants, the Oaxaca leaves were placed in a new genus, *Mexiglossa* (Fig. 13-36A and D). The possibility also remains that the Mexican leaves represent a remnant of the earlier Gondwana floral province that migrated northward to what is now Oaxaca during the Triassic and early Jurassic.

Associated with *Mexiglossa* was an interesting pollen-producing organ that may have been part of the plant that bore *Mexiglossa* foliage. *Perezlaria* is reconstructed as an axis that bears laterals with whorls of saclike bodies that were probably pollen sacs (Fig. 13-39C). Each sporangium is about 3.0 mm long, and they apparently dehisced as units. Morphologically, the paniclelike reproductive structure bears some resemblance to the seed fern pollen organ *Caytonanthus.* Whether these two plant parts represent organs of the same biological species or merely demonstrate the fortuitous association of isolated parts cannot be determined at this point.

PALEOZOIC FOLIAGE

Probably the most widespread and conspicuous plant fossils of the Carboniferous are the abundant impression-compression remains of fernlike foliage. The presence of what was thought to represent a diverse flora resulted in the Carboniferous being referred to as the Age of Ferns. However, this designation was applied before it was known that some of the fernlike foliage was produced by seed plants (members of the Pteridospermophyta). Historically, there have been several important attempts to classify fern foliage types on the basis of shape, size, venation pattern, and how the ultimate foliar segments were attached to the stem. Many of the genera and species used today were initially delimited by such noted paleobotanists as Brongniart (1828), Sternberg (1820–1838) (Fig. 13-9B), Goeppert (1836), Stur (1875, 1877), and Zeiller (Fig. 13-19B). In North America, much of the early work with compression floras of the Carboniferous can be attributed to the detailed studies of Lesquereux (1880, 1884) (Fig. 13-40A) and White (1900, 1936, 1937) (Fig. 13-40B). These form genera, which have become widely established in paleobotanical literature,

Figure 13-40 A. Leo Lesquereux. B. Charles David White.

almost always consist of sterile specimens. In cases where reproductive parts are found attached to folaige, some authors have adopted the practice of assigning the generic name of the fructification in place of the name of the vegetative foliage. It is important for the reader to understand the biological implications of dealing with Paleozoic foliage types. In several instances, a single genus may be known to represent the foliage of widely disparate plants, as in the case of *Sphenopteris,* which has been identified as the foliage of several different seed ferns as well as true ferns. Nowhere is the species problem more complex in paleobotany than in dealing with fern foliage types, where many of the "species" undoubtedly represent foliage or simply the variation inherent in a biological species from different parts of the frond at different stages of development. Despite these limitations, numerous Paleozoic foliage types have been used successfully in subdividing portions of the Carboniferous into recognizable divisions of geologic time. In some instances, stratigraphic levels can be recognized by a single index species, while in other cases, an assemblage of species has proved most useful in identifying particular time stratigraphic units. For example, several well-defined floral zones (Mississippian −3, Pennsylvanian −8, and Permian −3) have been determined in the Upper Paleozoic of the United States by Read and Mamay (1964), while Kidston (1923–1925) was initially responsible for subdividing the Coal Measures in Great Britain and continental Europe using foliage types. More recently, Wagner (1966) has successfully used Paleozoic foliage form genera to divide the Carboniferous in Spain.

The basic organization, or architectural plan, of the fossil fern leaf, or frond, is similar in most instances to the leaf of a living fern. The frond was attached to the primary stem by the stipe or petiole; in some instances the stipe was considerable in size. Branching may have assumed a variety of forms, with the main ribs of the frond termed the rachis. First-order subdivisions of the rachis are termed pinnae, and these may be opposite, subopposite, or alternate, and all in the same plane (biseriate). In a few Paleozoic fernlike plants (e.g., Zygopteridales), pinnae were borne at right angles to each other, a condition

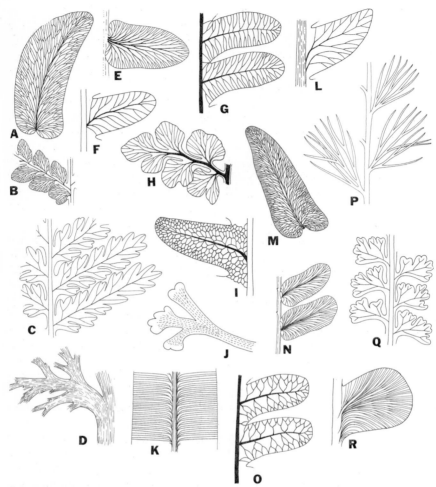

Figure 13-41 A. *Linopteris*. B. *Mariopteris*. C. *Sphenopteris*. D. Aphlebia. E. *Mixoneura*. F. *Pecopteris*. G. *Alethopteris*. H. *Eusphenopteris*. I. *Lochopteris*. J. *Kankakeea*. K. *Taeniopteris*. L. *Lescuropteris*. M. *Reticulopteris*. N. *Neuropteris*. O. *Lochopteridium*. P. *Rhodea*. Q. *Alloiopteris*. R *Odontopteris*.

termed quadriseriate. The ultimate foliar segments of the frond are the pinnules. If the main rachis lacks pinnae, only producing pinnules, the frond is said to be simply pinnate. When pinnules are borne on pinnae, the frond is bipinnate, tripinnate, or quadripinnate depending on the number of frond subdivisions.

Although many fern fronds have been described, most of the Paleozoic foliage is represented by pinnae and pinnules, and it is principally on pinnule morphology that the various form genera have been delimited. Following is a brief description of some of the most commonly encountered Paleozoic foliage genera.

Pecopteris   The genus *Pecopteris* (Fig. 13-41F) is one of the more commonly encountered foliage forms. The pinnules are typically small and stand free from one another (see Fig. 13-17E). They are attached along the entire width of the base and have parallel or nearly parallel margins. A single vein enters the base and extends almost to the rounded pinnule tip. The lateral veins are straight or slightly arched and simple or forked near the margin. *Pecopteris* is the foliage type present on the Carboniferous marattialean fern *Psaronius,* several true ferns, and also at least one seed fern (*P. pluckenetii*). The genus extends from the Lower Pennsylvanian (possibly Mississippian) into the Permian.

Alethopteris Pinnules of *Alethopteris* (Fig. 13-41G) are often quite large, with some species ranging up to 5.0 cm long. They are borne at an acute angle from the pinna midrib, with the base characteristically decurrent (flared) on the lower side. Each pinnule is vascularized by a single trace that generally forks to produce steeply arched secondary veins (subsidiary veins). In some species, the secondary veins arise from the pinna midrib along the decurrent base. All species of *Alethopteris* are believed to have been borne by medullosan pteridosperms.

Lonchopteris The morphology of *Lonchopteris* pinnules is similar to that of *Alethopteris,* except that in *Lonchopteris* the venation pattern is reticulate (Fig. 13-41I). Specimens are rare and are believed to have been produced by seed ferns.

Callipteridium Specimens of *Callipteridium* are similar to those of *Alethopteris* and, in some instances, have been confused with it. Pinnules of *Callipteridium* are typically smaller, and they insert at right angles to the pinna midrib. They are often slightly bilateral in symmetry, with the base generally less decurrent. A single vein enters the pinnule and becomes less distinct well below the pinnule apex, often forming subsidiary veins. Some secondary veins may enter the base from the rachis. The genus is believed to have been produced by seed ferns on the basis of the discovery of seeds near the pinnule bases of *C. koraiense.*

Neuropteris *Neuropteris* is another rather common Carboniferous foliage genus. The most characteristic feature is the narrow, constricted point with which the pinnule was attached to the pinna rachis (Fig. 13-41N). Pinnules of this type often have rounded tips. Each pinnule is supplied by a single vein, from which arise arched, dichotomously branched secondary veins. In some species, such as *N. scheuchzerii,* two round basal lobes are associated with each pinnule; covering the surface are numerous hairs. Pinnules of *Neuropteris* are known to have been associated with seeds and pollen organs borne on medullosan seed fern stems.

Odontopteris The pinnules of *Odontopteris* are generally small and slightly constricted at the base. They are attached along the entire length of the base, with several prominent veins (Fig. 13-41R) entering the lamina from the pinna rachis. Each of these veins may dichotomize several times before reaching the pinnule margin. The genus is believed to have been borne by some seed ferns of the Pennsylvanian. *Lescuropteris* is a generic name often used for odontoperid pinnules that exhibit reticulate venation (Fig. 31-41L).

Mixoneura Pinnules placed in the genus *Mixoneura* typically exhibit characteristics that are intermediate between those of *Neuropteris* and

Odontopteris. The pinnules are similar to those of *Neuropteris* in that they are narrowly attached and rounded at the tip. However, they possess a venation pattern similar to *Odontopteris,* with several veins entering the pinnule from the rachis midrib.

Linopteris   Specimens of *Linopteris* (Fig. 13-41A) are relatively rare, but those recovered are morphologically similar to pinnules assigned to the genus *Neuropteris.* They are, however, generally smaller and may be characterized by a reticulate venation pattern in which the secondary veins anastomose as they pass toward the pinnule margin (Fig. 13-16D). *Reticulopteris* (Fig. 13-41M) is another genus that has been used by some workers for pinnules that demonstrate a reticulate venation pattern. Some authorities believe the two may be distinguished by the pseudoreticulate venation in *Reticulopteris,* in which the veins bend toward one another but do not actually anastomose. Others have suggested that the two taxa merely represent variations of a single genus. At least one *Linopteris* species is thought to have been produced by the medullosan seed fern *Sutcliffia.*

Cyclopteris   *Cyclopteris* is a morphologic foliage type that is often found associated at the bases of some fronds, especially those of the neuropterid group (*Neuropteris, Odontopteris, Linopteris,* and *Reticulopteris*). These "pinnules" are rounded with the veins radiating outward from the point of attachment, forming an open dichotomous pattern (see Fig. 13-17G).

Spiropteris   *Spiropteris* is the generic name used for the coiled immature leaves (circinate vernation) of various fossil ferns.

Kankakeea   The genus *Kankakeea* has been used for for small, thalloid-lobed tips of pinna rachides that sometimes are dichotomously branched (Fig. 13-41J). They are often found attached to pinnae bearing other foliage types and have been suggested as some form of vegetative reproductive structure. The genus has been reported from the Pennsylvanian of North America and the Upper Carboniferous of France.

Mariopteris   Some species of *Mariopteris* (see Fig. 13-17B) closely approximate the pinnule morphology of *Pecopteris.* In general, the pinnules are attached broadly to the pinna axis, somewhat obliquely. They taper toward the tip, and many species are multilobed. Each pinnule contains a prominent midvein from which laterals depart in an acute angle (Fig. 13-41B). One species has been found associated with the seed fern stem *Schopfiastrum.*

Sphenopteris   Pinnules of *Sphenopteris* (see Fig. 13-17C) are generally constricted at the base and often are attached by a short stalk. They are oval in outline, with the margin lobed or variously toothed. The midvein may be relatively straight or flexuous, with the laterals departing in a steep angle as they pass toward the lobes of the margin singly or in small groups. *Sphenopteris* (Fig. 13-41C) foliage was relatively common during the Pennsylvanian, and it was associated with several true ferns (e.g., *Sermaya* and *Tedelea*), as well as seed ferns.

Megalopteris   The pinnules of *Megalopteris* are long and strap-shaped and sometimes bifurcated nearly to the base (Fig. 13-15D). The pinnule midrib is prominent, with many closely spaced laterals ascending from the margin in a steep angle. The end of the pinnule is often sharply pointed. Nothing is known about the plant that produced *Megalopteris* foliage, although it is thought to be the leaf of a seed fern, a hypothesis strengthened by the similarity of the epidermis and stomata to that of *Neuropteris* and a general morphology like that of *Alethopteris*. Although *Megalopteris* represents a rather rare Paleozoic foliage type, the genus has been reported in abundance from an early Pennsylvanian flora, of which a large percentage of the taxa are included in the noeggerathians. Because of its rare occurrence with other Paleozoic foliage form genera, *Megalopteris* is sometimes considered to be an indicator of upland habitats.

Allioiopteris   In the genus *Alloiopteris,* the frond is at least three times pinnate, with the pinnae bearing alternately arranged pinnules. The pinnules are strongly decurrent and typically fused at their bases. Each pinnule is vascularized by a prominent vein that may divide several times to produce laterals that extend to the pinnule margin. Pinnule lobes are prominent and may be lobed (Fig. 13-41Q) or have teeth. Morphologically similar foliage-bearing abaxial sporangia are called *Corynepteris,* and a recent study has demonstrated that *Alloiopteris* pinnules were produced by some plants with a *Zygopteris* type of anatomy.

Rhodea   The pinnules of *Rhodea* are represented by dichotomous subdivisions of narrow segments in which distinct lamina are all but absent (Fig. 13-41P). The genus is similar to some species of *Sphenopteris,* which are highly dissected, or to *Diplothmema,* which is distinguished on the basis of the forking of the petiole. Partially petrified axes bearing foliage of the *Rhodea* type recently have been shown attached to stems with *Heterangium* anatomy.

Eremopteris   Pinnules of *Eremopteris* (see Fig. 13-13A) are similar to some species of *Sphenopteris,* but they may be distinguished by the lack of a midrib and dichotomous venation. The margin may be variable, but most species are characterized by uneven teeth or lobes. The genus is thought to have been produced by pteridosperms, with one species, *E. zamioides,* associated with bilaterally symmetrical seeds and small synangiate pollen organs.

Taeniopteris   *Taeniopteris* includes large leaves with a prominent midrib (see Fig. 13-41K); secondary veins depart at an angle of approximately 70° and branch once before they reach the entire margin. The genus extends from the Carboniferous into the Cretaceous and constitutes an excellent example of a form genus. In the Carboniferous (Pennsylvanian of Kansas), *Taeniopteris* foliage is known with small seeds attached to the abaxial surface, while in the Mesozoic, the taxon has been associated with the cycadeoid *Williamsoniella*.

Discopteris   *Discopteris* is a generic name used for both sterile and fertile pinnules that superficially resemble the pinnules of *Sphenopteris*. Pinnules are highly dissected and possess a prominent midvein; fronds possess basal aphlebiae that become more highly dissected at higher levels. In *D. karwinensis,* the fertile pinnules are rounded and characterized by a disk-shaped sorus at the end of the midvein consisting of between 50 and 70 annulate sporangia. Sporangial histology closely resembles a number of true ferns, including the genus *Botryopteris*.

Cycadophyta and Cycadeoidophyta

CYCADOPHYTA

In some classifications at least three different groups of plants (pteridosperms, cycads, and cycadeioids) are included in the Cycadophyta. In this book the division Cycadophyta includes only those plants which have traditionally been placed in the Cycadales. The division includes both modern and fossil forms that can be traced with confidence back to the Permian and possibly into the Upper Pennsylvanian. Cycads probably originated among the Paleozoic seed ferns, with the Medullosales as the most probable ancestral stock, although Andrews (1961) has pointed out that there is a broad gap in our understanding of the early evolution of the group. During the Mesozoic, cycads reached their maximum development, but they have been on the decline ever since. Today they are represented by 10 genera and approximately 100 species. At one time they were worldwide in distribution, but today they are restricted to the geographic regions of Central America, South Africa, Australia, and eastern Asia.

Modern cycads may be characterized by tuberous, short, squat trunks; others resemble tree ferns or palms. Most of the arborescent types are unbranched. On the surface of the stems are persistent leaf bases surrounded by reduced, scalelike leaves termed cataphylls. Distally they exhibit a crown of pinnately compound leaves. The stems consist of a massive pith and cortex containing resin canals and a relatively small amount of manoxylic secondary xylem. All cycads are dioecious, with the seeds borne on reduced, modified leaves that are aggregated into cones or strobili; in *Cycas,* the megasporophylls are borne in the same phyllotactic spiral as the leaves and not aggregated into cones. Seeds are produced along the two edges of the petiole, with the terminal expanded portion of the leaf pinnately divided in some species. In other genera, the distal end of the megasporophyll is reduced or missing and tangentially expanded to form a peltate structure, with the two ovules borne on the inner surface. The pollen cones are small and compact; sporangia are attached to the lower surface of the microsporophylls. Pollen grains are boat-shaped, thin walled, and typically devoid of any ornamentation. The exine is honeycombed or alveolate.

In his comprehensive review of fossil cycads, Mamay (1976) suggests that the earliest cycads had simple rather than compound leaves. The genus *Spermopteris* (Fig. 14-1A), a pteridosperm from the Upper Pennsylvanian and Lower Permian, offers clues about the origin of the seed-bearing structures of later-appearing cycads (see Fig. 14-2). *Spermopteris* is characterized by elongate, simple leaves that are included in the Paleozoic to Mesozoic foliage genus *Taeniopteris* (see Fig. 13-41K). The seeds are arranged in a row on the abaxial surface near the margin (Fig. 14-2). The arrangement of the seeds and the general morphology of the leaf of *Spermopteris* are only slightly removed from the Lower Permian megasporophyll that Mamay named *Phasmatocycas* (Fig. 14-3A). The genus is based on compression specimens that include a fertile axis bearing two rows of sessile, broadly attached gymnospermous ovules. In *P. spectabilis* (Fig. 14-4A), the fertile axis is more than 20.0 cm long and contains more than 60 seeds. The seeds are typically preserved as flattened molds (Fig. 14-4B), with each containing a double seed cuticle and megaspore membrane. Between the ovules and on the lamina (Fig. 14-1B) are numerous glands that

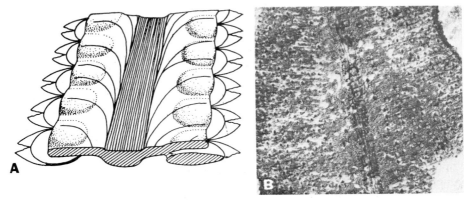

Figure 14-1 A. Suggested reconstruction of a portion of a fertile leaf of *Spermopteris coriacea* with ovule micropyles directed away from lamina. B. *Taeniopteris* sp. leaf with numerous glandlike structures. ×5. *(A from Cridland and Morris, 1960; B from Mamay, 1976.)*

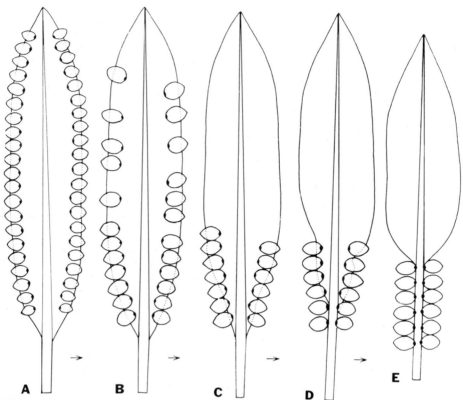

Figure 14-2 Suggested stages in the evolution of a *Cycas* megasporophyll (E). A. Early form similar to *Spermopteris* with a large number of ovules. B–D. Intermediate stages showing progressive reduction in number of ovules and leaf lamina. *(Modified from Mamay, 1976.)*

may represent nectaries associated with an early insect pollination syndrome. As several authors have noted, although insects do not appear to be the primary pollinators of modern cycads, they are associated with them and may represent the remnants of a once more widespread pollination system.

Archaeocycas is another Lower Permian cycad megasporophyll. In *A. whitei*, ovules were borne in opposite pairs along the stalk of the megasporophyll, with the lamina of the sporophyll partially enclosing the ovules (Fig. 14-3B). Ovules ranged up to 3.0 mm long and are characterized by a small, circular attachment scar.

There are a number of reports of early Mesozoic cycads, although in several instances the fossils need to be more critically examined. One of these is the Upper Triassic genus *Dioonitocarpidium*, which is known from Bavaria. The genus is based on plants with simple taeniopterid sterile leaves and pinnate sporophylls, each bearing a pair of basal ovules. In *D. liliensternii*, the seeds are described as attached to only one side of the megasporophyll. Both the question of the accuracy of the observations and possibility that the sterile foliage and

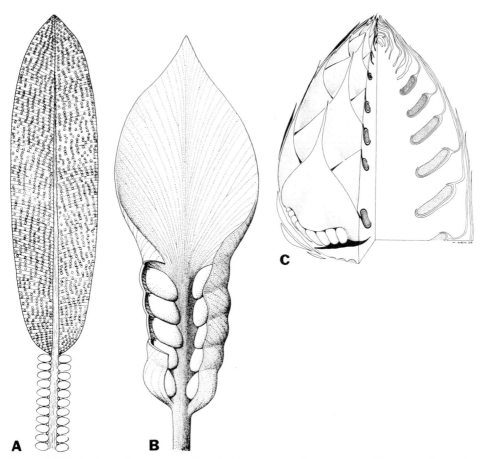

Figure 14-3 A. Suggested reconstruction of the megasporophyll of *Phasmatocycas*. B. Suggested reconstruction of *Archaeocycas* megasporophyll with partially enrolled lamina. C. Suggested reconstruction of the pollen cone *Lasiostrobus polysacci*. *(A from Mamay, 1976; B from Taylor and Millay, 1979; C from Taylor, 1970.)*

megasporophylls represent parts of different plants have caused some workers to discount the genus.

Another Upper Triassic cycad that was reconstructed on the basis of fragmentary evidence is *Bjuvia simplex*. The plant was reconstructed as a tree bearing large, entire leaves assignable to *Taeniopteris gigantea*. Megasporophylls with an ovate distal lamina were placed in the genus *Palaeocycas*. Two pairs of lateral protrusions believed to represent the stalks of seeds provided the basis of Florin's reconstruction of a megasporophyll as a leaflike appendage bearing four basal seeds attached to the naked stalk. Because of the association of the two organs and the similar epidermal pattern of both, the sporophylls and leaves were used to reconstruct a plant with a stout, heavily armored trunk with persistent leaf bases and a terminal crown of leaflike megasporophylls that

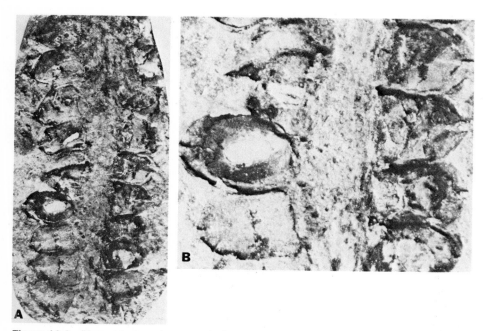

Figure 14-4 *Phasmatocycas kansana.* A. Axis with two lateral rows of seeds. ×4. B. Close-up showing morphology of seeds and manner of attachment. ×9. *(From Mamay, 1976.)*

superficially resemble those of *Cycas*. In the case of this fossil, the fragmentary nature of the remains, the absence of seeds, and the simple organization of the fronds are all features that have caused some skepticims regarding Florin's original interpretation.

One Upper Triassic cycadophyte that has been reconstructed on the basis of stem, leaves, and possible pollen-producing cones is *Leptocycas*. It is unlike modern cycads in that the stem was rather smooth and probably no more than 5.0 cm in maximum diameter. Based on the size of the leaves and the diameter of the stem, *L. gracilis* is thought to have been approximately 1.5 m tall. Along the stem, the leaf bases were widely separated; at the apex, there was a loose crown of pinnately compound leaves of the *Pseudoctenis* type associated with cataphylls. Individual fronds were petiolate and exceeded 20.0 cm in length; cuticle fragments indicate that the stomata are characteristically cycadalean with haplocheilic guard cell ontogeny. Attached to one stem is a slender strobilus that morphologically resembles a pollen cone. One of the interesting features of *L. gracilis* is the pinnate compound nature of the fronds; all the other pre-Jurassic cycads appear to have entire leaves. Mamay (1976) has suggested that the entire leaf is primitive among cycads, with the pinnately compound form derived (Fig. 14-5). The modification of the entire taeniopterid form involved the gradual dissection of the margin. Such a concept appears to have merit, but must await the discovery of additional late Paleozoic and early Mesozoic foliage types known to have been produced by cycads.

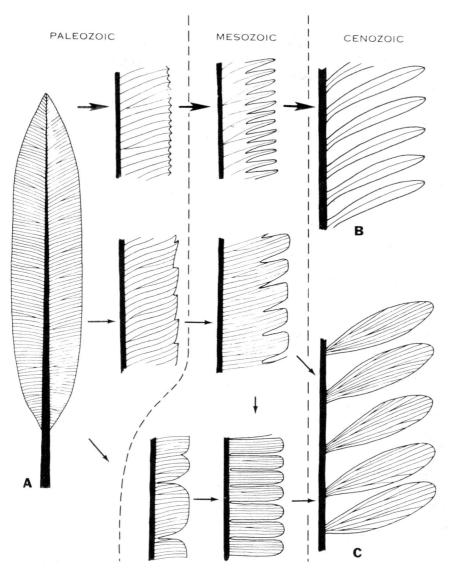

Figure 14-5 Suggested evolution of cycadalean leaves beginning with entire margined ancestral taeniopterid type (A) and extending to forms with more incised margins leading to the cycadaceous (B) and zamiaceous (C) types. *(Modified from Mamay, 1976.)*

One reproductive structure that has been suggested as cycadalean is a petrified pollen cone *Lasiostrobus* (Fig. 14-3C). It consists of helically arranged microsporophylls that are broadly attached at the base and distally upturned. Extending through the fleshy cone axis are six tangentially flattened vascular bundles that provide pairs of traces to the microsporophylls. On the lower surface of each sporophyll are 7 to 10 elongate, thick-walled pollen sacs (Fig.

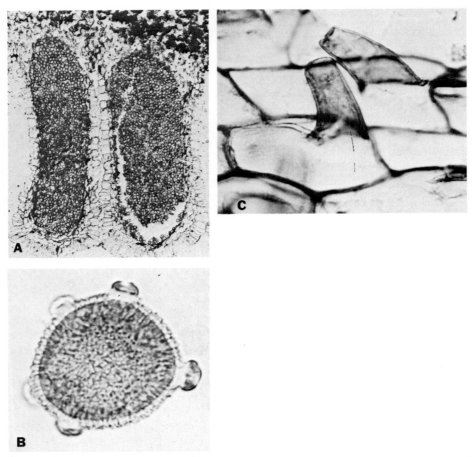

Figure 14-6 *Lasiostrobus polysacci.* A. Longitudinal section of two pollen sacs. ×55. B. Pollen grain with five sacci. ×1500. C. Hairlike extensions of abaxial surface epidermal cells. ×600. *(From Taylor, 1970.)*

14-6A). Slightly sunken cycadalean stomata and blunt trichomes are also present on the lower surfaces of the microsporophylls (Fig. 14-6C). The pollen of *L. polysaccii* is small (20 to 29 μm) and inaperturate; a few grains have been identified with trilete surtures. Extending from the surface of the grain are three to eight subequatorial small sacci (Fig. 14-6B). The ultrastructural organization of the exine is tectate. One interesting feature of the pollen grains concerns the apparent shedding in the microspore stage of development, a feature regarded as highly advanced because of the reduced nature of the microgametophyte. An analysis of the fossil cones, including pollen, apex, vascularization, epidermis, sporangia, and histology, shows features in common with both the cycads and conifers. *Lasiostrobus* also has been suggested as an early ginkgophyte on the basis of the unusual vascular system of the microsporophylls. Regardless of the ultimate systematic position of this interesting pollen cone, its relatively modern appearance does little to explain the evolutionary history of the pollen-producing organs of either the cycads or conifers.

Numerous fossil cycads are known from the Middle Jurassic of Yorkshire, England. *Beania* is the name used for ovulate cones consisting of an axis bearing widely separated megasporophylls, each with a distally expanded, peltate portion that resembles the megasporophylls of certain extant cycads (e.g., *Zamia*). Attached to the inner surface of each megasporophyll are two sessile, orthotropous seeds. The nucellus and integument of the seed are adnate in the lower two-thirds. Because the genus is known only from compressed specimens, features of the vascular system and histology of the ovules remain to be determined. Specimens of *B. mamayii* are known in which the axis is at least 18.0 cm long. Associated with the megasporophylls are strap-shaped leaves up to 80.0 cm long with a prominent midvein and entire margin. On the lower surface between the veins are scattered stomata with slightly sunken guard cells. Trichomes are common along the veins. Leaves are of the *Nilssonia tenuinervis* type. The pollen cones believed to be part of this cycad are typically about 7.5 cm long and appear to consist of helically arranged, imbricate microsporophylls. On the lower surface of each microsporophyll are numerous pollen sacs about 0.5 mm in diameter. The pollen of *Androstrobus wonnacottii* is monosulcate, smooth-walled, and less than 30 μm in diameter. The entire plant was reconstructed by Harris, but it did not look much like a modern cycad. Rather, the leaves and strobili were borne at the ends of slender, branched axes. It is not known whether the pollen and ovule-bearing cones were borne on the same plant or on different plants, as in modern cycads.

Although *Leptocycas, Bjuvia,* and *Beania* are the only attempts at reconstructing entire cycads, other remains are known from Triassic deposits. One of these is *Lyssoxylon grigsbyii,* a petrified stem known from the Chinle Formation of Arizona and New Mexico. It was initially described as a cycadeoid (Williamsoniaceae) axis, but additional specimens have proved beyond any doubt that the anatomy is more cycadalean. The silicified stem consists of a central pith surrounded by a manoxylic vascular cylinder containing a few growth rings (Fig. 14-7A). In transverse section, the tracheids are square; biseriate alternate pits are present on the radial walls (Fig. 14-7B). Extending through the wood are conspicuous vascular rays. Arising from the epidermis are bicelled hairs that form a dense mat around the petiole bases. One characteristic that substantiates the cycadalean affinities of *Lyssoxylon* is the girdling pattern of the leaf traces. Preservation is so excellent that many ray parenchyma cells contain nuclei and cytoplasm. The available evidence suggests that Triassic and Jurassic cycad stems were relatively slender and often branched, but *Lyssoxylon* appears to be an exception. Although it was several times larger in diameter than other fossil cycad stems, *Lyssoxylon* is still considerably smaller than most extant cycads. It is interesting, however, that there is more secondary xylem and less ground tissue, including cortex, than in a living cycad stem. If the modern cycads are descendents of the Paleozoic seed ferns, as some believe, then there has been a gradual reduction in wood accompanied by an increase in ground tissue production.

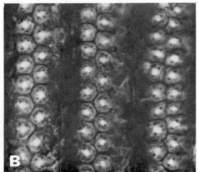

Figure 14-7 *Lyssoxylon grigsbyi.* A. Transverse section of trunk. ×1.7. B. Bordered pitting on radial walls of secondary xylem tracheids. ×560. *(From Gould, 1971.)*

Another silicified Triassic stem that is believed to be a member of the Cycadophyta is *Michelilloa waltonii* from the Ischigualasto Formation of northern Argentina. Although the entire stem was not preserved, it is estimated to have been about 10.0 cm in diameter. In the central portion is a massive pith with scattered mucilage ducts. The secondary xylem consisted of tracheids with multiseriate pits and numerous vascular rays. The structure of the leaf gap and presence of long filamentous hairs on the surface of the stem are features that *Michelilloa* shares with the extant cycad *Dioon.*

Fascisvarioxylon is a structurally preserved axis from the Rajmahal Hills of India that is regarded as a cycadalean stem. The stem measures 1.8 to 2.3 cm in diameter and is covered by an armor of leaf bases. Surrounding the pith are a series of mesarch primary strands and a zone of secondary xylem approximately 2.0 mm thick. Medullary rays are uni- or biseriate and up to 30 cells high.

Modern cycads typically consist of short, squat stems that bear helically arranged fronds. All the modern taxa are dioecious with pollen and seed cones produced on different plants. It is becoming increasingly apparent that the Mesozoic ancestors of the cycads were more treelike in appearance, consisting of relatively narrow stems that branched repeatedly. *Leptocycas,* a cycad, and *Ischnophyton,* a cycadeoid, both from the same Upper Triassic locality, exhibit the same general plant habit, consisting of slender branching axes. A similar growth pattern was present among the Paleozoic seed ferns, the group that most believe was ancestral to cycads and cycadeoids. Among the cycadeoids, the slender branching habit appears to have persisted in the Triassic and Jurassic Williamsoniaceae, while the later Cretaceous members of the Cycadeoideaceae are all known from plants with short, squat trunks. The fossil record provides no information about the subsequent evolution of modern cycads from their Mesozoic ancestors, but it is interesting that the same shift from slender branching axes appears to have occurred along the cycad line of evolution as well. This abrupt shift in the general habit of the plant may have been triggered by distinct shifts in the Cretaceous climate.

CYCADOPHYTA AND CYCADEOIDOPHYTA FOLIAGE

The Mesozoic is sometimes referred to as the "Age of Cycads" because of the abundance of foliage (Fig. 14-8A through C) that is believed to have been produced by members of the Cycadophyta and Cycadeoidophyta. The leaves

Figure 14-8 Mesozoic foliage types. A. *Zamites.* B. *Ptilophyllum.* C. *Nilssonia.*

occur as impressions and compressions, varying from a few centimeters in length to over a meter. They are typically once pinnate, although some may be entire and many appear to have been rather coriaceous with a thick cuticular layer. Although the importance of cuticular features in these leaves was understood as early as 1856 by Bornemann, the comprehensive studies of Nathorst (1902) and, later, Thomas and Bancroft were primarily responsible for demonstrating the existence of two major groups of Mesozoic cycadophytes—the Cycadophyta and Cycadeoidophyta. Thomas and Bancroft (1913) established two orders (Nilsson-iales and Bennettiales) that correspond rather closely to the Cycadophyta and Cycadeoidophyta, respectively. In distinguishing the two basic foliage types, one of the important epidermal characters was the stomatal apparatus. In the nilssonialean type, the two guard cells have their origin from a common cell, while the adjacent subsidiary cells are derived from other epidermal cells. This type of stomatal ontogeny has been termed haplocheilic and is typical of members of the Cycadophyta. Leaves with haplocheilic stomata also exhibit a relatively thin layer of cutin, especially over the guard cells. Other characteristics that have been useful in identifying cycadalean leaves but are less consistent include the irregular orientation of the stoma and the fact that the straight-walled epidermal cells are not in well-delineated rows.

The second pattern of stomatal ontogeny, which is slightly more complex, is termed syndetocheilic and is found in the Cycadeoidophyta. In this pattern, the two guard cells and subsidiary cells all have their origin from the division of a single cell. Syndetocheilic stomata have a thicker cuticle on the outer and dorsal (wall opposite the stoma) walls of the guard cells. Secondary characteristics include stomata aligned in distinct rows with the stomatal axes oriented at right angles to veins and the general sinuous margins of the epidermal cells. Harris (1969) noted that one interesting feature of the bennettitalean cuticle is the rather consistent crumbly nature of the thicker, upper cuticle, which often makes it impossible to obtain satisfactory cuticle preparations. This may suggest some basic difference in the biochemistry of the cutin. These two patterns are not unique to cycadophytes; the haplocheilic type also is present in seed ferns, cordaites, conifers, ginkgophytes, *Ephedra,* and some angiosperms, and the syndetocheilic pattern also is found in some angiosperms, *Gnetum, Welwitschia,* and the cycadeoides.

Although these two patterns are especially important at the ordinal level and provide an important systematic characteristic for fossil foliage types, recent studies with extant plant cuticles indicate that caution must be exercised when using such features. For example, syndetocheilic stomata have been found on the leaves on some species of the Magnoliaceae, a haplocheilic pattern on the floral parts (Paliwal and Bhandari, 1962). In other plants, the difference between the two types appears to be based on the degree of development.

Following is a brief description of some of the more common Mesozoic foliage genera that are believed to have been produced by members of the Cycadophyta and Cycadeoidophyta.

Nilssoniales

Nilssonia   The leaves of this genus are linear to oblanceolate, with the lamina occasionally segmented into various sizes and shapes (Fig. 14-8C). The lamina is attached to the upper edge of the rachis and may cover it. Veins are simple and depart from the midvein at right angles; the veins may contain resin bodies between them. Stomata and trichomes are present on the lower surface.

Ctenis   Some of the leaves assigned to this genus exceed a meter in length and are similar to those of some modern cycads in that pinnae are attached broadly to a prominent rachis. Pinnae are long and ascending, with several parallel veins entering the lamina; some veins may be interconnected. Stomata are confined to the lower surface and are organized into broad zones.

Pseudoctenis   The leaves included in this genus are morphologically identical to those of *Ctenis,* but they may be distinguished by the consistent absence of intervein connections. Pinnae are hypostomatic, with the stomata scattered.

Doratophyllum   This leaf is similar to that of *Nilssonia,* but it may be distinguished by the origin of the lamina from the sides of the midrib.

Macrotaeniopteris   The main characteristic of this leaf type is its size, with some forms exceeding a meter in length. The margin is entire.

Deltolepis   This leaf is broadly triangular and contains numerous parallel veins. Morphologically the leaves appear identical to the scale leaves of modern cycads.

Bennettitales

Pterophyllum   The pinnae of this leaf type are slender and have parallel margins. They are attached broadly at the base and borne at right angles to the pinna rachis. Morphologically they resemble *Nilssonia,* and in the absence of epidermal characters, the two are difficult to distinguish. The cell walls tend to be straight and not sinuous like typical bennettitalean leaves.

Ptilophyllum   The pinnae in this leaf are variable in their oblique angle of attachment (Fig. 14-8B), but all are borne from the upper surface of the rachis. The base is rounded, and the pinnae occasionally overlap.

Zamites   Pinnae are linear or lanceolate, and they are attached to the upper surface of the rachis (Fig. 14-8A). The pinna base is greatly constricted, and the venation pattern includes parallel or slightly divergent veins. Stomata are confined to the upper surface.

Otozamites   Pinnae of this form have constricted asymmetrical bases and are attached to the upper surface of the rachis. They are broadly oval with the anterior pinna lobe pronounced. Veins entering pinnae typically spread out, but in some species, they are almost parallel.

Dictyozamites   The bases of the pinnae are constricted in this form; they attach to the upper surface of the rachis and often overlap. The genus may be distinguished by the anastomosing pattern of the veins.

Pseudocycas The pinnae exhibit a single midrib, but lack lateral veins. Each leaf is attached broadly to the base, with the posterior margin slightly decurrent.

Nilssoniopteris Morphologically this leaf type resembles those of *Taeniopteris,* but with syndetocheilic stomata. The lamina is undivided; veins pass to the margin at right angles.

Anomozamites Morphologically these leaves are similar to *Pterophyllum* and sometimes are included in that genus. Harris (1932) listed several epidermal features, including the arrangement of the stomata, that can be used to distinguish the two.

CYCADEOIDOPHYTA

The Cycadeoidophyta is represented by the single order Cycadeoidales (Bennettitales to some authors). Judging from the abundant foliage, they were a conspicuous portion of the flora from the Triassic well into the Cretaceous. The order is subdivided into two families (Cycadeoidaceae and Williamsoniaceae), principally on the basis of the degree of branching and, to a lesser extent, the organization of the reproductive structures.

Cycadeoidaceae

The best-known genus of the Cycadeoidaceae is *Cycadeoidea,* known principally from silicified trunks (Fig. 14-9A). Numerous specimens have been collected from throughout the world, but possibly the most specimens have been recovered from the famous early Cretaceous sediments of the Black Hills of South Dakota. Most notable of the early researchers on fossil cycadeoids is G.

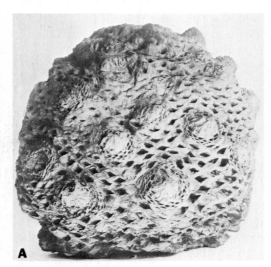
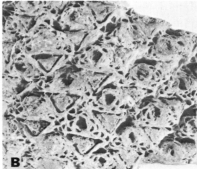

Figure 14-9 A. *Cycadeoidea dacotensis* trunk with several protruding cones. B. Portion of *Monanthesia* trunk. ×0.3. *(A courtesy of J. Schabilion.)*

R. Wieland (see Fig. 14-12C), who, while at Yale University, amassed numerous cycadeoid trunks in the preparation of his two-volume work entitled *American Fossil Cycads*. Other extensive collections of cycadeoids are housed at the University of Iowa and the Smithsonian Institution.

The petrified trunks of *Cycadeoidea* are similar in general habit to many modern cycads. They are typically cylindrical to columnar and usually less than a meter tall. Most trunks are unbranched, although a few apparently branched profusely. The unbranched trunks look much like old-fashioned straw beehives. Covering the surface were helically arranged persistent leaf bases and tongue-shaped, multicellular scale-like hairs that formed a ramentum. No mature leaves have ever been found attached to the trunks, although immature foliage of *Zamites* has been discovered attached to a *Cycadeoidea* stem. Reconstructions show a crown of helically arranged pinnate leaves extending from the distal end of the trunk (Fig. 14-10). Reproductive organs consisted of bisporangiate cones embedded in the trunk among the leaf bases.

In transverse section, the vascular cylinder of *Cycadeoidea* consists of a large pith with secretory structures surrounded by a dictyostele of secondary xylem and phloem. Primary xylem development is endarch. Secondary xylem is composed of scalariform tracheids and uni- and biseriate vascular rays. Surrounding the vascular cylinder is a broad cortex of thin-walled parenchyma and secretory cells. Leaf traces are arcuate in transverse section, becoming

Figure 14-10 Suggested reconstruction of a *Cycadeoidea* plant with attached leaves. *(From Delevoryas, 1971.)*

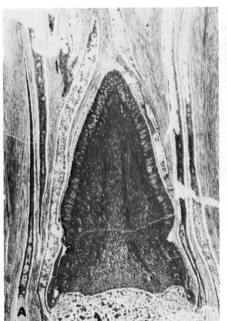
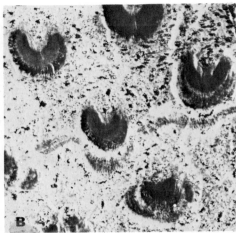

Figure 14-11 A. Longitudinal section through a *Cycadeoidea* cone in which the microsporangiate organs have disintegrated. ×3. B. Tangential section of *Cycadeoidea* sp. showing traces in the cortex. ×4. *(A from Crepet, 1974; B courtesy of J. Schabilion.)*

C-shaped in the cortex (Fig. 14-11B) and containing secondary tissues. The vascular system of the cone is derived from several leaf traces that form a cylinder in the outer cortex. At a higher level, one segment of the cylinder separates to vascularize a subtending leaf, the remaining vascular tissue extending into the cone peduncle.

The cones of all members of the Cycadeoideaceae were borne on short lateral branches or peduncles and did not extend above the level of the trunk surface (Fig. 14-9A). It is now known that some cycadeoids produced cones that were nonsynchronous in development, while other species produced cones that all appear to have matured at about the same time.

In another genus, *Monanthesia* (Fig. 14-9B), each leaf contains a cone in the axil. In *M. magnifica,* the vascular system of the cone is derived from the fusion of two cortical bundles that develop from two leaf traces, neither of which supplied the subtending leaf. This suggests that *Monanthesia* may be derived, while *Cycadeoidea* is more primitive.

Despite work on *Cycadeoidea* cones as early as 1870 by Carruthers, only within the last several years have we begun to accurately understand their structure, development, and function. Principally from the studies of Wieland (Fig. 14-12C), cycadeoids were hypothesized as angiosperm ancestors, a concept that had as its focal point the "flowerlike" nature of the cycadeoid reproductive

Figure 14-12   A. Transverse section of two synangia of *Cycadeoidea dacotensis*. ×20. B. *Cycadeoidea dacotensis* pollen grain. ×2500. C. George R. Wieland. *(B from Taylor, 1973; C courtesy of T. Delevoryas.)*

structure. Wieland suggested that the microsporophylls that were attached in a whorl to the base of an ovule-bearing receptacle opened at maturity. An exquisite glass reconstruction of his flower is on display at the Field Museum of Natural History in Chicago. Since Wieland's original interpretation of the *Cycadeoidea* reproductive structure, two subsequent ideas have been presented. Delevoryas (1968b) suggested that the cone contained an ovulate receptacle surrounded by pollen-bearing microsporophylls. Delevoryas reconstructed the microsporophylls like wedges of an orange with trabeculae extending between the dorsal and ventral surfaces to which were attached synangia containing pollen sacs. He viewed the entire cone as remaining closed, the microsporophylls never opening, as had earlier been suggested. A slight modification of this interpretation recently has been suggested by Crepet (1974). His studies utilizing cones representing several stages of development show that each cone consists of conical or dome-shaped, fleshy ovule-bearing receptacles, depending on the species, that may contain numerous stalked ovules and tightly packed sterile, interseminal scales. Arising from near the base of the receptacle was a whorl of microsporophylls that was in turn subtended by helically arranged bracts. The

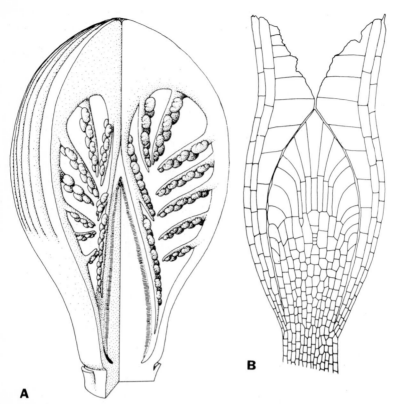

Figure 14-13 Suggested reconstruction of a *Cycadeoidea* cone with the sporophyll on the left cut transversely, the one on the right illustrated in radial view. B. Idealized longitudinal section of a young *Cycadeoidea* ovule shortly after megasporogenesis. *(A modified after Crepet, 1974; B from Crepet and Delevoryas, 1972.)*

microsporophylls were interpreted as a pinnate frond bent so that the distal tip would be adjacent to the base, with the pinnae folded into place of the rachis and similar to the trabecular arrangement suggested earlier (Fig. 14-13). The principal difference between these two ideas is that in the latter one, the pinnae (trabeculae) are attached to the rachis at only one side, and they are appressed or ontogenetically fused at the other. Despite what appears to have been free pinnae bearing synangia in *Cycadeoidea,* it is doubtful that the structure ever expanded, as was originally hypothesized by Wieland. Fusion of the distal tips of the microsporophylls, adhesion between proximal and distal portions of the pinnae, and the mass of sterile tissue at the distal end of the cone at a position of the maximum curvature of the microsporophylls (Fig. 14-14B) all would have posed structural problems relative to the unit ever opening.

The mature, thick-walled synangia of *Cycadeoidea* are kidney-shaped and contain 8 to 20 tubular sporangia that are arranged within the periphery of the synangium and at right angles to the long axis (Fig. 14-12A). Pollen grains of *C. dacotensis,* a common species, are broadly bilaterally symmetrical and up to 25 μm long (Fig. 14-12B). On the distal surface is a elongated sulcus; ornamentation is psilate to punctate. What were originally interpreted as cells of a microgametophyte have been shown to be folds of the thin exine.

One of the factors that has presented problems in the interpretation of cycadeoid cones is the occurrence of some ovulate cones that were believed to be dioecious because they were never found with microsporangiate parts attached. Subsequent studies, however, have indicated that these small ovulate cones are in fact bisporangiate like the larger ovulate receptacles, but that they represent a stage of development after the microsporangiate structures has shed pollen and disintegrated.

The larger, more common cones with the conical ovulate receptacle are known in varying stages of development ranging from undifferentiated tissue of the ovulate receptacle to cones with hundreds of seeds containing well-developed embryos. Immature ovules are stalked (Fig. 14-14A) and surrounded by five or six scales. As ovule development and megasporogenesis continued, the ovule stalks elongated, with the ovulate receptacle becoming more club-shaped. Mature seeds are small (2.0 mm long), slightly flattened, and characterized by an elongate extension of the distal end of the integument that forms a

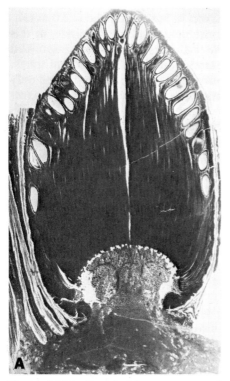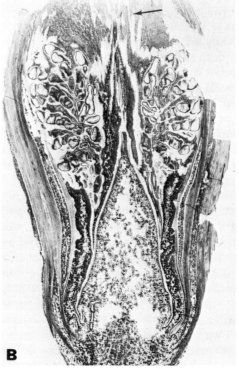

Figure 14-14 *Cycadeoidea* sp. cones. A. Longitudinal section through mature cone with dome-shaped receptacle and elongate seed stalks. ×3. B. Longitudinal section through mature cone showing the mass of sterile tissue in the position of maximum curvature of the rachis *(arrow)*. ×3. *(From Crepet, 1974.)*

micropylar tube. The integument is three-parted, with the nucellus and seed coat fused to near the micropylar region.

Crepet's discovery that all *Cycadeoidea* cones were bisporangiate eliminated some of the confusion that existed relative to how pollination took place in the genus. Structural features of the microsporophylls already mentioned suggest that the units did not open, but rather disintegrated (Fig. 14-14A) internally, ensuring that the ovules were self-pollinated. In addition, many *Cycadeoidea* cones show evidence of insect borings in the receptacle regions of synangia, which suggests the possibility of beetles acting as secondary pollinators in the self-pollinating system of these plants. Crepet (1974) has suggested that both pollination systems may have contributed to the rapid decline of the cycadeoids during the Cretaceous. Self-pollination ensures a homozygous population that would not be well suited to the climatic changes occurring during the Cretaceous. Another reason the cycadeoids rapidly declined may have been in response to the shifting of their insect pollinators to the angiosperms, which were rapidly evolving during the early Cretaceous.

Williamsoniaceae

Members of the Williamsoniaceae had cones that were often stalked, but not borne among leaf bases. The plants are believed to have been about 2.0 m tall. As with some of the cycads, however, reconstructions of entire plants in this family are based on fragmentary evidence. Nevertheless, information assembled to date suggests that the stems were quite slender and branched several times; leaves were widely separated. Some cones assigned to this group produced only ovules or pollen sacs; others were apparently bisporangiate like *Cycadeoidea*, but differed in opening at maturity.

One of the most frequently reproduced members of the Williamsoniaceae is *Williamsonia sewardiana* (see Fig. 14-16B), a petrified species described by Sahni (1932) from the Upper Gondwana (Jurassic) beds of India. It was reconstructed as a small tree (approximately 2.0 m tall) with persistent, helically arranged leaf bases; at the distal end of the trunk was a crown of pinnate leaves assignable to *Ptilophyllum*. Between the larger leaf scars on the trunk were smaller scars that marked the former position of scale leaves. Attached to short lateral branches, also bearing leaves, were ovulate cones, each borne on a long peduncle covered by hairy bracts. The ovules were elongate, with the distal end of the integument attenuated to form an elongate funnel or micropylar tube. The vascular system of the peduncle consisted of a narrow ring of scalariform tracheids that surrounded a massive pith.

Another species, *W. gigas,* was reconstructed as an unbranched, erect plant with a stem covered by rhombic leaf scars. Leaves of *Zamites* were produced in a crown. The taxon was based on such fragmentary material that the actual appearance of the plant continues to be questionable.

Ischnophyton is an Upper Triassic cycadeoid characterized by a slender stem (1.0 cm in diameter) bearing simple, compound fronds. The surface of the stem is slightly wrinkled, with persistent leaf bases absent. The leaves are about 20.0 cm long with pinnae attached to the upper surface of the rachis. Several veins enter the pinna base and dichotomize; stomata are syndetocheilic. When compared with cycadeoid foliage types, the leaves of *I. iconicum* appear to share features with forms assigned to both *Otozamites* and *Zamites*. Nothing is known about the reproductive parts of the plant.

Bucklandia is the name used for Mesozoic stems bearing relatively large leaf scars and thought to have been the stems of several cycadeoids. The name encompasses a variety of preservational states including compressions, casts, and petrifactions.

The genus *Williamsonia* is used for ovulate cones that include both impression-compressions and petrified forms; they may assume a variety of configurations depending on how they were preserved. The cone is generally rounded and consists of a dome-shaped receptacle bearing numerous small seeds and tightly packed interseminal scales. The elongate micropylar tubes of the seeds extend above the level of the scales. Subtending the seed-bearing receptacle is a whorl of bracts. One of the more common williamsonian cones from the Jurassic of Oaxaca, Mexico, is *W. netzahualcoyotlii* (Fig. 14-15A). Specimens range from 2.0 to 3.0 cm in diameter and at the base exhibit a small peduncle scar. The number of ovules present on the receptacle is estimated to have been between 25 and 50 (Fig. 14-15B); apparently not all reached maturity at the same time. At the distal end of the cone is a ring of fused scales that has been termed the corona. In *W. huitzilopochtilii,* also from the Jurassic of Oaxaca, the ovulate cone is subtended by a whorl of six to eight basally fused bracts, each 2.5 cm long. The ovulate receptacle is small (6.0 to 8.0 mm in diameter) with interseminal scales with polygonal heads. *Williamsonia diquiyuii* is a petrified specimen with a conical receptacle bearing tightly packed interseminal scales and elongate seed stalks up to 1.0 cm long. Seed are roughly circular in transverse section and contain dicotyledonous embryos.

Weltrichia (Fig. 14-16A) is the name now used for pollen-producing cones of the Williamsoniaceae that had earlier been considered pollen cones of *Williamsonia.* Earlier interpretations that the ovulate cones contained micro-

Figure 14-15 *Williamsonia netzahualcoyotlii.* A. Suggested reconstruction of a cone. ×1.8. B. Impression of cone at apex. ×1. *(From Delevoryas and Gould, 1973.)*

B

Figure 14-16 Compressed *Weltrichia* sp. cone. ×1. B. Suggested reconstruction of *Williamsonia sewardiana. (B from Delevoryas, 1971.)*

sporophylls like those of *Cycadeoidea* are now known to have been in error. The pollen cones appear to exhibit more morphologic variability than their ovule-bearing counterparts, including the position and shape of the pollen sacs and number and size of the sterile bracts. *Weltrichia sol* (= *Williamsonia gigas*) from the Jurassic of Yorkshire is a large pollen cone that consists of an open urn or cup-shaped receptacle approximately 10.0 cm in diameter. Extending from the rim of the cup are approximately 30 microsporophylls, each about 6.0 cm long. They are distally tapered and bear numerous pollen sacs on the inner surface. Pollen grains are thin-walled, monosulcate, and about 46 μm long. On the inner surface of the cup are numerous semicircular structures borne on short stalks. They have been referred to as "resinous sacs," but may have functioned as some form of attractant associated with the pollination syndrome of these plants. The uniformity of the stomatal pattern and consistent occurrence of *W. sol* cones, bracts of *Williamsonia gigas,* and leaves of *Zamites gigas* have been used to suggest that these parts represent organs of the same biological species. In *Weltrichia pecten,* the basal cup is smaller (4.0 cm wide), and the edge is dissected into only 10 to 12 microsporophylls. Synangia are borne in two rows on the inner surface of the microsporophyll. These pollen cones are continuously associated with *Ptilophyllum pecten* foliage.

    Williamsoniella is a Jurassic member of the family characterized by dichotomously branched stems bearing leaves of the *Nilssoniopteris* type. One of the distinguishing features of *Williamsoniella* is the bisporangiate nature of the cones. They are apparently borne in an axillary position on slender peduncles, although earlier accounts suggest that they were borne in the angles of branch dichotomies. Each cone consists of a central ovule-bearing receptacle with tightly packed interseminal scales and sessile ovules. Arising from the peduncle are several elongate sterile bracts bearing numerous trichomes. The distal end of the receptacle is slightly flattened and crownlike in morphology. Attached to the base of the receptacle are 12 to 14 wedge-shaped microsporophylls, each bearing short stalks terminating in a pollen capsule that was probably synangiate in organization. Pollen is described as monocolpate.

The pollen of *W. lignierii* has been thoroughly investigated by Harris (1974) and compared with dispersed grains of *Exesipollenites*. The grains are about 25 μm in diameter and are described as monoporate.

Cycadolepis is the name given to large lanceolate to circular scale leaves that may represent the sterile bracts of some cycadeoid cones. Species have been erected on the basis of various epidermal features that in several instances have been related to foliage leaves and epidermal patterns on cone parts.

CONCLUSIONS

Several authors have suggested a relationship between the synangiate pollen sacs of the cycadeoids and the pollen organs of the Paleozoic seed ferns. The recent discovery that the synangia in *Cycadeoidea* were attached to pinnate microsporophylls further supports the relationship between these two groups. Many of the synangiate pollen organs of the Medullosales are complex, multiple structures that were formed by the plication and aggregation of laminar-borne simple synangia. Exactly how and where these organs were borne on the Paleozoic seed ferns is not known in most instances, although the simple synangia of *Aulacotheca* are known to have been borne on a three-dimensional branching structure that could be considered homologous with the microsporophylls of a *Weltrichia* cone. It is far more difficult to derive the ovulate receptacle of a cycadeoid cone from a seed fern ancestor. In the Paleozoic pteridosperms, seeds are borne in cupules or solitary on leaves and not aggregated on specialized receptacles. One idea suggests that the *Cycadeoidea* cone was part of a foliar system that became phylogenetically telescoped to its position as the trunk was modified from a more elongate, ancestral stem type. One major problem in such an interpretation involves the different origin of the vegetative branch stele from that of the cone, suggesting that these two types of appendages (leaves and cones) are not morphologic equivalents.

The cycadeoids are characterized by both monosporangiate and bisporangiate cones, with monosporangiate forms (*Williamsonia* and *Weltrichia*) occurring earlier geologically (Triassic and Jurassic) than the bisporangiate (Cretaceous) types (*Cycadeoidea*). Among the Paleozoic seed ferns, no seed- and pollen-bearing structures were produced in the same fertile structure, although it appears that both types of organs were produced on the same plant. The fossil evidence is inconclusive; so it is difficult to determine whether all the cycadeoids were monecious, although judging by the bisporangiate cones of some taxa, it appears they were.

One of the interesting questions emerging about members of the Cycadeoi-dophyta and Cycadophyta concerns how the reproductive organs functioned at the time pollen and seeds ripened. There is increasing evidence that these seed plants had developed more than chance associations with insects, which may have served as secondary pollinators as early as the Pennsylvanian. For example, in the Permian associated with the *Taeniopteris* foliage and between the ovules on the *Phasmatocycas* megasporophyll are small bodies that Mamay suggests may have functioned as attractants. Similar structures have been noted in the cup of the pollen cone *Weltrichia*. While the pollination system of *Cycadeoidea* appears to have been one primarily of selfing, that of the Williamsoniaceae structurally appears to have been capable of outcrossing. In both *Williamsonia* and *Weltrichia,* the evidence is overwhelming that the fingerlike microsporo-phylls were expanded at maturity so that pollen could be easily transported from pollen sacs to ovule micropyles, probably via wind. In *Williamsoniella,* the cones appear to have been functionally bisporangiate, but there is strong evidence that the microsporophylls actually opened and/or became detached from the cone peduncle at maturity. Thus, although these cones were capable of self-pollinating, the timing of ovule and pollen development may have represented an early method of outcrossing. The high frequency of detached *Williamsonia* cones at a relatively early stage of development also may indicate that pollination and fertilization occurred after the cones fell from the parent plant. There is also indirect evidence that suggests that the earliest cycadeoids (*Williamsonia* and *Weltrichia*) were evolving in the direction of sporophyll closure, possibly in response to insect predation. In this regard, the organization of a *Williamsoniella* cone is only slightly removed from the self-pollination phenomenon of *Cycadeoidea.* Such a situation appears to be supported by the Jurassic age of the monosporangiate cone types.

The cycadeoids stand as a distinct group of Mesozoic cycadophytes that apparently became extinct near the end of the Cretaceous, giving rise to no other seed plant groups. Despite the many gaps in our knowledge about transitional forms to the Paleozoic ancestors, they do provide some interesting insight into the evolution of a specialized reproductive system.

Chapter 15

Ginkgophyta

The Ginkgophyta is represented today by a single species of the maidenhair tree, *Ginkgo biloba*. This taxon is sometimes referred to as a "living fossil" because it was widespread throughout the world beginning in the Mesozoic; today it is widely planted as an ornamental in temperate areas of the world because of its beauty and extreme resistance to attacks by fungi and insects. There is some question among scientists as to whether the stands of trees that today grow in southeastern China are native or were cultivated.

Although it is an extremely slow grower, *Ginkgo biloba* is an attractive stately tree that may reach a height of almost 30 m. Shoot dimorphism is a characteristic feature of the genus, with the spur shoots produced in the axile of leaves on the long shoots. Both long and spur shoots are developmentally reversible, with the secondary xylem composed of thin-walled tracheids and narrow vascular rays. Tracheal pitting is circular bordered and restricted to the radial walls. One of the distinctive morphologic features of the genus is the fan-shaped leaf with an open dichotomous venation pattern, although most leaves show vein anastomoses. There is a considerable amount of variability to the leaf margin, ranging from entire to deeply notched. *Ginkgo biloba* is dioecious with ovulate and pollen-bearing structures borne on different plants. The microsporangiate structures resemble catkins and are borne in the axils of leaves on the spur shoots. Attached to the stroboloid axis are numerous fertile appendages that have been termed sporangiophores, each bearing two to four microsporangia at the tip. The pollen is prolate and germinates from the distal surface. Seed-bearing structures also are borne on the short shoots and consist of a peduncle or stalk that terminates in two or three ovules. Surrounding each ovule at its base is a rimlike segment of tissue termed a collar that was at one time regarded as homologous with a megasporophyll. The mature ovule is anatomically similar to the seed of a cycad, but with a thick outer integumentary layer that smells like rancid butter upon decay.

The genus appears to have persisted relatively unchanged morphologically since the Mesozoic, with numerous reports of ginkgophyte foliage from many stratigraphic levels and geographic regions of the Northern Hemisphere. There are a few reports of ginkgophyte remains in the Paleozoic, although none of these has been conclusively associated with the Ginkgophyta. Only a few reproductive structures of this group have been described, and their inclusion is based only on association in the same beds that have provided vegetative remains.

One of the oldest probable ginkgophytes is *Trichopitys,* known from the Lower Permian of southern France. Compressed specimens consist of vegetative shoots with helically arranged, nonlaminar leaves. The leaves are slightly decurrent at the base and up to 10.0 cm long; each leaf is dissected into four to eight segments. Along some of the vegetative axes are zones of fertile structures, each borne in the axil of a leaf. Florin (1949) described these structures in *T. heteromorpha* as axillary sporangial trusses. Each consists of a poorly defined axis bearing two to six helically arranged branches terminated by a single recurved ovule (Fig. 15-1A). Ovules are slightly flattened and about 6.0 mm

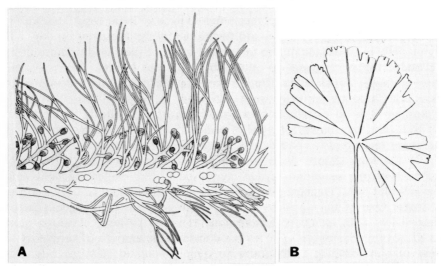

Fig. 15-1 A. Fertile shoot of *Trichopitys heteromorpha.* B. Leaf of *Ginkgoites acosmia. (A reproduced from* Studies in Paleobotany *with permission of John Wiley, Inc.; B from Harris, 1935.)*

long. The ovule-bearing branches of *Trichopitys* are morphologically similar to some abnormal ovulate structures known from *Ginkgo biloba* in which there may be up to 15 stalked ovules per shoot. Florin suggested that *Trichopitys* represents a primitive member of the ginkgophyte line based on the nature and organization of the ovulate-bearing structures and vegetative leaves. He considered the genus as demonstrating parallel evolution with the early cordaites and conifers.

Another possible representative of the ginkgophyte line that can be traced from the Lower Permian well into the Cretaceous is *Sphenobaiera*. This genus is based on wedge-shaped leaves that lack a distinct petiole and exhibit dichotomous venation of the segmented lamina. One of the better-known species is *S. longifolia* (Fig. 15-2B), common in the Jurassic of Yorkshire. Specimens are characterized by long (13.0 cm), wedge-shaped leaves that are divided at least four times into narrow ultimate segments. The cuticle is amphistomatic and thickest on the adaxial surface. Stomata on the upper surface are irregularly oriented in bands, with the guard cells surrounded by six papillate subsidiary cells. In *S. ophioglossum*, some leaves are 185.0 mm long and typically divided

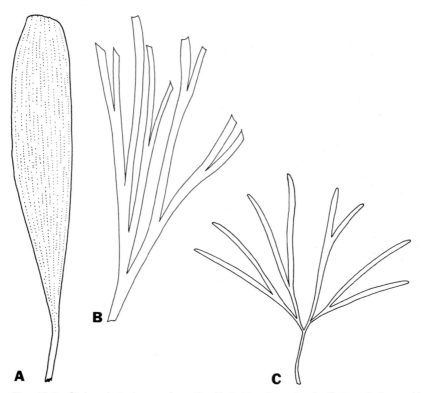

Fig. 15-2 Ginkgophyte leaves from the Yorkshire Jurassic. A. *Eretmophyllum whitbiense.* B. *Sphenobaiera longifolia.* C. *Baiera furcata. (Redrawn from Harris and Miller, 1974.)*

into two or four wide lobes. Oblanceolate leaves with an entire margin and closely spaced dichotomizing veins have been placed in the genus *Erethmophyllum* (Fig. 15-2A).

Another common Mesozoic genus believed related to the ginkgophytes is *Baiera* (Fig. 15-2C). The characteristic feature of this taxon is a distinct petiole, a feature lacking in *Sphenobaiera* and *Eretmophyllum*.

Relatively few ginkgophyte reproductive structures have been identified. Seeds almost 1.0 cm long and containing stomata similar to those of some ginkgophytes on the integument have been referred to as *B. furcata*. Other seeds from the Jurassic of Yorkshire are referred to as *Ginkgo huttonii* because of the consistent association of this foliage species in the same beds. The outer cuticle of the integument of these seeds is preserved and exhibits impressions of epidermal cell patterns. A pollen cone also has been described for this species. It is about 6.0 mm long and consists of loosely arranged, once dichotomized appendages, each terminated by what is believed to be a microsporangium. Adhering pollen grains are elongate (29 to 42 μm long) and ornamented with a sulcus on the presumed distal surface. *Stenorachis* is the name used for an axis bearing helically arranged ovate structures thought to be ginkgophyte microsporangia. Several species have been described from Cretaceous rocks, but none is preserved in sufficient detail to conclusively demonstrate the ginkgophyte affinities of the taxon.

There are numerous reports of foliage types that are indistinguishable from the leaves of the modern *Ginkgo biloba*. Some of these have been referred to the extant taxon, while others have been designated as *Ginkgoites* (Fig. 15-1B). Harris and Millington (1974) have recently suggested the abandonment of *Ginkgoites* because the genus is ill-defined and cannot be applied with consistency to all the morphologic forms known to have existed within a single species. *Ginkgo digitata* is a relatively common Jurassic species that includes a wedge-shaped lamina with the distal margins dissected by shallow indentations. In this species, the veins are numerous, and small resin bodies are common in the intervein areas. Stomata are crowded on the lower surface in the intervein areas; trichomes are present along the veins. A species that is similar to *G. digitata*, but characterized by more deeply divided leaves, is *G. huttonii*. In this species, the lamina is wedge-shaped with crowded veins. Another species from the early Cretaceous of Montana is *G. pluripartita*. The leaves of this form are relatively small, the largest about 2.0 cm long. The lamina is typically divided into four or six segments, with the central sinus most prominent. Stomata are present only on the lower surface and confined to the intervein areas. Subsidiary cells reveal prominent, overarching papillae.

Tralau (1968) suggested that there are three distinct phylogenetic groups of ginkgophyte foliage types and that foliar polymorphism was most prominent during the Cretaceous. Based on morphologic and anatomic features, it appears that *G. adiantoides* is the foliage type most closely related to the leaf form present on the modern *G. biloba* tree. An analysis of the stratigraphic and geographic distribution of ginkgophyte foliage suggests that the present-day East Asiatic home of *Ginkgo* was probably established during the Pleistocene.

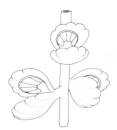

Fig. 15-3 Suggested reconstruction of *Leptostrobus cancer. (Redrawn from Harris and Miller, 1974.)*

Several genera of unusual gymnosperms reveal certain ginkgophyte features, and this has prompted some authors to include them within the Ginkgophyta. More recently, the group has been established as an order on the basis of the discovery of the ovulate organs. Today the Czekanowskiales include Jurassic and Cretaceous plants with persistent leaves borne on caducous spur shoots surrounded by scalelike leaves. The foliage leaves of this group were elongate with a single vein that entered the base and dichotomized several times before reaching the leaf margin. This feature has been useful in separating *Czekanowskia* leaves from those of *Ginkgo,* in which two vascular strands enter the base. In some species, laminar dissection is so pronounced that the leaves appear to be aggregated into fasicles. Cuticle preparations from the Yorkshire Jurassic indicate that the leaves were amphistomataic. *Solenites* is a genus included in the order that may be distinguished by distinct bundles of 11 to 16 elongated leaves. These are borne on short shoots and contain longitudinally oriented stomata on both surfaces. Leaves of *Sphenarion* are narrowly wedge-shaped with no distinction between the petiole and lamina. They are distinguished from *Czekanowskia* and *Solenites* in being wider than 1.0 mm.

Species of the ovulate cone *Leptostrobus* have been associated with foliage of the *Czekanowskia, Sphenobaiera,* and *Solenites* type. This association has been based on their common occurrence in the same fossil beds, the morphologic similarity with scale leaves, and the similarity of the cuticles. The strobilus *Leptostrobus cancer* is imperfectly known; some incomplete specimens are at least 15.0 cm in length. Helically attached to the axis at regular intervals of about 5.0 mm are flattened, globose capsules (Fig. 15-3), each approximately 5.0 mm long. Each capsule consists of two valves, with the outer surface of some species crenulated (Fig. 15-4B). The outer margin of the valve is slightly enrolled to form a broad flange that partially protects the enclosed seeds. Up to five seeds per valve have been recorded, each attached to the rim of the valve so that the micropyles were directed away of the cone axis toward the open portion of the capsule. Nothing is known about the tissue organization of the seeds, but macerated megaspore membranes suggest that the ovules were of a basic gymnospermous type. Although numerous pollen types have been identified in association with the seed micropyles, none occurs with sufficient frequency to be regarded conclusively as the pollen of *Leptostrobus.* Some grains appear to possess an encircling monosaccus, while others are distinctly bisaccate.

Ixostrobus is the name of a pollen cone believed by some workers to be the strobilus of *Czekanowskia.* Harris and Miller (1974), however, believe that

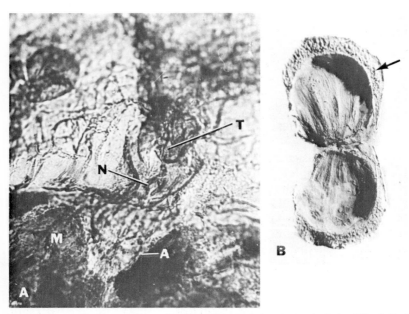

Fig. 15-4 A. Portion of the pollen chamber and megagametophyte (M) of *Karkenia* sp. (= *Sphenobaiera*) showing a pollen grain with tube (T) penetrating the neck cell (N) of an archegonium (A) at the time of fertilization. ×175. B. Opened capsule of *Leptostrobus stigmatoideus* showing the marginal stigmatic flange *(arrow).* ×3. *(Courtesy of V. Krassilov.)*

Ixostrobus more probably was produced by the plant that contained the ribbon-shaped foliage of the *Desmiophyllum* type. Specimens of *I. whitbiensis* (Jurassic of Yorkshire) exceed 10.0 cm in length and contain irregular whorls of six to eight coriaceous sporangium-bearing structures. At the end of each unit are four oval pollen sacs that are laterally fused to form a cup-shaped structure. Pollen is circular-oval, with a conspicuous sulcus on the distal surface. Grains range from 35 to 40 μm in diameter and, based on the description, may have possessed a tectate sporoderm.

Some authors, notably Krassilov (1977), view the Czekanowskiales as a group of Jurassic and Cretaceous proangiosperms rather than having affinities with other groups of ginkgophytes.

The ginkgophytes are an interesting group of gymnosperms that were at one time widespread throughout the world. For a long time the evolutionary relationships of the group were debated, some believing that they are related to the cycads on the basis of the similarity of the seeds, wood, and motile sperm of *Ginkgo biloba*. It appears, however, that the ginkgophytes are more closely related to some members of the Coniferopsida, and that the conifers, taxads, ginkgophytes, and cordaites represent parallel stages of gymnosperm evolution that may have become separated as early as the Devonian.

Chapter 16

Problematic Gymnosperms

There are a number of problematic gymnospermous plants that deserve mention because of their interesting morphology and, in some instances, unusual structure. Some of these are known from a very few collections and are restricted both geographically and stratigraphically. In other instances, the plants are known in some detail, but their affinities continue to remain obscure. Still others, such as the living gnetophytes, are well understood. The fossil record of this group, however, is almost entirely barren, which results in the absence of a precise classification for these plants or an understanding regarding their evolution. There can be little doubt that as paleobotanical studies are continued and additional specimens of existing taxa are uncovered, together with the discovery of new genera and species, some of the problematic taxa of today will be more completely understood and ultimately reclassified. Moreover, there are other taxa that need to be more completely understood relative to their anatomy and morphology. When this occurs, these taxa may be viewed as distinct taxonomic groups with no obvious relationship to any existing assemblage of extant or fossil plants.

GNETALES

The gnetophytes consist of a small group of extant gymnospermous plants that are represented by 3 genera (*Ephedra, Gnetum,* and *Welwitschia*) and approximately 66 species. The plants are unique because they possess vessels in the xylem and have reproductive structures that are compound in organization. Some authorities (e.g., Pulle, 1938) placed the gnetophytes within a transitional group of seed plants, the Chlamydospermae, on the basis of the bitegumented nature of the ovules. A more conventional approach has been to place each genus in a separate order within the class Gnetopsida.

Ephedra is a profusely branched shrub confined to cool arid and dry desert regions; a few of the approximately 35 species exist as small trees. The leaves of *Ephedra* vary from decussate to whorled and range from scalelike to needles up to 3.0 cm long. The reproductive organs of *Ephedra* are dioecious and consist of an axis that bears pairs of bracts that subtend either the microsporangiate unit or the seed-bearing structure. The pollen of *Ephedra* is ellipsoidal and ornamented with a series of striations that extend from one end of the grain to the other.

Almost all the species of *Gnetum* consist of lianas that inhabit the tropical rain forests in Asia, South America, and Africa. One of the interesting features is their pinnate reticulate venation pattern, which superficially resembles the leaves of many dicotyledons. The pollen grains are relatively small (16 to 20 μm) and typically spherical; some are ornamented with delicate spines.

The third genus of this group is the monotypic species *Welwitschia mirabilis,* which is confined to arid areas of West Africa. Morphologically the plant is unusual in that it consists of cone with two strap-shaped leaves that arise from the rim, and a deep-seated tap root. The microsporangiate structure consists of four ranks of decussate bracts that subtend a simple strobilus containing pollen sacs; the seed-bearing strobilus is similarily constructed and contains a bitegumented seed with conspicuous lateral wings formed by the fusion of a pair of bracts. Pollen of *Welwitschia* is like that of *Ephedra* but appears to possess a permanent leptoma.

At the present time, there is no bona fide megafossil record of any of the gnetophyte genera. There are, however, a number of pollen grains (Fig. 16-1A, and B) from sediments ranging from the Permian to the Recent that morphologically resemble the pollen of *Epherda* (Fig. 16-1C) and *Welwitschia*. Grains of *Ephedripites* from the Middle Cretaceous of Peru range up to 40 μm long and, depending on the species, possess a variable number of longitudinal ridges on

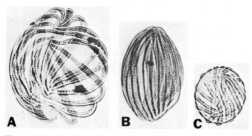

Figure 16-1 *Ephedra* pollen. A. *Ephedra chinleana.* ×325. B. *Ephedra chinleana* (Triassic) grain with relatively straight ridges. ×325. C. Recent grain of *Ephedra wraithiana.* ×325. *(From Scott, 1960.)*

their surfaces (Brenner, 1968). Other palynomorph genera described as gnetophyte types include *Gnetaceaepollenites, Vittatina,* and *Costapollenites.*

Despite the absence of a megafossil record for these interesting plants, most authors regard them as highly specialized gymnosperms. Martens (1971), after extensively examining the three genera, believes that there are more dissimilar features among the taxa than the characters they have in common and therefore regards them as a highly artificial and heterogeneous assemblage. Other workers believe that the major shared features (vessels and compound reproductive structures) indicate a close relationship between the three genera. Singh (1978), using embryologic data, suggests the inclusion of *Ephedra* with the other gymnosperms, while he regards *Gnetum* and *Welwitschia* as having an independent phyletic lineage.

VOJNOVSKYALES

The Vojnovskyales constitute an order erected by Neuburg (1965) for an interesting plant that was initially described from a Lower Permian specimen collected from the Pechora Basin of Russia. The original specimen of *Vojnovskya paradoxa* (Fig. 16-2) consists of an axis about 13.0 cm long and 2.0 cm in diameter; on the surface of the compressed specimen are large scars that mark the former position of the fan-shaped leaves of the *Nephropsis* type. The

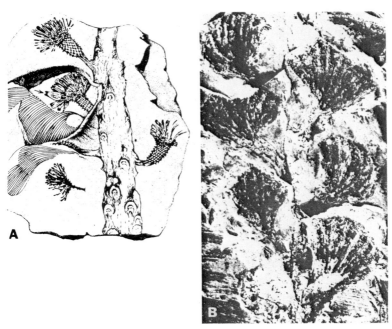

Figure 16-2 A. Fragmentary specimen of *Vojnovskya paradoxa* showing leaves and several reproductive organs. B. Several leaves of *Sandrewia texana* attached to an axis. ×1.7. *(From Mamay, 1976.)*

reproductive organs consists of fertile branches or cones, each about 3.0 cm long, that are scattered on the vegetative branches. Each cone is believed to have contained both ovules and pollen-containing organs; flattened seeds are attached to the basal region of the unit. What have been interpreted as the microsporophylls are borne in the apical region of the cone, although features of the microsporangia continue to remain obscure. Based on this limited material, *Vojnovskya* was suggested as being a shrubby or possibly arborescent gymnosperm.

Recently, Mamay (1976) has described a stroboloid axis from the Lower Permian of the southwestern United States that morphologically resembles Neuburg's original material of *Vojnovskya*. The conelike unit is about 5.0 cm long, with the apical portion containing an aggregation of about 30 slender appendages that may represent microsporophylls. Near the basal region of the unit are several flattened seeds, each with a notched apex. In an earlier paper, Mamay (1975) described some Lower Permian flabelliform-shaped leaves under the binomial *Sandrewia texana* (Fig. 16-2B), and these forms closely correspond to foliar units of *Nephropsis*. Strengthening the probability that *Sandrewia* is a vojnovskyalean is the constant association of platyspermic triangular seeds up to 1.0 cm long with a notched micropylar end. These seeds morphologically resemble the ovules described on the cones of *V. paradoxa*. Based in part on the North American material, Mamay suggested that the spines described on the cones of *V. paradoxa* represent seed stalks.

In order to more accurately speculate as to the natural affinities of this interesting assemblage of fossils, it will be especially important to have a more complete understanding of the apical region of the "cone" and whether the slender units do in fact represent microsporophylls. On the basis of the limited information currently available, both the cordaites and the cycadeoids have been suggested as potential ancestors of this group. For the present, however, Mamay's (1976) assessment of the Vojnovskyales as a "bizarre, short-lived group of the Late Paleozoic gymnosperms" will have to suffice.

PENTOXYLALES

The Pentoxylales constitute a small group of Jurassic gymnosperms, many of which are known from structurally preserved specimens. The first report of these interesting plants was made by the distinguished Indian paleobotanist Birbil Sahni in 1948 from plant remains collected from the Rajmahal Hills of northeastern India. Since the initial report, other specimens have been recovered from these same deposits, as well as from the Mesozoic (Tithonian or Neocomian) of New Zealand. The plants included in this order combine a variety of unusual characters, including some that suggest affinities with extant and fossil cycads and conifers and others that appear to be unique to the group (e.g., organization of the reproductive parts and stem anatomy).

Although the exact habit of these plants is not known, many workers consider them to have been small trees or shrubs that possessed both long and short shoots. *Pentoxylon* is the generic name of one stem type known from

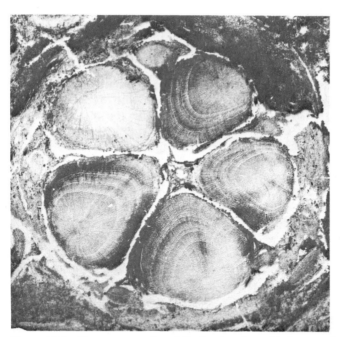

Figure 16-3 Transverse section of *Pentoxylon* stem with five vascular segments. *(Courtesy of R. Stockey.)*

specimens at least 2.0 cm in diameter. In transverse section, the stem consists of five or six roundly triangular vascular segments (Fig. 16-3) or sympodia that are embedded in a thin-walled ground tissue of pith and cortex. In some descriptions, these vascular segments are referred to as steles of a polystelic stem, but in light of the study by Basinger et al. (1974) regarding the vascular organization of *Medullosa,* it may be more appropriate to abandon the polystelic terminology for this group until the pattern of leaf trace production can be worked out in detail for an extended length of stem. Each xylem wedge consists of a mesarch primary xylem strand surrounded by dense secondary xylem arranged in conspicuous growth rings. In *Pentoxylon sahnii,* the most common species, the vascular cambium apparently functioned in a slightly different manner, so that in older stems there was a strongly endocentric development to the secondary xylem with more wood produced toward the pith region of the stem. In several features, the wood of *Pentoxylon* is coniferous, with uni- or biseriate circular bordered pits on the radial walls of the tracheids and uniseriate medullary rays up to seven cells high. Wood parenchyma, ray tracheids, and resin canals do not appear to have been a component of this wood type. Pith and cortex consists of thin-walled parenchyma with nests of sclerotic cells. In a few stems, the cortex contains radial rows of cells suggestive of a periderm. Alternating with the stem sympodia are an equal number of smaller xylem strands that are composed principally of wood. Some of these strands divide radially and have been suggested as the traces that supplied either the spur shoots or the reproductive organs. *Napanioxylon,* another genus, has been used for stems with a larger number of xylem wedges, but with a more concentric development of the secondary xylem. It is quite probable that the genus represents a different developmental stage of *Pentoxylon.*

Young shoots of *Pentoxylon* less than a centimeter in diameter contain only primary vascular bundles in the pith and cortex. Each bundle produced a strand from the inner margin that repeatedly branches to form the leaf traces. The outer surface of these spur shoots is ornamented with helically arranged, rhomboidal leaf cushions, each bearing seven to nine vascular bundle scars. Scars of two different sizes have been described as occurring in zones on the same stem, with the smaller ones thought to have been scale leaves.

Leaves of *Pentoxylon* are strap-shaped and about 7.0 cm long (Fig. 16-4A). They exhibit a prominent midrib and, in general features, are identical to those of the common Mesozoic genus *Taeniopteris.* Because the pentoxyloid leaves were structurally preserved, the generic name *Napaniophyllum* was instituted for the Rajmahal Hill foliage. Leaves of *N. raoi* are about 1.0 cm wide and are characterized by a shortened petiole. The midrib is broad and consists of several parallel veins that terminate at the rounded apex; lateral veins are borne at right angles, occasionally branching and fusing near the leaf margin. In transverse section, the petiole has five to nine traces. Each trace consists of both centripetal and centrifugal xylem separated from the protoxylem by a thin band of parenchyma and identical to the "diploxylic" pattern of leaf traces present in the leaves of extant cycads. In general, the stomata are sunken and confined to the abaxial surface. They appear to lack any type of orientation, although in a few specimens at least some stomata are arranged in rows. The position of the subsidiary cells on either side of some guard cells was initially interpreted as a syndetocheilic arrangement similar to that found in members of the Cycadeoido-phyta, but in others, each pair of guard cells is surrounded by a ring of subsidiary cells that reflects a closer relationship to the haplocheilic stomata found in living cycads.

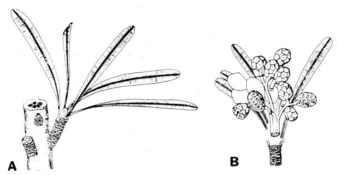

Figure 16-4   A. Suggested reconstruction of *Pentoxylon sahnii* showing *Taeniopteris*-type leaves attached to spur shoot. B. Suggested reconstruction of seed cones *(Carnoconites)* of *Pentoxylon sahnii. (From Sahni, 1948.)*

The microsporangiate organs are described by the binomial *Sahnia nipaniensis*. These pollen cones consist of numerous branches, which have been termed microsporophylls (approximately 24), that are fused at their bases to form a shallow ring around a dome-shaped receptacle at the end of the spur shoot. Each microsporophyll is about 1.5 cm long and contains numerous, helically arranged branches. At the end of each branch are several stalked sporangia. The sporangium wall is a single cell layer thick, with some cells radially thickened, suggesting a possible site of dehiscence. Pollen grains are prolate and about 25 μm long. On the distal surface is a elongate aperture; it is not known whether pollen tubes were produced in *Sahnia*.

The seed-bearing organs of the Pentoxylales have been termed infructescences, female flowers, seed-bearing fruits, and seed-bearing cones. Specimens of *Carnoconites* consist of a central branching peduncle or axis with each branch terminating in a cone (Fig. 16-4B). Each cone of *C. compactum* is about 2.0 cm long and contains approximately 20 tightly packed seeds. The seeds are platyspermic and apparently attach directly to the axis of the cone with the micropyles directed away from the axis. The outer integument consists of a thick, fleshy sarcotesta that surrounds the sclerotestal layer of the integument. The vascular tissue of the seed extends through the sclerotesta. In *C. cranwellii* from the Mesozoic of New Zealand, the seeds are about 2.0 mm long and rhomboidal in section view.

The Pentoxylales represent a unique group of gymnospermous seed plants that have no easily recognizable, closely related fossil ancestors. Certain features of the ovules (bilateral symmetry, thick sclerotesta) are similar to those of the Cycadeoidophyta, although the seeds of the cycadeoids were associated with conspicuous interseminal scales. Both haplocheilic and syndetocheilic stomatal types are present. Superficially the vascular system is like that of the Medullosales, although detailed studies must be undertaken to determine whether *Pentoxylon* was truly polystelic or more like the smypodial arrangement present in *Medullosa*. The pollen-bearing units possess a strong morphologic resemblance to those of modern *Ginkgo*, a similarity further supported by the monsulcate pollen grains. At the present time, the phylogenetic relationships of the Pentoxylales remain obscure. They possibly represent a dead end group of Jurassic gymnosperms from which the main coniferophytic and cycaophytic lines evolved, or they may demonstrate a combination of features that further underscore patterns of convergent evolution within the gymnosperms.

Coniferophyta

Included in the Coniferophyta are the members of the Cordaitopsida and Coniferopsida. The Cordaitopsida (cordaites) were one of the dominant groups of gymnospermous seed plants during the Carboniferous, and together with the Coniferopsida (conifers), they are believed to have evolved from some progymnospermous ancestor. By the Triassic, the conifers were highly diversified, with all the modern families, with the possible exception of the Cephalotaxaceae, represented. In general, both living and fossil representatives may be characterized as woody perennials with pycnoxylic secondary xylem and naked platyspermic seeds.

CORDAITOPSIDA

Cordaitales: Carboniferous to Permian

CONIFEROPSIDA

Voltziales: Pennsylvanian to Cretaceous
Coniferales

PALISSYACEAE: Triassic to Jurassic
PODOCARPACEAE: Triassic to Recent

ARAUCARIACEAE: Triassic to Recent
CUPRESSACEAE: Triassic to Recent
TAXODIACEAE: Triassic to Recent
PINACEAE: Triassic to Recent
CEPHALOTAXACEAE: Jurrassic to Recent

Taxales: Triassic to Recent

CORDAITOPSIDA

The Cordaitopsida constitute a group of Carboniferous and Permian coniferophytic gymnosperms that probably evolved from members of the Progymnospermophyta. The order has been especially important in demonstrating an early stage in the evolution of the conifer seed cone. Members of this order were arborescent, with some trees up to 40 m tall. The fossil record suggests that the cordaites represented the dominant vegetation type in some areas during the Pennsylvanian and well into the Permian. The trees consisted of monopodial trunks with distally produced straplike leaves; at the trunk bases were stiltlike roots suggestive of the basal portions of modern mangrove species. Pollen- and seed-producing organs were complex and borne on distal leaf-bearing branches. The pollen was saccate, and the seeds were typically bilateral or had conspicuous lateral wings.

Although the name *Cordaites* was initially used for foliage, the genus also has been used to designate structurally preserved stems and the entire tree. *Pennsylvanioxylon* (Fig. 17-1A) is the generic name now used for structurally preserved stems that had earlier been referred to as *Cordaites*. Stems of *Pennsylvanioxylon* contain a rather large parenchymatous pith surrounded by a small number of separate primary xylem strands (sympodia). The pith constitutes a conspicuous portion of the stem, with some specimens possessing a pith in excess of 10.0 cm in diameter. It consists of rather evenly spaced horizontal septations or diaphragms (Fig. 17-1A) that alternate with lacunae formed during the elongation of the stem tip. Some of the pith cells contain amorphous contents, which suggests to some workers that the pith tissue was secretory. Because of the transverse septations in *Pennsylvanioxylon*, pith casts are relatively easy to distinguish. In the early 1800s, the generic name *Sternbergia* was established by Artis for cordaitean pith casts in honor of his friend and colleague Sternberg (see Fig. 13-9B). At about the same time, Sternberg published a description of the pith casts in honor of Artis. Because *Sternbergia* also is the generic name of an extant flowering plant within the family Amaryllidaceae, cordaite pith casts are today referred to by the name *Artisia*.

The primary xylem of a cordaite stem is relatively inconspicuous, composed of just a few tracheids in the form of discrete sympodia at the ends of the narrow wedges of secondary xylem. Pitting of the primary xylem tracheids includes annular, spiral, scalariform, reticulate, and circular with little distinction between primary and secondary xylem tracheids. When the structurally

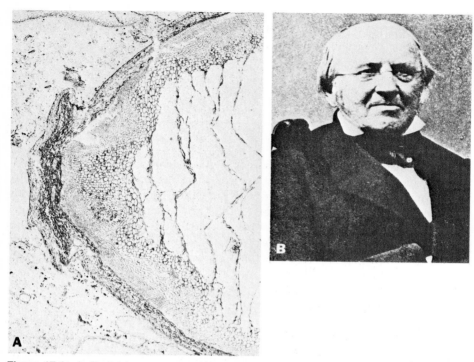

Figure 17-1 A. Partial transverse section of *Pennsylvanioxylon* stem showing pith septations. ×12. B. Heinrich Robert Goeppert. *(B reproduced from* Geschichte der Botanik *with permission of Gustav Fischer Verlag.)*

preserved stems were initially described by Renault (1896), the primary xylem was noted as endarch. Later, cordaitean axes were discovered in English coal balls, and the genus *Mesoxylon* was established for specimens with mesarch primary xylem strands. Although the distinction between this genus and *Pennsylvanioxylon* is rather slight and may simply reflect minor differences in development, a recently completed study indicates that in *Mesoxylon* there is a consistent presence of some centripetal primary wood in the pairs of leaf traces at the edge of the pith. Moreover, in *Mesoxylon,* the vascular system consists entirely of pairs of leaf traces at the perimedullary boundary, while in *Pennsylvanioxylon,* the primary vascular system consists of a number of primary xylem strands organized into sympodial complexes, with one strand of each complex serving as a leaf trace.

Secondary xylem in cordaites was extensive and rather simple, consisting only of tracheids and uniseriate rays that were variable in height. Xylem parenchyma and resin canals were absent. Ray cells were thin-walled and often preserved with amorphous cell contents. Secondary xylem tracheids exhibited closely spaced vertical rows of hexagonal pits. In some specimens, abrupt changes in tracheid diameter produced patterns in the secondary xylem that resemble growth rings. Large isolated pieces of secondary xylem have been described by the name *Dadoxylon*. Such wood is believed to have been produced by cordaiteans, but the wood is not sufficiently preserved to show the positions of protoxylem stands or leaf traces.

The cortex of the cordaiteans was of the "dictyoxylon" type, with longitudinally oriented sclerenchyma bands interspersed with patches of parenchyma. In some specimens, rectangular radially oriented cells have been described as the phloem.

The compressed leaves of the cordaites represent the most frequently encountered parts of the plant. They are strap-shaped (Fig. 17-2A), with some reaching a length of about 1.0 m. Most, however, are in the 10 to 20 cm size range. The distal end is bluntly rounded, and they are broadly attached at the base. Cordaitean leaves lack a midrib; instead they consist of parallel veins that occasionally dichotomize. The superficial appearance of parallel venation is a feature that earlier workers believed aligned the cordaites with the palms. Often, subgeneric names (e.g., *Eu-Cordaites, Dory-Cordaites,* and *Poa-Cordaites*) are used to distinguish impression and compression foliage specimens based on the external morphology and ribbing patterns on their surfaces. The leaves of the cordaites are helically arranged, and many species probably closely resembled certain modern species of *Podocarpus* and *Araucaria*.

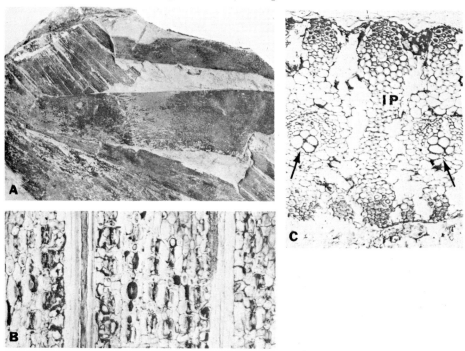

Figure 17-2 A. Compressed cordaitean leaves. ×0.5. B. Paradermal section of lower epidermis of *Cordaites felicis* showing stomatal bands. ×130. C. Transverse section of *Cordaites felicis* leaf showing intervein partition (IP) between vascular bundles *(arrows)*. ×60. *(B and C from Good and Taylor, 1970.)*

Various species of cordaitean leaves have been based on differences in the distribution of cell types and tissue systems in the petrified forms. For example, Harms and Leisman (1961) distinguished 10 species. Anatomically, the leaves are rather similar, consisting of well-differentiated palisade and spongy mesophyll. In some species, the distinction between these two tissues is difficult to determine; in others, either tissue may be absent. In some species, the most conspicuous anatomic features are the epidermisto-epidermis partitions between the veins; these resemble structural I beams (Fig. 17-2C). The presence and extent of these fibrous partitions have been useful in delimiting species, but it is important to examine these features at different locations along a leaf to be able to determine ontogenetic variability from true species differences. In the Lower Pennsylvanian species *Cordaites felicis,* the number of veins ranges from 10 to 25 per centimeter, with masses of hypodermal fibers above and below the veins. The vascular elements are surrounded by a sheath of thin-walled cells four to seven cell layers thick, and maturation of the bundles is mesarch. Most cordaitean leaves have been described with rows of stomata only on the lower surfaces. But in *C. felicis,* stomatiferous bands are present on both surfaces (Fig. 17-2B), and it is probable that most species were amphistomatic. In general, the stomatal apparatus is simple, consisting of two bean-shaped guard cells, two bean-shaped lateral subsidiary cells, and a terminal cell at the end of each stoma. The guard cells are slightly sunken below the surrounding subsidary cells, and in most species, the cuticle is thick, not extending into the substomatal chamber.

The roots of cordaites have been suggested as morphologically similar to the stiltlike roots of modern mangroves. Structurally preserved forms are included in the genus *Amyelon,* which includes both protostelic and siphonostelic forms. Organically attached *Amelon* roots have been identified on stems of *Mesoxylon nauertianum.* The protostelic specimens range from diarch to pentarch and exhibit spiral to multiseriate pitting. The secondary xylem is composed of uniseriate rays and radially aligned tracheids with one to five rows of bordered pits on the radial walls. A complex phloem has been described that contains sieve elements, phloem parenchyma, phloem fibers, and rays, with the outer zone loosely constructed and possibly aerenchymatous. Surrounding the secondary phloem zone is a layer of phelloderm that is also loosely arranged and a compact layer of phellem with lenticels. Lateral roots are borne in large clusters from phellem-covered protuberances on the larger roots. They show no definite arrangement, but appear to have been borne on only one side of the primary root. They possess the same complement of tissues as the main roots, but they have a well-developed endodermis. Although mycorrhizal fungi have been reported in the roots of some European cordaitean specimens, it is difficult to determine whether the fungi were true symbionts, or whether they invaded the tissues after the death of the plant.

Some cordaitean roots have been included in the genus *Premnoxylon* on the basis of the presence of a central pith with scattered tracheids. Surrounding the pith are numerous exarch bundles that are separated from the secondary xylem by several rows of parenchyma cells. Some specimens of *P. iowense* appear protostelic, and it has been suggested that *Premnoxylon* may represent a developmental stage of *Amyelon*.

The reproductive organs of the cordaiteans are believed to have been borne among the leaves on distal branches; reconstructions typically show them helically arranged and in the same organographic spiral as the leaves. However, their position has not been accurately demonstrated. Most of the reproductive structures have been assigned to the genus *Cordaianthus* (Fig. 17-3C), whether they ultimately produced pollen or seeds. Morphologically, they have been termed compound strobili or lax inflorescences. The reproductive organ consists of a primary axis that bears distichously arranged secondary shoots (cones) (Fig. 17-3C) in the axils of modified leaves (bracts) (Fig. 17-4A). In some of the most extensive compression specimens, the primary axis is about 30.0 cm long; the largest structurally preserved *Cordaianthus* is about 5.0 cm long. In transverse section, the primary axis is flattened and contains a centrarch or endarch medullated stele. Tracheids toward the periphery of the stele are radially aligned and exhibit scalariform pitting on both the radial and tangential walls. Traces

Figure 17-3   A. Portion of a *Cordaianthus* fertile axis bearing stalked ovules. B. Rudolph Florin. C. Compressed *Cordaianthus* cone from the Pennsylvanian of Illinois. ×1. *(A from Taylor and Millay, 1979; B from Lundblad, 1966.)*

depart alternately from two areas at opposite ends of the oval stele to the regularly arranged, four-ranked bracts. Thus it has been suggested that the apical meristem of *C. concinnus,* and probably all species, was bilateral.

Typically, the axil of each bract contains a small determinate cone that in some species (*C. concinnus,* Middle Pennsylvanian) is at least 1.6 cm long. Rothwell (1977) has demonstrated that the cones were absent from some axils owing to mechanical disruption; others were not formed owing to the early

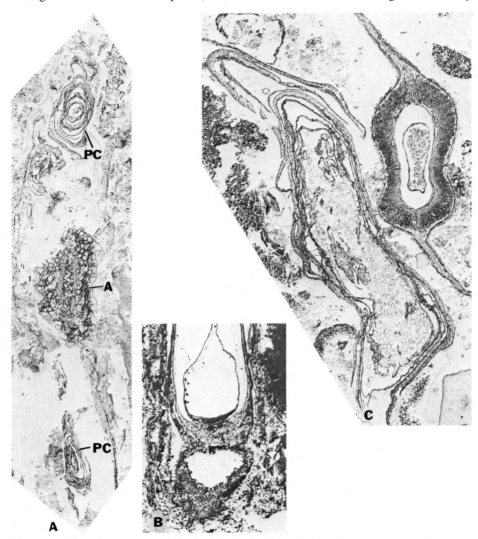

Figure 17-4   A. Transverse section of *Gothania lesliana* primary axis (A) with two pollen cones (PC). ×11.5. B. Longitudinal section through chalazal chamber of *Kamaraspermum leeanum.* ×10. C. Transverse section through mature pollen cone of *Gothania lesliana.* Seed in upper right-hand corner is *Mitrospermum compressum.* ×14. *(A and C from Daghlian and Taylor, 1979.)*

abortion of the shoot primordia. Each of the cones or secondary shoots contain axial bundles (sympodia) that increased in number distally like the eusteles of gymnosperms. The largest number of axial sympodia in *C. concinnus* cones is eight, with each giving rise to a scale trace. Surrounding the cone axis is a variable number of helically arranged modified leaves (scales), with all but the most distal ones sterile. In *C. schulerii* from the Middle Pennsylvanian of Iowa, the number of sterile scales per cone is estimated at about 95, while in *C. concinnus* and *C. compactus,* the number is closer to 30. Only the more distal 5 to 10 scales contain sporangia (pollen sacs) in *Cordaianthus.* Each fertile scale contains three to six elongate sporangia, each about 1.0 mm long. In *C. concinnus,* the six sporangia are arranged in pairs, with dehiscence taking place toward the center of the cluster. The sporangium wall is a single cell thick, and dehiscence is longitudinal. Each of the pollen sacs is vascularized by a small trace that departs from the vascular bundle of the fertile scale.

Pollen grains extracted from *Cordaianthus* sporangia are monosaccate, consisting of a central body (corpus) surrounded by a saccus or air bladder attached to both the proximal and distal surfaces. In *C. concinnus,* the grains measure 65×45 μm and exhibit conspicuous ornamentation (endoreticulations) on the inner surface of the saccus; the outer surface is relatively smooth. Other species possess pollen grains that approach 100 μm in diameter. Pollen of *Cordaianthus* is identical to the *sporae dispersae* grain type *Florinites* (Fig. 17-5B), which is a common Carboniferous palynomorph. Florin (1936) described some pollen grains from the pollen sacs of several silicified *Cordaianthus* cones of the Upper Carboniferous that contained what he believed were sterile jacket cells surrounding a row of lenticular cells inside the corpus. Subsequent studies have indicated that the sterile jacket cells were probably an artifact caused by folds in the corpus wall. However, there can be little doubt that the

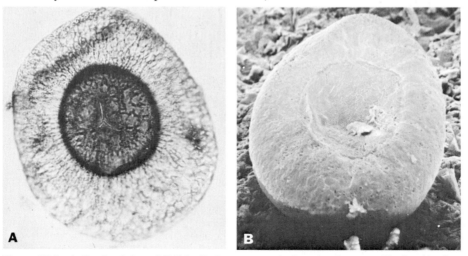

Figure 17-5   A. Proximal view of *Felixipollenites macroreticulata* showing central body with trilete and encircling monosaccus. ×500. B. Proximal surface of *Florinites* sp. pollen grain. ×1000.

lenticular cells represent stages in the development of the microgametophyte in the form of axially aligned prothallial cells. Although haptotypic markings are generally absent from the proximal surfaces of *Florinites* pollen, the ultrastructure and thin exine suggest that germination probably took place from the distal surface. It is not known whether pollen tubes were produced in this grain type.

Another pollen-bearing cone included within the Cordaitales is *Gothania* (Fig. 17-4A and C). The genus was delimited by Hirmer (1933) for cordaitean fructifications believed associated with the European stem genus *Mesoxylon multirame*. Recently, specimens have been discovered in Lower Pennsylvanian strata in eastern Kentucky. Morphologically, they are almost identical to specimens of *Cordaianthus,* differing in certain minor histologic features. The primary basis of distinguishing the two taxa involves differences in the types of pollen produced (Fig. 17-4C). In *Gothania lesliana,* the pollen grains are included in the *sporae dispersae* genus *Felixipollenites* (Fig. 17-5). The monosaccate pollen of this type ranges up to 180 μm in diameter and differs from the *Florinites* pollen of *Cordaianthus* in possessing a conspicuous, complex trilete suture on the proximal surface. Saccus to corpus attachment occurs at both poles except late in development when separation occurs at the distal pole, and the inner surface of the saccus contains prominent endoreticulations.

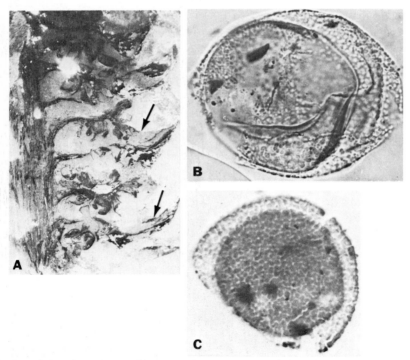

Figure 17-6   A. Portion of *Cladostrobus lutuginii* axis with sporophylls *(arrow).* ×5. B. *Cladostrobus lutuginii* spore. ×1000. C. *Cladaitina dibnerae,* the name used for isolated spores of *Cladostrobus.* ×1400. *(From Maheshwari and Meyen, 1975.)*

Cladostrobus (Fig. 17-6A) is an Upper Paleozoic pollen cone included with the cordaites principally on the association of the cones with presumed cordaite leaf *Rufloria*. The pollen cones consist of helically arranged microsporophylls with rhomboidal distal laminae. Clusters of sporangia are attached to the stalk of the sporophyll and appear to have been borne in pairs. Pollen grains about 30 μm in diameter are oval, and a weakly developed saccus covers the central body, except for a small region on the distal face (Fig. 17-6B). The pollen has been assigned to the *sporae dispersae* genus *Cladaitana* (Fig. 17-6C).

The seed-bearing reproductive units of the cordaites also are given the generic name *Cordaianthus* (Fig. 17-3A) and are morphologically identical to the pollen cones. Some compression specimens have been discovered that reach a length of at least 30.0 cm. In the axially produced seed cones, the distal fertile scales are divided and attenuated into long stalks, each terminating in a cordate-shaped seed (Fig. 17-3A). In some species, the ovule-bearing stalks are short, and the ovules are borne down among the scales. It has been suggested that these reproductive units were immature, and that during the development of the seed-bearing cones, the ovule stalks elongated to provide a more receptive position for the anemophilous (wind-borne) pollen. It is interesting that few structurally preserved seed cones have ever been discovered, even at those localities which have yielded numerous pollen cones and isolated seeds. It is quite probable that during pollination the ovules were exposed for a relatively short time and then were shed from the stalk, so that in reality some of the "pollen cones" represent seed cones that have shed their ovules.

As was noted in Chap. 12, isolated seeds thought to belong to the cordaites are included in the form order Cardiocarpales. Unlike most seed fern seeds, the ovules of the cordaites are bilaterally symmetrical, some with conspicuous lateral extensions of the integument in the form of wings. One of the more common Carboniferous seed taxa thought to have been produced by *Cordaianthus*-like reproductive structures is *Cardiocarpus*. Seeds of this type are so common in some coal ball localities in Iowa that hundreds could be pried from weathering coal balls in a relatively short time. Specimens of *C. spinatus* (Fig. 17-7D), the most common Pennsylvanian species, are about 2.0 cm long, with their apices attenuated into micropylar canals and their bases rounded or cordate-shaped. They are about 1.0 cm wide in the primary plane and approximately half the size when measured in the secondary plane. The integument is three-parted, consisting of an outer sarcotesta of large, irregularly shaped parenchyma cells. The middle layer of the integument, or sclerotesta, is constructed of thick-walled fibrous cells that are uneven and give the layer a spinous appearance when the seeds are sectioned transversely. The innermost integumentary component consists of a uniseriate, thin-walled layer termed the endotesta. In cordiate seeds, the integument and nucellus are adnate only at the base, with a simple pollen chamber formed at the distal end of the nucellus. A single terete vascular strand enters the base of the seed, giving off two slightly flattened strands in the primary plane that extend distally through the sarcotesta. The main strand continues to the base of the nucellus and flares slightly to form a

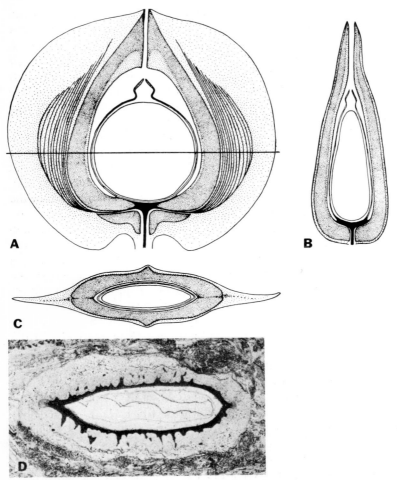

Figure 17-7   A. Longitudinal section (primary plane) of *Mitrospermum compressum*. B. *Mitrospermum compressum* (secondary plane). C. Transverse section of *Mitrospermum compressum* (through line in A). D. Transverse section of *Cardiocarpus spinatus.* ×3.

shallow disk of tracheids. No cordaite seeds are known in which the nucellus is vascularized. Several *C. spinatus* ovules have been described with exquisitely preserved megagametophytes filling the megaspore membrane, some with distally borne archegonia identified by their jacket cells. One of the truly outstanding cases of fossil preservation was demonstrated by Baxter (1964), who described starch grains (see Fig. 1-7A), each with a hilum, within the megagametophyte cells of a *C. spinatus* ovule. *Cardiocarpus oviformis* and *C. magnicellularis* are two additional cordaitean ovules that differ slightly in size and the disposition of cells of the integument. *Cardiocarpus florinii* (Pennsylvanian of Iowa), a slightly smaller species, may represent a developmentally younger form of another species.

Kamaraspermum leeanum is another cordaitean seed about 1.0 cm long and distinctly bilateral. The sclerotesta is rather thin on the flanks of the seed, but conspicuously developed in the basal region. One of the interesting features of *Kamaraspermum* is the presence of a chamber located in the base of the seed below the nucellus (Fig. 17-4B). In this taxon, the integument is more complex, consisting of two distinct zones of fibers. A recent paper by Baxter (1971) suggests that *Kamaraspermum* is identical to a seed described earlier under the generic name *Mitrospermum*.

One of the common European seeds assigned to the Cardiocarpales is the genus *Mitrospermum* (Fig. 17-7A through C). Specimens are about 7.5 mm long and about the same size in the primary plane. Lateral extensions of the sarcotesta form conspicuous wings in the primary plane of the seed (Fig. 17-7C). The vascular system consists of a small terete strand that enters the base of the seed and extends to the level of the nucellus. Two strands are given off, one on each side of the major seed plane, and they extend down toward the base and through the sclerotesta before arching upward to vascularize the integument. Once in the integument, the vascular strands become flattened. The consistent occurrence of pollen grains of the *Felixipollenites* type in the micropyle of *Mitrospermum compressum* seeds suggests that *Gothania* and *Mitrospermum* may have been components of the same biological species (Fig. 17-4C).

CONIFEROPSIDA

Most plants in the Coniferopsida are of enormous size and today represent the dominant and most conspicuous members of the gymnosperms. With the exception of a few deciduous taxa, all are evergreen and their foliage functions for more than a single season, except *Larix* and *Metasequoia*. A few taxa are characterized by long and short (spur) shoots; leaves are typically in the form of scales or needles. Reproductive structures are organized in cones that produce either pollen or ovules. Pollen cones contain sporangia on the abaxial surfaces of microsporophylls; seed cones contain flattened ovules that are attached to the upper surface of an ovuliferous scale and are subtended by a bract.

Voltziales

Members of the Voltziales can be traced from the Pennsylvanian, where they existed with the Cordaitales, into the Mesozoic. The taxa placed in this order were woody trees with generally small, helically arranged leaves. The reproductive organs were morphologically intermediate between those of the Cordaitales and the cones of modern conifers, and for this reason, the Voltziales are sometimes called the "transition conifers." Although most of the information about the group is known from compression specimens, certain members of the Voltziales have been important in morphologic interpretations of the extant conifer cone-scale complex.

Two of the best-known genera of the order are *Lebachia* (Fig. 17-8A) and *Ernestiodendron,* foliage types earlier included in *Walchia* (Fig. 17-8B and C), a genus retained for poorly preserved specimens in which cuticular features are

Figure 17-8   A. *Lebachia piniformis*. B. *Lebachia hypnoides*. C. *Walchia sternbergia*.

absent. *Lebachia* is believed to have been a tree that produced pinnately arranged branches covered with needlelike leaves only a few millimeters long. They were helically arranged and variable in form, with those on fertile branches usually forked at the tip. Each leaf was closely appressed to the branch and amphistomatic, with the bands on the adaxial surface extending from near the base to the leaf tip. Stomata were of the haplocheilic type, with 4 to 10 papillate subsidiary cells. Like *Lebachia*, *Ernestiodendron* produced leaf-bearing branches in a whorled arrangement. Branches with leaf scars suggest that the leaves of *Ernestiodendron* dropped more easily. The individual leaves in this genus extended out from the axis at almost right angles and were not flared at the base. In *Ernestiodendron filiciforme* (Lower Permian), the stomata are borne on both surfaces of the leaf, but are arranged in isolated rows. Each stoma is surrounded by four to eight papillate subsidiary cells. In addition to leaves on the ultimate axes, both genera are characterized by slightly larger, more widely spaced leaves on the penultimate axes. These leaves were generally bifurcated at the tips and oriented in various directions. Although detailed anatomic features remain to be determined for the branches of *Lebachia* and *Ernestiodendron*, it is known that the stems were eustelic with weakly developed endarch primary xylem. Secondary xylem consisted of tracheids with bordered pits on the radial walls in one to three rows; wood parenchyma and resin canals were not present. In general, the branching pattern and type of leaf resembled the living conifer *Araucaria heterophylla* (Norfolk Island Pine).

Specimens assigned to *Walchia*, but probably representing a species of *Lebachia*, may represent the oldest conifer remains described to date and consist of coalified needlelike leaves (1 to 5 mm long) from the Westphalian B (Upper

Carboniferous) of Yorkshire. With the aid of the scanning electron microscope, monocyclic stomata are seen in two bands on the lower surface of the leaf.

Buriadia is another Paleozoic conifer known from leafy shoots, some with secondary xylem. In this genus, flattened, dichotomized leaves are borne on irregularly arranged branches, unlike the two-ranked arrangement in *Lebachia* and *Ernestiodendron*. The leaves are helically arranged and are attached by broad decurrent bases. The lamina may be pointed or forked. The secondary xylem is of the pycnoxylic type with uniseriate rays. On some specimens of *B. heterophylla* from the Permian of India, single stalked ovules are laterally attached to shoots between the leaves, not aggregated into clusters as in other conifers. Seeds appear to have been bilaterally symmetrical, with the micropyle slightly recurved. On the tip of the nucellus in some specimens are oval, nonsaccate pollen grains. Pant and Nautiyal (1967) suggest that *Buriadia* is an ancestral voltzialean (e.g., *Labachia*), while Meyen (1968) regards the differences in the pollen, lack of cuticle associated with the megaspore of *Buriadia,* and the time-space relationship between the taxa as indicating affinities with an independent, presently ill-defined group of coniferous gymnosperms.

Reproductive organs of the Paleozoic conifers consisted of stroboloid structures borne at the ends of leafy branches. Like the cordaites, they were monosporangiate, with pollen and seed-producing cones probably borne on separate shoot systems. In at least one species, *L. hypnoides* (Fig. 17-8B), the reproductive structures were terminally positioned on lateral axes of the penultimate order. The seed-producing strobili of *Lebachia* (Fig. 17-9A) consist

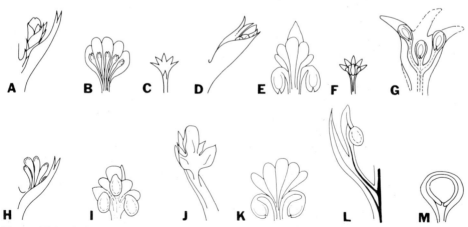

Figure 17-9 A. Cone-scale complex of *Lebachia piniformis.* B. Face view of cone-scale complex of *Voltziopsis africana.* C. Abaxial surface of cone-scale complex of *Swedenborgia cryptomerioides.* D. Cone-scale complex of *Moyliostrobus texanum.* E. Cone-scale complex of *Glyptolepis keuperiana.* F. Adaxial surface of *Swedenborgia cryptomerioides* cone-scale complex G. Cone-scale complex of *Tricranolepis frischmannii.* H. Lateral view of *Ernestiodendron filiciforme* cone-scale complex. I. Cone-scale complex of *Voltzia* sp. J. *Pseudovoltzia liebeana* bract and scale lacking seeds. K. Cone-scale complex of *Glyptolepis hungarica.* L. Lateral view of *Pseudovoltzia liebeana* bract and scale. M. *Ullmannia bronnii* with single recurved ovule and reduced cone-scale complex. *(From Miller, 1977.)*

of a central axis bearing helically arranged, fleshy bracts with forked distal ends. In the axil of each bract is a dwarf shoot that contains helically arranged, broadly decurrent scales. Unlike the arrangement of the ovule-bearing cone of the cordaites, in *Lebachia piniformis,* only one ovule is produced per cone. The fertile scale is the same organotactic spiral as the other sterile scales on the dwarf shoot axis. In other species (e.g., *L. goeppertiana* and *L. hypnoides*), although still constructed of helically arranged scales, the entire fertile unit is slightly flattened. The primary axis of the *Ernestiodendron* (Fig. 17-9H) ovulate strobilus contains helically arranged bifid scales. The seed cones are constructed of about 30 scales, with only the distal four to six bearing ovules. In *E. germanica,* no sterile scales are present, the ovules being subtended by a forked bract. The seed cone is also distinctly flattened. Some species appear to have had ovules that were orthotropous (with the micropyle directed away from the point of attachment), while others had ovules that were recurved (with the micropyle directed toward the region of attachment).

Moyliostrobus (Fig. 17-9D) is a structurally preserved cone of the Lower Permian in which the cone-scale complex consists of dwarf shoots subtended by a nonbifurcate bract. The dwarf shoot is flattened and contains a single ovule and 25 to 50 sterile scales. Each seed is about 1.2 cm long and about 6.0 mm wide. The integument is three-parted and consists of a parenchymatous sarcotesta, fibrous sclerotesta, and uniseriate endotesta. The nucellus is adnate with the integument at the base; nothing is known about the organization of the pollen chamber. No cells of the megagametophyte were preserved, but two seeds contain identifiable embryos. The embryos of *M. texanum* consist of an elliptical parenchymatous structure with annular tracheids.

Pseudovoltzia (Fig. 17-9J and L) is an Upper Permian genus in which the basic morphology of the dwarf shoots is similar to that of the previously discussed taxa, but with the number of scales reduced (probably five) in *P. liebeana.* The central and two lateral scales are slightly larger, with the entire unit fused at the base to the subtending bract. Each of the large scales bears one ovule. Structurally preserved specimens of *Pseudovoltzia* indicate that the ovules are fused to the larger scales and not borne on stalks, as was initially thought.

In *Voltzia andrewsii* (Upper Triassic of North Carolina), there are five fused scales and three ovules, with the ovule stalks fused to the sterile lobes. A further reduction of the dwarf shoot is suggested by the Upper Permian genus *Ullmannia.* In *U. brownii,* the dwarf shoot is disk-shaped and forms by the fusion of five wedge-shaped scales. This disk-shaped structure bears one anatropously directed ovule. It is thought that the fertile scale (disk) and bract were not fused, but it is not known whether the ovule axis was fused to the fertile scale.

Glyptolepis (Fig. 17-9E and K) is a genus known from deposits of the Permian and Triassic. The Permain forms bear rather large dwarf shoots (cones) in the axils of exserted bracts, while the Triassic species appear to bear smaller cones with short, rounded bracts. The cone scales are distinctly flattened, and they are constructed of two recurved seeds and five or six sterile scales. The genus *Voltziopsis* (Fig. 17-9B) (Permian to Upper Triassic) is known only from the Southern Hemisphere and includes both vegetative remains and seed cones. Branches bear dimorphic leaves, and the smaller scalelike ones are triangular and about 3.0 mm long; larger leaves (3.0 cm) extend out from the stems, in two rows and are slightly twisted. Ovule-bearing strobili are borne at the ends of short branches. Each strobilus consists of about 25 units (bract and ovuliferous scale), and the scales are five-lobed, each lobe bearing a single recurved ovule (Fig. 17-9B). In *Tricranolepis* (late Triassic to early Jurassic) seed cones, there is one scale with three large lobes, and each lobe is fused to the stalk of a recurved ovule (Fig. 17-9G). A similar scale morphology is seed in *Swedenborgia* (Fig. 17-9C and F), except that there are five scale lobes and an equal number of recurved ovules.

Through the detailed research efforts of the Swedish paleobotanist Florin (Fig. 17-3B), the evolutionary relationship between the cordaitean seed-bearing reproductive structure and the seed cone of modern conifers has been elucidated. During the evolution of the seed cone, several distinct morphologic changes took place, and the intermediate stages of these changes are represented by members of the Voltziales. This is certainly not to imply that there is a direct evolutionary lineage between the various taxa, but rather demonstrates the manner by which the seed-scale complex in a modern conifer seed cone may have evolved. Morphologically, the primary axis of the *Cordianthus* reproductive unit and the cone axis of a modern pine seed cone are homologous. Attached to the *Pinus* seed-cone axis are helically arranged seed-scale complexes that consist of an ovuliferous scale subtended by a bract. Seeds are attached to the upper surface of the ovuliferous scale. The major changes from the *Cordaianthus* reproductive unit to the conifer seed cone involved modifications of the dwarf shoots. One of these changes was the reduction in the number of sterile scales and a shift from a radially symmetrical structure to one that was slightly flattened. In geologically younger seed cones, the sterile scales became further reduced in number and fused to form a disk or scalelike structure. In some taxa the number of scales that became fused can be determined by the number of distal lobes. As the ovuliferous scale (Fig. 17-10E) was evolving, changes also were taking place relative to the ovules. In the earliest forms, the ovules were terminal at the ends of elongate stalks; in later taxa, the number of ovules was smaller, with the stalks adnate to the scales and the ovules recurved (Fig. 17-9M). The bract that subtends the ovuliferous scale also was continually modified, becoming smaller and, in some instances, fused to the lower surface of the ovuliferous scale.

The pollen organs of the Voltziales were relatively modern in appearance. Unlike the seed cones, they were always borne terminally on leafy branches. The cone consisted of a central axis surrounded by numerous helically arranged, flattened microsporophylls. Each sporophyll had an upturned distal segment

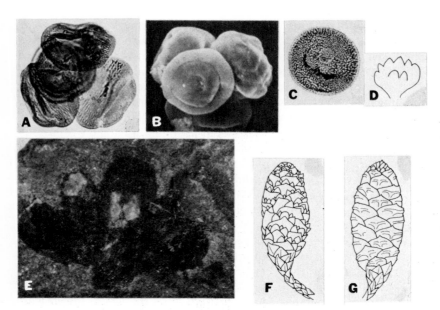

Figure 17-10 A. Tetrahedral tetrad of *Classopollis* pollen grains. ×900. B. Tetrahedral tetrad of *Classopollis* pollen grains as seen with the scanning electron microscope. Compare with Figure 17-10A. ×1000. C. Single *Classopollis echinatus* grain. ×1000. A–C from the Upper Albian of Texas. D. Detached scale of *Hirmerella muensteri* cone. E. Compressed cone-scale complex of *Voltzia liebeana*. F. Suggested reconstruction of *Hirmerella muensteri* before seed-scale dispersal. G. *Hirmerella muensteri* after seed scales dispersed. *(A–C from Srivastava, 1976; D, F, and G from Miller, 1977.)*

that overlapped the sporophyll above and a small basal projection that partially covered the pollen sacs. The lower surface of the microsporophyll contained two elongate microsporangia (pollen sacs) that dehisced longitudinally. The pollen grains of the earliest members of the Voltziales (*Lebachia* and *Ernestiodendron*) were monosaccate and ranged from 50 to 90 μm in the longest dimension. The saccus was internally ornamented with endoreticulations; the outer surface was relatively smooth. No haptotypic markings were present on the proximal surface, germination probably taking place through a thin area on the distal face. Pollen grains of the Upper Permian members (e.g., *Ullmannia*) were smaller and, in some species, bisaccate like certain extant conifers (e.g., *Pinus* and *Abies*). In the earliest forms, however, there was no obvious differentiation between the proximal and distal poles relative to the organization of the exine. These early grains also had sacci that were not distally inclined. Thus, although the seed cones of the Voltziales can be traced phylogenetically from the Carboniferous and Permian Cordaitales, the pollen cones are quite a different matter. The earliest forms in the Voltziales are morphologically modern in appearance and more similar to the pollen cones of extant conifers than they are to the pollen-producing organs of the Cordaitales. If the radial *Cordaianthus* dwarf shoots or pollen cones with elongate terminal sporangia represented the morphologic structure that gave rise to the voltzialean pollen cone, then the structural modifications appear to have taken place in far less time than those of the seed cones. While the pollen cones are quite modern in appearance, some of the voltzialean pollen is almost identical in morphology to the pollen grains present in the cordaitalean forms *Florinites* and *Felixipollenites*.

Some authorities divide the Voltziales into two families, the Voltziaceae and the Hirmerelliaceae (= Cheirolepidaceae), based primarily on differences in the reproductive structures. One member of the Hirmerellaceae is *Hirmerella*, considered by most to have been an arborescent conifer. The branches contained small, helically arranged leaves up to 3.0 mm long, each with a single vascular trace. In transverse section, the branches are eustelic, with tracheids of the secondary xylem ornamented with uniseriate circular bordered pits on the radial walls. The cortex consists of large parenchyma cells and bands of fibers that alternate with rows of haplocheilic stomata on the surface. Resin canals are absent. The ovule-producing cones of *Hirmerella* (= *Cheirolepis*) consists of a seed-scale complex of 6 to 10 sterile scales that extends out between the bracts and, because of its length, is partially visible on the cone surface (Fig. 17-19F). Each scale subtends two inverted ovules (Fig. 17-10D). The ovuliferous scales of *Hirmerella* were apparently shed at maturity, while the larger bracts were retained (Fig. 17-10G). The pollen cones consist of helically arranged microsporophylls that are upturned distally to form a peltate head. They are narrowly attached to the cone axis and cordate in shape. Specimens from south Wales suggest that the number of pollen sacs attached to the abaxial surface of the sporophyll is 2 rather than 12, as was originally suggested. Each sporangium is about 3.0 mm long and contains circular grains 20 to 29 μm in diameter. It is quite probable that the grains had a monosaccus, although this is not indicated in descriptions. On the proximal surfaces of some specimens are faint trilete marks; the distal face may have had a leptoma (thin area of the wall through which germination took place). The saccus is endoreticulate.

Lower Cretaceous leafy shoots from Argentina were initially described by the name *Tomaxellia*. These woody plants bear sharply tapered, helically arranged decurrent leaves up to 1.3 cm long. The leaves are amphistomatic, with the guard cells sunken, and surrounded by four to five subsidiary cells. Pollen cones are about 3.0 mm long and 1.0 mm in diameter; they are attached both laterally and at the tip of branches. Microsporophyll arrangement and the number of pollen sacs are not known. The pollen extracted from the cones conforms to the genus *Classopollis* (Fig. 17-10A), a genus that contains numerous morphologic species established for various stratigraphic periods.

Grains of *Classopollis* are unique in having two types of apertures. The proximal surface has a trilete tetrad scar, while the distal surface exhibits a cryptopore. Encircling the grain between the equator and distal pole is a circumpolar canal or zonisulcus (Fig. 17-10B) and a thickened band of sporoderm. Pollen of the *Classopollis* type is tectate, with the surface ornament (supratectal ornamentation) ranging from smooth to spinulose (Fig. 17-10C). This worldwide form genus that extends from the Triassic to the Middle

Cretaceous is known from several different reproductive structures, all probably representing extinct conifers.

The ovule-bearing cones of *Tomaxellia* are about 3.0 cm long and consist of bract-scale complexes arranged in a helix around an axis. Bracts are ovate, decurrent at the base, and partially surround the axis. The shorter scale is partially fused to the bract and exhibits a lobed margin. Two circular scars near the scale base are thought to represent the positions of the ovules. Isolated ovuliferous scales of *Tomaxellia* also have been found, suggesting that it, like *Hirmerella,* shed its scales at maturity.

Coniferales

Members of the Coniferales are generally arranged into seven families, with all but one, the Palissyaceae, having extant representatives. In some classifications, another family, the Taxaceae, is also included; but because the members of this group do not produce seeds in cones, they are treated as a separate order in this book. All the conifer families appear to have been highly diversified by the Jurassic, with several traceable to the Triassic. Today the modern conifers are widespread in both the Northern and Southern Hemispheres and include 51 genera and approximately 550 species.

Palissyaceae The Palissyaceae constitute a small family of Triassic and Jurassic conifers that has highly distinctive cone-scale complexes. *Palissya* is believed to have been a woody plant with alternately arranged, vegetative branches that bear persistent, helically arranged linear leaves. The stomata were confined to narrow bands on the lower surfaces of the leaves, one on each side of the midrib. In *P. sphenolepis,* the stomata are aligned longitudinally, and the subsidiary cells contain an overarching papilla. Ovulate cones are borne singly at the terminal end of lateral branches. Each cone is about 10.0 cm long and contains a peduncle that bears a few vegetative leaves. The axis contains helically arranged double cone scales, each with about 10 stalks (megasporophylls) that bear single ovules (Fig. 17-11A). The seeds are orthotropous and partially surrounded by an asymmetrical, cuplike aril that is well-developed on the side away from the cone axis. On some specimens, a circular scar can be identified at the base of the aril, and this marks the former position of the seed. The seed of *Palissya* is ovate and about 2.5 mm long. Nothing is known about the pollen-producing organs.

Another genus included in this family is *Stachyotaxus,* a late Triassic plant known only from Greenland, Switzerland, and southern Sweden. Leaves of *S. elegans* are morphologically similar to those of *Palissya,* but they appear to be borne in a two-ranked arrangement. Stomata are scattered on the lower surface and lack papillae on the subsidiary cells. The principal difference between the two genera lies in the ovulate cones. In *Stachyotaxus,* the cone-scale complexes are less complex, consisting of a pair of fused ovuliferous scales that terminates in a single ovule (Fig. 17-11F). Like *Palissya,* the aril of *Stachyotaxus* is a slightly asymmetrical. Macerated *S. elegans* ovules suggest that the nucellus and integument are fused only at the base.

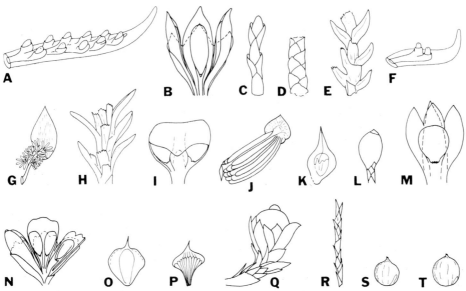

Figure 17-11 A. Cone-scale complex of *Palissya sphenolepis*. B. Cone scale of *Rissikia apiculata*. C. Vegetative shoot of *Cupressinocladus ramonensis*. D. Vegetative shoot of *Brachyphyllum macrocarpum*. E. Vegetative shoot of *Pagiophyllum veronense*. F. Cone scale of *Stachyotaxus elegans*. G. Microsporangiate organ of *Voltziostrobus mougeotii*. H. Vegetative shoot of *Elatocladus zignoi*. I. Cone-scale complex of *Mataia podocarpoides*. J. Microsporophyll of *Masculostrobus cordiformis*. K. Cone scale of *Araucarites cutchensis*. L. Terminal ovule of *Marksea thomasiana*. M. Recurved ovule and cone scale of *Nothodacrium warrenii*. N. Cone-scale complex of *Rissikia media*. O. Cone scale of *Araucarites columnaris*. P. Cone scale of *Doliostrobus acicularis*. Q. Terminal ovule of *Palaeotaxus rediviva*. R. Vegetative shoot of *Sphenolepis*. S and T. Seeds of *Vesquia tournaisii*. *(From Miller, 1977.)*

Pollen cones recovered from the same sediments are thought to be the microsporangiate organs of *Stachyotaxus*. Morphologically they resembled small catkins with helically arranged microsporophylls, each containing two elongate pollen sacs on the abaxial surface. Dehiscence is apparently longitudinal, with the pollen grains spherical and lacking sacci.

The morphology of the cone-scale complexes of *Palissya* and *Stachyotaxus* approximate the ovulate structures in the modern conifers *Cephalotaxus* and *Dacrydium*, prompting some authors to suggest affinities with these groups. Florin (1958), however, suggested that the two genera were probably distinct from any living conifers, possibly evolving directly from the voltzialean *Ernestiodendron*. Schweitzer (1963), on the other hand, believes that the taxa constitute a reduction series landing to the extant *Cephalotaxus*.

Podocarpaceae Members of this family are trees and shrubs with helically arranged leaves that may range from scalelike to linear or broad. Today the family is restricted to the Southern Hemisphere with approximately 150 species grouped into 7 genera. The pollen cones contain two sporangia per sporophyll; pollen grains are characterized by reduced sacci. Seed cones in this family are variable in morphology, but uniform in their attachment to a primary axis at the ends of lateral shoots. Each cone consists of an axis with a small number of sterile scales and one or two ovules. In many species, the scales develop into a fleshy structure (epimatium) that surrounds the ovule.

Fossils assignable to the Podocarpaceae are known from the Lower Triassic and extend throughout the Mesozoic. Possibly the oldest podocarpaceous remains include leafy twigs and detached pollen and seed cones from the Triassic of Africa and Australia. *Rissikia* bears spur shoots, each about 6.0 cm long, that are thought to have been deciduous on the basis of the presence of abscission scars. At the base of each spur shoot are several small, scalelike leaves; the remainder of the shoot contains 30 flattened, helically arranged leaves, each about 1.0 cm long. Stomata are arranged in four rows on the lower surface, with the guard cells slightly sunken. Arching over the stomatal pit are cuticular projections or papillae that originate from the subsidiary cells. The pollen cones of *R. media* are about 1.0 cm long and contain approximately 25 microsporophylls, each with two elongate, abaxially oriented pollen sacs. The sacs are thick-walled and partially protected by the upturned distal end of the sporophyll. Pollen grains possess distally inclined sacci. The grains are about 50 μm long and contain widely spaced endoreticulations on the inner surface of the saccus wall. On the distal surface is a slightly thinner region (leptoma); proximally the cappus exhibits numerous parallel striations. Similar *sporae dispersae* grains are included in the genus *Taeniasporites*. Seed cones range up to 6.0 cm long, each with a varible number of cone-scale complexes (Fig. 17-11B) identified by a trifid bract that subtends the cone scale (Fig. 17-11N). Extending from the lobe of each cone scale are two elongate ovules.

Another woody conifer from the Jurassic of Australia and New Zealand is *Mataia*. The leaves of this plant are helically arranged but twisted at the base to form two rows. The leaves are about 1.5 cm long and have rows of monocyclic stomata on their lower surfaces. The seed cones of *M. podocarpoides* measure about 3.0 cm long and contain basal foliage leaves that subtend a zone of 8 to 12 helically arranged cone-scale complexes. The bract is triangular in outline. The tip of the ovuliferous scale is recurved and produces two stalked ovules from the adaxial surface (Fig. 17-11I). Both the seed cones of *Rissikia* and *Mataia* suggest that the bract- and seed-bearing cone scales of some extant podocarps are equivalent to one of the scale lobes of the fossils. According to this idea, the epimatium represents a single bivascularized unit rather than two structures that have fused together.

Nothodacrium is a Jurassic conifer from Antarctica that is regarded as a member of the Podcarpaceae. In this woody conifer, there is no division of the vegetative parts into long and short shoots. Superficially, the axes appear pinnately arranged, although they were probably produced in a helical pattern. The leaves are borne somewhat like those of *Ernestiodendron,* diverging in several directions from the axis. Each is about 3.0 mm long and rhomboidal in transverse section. Ovule-bearing cones are borne at the ends of branches, each cone consisting of 10 to 15 cone-scale complexes. The ovuliferous scale is trilobed (Fig. 17-11M), but only a single recurved seed is produced. Pollen cones assignable to the form genus *Masculostrobus* (Fig. 17-11J) are known from the same sediments, but none have been found attached to leaf-bearing branches. Pollen grains have three sacci and are about 110 μm in diameter. Similar Jurassic pollen is included in the *sporae dispersae* taxon *Tsugaepollenites*. Structurally preserved pollen cones from the Jurassic of India that were formerly assigned to *Masculostrobus* are now included in *Podostrobus*. Pollen of this podocarpaceous cone is both bi- and trisaccate.

Helically arranged leaves approximately 6.0 mm long that leave a rhomboidal scar when detached from the twigs are described as *Trisacocladus* (Lower Cretaceous of Argentina). Both pollen and seed cones are assigned to this taxon. The largest ovule-bearing cone is about 2.0 cm long and consists of a fleshy axis that bears the ovules; none of the specimens contain bracts or scales. Ovules of *T. tigrensis* are orthotropous and about 3.0 mm long. The pollen cones produce helically arranged microsporophylls with probably two pollen sacs on each abaxial surface. Pollen grains are small (12 to 32 μm in diameter), and they are characterized by three sacci extending from the distal hemisphere of the grain. *Apterocladus* is the generic name of vegetative axes and pollen-producing cones from the same Lower Cretaceous formation in Argentina. Vegetative remains are distinguished by epidermal features (stomatal organization and pattern); pollen cones contain saccate pollen. Nothing is known about the ovule-bearing cones.

The Northern Hemisphere record of Mesozoic podocarps is relatively meager, including a few pollen grains and some megafossil remains from the Eocene of Tennessee. These specimens consist of stout stems with helically arranged, needle-shaped, amphistomatic leaves with thickened rings of cutin surrounding the stomata. These cuticular features clearly indicate the affinities of the leafy shoots with ancient members of the Podocarpaceae.

Several generic names have been applied to isolated pieces of structurally preserved woods thought to be podocarpaceous. These include *Podocarpoxylon, Paraphyllocladoxylon,* and *Phyllocladoxylon.* The origin of the family is believed to be associated with the late Paleozoic members of the Voltziales. This inference is based principally on the transition features of seed cones found in the fossils *Rissikia* and *Mataia.* Both genera demonstrate a reduction of the seed-scale complex and number of ovules, and suggest that the origin of the epimatium is a single enveloping scale. Although the Podocarpaceae are believed to have been restricted to the Southern Hemisphere throughout their geologic history, megafossil evidence, together with scattered Northern Hemisphere reports of pollen, suggests that early in the evolution of the family, some taxa may have been more cosmopolitan in distribution.

Araucariaceae This family of ancient conifers today consists of 2 genera, *Araucaria* and *Agathis,* and approximately 40 species. All the extant species are evergreen and lack shoot dimorphism. Leaves may be helically arranged or opposite, linear or broad. The reproductive structures are in the form of strobili that are typically large. Throughout the family, the number of pollen sacs varies from 5 to 20, with pollen grains typically nonsaccate. The ovuliferous scale and bract are fused, usually with one ovule produced per complex. The two genera are confined to the Southern Hemisphere today, but like the Podocarpaceae, they were present to a limited extent in the Northern Hemisphere during the Mesozoic. Although there are few reports of araucarian fossils in the Paleozoic, unquestionable specimens are known from the Upper Triassic, with the greatest period of radiation apparently during the Jurassic. Fossil evidence suggests that from the Cretaceous to the present, the family has gradually declined in numbers of taxa and geographic distribution.

Some living araucarians are represented by trees that exceed 60 m in height, with the folaige produced on branches forming a dense crown. Because of the enormous size of some of these trees and the large amount of wood produced, it is no wonder that one of the most common fossils assignable to the family is secondary xylem referred to as *Araucarioxylon.* One of the best-known sources of this wood is the Petrified Forest of Arizona, where silicified logs of *Araucarioxylon* are scattered over many miles. The genus is not a natural one, and it includes secondary xylem that contains both uniseriate and multiseriate bordered pits on the radial walls of tracheids. There is no xylem parenchyma, nor have resin canals been described in wood of this type. The vascular rays are uniseriate, with the individual cells pitted on the radial walls. In some instances, *Araucarioxylon* wood is difficult to distinguish from specimens of *Dadoxylon,* a genus that no doubt contains specimens of cordaitean secondary xylem. No foliage or reproductive organs have ever been found in association with *A. arizonicum* specimens; the logs are thought to have been rafted to the site of burial. In well-preserved specimens, a small pith is present, and this is surrounded by secondary xylem with weakly developed growth rings.

Brachyphyllum (Fig. 17-12C) is the name of shoots bearing helically arranged leaves that consist of a basal cushion that is wider than the free part of the leaf. Some specimens assigned to the genus no doubt represent the foliage of other conifers, but in the case of *B. mamillare* (Jurassic of Yorkshire), cuticle structure (stomatal organization) was used to demonstrate the association with the seed-cone scale of *Araucarites phillipsii.* The pollen cone of *B. mamillare* is about 1.2 cm long and contains three elongate pollen sacs on the lower surface of each microsporophyll. Pollen is smooth-walled, inaperturate, and in the 56 to 84 μm size range.

The generic name *Araucarites* has been used for cones, isolated ovuliferous scales (Fig. 17-11K and O), and sterile twigs, suggesting araucarian affinities. More recently, the name has been restricted to cones and cone parts. *Araucarites cutchensis* (Fig. 17-11K) is the name applied to detached, wedge-shaped seed scales up to 3.5 cm long ranging from the Upper Jurassic to the Lower Creataceous of India. Partially embedded in the upper scale surface is a single ovoid seed. One of the characteristic features of an extant araucarian seed-scale complex is the ligule, in this case the free extension of the ovuliferous scale that is not fused to the bract. Many of the presumed seed scales of

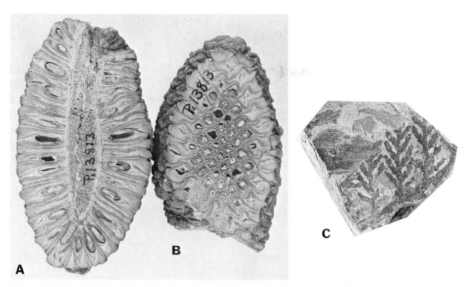

Figure 17-12   Median longitudinal section of *Araucaria mirabilis*. ×1. B. Tangential section of *A. mirabilis* showing cone scales. ×1. C. *Brachyphyllum hondurense*. ×0.8. *(A and B courtesy of R. Stockey; C courtesy of T. Delevorgas.)*

Araucarites do not exhibit a ligule. *Doliostrobus* (Fig. 17-11P) is the name applied to Cretaceous and Tertiary seed scales that morphologically resemble those of *Agathis*.

Some of the most spectacular and beautifully preserved araucarian fossils are silicified cones (Fig. 17-12A and B) found in the Cerro Cuadrado Petrified Forest of Patagonia. The precise stratigraphic position of these cones is not known, although most workers today regard the sediments as late Jurassic. Cones of *Araucaria mirabilis* are completely silicified by alpha quartz and range from spherical to elipsoidal. The largest specimens are almost 10.0 cm in diameter and consist of a central axis with helically arranged cone-scale complexes. Each unit is constructed of an ovuliferous scale subtended by a woody, winged bract (Fig. 17-13A). The axis of the cone contains a parenchyma-tous pith surrounded by a ring of fused bundles that become separate at higher levels. Each cone-scale complex is vascularized by a double set of bundles that provide traces to the bract and ovuliferous scale. Resin canals are associated with each vascular strand. Anatomic features of the patagonian cones suggest affinities with the section *Bunya* of the genus *Araucaria*. Mature seeds of *A. mirabilis* are up to 1.3 cm long and about half as wide. Each ovuliferous scale bears one seed, partially embedded on the upper surface. The integument of the seed is composed of three distinct tissue systems: parenchymatous sarcotesta, fibrous sclerotesta, and partially preserved endotesta. The seed coat and nucellus are adnate only at the base. Megagametophyte tissue is common, and in a few specimens, elliptical cavities suggestive of archegonia have been identified.

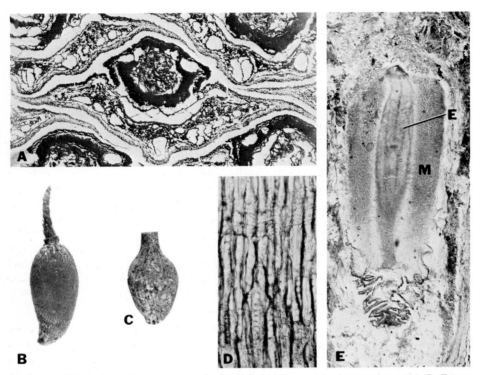

Figure 17-13   A. Tangential section of *Araucaria mirabilis* cone-scale complex. ×15. B. Extant seedling of *Araucaria bidwillii* with swollen hypocotyl. ×1. C. Fossil seedling of *Araucaria mirabilis*. ×1. D. Uniseriate pits on cone axis tracheids of *Pararaucaria patagonica*. ×250. E. Longitudinal section of *Araucaria mirabilis* embryo (E) embedded in tissue of the megagametophyte (M). ×20. *(A from Stockey, 1978; B and C from Stockey and Taylor, 1978; D from Stockey, 1977.)*

One of the interesting features of the araucarian seeds is the occurrence of dicotyledonous embryos embedded within the megagametophyte (Fig. 17-13E). They are typically in the telostage period of development and, in longitudinal section, clearly exhibit shoot apex, cotyledons, root meristem, vascular system, columella, and calyptroperiblem. Cellular preservation within these embryos is so good that nuclei appear to be present in some of the cells. The remnants of a highly coiled suspensor are also visible in some of the sections.

Rarely does the fossil record provide any easily identifiable evidence of postfertilization stages or embryo and seedling development. Several specimens that have been compared with extant araucarian seedlings (Fig. 17-13C) have been found among the Cerro Cuadrado fossil remains. These range from top-shaped to turbinate, the largest being about 3.5 cm long. Like the seedlings of living araucarians (Fig. 17-13B), the Cerro Cuadrado specimens have a swollen hypocotyl comprised of a parenchymatous cortex with patches of resin canals. In the central portion of the axis is a pith surrounded by radial files of vascular elements. Near the base of the seedling, the vascular cylinder consists of an elliptical xylem strand. The presence of fossil seedlings and embryos in one biological species provides not only an opportunity to detail a more complete developmental sequence for a fossil plant, but also an additional basis upon which to consider phylogeny within a conifer family.

Despite the numerous ovulate cones discovered in the Cerro Cuadrado sediments, it is interesting that to date no pollen cones referrable to the family have been identified. Similarly, no pollen grains or evidence of pollen tubes have been found within the seeds. This is especially unusual because in the Araucariaceae, the pollen tubes are quite erosive and typically leave conspicuous channels in the seed tissues. The absence of pollen in the sediments is believed by some workers to indicate that the forest was covered by volcanic ash prior to the ontogenetic development of the cones; the presence of embryos suggests that the cones may have developed parthenogenetically. Interestingly, pollen cones within the Araucariaceae are quite rare in the fossil record. Several specimens of the Jurassic have been identified in England associated with foliage of *Pagiophyllum* (Fig. 17-14), but poor preservation has obscured important features, including the position and number of pollen sacs. Associated pollen grains range up to 30 μm in diameter and are smooth-walled.

Cupressaceae   The Cupressaceae constitute the largest of the conifer families in terms of numbers of extant genera, with many cultivated as ornamentals. All species are evergreen and characterized by small, scalelike linear leaves that are borne oppositely or in whorls. Pollen-producing cones contain whorled microsporophylls with from three to six spherical pollen sacs.

Figure 17-14   Vegetative branch of *Pagiophyllum* sp. ×1.

Ovulate cones are typically small, with the bract and cone scale fused throughout. Ovule number is typically 2 to 3 per cone scale, but in some species of *Cupressus,* the number may vary from 6 to 20. At one time, the family was thought to have had a relatively short geologic history, but within recent years, several well-preserved specimens have been discovered that indicate cupressoid remains in the early Mesozoic.

The oldest recognized examples of the family are based on leafy twigs, fragments of secondary xylem, and ovulate cones from the late Triassic of France. Wood is typically assigned to *Cupressinoxylon* and *Juniperoxylon;* ovulate cones exhibit decussate bract-scale complexes that morphologically resemble those of the modern genera *Cupressus* and *Cryptomeria* (Taxodiaceae).

Cupressinocladus ramonensis (Fig. 17-11C) is the name given to compressed leafy shoots from the Jurassic black shales of Israel. The specimens consist of small decussate, regularly spaced leaves with decurrent bases. On the upper surface, stomata are arranged in a few widely spaced rows; on the lower surface, the number of stomatiferous rows may extend up to 15. Stomata are monocyclic, with four to six subsidiary cells (Fig. 17-15); the remaining epidermal cells possess distinct cuticular papillae. Nothing is known about the reproductive organs of this plant.

Another genus sometimes included in the Cupressaceae because of the resemblance to the modern genus *Callitris* is *Frenelopsis*. Other authors have placed this genus in the family Hirmerelliaceae (= Cheirolepidiaceae). *Frenelopsis* is common in the Cretaceous, but also has been reported from the Upper Jurassic of Spain. *Frenelopsis alata* is known from specimens that exhibit at least three orders of branching. Triangular-shaped leaves, each about 0.6 mm long, are produced in whorls of three. Recently, Alvin and Hlustik (1979) have demonstrated that a modified form of axillary branching is present in specimens of *F. alata* that is not known to occur in conifers. In *F. teixeirae* (Lower Cretaceous of Portugal), the leaves exhibit an opposite, decussate arrangement.

Figure 17-15   Cuticle preparation of *Cupressinocladus ramonensis.* ×250. *(Courtesy of J. Lorch.)*

Manica is the name used for *Frenelopsis*-like shoots with helically arranged leaves. When the sites where *Frenelopsis* has been found are plotted geographically, it becomes apparent that the genus inhabited the lower latitudes. *Pseudofrenelopsis* is a closely related genus that morphologically is similar to *Frenelopsis*. In *F.* (= *Pseudofrenelopsis*) *varians* (see Fig. 1-2A and B) from the Cretaceous of Texas, the cuticle is quite thick and consists of five to six subsidiary cells with papillae overarching the stomatal chamber. Based on the reduced leaf size, thick cuticle, and minerologic composition of the sediment, the central Texas species is believed to have been a salt marsh inhabitant where high rates of evaporation and salinity were common. Small cones (4.0 to 5.0 mm in diameter) containing helically arranged microsporophylls have recently been found associated with twigs of *P. parceramosa*. Specimens of *Classostrobus* have three cylindrical pollen sacs on the lower surface, each containing pollen of the *Classopollis* type. *Classoidites,* a pollen type similar to *Classopollis,* also has been found in the cone *F. oligostomata* discovered in Cretaceous sediments from Portugal.

Cupressoid fossils of *Hellia salicorniodes* are widely distributed in Tertiary floras of Europe and have been included in the family because of their similarity to the extant genus *Tetracilinis*. Specimens from the Middle Miocene of Denmark include beautifully preserved branchlets with leaves that were easily embedded in paraffin and sectioned with a rotary microtome. The leaves are amphistomatic and reveal monocyclic stomata arranged in two narrow bands.

Ovulate cones up to 3.5 cm long (Upper Cretaceous of Massachusetts) are included in the genus *Cupressinostrobus*. The number of oppositely arranged cone-scale complexes ranges from 14 to 24 with each producing two seeds. In transverse section, each scale contains three or four pairs of vascular strands along the upper surface. Associated with the seed cones were smaller strobili believed to be the pollen cones, although pollen sacs were not observed. In addition, the flora contained several wood types placed in the form genera *Widdringtonoxylon, Thujoxylon,* and *Libocedroxylon*.

Taxodiaceae   The members of this family, possibly more than any other conifer line, demonstrate a once diverse and extensive group of conifers that are represented by numerous fossil representatives, but relatively few extant species. The 15 modern species are classified in 10 genera with none on more than a single continent. Among the living members are found the largest organisms on the face of the earth (*Sequoiadendron*). The leaves are helically arranged and range from scalelike to broad; in some taxa, flattened determinate branchlets are seen. Cones are typically small, with the pollen cones bearing two to seven microsporangia per sporophyll. The pollen in this family lacks sacci. Within the family, two to seven ovules are produced on the upper surface of each ovuliferous cone scale.

Pararaucaria is a small cone (2.3 × 1.3 cm) from the Cerro Cuadrado Petrified Forest of Patagonia that, despite the generic name, probably was not involved in the evolution of the Araucariaceae. The ovulate cones from the

Patagonian site are delimited by the large woody, ovuliferous scales and small partly fused, flattened bracts. Each scale contains a single cordate-shaped seed about 6.0 mm long. Extending from the surface are two seed wings composed of anastomosing rows of glandular hairs that are continuous with the upper surface of the ovuliferous scale. Morphologic and histologic (Fig. 17-13D) features of the *P. patagonica* ovulate cones do not conform to any fossil or living conifer genus, but rather appear to combine a number of features of at least five different families. Several authors have suggested that *Pararaucaria* represents a cone type that is intermediate between some members of the Pinaceae and the Taxodiaceae.

Another Jurassic conifer which is included within the Taxodiaceae is *Sewardiodendron*. It was a woody plant with the foliage leaves helically arranged but appearing two-ranked and spread in various directions because of their twisted bases. Stomata were confined to the lower surface in distinct bands, with the subsidiary cells possessing overarching papillae. Also present were helically arranged scale leaves at the bases of lateral shoots. Nothing is known about the reproductive organs of this plant.

Elatocladus (Fig. 17-11H) is a name given conifer foliage types for which the exact affinities cannot be determined. Some of the Jurassic specimens morphologically resemble the narrowly attached leaves of the extant taxodiaceous genus *Cunninghamia;* others have been placed in the Cephalotaxaceae.

Sciadopitytes variabilis includes foliar and reproductive remains from the Lower Cretaceous of the Arctic. The linear leaves of this conifer are about 1.5 cm long and exhibit a slightly swollen base. Stomata are produced in bands in a definite groove on the lower surface. Each band is about five to eight stomata wide, with cuticular papillae prominent along the flanks of the stomatal groove. The guard cells are greatly thickened and not sunken beneath the surface. Pollen grains obtained from the same macerations are spherical and up to 48 μm in diameter. They appear almost identical to the pollen of modern *Sciadopitys* species.

Sciadopitophyllum is the name used for compressed shoots and leaves that range from the late Cretaceous to the Paleocene of western Canada. The specimens of *S. canadense* consist of foliar shoots bearing 8 to 12 lanceolate leaves, each up to 16.0 cm long. Not all the fossil leaves have the apical notch at the tip characteristic of the genus *Sciadopitys;* however, this feature apparently becomes obscured even in extant specimens as development continues.

To date the only modern taxodiaceous genus from the Jurassic is *Sequoia jeholensis* (Manchuria). The taxon is delimited on impression specimens of vegetative remains that superficially resemble the extant species *S. sempervirens.*

Elatides is a generic name used principally for ovulate cones, although some authors have extended the taxonomic designation to include vegetative remains and pollen-producing cones as well. Specimens are known from a number of geographic localities that range from the Middle Jurassic well into the Cretaceous. In *E. bommeri* (Cretaceous of Englnad), the vegetative axes are irregularly branched, with leaves about 3.0 mm long borne in a tight helix. In section view, the leaves are rhomboidal and characterized by a single, large resin canal and fibrous hypodermis. Stomata are arranged in rows, with the individual guard cells slightly sunken. Papillae are absent on the subsidiary cells. Ovule-bearing cones are borne terminally on the vegetative branches. The cone scales are stalked, terminating in a conspicuous distal spine. The seeds are about 3.0 mm long and lack distinct wings. In *E. williamsonii* (Jurassic of Greenland), the pollen cones are borne in clusters at the ends of vegetative branches. Each microsporophyll contains three pollen sacs on the abaxial surface; pollen is oval and contains a distal aperture.

Sphenolepis is another taxodiaceous conifer from the Cretaceous that includes structurally preserved wood, foliage (Fig. 17-11R), and ovulate cones. The wood most closely approximates that of *Cupressinoxylon,* with a narrow pith composed of pitted parenchyma cells. Secondary xylem tracheids contain uniseriate pits at either end of the cell and numerous narrow wood rays only a few cells high. No resin canals are present. The leaves are scalelike and triangular in transverse section. At their base they flare to form a cushion. The banded stomata are characterized by contiguous subsidiary cells. The ovule-producing cones of *S. kurriana* are about 1.2 cm long and consist of flattened, wedge-shaped cone scales that bear up to six seeds arranged in two rows.

With the exception of *Sequoiadendron,* all the modern genera in the Taxodiaceae are known from the Mesozoic (Miller, 1977). Many of these reports are based on impression foliage that morphologically resembles extant taxa, but provide no information on cuticular structure and organization.

Athrotaxis tasmanica consists of leafy shoots about 5.0 mm in diameter with helically arranged, triangular-shaped leaves. The leaves are thickest in the middle and amphistomatic, and the stomata are arranged in zones, but show no particular orientation. Elongate, fingerlike cutinized cells along the edge of the leaf give it a serrate margin.

Cunninghamiostrobus is an ovulate cone from the Lower Cretaceous of California that is associated with needlelike leaves that closely resemble extant specimens of *Cunninghamia.* The needles are helically arranged on stems, which contain summer-wood tracheids in the outer third of the axis. Resin canals are conspicuous and are arranged in a ring around the vascular tissue. The needles are broken, with the longest ones about 8.0 mm long. They contain a palisade mesophyll surrounded by a fibrous hypodermis. Ovule-bearing cones of *C. hueberi* are attached both laterally and terminally to the structurally preserved stems. They are ellipsoidal and consist of a central axis about 2.5 cm long with helically arranged cone-scale complexes. The presence of a partial growth ring in the cone axis indicates that the development of the cones required more than a single growing season to complete, much like some modern species of the family. In *C. hueberi,* the bract is conspicuous, with the ovuliferous scale reduced to a pad of tissue about one-third the size of the bract. On the upper surface of each scale are three flattened seeds.

An interesting member of the Taxodiaceae from the Cretaceous of Alaska is *Parataxodium.* The taxon was established for pollen and seed cones, as well as

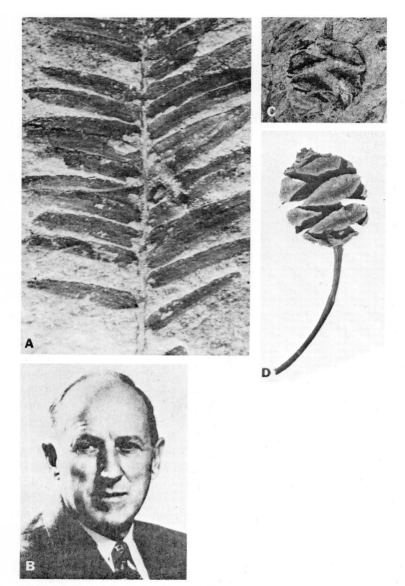

Figure 17-16 A. Vegetative shoot of *Metasequoia*. ×2. B. Ralph Works Chaney. C. Fossilized *Metasequoia* cone. ×0.6. D. Extant *Metasequoia* cone. ×0.6. *(B reproduced with permission of the Geological Society of America, courtesy J. Gray.)*

leaf-bearing twigs. Both long and short shoots are apparent on *P. wigginsii,* with entire leaf-bearing shoots apparently shed annually like those of *Taxodium* and *Metasequoia.* The leaves are attached by a short stalk and appear to have been alternate in arrangement. The leaf tip is generally blunt, with a small mucro at the tip. Detached seed cones thought to belong to *Parataxodium* are about 1.3 cm long and contain helically arranged flattened scales; the number of seeds produced per scale is not known. Pollen-producing cones (2.0 mm long) also were present in the matrix, but they were not histologically preserved; none contained pollen.

The genus *Metasequoia* (Dawn Redwood) presents an interesting example of a plant that was initially described from fossil remains, only later to be found living in central China. *Metasequoia* was described by Miki in 1941 from vegetative remains and cones collected in Pliocene clays and lignite beds. The distinguishing feature of *M. glyptostroboides* includes the deciduous, decussate leafy shoots that are borne in opposite pairs along the branches. The needles are twisted and also opposite (Fig. 17-16A); stomata are arranged in parallel rows on either side of the midrib. The leaves are petiolate and diverge at an acute angle from the axis. Possibly the best taxonomic characteristic for the genus is the decussate arrangement of the pollen and seed-cone scales (Fig. 17-16C and D). In *Sequoia* and *Taxodium,* the two genera most often confused with *Metasequoia,* the cone scales are arranged helically. Several years earlier, Endo (1928) realized that fossil cones described from Oligocene sediments as *Sequoia langsdorfii* were improperly designated because the cones possessed decussate cone scales. He also noted the blunt apices of the needles and the short penduncle of the cones, two characteristics that today are used to distinguish *Metasequoia.* In 1944 T. Wang, a forester, collected some specimens of a tree in central China with which he was not familiar. These specimens were analyzed and compared with the published descriptions of the fossil *Metasequoia,* resulting in the "discovery" of the living representatives. We know now that many of the fossil specimens origianlly described as species of *Sequoia* are in fact specimens of *Metasequoia* and that the genus was rather widespread in North America during the Cretaceous and Tertiary. One final note regarding this most important contribution should be mentioned. Beginning in about 1948, seeds of *Metasequoia* were obtained through the efforts of Merrill and Chaney (Fig. 17-16B) and were widely planted throughout North America and Europe, so that today the "fossil that came to life" may be appreciated by all.

Metasequoia milleri is a structurally preserved pollen cone described from Eocene sediments in British Columbia (Fig. 17-17). The cones have a maximum length of about 3.0 mm and are constructed of approximately 30 helically arranged sporophylls. Three pollen sacs are attached to the lower surface of each sporophyll and individual sporangia are a single cell layer thick. Pollen grains are subspheroidal in shape and are characterized by an erect papilla. In many features, the Eocene cones appear remarkably similar to the modern pollen cones of *M. glyptostroboides,* differing only in minor histologic characteristics and pollen morphology.

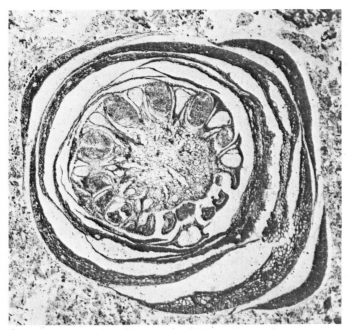

Figure 17-17   A. Transverse section of the pollen cone *Metasequoia milleri* from the Eocene of British Columbia. ×35. *(From Rothwell and Basinger, 1979.)*

Coniferous woods of taxodiaceous affinities have been reported from several Cretaceous and Tertiary localities. In *Taxodioxylon taxodii* (Fig. 17-18) (Upper Cretaceous of western Canada), the tracheids are large with characteristic cross-field pit patterns. The xylem rays are uni-to biseriate, with the rays up to 35 cells high. Sieve elements have been described from taxodiaceous bark of the Upper Cretaceous from the same general geographic area under the binomial *Taxodioxylon gypsaceum.*

Margeriella cretacea is the name of Upper Cretaceous silicified wood and leaves collected in central California and believed to be closely related to the Taxodiaceae. The leaves are helically arranged and about 4.0 cm long. They are apetiolate, and reveal a triangular point at their tips. Stomata are present on both surfaces, and clusters of thick-walled fibers are scattered throughout the leaf. The wood consists of tracheids with a single row of bordered pits on the radial walls and low uniseriate rays. In general, the histology of the wood is similar to the form genus *Cupressinoxylon,* a type found in members of the Podocarpaceae, Taxodiaceae, and Cupressaceae.

Pinaceae   Today the Pinaceae constitute principally a north temperate family that includes the most common conifers (e.g., firs, spruces, hemlocks, and pines). It represents the largest family of modern conifers, with 10 genera

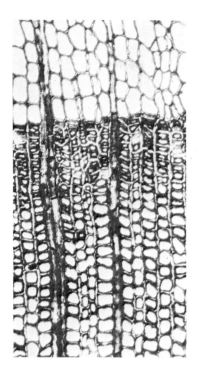

Figure 17-18 Transverse section of *Taxodioxylon* sp. from the Upper Cretaceous of Alberta, Canada. ×125. *(Courtesy of R. Stockey.)*

and about 200 species. The leaves are linear; the wood is pycnoxylic and commercially valuable. Both pollen-producing and seed cones are borne on the same plant (monoecious). Ovule-bearing cones consist of helically arranged ovuliferous scales bearing two seeds on the upper surfaces (Fig. 17-19C). Each scale is subtended by a bract. The pollen cones are composed of sporophylls arranged helically on an axis; each microsporophyll bears two elongate pollen sacs on the abaxial surface. In some of the Pinaceae, the pollen grains are bisaccate, and the saccus wall is internally ornamented with endoreticulations. It has not been possible to determine exactly when the family evolved, but judging from the diversity of the seed cones present during the Cretaceous, the group must have been well established early in the Mesozoic.

One of the oldest fossils that may be a member of the Pinaceae is *Compsostrobus,* an ovulate cone from the late Triassic of North Carolina. The specimens were preserved as compressions, but sufficient details are present that characteristics of the family can be identified. The largest cone is about 13.0 cm long and contains loosely arranged bracts and axillary ovuliferous scales. The scales are spatulate in outline and contain two flattened seeds on the upper surface. Associated with the ovulate cones are shoots bearing linear leaves. It has been suggested that they persisted for some time, because they were observed on axes of varying diameter. Also associated with the ovulate cones

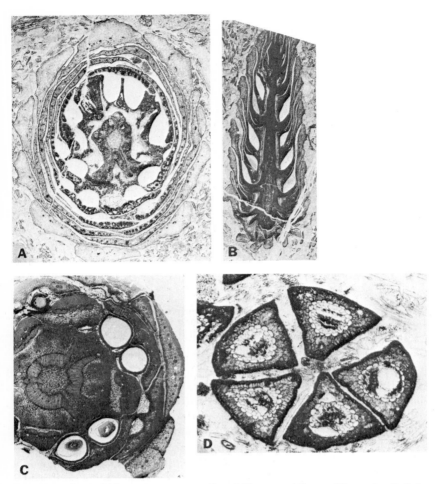

Figure 17-19 A. Oblique transverse section of *Pinus arnoldii* cone (Eocene). ×3. B. Longitudinal section of *Pinus arnoldii*. ×1. C. Transverse section of the seed cone *Pinus burtii*. ×1. D. Transverse section of a cluster of five needles of *Pinus similkameenensis*. ×30. *(A courtesy of R. Stockey; B and D from Miller, 1973; C from Miller, 1978.)*

were several slender pollen cones with apparently two pollen sacs per sporophyll. Masses of pollen grains were recovered; each grain is bisaccate and approximately 75 × 65 μm.

The genus *Abiocaulis* is used for structurally preserved stems that exhibit anatomic features similar to those of *Abies*. Specimens of *A. verticillatus* (Cretaceous of Belgium) consist of long shoots with helically arranged, decurrent leaf bases; no leaves were found attached to the stems. In section view, the stems contain a distinct zone of periderm that follows the outline of the leaf bases. Nests of irregular sclerids are present in both the pith and outer portion of the cortex. Anatomic features of the wood, including spiral checking of the tracheid walls and pattern of rays, suggest a wood of the *Cedroxylon* type. Wood of this type is similar to that produced by extant species of *Keteleeria* and *Abies*. The presence of persistent bud scales on the fossil specimens further supports the affinities within the Pinaceae. Associated with the stems were numerous leaves of the *Elatocladus* type, although none were found attached.

Cedrus-like silicified wood from the Lower Cretaceous of Alaska has been given the binomial *C. alaskensis*. The wood contains widely spaced growth rings, with spring wood constructed of hexagonal-shaped tracheids in cross section and horizontally disposed resin canals. Pitting on the tracheids is opposite, and the pit torus is large; distinct crassulae are present between the pits. No ray tracheids are present, but vascular rays are narrow and have simple pits on the horizontal cell walls.

Although there are numerous reports of the genus *Pinus* in the literature, many of these are not known in sufficient detail to provide information about the evolutionary history of the taxon. There have been several excellent studies of pinaceous ovulate cones in recent years, and these have provided important information about the evolution of the family in general, and seed-producing cones in particular. Today there are 23 species of structurally preserved ovulate cones that may be referred to the Pinaceae (Miller, 1976). The diversity exhibited by the seed cones in the early Cretaceous is regarded as evidence that the family had a significant pre-Cretaceous geologic history, possibly evolving during the Triassic. The oldest cone believed to be associated with the Pinaceae is *Pinus belgica,* a lignitic cone from the Lower Cretaceous of Belgium. The cones are about 4.5 cm long and include a small triangular bract that subtends a large (2.0 cm long) ovuliferous scale. The seeds possess a thin membraneous wing, and one seed per cone scale is most common. Histologically, the cone scale is similar to the modern cone of *P. sylvestris,* with abundant sclerenchyma and resin canals. Foliage of the subgenus *Pinus* has been reported from the late Cretaceous and includes dwarf shoots and fascicles of two-, three-, and four-needled forms.

The genus *Prepinus* was originally established for dwarf shoots and attached needle bases that were thought to represent a transition stage between the Paleozoic cordaites and modern members of the Pinaceae. A recent study (Robison, 1977) suggests that *Prepinus* should be regarded as a natural genus that combines vegetative features of several modern pinaceous genera, rather than leading to the vegetative organization demonstrated by *Pinus.*

The many cones described from Mesozoic sediments and believed to be related to the Pinaceae have been separated into two broad categories. One of these includes those forms such as *Pinus belgica* which can be assigned to modern genera. Of the remaining structurally preserved cones, most can be included in the organ genus *Pityostrobus* if they cannot be related to a modern genus. The others are placed into *Pseudoaraucaria.* Specimens of *Pseudoaraucaria* are up to 6.0 cm long and are characterized by a prominent scale apex. Each scale bears two seeds that are separated by a ridge of tissue, giving the impression that the seeds are embedded like those of *Araucaria.* In

Pityostrobus, numerous combinations of anatomic features are often used to separate extant cone types. Most of the anatomic and morphologic characteristics appear to be those present in the genus *Pinus.* For example, Miller (1976) notes that all species of *Pityostrobus* except one have at least one feature in common with modern *Pinus* cones, and nine species have at least two. Thus, at the present, it remains an impossible task to determine whether the pityostroboid cones represent a plexus from which modern *Pinus* cones evolved or divergent lines of seed cone evolution that have combined features of the ancestral cone types. For example, in *Pityostrobus hallii* (late Cretaceous of Maryland), the ovuliferous scales are very thin, like modern species of *Picea,* while the vascular trace pattern is similar to that of *Pinus.* Bract and scale fusion are more similar to the modern genera *Abies, Larix,* and *Tsuga. Pityostrobus palmeri* has seed scales like those of *Pinus,* but a vascular system more similar to the ovulate cones of *Cedurs.*

In the Tertiary, cone characteristics appear to be more consistent with extant genera. *Pinus arnoldii* (Fig. 17-19A and B) is a silicified cone from the Eocene of British Columbia. The cones are thought to be closely related to certain extant species (subgenus *Pinus*) of the genus on the basis of the abaxial position of resin canals in the seed scale, the inflated scale apices, and the strong curvature of the scale vascular strands. Occurring in the same sediments were stems, dwarf shoots, and needles that have been assigned to *P. similkameenensis* (Fig. 17-19D). The spur shoots are about 1.5 mm in diameter and up to 2.0 mm long. Each bears a fascicle of five needles that are anatomically identical to the leaves of extant white pines (*P. strobus*). In transverse section, they assume the configuration of an equilateral traingle, and the stomata are slightly sunken in two or three rows on the ventral faces. Stems possess well-developed growth rings and abundant resin canals.

Cephalotaxaceae This family consists of a single genus, *Cephalotaxus,* including about six species of small trees and shrubs. The leaves are opposite and needlelike. Most species appear to be dioecious, with the small ovulate cones producing one or two erect ovules that morphologically appear similar to those of some taxads. The pollen cones consist of irregularly shaped masses with three to eight pollen sacs per microsporophyll. Pollen grains are small, and they are characterized by a small distal leptoma. The family can be traced from the Jurassic with some confidence, but the total number of fossil taxa is relatively small.

Thomasiocladus is the name used for Jurassic impression-compression specimens from England. Only vegetative remains are known, and these consist of branches up to 5.0 cm long with helically arranged, two-ranked linear leaves. Stomata are haplocheilic and confined in rows on the abaxial surface. Each of the subsidiary cells contains a small papilla; guard cells are sunken. Miller (1977) notes that similar vegetative remains also have been placed in the extant genus *Cephalotaxus,* with specimens known from numerous geographic regions of both the Jurassic and Cretaceous.

Reproductive structures tentatively assigned to this group include *Cephalotaxospermum* and *Cephalotaxites*. *Cephalotaxospermum* is the name used for Cretaceous drupelike structures (1.3 cm long) constructed of an outer fleshy zone that surrounds a more sclerotic inner integument. Several authors have suggested that these fossils also may represent specimens of *Podocarpus*.

Taxales

Extant members of the Taxales are evergreen shrubs or small trees with helically arranged leaves. Pollen-bearing cones consist of sporophylls with three to nine pollen sacs. Members of this group differ from other conifers in having a single ovule (two ovules are occasionally produced) that is terminal on a modified shoot. Below the ovule are scales, but there is no evidence of the cone-scale complex that characterizes other conifers. In the genus *Taxus,* the ovule is partially surrounded by a fleshy envelop or aril. Pollen in the group is nonsaccate. Most authorities recognize 5 extant genera and about 20 species.

Possibly the best-known fossil member of the order is *Palaeotaxus,* a genus known from the Lower Jurassic (Fig. 17-11Q). Both vegetative and ovulate parts have been discovered. The foliage consists of linear needles twisted near the base so that they lie in a single plane, much like the leaves of modern *Taxus.* Leaves are hypostomatic, and the haplocheilic stomata are arranged in two rows, one on either side of the midrib. Subsidiary cells lack papillae, and trichomes are absent. The fine, undulating, anticlinal cell walls with irregular thickenings have been used to separate the fossils from extant taxa. The ovule-bearing shoots are radially symmetrical in cross section and are borne in the axils of vegetative leaves. The axis is covered with helically arranged acuminate scales, and it terminates in an ellipsoid, orthotropous ovule (5.0 mm long by 3.0 mm in diameter). The compressed nature of the specimens makes it difficult to determine the presence or absence of an aril.

Tomharrisia is a Middle Jurassic taxad that exhibits horizontally spreading vegetative shoots with persistent, two-ranked leaves. The leaves are hypostomatic, and the haplocheilic stomata are surrounded by four to six papillae that bear subsidiary cells. The genus *Bartholinodendron,* also from the Middle Jurassic, consists of single-veined leaves about 2.0 mm wide that reveal three to six irregular rows of stomata on the lower surface.

Marskea (Middle Jurassic) had leaves almost identical to those of living species of *Taxus,* differing only in the wavy epidermal cell walls of the fossil. The ovulate organ consists of a terminal ovule about 7.0 mm long and 3.0 mm in diameter (Fig. 17-11L). The faint outline of an aril is present on the fossil. The stalk of the ovule is smooth, except near the base of the seed, where there is a whorl of scales. The pollen-bearing organ of *Marskea* is believed to have consisted of sporophylls with upturned tips and three pollen sacs attached to the lower surface in a row. Pollen grains are round and similar to grains of the extant genus *Torreya* in that the exhibit a thin, distal germination site.

Vesquia is the name applied to Cretaceous fossil seeds thought to be most closely related to *Torreya.* Specimens of *V. tournaisii* (Fig. 17-11S and T) are about 1.0 cm in diameter and lignitic. The integument is composed of angular stone cells with numerous pits in the wall. The distal end of the seed is attenuated into a micropylar canal; in the lower third of the seed are two grooves, one on either side of the integument through which vascular tissue may have passed. The megaspore membrane is smooth, unlike the granulose texture of the membrane in most gymnosperms. However, this may simple reflect the stage of development prior to fossilization.

Several genera of fossil woods have been included in the Taxales. In *Taxaceoxylon,* there are distinct growth rings with helical thickenings on the tracheid walls. Bordered pits are uniseriate on the radial tracheid walls. The rays are generally homogenus with cross-field pits on the horizontal and tangential walls. Xylem parenchyma and resin canals are not present.

The earliest fossils assignable to the Taxales exhibit foliage and reproductive structures almost identical with extant forms, making it nearly impossible to trace the origins of the group. Harris (1976) has suggested that the terminal ovule of the taxads might be related to a Carboniferous ancestor in which the dwarf shoots (ovule-bearing cones) were not borne on a primary axis, but rather were distributed on leafy shoots. Such reproductive units would morphologically resemble *Lebachia* seed cones, but with two or three stalked ovules and a reduced number of sterile scales. The sequence would culminate with the cone producing a single terminal ovule. Although nothing is known about the origin of the aril, the development of such a structure from a plate meristem, possibly functioning for protection or as an attracting structure for seed dispersal, is not difficult to envision.

Mesozoic Conifer Foliage

Some authors have suggested that sterile Mesozoic conifer foliage be placed in one of a number of form genera rather than being assigned to extant taxa in the absence of reproductive parts. The eight morphologic types suggested by Harris (1979) are briefly described as follows.

Brachyphyllum   Helically arranged leaves with basal cushion and minute free end; total length of free part less than width of cushion (Fig. 17-11D).

Cupressinocladus   Shoot with decussate leaves or alternating pairs. Leaves scalelike, dorsiventrally flattened, but not constricted into petiole (Fig. 17-11C).

Cyparissidium   Helically arranged leaves with the free part of the leaf contracting gradually from the basal cushion. Leaves appressed to stem, longer than width of cushion.

Elatocladus   Helically or occasionally opposite leaves that are elongate and dorsiventrally flattened (Fig. 17-11H). Base forming small petiole attached to cushion.

Geinitzia   Needlelike helically arranged leaves arising gradually from cushion.

Pagiophyllum   Helically arranged leaves arising gradually from broad cushion with free part spreading. Leaf broader than thick and longer than width of cushion (Fig. 17-11E).

Pityocladus   Long shoot bearing spur shoots that in turn produce crowded needlelike leaves.

Podozamites   Leaves borne on caducous shoots of limited growth in helically or alternate pattern. Leaves lanceolate with narrow base and numerous parallel veins that are reduced to one at both the base and tip.

Anthophyta

The angiosperms, or flowering plants, represent the dominant plants of the world today and include some 300 to 400 families and nearly 300,000 species. With the possible exception of bacteria and pathogenetic fungi, the angiosperms constitute those organisms which most directly affect human existence on the earth today. Angiosperms include nearly all crop plants (e.g., wheat, rice, and corn) that form the basic food supply of the world. They are also necessary to human survival in the form of wood as a building material, drugs, and fibers. They demonstrate tremendous variation, ranging from stemless, free-floating plants such as duckweed to trees such as oaks and beeches. Structurally, they are adapted to a terrestrial environment, and some forms, such as the cacti, are able to tolerate the exceptionally dry environments of the desert.

Features used to separate angiosperms from other seed plants include the enclosed nature of the ovary, the presence of flowers, the specialized conducting elements (vessels) in the wood, double fertilization, the double integument of the ovule, the endosperm, and tectate pollen, to name only a few. Because of the unparalleled diversity within the group, there are exceptions to almost all the "angiosperm features," with the possible exception of double fertilization and endosperm formation.

Flowering plants have been subdivided into two groups, the monocotyledons and dicotyledons, but despite the names, the number of cotyledons represents only one of the features used to distinguish these plants. Monocots and dicots are also characterized by the arrangement of their vascular tissues [scattered in monocots (see Fig. 18-18A and B), forming a cylinder in dicots], presence (dicots) or absence (monocots) of a vascular cambium, venation pattern of the leaves [parallel or striate in monocots (see Fig. 18-20), reticulate in dicots (see Fig. 18-17A and B)], and the number of floral parts (three in monocots, four or five in dicots). It has been estimated that there are about 55,000 species of monocots and approximately 165,000 species of dicots.

For years scholars in many disciplines have been interested in the origin of angiosperms. Much has been written and debated about ancestral angiosperm stock, migration routes, and subsequent evolution to modern taxa. In the opinion of some, little or no progress has been made in resolving many of the questions about the evolution of flowering plants. Others have taken a far less pessimistic viewpoint, pointing to some Mesozoic and even Paleozoic nonangiospermous plants as possible ancestors. Such discussions continue today among paleobotanists, and newer techniques and approaches to the study of fossil flowering plants are yielding exciting information.

Central to any discussion concerning the evolution of angiosperms is the definition of precisely what an angiosperm is, and what features may be considered primitive. Both questions remain difficult problems that do not have simple solutions. Several of the classical angiosperm characteristics have already been noted. Many of these, at least in part, overlap and are found in other groups of vascular plants. For example, vessels are known in some gymnosperms and vascular cryptogams, while some gymnosperms, such as *Araucaria,* have superficially enclosed ovules at some stages of their development. Other angiosperm features, such as double fertilization and endosperm formation, characteristics that some believe represent the only consistent features of the group, by their very nature may be impossible to distinguish in the fossil record (see Fig. 15-4A). Using the comparative morphology of extant angiosperms as their basis, many workers believe that angiosperms with vesselless wood, leaflike stamens, monosulcate pollen, partially closed carpels, and numerous, free, helically arranged floral parts are primitive forms. Such studies have considered certain characteristics to be primitive because they occur in nonangiospermous groups. The basis of a great many of these studies involves a certain amount of circular reasoning in which primitive features are those characters which may be found in primitive taxa. In a few instances, the fossil record of the earliest angiosperms tends to support some long-held ideas about primitive angiosperms; in other cases, the fossil record has neither disputed nor substantiated the evolutionary level of a certain feature. In recent years, the discovery of several angiosperm reproductive structures has greatly modified a number of early ideas about primitive flower types. One fact that has a direct bearing on the question of angiosperm origin concerns the abundance of taxa that suddenly appeared during the Cretaceous. Without question, this sudden and expansive radiation of flowering plants during the early Cretaceous has been the impetus for paleobotanists to look to earlier geologic periods for fossils that demonstrate transitional features from their presumed gymnospermous ancestors. Historically, numerous pre-Cretaceous fossil plants have been regarded as early angiosperms. Some of these have now been placed in other taxonomic groups, while others have presented more difficult problems to resolve.

PRE-CRETACEOUS "ANGIOSPERMS"

One of the stratigraphically oldest fossils that has been regarded as an angiosperm is *Sanmiguelia* (Fig. 18-7E), a genus established for palmlike leaves collected from the Triassic of Colorado (Brown, 1956). Since the initial description, additional specimens have been discovered in place (Tidwell, Simper, and Thayn, 1977) and suggest that the plants were about 60.0 cm tall and consisted of helically arranged leaves attached to a conical stem. The leaves are broadly elliptical and are characterized by an acute apex and clasping base. The lamina is plicate and has parallel veins extending to the apex. Unfortunately, *Sanmiguelia* is known only from impressions, and nothing is known about cuticular features, especially the stomata. Information about the arrangement and organization of the stomata could certainly aid in clarifying the systematic position of this Triassic plant. To date, *Sanmiguelia lewisii* has been assigned to several groups of plants, including the Sphenophyta, because of its superficial resemblance to *Schizoneura*. The foliage also has been assigned to both the Cycadales and the Cycadeoidales. The angiospermous features of this Triassic plant have been underscored by several workers, although several of the important characteristics used to suggest affinities with the monocots have recently been challenged (Read and Hickey, 1972). One of these involves the plications, or folds, on the leaves, which alone are not regarded as being sufficient to identify the plant as a palm. In addition, the leaf of *Sanmiguelia* appears to lack a midrib, a character that appears to be consistent, even in juvenile palm foliage. Last, the genus appears to fall short of the status of a palm or member of the Liliaceae (*Veratrum*) in that it lacks several orders of venation in the form of cross-veins between the major veins.

Another pre-Cretaceous plant that has captured the imagination of paleobotanists as a possible early angiosperm is *Furcula*. The genus is known from the Triassic (Rhaetian) of Greenland and consists of lanceolate-shaped leaves that usually dichotomize at the middle. Some leaves are 15.0 cm long; all have entire margins. The venation consists of a prominent midrib from which are produced lateral veins about every 2.0 mm. Between these veins are smaller veinlets that anastomose to form a reticulate pattern characteristic of modern dicots. Cuticle preparations of *F. granulifera* suggest a rather simple epidermal pattern of slightly sunken stomata surrounded by a ring of six subsidiary cells. Based on cuticular features, *Furcula* possesses syndetocheilic stomata, typical of a number of plant groups, including angiosperms. Although *Furcula* has been regarded as a pre-Cretaceous angiosperm by some, others believe that features of the venation pattern more strongly indicate affinities with some seed fern groups.

Problematospermum is an interesting Jurassic fossil that was initially described as a gymnosperm. Specimens of *P. ovale* consist of small, ovoid structures about 2.5 cm long with a pappus on one end. A few pollen grains have been found on the pappus tube. Morphologically, specimens resemble the achene and pappus of certain composites, but they also have been compared to certain pteridosperm seeds that are known to have possessed integumentary-borne processes or plumes (e.g., *Gentopsis*).

In addition to megafossils, pollen grains also have been widely used to support the existence of angiosperms before the Cretaceous. One such pollen type is *Eucommiidites*, a grain originally described from Jurassic sediments in Sweden. Subsequent reports have extended the taxon from the Triassic well into the Cretaceous. The smooth-walled grains of *E. troedssonii* are boat-shaped and range from 30 to 40 μm long. On one surface is a prominent furrow, or colpus. The apparent tricolpate organization of *Eucommiidites* is used to suggest affinities with the modern dicot genus *Eucommia,* in which the colpi are of slightly unequal size. Subsequent studies of *Eucommiidites* have substantiated that the grains possess a single colpus, with the remaining "colpi" formed by a proximally positioned zonosulcus that surrounds the bilaterally symmetrical grain. More recently, several reports (e.g., Brenner, 1967) have confirmed the presence of *Eucommiidites*-type pollen grains, which are unmistakably gymnospermous, in the micropyle and pollen chamber of ovules (*Spermatites* and *Allicospermum*). Pollen of *Eucommiidites* also has been found in the Jurassic cycadalean cone *Hastystrobus* (Van Koinjneburg-Van Cittert, 1971). A detailed ultrastructural study of *Eucommiidites* pollen also supports the gymnosperm affinities of this pollen type.

EARLY ANGIOSPERM POLLEN

In sediments of the Cretaceous there are several pollen grains that appear to represent early angiosperm types. One of these is *Retimonocolpites*, a small (14 to 25 μm) monosulcate grain. The surface is coarsely reticulate, a feature that was responsible in part for the initial consideration of this grain as a monolete fern spore. *Retimonocolpites* lacks the tectate exine characteristic of most modern angiosperms. In *Stellatopollis* (Fig. 18-1B and C), another early Cretaceous monosulcate pollen type, the exine is semitectate. These genera, together with one additional form, *Clavatipollenites* (Fig. 18-1D), are regarded as the earliest acceptable angiosperm pollen types. Another common Lower Cretaceous pollen type that may represent a morphotype of *Clavatipollenites* is *Liliacidites*. Specimens of *Clavatipollenites* have been reported from the Lower Cretaceous of several geographic areas (e.g., England, Argentina, United States, Africa, and Israel), and because of their morphologic variability, they have been suggested as representing the pollen of several different taxa. These monosulcate grains are generally less than 30 μm long; in a few morphotypes, a Y-shaped aperture termed a trichotomosulcus replaces the single furrow. The structure of the exine in *Clavatipollenites* is variable, but in some forms the

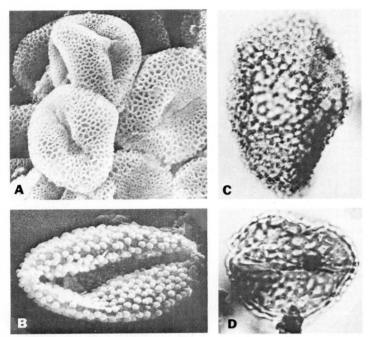

Figure 18-1 Cretaceous pollen. A. Several grains of *Tricolpites minutus.* ×750. B. Monosulcate pollen grain *Stellatopollis barghoornii.* ×1000. C. *Stellatopollis* sp. ×1200. D. *Clavatipollenites hughesii.* ×1200. *(A and B from Doyle, Van Campo, and Lugardon, 1975; C and D from Doyle et al., 1977.)*

radially disposed rods of sporopollenin are fused at their summits to form a nearly continuous outer layer or tectum. Although there are several nonangio-spermous pollen types that morphologically resemble *Clavatipollenites* (e.g., *Ginkgo, Cycadeoidea,* and certain seed ferns), none demonstrates the tendency toward a tectate exine, a feature regarded by many palynologists as unique to angiosperms.

The first distinctly tricolpate pollen appears at about the middle of the Albian stage. Grains of this type have been described by the generic names *Tricolpites* (Fig. 18-1A) and *Tricolpopollenites,* and some have been found preserved in pollen sacs (see Fig. 18-22C). They are small (less than 25 μm) and reveal equidistantly spaced colpi and a semitectate exine. The pollen record indicates that from the Albian into younger sediments there was a rapid evolution of numerous pollen features, including size, shape, exine structure, and aperture site. Some of these hypothesized trends are summarized in the detailed studies of Doyle (1973), Doyle and co-workers (1975), and Muller (1970).

There can be little doubt that one important area of future research with early fossil angiosperms will involve the continued ultrastructural analysis of both extant and fossil pollen types. Such studies may be especially rewarding in focusing attention of potential angiosperm ancestors.

CRETACEOUS ANGIOSPERM LEAVES

The most common Cretaceous angiosperm fossils are numerous impression and compression remains of leaves. During the late nineteenth and early twentieth centuries, numerous paleobotanists attempted to make direct comparisons between fossil angiosperm foliage types and the leaves of modern flowering plants. Most of these studies relied on leaf size, shape, and margin, and, to a lesser degree, the pattern of venation as the principal taxonomic characteristics. Almost no attempt was made to place the fossil leaves in any developmental pattern that reflected their stage of maturity at the time they were fossilized. As a consequence, many of these early studies represent what has been termed "picture matching" attempts to relate the fossil leaves with modern counterparts. The use of additional characters and newer techniques indicate that many of the earlier identifications were incorrect. This is not to suggest that all the early angiosperm leaf studies were not completed with an attempt to utilize a set of taxonomically useful and reliable characteristics to describe the taxa. For example, one need only examine the voluminous contributions of Von Ettinghausen (for example, 1854, 1856, 1858, 1865) to realize that he was aware of the importance of venation as a systematic character. Other paleobotanists, such as Berry, Lesquereux, and Hollick, incorporated some of the terminology developed by Von Ettinghausen, but in general, Von Ettinghausen's use of wideranging characteristics did not gain universal acceptance.

It also should be pointed out that many of the early collections of angiosperms were made under circumstances in which the precise stratigraphic position of the fossils was either not recorded or not known to the collector. In the absence of detailed stratigraphic control, many of these collections became useless as investigators attempted to trace angiosperm taxa through time.

In recent years, there has been a rebirth of interest in angiosperm paleobotany, in part reflecting the incorporation of new techniques to the study of these fossils. Possibly of greater importance, however, are the new ideas that have developed that reflect attempts to more accurately define the taxonomic limits of angiosperm leaf taxa. One such approach involves the definition, development, and classification of leaf characteristics on the basis of what has been described as leaf architecture. According to this philosophy, emphasis is placed on those elements which constitute the outward expression of leaf structure, including such features as shape, venation pattern, configuration of the margin, and presence or absence of such structures as glands. As a basis for the development of this classification scheme, Hickey (1973) examined 1212 genera representing 135 families of dicots. Particular emphasis was directed at what has been termed lower-order features, those which would have an increased probability of expression on fossilized leaves. Using these characteristics as base-level data, it was then possible to critically examine early Cretaceous angiosperm leaves in an attempt to identify those characteristics which may be regarded as primitive. This approach is especially important in that it provides a method whereby certain ontogenetic stages of the fossils can be studied. Because certain leaf features appear to have evolved in combination, it has been possible for researchers to consider certain aspects of the phylogeny of larger taxonomic groups.

One of the most important features successfully used in these studies is the pattern of the veins. Four distinct venation patterns have been recognized. These include first-rank forms, in which the secondary and higher-order veins are irregular and the spaces between the veins (intercostal areas) are irregular in size and shape. In leaves of the next order, the secondary veins are more regular, but the tertiary veins and intercostal areas remain irregular. Most dicot leaves are represented by third-rank leaves. In these forms, the tertiary veins are regular and the aeroles are irregular in size and orientation. Aeroles of uniform morphology are found in fourth-rank leaves according to this classification. It should be remembered, however, that not all features of leaves can be interpreted as stages of evolution; some may constitute an expression of the environment the plant was living in.

In recent years, the anatomy of fossil leaves, in particular the cuticle, has been demonstrated to be an important and powerful research tool in the identification and analysis of fossil angiosperm leaves (Dilcher, 1974). The cuticle represents a number of important characteristics that may be useful in determining relationships at the species, genus, and family levels. These include the thickness and chemical composition of the cuticle, the morphology of the epidermal cells, the presence of trichomes, glands, and scales, and the organization of the stomatal complex. A precise terminology has been developed to refer to the arrangement of the epidermal cells that surround the guard cells of the stomatal complex (Dilcher, 1974). In utilizing cuticular features, it is important to underscore that the total complement of characteristics must be utilized so that ontogenetic and ecologic influences are separated from those which may be of systematic importance.

CRETACEOUS LEAVES AND POLLEN

One important contribution to the study of early angiosperm was that of Hickey and Doyle (1977), who examined both the leaf and pollen record from early Cretaceous sediments (Potomac) of eastern North America (Fig. 18-2). Using well-defined pollen zones, these authors were able to correlate leaf type in order to provide a stratigraphic analysis of leaf architecture features throughout the Cretaceous. The angiosperm remains in Zone I of the Potomac sequence are rather rare, with most of the pollen types consisting of monosulcate forms. Only in the upper part of the zone were there a few tricolpates. The angiosperm leaves (Fig. 18-3A and B) of this zone are characterized by a lack of differentiation between the lamina and petiole (Fig. 18-4C) and a disorganized

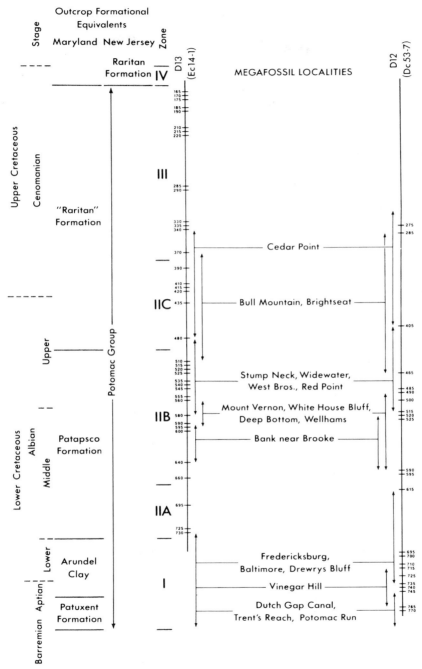

Figure 18-2 Subdivisions of the early Cretaceous Potomac Group based on the megafossil and pollen study of Hickey and Doyle. *(From Hickey and Doyle, 1977.)*

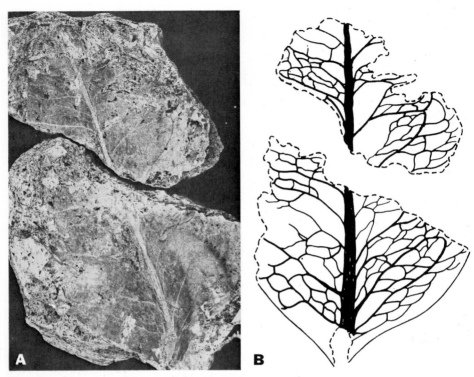

Figure 18-3   A. *Ficophyllum crassinerve.* ×1. B. Diagram of *Ficophyllum crassinerve* showing pattern of venation. ×0.7. *(From Hickey and Doyle, 1977.)*

pattern of venation (Fig. 18-4B). These leaves are generally elliptical in outline (Fig. 18-4A and B), with later-appearing forms characterized by asymmetrical bases. In addition, a high percentage of these leaves exhibit entire margins. In the next zone (IIB), there are many more tricolpates and monocolpates that have reticulate exine patterns. This is also the first appearance of tricolporoidates and grains that are more triangular in outline. The leaves of this zone are much more variable in shape, and it is here that the first palmately veined forms can be found (Fig. 18-5A and B). In many of these leaves, the primary veins dichotomize to form symmetrical loops within the margin (Fig. 18-5C). It is at this level that both pinnately (Fig. 18-6A) and palmately lobed forms make their first appearance. Other leaves indicate the initial appearance of various types of glands. In Zones IIC and III, the pollen flora includes greater numbers of tricolporoidate types. Leaves of the platanoid type (Fig. 18-6B) dominate at this level, with the venation pattern (Fig. 18-6C), especially the tertiary veins, more well-developed (Fig. 18-5D). In addition, the leaves in these zones often have expended petiole bases, which are suggestive of abscission zones in deciduous leaves. Despite an incomplete fossil record of the earliest angiosperms, Hickey and Doyle have suggested that during the Albian and early Cenomanian there was a major diversification in angiosperm leaf features. Studies of this type have

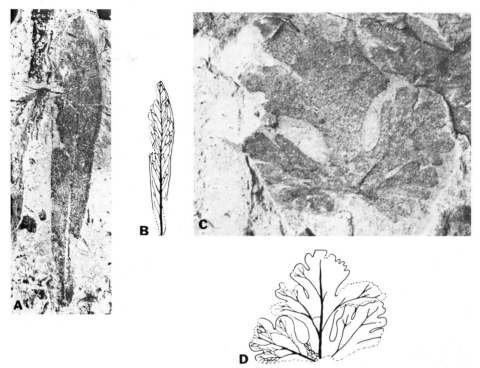

Figure 18-4 A. *Rogersia angustifolia* (Zone I). ×1. B. *Rogersia angustifolia* showing venation pattern. ×1. C. *Vitiphyllum multifidum* (Zone I). ×2. D. Leaf margin and venation of *Vitiphyllum multifidum*. *(From Hickey and Doyle, 1977.)*

provided a rational basis for interpreting the evolution of earlier leaf types. For example, the origin of the dicot leaf is now postulated as beginning with a compound leaf that underwent a reduction of the lamina associated with the semiarid environment. Based on the earliest appearing angiosperms, the first of these leaves were small and simple and represented the prototype from which later forms evolved. With the development of a later, more mesic environment, expansion of the lamina resulted in an increased blade size and venation pattern (Fig. 18-5E).

TERTIARY FLORAS

Several extensively investigated Tertiary floras occur in volcanic ash and fine-grained clays in the Columbia Plateau region of the Pacific Northwest. Through the pioneering work of Ralph Chaney (Fig. 17-16B) and the subsequent contributions of others, we now have a rather accurate picture of the vegetational history of the region during the Upper Miocene based on both geologic and biological information. The geology of the area indicates that as a consequence of the mountain-building activity associated with the formation of

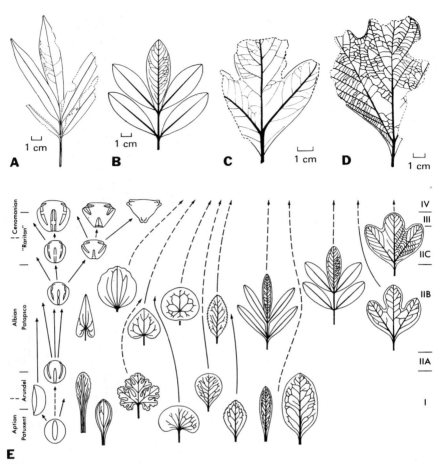

Figure 18-5   A. *Sapindopsis* leaf from Zone IIB. B. Pinnately compound *Sapindopsis* leaf from the upper part of Zone IIB. C. *Sassafras potomacensis,* a member of the "platanoid" sequence from the upper part of Zone IIB. D. *Araliopsoides cretaceae* from Zones IIC and III. E. Summary of basic leaf and pollen types plotted against Lower Cretaceous stratigraphic units. *(From Hickey and Doyle, 1977.)*

the Cascade Range, the previous drainage patterns became greatly modified, and this resulted in the formation of numerous swamps and lakes. Extensive precipitation from Pacific-borne winds resulted in the establishment of an extensive mixed deciduous forest that today is represented in the numerous basins where volcanic ash and upland sediment entombed the vegetative and reproductive parts of this extensive flora. Near the end of the Miocene, the Cascade Range was of sufficient height that the heavy precipitation was eliminated as a climatic factor in the area, resulting in increasing aridity. Near the close of the Pliocene, the composition of the flora in the region approximated the vegetation present today. To this extensive and highly diverse forest that inhabitated the Columbia Plateau during the Miocene, Chaney (1959) applied the name Arcto-Tertiary Geoflora.

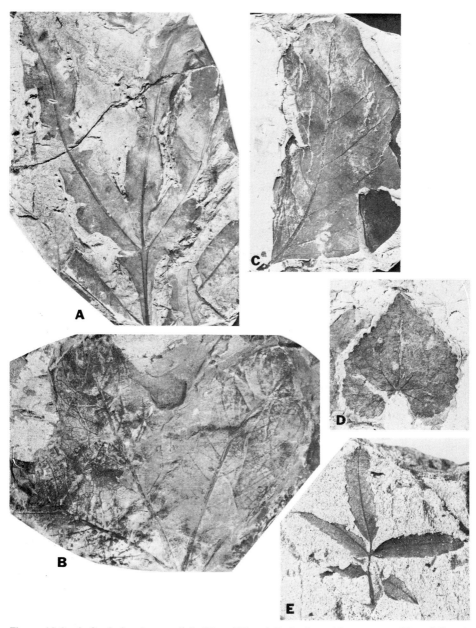

Figure 18-6 A. *Sapindopsis magnifolia* (Zone IIB). ×1. B. *Araliopsoides cretacea* (Zone IIC). ×1. C. *Andromeda parlatorii*-like leaf from Zone III. ×1. D. *Populus potomacensis*-like leaf from Zone IIB. ×1. E. *Sapindopsis* leaf with toothed margin (Zone IIB). ×2. *(From Hickey and Doyle, 1977.)*

Numerous floras of this extensive forest are known from Idaho, Washington, and Oregon, with the largest number of described floras concentrated in east central Oregon. One of the most extensively studied paleofloras of the Columbia Plateau is the Succor Creek flora located near the Idaho and Oregon border in southeastern Oregon. The vegetational composition of this important Upper Miocene flora includes representatives of 47 families, consisting of 60 genera and approximately 70 species (Graham, 1965). The most commonly occurring taxa include species of *Quercus, Cedrela, Acer, Woodwardia, Platanus, Ulmus,* and *Picea.* Morphologic analysis of the fossil specimens indicates that the closest extant taxa occur principally in eastern America and the eastern Asian deciduous hardwood forests. Using climatic tolerance limits of *Cedrela,* one of the common fossil elements, the climate during the Upper Miocene has been suggested as having winter temperatures not falling below freezing for any extended period of time. Based on the sedimentation cycle, regional geology, and taxa present at the Succor Creek sites, Graham (1965) has postulated that the flora was deposited in a freshwater lake that existed at an elevation of about 2000 feet.

An analysis of the composition of the Succor Creek flora suggests the presence of several identifiable plant communities in the area. Surrounding the lake in a narrow band was a herbaceous marsh vegetation that included species of *Equisetum, Typha,* and *Potamogeton.* One of the more common elements of the lowland community was *Glyptostrobus,* an Asiatic genus of plants that grows in the evergreen broad-leaved forests of China. At the Succor Creek site, the upland community was dominated by species of oak, together with *Acer, Alnus, Betula, Fagus,* and several other taxa. The palynology of sediments from higher elevations showed high concentrations of *Abies* and *Picea* pollen. The presence of some grass pollen together with the remains of grazing animals led Graham (1965) to speculate that open grasslands were present in the forest community.

This brief description of one of the well-documented Columbia Plateau Miocene floras serves as an excellent example of the necessary interfacing of biological and geologic principles needed in the complete analysis of fossil plant communities and the important role such studies play in tracing vegetational history. The interested reader is encouraged to examine some of the original papers describing these floras (e.g., Chaney, 1959, 1967; Chaney and Axelrod, 1959; Cranwell, 1964; Graham, 1965). Space does not permit a discussion of some of the over 220 exquisitely preserved Tertiary floras that have been described throughout the world; however, discussions of several of the more extensive ones can be found in the following sources: Pliocene, Axelrod (1944, 1956) and Dorf (1930); Miocene, Brown (1935) and Wolfe (1964); Oligocene, Becker (1961, 1973) and MacGinitie (1953); Eocene, Axelrod (1966) and MacGinitie (1941, 1969); and Paleocene, Brown (1962) and Koch (1963).

EOCENE ANGIOSPERMS

Another approach to the study of angiosperm fossils that has proven successful involves the analysis of morphologic and anatomic features of plants that are well-defined stratigraphically and geographically. One assemblage of fossil angiosperms that has received considerable attention in recent years is the Eocene flora of western Kentucky and Tennessee. These areas, which are now regarded as Middle Eocene (Claiborne Formation) based on pollen data, include leaf-bearing clay lenses that were apparently deposited in oxbow lake sediments. In one study, a large number of lobed leaves with palmate venation that had been assigned to the genus *Aralia* were critically examined. Included in the study were forms with three or five lobes and comptodrome secondary veins. Cuticle preparations demonstrated that stomata were confined to the lower leaf surface and consisted of three subsidiary cells surrounding the pair of guard cells; papillae were present on the other epidermal cells. Based on these detailed studies, the fossils were transferred to the genus *Dendropanax* and a diagnosis developed that reflected the variability within the characteristics of the taxon.

One interesting approach to the study of these Middle Eocene floras has been the utilization of multivariate statistics in handling several taxonomic characteristics (Dolph, 1975). The application of statistical methodology in the analysis of fossil specimens has several important advantages. These include ease of handling, storage, retrieval, and the opportunity to develop a nonbiased classification. Possibly the most important advantage in using multivariate statistics in paleobotany is that consistent results can be generated and compared with other data developed in a similar manner. However, despite the value of a statistical approach in the analysis of fossil plants, it remains the job of the paleobotanist to first carefully select and then interpret those characteristics which will be the data-base source, for if the characteristics are not evaluated in a total biological context, the statistics will have little substantive significance.

The Claiborne Formation clay pits also have provided a wealth of information about several taxa that have previously been unreported in the fossil record. One of these is *Philodendron* (Fig. 18-7A), which is almost indistinguishable from extant species on the basis of cuticular features and venation pattern (Fig. 18-7C and D). In fact, an analysis of the fossil monocots from these Eocene localities indicates that all are quite similar to their extant counterparts. However, the dicots from the same localities cannot be related to modern taxa with the same degree of confidence. The family to which *Phildodendron* belongs, the Araceae, is rather incompletely known, but the morphologic and anatomic similarities between the Eocene specimens and the extant counterparts indicate that this family must have had a relatively early origin and that evolution within the family must have been quite rapid. In the case of *P. limnestis* (Fig. 18-7B), knowledge of the depositional environment and the frequency in which these fossils are found has provided an opportunity to consider how and where the plants grew. In this instance, *Philodendron* has been suggested as growing as a herbaceous shrub in wet areas on floodplains. Because several leaves, presumably from the same plant, were found oriented in the same direction and surrounded by thin clay partings. it was suggested that the plants were washed into sediment laden waters and incorporated in these ancient basins.

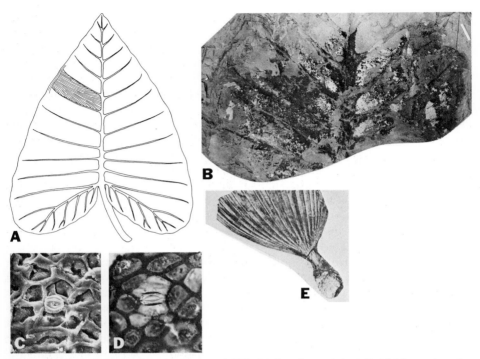

Figure 18-7 A. Suggested reconstruction of *Philodendron limnestis* leaf. B. Middle portion of a large *Philodendron limnestis* leaf. ×0.7. C. Lower epidermis of *Philodendron limnestis* leaf showing stomatal complex. ×200. D. Upper epidermis of *Philodendron limnestis* as seen in transmitted light. ×425. E. *Sanmiguelia lewisi* leaf and petiole. ×0.1. *(A, B, and D from Dilcher and Daghlian, 1977; C courtesy of D. Dilcher; E from Brown, 1956.)*

    In many instances, a careful analysis of a fossil flora provides an opportunity to offer generalizations regarding the climatic conditions of the area. Sufficient specimens have been collected and described from the Claiborne sites of Tennessee that an analysis of the community provides a potential for extrapolating paleoclimates. However, these Eocene communities provide an excellent example of why caution and careful evaluation of the fossils must precede generalizations about past climates. For example, there are several genera (*Sabal, Philodendron, Ficus,* and *Ocotea*) that by their presence suggest a lowland tropical environment. Associated with these fossils are other floral elements that are common in montane areas (e.g., *Podocarpus,* pine pollen, and *Dryophyllum*). These contemporary genera underscore not only the necessity for accurate, detailed analyses of the taxa, but also the need to thoroughly record all fossil plants present at a particular site. An analysis of the community structure of the Eocene plants in the southeastern United States suggests a collection of plants that may reflect nothing more than a similar tolerance to a particular environment. Obviously, as morphologic and anatomic features were changing, physiological levels were being modified as well.

Historically, leaf margin and size have provided a rough estimate of climate that is independent of taxonomy. Such studies have their foundation in the work of Sinnott and Bailey (1915), who graphically pointed out that many of the leaves of woody dicots are generally entire in tropical, arctic, and xeric regions and nonentire in temperate zones. The reduced size of leaves also has been correlated with a decrease in moisture and temperature. The Eocene sites in the Mississippian embayment have been regarded as representative of a tropical rain forest, based principally on the identification of certain taxa. An analysis of the area based on foliar physiogamy suggests, to the contrary, that during the Eocene the area was a seasonally dry to slightly moist, warm temperate to cool subtropical regime.

An analysis of the flora (Hickey, 1977) from the early Tertiary (Golden Valley Formation) of western North Dakota underscores the necessity of using more than a single leaf characteristic to develop a paleoclimatic profile for an area. Using the climatic tolerances of modern leaves to interpret the fossils, the data from this area suggest that the climate of the area was subtropical. Using leaf margin features and size, the fossils indicate that the plants grew in a rather cool climate. This disparity clearly indicates that although leaf margin analysis is valuable in corroborating climatic conditions, such an analysis cannot be used as the only method. One generally neglected, but important parameter in most paleofloristic studies involves the analysis of the sedimentary cycle and depositional history of the area. In the case of the Golden Valley Formation, the absence of salt crystals and gypsum deposits or red beds provides additional evidence that the plants were growing and fossilized in a humid climate.

SITE OF ORIGIN

Another interesting problem concerns defining the geographic region from which the earliest angiosperms are believed to have originated. At one time, the presence of various angiosperm leaf remains from what were originally interpreted as Lower Cretaceous sediments in Greenland was used to support the thesis that flowering plants originated in the Arctic. This idea has been generally discounted in light of the Upper Cretaceous age of the fossils and numerous Arctic floras that indicate a total absence of angiosperms until the Upper Cretaceous (Cenomanian).

The more widely held view is that flowering plants originated in the tropics, spreading poleward during their rapid diversification. This view has been supported by the high percentage of primitive modern taxa in the southwestern Pacific and southeastern Asia and by a number of fossil records. Using tricolpate pollen as the basis, Brenner (1976) has supported this idea with evidence that indicates that there is a greater frequency of tricolpates in continually younger sediments as one proceeds to higher latitudes on both sides of the equator. An analysis of angiosperm pollen during the Middle Cretaceous suggests the existence of four major floral provinces (Northern Laurasian, Southern Laurasian, Northern Gondwana, and Southern Gondwana). The Northern Laurasian province includes the Arctic and is characterized by bisaccate types; numerous smooth-walled, trilete forms associated with several modern fern families; and a number of grains that suggest temperate conditions. In the Southern Laurasian province (middle latitudes of North America and Europe), the palynomorphs suggest a warm temperate to subtropical climate. The northern parts of Africa and South America are grouped in the Northern Gondwana province and include pollen and spores indicative of semiarid conditions. Bisaccate grain types are characteristically absent from this province, with gymnosperms represented by various araucarians and members of the Podocarpaceae. A high percentage of the palynomorphs from this province include monosulcate cycadophyte grains; this province also has provided the oldest tricolpates. The fourth province (Southern Gondwana) is represented by South Africa, Australia, New Zealand, India, and Argentina. This province is postulated to have had a climate with abundant humidity. Bisaccate pollen referable to the podocarps is present in abundance in these sediments, together with various fern spores thought to belong to the Schizaeaceae.

Other authors (Doyle, 1969; Muller, 1970) argue that the pollen record does not unidirectionally demonstrate that angiosperms originated and spread poleward from an origin in the tropics. Further compounding the problem of origin and migration is the apparent uniformity of the Cretaceous climate, the difficulty in determining the equatorial regions during the Cretaceous, especially in light of continental movements, and the possibility that angiosperms originated polyphyletically. Moreover, it may be highly probable that some of the so-called gymnospermous cycadophytes do in fact represent early angiosperm monosulcates, and that the pollen record is not being interpreted using all the data.

In general, the pollen and megafossil data appear to indicate the origin of angiosperms during the latter stages of the Jurassic or very early Cretaceous. As several workers have suggested, these earliest angiosperms were represented by a relatively small group of plants that were still dominated by gymnosperms and ferns. The pollen record appears to indicate that these early angiosperms were not highly diversified. A second phase of morphologic diversity has been postulated as occurring around the Cenomanian. This phase, which may have lasted from 5 million to 10 million years, is characterized by the appearance of tricolporate and triporate pollen types. During the Turonian-Senonian, the flowering plants became the dominant floral element with extensive geographic differentiation and diversification and the establishment of modern families and genera. From the Paleocene to the Eocene, there was increased geographic differentiation and the extinction of some Cretaceous groups. Pollen evidence suggests that beginning in about the Oligocene, there was a rapid approach to a modern flora. This gradual appearance during the early part of the Cretaceous seems to coincide with a climatic stabilization that was influenced by seafloor spreading. Axelrod (1970) has suggested that it is possible to recognize three major periods of angiosperm evolution in response to dry climates. These include seasonal drought in tropical uplands on Gondwanaland during the

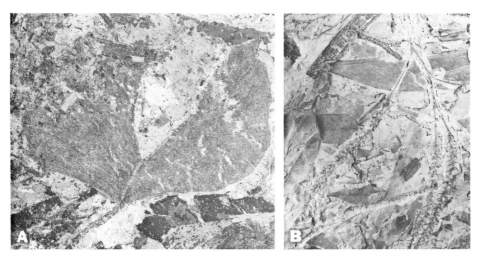

Figure 18-8 A. Cretaceous *Liriophyllum*-type leaf with deeply lobed blade. ×0.5. B. Large raceme of distantly alternating, elongate, unisexual multifollicles. ×0.8. *(Courtesy of D. Dilcher.)*

Permian and Triassic and a second surge of angiosperm evolution that took place during the Triassic and Jurassic that includes taxa found today in warm deserts and in dry areas at lower latitudes. The third radiation is hypothesized as being continuous since the Cenomanian, initially in dry valley bottoms on the southwestern parts of the continents, then spreading since the Paleocene. Changes in the position, configuration, size, and altitude of the continents and continental drifting have continued throughout the history of angiosperms. This has resulted in the conversion of desert lands into tropical areas, the disjointing of connected land masses, and the formation of mountainous regions where continental plates have collided. These physical modifications associated with the continents and the alteration of climates resulted in greater genetic variability, and that, in turn, provided the principal stimulus for the evolution of angiosperm floras.

Another unresolved question regarding early angiosperms concerns what the plants actually looked like. Early ideas based on an analysis of modern tropical fruits suggested that the earliest angiosperms were mesophytic, tropical trees with pinnate leaves and clusters of large, arillate follicles. Another idea based on living angiosperms suggested that they were broadleaf trees in tropical uplands. Takhtajan (1969) views early angiosperms as small, woody evergreen trees with simple, entire, pinnately veined leaves with flowers pollinated by insects and seeds distributed by animals. Another recently presented view regards the earliest angiosperms as small-leafed shrubs of seasonally arid climates that migrated to more mesic regions as riparian weeds. The most recent idea suggests that some early angiosperms or angiosperm ancestors may have been microphyllous halophytes and that mangrove environments were critical to their dispersal and early succession as they moved to upland sites and disturbed

Figure 18-9 A. Cretaceous reproductive axis with helically arranged carpels. ×0.9. B. Axis covered by carpels. ×0.9. *(Courtesy of D. Dilcher.)*

areas along the edges of stream valleys and coasts. These plants are believed to have been pollinated initially by wind (Fig. 18-8B) and water, only later becoming associated with various animals as the principal pollinating vectors. Much of the evidence for this theory comes from the discovery of several interesting ovulate reproductive organs (Fig. 18-9A and B) collected from Middle Cretaceous sediments in central Kansas.

It is quite probable that we may never know which of these hypotheses most accurately describes the very earliest angiosperms, and in fact, there are many who believe that the condition of "angiospermy" arose more than one time. Still others favor a monophyletic origin of angiosperms, with the earliest forms morphologically resembling small, woody shrubs or subshrubs.

PROANGIOSPERMS

Historically, almost every group of fossil vascular plants has at one time or another been suggested as giving rise to angiosperms. Throughout the years, many of these ideas have been discounted as more information about the fossils has been realized. Today the Mesozoic gymnosperms, especially the seed ferns, are receiving the most attention as possible proangiosperms. One order that has been repeatedly suggested as demonstrating angiospermous features is the Caytoniales (see Chap. 13). These plants, which were initially described by Thomas as potential angiosperms of the Jurassic, have been studied more intensely in recent years and are regarded as seed ferns by most authorities. The intriguing feature of this group involves their seed-bearing cupules, which contain a large number of ovules enclosed in a thinly cutinized inner sac. Proponents of the Caytoniales as angiosperm ancestors point to the almost sealed cupule as indicating a way in which the carpel may have evolved. Supporting this hypothesis is evidence that the outer edge or lip of the cupule was connected to the ovules by a cutinized tube subdivided into a number of channels corresponding to the number of seeds. In *Caytonia,* pollen grains apparently found their way to the seed micropyles via these channels. In the case of the transition from gymnosperm to angiosperm, these tubes would have functioned as "style" mechanisms prior to the evolution of rapidly growing pollen tubes. The Caytoniales also exhibit leaves with a netlike pattern of venation and loculate sporangia that superficially resemble anthers.

Another group of Jurassic seed plants regarded by some as early angiosperms is the Czekanowskiales (see Chap. 15). The leaves of this order were linear and attached to short shoots. Like the Caytoniales, they possessed seed cupules (capsules) that contained a papillate flange that superficially resembled a stigmatic surface. Pollen grains landed directly on the micropyle of the ovule, indicating that the capsule was not entirely closed. At least with reference to carpel closure, these Jurassic gymnosperms parallel the condition seen in several angiosperms thought to be primitive, where the carpel remains partially open (e.g., *Drimys, Degeneria, Bubbia,* and *Exospermun*). The formation of a carpel by the closure of cupules has been advanced for several Paleozoic seed ferns, with the ovules of *Anasperma* that were anatropously borne on the inner surface of the cupule being the most convincing.

The glossopterids represent another group of gymnosperms that have long been considered by some as angiosperm progenitors. The recent discovery of structurally preserved seeds borne on the surface of a partially enrolled megasporophyll strengthens this assumption. Histologically, the megasporophyll is identical to a typical *Glossopteris* leaf, but it lacks sclerenchyma. Again the manner in which the seeds of the glossopterids were borne superficially resembles an angiosperm carpel. The pollen of this group is bisaccate and unlike the hypothesized early angiosperm pollen types.

The cycadeoids also constitute a group that has been repeatedly suggested as involved in the evolution of flowering plants. This assumption has been based primarily on the nature and organization of the reproductive structures, which were initially believed to have opened like flowers. The "flower" consisted of a basal receptacle to which were attached a whorl of microsporophylls and in the center numerous stalked ovules. Between the ovules were large interseminal scales, and these were hypothesized as fusing to enclose the ovules, thus achieving a carpellike structure.

Recently, Krassilov (1975) has proposed a new family of proangiosperms, the Dirhopalostachyaceae, that is based on ovuliferous fructifications containing paired capsules (Fig. 18-22A), each with a flattened seed (Fig. 18-22D). On the basis of the constant association with ovuliferous reproductive units (*Dirhopalostachys*), it is believed that the foliage of these trees or shrubs was of the *Nilssonia* type. Based on the organization of the ovule-bearing unit and similarities in cuticle structure, the affinities of this late Jurassic to early Cretaceous family are suggested as being with the cycadalean *Beania*.

It should be noted that the enclosure of ovules to form a carpellike structure is but one of many features that characterize the flowering plants. Judging from the morphologic organization of the seed-bearing units in a number of Mesozoic gymnosperms, it appears quite probably that the enclosure of seeds may have evolved in several groups. Unfortunately, the fossil record does not provide much evidence relative to the evolution of the other so-called angiosperm features.

Any discussion of fossil angiosperms must consider not only the potential progenitors, but also why the pre-Cretaceous record appears so barren of angiosperm remains. One of the earliest ideas suggested to explain the absence of bona fide angiosperm fossil record prior to the Cretaceous has been termed the "upland origin" hypothesis. According to this idea, angiosperms initially evolved in rolling hilly tracts and lower to middle slopes of mountains in the ancient tropics. Because these sites were far from the depositional basins, the proponents of this theory argued, the opportunity for plants to be fossilized was extremely low. Others have countered that in spite of the absence of a megafossil record, some pollen grains produced by these upland plants should be preserved in the record. Supporters cite the probable delicate nature of the exine as a reason for the absence of pollen grains, or the difficulty in distinguishing these grains from those of nonangiosperm (gymnosperm) types. Other reasons advanced include the initial small population size, the elimination of the original sites owing to various physical processes, and in the case of pollen, the very small amount produced by the presumably insect-pollinated plants.

Another often used explanation merely underscores the difficulty in interpreting precisely what an angiosperm is and when a sufficient suite of characters is present to achieve the level of angiospermy. If one adheres tenaciously to a particular set of characteristics that have been assembled from modern flowering plants, as is repeatedly done, then those features which appear to be unique in angiosperms (double fertilization and endosperm development) by their nature may never be identified in the fossil record. Perhaps a more realistic and rewarding avenue of investigation would be to view fossil angiosperms as representing a particular level of evolution, with the earliest forms not demonstrating the total complement of modern angiosperm characters. There can be little doubt that most angiosperm paleobotany has been directed at attempting to identify pre-Cretaceous flowering plants using criteria from modern organisms that have had many millions of years to evolve. Some may argue that such an approach merely begs the question, that no pre-Jurassic group of plants can be singled out as angiosperm precursors. Nevertheless, as Krassilov (1977) and others have suggested, there appears to have been the necessary "gene pool" from which the complement of modern angiosperm characters could be drawn. A slightly different view was adopted by Melville (1960), who suggested that the earliest angiosperms may have looked so different from ideas about them that if they were found as fossils, they probably would not be recognized.

RECENT ADVANCES IN ANGIOSPERM PALEOBOTANY

Despite what may appear to be a rather bleak outlook for ever identifying pre-Cretaceous angiosperms, there have been many exciting discoveries in recent years that have contibuted a wealth of information about fossil flowering plants. Some of these have been brought about by the utilization of new techniques, others by the discovery of new and exciting fossils, and still others by the use of peripheral information sources and alternative approaches to problem solving. A few of these are discussed in the following paragraphs.

In recent years, some outstanding advances in angiosperm paleobotany have been made because of the application of new techniques. Some of these, such as transmission and scanning electron microscopy (see Fig. 18-19B), have already been alluded to in earlier discussions of other groups of plants. One need only cite the role that scanning electron microscopy has played in the elucidation of complex morphologic features and ornamentation patterns of pollen. In a similar manner, a previously unrecognized information source has been assembled as a result of the application of transmission electron microscopy to the study of fossil plants.

One technique that has been used effectively with angiosperm fossils and promises to provide important advances in the future involves the use of organic chemical profiles. Although chemosystematics have been used widely with extant plants and today constitute a basic and almost routine technique in plant

Figure 18-10 Fossil and extant *Quercus* leaves from which flavonoids and other compounds were extracted. A. *Quercus comsimilis* (fossil). B. *Quercus myrsinaefolia* (extant). ×0.7. *(From Niklas and Giannasi, 1978.)*

A   B

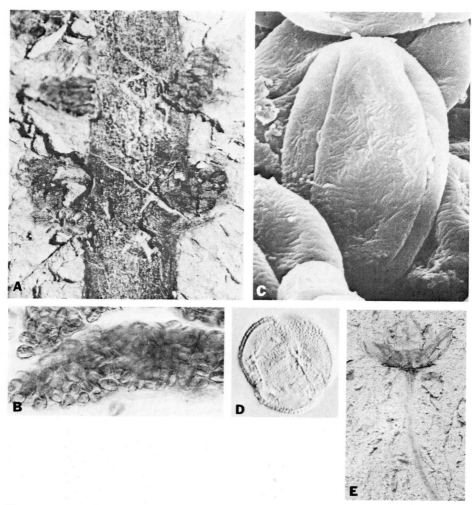

Figure 18-11 A. Several castaneoid lateral florets. ×20. B. A mass of pollen from an isolated anther. ×400. C. Fossil castaneoid pollen grain showing two colpi. ×5080. D. Tricolpate pollen grain macerated from the anther of a Middle Eocene flower. ×950. E. Small, regular Eocene flower. ×5. *(A–C from Crepet, 1980; D and E from Crepet, 1979.)*

systematics, the application of these techniques to the study of fossil plants has only recently been attempted on a sophisticated scale. In one study (Fig. 18-10A and B), Miocene (Succor Creek) leaf specimens of five genera (*Acer, Celtis, Quercus, Ulmus,* and *Zelkova*) were morphologically and chemically compared with extant counterparts. Flavonoid chemistry, together with other chemical constituents of the fossils (paraffins, steranes, triterpanes, and fatty acids), indicated a high degree of correlation between the fossils and modern species. In the case of some fossil oak species, chemical profiles provided a more definitive means by which to separate closely related taxa than was possible with megascopic methods. In another instance, leaves with similar morphologies were identified on the basis of chemical differences that could be compared with extant relatives. As studies of this type are continued, it will be important to pay particular attention to various features associated with sediment diagenesis. If the physical processes associated with fossilization can be evaluated so that the chemical profiles of the fossil plants reflect uniformity, then such profiles, especially of leaves, may provide an important tool with which to aid paleofloristic interpretations. Chemical data that are extended both stratigraphically and geographically also may prove to be useful in focusing attention on problems of angiosperm origins.

Despite the very fragile nature of floral parts, some fossil flowers have been described. Most of these have been impressions and compressions (Fig. 18-11A and C through E) in which the quality of preservation rarely provides an opportunity to make detailed observations and accurate identifications. Some of the most spectacular flowers that have been described include those preserved in the famous Oligocene Baltic amber (Czeczott, 1960). During the last several years, there has been considerable interest in the floral parts of early angiosperms. Newly discovered specimens of flowers, together with the application of new techniques, have provided considerable information that promises to be especially illuminating as angiosperm paleobiology expands. Some of the studies already completed challenge early ideas about floral morphology and primitive versus advanced characteristics. If adequately preserved, fossil flowers also provide a method of investigating in situ pollen types (Fig. 18-11B). These may then be compared with dispersed grains in order to gain a more accurate perspective of the evolution of certain pollen characteristics. The study of fossil flowers also makes it possible to discuss such ephemeral subjects as the pollination systems of these ancient flowering plants.

One interesting study involves a staminate catkinlike flower from the Middle Eocene of Tennessee (Fig. 18-12A). The specimens consist of an axis about 6.0 cm long, with widely spaced, helically arranged flowers (Fig. 18-12B). The flowers are bilaterally symmetrical, each constructed of a three-lobed bract and a three-parted floral envelope (Fig. 18-12C). Cuticular preparations indicate that the surfaces of the perianth parts contain large peltate scales (Fig. 18-12E). Extending down from the elongate floral receptacle are 10 to 15 stamens. The pollen of *Eokachyra aeolia* is triporate and about 20 μm in diameter through the equator (Fig. 18-12D). Based on a comparison with extant flowers, the specimens of *E. aeolia* closely resemble the flowers of *Engelhardia*, *Oreomunnea*, and *Alfaroa* of the Juglandaceae. The morphologic arrangement of the parts, coupled with the type of pollen, suggest that like the closely related extant taxa, the fossil specimens were probably pollinated by wind.

A Middle Eocene flower that appears to be closely related to the Araceae is *Acorites*. It consists of helically arranged florets (Fig. 18-13A), each characterized by a trilocular ovary and orbicular stigma (Fig. 18-13B). The cuticular pattern present is of a paracytic type (Fig. 18-13C), a feature that was used to establish affinities with the Araceae. Nothing is known about the pollen

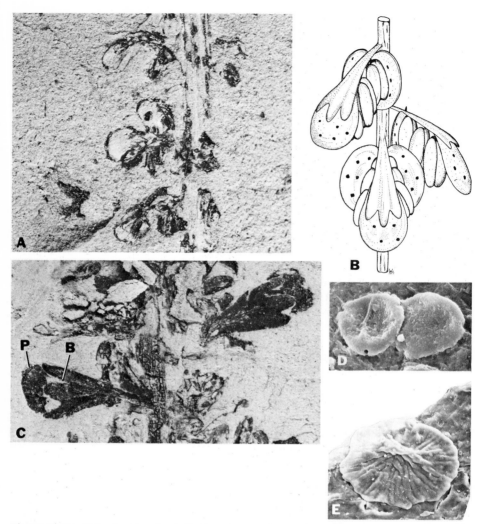

Figure 18-12 *Eokachyra aeolia.* A. Portion of a catkin showing several individual flowers. ×7. B. Suggested reconstruction of several flowers. C. Specimen showing three-lobed bract (B) and perianth parts (P) of an individual flower. ×8. D. Triporate pollen grains. ×1250. E. Peltate scale recovered from cuticle of perianth. ×250. *(From Crepet, Dilcher, and Potter, 1975.)*

produced by these flowers, but by comparison with other extant taxa, the pollination vector has been suggested as dipteran.

Structurally preserved flowers are far less frequently encountered, but a few have been described from Cretaceous and Eocene sediments (e.g., Stopes and Fujii, 1911; Chitaley and Kate, 1974; Chitaley and Patel, 1975). In many instances, preservation is not sufficient for establishment of their affinities. One structurally preserved Eocene flower that can be assigned to a modern family with a certain degree of confidence is *Paleorosa* (Fig. 18-14B and D). The flowers were preserved in silica and include two different stages of floral development. One of these is budlike, and the other is considered to be a more mature stage of development. *Paleorosa similkameenensis* is a perfect antinomorphic flower with five sepals and petals that are alternately inserted. The flower contains five free carpels (Fig. 18-14B), each with two ovules. The number of bilocular stamens is variable, ranging from 13 to 19; pollen grains were not recovered. Features of the flowers suggest that there are more primitive characteristics in *Paleorosa* than in any living member of the Rosaceae. The discovery of this structurally preserved rosaceous flower is important because it provides a basis from which to consider the evolution of both anatomic and morphologic features in extant members.

Various types of presumed angiosperm fruits are relatively common beginning in the Upper Cretaceous (Fig. 18-15A and C). Some of these have been related to extant families; others have been assigned to form taxonomic categories until their affinities can be accurately determined. One early angiosperm fruit type known from Barremian and Albian strata, as well as Upper Cretaceous and Tertiary sediments, is *Onoana californica*. The fruit consists of an endocarp about 2.0 cm long that is slightly pointed at one end. Scattered over the surface are numerous irregular pits that do not extend through the endocarp. In section view, the endocarp is composed of radially aligned parenchyma cells that form a layer about 3.0 mm thick. Internally there is a single locule and a partially preserved seed. The specimens have been suggested as belonging to the Icacinaceae, a family of tropical trees and lianas believed to be relatively advanced on the basis of an analysis of modern representatives.

Trochodendrocarpus (Figs. 18-15A and 18-22B) is the name used for a

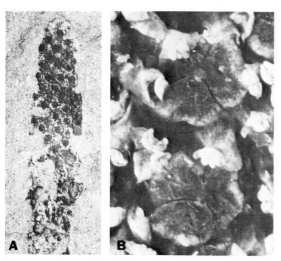

Figure 18-13 A. Spadix of *Acorites heeri* with helically arranged florets. ×5. B. Several florets of the extant taxon *Acorus calamus.* ×25. *(From Crepet, 1978.)*

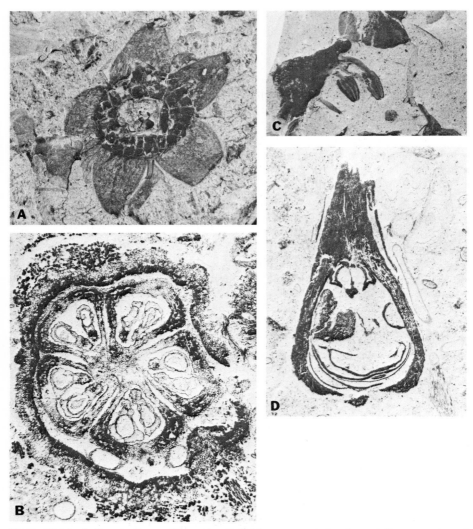

Figure 18-14 A. Regular flower (Eocene). ×6. B. Transverse section through the gynoecium of *Paleorosa similkameenensis* showing two ovules per carpel. ×40. C. Two stamens from the Cretaceous. ×1.5. D. Longitudinal section of gynoecium of *Paleorosa similkameenensis*. ×40. *(A from Crepet, 1979; B and D courtesy J. Basinger; C courtesy D. Dilcher.)*

rather common Upper Cretaceous compound fruit type that closely resembles that of *Trochodendron*. Other names that have appeared in the literature for similar structures include *Nyssa*, *Leguminosites*, *Berrya*, and *Cercidophyllum*. Each fruit is borne on a stalk about 30.0 cm long that bears alternately arranged branches. Eight to 14 helically arranged pods are attached singly or in pairs to each branch. The elliptical pods are 3.0 cm long and contain a short style at one end. The seeds are small (2.0 mm) and are characterized by a narrow wing.

Paraoreomunnea (Fig. 18-16A and C) is the name used for Middle Eocene

Figure 18-15 A. *Cercidophyllum* fruits. B. *Fraxinopsis.* C. Portion of a legume pod from the Oligocene of Texas.

trilobate winged fruits that have been placed in the Juglandaceae (Fig. 18-16D and E). Each of the three lobes has a distinct midvein and two subordinate veins. On the cuticle are numerous discoid, peltate trichomes. Another taxon from the same locality, *Paleooreomunnea,* was also a winged juglandaceous fruit (Fig. 18-16B), but with shallow sinuses between the lobes. Covering a large, bilobed nut is another lobe vascularized by up to 10 major veins. These two forms, together with several other genera, suggest that the plants grew in a variety of environments, with the winged fruits variously adapted for dispersal. Some, such as *Paleooreomunnea,* which are believed to be related to *Oreomunnea,* were apparently much more widespread during the Eocene than is reflected by extant members, which today are restricted to the Western Hemisphere.

Of the many paleobotanical floras described, few rival the extensive treatment of fruits and seeds represented in the London Clay Flora by Reid and Chandler. These fossils, long collected by amateurs from numerous localities in southeastern England, are early Eocene in age. The flora is dominated by angiosperms, with approximately 234 species identified, but only 29 of the approximately 100 genera referrable to extant forms. Many of the taxa are tropical in distribution, and the most closely comparable modern flora is that of the forests of the Malay Islands.

One interesting aspect of the study of early angiosperms concerns the very high percentage of fossils that are related to dicotyledonous families (Fig. 18-17A and B). The absence of a large number of fossil monocots probably reflects the higher percentage of dicot genera within the flowering plants, much

Figure 18-16 Juglandaceous winged fruits. A. Venation of one lobe of *Paraoreomunnea puryearensis*. ×7. B. Bilobed nut and adaxial bract of *Paleooreomunnea stoneana*. ×1.5. C. Winged fruit of *Paraoreomunnea puryearensis*. ×1.5. D. Cleared bracts of the extant taxon *Engelhardia roxburghiana*. ×1.5. *(A courtesy D. Dilcher; B–D from Dilcher, Potter, and Crepet, 1976.)*

as it does among extant genera today. However, despite the greater number of fossil dicots, several monocotyledonous fossils are known (Fig. 18-18). Daghlian (1981) provides an excellent review of the known fossil monocot families, noting that of the approximately 20 families recognized in sediments of various age, 4 have a fossil record that extends back into the Cretaceous. Using paleoclimatic data plotted against the occurrence of monocot taxa, Daghlian suggests that

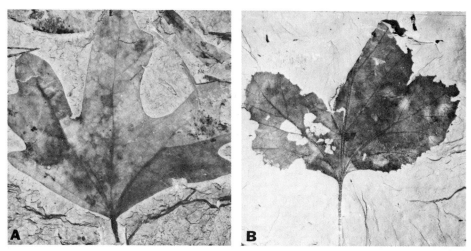

Figure 18-17 A. *Acerites multiformis*-type leaf from the Cretaceous of Kansas. ×0.9. B. *Platanus*-type leaf from the Cretaceous of Kansas. ×0.4. *(Courtesy of D. Dilcher.)*

there were at least three general phases of monocot evolution that can be recognized. The first phase appears to have been initiated during the Lower Cretaceous (Aptian-Albian) and extended to about Maastrichtian time. The climate during this phase is postulated as initially cool (approximately 15°C) and gradually becoming warmer (18 to 24°C) in the Upper Cretaceous. Fossil angiosperms collected from these sediments indicate that there were few plants identifiable with modern taxa, although several were obviously monocots. During the second phase, which extended from the Maastrichtian through the Eocene, the warming trend generally continued, with several of the tropical and subtropical monocot species expanding their geographic ranges. It was also at this time that many of the modern monocotyledonous groups made their first appearance. The third stage in monocot evolution extended from the Oligocene to the Neogene and is marked by overall climatic deterioration. Those monocots which were widely distributed in the Paleocene now became geographically restricted, while some of the taxa that made their initial appearance during the Eocene became more widespread with the beginning of cooler and drier conditions. It was during this period that the grasses and sedges underwent their major radiation. Daghlian postulates that such climatic conditions favored wind-pollinated plants rather than those forms which relied on insects as pollination vectors; he further postulates that the combination of wind pollination and a rhizomatous habit were features that allowed the grasses and sedges to spread rapidly during a time when the climate was generally unfavorable.

Despite the fact that the fossil record provides no corroborative evidence concerning the implied evolutionary relationships between monocots and dicots (Fig. 18-19A), there can be little doubt that detailed studies of fossil monocotyledons offer promising new sources of information concerning evolution within

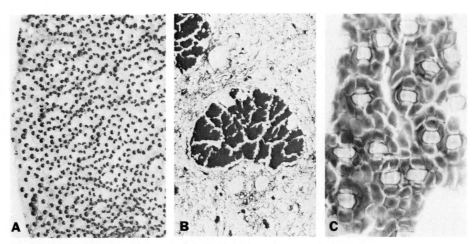

Figure 18-18 A. Transverse section of silicified *Palmoxylon* wood. ×1. B. Transverse section of a single vascular bundle and fiber cap of *Palmoxylon*. ×32. C. Stomatal complexes of the Eocene palm *Sabal dortehii*. ×200. *(C courtesy of C. Daghlian.)*

the angiosperms. For example, investigations of Eocene palms (Fig. 18-20) indicate that the modern genus *Sabal* and the closely related form *Sabalites* share unique combinations of foliar features that provide a basis for demonstrating evolutionary trends from the Cretaceous palms to the modern counterparts (Daghlian, 1978). Of particular significance in Daghlian's comprehensive review of the monocots is the demonstration of an approach in paleobotany that utilizes information from several areas of the biological and geologic sciences that is directed to the solution of major evolutionary questions about plants.

Fossil grasses (Gramineae) have been described by a number of authors from sediments of the late Tertiary from the plains of central North America. Generally the fossils consist of silicified three-dimensional specimens of lemma or palea that reveal important systematic epidermal features when examined with the aid of the scanning electron microscope. For example, the sinuous interlocking epidermal cell walls in late Miocene to early Pliocene specimens of *Panicium* not only establish the earliest geologic record of the genus, but also provide a basis for discussing the evolution within the genus.

The study of anatomically preserved Pliocene grasses from California has recently been used to suggest important physiologic parameters for the fossils (Nambudiri et al., 1978). The Kranz symdrome is a collection of anatomic and physiologic characteristics that occur together in certain angiosperms, especially grasses, that reveal a high level of CO_2 assimilation. The Kranz symdrome is present in all plants that fix CO_2 by phosphoenolpyruvate carboxylase in the mesophyll and subsequently produce Calvin-Benson cycle intermediates in the bundle sheath. These physiologic processes in C4 plants are closely related to a specific anatomy that includes prominent bundle sheath, low intervein distance,

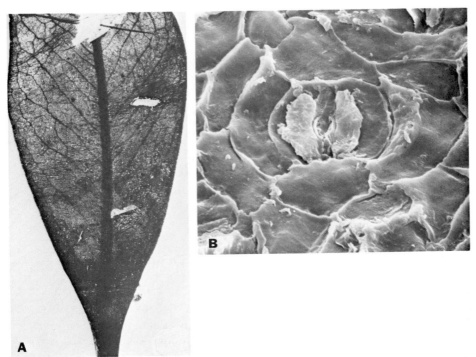

Figure 18-19 A. Cleared leaf of *Magnoliaephyllum* sp. to show the venation pattern (Cretaceous). ×3.3. B. Stomatal complex of a fossil angiosperm leaf. ×1000. *(Courtesy of D. Dilcher.)*

and radiating parenchyma in the mesophyll. Based on isotopic analysis and anatomic features, the Pliocene grasses are suggested as having possessed a C4 photosynthesis pathway. Studies such as these, which correlate physiologic and developmental patterns with anatomic and morphologic features, hold promise for opening new avenues of research in the biology of fossil plants.

One recent approach in angiosperm paleobotany has involved the consideration of floral morphology in conjunction with the probable pollination syndrome of the plant. Well-documented cases of coevolution between insects and plants are known, but these have been detailed primarily from modern associations. Beginning in the Paleozoic, there were apparently appropriate selective pressures operative so that insect-plant interactions were common. No doubt many of these came about as insects gained greater mobility and began feeding on spores, pollen, and possibly even ovules. In recent years, attention has been focused on the reproductive biology of several different kinds of fossil plants, so that today the reproductive systems of many ancient plants are fairly well understood. Observation of such features as pollen size and exine structure, sterile tissue surrounding pollen organs and seeds, insect-damaged reproductive structures, and the arrangement of reproductive units has contributed useful

Figure 18-20 Portion of the leaf of the Eocene palm *Palustrapalma agathae.* ×1. *(Courtesy of C. Daghlian.)*

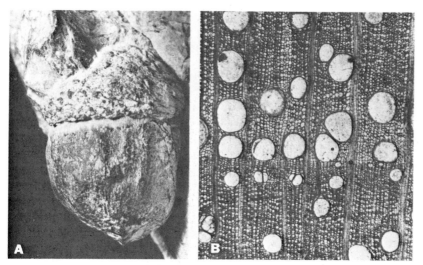

Figure 18-21 A. Fossil acorn from the Middle Eocene of Oregon. ×2. B. Transverse section of *Triplochitioxylon oregonensis* secondary xylem, an Eocene member of the Malvales. ×26.5. *(A courtesy of S. Manchester; B from Manchester, 1979.)*

information to discussions of these reproductive systems. Although color, potential attractants, and nutritional awards are important in determining a particular system of insect pollination, the most important element for angiosperms is floral morphology. Eocene sediments, especially from the southeastern United States, have yielded a large number of well-preserved flowers and fruits (Fig. 18-21A) of a variety of morphologic types that can be related to modern families and subfamilies (e.g., Fagaceae, Araceae, Juglandaceae, and Mimosoideae). An analysis of these flower types has already provided information that suggests the presence of beetle, fly, bee, and butterfly pollinators by the Middle Eocene. In an excellent review of the subject, Crepet (1979) notes that by the Middle Eocene, nectar production was already an important food source and that floral morphology had already evolved to the level of excluding certain insects. In addition, the number of stamens and perianth parts was reduced, with the latter whorled and fused in certain taxa. All these features are believed to have been acquired with the increasing specialization associated with insect pollination. Studies of this type suggest that although insects were important pollinators in several groups at this time, the pollination syndromes present today were not achieved by the Middle Eocene and several specialized insect flower types had not yet evolved.

Research with fossil angiosperms is moving forward on many fronts with exciting results. Only a few have been mentioned here to underscore the diversity of approaches being used today. Paleobotanists appear to have moved beyond the preoccupation of looking only for ancestral angiosperm stock (Fig. 18-22D) and are now engaged in research endeavors that may ultimately be far more rewarding. In recent years, a broad-based symposium ["The Bases of

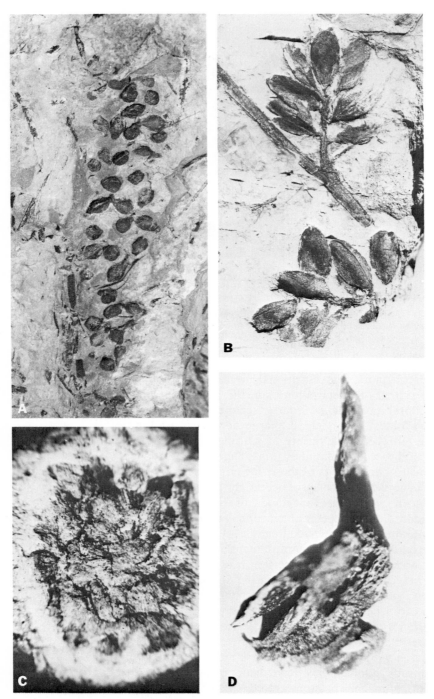

Figure 18-22 A. Portion of a strobilus of *Dirhopalostachys rostrata* from the Lower Cretaceous of Bureja Basin. ×1. B. A panicle of *Trochodendrocarpus arcticus* fruits from the Upper Cretaceous of Amur Basin. ×1. C. Staminate head of *Tricolpopollianthus burejensis*. ×7. D. Capsule of *Dirhopalostachys rostrata* showing pronounced adaxial keel. ×10. *(B from Krassilov, 1973; A, C, and D courtesy of V. Krassilov.)*

Angiosperm Phylogeny" (Walker, 1975)] and two excellent books [*Paleobiology of Angiosperm Origin* (Hughes, 1976) and *Origin and Early Evolution of Angiosperms* (Beck, 1976)] directed at angiosperm phylogeny have been published. The authoritative papers in these important contributions represent an excellent starting point for any serious student interested in angiosperm paleobotany.

Bibliography

GENERAL REFERENCES

Andrews, H. N., Jr. 1947. *Ancient plants and the world they lived in.* Comstock, Ithaca, N.Y. 279 pages.

———. 1955. *Index of generic names of fossil plants, 1820–1950.* U.S. Geological Survey Bulletin 1013. 262 pages.

———. 1961. *Studies in paleobotany.* Wiley, New York. 487 pages.

———. 1970. *Index of generic names of fossil plants, 1820–1965.* U.S. Geological Survey Bulletin 1300. 354 pages.

———, C. A. Arnold, E. Boureau, J. Doubinger, and S. Leclercq. 1970. *Traité de Paléobotanique,* vol. IV, part I: *Filicophyta.* Masson et Cie, Paris. 519 pages.

Arnold, C. A. 1947. *An introduction to paleobotany.* McGraw-Hill, New York. 433 pages.

Balfour, J. H. 1872. *Introduction to the study of palaeontological botany.* A. & C. Black, Edinburgh. 118 pages.

Banks, H. P. 1970. *Evolution and plants of the past.* Wadsworth, Belmont, Calif. 170 pages.

Bierhorst, D. W. 1971. *Morphology of vascular plants.* Macmillan, New York. 560 pages.

Boureau, E. 1964. *Traité de Paléobotanique,* vol. III: *Sphenophyta, Noeggerathiophyta.* Masson et Cie, Paris. 544 pages.

———, and J. Doubinger. 1975. *Traité de Paléototanique,* vol. IV, part II: *Pteridophylla* (part 1). Masson et Cie, Paris. 768 pages.

———, S. Jovet-Ast, O. A. Höeg, and W. J. Chaloner. 1967. *Traité de Paléobotanique,* vol. II: *Bryophyta, Psilophyta, Lycophyta.* Masson et Cie, Paris. 845 pages.

Bower, F. O. 1908. *The origin of a land flora.* Macmillian, London. 727 pages.

———. 1935. *Primitive land plants.* Macmillian, London. 658 pages.

Copeland, E. B. 1947. *Genera Filicum (The genera of ferns).* Chronica Botanica, Waltham, Mass.

Darrah, W. C. 1939. *Textbook of paleobotany.* Appleton-Century, New York. 441 pages.

———. 1960. *Principles of paleobotany.* Ronald, New York. 295 pages.

Delevoryas, T. 1962. *Morphology and evolution of fossil plants.* Holt, New York. 189 pages.

Emberger, L. 1968. *Les Plantes Fossiles.* Masson et Cie, Paris. 758 pages.

Gothan, W., and H. Weyland. 1964. *Lehrbuch der Paläobotanik.* Akademie-Verlag, Berlin. 594 pages.

Hirmer, M. 1927. *Handbuch der Paläobotanik.* R. Oldenbourg, Munich. 708 pages.

Holttum, R. 1947. A revised classification of the leptosporangiate ferns. *J. Linn. Soc. London, Bot.* **53:**123–158.

Knowlton, F. H. 1927. *Plants of the past.* Princeton, Princeton, N.J. 275 pages.

Krassilov, V. A. 1975. *Paleoecology of terrestrial plants. Basic principles and techniques.* Wiley, New York. 283 pages.

Lindley, J., and W. Hutton. 1881–1883. *The fossil flora of Great Britain; or, figures and descriptions of the vegetable remains found in a fossil state in this country,* vol. 1. J. Ridgway, London. 218 pages.

——— and ———. 1883–1885. *The fossil flora of Great Britain; or, figures and descriptions of the vegetable remains found in a fossil state in this country,* vol. 2. J. Ridgway, London. 208 pages.

——— and ———. 1887. *The fossil flora of Great Britain; or, figures and descriptions of the vegetable remains found in a fossil state in this country,* vol. 3. J. Ridgway, London. 204 pages.

Pichi-Sermolli, R. E. G. 1958. The higher taxa of the Pteridophyta and their classification. In O. Hedberg (ed.), *Systematics of Today.* Almquist and Wiksells, Uppsala, pp. 70–90.

Reid, E. M., and M. E. J. Chandler. 1933. *The London clay flora.* British Museum (Natural History), London. 561 pages.

Remy, W., and R. Remy. 1959. *Pflanzenfossilien.* Akademie-Verlag, Berlin. 285 pages.

Schimper, W. P. 1869. *Traité de Paléontologie Végétale ou la Flore du Monde Primitif,* vol. I. 740 pages; vol. II. 1870–1872. 966 pages; vol. III. 1874. 896 pages.

Scott, D. H. 1920. *Studies in fossil botany,* vol. I: *Pteridophyta.* A. & C. Black, London. 434 pages.

———. 1923. *Studies in fossil botany,* vol. II: *Spermophyta.* A. & C. Black, London. 446 pages.

———. 1924. *Extinct plants and problems of evolution.* Macmillian, London. 239 pages.

Seward, A. C. 1898. *Fossil plants,* vol. I. 452 pages; vol. II. 1910. 624 pages; vol. III. 1917. 656 pages; vol. IV. 1919. 543 pages. Cambridge, Cambridge, England.

———. 1931. *Plant life through the ages.* Cambridge, Cambridge, England. 601 pages.

Solms-Laubach, H. Graf. 1891. *Fossil botany*. Claredon, Oxford. 401 pages.

Stopes, M. C. 1910. *Ancient plants*. Blackie & Son, Glasgow. 198 pages.

Wagner, W. H., Jr. 1969. The construction of a classification. In *Systematic Biology*. Publ. 1962, Nat. Acad. Sci., Washington, D.C., pp. 67–103.

Walton, J. 1953. *An introduction to the study of fossil plants*. A. & C. Black, London. 201 pages.

Zeiller, R. 1900. *Éléments de Paléobotanique*. Carré & Naud, Paris, 421 pages.

CHAPTER 1: Introduction

Bartholomew, R. L., L. C. Matten, and E. F. Wheeler. 1970. Staining silicified woods. *J. Paleo.* **44**:905–907.

Beck, C. B. 1955. A technique for obtaining polished surfaces of sections of pyritized plant fossils. *Bull. Torrey Bot. Club* **82**:286–291.

Bennett, C. L. 1979. Radiocarbon dating with accelerators. *Amer. Sci.* **67**:450–457.

Gillespie, W. H., and H. W. Pfefferkorn. 1979. Distribution of commonly occurring plant megafossils in the proposed Pennsylvanian system stratotype. In: K. J. Englund et al. (eds.), *Proposed Pennsylvanian system stratotype Virginia and West Virginia. Field Trip No. 1.* 9th Int. Cong. Carb. Strat. Geol., Amer. Geol. Inst. Guidebook Ser. No. 1, pp. 87–96.

Gray, L. R., and T. N. Taylor. 1967. Palynology of the Schultztown coal in western Kentucky. *Trans. Amer. Micros. Soc.* **86**:502–506.

Hall, J. W. 1971. A spore with cytoplasm-like contents from the Cretaceous of Minnesota, USA. *Pollen Spores* **13**:163–164.

Harper, C. T. 1973. *Geochronology: Radiometric dating of rocks and minerals*. Benchmark Papers in Geology. Dowden, Hutchinson & Ross, Stroudsburg, Pa.

Langenheim, J. H. 1967. Preliminary investigations of *Hymenaea courbaril* as a resin producer. *J. Arnold Arbor.* **48**:203–227.

———. 1969. Amber: A botanical inquiry. *Science* **163**:1157–1169.

———, and J. W. Beck. 1968. Catalogue of infrared spectra of fossil resins (ambers). I. North and South America. *Bot. Mus. Leaflets, Harvard Univ.* **22**:65–120.

Moore, P. D., and J. A. Webb. 1978. *An illustrated guide to pollen analysis*. Hodder, London. 133 pages.

Moore, R. C., et al. 1968. Developments, trends, and outlooks in paleontology. *J. Paleo.* **42**:1327–1377.

Navale, G. K. B. 1963. Coal—A palyno-petrographic approach. *J. Geol. Soc. India* **4**:68–78.

Niklas, K. J., R. M. Brown, Jr., R. Santos, and B. Vian. 1978. Ultrastructure and cytochemistry of Miocene angiosperm leaf tissues. *Proc. Nat. Acad. Sci.* **75**:3263–3267.

Phillips, T. L., R. A. Peppers, M. J. Avcin, and P. F. Laughnan. 1974. Fossil plants and coal: Patterns of change in Pennsylvanian coal swamps of the Illinois Basin. *Science* **187**:1367–1369.

Schopf, J. M. 1975. Modes of fossil preservation. *Rev. Palaeobot. Palynol.* **20**:27–53.

Scott, A. C. 1979. The ecology of Coal Measure floras from northern Britain. *Proc. Geol. Assoc.* **90**:97–116.

———, and M. E. Collinson. 1978. Organic sedimentary particles: Results from scanning electron microscope studies of fragmentary plant material. In: W. B. Whalley (ed.), *Scanning electron microscopy in the study of sediments.* Geo. Abstracts, Norwich, England, pp. 137–167.

Stewart, W. N., and T. N. Taylor. 1965. The peel technique. In: B. Kummel and D. Raup (eds.), *Handbook of paleontological techniques.* Freeman, San Francisco, pp. 224–232.

Strümer, W., and S. Schaarschmidt. 1980. Pflanzen im Hunsrückschiefer. In: *Versteinertes Leben im Röntgenlicht.* Klein Senckenberg-Reihe Nr. ll., Kramer, Frankfurt.

Wagner, R. H. 1966. Palaeobotanical dating of Upper Carboniferous folding phases in N. W. Spain. *Mem. Inst. Geol. Min. Espana* **66**:1–169.

———, A. C. Higgins, and S. V. Meyen. 1979. *The Carboniferous of the U.S.S.R.* Yorkshire Geol. Soc. Occas. Publ. No. 4. (Reports presented at the I.U.G.S. subcommission on Carboniferous Stratigraphy at the 8th Int. Cong. on Carb. Strat. Geol. held at Moscow, 1975.)

CHAPTER 2: Precambrian Biology

Awramik, S. M., and E. S. Barghoorn. 1977. The Gunflint microbiota. *Precambrian Res.* **5**:121–142.

Barghoorn, E. S., and S. A. Tyler. 1965. Microorganisms from the Gunflint chert. *Science* **147**:563–577.

Cloud, P. E., Jr. 1965. Significance of the Gunflint (Precambrian) mircoflora. *Science* **148**:27–35.

Förster, R., and H. Wachendorf. 1977. Stromatolites from the Precambrian Transvaal Dolomite of N.E.-Transvaal, South Africa. In: E. Flügel (ed.), *Fossil algae: Recent results and developments.* Springer-Verlag, Berlin, pp. 66–73.

Hoffman, P. 1973. Recent and ancient algal stromatolites: Seventy years of pedagogic cross-pollination. In: R. N. Ginsburg (ed.), *Evolving Concepts in Sedimentology.* Johns Hopkins, Baltimore, pp. 178–191.

Hofmann, H. J. 1974. Mid-Precambrian prokaryotes (?) from the Belcher Islands, Canada. *Nature* **249**:87–88.

Knoll, A. H., and E. S. Barghoorn. 1975. Precambrian eukaryotic organisms: A reassessment of the evidence. *Science* **190**:52–54.

——— and ———. 1977. Archean microfossils showing cell division from the Swaziland System of South Africa. *Science* **198**:396–398.

Licari, G. R., and P. E. Cloud, Jr. 1968. Reproductive structures and taxonomic affinities of some nannofossils from the Gunflint Iron Formation. *Proc. Nat. Acad. Sci.* **59**:1053–1060.

Muir, M. D. 1976. Proterozoic microfossils from the Amelia Dolomite, McArthur Basin, Northern Territory. *Alcheringa* **1**:143–158.

Nagy, L. A. 1974. Transvaal stromatolite: First evidence for the diversification of cells about 2.2 × 10⁹ years ago. *Science* **183**:514–515.

———. 1978. New filamentous and cystous microfossils, ∼ 2,300 M.Y. old, from the Transvaal sequence. *J. Paleo.* **52**:141–154.

Nautiyal, A. C. 1976. First record of filamentous algal remains from the Late Precambrian rocks of Random Island (Trinity Bay), eastern Newfoundland, Canada. *Curr. Sci.* **5**:609–611.

Oehler, D. Z. 1978. Microflora of the Middle Proterozoic Balbirini Dolomite (McArthur Group) of Australia. *Alcheringa* **2**:269–309.

Oehler, J. H., D. Z. Oehler, and M. D. Muir. 1976. On the significance of tetrahedral tetrads of Precambrian algal cells. *Origins of Life* **7**:259–267.

Schopf, J. W. 1968. Microflora of the Bitter Springs Formation, Late Precambrian, central Australia. *J. Paleo.* **42**:651–688.

———. 1970a. Precambrian micro-organisms and evolutionary events prior to the origin of vascular plants. *Biol. Rev.* **45**:319–352.

———. 1970b. Electron microscopy of organically preserved Precambrian microorganisms. *J. Paleo.* **44**:1–6.

———. 1975. Precambrian paleobiology: Problems and perspectives. *Annu. Rev. Earth Planet. Sci.* **3**:213–249.

———. 1976. Are the oldest "fossils," fossils? *Origins of Life* **7**:19–36.

———, and E. S. Barghoorn. 1969. Microorganisms from the Late Precambrian of South Australia. *J. Paleo.* **43**:111–118.

———, and J. M. Blacic. 1971. New microorganisms from the Bitter Springs Formation (Late Precambrian) of the north-central Amadeus Basin, Australia. *J. Paleo.* **45**:925–959.

———, B. N. Haugh, R. E. Molnar, and D. F. Satterthwait. 1973. On the development of metaphytes and metazonas. *J. Paleo.* **47**:1–9.

———, and D. Z. Oehler. 1976. How old are the eukaryotes? *Science* **193**:47–49.

———, D. Z. Oehler, R. J. Horodyski, and K. A. Kvenvolden. 1971. Biogenicity and significance of the oldest known stromatolites. *J. Paleo.* **45**:477–485.

———, and K. N. Prasad. 1978. Microfossils in Collenia-like stromatolites from the Proterozoic Vempalle Formation of the Cuddapah Basin, India. *Precambrian Res.* **6**:347–366.

———, and Y. K. Sovietov. 1976. Microfossils in *Conophyton* from the Soviet Union and their bearing on Precambrian biostratigraphy. *Science* **193**:143–146.

Shimizu, A., K. Imahori, and S. Yuasa. 1977. Filamentous microfossils from the Gunflint chert, the Middle Precambrian sediments of Ontario (Canada). *Sci. Rep.* **26**:29–37.

———, ———, and ———. 1978. Examination of the Gunflint microfossils by scanning electron microscopy. *Origin of Life.* Proceedings of the Second ISSOL Meeting and the Fifth ICOL Meeting (ed. by H. Noda), Center of Academic Publications of Japan, Japan Scientific Society Press, pp. 527–532.

Siegel, S. M., and B. Z. Siegel. 1968. A living organism microfossils from the Gunflint chert, the Middle Precambrian sediments of Ontario (Canada). *Sci. Rep.* **26**:29–37.

Tyler, S. A., and E. S. Barghoorn. 1954. Occurrence of structurally preserved plants in pre-Cambrian rocks of the Canadian Shield. *Science* **119**:606–608.

Walter, M. R. (ed.). 1976. *Stromatolites.* Developments in Sedimentology 20. Elsevier, New York. 790 pages.

CHAPTER 3: Fungi and Bacteria

FUNGI

Agashe, S. N., and S. T. Tilak. 1970. Occurrence of fungal elements in the bark of arborescent Calamite roots from the American Carboniferous. *Bull. Torrey Bot. Club.* **97**:216–218.

Alvin, K. L., and M. D. Muir. 1970. An epiphyllous fungus from the Lower Cretaceous. *Biol. J. Linn. Soc.* **2**:55–59.

Andrews, H. N., Jr. 1948. A note on *Fomes idahoensis* Brown. *Ann. Missouri Bot. Gard.* **35**:193–207.

————, and L. W. Lenz. 1943. A mycorrhizome from the Carboniferous of Illinois. *Bull. Torrey Bot. Club* **70**:120–125.

———— and ————. 1947. Fossil polypores from Idaho. *Ann. Missouri Bot. Gard.* **34**:113–114.

Batra, L. R., R. H. Segal, and R. W. Baxter. 1964. A new Middle Pennsylvanian fossil fungus. *Amer. J. Bot.* **51**:991–995.

Baxter, R. W. 1975. Fossil fungi from American Pennsylvanian coal balls. *Univ. Kansas Paleontol. Contr.* **77**:1–6.

Berry, E. W. 1916. Remarkable fossil fungi. *Mycologia* **8**:73–79.

Boullard, B., and Y. Lemoigne. 1971. Les champignons endophytes du *Rhynia gwynne-vaughanii* K. et L. Étude morphologique et déductions sur leur biologie. *Botaniste* **54**:49–89.

Brown, R. W. 1938. Two fossils misidentified as shelf-fungi. *J. Wash. Acad. Sci.* **28**:130–131.

————. 1940. A bracket fungus from the late Tertiary of southwestern Idaho. *J. Wash. Acad. Sci.* **30**:422–424.

Cridland, A. A. 1962. The fungi in Cordaitean rootlets. *Mycologia* **54**:230–234.

Daghlian, C. P. 1978. A new melioloid fungus from the early Eocene of Texas. *Palaeontology* **21**:171–176.

Davis, B., and G. A. Leisman. 1962. Further observations on *Sporocarpon* and allied genera. *Bull. Torrey Bot. Club.* **89**:97–109.

Dennis, R. L. 1969. Fossil mycelium with clamp connections from the Middle Pennsylvanian. *Science* **163**:670–671.

————. 1970. A Middle Pennsylvanian basidiomycete mycelium with clamp connections. *Mycologia* **62**:578–584.

————. 1976. *Palaeosclerotium,* a Pennsylvanian age fungus combining features of modern ascomycetes and basidiomycetes. *Science* **192**:66–68.

Dilcher, D. L. 1965. Epiphyllous fungi from Eocene deposits in western Tennessee, U.S.A. *Palaeontographica* **B116**:1–54.

Elsik, W. C. 1971. Microbiological degradation of sporopollenin. In: J. Brooks et al. (eds.), *Sporopollenin.* Academic Press, New York, pp. 480–511.

————, and D. L. Dilcher. 1974. Palynology and age of clays exposed in Lawrence clay pit, Henry County, Tennessee. *Palaeontographica* **B146**:65–87.

————, and J. Jansonius. 1974. New genera of Paleogene fungal spores. *Can. J. Bot.* **52**:953–958.

Fry, W. L., and D. J. McLaren. 1959. Fungal filaments in a Devonian limestone from Alberta. *Geol. Surv. Can. Bull.* **48**:1–9.

Graham, A. 1971. The role of Myxomyceta spores in palynology (with a brief note on the morphology of certain algal zygospores). *Rev. Palaeobot. Palynol.* **11**:89–99.

Kidston, R., and W. H. Lang. 1921. On Old Red Sandstone plants showing structure, from the Rhynie Chert Bed, Aberdeenshire. Part V. The Thallophyta occurring in the peat-bed, the succession of the plants through a vertical section of the bed, and the conditions of accumulation and preservation of the deposit. *Trans. Roy. Soc. Edinburgh* **52**:885–902.

Lange, R. T. 1969. Recent and fossil epiphyllous fungi of the *Manginula-Shortensis* group. *Australian J. Bot.* **17**:565–574.

McLaughlin, D. J. 1976. On *Palaeosclerotium* as a link between ascomycetes and basidiomycetes. *Science* **193**:602.

Millay, M. A., and T. N. Taylor. 1978. Chytrid-like fossils of Pennsylvanian age. *Science* **200**:1147–1149.

Oliver, D. L. 1978. *Retiarius* gen. nov.: Phyllosphere fungi which capture wind-borne pollen grains. *Trans. Br. Mycol. Soc.* **71**:193–201.

Pflug, H. D. 1978. Yeast-like microfossils detected in oldest sediments of the earth. *Naturwissenschaften* **65**:611–615.

———, and H. Jaeschke-Boyer. 1979. Combined structural and chemical analysis of 3,800-Myr-old microfossils. *Nature* **280**:483–486.

Pirozynski, K. A., and D. W. Malloch. 1975. The origin of land plants: A matter of mycotrophism. *BioSyst.* **6**:153–164.

———, and L. K. Weresub. 1979. The classification and nomenclature of fossil fungi. In: B. Kendrick (ed.), *The whole fungus*. National Museum of Natural Sciences, National Museum of Canada, and Kananaskis Foundation, Ottawa, pp. 653–772.

Ramanujam, C. G. K., and P. Ramachar. 1963. *Sporae dispersae* of the rust fungi (Uredinales) from the Miocene lignite of South India. *Curr. Sci.* **32**:271–272.

Rothwell, G. W. 1972. *Palaeosclerotium pusillum* gen. et sp. nov.: A fossil eumycete from the Pennsylvanian of Illinois. *Can. J. Bot.* **50**:2353–2356.

Schopf, J. W. 1970. Electron microscopy of organically preserved Precambrian microorganisms. *J. Paleo.* **44**:1–6.

———, and E. S. Barghoorn. 1969. Microorganisms from the Late Precambrian of South Australia. *J. Paleo.* **42**:111–118.

Sheffy, M. W., and D. L. Dilcher. 1971. Morphology and taxonomy of fungal spores. *Palaeontographica* **B133**:34–51.

Singer, R. 1977. An interpretation of *Palaeosclerotium*. *Mycologia* **69**:850–854.

Srivastava, S. K. 1976. Biogenic infection in Jurassic spores and pollen. *Geosci. Man* **15**:95–100.

Stidd, B. M., and K. Cosentino. 1975. *Albugo*-like oogonia from the American Carboniferous. *Science* **190**:1092–1093.

Wolf, F. A. 1969. A rust and an alga in Eocene sediment from western Kentucky. *J. Elisha Mitchell Soc.* **85**:57–58.

Xinan, M. 1977. Upper Permian fossil fungi from Anshun of Guizhou. *Acta Palaeontol. Sinica* **16**:151–158.

BACTERIA

Awramik, S. M., and E. S. Barghoorn. 1977. The Gunflint microbiota. *Precambrian Res.* **5**:121–142.

Banks, H. P., K. I. M. Chesters, N. F. Hughes, G. A. L. Johnson, H. M. Johnson, and L. R. Moore. 1967. *The fossil record—Thallophyta.* Geol. Soc. London, pp. 163–180.

Barghoorn, E. S., and J. W. Schopf. 1966. Microorganisms three billion years old from the Precambrian of South Africa. *Science* **152:**758–763.

Bertrand, C. E. 1903. Les coprolithes des Bernissart. *Mém. Mus. Roy. Hist. Nat. Belgique* **1:**10–154.

Bradley, W. H. 1946. Coprolites from the Bridger Formation of Wyoming: Their composition and microorganisms. *Amer. J. Sci.* **244:**215–239.

———. 1963. Unmineralized fossil bacteria. *Science* **141:**919–921.

Dombrowski, H. J. 1963. Bacteria from Paleozoic salt deposits. *Ann. N.Y. Acad. Sci.* **108:**453–460.

Ellis, D. 1914. Fossil microorganisms from the Jurassic and Cretaceous rocks of Great Britain. *Proc. Roy. Soc. Edinburgh* **35:**110–133.

Renault, B. 1900. Sur quelques microorganismes des combustibles fossiles. *Soc. Ind. Min. St.-Étienne Bull.* **14:**1–460.

Schopf, J. M., E. G. Ehlers, D. V. Stiles, and J. D. Birle. 1965. Fossil iron bacteria preserved in pyrite. *Proc. Amer. Phil. Soc.* **109:**288–308.

CHAPTER 4: Algae and Lichens

CYANOCHLORONTA

Bold, H. C., and M. J. Wynne. 1978. *Introduction to the algae. Structure and reproduction.* Prentice-Hall, Englewood Cliffs, N.J. 706 pages.

Cloud, P. E., Jr., and G. R. Licardi. 1972. Ultrastructure and geologic relations of some two-aeon old Nostocacean algae from Northeastern Minnesota. *Amer. J. Sci.* **272:**138–149.

———, M. Moorman, and D. Pierce. 1975. Sporulation and ultrastructure in a Late Proterozoic cyanophyte: Some implications for taxonomy and plant phylogeny. *Quart. Rev. Biol.* **50:**131–150.

Croft, W. N., and E. A. George. 1959. Blue-green algae from the Middle Devonian of Rhynie, Aberdeenshire. *Bull. Brit. Mus. (Nat. Hist.) Geol.* **3:**339–353.

Flügel, E. 1977. *Fossil algae: Recent results and developments.* Springer-Verlag, Berlin. 375 pages.

Knoll, A. H., E. S. Barghoorn, and S. Golubic. 1975. *Paleopleurocapsa wopfnerii* gen. et sp. nov.: A Late Precambrian alga and its modern counterpart. *Proc. Nat. Acad. Sci.* **72:**2488–2492.

Moorman, M. 1974. Microbiota of the Late Proterozoic Hector Formation, Southwestern Alberta, Canada. *J. Paleo.* **48:**524–539.

Schopf, J. W. 1968. Microflora of the Bitter Springs Formation, Late Precambrian, central Australia. *J. Paleo.* **42:**652–688.

———. 1970. Precambrian microorganisms and evolutionary events prior to the origin of vascular plants. *Biol. Rev.* **45:**319–352.

————, and J. M. Blacic. 1971. New microorganisms from the Bitter Springs Formation (Late Precambrian) of the north-central Amadeus Basin, Australia. *J. Paleo.* **45**:925–960.

————, and Y. K. Sovietov. 1976. Microfossils in *Conophyton* from the Soviet Union and their bearing on Precambrian biostratigraphy. *Science* **193**:143–146.

Wicander, E. R., and J. W. Schopf. 1974. Microorganisms from the Kalkberg Limestone (Lower Devonian) of New York state. *J. Paleo.* **48**:74–77.

CHLOROPHYCOPHYTA

Baschnagel, R. A. 1966. New fossil algae from the Middle Devonian of New York. *Trans. Amer. Microsc. Soc.* **85**:297–302.

Basson, P. W., and H. S. Edgell. 1971. Calcareous algae from the Jurassic and Cretaceous of Lebanon. *Micropaleontology* **17**:411–433.

————, and J. M. Wood. 1970. *Algites enteromorphoides* sp. nov.: A filamentous alga of Devonian age from Missouri. *Amer. Midl. Natur.* **83**:283–290.

Bassoullet, J. P., P. Bernier, R. Deloffre, P. Genot, M. Jaffrezo, A. F. Poignant, and G. Segonzac. 1977. Classification criteria of fossil Dasycladales. In: E. Flügel (ed.), *Fossil Algae: Recent Results and Developments.* Springer-Verlag, Berlin, pp. 154–166.

Black, M. 1965. Coccoliths. *Endeavour* **24**:131–137.

Blackburn, K. B. 1936. *Botrycoccus* and the algal coals. Part I: A reinvestigation of the alga *Botryococcus braunii* Kützing. *Trans. Roy. Soc. Edinburgh* **58**:841–854.

Bold, H. C. 1973. *Morphology of plants,* 3rd ed. Harper & Row, New York. 668 pages.

Boureau, E. 1979. Louis Grambast (1927–1976). *Rev. Palaeobot. Palynol.* **28**:95–102.

Combaz, A. 1973. La matière algaire et l'origine du pétrole. In: B. Tissot and F. Bienner (eds.), *Advances in organic geochemistry.* Technip, Paris, pp. 423–438.

Croft, W. N. 1952. A new *Trochiliscus* (Charophyta) from the Downtonian of Podolia. *Bull. Brit. Mus. (Nat. Hist.) Geol.* **1**:187–220.

Elliott, G. F. 1978. Ecologic significance of post-Paleozoic green calcareous algae. *Geol. Mag.* **115**:437–442.

Evitt, R. 1963. Occurrence of freshwater alga *Pediastrum* in Cretaceous marine sediments. *Amer. J. Sci.* **261**:890–893.

Flajs, G. 1977. Die Ultrastrukturen des Kalkalgenskeletts. *Palaeontographica* **B160**:69–128.

Grambast, L. 1967. La série évolutive *Perimneste-Aptopchara* (Charophytes). *C.R. Acad. Sci. Paris* **D264**:581–584.

————. 1974. Phylogeny of the Charophyta. *Taxon* **23**:463–481.

Gray, J. 1960. Fossil Chlorophycean algae from the Miocene of Oregon. *J. Paleo.* **34**:453–463.

Herak, M., V. Kochansky-Devide, and I. Gusic. 1977. The development of the Dasyclad algae through the ages. In: E. Flügel (ed.), *Fossil algae: Recent results and developments.* Springer-Verlag, Berlin, pp. 143–153.

Hillis-Colinvaux, L. 1980. *Ecology and Taxonomy of Halimeda: Primary Producer of Coral Reefs.* Adv. Marine Biol. Vol. 17. Academic, New York.

Jux, U. 1968. Über den Feinbau der Wandung *Tasmanites* Newton. *Palaeontographica* **B124**:112–124.

Kjellström, G. 1968. Remarks on the chemistry and ultrastructure of the cell wall of some Paleozoic leiospheres. *Geol. Föreningens i Stockholm Förhandlingar* **90**:221–228.

Newton, E. T. 1875. On "Tasmanite" and Australian "White Coal." *Geol. Mag.* (2)**2**:337–342.

Niklas, K. J. 1976*a*. Morphological and chemical examination of *Courvoisiella ctenomorpha* gen. and sp. nov., a siphonous alga from the Upper Devonian, West Virginia, U.S.A. *Rev. Palaeobot. Palynol.* **21**:187–203.

———. 1976*b*. The chemotaxonomy of *Parka decipiens* from the Lower Old Red Sandstone, Scotland (U.K.). *Rev. Palaeobot. Palynol.* **21**:205–217.

———. 1976*c*. Morphological and ontogenetic reconstruction of *Parka decipiens* Fleming and *Pachytheca* Hooker from the Lower Old Red Sandstone, Scotland. *Trans. Roy. Soc. Edinburgh* **69**:483–499.

Nitecki, H. 1970. North American Cyclocrinitid algae. *Fieldiana Geol.* **21**:1–182.

———. 1971. *Ischadites abbottae,* a new North American Silurian species (Dasycladales). *Phycologia* **10**:263–275.

———. 1972. North American Silurian receptaculitid algae. *Fieldiana Geol.* **28**:1–108.

———, and C. C. Dapples. 1975. Silurian *Ischadites tenuis* n. sp. (Receptaculitids) from Indiana. *Fieldiana Geol.* **35**:11–20.

Obrhel, J. 1968. Die Silur- und Devonflora des Barrandiums. *Paläont. Abh.* **B2**:635–793.

Peck, R. E. 1957. North American Mesozoic Charophyta. *U.S.G.S. Prof. Paper* **A294**:1–44.

———, and J. A. Eyer. 1963. Pennsylvanian, Permian and Triassic Charophyta of North America. *J. Paleo.* **37**:835–844.

Rietschel, S. 1977. Receptaculitids are calcareous algae but no Dasyclads. In: E. Flügel (ed.), *Fossil algae: Recent results and developments.* Springer-Verlag, Berlin, pp. 212–214.

Wilson, L. R., and W. H. Hoffmeister. 1953. Four new species of fossil *Pediastrum.* *Amer. J. Sci.* **251**:753–760.

CHRYSOPHYCOPHYTA

Hoops, H. H., and G. L. Floyd. 1979. Ultrastructure of the centric diatom *Cyclotella meneghiniana:* Vegetative cell and auxospore development. *Phycologia* **18**:425–436.

Lohman, K. E. 1941. Geology and biology of North Atlantic deep-sea cores between Newfoundland and Ireland. Part 3. Diatomaceae. *U.S.G.S. Prof. Paper* **B196**:57–86.

Sieburth, J. M. 1979. *Sea microbes.* Oxford, New York.

Van Landingham, S. L. 1967–1971. *Catalogue of fossil and recent genera and species of diatoms and their synonyms,* vol. I. 1967; vol. II. 1968; vol. III. 1969; vol. IV. 1971. J. Cramer, Lehre, Germany.

RHODOPHYCOPHYTA

Basson, P. W. 1972. *Algites hakelensis* sp. nov.: A Cretaceous foliose alga from Lebanon. *Amer. Midl. Natur.* **88**:506–511.

DiMichele, W. A., and T. L. Phillips. 1976. *Thallites dichopleurus* sp. nov., from the Middle Pennsylvanian Mazon Creek Flora. *Bull. Torrey Bot. Club* **103**:218–222.

Elliott, G. F. 1964. Tertiary solenoporacean algae and the reproductive structures of the Solenoporaceae. *Palaeontology* **7**:695–702.

———. 1973. A Miocene solenoporoid alga showing reproductive structures. *Palaeontology* **16**:223–230.

Fry, W. L., and H. P. Banks. 1955. Three new genera of algae from the Upper Devonian of New York. *J. Paleo.* **29**:37–44.

Johnson, J. H. 1954. Fossil calcareous algae from Bikini Atoll. *U.S.G.S. Prof. Paper* **M260**:537–545.

———. 1962. The algal genus *Lithothamnium* and its fossil representatives. *Colorado Sch. Mines Quart.* **57**:1–111.

———, and O. A. Køeg. 1961. Studies of Ordovician algae. *Colorado Sch. Mines Quart.* **56**:1–120.

———, and K. Konishi. 1959. A review of Silurian (Gotlandian) algae. *Colorado Sch. Mines Quart.* **54**:2–114.

Mamay, S. H. 1959. *Litostroma,* a new genus of problematical algae from the Pennsylvanian of Oklahoma. *Amer. J. Bot.* **46**:283–292.

Parker, B. C., and E. Y. Dawson. 1965. Non-calcareous marine algae from California Miocene deposits. *Nova Hedwig.* **10**:273–295.

Poignant, A. F. 1977. The Mesozoic red algae: A general survey. In: E. Flügel (ed.), *Fossil algae: Recent results and developments.* Springer-Verlag, Berlin, pp. 177–189.

Wray, J. L. 1977. Late Paleozoic calcareous red algae. In: E. Flügel (ed.), *Fossil algae: Recent results and developments.* Springer-Verlag, Berlin, pp. 167–176.

PHAEOPHYCOPHYTA

Arnold, C. A. 1952. A specimen of *Prototaxites* from the Kettle Point Black Shale of Ontario. *Palaeontographica* **B93**:45–56.

Niklas, K. J. 1976*a*. Chemotaxonomy of *Prototaxites* and evidence for possible terrestrial adaptation. *Rev. Palaeobot. Palynol.* **22**:1–17.

———. 1976*b*. Organic chemistry of *Protosalvinia* (= *Foerstia*) from the Chattanooga and New Albany Shales. *Rev. Palaeobot. Palynol.* **22**:265–279.

———, and T. L. Phillips. 1976. Morphology of *Protosalvinia* from the Upper Devonian of Ohio and Kentucky. *Amer. J. Bot.* **63**:9–29.

———, ———, and A. V. Carozzi. 1976. Morphology and paleoecology of *Protosalvinia* from the Upper Devonian (Famennian) of the Middle Amazon Basin of Brazil. *Palaeontographica* **B155**:1–30.

Phillips, T. L., K. J. Niklas, and H. N. Andrews, Jr. 1972. Morphology and vertical distribution of *Protosalvinia* (*Foerstia*) from the New Albany Shale (Upper Devonian). *Rev. Palaebot. Palynol.* **14**:171–196.

Schmid, R. 1976. Septal pores in *Prototaxites,* an enigmatic Devonian plant. *Science* **191**:287–288.

Schopf, J. M. 1978. *Foerstia* and recent interpretations of early, vascular land plants. *Lethaia* **11**:139–143.

PYRRHOPHYCOPHYTA

Damassa, S. P. 1979. Danian dinoflagellates from the Franciscan complex, Mendocino County, California. *Palynology* **3**:191–207.

Evitt, W. R. 1961. Observations on the morphology of fossil dinoflagellates. *Micropaleontology* **7**:385–420.

————. 1963*a*. A discussion and proposals concerning fossil dinoflagellates, hystricho-spheres, and acritarchs, part I. *Proc. Nat. Acad. Sci.* **29**:158–164.

————. 1963*b*. A discussion and proposals concerning fossil dinoflagellates, hystricho-spheres, and acritarchs, part II. *Proc. Nat. Acad. Sci.* **49**:298–302.

Hutter, T. 1979. *Alpenachitina crameri,* a new chitinozoan from the Middle Devonian of Egypt. *Palynology* **3**:23–29.

Rasul, S. M. 1979. Acritarch zonation of the Tremadoc Series of the Shineton Shales, Wrekin, Shropshire, England. *Palynology* **3**:53–72.

Wall, D., and B. Dale. 1967. "Living fossils" in western Atlantic plankton. *Nature* **211**:1025–1026.

Whitney, B. L. 1979. A population study of *Alterbia acutula* (Wilson) Lentin and Williams from the Maestrichtian (Upper Cretaceous) of Maryland. *Palynology* **3**:123–128.

LICHENS

Hallbauer, D. K., and M. H. Jahns. 1977. Morphological and anatomical observations on some Precambrian plants from the Witwatersrand, South Africa. *Geol. Rundschau* **66**:477–491.

CHAPTER 5: Bryophytes

Andrews, H. N., Jr. 1960. Notes on Belgium specimens of *Sporogonites. Palaeobotanist* **7**:85–89.

Boureau, E., S. Jovet-Ast, O. A. Höeg, and W. J. Chaloner. 1967. *Traité de Paléobotanique,* vol. II: *Bryophyta, Psilophyta Lycophyta.* Masson et Cie, Paris. 845 pages.

Brown, J. T., and C. R. Robison. 1974. *Diettertia montanensis,* gen. et. sp. nov., a fossil moss from the Lower Cretaceous Kootenai Formation of Montana. *Bot. Gaz.* **135**:170–173.

———— and ————. 1976. Observations on the structure of *Marchantiolites blairmorensis* (Berry) n. comb. from the Lower Cretaceous of Montana, U.S.A. *J. Paleo.* **50**:309–311.

Edwards, D. 1979. A Late Silurian flora from the Lower Old Red Sandstone of South-West Dyfed. *Palaeontology* **22**:23–52.

Grambast, L. J., and W. S. Lacey. 1967. Bryophyta and Charophyta. In: *The fossil record,* Geological Society of London and Northern Ireland, pp. 211–217.

Halle, T. G. 1916. Lower Devonian plants from Röragen in Norway. *Kungl. Svenska Vet. Handl.* **57**:3–46.

Harris, T. M. 1938. *The British rhaetic flora.* British Museum (Natural History), London.

Hibbert, F. A. 1967. The use of scanning electron microscopy in the study of Carboniferous miospores. *New Phytol.* **66**:825–826.

Hueber, F. M. 1961. *Hepaticites devonicus,* a new fossil liverwort from the Devonian of New York. *Ann. Missouri Bot. Gard.* **48**:125–132.

Janssens, J. A. P., D. G. Horton, and J. Basinger. 1979. *Aulacomnium heterostichoides,* sp. nov., an Eocene moss from south central British Columbia. *Can. J. Bot.* **57:**2150–2161.

Krassilov, V. A. 1970. Leafy liverworts from the Jurassic (USSR). *Akad. Nauk SSSR. Paleontological J.* **3:**131–142 (in Russian).

―――. 1973. Mesozoic bryophytes from the Bureja Basin, Far East of the USSR. *Palaeontographica* **B143:**95–105.

Lacey, W. S. 1969. Fossil bryophytes. *Biol. Rev.* **44:**189–205.

Lemoigne, Y. 1966. Sur un sporogone de Bryale d'âge Dévonien. *Soc. Linn. Lyon Bull. Mensuel* **35:**13–16.

Lundlbad, B. 1954. Contributions to the geological history of the Hepaticae. Fossil Marchantiales from the Rhaetic-Liassic coal mines of Skromberga (Prov. of Scania), Sweden. *Svensk Bot. Tidskrift* **48:**381–417.

Neuburg, M. F. 1960. Leafy mosses from the Permian deposits of Angaraland. *Trudy Geol. Inst.* **19:**1–104 (in Russian).

Savicz-Ljubitzkaja, L. I., and I. I. Abramov. 1959. The geological annals of Bryophyta. *Rev. Bryol. Lichen.* **28:**330–342.

Schuster, R. M. 1966. *The Hepaticae and Anthocerotae of North America east of the hundredth meridian,* vol. I. Columbia, New York.

Steere, W. C. 1946. Cenozoic and Mesozoic bryophytes of North America. *Amer. Midl. Natur.* **36:**298–324.

Thomas, B. A. 1972. A probable moss from the Lower Carboniferous of the Forest of Dean, Gloucestershire. *Ann. Bot.* **36:**155–161.

Walton, J. 1925. Carboniferous Bryophyta, part I: Hepaticae. *Ann. Bot.* **39:**563–572.

CHAPTER 6: The Evolution of Vascular Plants

Esau, K. 1965. *Plant anatomy,* 2d ed. Wiley, New York.

―――. 1977. *Anatomy of seed plants,* 2d ed. Wiley, New York.

Fahn, A. 1967. *Plant anatomy,* 2d ed. Pergamon, New York.

CHAPTER 7: Early Vascular Plants

Andrews, H. N., Jr. 1974. Paleobotany 1947–1972. *Ann. Missouri Bot. Gard.* **61:**179–202.

―――, and S. A. Stepanov. 1968. Finds of sporiferous organs in *Psilophyton princeps* Dawson emend. Halle in the Lower Devonian of the southern Minusinsk Trough, Western Siberia. In: *New materials on the stratigraphy and paleontology of the Lower and Middle Paleozoic of Western Siberia.* Tomsk State Univ., *Trudy* **202:**30–46.

————, P. G. Gensel, and A. E. Kasper. 1975. A new fossil plant of probable intermediate affinities (Trimerophyte-Progymnosperm). *Can. J. Bot.* **53**:1719–1728.

————, A. Kasper, and E. Mencher. 1968. *Psilophyton forbesii,* a new Devonian plant from northern Maine. *Bull. Torrey Bot. Club* **95**:1–11.

Banks, H. P. 1965. Some recent additions to the knowledge of the early land flora. *Phytomorphology* **15**:235–245.

————. 1967. Anatomy and affinities of a Devonian *Hostinella. Phytomorphology* **17**:321–330.

————. 1968. The early history of land plants. In: E. T. Drake (ed.), *Evolution and environment.* Yale, New Haven, pp. 73–107.

————. 1973. Occurrence of *Cooksonia,* the oldest vascular land plant macrofossil, in the Upper Silurian of New York State. *J. Indian Bot. Soc.* **A50**:227–235.

————, and M. R. Davis. 1969. *Crenaticaulis,* a new genus of Devonian plants allied to *Zosterophyllum,* and its bearing on the classification of early land plants. *Amer. J. Bot.* **56**:436–449.

————, S. Leclercq, and F. M. Hueber. 1975. Anatomy and morphology of *Psilophyton dawsonii,* sp. n., from the Late Lower Devonian of Quebec (Gaspé), and Ontario, Canada. *Palaeontographica Amer.* **8**:77–127.

Bierhorst, D. W. 1968. On the Stromatopteridaceae (Fam. Nov.) and on the Psilotaceae. *Phytomorphology* **18**:232–268.

Boullard, B., and Y. Lemoigne. 1971. Les champignons endophytes du *Rhynia gwynne-vaughanii* K. et L. Étude morphologique et déductions sur leur biologie. *Botaniste* ser. **54**:49–89.

Daber, R. 1960. *Eogaspesiea gracillis* n. g. n. sp. *Geologie* **9**:418–425.

Dawson, J. W. 1859. On fossil plants from the Devonian rocks of Canada. *Quart. J. Geol. Soc. London* **15**:477–488.

————. 1870. The primitive vegetation of the earth. *Nature* **2**:85–88.

————. 1871. The fossil plants of Devonian and Upper Silurian formations of Canada. *Geol. Surv. Can.* 1–92.

Doran, J. B. 1979. A new species of *Psilophyton* from the Lower Devonian of northern New Brunswick, Canada. Ph.D. diss., Univ. Alberta, Edmonton.

Dorf, E. 1933. A new occurrence of the oldest known terrestrial vegetation, from Beartooth Butte, Wyoming. *Bot. Gaz.* **95**:240–257.

Edwards, D. 1969a. Further observations on *Zosterophyllum llanoveranum* from the Lower Devonian of South Wales. *Amer. J. Bot.* **56**:201–210.

————. 1969b. *Zosterophyllum* from the Lower Old Red Sandstone of South Wales. *New Phytol.* **68**:923–931.

————. 1970a. Fertile Rhyniophytina from the Lower Devonian of Britain. *Palaeontology* **13**:451–461.

————. 1970b. Further observations on the Lower Devonian plant, *Gosslingia breconensis* Heard. *Phil. Trans. Roy. Soc. London* **258**:225–243.

————. 1972. A *Zosterophyllum* fructification from the Lower Old Red Sandstone of Scotland. *Rev. Palaeobot. Palynol.* **14**:77–83.

————. 1976. The systematic position of *Hicklingia edwardii* Kidston and Lang. *New Phytol.* **76**:173–181.

————. 1979. A late Silurian flora from the Lower Old Red Sandstone of South-west Dyfed. *Palaeontology* **22**:23–52.

————, and E. C. W. Davies. 1976. Oldest recorded *in situ* tracheids. *Nature* **263**:494–495.

————, and J. B. Richardson. 1974. Lower Devonian (Dittonian) plants from the Welsh borderland. *Palaeontology* **17**:311–324.

Eggert, D. A. 1974. The sporangium of *Horneophyton lignieri* (Rhyniophytina). *Amer. J. Bot.* **61**:405–413.

El-Saadawy, W. E., and W. S. Lacey. 1979. Observations on *Nothia aphylla* Lyon ex Høeg. *Rev. Palaeobot. Palynol.* **27**:119–147.

Gensel, P. G. 1976. *Renalia hueberi,* a new plant from the Lower Devonian of Gaspé. *Rev. Palaeobot. Palynol.* **22**:19–37.

————. 1979. Two *Psilophyton* species from the Lower Devonian of eastern Canada with a discussion of morphological variation within the genus. *Palaeontographica* **B168**:81–99.

————, A. Kasper, and H. N. Andrews, Jr. 1969. *Kaulangiophyton,* a new genus of plants from the Devonian of Maine. *Bull. Torrey Bot. Club* **96**:265–276.

Granoff, J. A., P. G. Gensel, and H. N. Andrews, Jr. 1976. A new species of *Pertica* from the Devonian of Eastern Canada. *Palaeontographica* **B155**:119–128.

Hartman, C. M., and H. P. Banks. 1980. Pitting in *Psylophyton dawsonii,* an early Devonian trimerophyte. *Amer. J. Bot.* **67**:400–412.

Hébant, C. 1977. *The Conducting Tissues of Bryophytes.* J. Cramer, Vaduz, Germany.

Hopping, C. A. 1956. On a specimen of *"Psilophyton robustius"* Dawson, from the Lower Devonian of Canada. *Proc. Roy. Soc. Edinburgh* **B66**:10–28.

Hueber, F. M. 1964a. The Psilophytes and their relationship to the origin of ferns. *Torrey. Bot. Club Mem.* **21**:5–9.

————. 1964b. New data on the morphology of Devonian Psilopsida and Lycopsida. *10th Int. Bot. Cong. Edinburgh, Abstr.,* p. 17.

————. 1968. *Psilophyton:* The genus and the concept. *Int. Symp. Devonian Syst.,* vol. II. Alberta Soc. Petrol. Geol., Calgary (D. H. Oswald, ed.), pp. 815–822.

————. 1970. *Rebuchia:* A new name for *Bucheria* Dorf. *Taxon* **19**:822.

————. 1971. *Sawdonia ornata:* A new name for *Psilophyton princeps* var. *ornatum. Taxon* **20**:641–642.

————. 1972. *Rebuchia ovata,* its vegetative morphology and classification with the Zosterophyllophytina. *Rev. Palaeobot. Palynol.* **14**:113–127.

————, and H. P. Banks. 1967. *Psilophyton princeps:* The search for organic connection. *Taxon* **16**:81–85.

————, and J. D. Grierson. 1961. On the occurrence of *Psilophyton princeps* in the early Upper Devonian of New York. *Amer. J. Bot.* **48**:473–479.

Kasper, A., and H. N. Andrews, Jr. 1972. *Pertica,* a new genus of Devonian plants from northern Maine. *Amer. J. Bot.* **59**:897–911.

————, ————, and W. H. Forbes. 1974. New fertile species of *Psilophyton* from the Devonian of Maine. *Amer. J. Bot.* **61**:339–359.

Kidston, R., and W. H. Lang. 1917. On Old Red Sandstone plants showing structure, from the Rhynie Chert Bed, Aberdeenshire, part 1: *Rhynia gwynne-vaughani,* K. and L. *Trans. Roy. Soc. Edinburgh* **51**:761–784.

———— and ————. 1920. On Old Red Sandstone plants showing structure, from the Rhynie Chert Bed, Aberdeenshire, part 2: Additional notes on *Rhynia gwynne-vaughani,* K. and L.; with descriptions of *Rhynia major,* n. sp., and *Hornea lignieri,* n.g., n. sp. *Trans. Roy. Soc. Edinburgh* **52**:603–627.

———— and ————. 1921. On Old Red Sandstone plants showing structure from the Rhynie Chert Bed, Aberdeenshire, part 4: Restorations of the vascular cryptogams, and discussion of their bearing on the general morphology of the Pteridophyta and the origin of the organization of land-plants. *Trans. Roy. Soc. Edinburgh* **52**:831–854.

———— and ————. 1923. Notes on fossil plants from the Old Red Sandstone of Scotland, part I: *Hicklingia edwardii,* K. and L. *Trans. Roy. Soc. Edinburgh* **53**:405–407.

Lele, K. M., and J. Walton. 1961. Contributions to the knowledge of *"Zosterophyllum myretonianum"* Penhallow from the Lower Old Red Sandstone of Angus. *Trans. Roy. Soc. Edinburgh* **64**:469–475.

Lundblad, B. 1972. A reconsideration of *Psilophyton (?) hedei* Halle, Silurian of Gotland (Sweden). *Rev. Palaeobot. Palynol.* **14**:135–139.

Remy, W. 1978. Der Dehiszenzmechanismus der Sporangien von *Rhynia. Argumenta Palaeobot.* **5**:23–30.

————, and R. Remy. 1980. Devonian gametophytes with anatomically preserved gametangia. *Science* **208**:295–296.

Skog, J. E., and H. P. Banks. 1973. *Ibyka amphikoma,* gen. et sp. n., a new protoarticulate precursor from the Late Middle Devonian of New York State. *Amer. J. Bot.* **60**:366–380.

Stevenson, D. W. 1974. Ultrastructure of the nacreous leptoids (sieve elements) in the polytrichaceous moss *Atrichum undulatum. Amer. J. Bot.* **61**:414–421.

Zimmermann, W. 1952. Main results of the "Telome Theory." *Palaeobotanist* **1**:456–470.

CHAPTER 8: Lycophyta

PROTOLEPIDODENDRALES

Andrews, H. N., Jr., C. B. Read, and S. H. Mamay. 1971. A Devonian lycopod stem with well-preserved cortical tissues. *Palaeontology* **14**:1–9.

Banks, H. P. 1960. Notes on Devonian lycopods. *Senckenberg Lethaea* **41**:59–88.

————. 1965. Some recent additions to the knowledge of the early land flora. *Phytomorphology* **15**:235–245.

————. 1967. The stratigraphic occurrence of early land plants and its bearing on their origin. *Int. Symp. Devonian Syst.* vol. II (D. H. Oswald, ed.), Alberta Soc. Petrol. Geol., Calgary, pp. 721–730.

————, and J. D. Grierson. 1968. *Drepanophycus spinaeformis* Göppert in the Early Upper Devonian of New York state. *Palaeontographica* **B123**:113–120.

————, P. M. Bonamo, and J. D. Grierson. 1972. *Leclercqia complexa* gen. et sp. nov., a new lycopod from the Late Middle Devonian of Eastern New York. *Rev. Palaeobot. Palynol.* **14**:19–40.

Boureau, E., S. Jovet-Ast, O. Höeg, and W. J. Chaloner. 1967. *Traité de Paléobotanique,* vol. II: *Bryophyta, Psilophyta, Lycophyta.* Masson et Cie, Paris.

Fairon-Demaret, M., and H. P. Banks. 1978. Leaves of *Archaeosigillaria vanuxemii,* a Devonian lycopod from New York. *Amer. J. Bot.* **65**:246–249.

Grierson, J. D., and H. P. Banks. 1963. Lycopods of the Devonian of New York state. *Palaeontographica Amer.* **4**:220–295.

————, and P. M. Bonamo. 1979. *Leclercqia complexa:* Earliest ligulate lycopod (Middle Devonian). *Amer. J. Bot.* **66**:474–476.

Kidston, R., and W. H. Lang. 1920. On Old Red Sandstone plants showing structure from the Rhynie Chert Bed, Aberdeenshire, part 3: *Asteroxylon mackiei,* K. and L. *Trans. Roy. Soc. Edinburgh* **52**:643–680.

Lacey, W. S. 1962. Welsh Lower Carboniferous plants, part I: The flora of the Lower Brown Limestone in the Vale of Clwyd, North Wales. *Palaeontographica* **B111**:126–160.

Lang, W. H., and I. C. Cookson. 1935. On a flora, including vascular land plants, associated with *Monograptus,* in rocks of Silurian age, from Victoria, Australia. *Phil. Trans. Roy. Soc. London* **B224**:421–449.

Lyon, A. G. 1964. Probable fertile region of *Asteroxylon mackiei,* K. and L. *Nature* **203**:1082–1083.

Schweitzer, H. 1965. Über *Bergeria* and *Protolepidodendron pulchra* aus dem Devon Westspitzbergens. *Palaeontographica* **B115**:117–138.

————. 1966. Die Mitteldevon-Flora von Lindlar (Rheinland), part 1: Lycopodiinae. *Palaeontographica* **B118**:93–112.

LEPIDODENDRALES

Andrews, H. N., Jr., and W. H. Murdy. 1958. *Lepidophloios*—And ontogeny in arborescent lycopods. *Amer. J. Bot.* **45**:552–559.

Balbach, M. K. 1967. Paleozoic lycopsid fructifications, part III: Conspecificity of British and North American *Lepidostrobus* petrifactions. *Amer. J. Bot.* **54**:867–875.

Brack, S. D. 1970. On a new structurally preserved arborescent lycopsid fructification from the Lower Pennsylvanian of North America. *Amer. J. Bot.* **57**:317–330.

Brack-Hanes, S. D. 1978. On the megagametophytes of two lepidodendracean cones. *Bot. Gaz.* **139**:140–146.

————, and J. C. Vaughn. 1978. Evidence of Paleozoic chromosomes from lycopod microgametophytes. *Science* **200**:1383–1385.

Delevoryas, T. 1957. Anatomy of *Sigillaria approximata. Amer. J. Bot.* **44**:654–660.

————. 1964. Ontogenetic studies of fossil plants. *Phytomorphology* **14**:299–314.

DiMichele, W. A. 1979a. Arborescent lycopods of Pennsylvanian age coals: *Lepidophloios. Palaeontographica* **B171**:57–77.

————. 1979b. Arborescent lycopods of Pennsylvanian age coals: *Lepidodendron dicentricum* C. Felix. *Palaeontographica* **B171**:122–136.

————, J. F. Mahaffy, and T. L. Phillips. 1979. Lycopods of Pennsylvanian age coals: *Polysporia. Can. J. Bot.* **57**:1740–1753.

Eggert, D. A. 1961. The ontogeny of Carboniferous arborescent Lycopsida. *Palaeontographica* **B108**:43–92.

————. 1972. Petrified *Stigmaria* of sigillarian origin from North America. *Rev. Palaeobot. Palynol.* **14**:85–99.

————, and N. Y. Kanemoto. 1977. Stem phloem of a Middle Pennsylvanian *Lepidodendron. Bot. Gas.* **138**:102–111.

Frankenberg, J. M., and D. A. Eggert. 1969. Petrified *Stigmaria* from North America, part I: *Stigmaria ficoides,* the underground portions of Lepidodendraceae. *Palaeontographica* **B128**:1–47.

Hanes, S. D. 1975. Structurally preserved lepidodendracean cones from the Pennsylvanian of North America. Ph.D. diss., Ohio Univ. 112 pages.

Jennings, J. R. 1972. A new lycopod genus from the Salem limestone (Mississippian of Illinois). *Palaeontographica* **B137**:72–84.

―――. 1973. The morphology of *Stigmaria stellata*. *Amer. J. Bot.* **60**:414–425.

―――. 1975. *Protostigmaria*, a new plant organ from the Lower Mississippian of Virginia. *Palaeontology* **18**:19–24.

Jonker, F. P. 1976. The Carboniferous "genera" *Ulodendron* and *Halonia*—An assessment. *Palaeontographica* **B157**:97–111.

Kräusel, R., and H. Weyland. 1929. Beiträge zur Kenntnis der Devonflora, part III. *Abh. Senckenberg Nat. Gesellsch.* **41**:317–359.

Leisman, G. A. 1970. A petrified *Sporangiostrobus* and its spores from the Middle Pennsylvanian of Kansas. *Palaeontographica* **B129**:166–177.

―――, and T. L. Phillips. 1979. Megasporangiate and microsporangiate cones of *Achlamydocarpon varius* from the Middle Pennsylvanian. *Palaeontographica* **B168**:100–128.

Mustafa, H. 1978. Beiträge zur Devonflora III. *Argumenta Palaeobot.* **5**:91–132.

Phillips, T. L. 1979. Reproduction of heterosporous arborescent lycopods in the Mississippian-Pennsylvanian of Euramerica. *Rev. Palaeobot. Palynol.* **27**:239–289.

―――, M. J. Avcin, and J. M. Schopf. 1975. Gametophytes and young sporophyte development in *Lepidocarpon*. *Bot. Soc. Amer., Abstr.*, p. 23.

Schopf, J. M. 1941. Contributions to Pennsylvanian paleobotany. *Mazocarpon oedipternum* sp. nov. and sigillarian relationships. *Ill. State Geol. Surv. Rept. Invest.* **75**:1–53.

Taylor, T. N., and S. D. Brack-Hanes. 1976. *Achlamydocarpon varius* comb. nov.: Morphology and reproductive biology. *Amer. J. Bot.* **63**:1257–1265.

―――, and D. A. Eggert. 1968. Petrified plants from the Upper Mississippian of North America, part II: *Lepidostrobus fayettevillense* sp. nov. *Amer. J. Bot.* **55**:306–313.

Thomas, B. A. 1966. The cuticle of the lepidodendroid stem. *New Phytol.* **65**:296–303.

―――. 1967a. The cuticle of two species of *Bothrodendron* (Lycopsida: Lepidodendrales). *J. Nat. Hist.* **1**:53–60.

―――. 1967b. *Ulodendron* Lindley and Hutton and its cuticle. *Ann. Bot.* **31**:775–782.

―――. 1970. Epidermal studies in the interpretation of *Lepidodendron* species. *Palaeontology* **12**:145–173.

―――. 1974. The lepidodendroid stoma. *Palaeontology* **17**:525–539.

―――. 1977. Epidermal studies in the interpretation of *Lepidophloios* species. *Palaeontology* **20**:273–293.

―――. 1978. Carboniferous Lepidodendraceae and Lepidocarpaceae. *Bot. Rev.* **44**:321–364.

―――, and J. Watson. 1976. A rediscovered 114-foot *Lepidodendron* from Bolton, Lancashire. *Geol. J.* **11**:15–20.

PLEUROMEIALES

Daugherty, L. H. 1941. The Upper Triassic flora of Arizona. *Carnegie Inst. Cont. Paleont. Publ.* **526**:1–108.

Dobruskina, I. A. 1974. Triassic lepidophytes. *Paleont. Zhur.* **3**:111–124.

Glaessner, M. F., and V. R. Rao. 1955. Lower Cretaceous plant remains from the vicinity of Mount Babbage, South Australia. *Trans. Proc. Roy. Soc. South Australia* **78**:134–140.

Kon'no, E. 1973. New species of *Pleuromeia* and *Neocalamites* from the Upper Scythian bed in the Kitakami Massif, Japan. *Sci. Rep. Tôhoku Univ., Sendai, Geol.* **43:**99–115.

Krassilov, V. A., and Yu. D. Zakharov. 1975. *Pleuromeia* from the Lower Triassic of the Far East of the U.S.S.R. *Rev. Palaeobot. Palynol.* **19:**221–232.

Miller, C. N., Jr. 1968. The lepidophytic affinities of the genus *Chinlea* and *Osmundites walkeri. Amer. J. Bot.* **55:**109–115.

Morbelli, M. A., and B. Petriella. 1973. *Austrostrobus ornatum* nov. gen. et sp. cono petrificado de Lycopsida del Triásico de Santa Cruz (Argentina). *Revta. Mus. La Plata 7, Sec. Paleont.* **46:**279–289.

Retallack, G. J. 1975. The life and times of a Triassic lycopod. *Alcheringa* **1:**3–29.

ISOETALES

Bose, M. N., and S. K. Roy. 1964. Studies on the Upper Gondwana of Kutch, part 2: Isoetaceae. *Palaeobotanist* **12:**226–228.

Brown, R. W. 1939. Some American fossil plants belonging to the Isoetales. *J. Wash. Acad. Sci.* **29:**261–269.

Karrfalt, E. E., and D. A. Eggert. 1977*a*. The comparative morphology and development of *Isoetes* L., part I: Lobe and furrow development in *I. tuckermanii* A. Br. *Bot. Gaz.* **138:**236–247.

——— and ———. 1977*b*. The comparative morphology and development of *Isoetes* L., part II: Branching of the base of the corm in *I. tuckermanii* A. Br. *Bot. Gaz.* **138:**357–368.

Pigg, K. B., and G. W. Rothwell. 1979. Stem-root transition of an Upper Pennsylvanian woody lycopsid. *Amer. J. Bot.* **66:**914–924.

LYCOPODIALES

Alvin, K. L. 1965. A new fertile lycopod from the Lower Carboniferous of Scotland. *Palaeontology* **8:**281–293.

Krassilov, V. A. 1978. Mesozoic lycopods and ferns from the Bureja Basin. *Palaeontographica* **B166:**16–29.

SELAGINELLALES

Darrah, W. C. 1938. A remarkable fossil *Selaginella* with preserved female gametophytes. *Bot. Mus. Leaflets, Harvard Univ.* **6:**113–136.

Fairon-Demaret, M. 1977. A new lycophyte from the Upper Devonian of Belgium. *Palaeontographica* **B162:**51–63.

Leisman, G. A. 1961. Further observations on the structure of *Selaginellites crassicinctus. Amer. J. Bot.* **48:**224–229.

Lundblad, B. 1950. On a fossil *Selaginella* from the Rhaetic of Hyllinge, Scania. *Svensk. Bot. Tidskrift* **44:**477–487.

Phillips, T. L., and G. A. Leisman. 1966. *Paurodendron,* a rhizomorphic lycopod. *Amer. J. Bot.* **53:**1086–1100.

Schlanker, C. M., and G. A. Leisman. 1969. The herbaceous Carboniferous lycopod *Selaginella fraiponti* comb. nov. *Bot. Gaz.* **130:**35–41.

CHAPTER 9: Sphenophyta

PSEUDOBORNIALES

Mägdefrau, K. 1973. *Geschichte der Botanik—Leben und Leistung grosser Forscher.* Gustav Fischer Verlag, Stuttgart.

Mamay, S. H. 1962. Occurrence of *Pseudobornia* Nathorst in Alaska. *Palaeobotanist* **11:**19–22.

Nathorst, A. G. 1894. Zur fossilen Flora der Polarländer. 1. Teil, 1. Lief. Zur paläozischen Flora der arktischen Zone. *Kgl. Svenska Vet. Akad. Handl.* **26:**1–80.

———. 1899. Uber die oberdevonische Flora (Die "Ursaflora") der Bäreninsel. *Bull. Geol. Inst. Upsala* **8:**1–5.

———. 1902. Zur fossilen Flora der Polarländer. 1. Teil, 3. Lief. Zur oberdevonischen Flora der Bäreninsel. *Kgl. Svenska Vet. Akad. Handl.* **26:**1–60.

Schweitzer, H. J. 1967. Die Oberdevon-flora der Bäreninsel, part 1: *Pseudobornia ursina* Nathorst. *Palaeontographica* **B120:**116–137.

SPHENOPHYLLALES

Abbott, M. L. 1958. The American species of *Asterophyllites, Annularia* and *Sphenophyllum. Bull. Amer. Paleo.* **38:**289–390.

Baxter, R. W. 1950. *Peltastrobus reedae:* A new sphenopsid cone from the Pennsylvanian of Indiana. *Bot. Gaz.* **112:**174–182.

Good, C. W. 1973. Studies of *Sphenophyllum* shoots: Species delimitation within the taxon *Sphenophyllum. Amer. J. Bot.* **60:**929–939.

———, and T. N. Taylor. 1972. The ontogeny of Carboniferous articulates: The apex of *Sphenophyllum. Amer. J. Bot.* **59:**617–626.

Hoskins, J. H., and A. T. Cross. 1943. Monograph of the Paleozoic cône genus *Bowmanites* (Sphenophyllales). *Amer. Midl. Natur.* **30:**113–163.

Leclercq, S. 1957. Étude d'une fructification de Sphénopside à structure conservée du dévonien supérieur. *Acad. Roy. Belgique* (2)**14:**1–39.

Leisman, G. A., and C. Graves. 1964. The structure of the fossil sphenopsid cone, *Peltastrobus reedae. Amer. Midl. Natur.* **72:**426–437.

Levittan, E. D., and E. S. Barghoorn. 1948. *Sphenostrobus thompsonii:* A new genus of the Sphenophyllales. *Amer. J. Bot.* **35:**350–358.

Mamay, S. H. 1959. A new bowmanitean fructification from the Pennsylvanian of Kansas. *Amer. J. Bot.* **46:**530–536.

Phillips, T. L. 1959. A new sphenophyllalean shoot system from the Pennsylvanian. *Ann. Missouri Bot. Gard.* **46:**1–17.

Remy, R., and W. Remy. 1961. Beitrage zur Flora des Autuniens, part II. *Mber. Dtsch. Akad. Wiss., Berlin* **3:**213–225.

Taylor, T. N. 1969. On the structure of *Bowmanites dawsoni* from the Lower Pennsylvanian of North America. *Palaeontographica* **B125:**65–72.

———. 1970. The morphology of *Bowmanites dawsoni* spores. *Micropaleontology* **16:**243–248.

EQUISETALES

Agashe, S. N. 1964. The extra-xylary tissues of certain *Calamites* from the American Carboniferous. *Phytomorphology* **14**:598–611.

———, and S. T. Tilak. 1970. Occurrence of fungal elements in the bark of arborescent calamite roots from the American Carboniferous. *Bull. Torrey Bot. Club* **97**:216–218.

Andrews, H. N., Jr. 1952. Some American petrified calamitean stems. *Ann. Missouri Bot. Gard.* **39**:189–218.

Arnold, C. A. 1956. A new calamite from Colorado. *Cont. Mus. Paleo. Univ. Mich.* **13**:161–173.

Batten, D. J. 1968. Probable dispersed spores of Cretaceous *Equisetites*. *Palaeontology* **11**:633–642.

Baxter, R. W. 1955. *Palaeostachya andrewsii*, a new species of calamitean cone from the American Carboniferous. *Amer. J. Bot.* **42**:342–351.

———. 1962. A *Palaeostachya* cone from southeast Kansas. *Univ. Kansas Sci. Bull.* **43**:75–81.

Brown, J. T. 1975. *Equisetum clarnoi*, a new species based on petrifactions from the Eocene of Oregon. *Amer. J. Bot.* **62**:410–415.

Chaphekar, M. 1963. Some calamitean plants from the Lower Carboniferous of Scotland. *Palaeontology* **6**:408–429.

———. 1965. On the genus *Pothocites* Paterson. *Palaeontology* **8**:107–112.

Delevoryas, T. 1955. A *Palaeostachya* from the Pennsylvanian of Kansas. *Amer. J. Bot.* **42**:481–488.

Eggert, D. A. 1962. The ontogeny of Carboniferous arborescent Sphenopsida. *Palaeontographica* **B110**:99–127.

Good, C. W. 1971*a*. The ontogeny of Carboniferous articulates: *Calamostachys binneyana*. *Bot. Gaz.* **132**:337–346.

———. 1971*b*. The ontogeny of Carboniferous articulates: Calamite leaves and twigs. *Palaeontographica* **B133**:137–158.

———. 1975. Pennsylvanian-age calamitean cones, elater-bearing spores, and associated vegetative organs. *Palaeontographica* **B153**:28–99.

———. 1976. The anatomy and three-dimensional morphology of *Annularia hoskinsii* sp. n. *Amer. J. Bot.* **63**:719–725.

———, and T. N. Taylor. 1974. The establishment of *Elaterites triferens* spores in *Calamocarpon insignis* microsporangia. *Trans. Amer. Micros. Soc.* **93**:148–151.

——— and ———. 1975. The morphology and systematic position of calamitean elater-bearing spores. *Geosci. Man.* **11**:133–139.

Harris, T. M. 1931. The fossil flora of Scoresby Sound East Greenland, part 1: Cryptogams (exclusive of Lycopodiales). *Medd. Gronland* **85**:1–102.

Hibbert, F. A., and D. A. Eggert. 1965. A new calamitean cone from the Middle Pennsylvanian of southern Illinois. *Palaeontology* **8**:681–686.

Jennings, J. R. 1970. Preliminary report on fossil plants from the Chester Series (Upper Mississippian) of Illinois. *Trans. Ill. Acad. Sci.* **63**:167–177.

Kosanke, R. M. 1955. *Mazostachys*—A new calamitean fructification. *Ill. State Geol. Surv. Rept. Invest.* **180**.

Lacey, W. S., and D. A. Eggert. 1964. A flora from the Chester Series (Upper Mississippian) of southern Illinois. *Amer. J. Bot.* **51**:976–985.

——— D. E. Van Dijk, and K. D. Gordon-Gray. 1975. Fossil plants from the Upper

Permian in the Mooi River district of Natal, South Africa. *Ann. Natal Mus.* **22:**349–420.

Leisman, G. A., and J. L. Bucher. 1971. On *Palaeostachya decacnema* from the Middle Pennsylvanian of Kansas. *Bull. Torrey Bot. Club* **98:**140–144.

Melchior, R. C., and J. A. Hall. 1961. A calamitean shoot apex from the Pennsylvanian of Iowa. *Amer. J. Bot.* **48:**811–815.

Pant, D. D., and P. F. Kidwai. 1968. On the structure of stems and leaves of *Phyllotheca indica* Bunbury, and its affinities. *Palaeontographica* **B121:**102–121.

Rothwell, G. W., and T. N. Taylor, 1971*a*. Studies of calamitean cones: *Weissia kentuckiense* gen. et sp. nov. *Bot. Gaz.* **132:**215–224.

———— and ————. 1971*b*. *Weissistachys kentuckiensis:* A new name for *Weissia kentuckiense* Rothwell and Taylor. *Bot. Gaz.* **132:**371–372.

Scott, D. H. 1897. On *Cheirostrobus,* a new type of fossil cone from the Lower Carboniferous strata (Calciferous Sandstone Series). *Phil. Trans. Roy. Soc. London* **189:**1–34.

Taylor, T. N. 1967. On the structure of *Calamostachys binneyana* from the Lower Pennsylvanian of North America. *Amer. J. Bot.* **54:**298–305.

Thomas, B. A. 1969. A new British Carboniferous calamite cone, *Paracalamostachys spadiciformis. Palaeontology* **12:**253–261.

Townrow, J. A. 1955. On some species of *Phyllotheca. Roy. Soc. New South Wales, J. Proc.* **89:**39–63.

White, D. 1937. Fossil flora of the Wedington Sandstone member of the Fayetteville Shale. *U.S.G.S. Prof. Paper* **B186:**13–40.

Wilson, M. L., and D. A. Eggert. 1974. Root phloem of fossil tree-sized arthrophytes. *Bot. Gaz.* **135:**319–328.

Zalessky, M. S. 1927. Flore permienne des limites ouraliennes de l'Angaride. *Comité Russe Géol. Mém. Leningrad* **176:**1–52.

CHAPTER 10: Pteridophyta

CLADOXYLOPSIDA

Bertrand, P. 1914. *État actuel de nos connaissances sur les genres Cladoxylon et Steloxylon.* C.R. Assoc. Fr. Avanc. Sci., Le Havre, pp. 446–448.

————. 1935. Contribution a l'étude des Cladoxylées de Saalfeld. *Palaeontographica* **B80:**101–170.

Bonamo, P. M., and H. P. Banks. 1966. *Calamophyton* in the Middle Devonian of New York. *Amer. J. Bot.* **53:**778–791.

Gothan, W., and H. Weyland. 1964. *Lehrbuch der Paläobotanik.* Akademie-Verlag, Berlin. 594 pages.

Hueber, F. M. 1960. Contributions to the fossil flora of the Onteora "Red Beds" (Upper Devonian) in New York State. Ph.D. diss., Cornell Univ. Mic. No. 61-1432, Univ. Microfilms, Inc., Ann Arbor, Mich.

Kräusel, R., and H. Weyland. 1926. Beiträge zur Kenntnis der Devonflora, part II. *Abh. Senckenb. Naturforsch. Ges.* **40**:115–155.

———— and ————. 1941. Pflanzenreste aus dem Devon von Nord-Amerika. *Palaeontographica* **B86**:1–78.

Leclercq, S., and H. P. Banks. 1962. *Pseudosporochnus nodosus* sp. nov., a Middle Devonian plant with Cladoxylalean affinities. *Palaeontographica* **B110**:1–34.

————, and K. M. Lele. 1968. Further investigation on the vascular system of *Pseudosporochnus nodosus. Palaeontographica* **B123**:97–112.

————, and H. J. Schweitzer. 1965. *Calamophyton* is not a sphenopsid. *Bull. Acad. Belg. Cl. Sci.* (5)**51**:1395–1403.

Long, A. G. 1968. Some specimens of *Cladoxylon* from the Calciferous Sandstone Series of Berwickshire. *Trans. Roy. Soc. Edinburgh* **68**:45–61.

Matten, L. C. 1974. The Givetian flora from Cairo, New York: *Rhacophyton, Triloboxylon* and *Cladoxylon. Bot. J. Linn. Soc.* **68**:303–318.

Read, C. B. 1935. An occurrence of the genus *Cladoxylon* in North America. *J. Wash. Acad. Sci.* **25**:493–497.

————, and G. Campbell. 1939. Preliminary account of the New Albany Shale Flora. *Amer. Midl. Natur.* **21**:435–453.

Scheckler, S. E. 1975. *Rhymokalon,* a new plant with cladoxylalean anatomy from the Upper Devonian of New York State. *Can. J. Bot.* **53**:25–38.

Schweitzer, H. J. 1968. Pflanzenreste aus dem Devon Nord-Westspitzbergens. *Palaeontographica* **B123**:43–75.

————. 1972. Die Mitteldevon-flora von Lindlar (Rheinland), part 3: Filicinae—*Hyenia elegans* Kräusel and Weyland. *Palaeontographica* **B137**:154–175.

————. 1973. Die Mitteldevon-flora von Lindlar (Rheinland), part 4: Filicinae—*Calamophyton primaevum* Kräusel and Weyland. *Palaeontographica* **B140**:117–150.

Unger, F. 1856. Beiträge zur Paleontologie des Thüringer Waldes, part II: Scheifer und Sandstein Flora. *K. Akad. Wiss. Wien Denkschr.* **11**:139–186.

RHACOPHYTOPSIDA

Anamiev, A. R. 1960. Studies in the Middle Devonian flora of the Altai-Sayan Mountain Region. *Bot. Zhur.* **45**:649–666 (in Russian).

Andrews, H. N., Jr., and T. L. Phillips. 1968. *Rhacophyton* from the Upper Devonian of West Virginia. *Bot. J. Linn. Soc.* **61**:37–64.

Cornet, B., T. L. Phillips, and H. N. Andrews, Jr. 1976. The morphology and variation in *Rhacophyton ceratangium* from the Upper Devonian and its bearing on frond evolution. *Palaeontographica* **B158**:105–129.

Crépin, F. 1875. Observations sur quelques plantes fossiles des dépots dévoniens rapportés par Dumont à l'étage quartzoschisteux inférieur de son système eifelien. *Bull. Soc. Roy. Bot. Belg* **14**:214–230.

Kräusel, R., and H. Weyland. 1941. Pflanzenreste aus dem Devon von Nord-Amerika, part II: Die oberdevonischen Floren von Elkins, West-Virginien und Perry, Maine, mit Berücksichtigung einiger Stücke von der Chaleur-Bai, Canada. *Palaeontographica* **B86**:1–78.

Leclercq, S. 1951. Étude morphologique et anatomique d'une fougère du dévonien supérieur, le *Rhacophyton zygopteroides* nov. sp. *Ann. Soc. Géol. Belg. Mem.* **40**:1–62.

————. 1954. An Upper Devonian zygopterid showing clepsydropsoid and etapteroid features. *Amer. J. Bot.* **41**:488–492.

Matten, L. C. 1974. The Givetian flora from Cairo, New York: *Rhacophyton, Triloboxylon* and *Cladoxylon. Bot. J. Linn. Soc.* **68:**303–318.

Scheckler, S. E. 1974. Systematic characters in Devonian ferns. *Ann. Missouri Bot. Gard.* **61:**462–473.

Schultka, St. 1978. Beiträge zur Anatomie von *Rhacophyton condrusorum* Crépin. *Argumenta Palaeobot.* **5:**11–22.

Schweitzer, H. J. 1968. Pflanzenreste aus dem Devon Nord-Westspitzbergens. *Palaeontographica* **B123:**43–75.

COENOPTERIDOPSIDA

Stauropteridales

Chaloner, W. G. 1958. Isolated megaspore tetrads of *Stauropteris burntislandica. Ann. Bot.* **22:**197–204.

Eggert, D. A. 1964. The question of the phylogenetic position of the Coenopteridales. *Mem. Torrey Bot. Club* **21:**38–57.

Lacey, W. S., K. W. Joy, and A. J. Willis. 1957. Observations on the aphlebiae and megasporangia of *Stauropteris burntislandica* P. Bertrand. *Ann. Bot.* **21:**621–625.

Scott, R. 1908. On *Bensonites fusiformis* sp. nov., a fossil associated with *Stauropteris burntislandica* P. Bertrand, and on the sporangia of the latter. *Ann. Bot.* **22:**683–687.

Surange, K. R. 1952. The morphology of *Stauropteris burntislandica* P. Bertrand and its megasporangium *Bensonites fusiformis* R. Scott. *Phil. Trans. Roy. Soc. London* **B237:**73–91.

Zygopteridales

Abbott, M. L. 1961. A coenopterid fern fructification from the Upper Freeport No. 7 coal in southeastern Ohio. *J. Paleo.* **35:**981–985.

Barthel, M. 1968. *"Pecopteris" feminaeformis* (Schlotheim) Sterzel und *"Araucarites" spiciformis* Andrae in Germar—Coenopterideen des Stephans und Unteren Perms. *Paläont. Abh.* **B2:**727–742.

Chaphekar, M., and K. L. Alvin. 1972. On the fertile parts of the coenopterid fern *Metaclepsydropsis duplex* (Williamson). *Rev. Palaeobot. Paylnol.* **14:**63–76.

Cridland, A. A. 1966. *Biscalitheca kansana* sp. n. (Coenopteridales, Zygopteridaceae), a compression from the Lawrence Shale (Upper Pennsylvanian), Kansas, U.S.A. *Amer. J. Bot.* **53:**987–994.

Darrah, W. C. 1941. The coenopterid ferns in American coal balls. *Amer. Midl. Natur.* **25:**233–269.

Dennis, R. L. 1974. Studies of Paleozoic ferns: *Zygopteris* from the Middle and Upper Pennsylvanian of the United States. *Palaeontographica* **B148:**95–136.

Galtier, J. 1963. Structure et ramification du phyllophore chez un *Dineuron* du Carbonifère inférieur. *Naturalia Monspel., Sér. Bot.* **15:**82–92.

———. 1964. Anatomie comparée et affinites de deux Zygopteridacées Carbonifère inférieur. *C.R. Acad. Sci. Paris* **259:**4764–4767.

———. 1966a. Un phyllophore de *Clepsydropsis* à ramification quadriseriée. *C.R. Acad. Sci. Paris* **263:**232–235.

———. 1966b. Observations nouvelles sur le genre *Clepsydropsis. Naturalia Monspel., Sér. Bot.* **17:**111–129.

————. 1968. Un nouveau type de fructification filicinéene du Carbonifère inférieur. *C.R. Acad. Sci. Paris* **D266:**1004–1007.

————, and L. Grambast. 1972. Observations nouvelles sur les structures réproductrices attribuées à *Zygopteris lacattei* (Coenopteridales de l'Autuno-Stéphanien français). *Rev. Palaeobot. Palynol.* **14:**101–111.

————, and J. Holmes. 1976. Un *Corynepteris* à structure conservée du Westphalien d'Angleterre. *C.R. Acad. Sci. Paris* **D282:**1265–1268.

————, and A. C. Scott. 1979. Studies of Paleozoic ferns: On the genus *Corynepteris*. A redescription of the type and some other European species. *Palaeontographica* **B170:**81–125.

Gordon, W. T. 1911*a*. On the structure and affinities of *Metaclepsydropsis duplex* (Williamson). *Trans. Roy. Soc. Edinburgh* **48:**163–190.

————. 1911*b*. On the structure and affinities of *Diplolabis römeri* (Solms). *Trans. Roy. Soc. Edinburgh* **47:**711–736.

Jennings, J. R. 1975. Lower Pennsylvanian plants of Illinois, part II: Structurally preserved *Alloiopteris* from the Drury Shale. *J. Paleo.* **49:**52–57.

Leclercq, S. 1931. Sur l'évolution des *Etapteris*. *Ann. Soc. Géol. Belgique* **55:**51–59.

Long, A. C. 1976. *Rowleya trifurcata* gen. et sp. nov., a simple petrified vascular plant from the Lower Coal Measures (Westphalian A) of Lancashire. *Trans. Roy. Soc. Edinburgh* **69:**467–481.

Mamay, S. H. 1957. *Biscalitheca,* a new genus of Pennsylvanian oeconopterids, based on its fructification. *Amer. J. Bot.* **44:**229–239.

Phillips, T. L. 1974. Evolution of vegetative morphology in coenopterid ferns. *Ann. Missouri Bot. Gard.* **61:**427–461.

————, and H. N. Andrews, Jr. 1968. *Biscalitheca* (Coenopteridales) from the Upper Pennsylvanian of Illinois. *Palaeontology* **11:**104–115.

Sahni, B. 1928. On *Clepsydropsis australis,* a zygopterid tree-fern with a *Tempskya*-like false stem, from the Carboniferous rocks of Australia. *Phil. Trans. Roy. Soc. London* **B217:**1–37.

————. 1930. On *Asterochlaenopsis,* a new genus of zygopterid tree-ferns from western Siberia. *Phil. Trans. Roy. Soc. London* **B218:**447–471.

————. 1932. On the structure of *Zygopteris primaria* (Cotta) and on the relations between the genera *Zygopteris, Etapteris* and *Botrychioxylon*. *Phil. Trans. Roy. Soc. London* **B222:**29–45.

Smoot, E. L., and T. N. Taylor. 1978. Sieve areas in fossil phloem. *Science* **202:**1081–1083.

Taylor, T. N., and M. A. Millay. 1977. Structurally preserved fossil cell contents. *Trans. Amer. Micros. Soc.* **96:**390–393.

FILICOPSIDA

Marattiales

Asama, L. 1960. Evolution of leaf forms through the ages explained by the successive retardation and neotony. *Sci. Rep. Tôhoku Univ., Geol. Spec.* (2)**4:**252–280.

Brousmiche, C. 1979. *Pecopteris (Asterotheca) saraei* P. Corsin, 1951, forme fertile de *Sphenopteris damesii* (Stur, 1885). *Géobios* **12:**75–97.

DiMichele, W. A., and T. L. Phillips. 1977. Monocyclic *Psaronius* from the Lower Pennsylvanian of the Illinois Basin. *Can. J. Bot.* **55:**2514–2524.

Ehret, D. L., and T. L. Phillips. 1977. *Psaronius* root systems—Morphology and development. *Palaeontographica* **B161:**147–164.

Harris, T. M. 1961. *The Yorkshire Jurassic Flora*, vol. I: *Thallophyta-Pteridophyta*. British Museum (Natural History), London.

Jennings, J. R., and M. A. Millay. 1978. A new permineralized marattialean fern from the Pennsylvanian of Illinois. *Palaeontology* **21**:709–716.

Klipper, K. 1964. Uber die Rät-Lias-Flora aus dem Nördlichen abfall des Albers-Gebirges in Nordiran, part 1: Bryophyta und Pteridophyta. *Palaeontographica* **B114**:1–78.

Knowlton, F. H. 1922. Revision of the flora of the Green River Formation, with description of new species. *U.S.G.S. Prof. Paper* **F131**:133–182.

Laveine, J. 1969. Quelques Pécopteridinées houillères à lumière de la palynologie. *Pollen Spores* **11**:619–685.

Lundblad, B. 1950. Studies in the Rhaeto-Liassic floras of Sweden, part I: Pteridophyta, Pteridospermae, and Cycadophyta from the mining district of NW Scania. *Kungl. Svenska Vet. Handl. Fjarde Ser.* **1**(8):1–82.

Millay, M. A. 1977. *Acaulangium* gen. n., a fertile marattialean from the Upper Pennsylvanian of Illinois. *Amer. J. Bot.* **64**:223–229.

———. 1978. Studies of Paleozoic marattialeans: The morphology and phylogenetic position of *Eoangiopteris goodii* sp. n. *Amer. J. Bot.* **65**:577–583.

———. 1979. Studies of Paleozoic marattialeans: A monograph of the American species of *Scolecopteris*. *Palaeontographica* **B169**:1–69.

Morgan, J. 1959. The morphology and anatomy of American species of the genus *Psaronius*. *Ill. Biol. Monogr.* **27**:1–108.

———, and T. Delevoryas. 1952a. An anatomical study of *Stipitopteris*. *Amer. J. Bot.* **39**:474–478.

——— and ———. 1952b. *Stewartiopteris singularis:* A new psaroniaceous fern rachis. *Amer. J. Bot.* **39**:479–484.

Pfefferkorn, H. W. 1976. Pennsylvanian tree fern compressions *Caulopteris, Megaphyton* and *Artisophyton* gen. nov. in Illinois. *Illinois State Geol. Surv. Circ.* **492**:1–31.

Seward, A. C., and B. Sahni. 1920. Indian Gondwana plants: A revision. *Mem. Geol. Surv. India (Palaeontologia Indica), N.S.* **7**:1–42.

Stidd, B. M. 1971. Morphology and anatomy of the frond of *Psaronius*. *Palaeontographica* **B134**:87–123.

———. 1974. Evolutionary trends in the Marattiales. *Ann. Missouri Bot. Gard.* **61**:388–407.

———, and T. L. Phillips. 1968. Basal stem anatomy of *Psaronius*. *Amer. J. Bot.* **55**:834–840.

Taylor, T. N. 1967. On the structure and phylogenetic relationships of the fern *Radstockia* Kidston. *Palaeontology* **10**:43–46.

Filicales

Botryopteridaceae

Delevoryas, T., and J. Morgan. 1954. Observations on petiolar branching and foliage of an American *Botryopteris*. *Amer. Midl. Natur.* **52**:374–387.

Dennis, R. L. 1968. *Rhabdoxylon americanum* sp. n., a structurally simple fern-like plant from the Upper Pennsylvanian of Illinois. *Amer. J. Bot.* **55**:989–995.

Galtier, J. 1967. Les sporanges de *Botryopteris antiqua* Kidston. *C.R. Acad. Sci. Paris* **D264**:897–900.

———, and T. L. Phillips. 1977. Morphology and evolution of *Botryopteris*, a

Carboniferous age fern, part 2: Observations on Stephanian species from Grand-Croix, France. *Palaeontographica* **B164**:1–32.

Holden, H. S. 1962. The morphology of *Botryopteris antiqua. Bull. Brit. Mus. (Nat. Hist.) Geol.* **5**:359–380.

Holmes, J. C. 1979. Further observations on the coenopterid fern genus, *Rhabdoxylon. Ann. Bot.* **44**:113–119.

————, and J. Galtier. 1976. Twin shoots borne on a *Botryopteris* frond from the British Upper Carboniferous. *Rev. Palaeobot. Palynol.* **22**:207–224.

Long, A. G. 1943. On the occurrence of buds on the leaves of *Botryopteris hirsuta* Will. *Ann. Bot.* **7**:133–146.

Millay, M. A., and T. N. Taylor. 1979. An unusual botryopterid sporangial aggregation from the Middle Pennsylvanian of North America. *Amer. J. Bot.* (in press).

Murdy, W. H., and H. N. Andrews, Jr. 1957. A study of *Botryopteris globosa* Darrah. *Bull. Torrey Bot. Club* **84**:252–267.

Phillips, T. L. 1970. Morphology and evolution of *Botryopteris*, a Carboniferous age fern, part 1: Observations on some European species. *Palaeontographica* **B130**:137–172.

————, and S. W. Russo. 1970. Spores of *Botryopteris globosa* and *Botryopteris americana* from the Pennsylvanian. *Amer. J. Bot.* **57**:543–551.

Anachoropteridaceae

Bancroft, H. 1915. A contribution to our knowledge of *Rachiopteris cylindrica* Will. *Ann. Bot.* **29**:532–565.

Delevoryas, T., and J. Morgan. 1952. *Tubicaulis multiscalariformis:* A new American coenopterid. *Amer. J. Bot.* **39**:160–166.

———— and ————. 1954*a*. A further investigation of the morphology of *Anachoropteris clavata. Amer. J. Bot.* **41**:192–198.

———— and ————. 1954*b*. An anatomical study of a new coenopterid and its bearing on the morphology of certain coenopterid petioles. *Amer. J. Bot.* **41**:198–203.

Eggert, D. A. 1959. Studies of Paleozoic ferns: *Tubicaulis stewartii* sp. nov. and evolutionary trends in the genus. *Amer. J. Bot.* **46**:594–602.

Galtier, J. 1971. La fructification du *Botryopteris forensis* Renault (Coenoptéridales du Stéphanien français): Précisions sur les sporanges et les spores. *Naturalia Monspel. Sér. Bot.* **22**:145–155.

Hall, J. W. 1961. *Anachoropteris involuta* and its attachment to a *Tubicaulis* type of stem from the Pennsylvanian of Iowa. *Amer. J. Bot.* **48**:731–737.

Holden, H. S. 1960. The morphology and relationships of *Rachiopteris cylindrica. Bull Brit. Mus. (Nat. Hist.)* **4**:51–69.

————, and W. Croft. 1962. The morphology of *Tubicaulis africanus* sp. nov., a fossil fern from Tanganyika. *Bull. Brit. Mus. (Nat. Hist.)* **7**:197–211.

Holmes, J. C. 1977*a*. The Carboniferous fern *Psalixochlaena cylindrica* as found in Westphalian A coal balls from England, part I: Structure and development of the cauline system. *Palaeontographica* **B164**:33–75.

————. 1977*b*. Variabilité morphologique et développement du système caulinaire de *Psalixochlaena cylindrica. C.R. Acad. Sci. Paris* **D284**:1761–1764.

————, and J. Galtier. 1975. Ramification dichotomique et ramification latérale chez *Psalixochlaena cylindrica,* fougère du Carbonifère moyen d'Angleterre. *C.R. Acad. Sci. Paris* **D280**:1071–1074.

Long, A. G. 1976. *Psalixochlaena berwickense* sp. nov., a Lower Carboniferous fern from Berwickshire. *Trans. Roy. Soc. Edinburgh* **69**:513–521.

Phillips, T. L., and H. N. Andrews, Jr. 1965. A fructification of *Anachoropteris* from the Middle Pennsylvanian of Illinois. *Ann. Missouri Bot. Gard.* **52**:251–261.

Sermayaceae

Eggert, D. A., and T. Delevoryas. 1967. Studies of Paleozoic ferns: *Sermaya*, gen. nov. and its bearing on filicalean evolution in the Paleozoic. *Palaeontographica* **B120**:169–180.

Phillips, T. L. 1974. Evolution of vegetative morphology in coenopterid ferns. *Ann. Missouri Bot. Gard.* **61**:427–461.

Rothwell, G. W. 1978. *Doneggia complura* gen. et sp. nov., a filicalean fern from the Upper Pennsylvanian of Ohio. *Can. J. Bot.* **56**:3096–3104.

Tedeleaceae

Andrews, H. N., Jr. 1956. A note on the nodal anatomy of *Ankropteris glabra* Baxter. *Ann. Missouri Bot. Gard.* **43**:379–380.

Baxter, R. W. 1951. *Ankropteris glabra,* a new American species of the Zygopteridaceae. *Amer. J. Bot.* **38**:440–452.

Eggert, D. A. 1959. Studies of Paleozoic ferns. The morphology, anatomy and taxonomy of *Ankyropteris glabra. Amer. J. Bot.* **46**:510–520.

———. 1963. Studies of Paleozoic ferns: The frond of *Ankyropteris glabra. Amer. J. Bot.* **50**:379–387.

———, and T. N. Taylor. 1966. Studies of Paleozoic ferns: On the genus *Tedelea* gen. nov. *Palaeontographica* **B118**:52–73.

Holden, H. S. 1930. On the structure and affinities of *Ankyropteris corrugata. Phil. Trans. Roy. Soc. London* **B218**:79–114.

Read, C. B. 1938. A new fern from the Johns Valley Shale of Oklahoma. *Amer. J. Bot.* **25**:335–338.

Osmundaceae

Archangelsky, S., and E. R. de la Sota. 1963. *Osmundites herbstii,* nueve petrifacacion Triasica de el Tranquillo, Provincia de Santa Cruz. *Ameghiniana* **3**:135–140.

Arnold, C. A. 1952. Fossil Osmundaceae from the Eocene of Oregon. *Palaeontographica* **B42**:63–78.

Brongniart, A. 1849. Tableux des genres des végétaux fossiles. *Dict. Univ. Hist. Nat.* **13**:35–36.

Daugherty, L. H. 1960. *Itopsidema,* a new genus of the Osmundaceae from the Triassic of Arizona. *Amer. J. Bot.* **47**:771–777.

Eichwald, E. 1860. *Lethaea Rossica ou Paléontologie de la Russie,* vol. I. part 1, pp. 1–681; part 2, pp. 682–1587. E. Schweizerbart, Stuttgart.

Gould, R. E. 1970. *Palaeosmunda,* a new genus of siphonostelic osmundaceous trunks from the Upper Permian of Queensland. *Palaeontology* **13**:10–28.

Gwynne-Vaughan, D. T. 1911. Some remarks on the anatomy of the Osmundaceae. *Ann. Bot.* **25**:525–536.

Herbst, R. 1975. On *Osmundacaulis carnieri* (Schuster) Miller and *Osmundacaulis braziliensis* (Andrews) Miller. In: K. S. Campbell (ed.), *Gondwana geology,* Australian University National Press, Canberra, pp. 117–123.

Hewitson, W. 1962. Comparative morphology of the Osmundaceae. *Ann. Missouri Bot. Gard.* **49**:57–93.

Miller, C. N., Jr. 1967. Evolution of the fern genus *Osmunda*. *Cont. Mus. Paleont. Univ. Mich.* **21:**139–203.

———. 1971. Evolution of the fern family Osmundaceae based on anatomical studies. *Cont. Mus. Paleont. Univ. Mich.* **23:**105–169.

Seward, A. C. 1907. Notes on fossil plants from South Africa. *Geol. Mag. N.S.* **4:**481–487.

Van Konijnenburg-Van Cittert, J. H. A. 1978. Osmundaceous spores *in situ* from the Jurassic of Yorkshire, England. *Rev. Palaeobot. Palynol.* **26:**125–141.

Zalessky, M. D. 1931*a*. Structure anatomique du stipe du *Petcheropteris splendida* n.g. et sp., un nouveau représentant des Osmundacées permiennes. *Bull. Acad. Sci. U.S.S.R., Cl. Sci., Math., Nat.* (7)**5:**705–710.

———. 1931*b*. Structure anatomique du stipe du *Chasmatopteris principalis* n.g. et sp., un nouveau représentant des Osmundacées permiennes. *Bull. Acad. Sci. U.S.S.R., Cl. Sci., Math., Nat.* (7)**5:**715–720.

Schizaeaceae

Bolchovitina, N. A. 1961. Fossil and modern spores of the Schizaeaceae family. *Akad. Nauk SSSR., Trudy Geol. Inst.* **40:**1–176 (in Russian).

Brown, R. W. 1943. A climbing fern from the Upper Cretaceous of Wyoming. *J. Wash. Acad. Sci.* **33:**141–142.

Chandler, M. E. J. 1955. The Schizaeaceae of the south of England in early Tertiary times. *Bull. Brit. Mus. (Nat. Hist.) Geol.* **2:**291–314.

Harris, T. M. 1961. *The Yorkshire Jurassic Flora* vol. I: *Thallophyta-Pteridophyta*. British Museum (Natural History), London.

Jennings, J. R., and D. A. Eggert. 1977. Preliminary report on permineralized *Senftenbergia* from the Chester Series of Illinois. *Rev. Palaeobot. Palynol.* **24:**221–225.

Gleicheniaceae

Abbott, M. L. 1954. Revision of the Paleozoic fern genus *Oligocarpia*. *Palaeontographica* **B96:**39–65.

Andrews, H. N., Jr., and C. S. Pearsall. 1941. On the flora of the Frontier Formation of southwestern Wyoming. *Ann. Missouri Bot. Gard.* **28:**165–192.

Bolchovitina, N. A. 1967. The fossil spores of the family Gleicheniaceae (morphology and taxonomy). *Rev. Palaeobot. Palynol.* **3:**59–64.

———. 1968. The spores of the family Gleicheniaceae ferns and their importance for the stratigraphy. *Acad. Nauk, SSSR., Geol. Inst. Trans.* **186:**1–116 (in Russian).

Halle, T. G. 1927. Palaeozoic plants from central Shansi. *Palaeont. Sinica* **2:**1–316.

Harris, T. M. 1931. The fossil flora of Scoresby Sound east Greenland, part 1: Cryptogams (exclusive of Lycopodiales). *Medd. Gronland* **85:**1–102.

Pant, D. D., and G. K. Srivastava. 1977. On the structure of *Gleichenia rewahensis* Feistmantel and allied fossils from the Jabalpur Series, India. *Palaeontographica* **B163:**152–161.

Rege, R. 1921. Note su alcuni del carbonifero della Cina. *Soc. Ital. Sci. Nat. Atti.* **59:**183–196.

Skarby, A. 1964. Revision of *Gleicheniidites senonicus* Ross. *Contr. Geol. Stockholm* **25:**59–77.

Dicksoniaceae

Harris, T. M. 1961. *The Yorkshire Jurassic flora,* vol. I: *Thallophyta-Pteridophyta.* British Museum (Natural History), London.

Thomas, H. H. 1911. On the spores of some Jurassic ferns. *Proc. Cambridge Phil. Soc.* **16**:384–388.

Wilson, S., and P. J. Yates. 1953. On two dicksoniaceous ferns from the Yorkshire Jurassic. *Ann. Mag. Nat. Hist.* (12)**6**:929–937.

Cyatheaceae

Arnold, C. A. 1945. Silicified plant remains from the Mesozoic and Tertiary of western North America, part 1: Ferns. *Mich. Acad. Sci.* **30**:3–34.

Menendez, C. A. 1961. Estípite petrificado de une nueva Cyatheaceae del Terciario de Neuquén. *Soc. Argentina Bot. Bol.* **9**:331–358.

Ogura, Y. 1927. On the structure and affinities of some fossil tree-ferns from Japan. *J. Fac. Sci. Imp. Univ. Tokyo* (3)**1**:351–380.

———. 1931–1932. On a fossil tree fern stem from the Upper Cretaceous of Iwaki, Japan. *Jpn. J. Geol. Geogr.* **9**:55–60.

Matoniaceae

Alvin, K. L. 1971. *Weichselia reticulata* (Stokes et Webb) Fontaine from the Wealden of Belgium. *Mem. Inst. Roy. Sci. Nat. Belgique* **166**:1–33.

Andrews, H. N., Jr., and C. S. Pearsall. 1941. On the flora of the Frontier Formation of southwestern Wyoming. *Ann. Missouri Bot. Gard.* **28**:165–192.

Arnold, C. A. 1956. Fossil ferns of the Matoniaceae from North America. *J. Palaeont. Soc. India* **1**:118–121.

Berry, E. W. 1919. A new *Matonidium* from Colorado, with remarks on the distribution of the Matoniaceae. *Bull. Torrey Bot. Club.* **46**:285–294.

Tralau, H. 1965. *Phlebopteris angustiloba* (Presl) Hirmer et Hörhammer (Matoniaceae) from "Olstrop" Shaft, Bjuv, Scania. *Bot. Not.* **118**:373–376.

Polypodiaceae

Arnold, C. A. 1964. Mesozoic and Teritary fern evolution and distribution. *Bull. Torrey Bot. Club* **21**:58–86.

———, and L. H. Daugherty. 1963. The fern genus *Acrostichum* in the Eocene Clarno Formation of Oregon. *Cont. Mus. Paleontol. Univ. Mich.* **18**:205–227.

——— and ———. 1964. A fossil dennstaedtioid fern from the Eocene Clarno Formation of Oregon. *Cont. Mus. Paleontol. Univ. Mich.* **19**:65–88.

Brown, R. W. 1962. Paleocene flora of the Rocky Mountains and Great Plains. *U.S.G.S. Prof. Paper* **375**:1–119.

Tidwell, W. D., S. R. Rushforth, and J. L. Reveal. 1967. *Astralopteris,* a new Cretaceous fern genus from Utah and Colorado. *Brigham Young Univ. Geol. Studies* **14**:237–240.

Tempskyaceae

Andrews, H. N., Jr., and E. M. Kern. 1947. The Idaho Tempskyas and associated fossil plants. *Ann. Missouri Bot. Gard.* **34**:119–186.

Arnold, C. A. 1945. Silicified plant remains from the Mesozoic and Tertiary of western North America, part I: Ferns. *Mich. Acad. Sci.* **30**:3–34.

──────. 1958. A new *Tempskya. Cont. Mus. Paleontol. Univ. Mich.* **14**:133–142.

Ash, S. R., and C. B. Read. 1976. North American species of *Tempskya* and their stratigraphic significance. *U.S.G.S. Prof. Paper* **874**:1–42.

Read, C. B., and R. W. Brown. 1937. American Cretaceous ferns of the genus *Tempskya. U.S.G.S. Prof. Paper* **F186**:105–109.

Marsileales

Sahni, B., and H. S. Rao. 1943. A silicified flora from the Intertrappean Cherts round Sausar in the Deccan. *Proc. Nat. Acad. Sci. India* **13**:36–75.

Salviniales

Arnold, C. A. 1955. A Tertiary *Azolla* from British Columbia. *Cont. Mus. Paleontol. Univ. Mich.* **21**:37–45.

Florin, R. 1940. Zur Kenntnis einiger fossiler *Salvinia*-arten und der früheren geographischen Verbreitung der Gattung. *Svensk. Bot. Tidskrift* **34**:265–292.

Hall, J. W. 1969. Studies of fossil *Azolla:* Primitive types of megaspores and massulae from the Cretaceous. *Amer. J. Bot.* **56**:1173–1180.

──────. 1974. Cretaceous Salviniaceae. *Ann. Missouri Bot. Gard.* **61**:354–367.

──────. 1975. *Ariadnaesporites* and *Glomerisporites* in the Late Cretaceous: ancestral Salviniaceae. *Amer. J. Bot.* **62**:359–369.

──────, and R. D. Bergad. 1971. A critical study of three Cretaceous salviniaceous megaspores. *Micropaleontology* **17**:345–356.

Hills, L. V., and B. Gopal. 1967. *Azolla primaeva* and its phylogenetic significance. *Can. J. Bot.* **45**:1179–1191.

Jain, R. K. 1971. Pre-Tertiary records of Salviniaceae. *Amer. J. Bot.* **58**:487–496.

──────, and J. W. Hall. 1969. A contribution to the Early Tertiary fossil record of the Salviniaceae. *Amer. J. Bot.* **56**:527–539.

Nasu, T., and K. Seto. 1976. Fossil macrospores and massulae of *Salvinia natans* from the Pliocene and the Quaternary sediments in the Kinki and Tokai Districts, Japan. *Bull. Osaka Mus. Nat. Hist.* **30**:37–48.

Sahni, B. 1941. Indian silicified plants, part I: *Azolla intertrappea* Sah. and H. S. Rao. *Proc. Indian Acad. Sci.* **14**:489–501.

CHAPTER 11: Progymnospermophyta

Andrews, H. N., Jr., T. L. Phillips, and N. W. Radforth. 1965. Paleobotanical studies in Arctic Canada, part I: *Archaeopteris* from Ellesmere Island. *Can. J. Bot.* **43**:545–556.

Barnard, P. D. W., and A. G. Long. 1975. *Triradioxylon*—A new genus of Lower Carboniferous petrified stems and petioles together with a review of the classification of early Pterophytina. *Trans. Roy. Soc. Edinburgh* **69**:231–249.

Beck, C. B. 1957. *Tetraxylopteris schmidtii* gen. et sp. nov., a probable pteridosperm precursor from the Devonian of New York. *Amer. J. Bot.* **44:**350–367.

———. 1960*a*. Connection between *Archaeopteris* and *Callixylon. Science* **131:**1524–1525.

———. 1960*b*. The identity of *Archaeopteris* and *Callixylon. Brittonia* **12:**351–368.

———. 1962. Reconstructions of *Archaeopteris* and further consideration of its phylogenetic position. *Amer. J. Bot.* **49:**373–382.

———. 1967. *Eddya sullivaneesis,* gen. et sp. nov., a plant of gymnospermic morphology from the Upper Devonian of New York. *Palaeontographica* **B121:**1–22.

———. 1970. The appearance of gymnospermous structure. *Biol. Rev.* **45:**379–400.

———. 1971. On the anatomy and morphology of lateral branch systems of *Archaeopteris. Amer. J. Bot.* **58:**758–784.

———. 1976. Current status of the Progymnospermopsida. *Rev. Palaeobot. Palynol.* **21:**5–23.

Bonamo, P. M. 1975. The Progynmospermopsida: Building a concept. *Taxon* **24:**569–579.

———. 1977. *Rellimia thomsonii* (Progymnospermopsida) from the Middle Devonian of New York State. *Amer. J. Bot.* **64:**1272–1285.

———, and H. P. Banks. 1967. *Tetraxylopteris schmidtii:* Its fertile parts and its relationships within the Aneurophytales. *Amer. J. Bot.* **54:**755–768.

Carluccio, L. M., F. M. Hueber, and H. P. Banks. 1966. *Archaeopteris macilenta,* anatomy and morphology of its frond. *Amer. J. Bot.* **53:**719–730.

Galtier, J. 1970. Recherches sur les végétaux á structure conservée du carbonifère inférieur français. *Paleobiol. Cont.* **1:**1–221.

Goldring, W. 1924. The Upper Devonian forest of seed ferns in eastern New York. *New York Mus. Bull.* **251:**50–72.

Kon'no, E. 1929. On genera *Tingia* and *Tingiostachya* from the Lower Permian and the Permo-Triassic beds in northern Korea. *Jap. J. Geol. Geogr.* **6:**113–147.

Kräusel, R., and H. Weyland. 1929. Beiträge zur Kenntnis der Devonflora III. *Abh. Senckenberg Naturf. Ges.* **41:**315–360.

——— and ———. 1935. Pflanzenreste aus dem Devon IX. Ein Stamm von *Eospermatopteris* Bau aus dem Mittledevon des Kirberges, Elberfeld. *Senckenbergiana* **17:**1–20.

Leary, R. L. 1973. *Lacoea,* a Lower Pennsylvanian Noeggerathialian cone from Illinois. *Rev. Palaeobot. Palynol.* **15:**43–50.

Leclercq, S., and P. M. Bonamo. 1971. A study of the fructification of *Milleria (Protopteridium) thomsonii* Lang from the Middle Devonian of Belgium. *Palaeontographica* **B136:**83–114.

——— and ———. 1973. *Rellimia thomsonii,* Lang 1926, emend. Leclercq and Bonamo 1971. *Taxon* **22:**435–437.

Mamay, S. H. 1954. A Permian *Discinites* cone. *J. Wash. Acad. Sci.* **44:**7–11.

Matten, L. C. 1973. The Cairo Flora (Givetian) from eastern New York, part I: *Reimannia,* terete axes, and *Cairoa lamanekii* gen. et sp. n. *Amer. J. Bot.* **60:**619–630.

Namboodiri, K. K., and C. B. Beck. 1968*a*. A comparative study of the primary vascular system of conifers, part I: Genera with helical phyllotaxis. *Amer. J. Bot.* **55:**447–457.

——— and ———. 1968*b*. A comparative study of the primary vascular system of conifers, part II: Genera with opposite and whorled phyllotaxis. *Amer. J. Bot.* **55:**458–463.

—— and ——. 1968*c*. A comparative study of the primary vascular system of conifers, part III: Stelar evolution in gymnosperms. *Amer. J. Bot.* **55**:464–472.

Nemejc, F. 1928. The Noeggerathiae and Archaeopterides in the Coal Basins of Central Bohemia—Palaeontographica Bohemiae. *Ceská Akad. véd a umeni.* **12**:47–82.

Phillips, T. L., H. N. Andrews, Jr., and P. G. Gensel. 1972. Two heterosporous species of *Archaeopteris* from the Upper Devonian of West Virginia. *Palaeontographica* **B139**:47–71.

Remy, W., and R. Remy. 1956. *Noeggerathiostrobus vicinalis* E. Weiss und Bemerkungen zu ahnlichen Fruktifikationen. *Abh. Deutsch. Akad. Wiss. Berlin, Biologie* **2**:1–11.

Scheckler, S. E. 1975. A fertile axis of *Triloboxylon ashlandicum,* a progymnosperm from the Upper Devonian of New York. *Amer. J. Bot.* **62**:923–934.

——. 1976. Ontogeny of progymnosperms, part I: Shoots of Upper Devonian Aneurophytales. *Can. J. Bot.* **54**:202–219.

——. 1978. Ontogeny of progymnosperms, part II: Shoots of Upper Devonian Archaeopteridales. *Can. J. Bot.* **56**:3136–3170.

——, and H. P. Banks. 1971*a*. Anatomy and relationships of some Devonian progymnosperms from New York. *Amer. J. Bot.* **58**:737–751.

—— and ——. 1971*b*. *Proteokalon,* a new genus of progymnosperms from the Devonian of New York state and its bearing on phylogenetic trends in the group. *Amer. J. Bot.* **58**:874–884.

Serlin, B. S., and H. P. Banks. 1978. Morphology and anatomy of *Aneurophyton,* a progymnosperm from the Late Devonian of New York. *Palaeontographica Amer.* **8**:343–359.

Walton, J. 1957. On *Protopitys* (Göppert): With a description of a fertile specimen *Protopitys scotica* sp. nov. from the Calciferous Sandstone Series of Dunbartonshire. *Trans. Roy. Soc. Edinburgh* **63**:333–340.

CHAPTER 12: The Origin and Evolution of the Seed Habit

Andrews, H. N., Jr. 1961. *Studies in paleobotany.* Wiley, New York.

——, P. G. Gensel, and W. H. Forbes. 1974. An apparently heterosporous plant from the Middle Devonian of New Brunswick. *Palaeontology* **17**:387–408.

Barnard, P. D. W., and A. G. Long. 1973. On the structure of a petrified stem and some associated seeds from the Lower Carboniferous rocks of East Lothian, Scotland. *Trans. Roy. Soc. Edinburgh* **69**:91–108.

Benson, M. 1904. *Telangium scotti,* a new species of *Telangium (Calymmatotheca)* showing structure. *Ann. Bot.* **18**:162–176.

Brauer, D. F. 1979. Barinophytacean plants from the Upper Devonian Catskill Formation of northern Pennsylvania. Ph.D. diss., SUNY at Binghamton.

Chaloner, W. G. 1967. Spores and land-plant evolution. *Rev. Palaeobot. Palynol.* **1**:83–93.

——, A. J. Hill, and W. S. Lacey. 1977. First Devonian platyspermic seed and its implications in gymnosperm evolution. *Nature* **265**:233–235.

Long, A. G. 1960*a*. On the structure of *Calymmatotheca kidstoni* Calder (emended) and *Genomosperma latens* gen. et sp. nov. from the Calciferous Sandstone Series of Berwickshire. *Trans. Roy. Soc. Edinburgh* **64**:29–44.

————. 1960*b*. *Stamnostoma huttonense* gen. et sp. nov.—A pteridosperm seed and cupule from the Calciferous Sandstone Series of Berwickshire. *Trans. Roy. Soc. Edingurgh* **64**:201–215.

————. 1960*c*. On the structure of *Samaropsis scotica* Calder (emended) and *Eurystoma angulare* gen. et sp. nov., petrified seeds from the Calciferous Sandstone Series of Berwickshire. *Trans. Roy. Soc. Edinburgh* **64**:261–280.

————. 1961*a*. On the structure of *Deltasperma fouldenense* gen. et sp. nov., and *Camptosperma berniciense* gen. et sp. nov., petrified seeds from the Calciferous Sandstone Series of Berwickshire. *Trans. Roy. Soc. Edinburgh* **64**:281–295.

————. 1961*b*. Some pteridosperm seeds from the Calciferous Sandstone Series of Berwickshire. *Trans. Roy. Soc. Edinburgh* **64**:401–419.

————. 1961*c*. *Tristichia ovensi* gen. et sp. nov., a protostelic Lower Carboniferous pteridosperm from Berwickshire and East Lothian, with an account of some associated seeds and cupules. *Trans. Roy. Soc. Edinburgh* **64**:477–492.

————. 1965. On the cupule structure of *Eurystoma angulare*. *Trans. Roy. Soc. Edinburgh* **66**:111–128.

————. 1966. Some Lower Carboniferous fructifications from Berwickshire, together with a theoretical account of the evolution of ovules, cupules, and carpels. *Trans. Roy. Soc. Edinburgh* **66**:345–375.

————. 1969. *Eurystoma trigona* sp. nov., a pteridosperm ovule borne on a frond of *Alcicornopteris* Kidston. *Trans. Roy. Soc. Edinburgh* **68**:171–182.

————. 1975. Further observations on some Lower Carboniferous seeds and cupules. *Trans. Roy. Soc. Edinburgh* **69**:267–293.

————. 1977*a*. Some Lower Carboniferous pteridosperm cupules bearing ovules and microsporangia. *Trans. Roy. Soc. Edinburgh* **70**:1–11.

————. 1977*b*. Lower Carboniferous pteridosperm cupules and the origin of angiosperms. *Trans. Roy. Soc. Edinburgh* **70**:13–35.

————. 1977*c*. Observations on Carboniferous seeds of *Mitrospermum, Conostoma,* and *Lagenostoma. Trans. Roy. Soc. Edinburgh* **70**:37–61.

Miller, C. N., Jr., and J. T. Brown. 1973. Paleozoic seeds with embryos. *Science* **179**:184–185.

Pettitt, J. M. 1965. Two heterosporous plants from the Upper Devonian of North America. *Bull. Brit. Mus. (Nat. Hist.) Geol.* **10**:81–92.

————. 1969. Pteridophytic features in some Lower Carboniferous seed megaspores. *Bot. J. Linn. Soc.* **62**:233–239.

————. 1970. Heterospory and the origin of the seed habit. *Biol. Rev.* **45**:401–415.

————, and C. B. Beck. 1968. *Archaeosperma arnoldii*—A cupulate seed from the Upper Devonian of North America. *Cont. Mus. Paleontol. Univ. Mich.* **22**:139–154.

————, and W. S. Lacey. 1972. A Lower Carboniferous seed compression from North Wales. *Rev. Palaeobot. Palynol.* **14**:159–169.

Schabilion, J. T., and N. C. Brotzman. 1979. A tetrahedral megaspore arrangement in a seed fern ovule of Pennsylvanian age. *Amer. J. Bot.* **66**:744–745.

Smith, L. 1964. The evolution of the ovule. *Biol. Rev.* **39**:137–159.

Stidd, B. M., and K. Cosentino. 1976. *Nucellangium:* Gametophytic structure and relationship to *Cordaites. Bot. Gaz.* **137**:242–249.

Taylor, T. N., and M. A. Millay. 1979. Pollination biology and reproduction in early seed plants. *Rev. Palaeobot. Palynol.* **27**:329–355.

CHAPTER 13: Pteridospermophyta

LYGINOPTERIDALES

Amerom, H. W. J., van. 1975. Die eusphenopteridischen Pteriophyllen. *Meded. Rijks Geol. Dienst.* (C-III) **1**(7):1–208.

Andrews, H. N., Jr. 1940. A new cupule from the Lower Carboniferous of Scotland. *Bull. Torrey Bot. Club* **67**:595–601.

―――. 1942. Contributions to our knowledge of American Carboniferous floras, part 5: *Heterangium. Ann. Missouri Bot. Gard.* **29**:275–282.

―――. 1954. Contributions to our knowledge of American Carboniferous floras, part VII: Some pteridosperm stems from Iowa. *Ann. Missouri Bot. Gard.* **32**:323–360.

―――, and S. Mamay. 1948. A *Crossotheca* from northern Illinois. *Ann. Missouri Bot. Gard.* **35**:203–204.

Barthel, M. 1962. Epidermisuntersuchungen an einigen inkohlten Pteridospermen-blättern des Oberkarbons und Perms. *Geologie* **33**:1–140.

Beck, C. B. 1960. Studies of New Albany Shale plants, part I: *Stenokoleos simplex* comb. nov. *Amer. J. Bot.* **47**:115–124.

―――. 1978. *Periastron reticulatum* Unger and *Aerocortex kentuckiensis,* n. gen. et sp., from the New Albany Shale of Kentucky. *Amer. J. Bot.* **65**:221–235.

Blanc-Louvel, C. 1966. Étude anatomique comparée des tiges et des pétioles d'une pteridospermée du Carbonifère du genre *Lyginopteris* Potonié. *Mem. Mus. Nat. Hist. N.S.* **18**:1–103.

Eggert, D. A., and T. N. Taylor. 1971. *Telangiopsis* gen. nov., an Upper Mississippian pollen organ from Arkansas. *Bot. Gaz.* **132**:30–37.

Gensel, P. G., and J. E. Skog. 1977. Two early Mississippian seeds from the Price Formation of southwestern Virginia. *Brittonia* **29**:332–351.

Gordon, W. T. 1912. On *Rhetinangium arberi,* a new genus of Cycadofilices from the Calciferous Sandstone Series. *Trans. Roy. Soc. Edinburgh* **48**:813–825.

―――. 1938. On *Tetrastichia bupatides:* A Carboniferous pteridosperm from East Lothian. *Trans. Roy. Soc. Edinburgh* **59**:351–370.

―――. 1941. On *Salpingostoma dasu:* A new Carboniferous seed from East Lothian. *Trans. Roy. Soc. Edinburgh* **60**:427–464.

Hall, J. W. 1952. The phloem of *Heterangium americanum. Amer. Midl. Natur.* **47**:763–768.

Jennings, J. R. 1976. The morphology and relationships of *Rhodea, Telangium, Telangiopsis* and *Heterangium. Amer. J. Bot.* **63**:1119–1133.

Leisman, G. A. 1964. *Physostoma calcaratum* sp. nov., a tentacled seed from the Middle Pennsylvanian of Kansas. *Amer. J. Bot.* **51**:1069–1075.

Long, A. G. 1944. On the prothallus of *Lagenostoma ovoides* Will. *Ann. Bot. NS* **8**:105–117.

―――. 1961. *Tristichia ovensi* gen. sp. nov., a protostelic Lower Carboniferous pteridosperm from Berwickshire and East Lothian, with an account of some associated seeds and cupules. *Trans. Roy. Soc. Edinburgh* **64**:477–492.

―――. 1963. Some specimens of *"Lyginorachis papilio"* Kidston associated with stems of *"Pitys." Trans. Roy. Soc. Edinburgh* **45**:211–224.

―――. 1964. On the structure of some petioles associated with *Rhetinangium* Gordon. *Trans. Roy. Soc. Edinburgh* **46**:1–7.

————. 1975. Further observations on some Lower Carboniferous seeds and cupules. *Trans. Roy. Soc. Edinburgh* **69**:267–293.

————. 1976. *Calathopteris heterophylla* gen. et sp. nov., a Lower Carboniferous pteridosperm bearing two kinds of petioles. *Trans. Roy. Soc. Edinburgh* **69**:327–336.

————. 1979. The resemblance between the Lower Carboniferous cupules of *Hydrasperma* cf. *tenuis* Long and *Sphenopteris bifida* Lindley and Hutton. *Trans. Roy. Soc. Edinburgh* **70**:129–137.

Mamay, S. H. 1954. Two new plant genera of Pennsylvanian age from Kansas coal balls. *U.S.G.S. Prof. Paper* **D245**:81–95.

Matten, L. C., and H. P. Banks. 1969. *Stenokoleos bifidus* sp. n. in the Upper Devonian of New York State. *Amer. J. Bot.* **56**:880–891.

Millay, M. A., and T. N. Taylor. 1977. *Feraxotheca* gen. n., a lyginopterid pollen organ from the Pennsylvanian of North America. *Amer. J. Bot.* **64**:177–185.

———— and ————. 1978. Fertile and sterile frond segments of the lyginopterid seed fern *Feraxotheca*. *Rev. Palaeobot. Palynol.* **25**:151–162.

Neely, F. E. 1951. Small petrified seeds from the Pennsylvanian of Illinois. *Bot. Gaz.* **113**:165–179.

Oliver, F. W., and E. J. Salisbury. 1911. On the structure and affinities of the Palaeozoic seeds of the *Conostoma* group. *Ann. Bot.* **25**:1–50.

————, and D. H. Scott. 1904. On the structure of the Palaeozoic seed *Lagenostoma lomaxi*, with a statement of the evidence upon which it is referred to *Lyginodendron*. *Phil. Trans. Roy. Soc. London* **B197**:193–247.

Pfefferkorn, H. W. 1978. Revision der Sphenopteriden *Discopteris karwinensis* Stur, *Discopteris vuellersi* Stur und der Gattung *Discopteris* Stur. *Argumenta Palaeobot.* **5**:167–193.

Potonié, H. 1899. *Lehrbuch der Pflanzenpaleontologie mit besondere Rücksicht auf die Bedürfnisse des Geologen.* Dümmber, Berlin, pp. 170–175, 230–233.

Reed, F. D. 1939. Structure of some Carboniferous seeds from American coal fields. *Bot. Gaz.* **100**:769–787.

Renault, B. 1885. *Cours de Botanique Fossile*, vol. 4: *Coniféres—Gnetacéees.* G. Masson, Paris.

Rothwell, G. W. 1971. Additional observations on *Conostoma anglo-germanicum* and *C. oblongum* from the Lower Pennsylvanian of North America. *Palaeontographica* **B131**:167–178.

————, and D. A. Eggert. 1970. A *Conostoma* with a tentacular sarcotesta from the Upper Pennsylvanian of Illinois. *Bot. Gaz.* **131**:359–366.

————, and T. N. Taylor. 1972. Carboniferous pteridosperm studies: Morphology and anatomy of *Schopfiastrum decussatum*. *Can. J. Bot.* **50**:2649–2658.

Schabilion, J. T., and N. C. Brotzman. 1979. A tetrahedral megaspore arrangement in a seed fern ovule of Pennsylvanian age. *Amer. J. Bot.* **66**:744–745.

Scott, D. H. 1917. The Heterangiums of the British Coal Measures. *J. Linn. Soc.* **44**:59–105.

Sellards, E. H. 1902. On the fertile fronds of *Crossotheca* and *Myriotheca*, and on the spores of other Carboniferous ferns, from Mazon Creek, Illinois. *Amer. J. Sci.* (4)**14**:195–202.

Shadle, G. L., and B. M. Stidd. 1975. The frond of *Heterangium*. *Amer. J. Bot.* **62**:67–75.

Skog, J. E., H. N. Andrews, Jr., and S. H. Mamay. 1969. *Canipa quadrifida,* gen. et sp.

nov., a synangial fructification from the Middle Pennsylvanian of West Virginia. *Bull. Torrey Bot. Club* **96**:276–287.

Taylor, T. N., and G. A. Leisman. 1963. *Conostoma kestospermum,* a new species of Paleozoic seed from the Middle Pennsylvania. *Amer. J. Bot.* **50**:574–580.

———, and M. A. Millay. 1980. Morphologic variability of Pennsylvanian lyginopterid seed ferns. *Rev. Palaeobot. Palynol.* (in press).

———, and R. A. Stockey. 1976. Studies of Paleozoic seed ferns: Anatomy and morphology of *Microspermopteris aphyllum. Amer. J. Bot.* **63**:1302–1310.

Williamson, W. C. 1887. On the organization of the fossil plants of the coal-measures, part 13: *Heterangium tiliaeoides* (Williamson) and *Kaloxylon hookeri. Phil. Trans. Roy. Soc. London* **B178**:289–304.

MEDULLOSALES

Andrews, H. N., Jr. 1940. On the stelar anatomy of the pteridosperms, with particular reference to the secondary wood. *Ann. Missouri Bot. Gard.* **27**:51–118.

———. 1945. Contributions to our knowledge of American Carboniferous floras, part 7: Some pteridosperm stems from Iowa. *Ann. Missouri Bot. Gard.* **32**:323–360.

———. 1948. Some evolutionary trends in the pteridosperms. *Bot. Gaz.* **110**:13–31.

———, and S. H. Mamay. 1953. Some American Medullosas. *Ann. Missouri Bot. Gard.* **40**:183–209.

Basinger, J. F., G. W. Rothwell, and W. N. Stewart. 1974. Cauline vasculature and leaf trace production in medullosan pteridosperms. *Amer. J. Bot.* **61**:1002–1015.

Baxter, R. W. 1949. Some pteridosperm stems and fructifications with particular reference to the Medullosae. *Ann. Missouri Bot. Gard.* **36**:287–352.

Brongniart, A. 1828. Prodrome d'une histoire des végétaux fossiles. *Dict. Sci. Nat.* **57**:16–212.

Cotta, B. 1832. *Die Dendrolithen in Beziehung auf Ihren Inneren Bau.* Arnoldische Buchhandlung, Dresden and Leipzig.

Cridland, A. A., and J. E. Morris. 1960. *Spermopteris,* a new genus of pteridosperms from the Upper Pennsylvanian Series of Kansas. *Amer. J. Bot.* **47**:855–859.

Delevoryas, T. 1955. The Medullosae-structure and relationships. *Palaeontographica* **B97**:114–167.

———, and T. N. Taylor. 1969. A probable pteridosperm with eremopterid foliage from the Allegheny Group of northern Pennsylvania. *Postilla* **133**:1–14.

Dennis, R. L., and D. A. Eggert. 1978. *Parasporotheca,* gen. nov. and its bearing on the interpretation of the morphology of permineralized medullosan pollen organs. *Bot. Gaz.* **139**:117–139.

Eggert, D. A., and R. W. Kryder. 1969. A new species of *Aulacotheca* (Pteridospermales) from the Middle Pennsylvanian of Iowa. *Palaeontology* **12**:414–419.

———, and G. W. Rothwell. 1979. *Stewartiotheca* gen. n. and the nature and origin of complex permineralized medullosan pollen organs. *Amer. J. Bot.* **66**:851–866.

Gastaldo, R. A., and L. C. Matten. 1978. *Trigonocarpus leeanus,* a new species from the Middle Pennsylvanian of southern Illinois. *Amer. J. Bot.* **65**:882–890.

Goeppert, H. R. 1936. Die fossilen Farrenkräuter (Systema filicum fossilium). *Nova Acta Leopoldina* **17**:1–486.

———, and G. Stenzel. 1882. Die Medulloseae. Eine neue Gruppe der fossilen Cycadeen. *Palaeontographica* **28**:111–128.

Halle, T. G. 1929. Some seed-bearing pteridosperms from the Permian of China. *Kungl. Svenska Vet. Handl.* **6**:3–24.

————. 1932. On the seeds of the pteridosperm *Emplectopteris triangularis. Geol. Soc. China Bull.* **11**:301–306.

————. 1933. The structure of certain fossil spore-bearing organs believed to belong to pteridosperms. *Kung. Svenska Vet. Handl.* (3)**12**:1–103.

Kidston, R. 1905. On the fructification of *Neuropteris heterophylla*, Brongniart. *Phil. Trans. Roy. Soc. London* **B197**:1–5.

————. 1923–1925. Fossil plants of the Carboniferous rocks of Great Britain. *Mem. Geol. Survey, Great Britain* **2**:parts 1–6.

Lacey, W. S., and D. A. Eggert. 1964. A flora from the Chester Series (Upper Mississippian) of southern Illinois. *Amer. J. Bot.* **51**:976–985.

Laveine, J. P., R. Coquel, and S. Loboziak. 1977. Phylogenie générale des Callipteridiaceae (Pteridospermopsida). *Géobios* **10**:757–847.

Leary, R. L. 1975. Early Pennsylvanian paleogeography of an upland area western Illinois USA. *Bull. Belg. Ver. Geologie* **84**:19–31.

Leisman, G. A. 1960. The morphology and anatomy of *Callipteridium sullivanti. Amer. J. Bot.* **47**:281–287.

————, and J. Peters. 1970. A new pteridosperm male fructification from the Middle Pennsylvanian of Illinois. *Amer. J. Bot.* **57**:867–873.

————, and J. Roth. 1963. A reconsideration of *Stephanospermum. Bot Gaz.* **124**:231–240.

Lesquereux, L. 1880. Description of the coal flora of the Carboniferous formation in Pennsylvania and throughout the United States. *Penn. 2d Geol. Surv. Rept. Prog. P* **1**:1–354; **2**:355–694 (Atlas 1879).

————. 1884. Description of the coal flora of the Carboniferous formation in Pennsylvania. *Penn. 2d Geol. Sur. Rept. Prog. P* **3**:695–977.

Mamay, S. H., and A. D. Watt. 1971. An ovuliferous callipteroid plant from the Hermit Shale (Lower Permian) of the Grand Canyon, Arizona. *U.S.G.S. Prof. Paper* **C750**:48–51.

Millay, M. A., and T. N. Taylor. 1979. Paleozoic seed fern pollen organs. *Bot. Rev.* **45**:301–375.

Newberry, J. S. 1853. Fossil plants from the Ohio coal basin. *Ann. Sci. Cleveland* **1**:106–108.

Phillips, T. L., and H. N. Andrews, Jr. 1963. An occurrence of the medullosan seed-fern *Sutcliffia* in the American Carboniferous. *Ann. Missouri Bot. Gard.* **50**:29–51.

Ramanujam, C. G. K., G. W. Rothwell, and W. B. Stewart. 1974. Probable attachment of the *Dolerotheca* campanulum to a *Myeloxylon-Alethopteris* type frond. *Amer. J. Bot.* **61**:1057–1066.

Read, C. B., and S. H. Mamay. 1964. Upper Paleozoic floral zones and floral provinces of the United States. *Geol. Survey Prof. Paper* **454K.**

Reihman, M. A., and J. T. Schabilion. 1976. Cuticle of two species of *Alethopteris. Amer. J. Bot.* **63**:1039–1046.

Rothwell, G. W., and K. L. Whiteside. 1974. Rooting structures of the Carboniferous medullosan pteridosperms. *Can. J. Bot.* **52**:97–102.

Scott, D. H. 1906. On *Sutcliffia insignis*, a new type of Medullosaceae from the Lower Coal Measures. *Trans. Linn. Soc. London*, (2)**7**:45–68.

————. 1923. *Studies in fossil botany*, part II, 3d ed. A. & C. Black, London.

Sellards, E. H. 1903. *Codonotheca*, a new type of spore-bearing organ from the Coal Measures. *Amer. J. Sci.* **16**:87–95.

Steidtmann. W. E. 1944. The anatomy and affinities of *Medullosa noei* Steidtmann, and associated foliage, roots, and seeds. *Cont. Mus. Paleont. Univ. Mich.* **6**:131–166.

Sternberg, G. K. 1820–1838. *Versuch einer geognostischen botanischen Darstellung der Flora der Vorwelt,* vol. 1, pp. 1–24 (1820); part 2, pp. 1–33 (1922); part 3, pp 1–39 (1823); part 4, pp. 1–48 (1825); vol. 2: parts 5 and 6, pp. 1–80 (1833); parts 7 and 8, pp. 81–220 (1838). Leipzig and Prague.

Stewart, W. N. 1951. A new *Pachytesta* from the Berryville locality of southeastern Illinois. *Amer. Midl. Natur.* **46:**717–742.

———. 1954. The structure and affinities of *Pachytesta illinoense* comb. nov. *Amer. J. Bot.* **41:**500–508.

———. 1958. The structure and relationships of *Pachytesta composita* sp. nov. *Amer. J. Bot.* **45:**580–588.

———, and T. Delevoryas. 1956. The medullosan pteridosperms. *Bot. Rev.* **22:**45–80.

Stidd, B. M. 1978*a.* The synangiate nature of *Dolerotheca. Amer. J. Bot.* **65:**243–245.

———. 1978*b.* An anatomically preserved *Potoniea* with *in situ* spores from the Pennsylvanian of Illinois. *Amer. J. Bot.* **65:**677–683.

———, G. A. Leisman, and T. L. Phillips. 1977. *Sullitheca dactylifera* gen. et sp. n.: A new medullosan pollen organ and its evolutionary significance. *Amer. J. Bot.* **64:**994–1002.

———, L. L. Oestry, and T. L. Phillips. 1975. On the frond of *Sutcliffia insignis* var. *tuberculata. Rev. Palaeobot. Palynol.* **20:**55–66.

Stur, D. R. J. 1875. Beiträge zur Kenntniss der Flora der Vorwelt-Die Culm Flora, part 1; Die Culm Flora des mährisch-schlischen Dachschiefers. *Kgl. geol. Reichsanst. Abh.* **8:**1–106.

———. 1877. Beiträge zur Kenntniss der Flora der Vorwelt-Die Culm Flora, part 2; Die Culm Flora der Ostrauer und waldenburger Schichten. *Kgl. geol. Teichsanst. Abh.* **8:**1–366.

Taylor, T. N. 1962. Additional observations on *Stephanospermum ovoides,* a middle Pennsylvanian seed. *Amer. J. Bot.* **49:**794–800.

———. 1965. Paleozoic seed studies: A monograph of the American species of *Pachytesta. Palaeontographica* **B117:**1–46.

———. 1966. Paleozoic seed studies: On the genus *Hexapterospermum. Amer. J. Bot.* **53:**185–192.

———. 1967. Paleozoic seed studies: On the structure of *Conostoma leptospermum* n. sp., and *Albertlongia incostata* n. gen. and sp. *Palaeontographica* **B121:**23–29.

———. 1971. *Halletheca reticulatus* gen. et sp. n.: A synangiate Pennsylvanian pteridosperm pollen organ. *Amer. J. Bot.* **58:**300–308.

———. 1976. The ultrastructure of *Schopfipollenites:* Orbicules and tapetal membranes. *Amer. J. Bot.* **63:**857–862.

———. 1978. The ultrastructure and reproductive significance of *Monoletes* (Pteridospermales) pollen. *Can. J. Bot.* **56:**3105–3118.

———, and T. Delevoryas. 1964. Paleozoic seed studies: A new Pennsylvanian *Pachytesta* from southern Illinois. *Amer. J. Bot.* **51:**189–195.

———, and D. A. Eggert. 1967. Petrified plants from the Upper Mississippian of North America, part I: The seed *Rhynchosperma* gen. n. *Amer. J. Bot.* **54:**984–992.

——— and ———. 1969. On the structure and relationships of a new Pennsylvanian species of the seed *Pachytesta. Palaeontology* **12:**382–387.

Wagner, R. H. 1965. Stephanian B flora from the Ciñera-Matallana coalfield (Léon) and neighbouring outliers, part III: *Callipteridium* and *Alethopteris. Notas Comuns. Inst. Geol. Minero España* **78:**5–70.

———. 1966. Palaeobotanical dating of Upper Carboniferous folding phases in NW Spain. *Mem. Inst. Geol. Min. Spain* **66:**5–169.

White, D. 1900. The stratigraphic succession of the fossil floras of the Pottsville Formation in the southern anthracite coal field, Pennsylvania. *U.S. Geol. Survey 20th Annu. Rept.* **2:**751–930.

———. 1936. Fossil flora of the Wedington sandstone member of the Fayetteville shale. *U.S. Geol. Survey Prof. Paper* **186B.**

———. 1937. Fossil plants from the Stanley shale and Jackfork sandstone in southeastern Oklahoma and western Arkansas. *U.S. Geol. Survey Prof. Paper* **186C.**

Zhang, S., and Z. Mo. 1979. New forms of seed-bearing fronds from the Cathaysia Flora in Henan, China. *9th Int. Cong. Carb. Strat. Geol.,* pp. 1–5.

CALLISTOPHYTALES

Delevoryas, T., and J. Morgan. 1954. A new pteridosperm from Upper Pennsylvanian deposits of North America. *Palaeontographica* **B96:**12–23.

Eggert, D. A., and T. Delevoryas. 1960. A new seed genus from the Upper Pennsylvanian of Illinois. *Phytomorphology* **10:**131–138.

Hall, J. W., and B. M. Stidd. 1971. Ontogeny of *Vesicaspora,* a Late Pennsylvanian pollen grain. *Palaeontology* **14:**431–436.

Millay, M. A., and D. A. Eggert. 1970. *Idanothekion* gen. n., a synangiate pollen organ with saccate pollen from the Middle Pennsylvanian of Illinois. *Amer. J. Bot.* **57:**50–61.

——— and ———. 1974. Microgametophyte development in the Paleozoic seed fern family Callistophytaceae. *Amer. J. Bot.* **61:**1067–1075.

Rothwell, G. W. 1971. Ontogeny of the Paleozoic ovule, *Callospermarion pusillum. Amer. J. Bot.* **58:**706–715.

———. 1972a. Pollen organs of the Pennsylvanian Callistophytaceae (Pteridospermopsida). *Amer. J. Bot.* **59:**993–999.

———. 1972b. Evidence of pollen tubes in Paleozoic pteridosperms. *Science* **175:**772–774.

———. 1975. The Callistophytaceae (Pteridospermopsida), part I: Vegetative structures. *Palaeontographica* **B151:**171–196.

———. 1977. Evidence for a pollination-drop mechanism in Paleozoic pteridosperms. *Science* **198:**1251–1252.

———. 1980. The Callistophytaceae (Pteridospermopsida), part II: Reproductive features. *Palaeontographica* (in press).

Stidd, B. M., and J. W. Hall. 1970a. *Callandrium callistophytoides,* gen. et. sp. nov., the probable pollen-bearing organ of the seed fern, *Callistophyton. Amer. J. Bot.* **57:**394–403.

——— and ———. 1970b. The natural affinity of the Carboniferous seed, *Callospermarion. Amer. J. Bot.* **57:**827–836.

CALAMOPITYALES

Beck, C. B. 1970. The appearance of gymnospermous structure. *Biol. Rev.* **45:**379–400.

———, and R. E. Bailey. 1967. Plants of the New Albany Shale, part III: *Chapelia campbellii* gen. n. *Amer. J. Bot.* **54:**998–1007.

Hoskins, J. H., and A. T. Cross. 1951. The structure and classification of four plants from the New Albany Shale. *Amer. Midl. Natur.* **46:**684–716.

——— and ———. 1952. The petrifaction flora of the Devonian-Mississippian black shale. *Palaeobotanist* **1:**215–238.

Kidston, R., and D. T. Gwynne-Vaughan. 1912. On the Carboniferous flora of Berwickshire, part I: *Stenomyelon tuedianum* Kidston. *Trans. Roy. Soc. Edinburgh* **48**:263–271.

Long, A. G. 1964. Some specimens of *Stenomyelon* and *Kalymma* from the Calciferous Sandstone Series of Berwickshire. *Trans. Roy. Soc. Edinburgh* **65**:435–447.

Matten, L. C., and L. J. Trimble. 1978. Studies on *Kalymma*. *Palaeontographica* **B167**:161–174.

Read, C. B. 1936*a*. The flora of the New Albany Shale, part 1: *Diichnia kentuckiensis*, a new representative of the Calamopityeae. *U.S.G.S. Prof. Paper* **185H.**

———. 1936*b*. A Devonian flora from Kentucky. *J. Paleo.* **10**:215–227.

———. 1937. The flora of the New Albany Shale, part 2: The Calamopityeae and their relationships. *U.S.G.S. Prof. Paper* **186H.**

Sebby, W. S., and L. C. Matten. 1969*a*. *Kalymma minuta* (Read) comb. nov. from the New Albany Shale. *Bull. Torrey Bot. Club* **96**:79–88.

——— and ———. 1969*b*. A reconstruction of the frond of *Kalymma*. *Trans. Illinois Acad. Sci.* **62**:356–361.

Skog, J. E., and P. G. Gensel. 1980. A fertile species of *Triphyllopteris* from the early Carboniferous (Mississippian) of southwestern Virginia. *Amer. J. Bot.* **67**:440–451.

Stein, W. E., and C. B. Beck. 1978. *Bostonia perplexa* gen. et sp. nov., a calamopityan axis from the New Albany Shale of Kentucky. *Amer. J. Bot.* **65**:459–465.

CAYTONIALES

Dilcher, D. L. 1979. Early angiosperm reproductions: An introductory report. *Rev. Palaeobot. Palynol.* **27**:291–328.

Harris, T. M. 1933. A new member of the Caytoniales. *New Phytol.* **32**:97–114.

———. 1940. *Caytonia. Ann. Bot.* **4**:713–734.

———. 1941. *Caytonanthus*, the microsporophyll of *Caytonia. Ann. Bot.* **5**:47–58.

Krassilov, V. A. 1977. Contributions to the knowledge of the Caytoniales. *Rev. Palaeobot. Palynol.* **24**:155–178.

Reymanówna, M. 1970. New investigations of the anatomy of *Caytonia* using sectioning and maceration. *Paläontol. Abh.* **B3**:651–655.

———. 1973. The Jurassic flora from Grojec near Kraków in Poland, part II: Caytoniales and anatomy of *Caytonia. Acta Palaeobot.* **14**:46–87.

Thomas, H. H. 1925. The Caytoniales, a new group of angiospermous plants from the Jurassic rocks of Yorkshire. *Phil. Trans. Soc. London* **B213**:299–363.

CORYSTOSPERMALES

Archangelsky, S. 1968. Studies on Triassic fossil plants from Argentina, part IV: The leaf genus *Dicroidium* and its possible relations to *Rhexoxylon* stems. *Palaeontology* **11**:500–512.

Bose, M. N., and S. C. Srivastava. 1971. The genus *Dicroidium* from the Triassic of Nidpur, Makhya Pradesh, India. *Palaeobotanist* **19**:41–51.

Brett, D. W. 1968. Studies on Triassic fossil plants from Argentina, part III: The trunk of *Rhexoxylon. Palaeontology* **11**:236–245.

Pant, D. D., and N. Basu. 1979. Some further remains of fructifications from the Triassic of Nidpur, India. *Palaeontographica* **B168**:129–146.

Townrow, J. A. 1962. On *Pteruchus,* a microsporophyll of the Corystospermaceae. *Bull. Brit. Mus. (Nat. Hist.) Geol.* **6:**289–320.

PELTASPERMALES

Harris, T. M. 1937. The fossil flora of Scoresby Sound East Greenland, part 5: Stratigraphic relations of the plant beds. *Medd. Gronland* **112:**1–114.

Thomas, H. H. 1933. On some pteridospermous plants from the Mesozoic rocks of South Africa. *Phil. Trans. Roy. Soc. London* **B222:**193–265.

———. 1955. Mesozoic pteridosperms. *Phytomorphology* **5:**177–185.

Townrow, J. A. 1960. The Peltaspermaceae, a pteridosperm family of Permian and Triassic age. *Palaeontology* **3:**333–361.

GLOSSOPTERIDALES

Chandra, S., and K. R. Surange. 1976. Cuticular studies of the reproductive organs of *Glossopteris,* part I: *Dictyopteridium feistmanteli* sp. nov. attached on *Glossopteris tenuinervis. Palaeontographica* **B156:**87–102.

Delevoryas, T., and R. E. Gould. 1971. An unusual fossil fructification from the Jurassic of Oaxaca, Mexico. *Amer. J. Bot.* **58:**616–620.

———, and C. P. Person. 1975. *Mexiglossa varia* gen. et sp. nov., a new genus of glossopterid leaves from the Jurassic of Oaxaca, Mexico. *Palaeontographica* **B154:**114–120.

Gould, R. E. 1975. A preliminary report on petrified axes of *Vertebraria* from the Permian of eastern Australia. In: K. Campbell (ed.), *Gondwana geology.* Australian University National Press, Canberra, pp. 109–115.

———, and T. Delevoryas. 1977. The biology of *Glossopteris:* Evidence from petrified seed-bearing and pollen-bearing organs. *Alcheringa* **1:**387–399.

Holmes, W. B. K. 1973. On some fructifications of the Glossopteridales from the Upper Permian of N.S.W. *Proc. Linn. Soc. New South Wales* **98:**132–141.

Lacey, W. S., D. E. Van Dijk, and K. D. Gordon-Gray. 1975. Fossil plants from the Upper Permian in the Mooi River district of Natal, South Africa. *Ann. Natal. Mus.* **22:**349–420.

Maheshwari, H. K. 1965. Studies in the *Glossopteris* flora of India—31. Some remarks on the genus *Glossopteris* Sternb. *Palaeobotanist* **14:**36–45.

———. 1972. Permian wood from Antarctica and revision of some Lower Gondwana wood taxa. *Palaeontographica* **B138:**1–43.

Pant, D. D. 1958. The structure of some leaves and fructifications of the *Glossopteris* flora of Tanganyika. *Bull. Brit. Mus. (Nat. Hist.) Geol.* **3:**125–175.

———. 1962. Some recent contributions towards our knowledge of the *Glossopteris* flora. *Proc. Summer Sch. Bot. Darjeeling* (P. Mahesewari, B. M. Johri, and I. K. Vasil, eds.):302–319.

———. 1968. On the stem and attachment of *Glossopteris* leaves. *Phytomorphology* **17:**351–359.

———, and K. L. Gupta. 1968. Cuticular structure of some Indian lower Gondwana species of *Glossopteris* Brongniart. *Palaeontographica* **B124:**45–81.

———, and D. D. Nautiyal. 1960. Some seeds and sporangia of *Glossopteris* flora from Raniganj Coalfield, India. *Palaeontographica* **B107:**41–64.

———, and K. B. Singh. 1968. On the genus *Gangamopteris* McCoy. *Palaeontographica* **B124**:83–101.

———, and R. S. Singh. 1968. The structure of *Vertebraria indica* Royle. *Palaeontology* **11**:643–653.

Plumstead, E. P. 1952. Description of two new genera and six new species of fructifications borne on *Glossopteris* leaves. *Trans. Geol. Soc. S. Africa* **55**:281–328.

———. 1956. Bisexual fructifications borne on *Glossopteris* leaves from South America. *Palaeontographica* **B100**:1–25.

Rigby, J. F. 1978. Permian glossopterid and other cycadopsid fructifications from Queensland. *Geol. Surv. Queensland. Palaeontol. Paper* **1–21.**

Royle, J. F. 1833. *Illustrations of the botany and other branches of natural history of the Himalayan Mountains, and of the flora of Cashmere.* Allen, London.

Schopf, J. M. 1965. Anatomy of the axis in *Vertebraria*. In: J. B. Hadley (ed.), *Geology and paleontology of the antarctic.* Antarctic Res. Ser. 6, pp. 217–228.

———. 1976. Morphologic interpretation of fertile structures in glossopterid gymnosperms. *Rev. Palaeobot. Palynol.* **21**:25–64.

Surange, K. R., and S. Chandra. 1972. Some male fructifications of Glossopteridales. *Palaeobotanist* **21**:255–266.

——— and ———. 1973. *Denkania indica* gen. et sp. nov.—A glossopteridean fructification from the Lower Gondwana of India. *Palaeobotanist* **20**:264–268.

——— and ———. 1975. Morphology of the gymnospermous fructifications of the *Glossopteris* flora and their relationships. *Palaeontographica* **B149**:153–180.

———, and H. K. Maheshwari. 1970. Some male and female fructifications of Glossopteridales from India. *Palaeontographica* **B129**:178–192.

Thomas, H. H. 1958. *Lidgettonia,* a new type of fertile *Glossopteris*. *Bull. Brit. Mus. (Nat. Hist.) Geol.* **3**:179–189.

CHAPTER 14: Cycadophyta and Cycadeoidophyta

CYCADOPHTYA

Archangelsky, S., and D. W. Brett. 1963. Studies on Triassic fossil plants from Argentina, part II: *Michelilloa waltonii* nov. gen. et spec. from the Ischigualasto Formation. *Ann. Bot.* **27**:147–154.

Bornemann, J. G. 1856. *Über organische Reste der Letterkohlengruppe Thüringens. Ein Beitrag zur Favena and Flora dieser Formation der Jetztweltlichen Cycadeegattungen,* vol. 9. Verlag Wilch Engelmann, Leipzig. 85 pages.

Delevoryas, T., and R. C. Hope. 1971. A new Triassic cycad and its phyletic implications. *Postilla* **150**:1–21.

Gould, R. E. 1971. *Lyssoxylon grigsbyi,* a cycad trunk from the Upper Triassic of Arizona and New Mexico. *Amer. J. Bot.* **58**:239–248.

Harris, T. M. 1941. Cones of extinct Cycadales from the Jurassic rocks of Yorkshire. *Phil. Trans. Roy. Soc. London* **231**:75–98.

———. 1961. The fossil cycads. *Palaeontology* **4**:313–323.

———. 1964. *The Yorkshire Jurassic flora*, vol. II: *Caytoniales, Cycadales, and Pteridosperms*. British Museum (Natural History), London.

———. 1969. *The Yorkshire Jurassic flora*, vol. III: *Bennettitales*. British Museum (Natural History), London, pp. 1–186.

Jain, K. P. 1964. *Fascisvarioxylon methae* gen. et sp. nov., a new petrified cycadean wood from the Rajmahal Hills, Bihar, India. *Palaeobotanist* **11**:138–143.

Mamay, S. H. 1973. *Archaeocycas* and *Phasmatocycas*—New genera of Permian cycads. *J. Res. U.S.G.S.* **1**:687–689.

———. 1976. Paleozoic origin of cycads. *U.S.G.S. Prof. Paper* **934**:1–48.

Nathorst, A. G. 1902. Beiträge zur Kenntnis einiger mesozoischen Cycadophytens. *K. Svenska Vetensk. Akad. Handl.* **36**:1–28.

Paliwal, G. S., and N. N. Bhandari. 1962. Stomatal development in some Magnoliaceae. *Phytomorphology* **12**:409–412.

Taylor, T. N. 1969. Cycads: Evidence from the Upper Pennsylvanian. *Science* **164**:294–195.

———. 1970. *Lasiostrobus* gen. n., a staminate strobilus of gymnospermous affinity from the Pennsylvanian of North America. *Amer. J. Bot.* **57**:670–690.

———, and M. A. Millay. 1977. The ultrastructure and reproductive significance of *Lasiostrobus* microspores. *Rev. Palaeobot. Palynol.* **23**:129–137.

——— and ———. 1979. Pollination biology and reproduction in early seed plants. *Rev. Palaeobot. Palynol.* **27**:329–355.

Thomas, H. H., and N. Bancroft. 1913. On the cuticles of some recent and fossil cycadean fronds. *Trans. Linn. Soc. London* **8**:155–204.

CYCADEOIDOPHYTA

Cycadeoidaceae

Carruthers, W. 1870. On fossil cycadean stems from the secondary rocks of Britain. *Trans. Linn. Soc.* **26**:675–708.

Crepet, W. L. 1974. Investigations of North American cycadeoids: The reproductive biology of *Cycadeoidea*. *Palaeontographica* **B148**:144–169.

———, and T. Delevoryas. 1972. Investigations of North American cycadeoids: Early ovule ontogeny. *Amer. J. Bot.* **59**:209–215.

Delevoryas, T. 1959. Investigations of North American cycadeoids: *Monanthesia*. *Amer. J. Bot.* **46**:657–666.

———. 1960. Investigations of North American cycadeoids: Trunks from Wyoming. *Amer. J. Bot.* **47**:778–786.

———. 1963. Investigations of North American cycadeoids: Cones of *Cycadeoidea*. *Amer. J. Bot.* **50**:45–52.

———. 1966. Investigations of North American cycadeoids: Microsporangiate structures and phylogenetic implications. *Palaeobotanist* **14**:89–93.

———. 1968*a*. Some aspects of cycadeoid evolution. *J. Linn. Soc. Bot.* **61**:137–146.

———. 1968*b*. Investigations of North American cycadeoids: Structure, ontogeny and phylogenetic considerations of cones of *Cycadeoidea*. *Palaeontographica* **B121**:122–133.

———. 1971. Biotic provinces and the Jurassic-Cretaceous floral transition. *Proc. N. Amer. Paleontol. Conv.* **L**:1660–1674.

————, and R. C. Hope. 1976. More evidence for a slender growth habit in Mesozoic cycadophytes. *Rev. Palaeobot. Palynol.* **21**:93–100.

Harris, T. M. 1932. The fossil flora of Scoresby Sound East Greenland, part 3: Caytoniales and Bennettitales. *Medd. Gronland* **85**:1–133.

————. 1969. *The Yorkshire Jurassic flora,* vol. III: *Bennettitales.* British Museum (Natural History), London.

Taylor, T. N. 1973. A consideration of the morphology, ultrastructure and multicellular microgametophyte of *Cycadeoidea dacotensis* pollen. *Rev. Palaeobot. Palynol.* **16**:157–164.

Wieland, G. R. 1906. *American fossil cycads.* Carnegie Institute, Washington, D.C.

————. 1916. *American fossil cycads,* vol. II. Carnegie Institute, Washington, D.C.

Williamsoniaceae

Asama, K. 1974. *Weltrichia* (male *Williamsonia*) from Ulu Endau, West Malaysia. *Geol. Palaeont. Southeast Asia* **14**:83–87.

Ash, S. R. 1968. A new species of *Williamsonia* from the Upper Triassic Chinle Formation of New Mexico. *J. Linn. Soc. Bot.* **61**:113–120.

Delevoryas, T., and R. E. Gould. 1973. Investigations of North American cycadeoids: Williamsonian cones from the Jurassic of Oaxaca, Mexico. *Rev. Palaeobot. Palynol.* **15**:27–42.

Harris, T. M. 1944. A revision of *Williamsoniella. Phil. Trans. Roy. Soc. London* **231**:313–328.

————. 1974. *Williamsoniella lignieri:* Its pollen and the compression of spherical pollen grains. *Palaeontology* **17**:125–148.

Sahni, B. 1932. A petrified *Williamsonia* (*W. sewardiana,* sp. nov.) from the Rajmahal Hills, India. *Palaeontologica Indica* **20**:1–19.

Sharma, B. D. 1976. Fruit development in *Williamsonia* Carr. (Bennettitales). *Geobios* **9**:503–507.

Thomas, H. H. 1915*a.* On some new and rare Jurassic plants from Yorkshire: the male flower of *Williamsonia gigas* (Lind. and Hutt.). *Proc. Cambridge Phil. Soc.* **18**:105–110.

————. 1915*b.* On *Williamsoniella,* a new type of bennettitalean flower. *Phil. Trans. Roy. Soc. London* **B207**:113–148.

Wieland, G. R. 1911. On the Williamsonian tribe. *Amer. J. Sci.* **32**:433–476.

CHAPTER 15: Ginkgophyta

Brown, J. T. 1975. Upper Jurassic and Lower Cretaceous Ginkgophytes from Montana. *J. Paleo.* **49**:724–730.

Florin, R. 1949. The morphology of *Trichopitys heteromorpha* Saporta, a seed-plant of Palaeozoic age, and the evolution of the female flowers in the Ginkgoinae. *Acta Horti Bergiani* **15**:79–109.

————. 1951. Evolution in cordaites and conifers. *Acta Horti Bergiani* **15**:285–389.

Harris, T. M. 1935. The fossil flora of Scoresby Sound East Greenland, part 4: Ginkgoales, Coniferales, Lycopodiales. *Medd. Gronland* **112**:3–176.

———. 1951. The fructification of *Czekanowskia* and its allies. *Phil. Trans. Roy. Soc. London* **B235**:483–508.

———. 1976. The Mesozoic gymnosperms. *Rev. Palaeobot. Palynol.* **21**:119–134.

———, and J. Miller. 1974. *The Yorkshire Jurassic flora*, vol. IV: *Czekanowskiales*. British Museum (Natural History), London, pp. 79–150.

———, and W. Millington. 1974. *The Yorkshire Jurassic flora*, vol. IV: *Ginkgoales*. British Museum (Natural History), London, pp. 2–78.

Kimura, T., and T. Ohana. 1978. *Czekanowskia nipponica* sp. nov., from the Upper Cretaceous Omichidani Formation, Ishikawa Prefecture in the Inner Zone of Central Japan. *Proc. Japan Acad.* **54**:595–600.

Krassilov, V. A. 1968. A new group of Mesozoic gymnosperms—Czekanowskiales. *Akad. Nauk SSSR. Doklady* **168**:942–945.

———. 1969. Approach to the classification of Mesozoic "Ginkgoalean" plants from Siberia. *Palaeobotanist* **18**:12–19.

———. 1977. The origin of angiosperms. *Bot. Rev.* **43**:143–176.

Pant, D. D. 1959. The classification of gymnospermous plants. *Palaeobotanist* **6**:65–70.

Tralau, H. 1968. Evolutionary trends in the genus *Ginkgo*. *Lethaia* **1**:63–101.

CHAPTER 16: Problematic Gymnosperms

Bharadwaj, D. C. 1963. Pollen grains of *Ephedra* and *Welwitschia* and their probable fossil relatives. *Mem. Indian Bot. Soc.* **4**:125–135.

Brenner, G. J. 1968. Middle Cretaceous spores and pollen from northeastern Peru. *Pollen Spores* **10**:341–383.

Gray, J. 1960. Temperate pollen genera in the Eocene (Claiborne) flora, Alabama. *Science* **132**:808–810.

Harris, T. M. 1962. The occurrence of the fructification *Carnoconites* in New Zealand. *Trans. Roy. Soc. New Zealand Geol.* **1**:17–27.

Mamay, S. H. 1975. *Sandrewia*, n. gen., a problematical plant from the Lower Permian of Texas and Kansas. *Rev. Palaeobot. Palynol.* **20**:75–83.

———. 1976. Vojnovskyales in the Lower Permian of North America. *Palaeobotanist* **25**:290–297.

Martens, P. 1971. *Les Gnétophytes. Handbuch der Pflanzenanatomie*, vol. 12. Gebrüder Borntraeger, Berlin.

Meyen, S. V. 1968. Conifer systematics and evolution—Relation to discovery of ovules in *Buriadia*. *Akad. Nauk SSSR Paleont. J.* **4**:28–31.

Neuburg, M. F. 1965. Permian flora of Pechora Basin, part III. *Akad. Nauk SSSR Geol. Inst. Trans.* **116**:1–44.

Pulle, A. 1938. The classification of the spermatophytes. *Chron. Bot.* **4**:109–113.

Sahni, B. 1948. The Pentoxyleae: A new group of Jurassic gymnosperms from the Rajmahal Hills of India. *Bot. Gaz.* **110**:47–80.

Scott, R. A. 1960. Pollen of *Ephedra* from the Chinle Formation (Upper Triassic) and the genus *Equisetosporites*. *Micropaleontology* **6**:271–276.

Sharma, B. D. 1974. Observations on the branching in *Pentoxylon sahnii* Srivastava. *Bull. Nat. Sci. Mus.* **17**:315–324.

Singh, H. 1978. *Embryology of Gymnosperms. Handbuch der Pflanzenanatomie,* vol. 10. Gebrüder Borntraeger, Berlin.

Vishnu-Mittre. 1953. A male flower of the Pentoxyleae with remarks on the structure of the female cones of the group. *Palaeobotanist* **2**:75–84.

———. 1958. Studies on the fossil flora of Nipania (Rajmahal Series), India— Pentoxyleae. *Palaeobotanist* **6**:31–46.

CHAPTER 17: Coniferophyta

CORDAITOPSIDA

Andrews, H. N., Jr., and C. J. Felix. 1952. The gametophyte of *Cardiocarpus spinatus* Graham. *Ann. Missouri Bot. Gard.* **39**:127–135.

Baxter, R. W. 1964. Paleozoic starch in fossil seeds from Kansas coal balls. *Trans. Kansas Acad. Sci.* **67**:418–422.

———. 1971. A comparison of the Paleozoic seed genera *Mitrospermum* and *Kamaraspermum. Phytomorphology* **21**:108–121.

Bhardwaj, D. C. 1953. Jurassic woods from the Rajmahal Hills, Bihar. *Palaeobotanist* **2**:59–70.

Cridland, A. A. 1962. The fungi in cordaitean rootlets. *Mycologia* **54**:230–234.

———. 1964. *Amyelon* in American coal balls. *Palaeontology* **7**:186–209.

Daghlian, C. P., and T. N. Taylor. 1979. A new structurally preserved Pennsylvanian cordaitean pollen organ. *Amer. J. Bot.* **66**:290–300.

Delevoryas, T. 1953. A new male cordaitean fructification from the Kansas Carboniferous. *Amer. J. Bot.* **40**:144–150.

Florin, R. 1936. On the structure of the pollen grains in the cordaitales. *Svensk Bot. Tidskrift* **30**:624–651.

———. 1944. Die Koniferen des Oberkarbons und des Unteren Perms. *Palaeontographica* **B85**(6):366–456.

———. 1950a. On female reproductive organs in the Cordaitinae. *Acta Horti Bergiani* **15**:111–134.

———. 1950b. Upper Carboniferous and Lower Permian conifers. *Bot. Rev.* **16**:258–282.

———. 1957. Notes on cordaitean fructifications from the Coal-Measures of North-Western Spain. *Acta Horti Bergiani* **17**:223–228.

Fry, W. L. 1956. New cordaitean cones from the Pennsylvanian of Iowa. *J. Paleo.* **30**:35–45.

Good, C. W., and T. N. Taylor. 1970. On the structure of *Cordaites felicis* Benson from the Lower Pennsylvanian of North America. *Palaeontology* **13**:29–39.

Harms, V. L., and G. A. Leisman. 1961. The anatomy and morphology of certain *Cordaites* leaves. *J. Paleo.* **35**:1041–1064.

Leisman, G. A. 1961. A new species of *Cardiocarpus* in Kansas coal balls. *Trans. Kansas Acad. Sci.* **64**:117–122.

Lundblad, B. 1966. Rudolf Florin. *Taxon* **15**:85–93.

Maheshwari, H. K., and S. V. Meyen. 1975. *Cladostrobus* and the systematics of cordaitalean leaves. *Lethaia* **8**:103–123.

Pierce, R. L., and J. W. Hall. 1953. *Premnoxylon,* a new cordaitean axis. *Phytomorphology* **3**:384–391.

Renault, B. 1893. Bassin houiller et permien d'Autun et d'Epinac, flore fossile, part 1, in *Études des gîtes minéraux de la France,* Fasc. 4. pp. 1–578. Imprimerie Nationale, Paris. (Atlas).

Rothwell, G. W. 1976. Primary vasculature and gymnosperm systematics. *Rev. Palaeobot. Palynol.* **22**193–206.

———. 1977. The primary vasculature of *Cordaianthus concinnus. Amer. J. Bot.* **64**:1235–1241.

Taylor, T. N., and W. N. Stewart. 1964. The Paleozoic seed *Mitrospermum* in American coal balls. *Palaeontographica* **B115**:51–58.

Traverse, A. 1950. The primary vascular body of *Mesoxylon thompsonii,* a new American cordaitean. *Amer. J. Bot.* **37**:318–325.

Vogellehner, D. 1964. Zur Nomenklatur der fossilen Holzgattung *Dadoxylon* Endlicher 1847. *Taxon* **13**:233–237.

———. 1965. Untersuchungen zur Anatomie and Systematik der verkieselten Holzer aus dem frankischen und sudthuringischen Keuper. *Erlanger Geol. Abh.* **59**:1–76.

Whiteside, K. L. 1974. Petrified cordaitean stems from North America. Ph.D. diss., Univ. of Iowa.

CONIFEROPSIDA

Voltziales

Archangelsky, S. 1966. New gymnosperms from the Ticó Flora, Santa Cruz Province, Argentina. *Bull. Brit. Mus. (Nat. Hist.) Geol.* **13**:259–295.

———, and J. C. Gamerro. 1966. Pollen grains found in coniferous cones from the Lower Cretaceous of Patagonia (Argentina). *Rev. Palaeobot. Palynol.* **5**:179–182.

Delevoryas, T., and R. C. Hope. 1975. *Voltzia andrewsii,* n. sp., and Upper Triassic seed cone from North Carolina, U.S.A. *Rev. Palaeobot. Palynol.* **20**:67–74.

Florin, R. 1938. Die Koniferen des Oberkarbons und Unteren Perms, part I. *Palaeontographica* **B85**:2–62.

———. 1939a. Die Koniferen des Oberkarbons und des Unteren Perms, part II. *Palaeontographica* **B85**:64–122.

———. 1939b. Die Koniferen des Oberkarbons und des Unteren Perms, part III. *Palaeontographica* **B85**:124–173.

———. 1939c. Die Koniferen des Oberkarbons und des Unteren Perms, part IV. *Palaeontographica* **B85**:176–241.

———. 1940. Die Koniferen des Oberkarbons und des Unteren Perms, part V. *Palaeontographica* **B85**:244–363.

———. 1945. Die Koniferen des Oberkarbons und des Unteren Perms, part VIII. *Palaeontographica* **B85**:655–729.

————. 1951. Evolution in cordaites and conifers. *Acta Horti Bergiani* **15**:285–389.

Harris, T. M. 1957. A Liasso-Rhaetic flora in South Wales. *Proc. Roy. Soc. London* **B147**:289–308.

————. 1979. *The Yorkshire Jurassic flora*, vol. V: *Coniferales*. British Museum (Natural History), London.

Jung, W. W. 1968. *Hirmerella muensteri* (Schank) Jung nov. comb., eine bedeutsame Konifere des Mesozoikums. *Palaeontographica* **B122**:55–93.

Mägdefrau, K. 1963. Die Gattungen *Voltzia* und *Glyptolepis* im Mittleren Keuper von Hassfurt (Main). *Geol. Bl. NO-Bayern* **13**:95–98.

Meyen, S. V. 1968. Some general questions concerning the systematics and evolution of conifers in connection with the open ovule of *Buriadia*. *Akad. Nauk SSSR. J. Paleo.* **4**:28–31.

Miller, C. N., Jr., and J. T. Brown. 1973. A new voltzialean cone bearing seeds with embryos from the Permian of Texas. *Amer. J. Bot.* **60**:561–569.

Pant, D. D., and D. D. Nautiyal. 1967. On the structure of *Buriadia heterophylla* (Feistmantel) Seward and Sahni and its fructification. *Phil. Trans. Roy. Soc. London, Ser. B,* **252**:27–48.

Schweitzer, H. J. 1963. Der weibliche Zapfen von *Pseudovoltzia liebeana* und seine Bedeutung für die Phylogenie der Koniferen. *Palaeontographica* **B113**:1–29.

Scott, A. 1974. The earliest conifer. *Nature* **251**:707–708.

Srivastava, S. K. 1976. The fossil pollen genus *Classopollis*. *Lethaia* **9**:437–457.

Townrow, J. A. 1967. On *Voltziopsis*, a southern conifer of Lower Triassic age. *Proc. Roy. Soc. Tasmania* **101**:173–188.

Coniferales

Palissyaceae

Florin, R. 1958. On Jurassic taxads and conifers from northwestern Europe and eastern Greenland. *Acta Horti Bergiani* **17**:257–402.

Harris, T. M. 1935. The fossil flora of Scoresby Sound, east Greenland, part 4: Ginkgoales, Coniferales, Lycopodiales and isolated fructifications. *Medd. Gronland* **112**:1–176.

Kraüsel, R. 1952. *Stachyotaxus sahnii* nov. spec., eine Konifere aus der Trias von Neuewelt bei Basel. *Palaeobotanist* **1**:285–288.

Nathorst, A. G. 1908. Paläobotanische Mitteilungen, part 7: Uber *Palissya, Stachyotaxus* und *Palaeotaxus*. *Kgl. Svenska Vet. Handl.* **43**:1–20.

Schweitzer, H. J. 1963. Der weibliche Zpfen von *Pseudovoltzia liebeana* und seine Bedeutung für die Phylogenie der Koniferen. *Palaeontographica* **B113**:1–29.

Podocarpaceae

Archangelsky, S. 1966. New gymnosperms from the Ticó Flora, Santa Cruz Province, Argentina. *Bull. Brit. Mus. (Nat. Hist.) Geol.* **13**:261–295.

Dilcher, D. L. 1969. *Podocarpus* from the Eocene of North America. *Science* **164**:299–301.

Playford, G., and M. F. Dettmann. 1978. Pollen of *Dacrydium franklinii* Hook. F. and comparable early Tertiary microfossils. *Pollen Spores* **20**:513–534.

Ramanujam, C. G. K. 1972. Fossil coniferous woods from the Oldham Formation (Upper Cretaceous) of Alberta. *Can. J. Bot.* **50**:595–602.

Townrow, J. A. 1967a. On *Rissikia* and *Mataia* Podocarpaceous conifers from the Lower Mesozoic of southern lands. *Proc. Roy. Soc. Tasmania* **101**:103–136.

———. 1967b. On a conifer from the Jurassic of east Antarctica. *Proc. Roy. Soc. Tasmania* **101**:137–146.

Araucariaceae

Archangelsky, S. 1966 New gymnosperms from the Ticó Flora, Santa Cruz Province, Argentina. *Bull. Brit. Mus. (Nat. Hist.) Geol.* **13**:261–295.

Bose, M. N., and H. K. Maheshwari. 1973. Some detached seed-scales belonging to Araucariaceae from the Mesozoic rocks of India. *Geophytology* **3**:205–214.

Kendall, N. W. 1949. A Jurassic member of the Araucariaceae. *Ann. Bot.* **13**:151–161.

———. 1952. Some conifers from the Jurassic of England. *Ann. Mag. Nat. Hist.* (12)**5**:583–594.

Krassilov, V. A. 1978. Araucariaceae as indicators of climate and paleolatitudes. *Rev. Palaeobot. Palynol.* **26**:113–124.

Sharma, B. D., and D. R. Bohra. 1977. Petrified araucarian megastrobili from the Jurassic of the Rahmahal Hills, India. *Acta Paleobot.* **18**:31–36.

Stockey, R. A. 1975. Seeds and embryos of *Araucaria mirabilis*. *Amer. J. Bot.* **62**:856–868.

———. 1978. Reproductive biology of Cerro Cuadrado fossil conifers: Ontogeny and reproductive strategies in *Araucaria mirabilis*. *Palaeontographica* **B166**:1–15.

———, and T. N. Taylor. 1978. On the structure and evolutionary relationships of the Cerro Cuadrado fossil conifer seedlings. *Bot. J. Linn. Soc.* **76**:161–176.

Cupressaceae

Alvin, K. L. 1977. The conifers *Frenelopsis* and *Manica* in the Cretaceous of Portugal. *Palaeontology* **20**:387–404.

———, and A. Hlustik. 1979. Modified axillary branching in species of the fossil genus *Frenelopsis:* A new phenomenon among conifers. *Bot. J. Linn. Soc.* **79**:231–241.

———, and J. J. C. Pais. 1978. A *Frenelopsis* with opposite decussate leaves from the Lower Cretaceous of Portugal. *Palaeontology* **21**:873–879.

———, R. A. Spicer, and J. Watson. 1978. A *Classopollis*-containing male cone associated with *Pseudofrenelopsis*. *Palaeontology* **21**:847–856.

Chaloner, W. G., and J. Lorch. 1960. An opposite leaved conifer from the Jurassic of Israel. *Palaeontology* **2**:236–242.

Daghlian, C. P., and C. P. Person. 1977. The cuticular anatomy of *Frenelopsis varians* from the Lower Cretaceous of central Texas. *Amer. J. Bot.* **64**:564–569.

Friis, E. M. 1977. Leaf whorls of Cupressaceae from the Miocene Fasterholt flora, Denmark. *Bull. Geol. Soc. Denmark* **26**:103–113.

Hlustik, A., and M. Konzalova. 1976a. Polliniferous cones of *Frenelopsis alata* (K. Feism.) Knobloch from the Cenomanian of Bohemia, Czechoslovakia. *Vestnik Ustredniho Ustavu Geologickeho* **51**:31–45.

——— and ———. 1976b. *Frenelopsis alata* (K. Feistm.) Knobloch (Cupressaceae) from the Cenomanian of Bohemia, a new plant producing *Classopollis* pollen. In: *Evolutionary biology*. Proceedings of Conference, 1975, Liblice, pp. 125–131.

Lemoigne, Y. 1967. Paléoflore à Cupressales dans le Trias-Rhétien du Cotentin. *C.R. Acad. Sci. Paris* **D264**:715–718.

Lorch, J. 1968. Some Jurassic conifers from Israel. *Bot. J. Linn. Soc.* **61**:177–188.

Penny, J. S. 1947. Studies on the conifers of the Magothy Flora. *Amer. J. Bot.* **34**:281–296.

Pons, D., and J. Broutin. 1978. Les organes réproducteurs de *Frenelopsis oligostomata*, (Cretace, Portugal). *Cong. Nat. Soc. Savantes, Sci.* **2**:138–159.

Taxodiaceae

Arnold, C. A. and J. S. Lowther. 1955. A new Cretaceous conifer from northern Alaska. *Amer. J. Bot.* **42**:522–528.

Bose, M. N. 1955. *Sciadopitytes variabilis* n. sp. from the Arctic of Canada. *Norsk Geol. Tidsskrift* **35**:53–68.

Chaney, R. W. 1951. A revision of fossil *Sequoia* and *Taxodium* in western North America based upon the recent discovery of *Metasequoia*. *Trans. Amer. Phil. Soc. N.S.* **40**:171–263.

Christophel, D. C. 1973. *Sciadopitophyllum canadense* gen. et sp. nov.: A new conifer from western Alberta. *Amer. J. Bot.* **60**:61–66.

Endo, A. 1928. A new Palaeocene species of *Sequoia*. *Jpn. J. Geol. Geog.* **6**:27–29.

Florin, R. 1958. On Jurassic taxads and conifers from northwestern Europe and eastern Greenland. *Acta Horti Bergiani* **17**:257–402.

Harris, T. M. 1953. Conifers of the Taxodiaceae from the Wealden Formation of Belgium. *Mem. Inst. Roy. Sci. Nat. Belgique* **126**:1–43.

Hu, H. H., and W. C. Cheng. 1948. On the new family Metasequoiaceae and on *Metasequoia glyptostroboides*, a living species of the genus *Metasequoia* found in Szechuan and Hupeh. *Bull. Fan Mem. Inst. Biol.* **1**:153–161.

Kimura, T., and J. Horiuchi. 1978. *Cunninghamia nodensis* sp. nov., from the Palaeogene Noda Group, Northeast Japan. *Proc. Jpn. Acad.* **54**:589–594.

Miki, S. 1941. On the change of flora in eastern Asia since Tertiary Period, part I: The clay or lignite beds flora in Japan with special reference to the *Pinus trifolia* beds in Central Hondo. *Jap. J. Bot.* **11**:237–303.

Miller, C. N., Jr. 1975. Petrified cones and needle-bearing twigs of a new taxodiaceous conifer from the early Cretaceous of California. *Amer. J. Bot.* **62**:706–713.

Page, V. M. 1973. A new conifer from the Upper Cretaceous of Central California. *Amer. J. Bot.* **60**:570–575.

Ramanujam, C. G. K., and W. N. Stewart. 1969*a*. Fossil woods of Taxodiaceae from the Edmonton Formation (Upper Cretaceous) of Alberta. *Can. J. Bot.* **47**:115–124.

——— and ———. 1969*b*. Taxodiaceous bark from the Upper Cretaceous of Alberta. *Amer. J. Bot.* **56**:101–107.

Rothwell, G. W., and J. F. Basinger. 1979. *Metasequoia milleri* n. sp., anatomically preserved pollen cones from the Middle Eocene (Allenby Formation) of British Columbia. *Can. J. Bot.* **57**:958–970.

Stockey, R. A. 1977. Reproductive biology of the Cerro Cuadrado (Jurassic) fossil conifers: *Pararaucaria patagonica*. *Amer. J. Bot.* **64**:733–744.

Townrow, J. A. 1967. The *Brachphyllum crassum* complex of fossil conifers. *Papers Proc. Roy. Soc. Tasmania* **101**:149–172.

Pinaceae

Alvin, K. L. 1953. Three Abietaceous cones from the Wealden of Belgium. *Mem. Inst. Roy. Sci. Nat. Belgique* **125**:1–42.

———. 1957. On *Pseudoaraucaria* Fliche emend., a genus of fossil Pinaceous cones. *Ann. Bot.* **21**:33–51.

————. 1960. Further conifers of the Pinaceae from the Wealden Formation of Belgium. *Mem. Inst. Roy. Sci. Nat. Belgique* **146**:1–39.

Arnold, C. A. 1953. Silicified plant remains from the Mesozoic and Tertiary of western North America. *Papers Mich. Acad. Sci. Arts Letters* **38**:9–20.

————. 1955. Tertiary conifers from the Princeton Coal Field of British Columbia. *Cont. Mus. Paleo. Univ. Mich.* **12**:245–258.

Delevoryas, T., and R. C. Hope. 1973. Fertile coniferophyte remains from the late Triassic Deep River Basin, North Carolina. *Amer. J. Bot.* **60**:810–818.

Jeffrey, E. C. 1908. On the structure of the leaf in Cretaceous pines. *Ann. Bot.* **22**:207–220.

Miller, C. N., Jr. 1972. *Pityostrobus palmeri,* a new species of petrified conifer cones from the Late Cretaceous of New Jersey. *Amer. J. Bot.* **59**:352–358.

————. 1973. Silicified cones and vegetative remains of *Pinus* from the Eocene of British Columbia. *Cont. Mus. Paleo. Univ. Mich.* **24**:101–118.

————. 1974. *Pityostrobus hallii,* a new species of structurally preserved conifer cones from the Late Cretaceous of Maryland. *Amer. J. Bot.* **61**:798–804.

————. 1976. Early evolution in the Pinaceae. *Rev. Palaeobot. Palynol.* **21**:101–117.

————. 1977. Mesozoic conifers. *Bot. Rev.* **43**:218–280.

————. 1978. *Pinus burtii,* a new species of petrified cones from the Miocene of Martha's Vineyard. *Bull. Torrey Bot. Club* **105**:93–97.

Robison, C. R. 1977. *Prepinus parlinensis.* sp. nov., from the Late Cretaceous of New Jersey. *Bot. Gaz.* **138**:352–356.

Cephalotaxaceae

Berry, E. W. 1919. Contributions to the Mesozoic flora of the Atlantic coastal plain, part 5. *Bull. Torrey Bot. Club* **37**:181–200.

Florin, R. 1958. On Jurassic taxads and conifers from northwestern Europe and eastern Greenland. *Acta Horti Bergiani* **17**:257–402.

Heer, O. 1883. Die fossile Flora der Polarlander. *Flora Fossilis Arctica, Zurich* **7**:1–275.

Taxales

Alvin, K. L. 1960. On the seed *Vesquia tournaisii* C. E. Bertrand, from the Belgian Wealden. *Ann. Bot.* **24**:508–515.

Florin, R. 1944. Die Koniferen des Oberkarbons und des Unteren Perms, part VII. *Palaeontographica* **B85**:459–654.

————. 1948. On the morphology and relationships of the Taxaceae. *Bot. Gaz.* **110**:31–39.

————. 1954. The female reproductive organs of conifers and taxads. *Biol. Rev.* **29**:367–389.

————. 1958. On Jurassic taxads and conifers from northwestern Europe and eastern Greenland. *Acta Horti Bergiani* **17**:257–402.

————. 1963. The distribution of conifer and taxad genera in time and space. *Acta Horti Bergiani* **20**:121–312.

Harris, T. M. 1976a. The Mesozoic gymnosperms. *Rev. Palaeobot. Palynol.* **21**:119–134.

————. 1976b. Two neglected aspects of fossil conifers. *Amer. J. Bot.* **63**:902–910.

Roy, S. K. 1972. Fossil wood of Taxaceae from the McMurray Formation (Lower Cretaceous) of Alberta, Canada. *Can. J. Bot.* **50**:349–352.

CHAPTER 18: Anthophyta

Axelrod, D. I. 1944. The Pliocene sequence in central California. *Carnegie Inst. Wash. Publ.* **553**(VIII):207–224.

———. 1956. Mio-Pliocene floras from west-central Nevada. *Univ. Calif. Bull. Dept. Geol. Sci.* **33**:1–321.

———. 1959. Poleward migration of early angiosperm flora. *Science* **130**:203–207.

———. 1961. How old are the angiosperms? *Amer. J. Sci.* **259**:447–459.

———. 1966. The Eocene Copper Basin flora of northeastern Nevada. *Univ. Calif. Publ. Geol. Sci.* **51.**

———. 1970. Mesozoic paleogeography and early angiosperm history. *Bot. Rev.* **36**:277–319.

Basinger, J. F. 1976. *Paleorosa similkameenensis,* gen. et sp. nov., permineralized flowers (Rosaceae) from the Eocene of British Columbia. *Can. J. Bot.* **54**:2293–2350.

Beck. C. B. 1976. Origin and early evolution of angiosperms: A perspective. In: C. B. Beck (ed.), *Origin and early evolution of angiosperms.* Columbia Univ. Press, New York, pp. 1–10.

Becker, H. F. 1961. Oligocene plants from the Upper Ruby River Basin, southwestern Montana. *Geol. Soc. Amer. Mem.* **82.**

———. 1972. *Sanmiguelia,* an enigma compounded. *Palaeontographica* **B138**:181–185.

———. 1973. The York ranch flora of the Upper Ruby River Basin, southwestern Montana. *Palaeontographica* **B143**:18–93.

Brenner, G. J. 1967. The gymnospermous affinity of *Eucommiidites* Erdtman, 1948. *Rev. Palaeobot. Palynol.* **5**:123–127.

———. 1976. Middle Cretaceous floral provinces and early migrations of angiosperms. In: C. B. Beck (ed.), *Origin and early evolution of angiosperms.* Columbia Univ. Press, New York, pp. 23–47.

Brown, R. W. 1935. Miocene leaves, fruits, and seeds from Idaho, Oregon, and Washington. *J. Paleo.* **9**:572–587.

———. 1956. Palmlike plants from the Dolores Formation (Triassic) in southwestern Colorado. *U.S.G.S. Prof. Paper.* **274**:205–209.

———. 1962. Paleocene flora of the Rocky Mountains and the Great Plains. *U.S. Geol. Survey Prof. Paper* **375.**

Chandler, M. E. J., and D. I. Axelrod. 1961. An early Cretaceous (Hauterivian) angiosperm fruit from California. *Amer. J. Sci.* **259**:441–446.

Chaney, R. W. 1959. Miocene floras of the Columbia Plateau, part I: Composition and interpretation. *Carnegie Inst. Wash. Publ.* **617**:1–134.

———. 1967. Miocene forests of the Pacific Basin: Their ancestors and their descendants. Jubilee Publ. Commem. Prof. Sasa, 60th Birthday, pp. 209–239.

———, and D. I. Axelrod. 1959. Miocene floras of the Columbia Plateau, part II: Systematic considerations. *Carnegie Inst. Wash. Publ.* **617**:135–229.

Chitaley, S. D., and U. R. Kate. 1974. *Deccanathus savitrii,* a new petrified flower from the Deccan Intertrappean beds of India. *Palaeobotanist* **21**:317–320.

———, and M. Z. Patel. 1975. *Raoanthus intertrappea,* a new petrified flower from India. *Palaeontographica* **183B**:141–149.

Cranwell, L. M. 1964. Ancient Pacific floras. In: L. M. Cranwell (ed.), *Tenth Pacific Science Congress Series.* University of Hawaii Press, Honolulu. 113 pages.

Crepet, W. L. 1978. Investigations of angiosperms from the Eocene of North America: An aroid inflorescence. *Rev. Palaeobot. Palynol.* **25**:241–252.

―――. 1979. Insect pollination: A paleontological perspective *BioSci.* **29**:102–108.

―――. 1980. Castaneoid inflorescences from the middle Eocene of Tennessee and the diagnostic value of pollen (at the subfamily level) within the Fagaceae. *Amer. J. Bot.* (in press).

―――, D. L. Dilcher, and F. W. Potter. 1974. Eocene angiosperm flowers. *Science* **185**:781–782.

―――, ―――, and ―――. 1975. Investigations of angiosperms from the Eocene of North America: A catkin with juglandaceous affinities. *Amer. J. Bot.* **62**:813–823.

Czeczott, H. 1960. The flora of the Baltic amber and its age. *Pr. Muz. Ziemi.* **4**:119–145.

Daghlian, C. P. 1978. Coryphoid palms from the Lower and Middle Eocene of southeastern North America. *Palaeontographica* **B166**:44–82.

―――. 1981. A review of the fossil record of the monocots. *Bot. Rev.* (in press).

Dilcher, D. L. 1973. A paleoclimatic interpretation of the Eocene floras of southeastern North America. In: A. Graham (ed.), *Vegetation and vegetational history of northern Latin America,* Elsevier, Amsterdam, pp. 39–59.

―――. 1974. Approaches to the identification of angiosperm leaf remains. *Bot. Rev.* **40**:1–157.

―――, and C. P. Daghlian. 1977. Investigations of angiosperms from the Eocene of southeastern North America: *Philodendron* leaf remains. *Amer. J. Bot.* **64**:526–534.

―――, and G. E. Dolph. 1970. Fossil leaves of *Dendropanax* from Eocene sediments of southeastern North America. *Amer. J. Bot.* **57**:153–160.

―――, F. W. Potter, and W. L. Crepet. 1976. Investigations of angiosperms from the Eocene of North America: Juglandaceous winged fruits. *Amer. J. Bot.* **63**:532–544.

Dolph, G. 1975. A statistical analysis of *Apocynophyllum mississippiensis.* *Palaeontographica* **B151**:1–51.

―――, and D. L. Dilcher. 1979. Foliar physiognomy as an aid in determining paleoclimate. *Palaeontographica* **B170**:151–172.

Dorf, E. 1930. Pliocene floras of California. *Carnegie Inst. Wash. Publ.* **412.**

Doyle, J. A. 1969. Cretaceous angiosperm pollen of the Atlantic coastal plain and its evolutionary significance. *J. Arnold Arbor.* **50**:1–35.

―――. 1973. The monocotyledons: Their evolution and comparative biology, part 5: Fossil evidence on early evolution of the monocotyledons. *Quart. Rev. Biol.* **48**:399–413.

―――, M. Van Campo, and B. Lugardon. 1975. Observations on exine structure of *Eucommiidites* and Lower Cretaceous angiosperm pollen. *Pollen Spores* **17**:429–486.

―――, and L. J. Hickey. 1976. Pollen and leaves from the Mid-Cretaceous Potomac Group and their bearing on early angiosperm evolution. In: C. B. Beck (ed.), *Origin and early evolution of angiosperms.* Columbia Univ. Press, New York, pp. 139–206.

―――, P. Biens, A. Doerenkamp, and S. Jardiné. 1977. Angiosperm pollen from the Pre-Albian Lower Cretaceous of equatorial Africa. *Bull. Cent. Rech. Explor.-Prod. Elf-Aquitaine* **1**:451–473.

Giannasi, D. E., and K. J. Niklas. 1978. Flavonoid and other chemical constituents of fossil Miocene *Celtis* and *Ulmus* (Succor Creek Flora). *Science* **197**:765–767.

Gould, R. E., and T. Delevoryas. 1977. The biology of *Glossopteris:* Evidence from seed-bearing and pollen-bearing organs. *Alcheringa* **1**:387–399.

Graham, A. 1965. The Sucker Creek and Trout Creek Miocene floras of southeastern Oregon. *Kent State Univ. Res. Ser. Bull.* **9.**

Harris, T. M. 1932. The fossil flora of Scoresby Sound, east Greenland, part 2:

Description of seed plants *Incertae sedis* together with a discussion of certain cycadophyte cuticles. *Medd. Gronland* **85:**1–112.

Hickey, L. J. 1973. Classification of the architecture of dicotyledonous leaves. *Amer. J. Bot.* **60:**17–33.

———. 1977. Stratigraphy and paleobotany of the Golden Valley Formation (Early Tertiary) of western North Dakota. *Geol. Mem.* **150:**1–181.

———. 1978. Origin of the major features of angiosperm leaf architecture in the fossil record. *Cour. Forsch. Inst. Senckenberg* **30:**27–34.

———, and J. A. Doyle. 1977. Early Cretaceous fossil evidence for angiosperm evolution. *Bot. Rev.* **43:**3–104.

Hughes, N. F. 1961. Further interpretation of *Eucommiidites* Erdtman. *Paleontology* **4:**292–299.

———. 1976. *Palaeobiology of angiosperm origins—Problems of mesozoic seed-plant evolution.* Cambridge Univ. Press, Cambridge, England.

———. 1977. Palaeo-succession of earliest angiosperm evolution. *Bot. Rev.* **43:**105–127.

Kemp, E. M. 1968. Probable angiosperm pollen from British Barremian to Albian strata. *Palaeontology* **11:**421–434.

Koch, B. E. 1963. Fossil plants from the lower Paleocene of the Agatdalen (Angmarttus-sut) area, central Nûgssuaq Peninsula, Northwest Greenland. *Medd. Gronland* **172.**

Krassilov, V. A. 1973. Mesozoic plants and the problem of angiosperm ancestry. *Lethaia* **6:**163–178.

———. 1975. Dirhopalostachyaceae—A new family of proangiosperms and its bearing on the problem of angiosperm ancestry. *Palaeontographica* **B153:**100–110.

———. 1977. The origin of angiosperms. *Bot. Rev.* **43:**143–176.

MacGinitie, H. D. 1941. A middle Eocene flora from the Central Sierra Nevada. *Carnegie Inst. Wash. Publ.* **534:**1–178.

———. 1953. Fossil plants from the Florissant beds. Colorado. *Carnegie Inst. Wash. Publ.* **599.**

———. 1969. *The Eocene Green River flora of northwestern Colorado and northeastern Utah.* Univ. California, Berkeley and Los Angesles. 203 pages.

Manchester, S. R. 1979. *Triplochitioxylon* (Sterculiaceae): A new genus of wood from the Eocene of Oregon and its bearing on xylem evolution in the extant genus *Triplochiton. Amer. J. Bot.* **66:**699–708.

Melville, R. 1960. A new theory of the angiosperm flower. *Nature* **188:**14–18.

Muller, J. 1970. Palynological evidence on early differentiation of angiosperms. *Biol. Rev.* **45:**417–450.

Nambudiri, E. M. V., W. D. Tidwell, B. N. Smith, and N. P. Hebbert. 1978. A C4 plant from the Pliocene. *Nature* **276:**816–817.

Niklas, K. J., and D. E. Giannasi. 1978. Angiosperm paleobiochemistry of the Succor Creek Flora (Miocene) Oregon, USA. *Amer. J. Bot.* **65:**943–952.

Pacltova, B. 1977. Cretaceous angiosperms of Bohemia—Central Europe. *Bot. Rev.* **43:**128–142.

Read, R. W., and L. J. Hickey. 1972. A revised classification of fossil palm and palm-like leaves. *Taxon* **21:**129–137.

Reid, M. E., and M. E. J. Chandler. 1933. *The flora of the London clay.* British Museum (Natural History), London.

Sinnott, E. W., and I. W. Bailey. 1915. Investigations of the phylogeny of the angiosperms, part 5: Foliar evidence as to the ancestry and early climatic environment of the angiosperms. *Amer. J. Bot.* **2:**1–22.

Stebbins, G. L. 1965. The probable growth habit of the earliest flowering plants. *Ann. Missouri Bot. Gard.* **52**:457–468.

Stopes, M. C., and K. Fujii. 1911. Studies on the structure and affinities of Cretaceous plants. *Phil. Trans. Roy. Soc. London* **201**:1–90.

Takhtajan, A. 1969. *Flowering plants origin and dispersal.* Oliver Boyd, Edinburgh. 310 pages.

Thomasson, J. R. 1978*a*. Observations on the characteristics of the lemma and palea of the late Cenozoic grass *Panicum elegans. Amer. J. Bot.* **65**:34–39.

———. 1978*b*. Epidermal patterns of the lemma in some fossil and living grasses and their phylogenetic significance. *Science* **199**:975–977.

Tidwell, W. D., A. D. Simper, and G. F. Thayn. 1977. Additional information concerning the controversial Triassic plant: *Sanmiguelia. Palaeontographica* **B163**: 143–151.

Van Konijnenburg-Van Cittert, J. H. A. 1971. In situ gymnosperm pollen from the Middle Jurassic of Yorkshire. *Acta Bot. Neerl.* **20**:1–96.

Von Ettinghausen, C. 1854. Über die Nervation der Blätter und blattartigen Organe bei den Euphorbiaceen, mit besonderer Rückischt auf die vorweltlichen Formen. *Sitz. Ber. Kaiserl. Akad. Wiss., Math Nat. Cl.* **12**:138–160.

———. 1856. Über die Nervation der Blätter bei den Celastrineen. *Sitz. Ber. Kaiserl. Akad. Wiss., Math. Naturw, Cl.* **22**:269–271.

———. 1858. Die Blattskelete der Apetalen, line Vorarbeit zur Interpretation der fossilen Pflanzenreste. *Denkschr. Kaiserl. Akad. Wiss., Math Nat. Cl.* **15**:181–272.

———. 1865. Beitrag zur Kenntnis der Nervation der Gramineen. *Sitz. Ber. Kaiserl. Akad. Wiss., Math Nat. Cl.* **32**:51–84.

Walker, J. W. (ed.). 1975. The bases of angiosperm phylogeny (a series of twelve papers including both extant and fossil materials). *Ann. Missouri Bot. Gard.* **62**:515–834.

Wolfe, J. A. 1964. Miocene floras from Fingerrock Wash, southwestern Nevada. *U.S. Geol. Survey Prof. Paper* **398B**:1–32.

———., J. A. Doyle, and V. M. Page. 1975. The bases of angiosperm phylogeny: Paleobotany. *Ann. Missouri Bot. Gard.* **62**:801–824.

Glossary

Abaxial   Lower surface.

Acritarchs   General terms for morphologically variable microfossils whose affinities cannot be determined.

Acrolamella   In certain heterosporous ferns, the elongate proximal region of the perispore.

Actinostele   A type of protostele in which the outer edge appears fluted or ridged in transverse section.

Acumen   A tapering point.

Adaxial   Upper surface.

Adventitious   A structure that arises from an unusual or abnormal position.

Aerial   Living above the surface of the ground or water.

Alveolate   A type of sporoderm infrastructure characterized by a honeycombed pattern.

Amber   Fossil resin.

Amphicribral   A concentric vascular bundle in which the phloem surrounds the xylem.

Amphiphloic   Arrangement in which phloem is present on both sides of the xylem.

Amphistomatic   Having stomata on both surfaces of a leaf.

Anatropous   A condition in which an ovule or seed is reflexed so that the micropyle is directed toward the point of attachment.

Anemophilous   Wind pollinated.

Anisophyllous   Producing more than one form of leaf.

Antheridium   A multicellular organ, except in algae and fungi, that produces sperm.

Antithetic (interpolation) theory   Idea that suggests how the alternation of generations in plants came about. According to this concept, the gametophyte is primitive, and the sporophyte is of secondary origin, having evolved through a delay in meiosis of a diploid zygote.

Aphlebia   Anomalous pinnae on the rachis of some ferns.

Apoxogenesis   Type of growth that results in the decrease in diameter of the primary xylem in distal parts of a plant.

Arborescent   Treelike.

Areoles   The smallest areas of the leaf tissue surrounded by veins which taken together form a contiguous field over most of the area of the leaf.

Aril   A fleshy and often colored outer envelope around a seed.

Ascoscarp   The sporocarp, or "fruiting body," in certain fungi that produces the asci and ascospores.

Autospore   Nonmotile algal spore that is a miniature of the cell from which it was derived.

Autotrophic   Capacity to synthesize protoplasm from inorganic substances.

Azonate   Lacking furrows that encircle the equator of a spore.

Bisaccate   A pollen grain processing two sacci.

Biseriate frond   Pinnae arranged in two rows and flattened in the same plane.

Bisporangiate   Reproductive organ that produces two types of spores.

Calyptroperiblem   The root cap of the embryo of certain conifers.

Camptodromous   A leaf-venation pattern characterized by secondary veins not terminating at the margin.

Cappus   The thickened proximal portion of a saccate pollen grain (e.g., *Pinus*).

Carinal canal   Elongate cavity in sphenophyte stems formed during stem elongation when protoxylem tracheids were ruptured.

Cast   Preservation type that forms in a mold.

Cataphyll   A rudimentary scalelike leaf that precedes the foliage leaf.

Centrarch   A type of primary xylem differentiation in which the protoxylem is central and surrounded by metaxylem.

Circinate vernation   Curled or coiled arrangement of leaves or leaflets in the bud.

Clamp connection   A small protuberance or outgrowth of a hyphal cell to an adjacent cell at the time of cell division in dikaryotic hyphae of the basidiomycetes.

Cleistothecium   A type of ascocarp that produces spores internally and that is enclosed at maturity.

Clepsydroid   Hourglass shaped in transverse section.

Coal ball   A type of petrifaction that occurs associated with Pennsylvanian peat accumulations in which the mineral matrix is typically microcrystalline calcite or dolomite.

Columella   A central column of sterile cells in a sporangium.

Compression   A type of preservation in which the organic material is represented by a thin film of carbon.

Connate   Joined into a single organ, e.g., leaves that are united at the base.

Coriaceous   Thick or leathery in texture.

Corpus   The central body of a saccate pollen grain.

Costa   A ridge or midrib.

Crassula (crassulae)   Thickenings of intercellular material and primary wall along the upper and lower margins of a pit pair in gymnosperm tracheids.

Cryptogam   A seedless plant.

Cryptopore   Pore covered by the tectum on the distal face of a *Classopollis* pollen grain.

Cupule   An accessory set of structures that may be free or united and surrounds one or more seeds.

Cuticle   The waxy layer that impregnates the walls of epidermal cells making them nearly impermeable to water.

Decussate   Pairs of appendages that occur alternately and at right angles to one another.

Determinate growth   Type of growth that has a fixed and definite limit (e.g., vegetative organs of the arborescent lycopods).

Dextral   Turned to the right; clockwise.

Diarch   Having two sites of protoxylem.

Diatomaceous earth   Sediment made up of siliceous diatom frustules.

Dichotomous   Divided into two branches; forking in pairs.

Dictyostele   A siphonostele or solenostele dissected by leaf gaps.

Dictyoxylon   Type of cortical organization characterized by a netted system of fibrous strands.

Dioecious   The condition in seed plants in which the pollen- and seed-producing organs are borne on separate plants.

Diploxylic   Having two or more vascular bundles in a leaf; a vascular bundle in which the centrifugal part of the wood is secondary.

Ectophloic   Arrangement in which phloem is external to the xylem.

Elater   Hygroscopic appendages present on the surface of many sphenophyte spores; twisted hygroscopic filament present in the capsule of some liverworts.

Enation   An outgrowth from any plant surface, but typically a stem.

Endarch   A type of primary xylem maturation in which the protoxylem elements are closest to the center of the axis or in which differentiation is centrifugal.

Endoreticulations   The reticulum or network of processes that are present lining the inner surface of the sacci of some pollen grains.

Endosporic   Gametophyte of heterosporous plants that is enclosed by the wall of the spore.

Endotesta   The delicate, innermost layer of the integument of some seeds.

Entomophilous   Pollination by insects.

Epidogenesis   Type of growth that results in an increase in the diameter of primary xylem at the base of an organ.

Epimatium   Fleshy outgrowth covering the ovule of podocarps.

Epithelial cells   A layer of parenchymatous cells that may be secretory and that surrounds an intercellular canal.

Equisetiform hair   Multicellular, uniseriate epidermal hair characterized by cell wall extensions of the end walls that give a toothlike appearance.

Eustele   Cylindrical stele constructed of discrete strands separated by parenchymatous tissue and, in some instances, leaf gaps.

Exannulate   Lacking an annulus.

Exarch   A type of primary xylem maturation in which the protoxylem elements are closest to the outside of the axis or in which differentiation is centripetal.

Exosporic   Gametophyte of homosporous plants that is free living and not enclosed by the spore wall.

False stem   Axis that morphologically resembles a true stem, but structurally has tissues organized in an atypical manner (e.g., stem of *Psaronius*).

Foliar member   General term used in descriptions of fossil ferns to refer to isolated frond parts that demonstrate bilateral symmetry and a branching pattern that is lateral and distichous.

Form genus   A genus that cannot be assigned to a family because there is no proof of the precise botanical affinities.

Frustule   Siliceous wall of a diatom.

Gametophore   A structure upon which gametes are borne.

Gametophyte   Gamete-producing plant.

Gemma   A specialized bud or cluster of cells that functions in vegetative (asexual) reproduction.

Glochidium   Elongate, hooked process that forms on the microspore massulae and serves to attach the mass of microspores to the megaspore massulae.

Gradate sorus   A sorus in which the sporangia mature from the center toward the periphery.

Graptolite   Extinct zoologic colonial organism that produced chitinous enclosing and supporting structures and regarded by some as hydrozoan or related to primitive chordates.

Gyrogonite   Fossilized charophyte oogonium.

Haplocheilic   Type of stomatal development in which the guard cells and subsidiary cells develop from different epidermal cells.

Haplostele   Cylindrical protostele that possesses a smooth margin when viewed in transverse section.

Haptotypic   Characters that develop on a pollen grain or spore in response to contact with its neighbors.

Haustorium   An absorptive structure such as a hyphal branch or pollen tube.

Herbaceous   A plant having little or no secondary development and thus not being woody.

Heterosporous   The production of spores of two sizes.

Heterotrichous   A type of algal thallus consisting of a prostrate portion from which extends a series of filamentous branches.

Homologous (transformation) theory   Idea that suggests how the alternation of generations in plants came about. According to this concept, the gametophyte is primitive, and the sporophyte is believed to be a modified gametophyte.

Homosporous   The production of spores of one size.

Hydathode   A glandular structure that exudes water from a leaf.

Hydroid   A water-conducting strand in aerial stems.

Hypostomatic   Possessing stomata only on the undersurface.

Hystrichosphere   General term for dinoflagellatelike microfossils with spherical central bodies that exhibit radiating processes.

Impression   Preservation type represented by the negative imprint of an organism.

Indusium (indusia)   A covering that protects the sorus of a fern.

Integument   Outer tissue that covers the megasporangium of an ovule.

Internode   Portion of an axis between nodes.

Isophyllous   Producing one type of leaf.

Isospore   General designation for the spores of homosporous plants.

Kerogen   The insoluble amorphous organic material present in sediments.

Lagenostome   Small extension at the distal end of the megasporangium of certain fossil seed plants.

Leptoids   Clusters of polygonal cells found in some bryophytes that resemble sieve tubes.

Leptoma   Aperturelike thin area on a pollen grain.

Liana   Woody climbing plant characteristically found in the tropics.

Ligule A small flap of tissue on the adaxial surfaces of leaves of certain members of the Lycophyta.

Lysigenous Having a cavity formed by the disorganization or dissolution of some cells.

Manoxylic General term for a wood type that contains abundant parenchyma.

Massula (massulae) Large masses of mucilaginous material that develop from the plasmodium in certain heterosporous ferns *(Azolla)* above the functional megaspore.

Medullated The presence of a pith or ground tissue.

Megaphyll Large leaf with many veins that typically is associated with a stele with gaps.

Megaspore Large spore that typically produces a megagametophyte.

Mesarch A type of primary xylem maturation in which the metaxylem surrounds the protoxylem.

Metaxylem Primary xylem formed after the protoxylem and after elongation is completed.

Microphyll Small leaf with a single trace that does not leave a gap when it departs from the stele.

Micropyle Channel through the integument of a seed through which the pollen or pollen tube may enter.

Microspore Small spore that typically produces a microgametophyte.

Miospore Neutral term for all spores less than 200 μm in diameter regardless of their function.

Mold Preservation type represented by a highly three-dimensional negative imprint.

Monarch Having a single protoxylem group.

Monocolpate Elongate furrow on a pollen grain that crosses the equator of the grain at right angles; sometimes used in place of monosulcate.

Monocyclic stomata Having a single row of subsidiary cells surrounding the guard cells.

Monoecious The condition in seed plants in which the pollen- and seed-producing organs are produced on the same plant.

Monolete Spore with a single straight scar on the proximal surface marking the position of contact with the other spores of the tetrad.

Monopodial One continuous main stem or axis.

Monopodial branching A pattern with one continuous main stem and branches arising laterally below the apex.

Monoporate Pollen grain with a single rounded pore or aperture.

Monosaccate A pollen grain with a single encircling saccus.

Monosporangiate Reproductive organ that produces a single type of spore.

Monosulcate Elongate furrow on the distal surface of a pollen grain.

Mycorrhiza Symbiotic relationship of a fungus and root or rootlike organ.

Nectary A nectar-secreting gland or organ.

Node Position on an axis where one or more parts are attached.

Nucellus The tissue that surrounds the megasporocyte of seed plants that is probably homologous with a megasporangium.

Nucule cast A type of preservation that occurs when sediment fills the inside of the seed integument or the inside of the nucellus.

Oogamy Sexual union of a small motile sperm and large nonmotile egg.

Oogonium A unicellular gametangium that contains an egg.

Operculum A lid covering the capsule in some bryophytes.

Orbicle Spherical structures composed of sporopollenin that are produced in the sporangia of some vascular plants that possess a secretory type of tapetum.

Organ genus A genus assignable to a family as defined by functionally related and commonly connected sets of biocharacters.

Organotaxis The system of organ arrangement on an axis or stem.

Orthotropous Ovule arrangement in which the micropyle is directed away from the point of attachment.

Ostiole A small opening or pore.

Ovule A megasporangium enclosed by an integument and developing into a seed after fertilization.

Palea (paleae) Scales that form the ramentum in ferns.

Paleobotany The study of fossil plants.

Palynology The study of pollen grains and spores; in a more general sense, the study of plant microfossils.

Palynomorph General term for all types of microfossils found in palynological preparations.

Paper coal Thin lens of organic material made up entirely of plant cuticle.

Paracytic stomata Type of stomatal pattern in which one or two cells adjacent to the guard cells are positioned with their long axes paralleling the long axes of the guard cells.

Periderm Outer tissue consisting of cork cells, cork cambium, and often parenchyma that develops in organs undergoing secondary growth.

Perispore The outermost extraexinous sporoderm layer in some spores that is formed as a result of the activity of the plasmodium.

Perithecium A type of ascoscarp that is enclosed at maturity except for a small opening or ostiole.

Pertifaction (permineralization) Type of preservation in which mineral material has permeated the cells and interstices soon after deposition.

Phelloderm A portion of the periderm that resembles cortical parenchyma and formed by the phellogen.

Phellogen A lateral meristem (cork cambium) that produces the periderm in the stems and roots of many plants.

Phyllophore Leaf-bearing organ.

Phyllotaxy The arrangement of leaves on an axis or stem.

Pinna (pinnae) Subdivision of a compound leaf or frond.

Pinnule The ultimate subdivision of pinnae of a compound leaf or frond.

Platyspermic Seed flattened in the transverse plane.

Plectostele A type of protostele that is dissected longitudinally into several platelike units.

Pollen A microspore in seed plants that contains the mature or immature microgametophyte.

Polystelic Axis containing more than one stele.

Prokaryotic Cell type having no unit-membrane-bound organelles.

Prolate Drawn out toward the poles; pollen grain in which the ratio of the polar axis to the equatorial diameter is between 1.25 and 2.0.

Prothallial cell One to several small cells produced during the development of the seed-plant microgametophyte and thought to represent the vestigial vegetative tissue of the male gametophyte.

Protostele Solid core of xylem surrounded by phloem.

Protoxylem The first-formed primary xylem.

Pseudomonopodial A type of branching with a single or primary axis that results from unequal development of a dichotomous system.

Pulvinus   A swelling or cushion at the base of a petiole that may act as a center of sensitivity.

Punctae   A type of ornamentation characterized by small pits.

Pycnoxylic   General term for wood that is compact, containing mostly vascular elements and little parenchyma.

Rachis   The axis of a compound leaf on which the leaflets are borne.

Radiometric dating   Quantitative determination of geologic age based on the uniform decay rate of certain radioactive nuclides.

Rhizoid   Unicellular or multicellular rootlike filament that functions to anchor and absorb.

Rhizome   A horizontal stem that may be subterranean.

Saccus   The air sacs or bladders on certain wind-borne pollen grains.

Salpinx   Extended distal end of the megasporangium in some fossil seeds that aided pollen capture.

Sarcotesta   The outer parenchymatous layer of the integument in some seeds.

Sclerotesta   The fibrous layer of the integument of some seeds.

Sclerotium   In certain fungi, a rounded, often hardened mass of hyphae.

Segment cell   First-order cells produced by the internal cutting faces of an apical cell.

Sextant cells   Derivatives of segment cells in the region of the apical meristem.

Sinistral   Turned to the left; counterclockwise.

Siphonogamous   Producing pollen tubes.

Siphonostele   A type of stele in which the xylem and phloem are arranged in a hollow cylinder that surrounds a central pith.

Solenostele   An amphiphloic siphonostele.

Sparganum   Type of cortical organization characterized by radiating fibrous bands vertically aligned without anastomoses.

Sporae dispersae   Pollen grains and spores that are found dispersed in sediments and not in situ in the organ that produced them.

Sporangium   A structure in which spores are produced.

Spore   A reproductive cell capable of germinating into a new organism. There are various types of spores identified among plants on the basis of their function in the life cycle (e.g., microspores, megaspores, isospores, teliospores, auxospores, etc.).

Sporoderm   General term for the entire pollen-grain wall or spore coat.

Sporophyte   Spore-producing asexual phase.

Sporopollenin   Oxidative polymers of carotenoides and/or carotenoide esters that make up the wall of pollen grains and spores.

Stele   Vascular tissue of axes.

Stipe   The petiole of a fern frond.

Stoma (stomata)   A pore in the epidermis surrounded by guard cells.

Stomium   Thin-walled cells of a sporangium along which rupture takes place.

Strobilus   Axis with short internodes containing spore-bearing units.

Stromatolite   Finely laminated, usually calcareous, organosedimentary structures resulting from the accretion of detrital and percipitated minerals on sheetlike mats formed by communities of microorganisms (filamentous blue-green algae).

Subsidiary cell   Epidermal cell associated with the guard cells of a stoma.

Symbiosis   Dissimilar organisms living together in a state of mutualism.

Sympodium   Discrete, axial vascular bundle from which leaf traces diverge at regular intervals.

Synangium   United sporangia.

Syndetocheilic   A type of stomatal development in which the guard cells and subsidiary cells originate from the same initial.

Tectate   A type of pollen-grain infrastructure in which the columns that arise from the inner layer of the exine are united across their tips.

Telome   Terminal segment of a dichotomously branched axis that may be fertile or sterile.

Telome theory   Theory advanced to explain the evolutionary development of many vascular plants and plant organs beginning with a three-dimensional branching system.

Tetrad   A cluster of four spores that have arisen by division from a common spore mother cell.

Tetrahedral tetrad   Spatial configuration in which one of the spores is positioned centrally over the other three; in contrast to the *tetragonal, rhomboidal,* and *decussate* tetrad types, in which the four spores are in the same plane.

Torus   The central thickened part of a bordered-pit membrane.

Trichome   A hair or hairlike outgrowth of the epidermis.

Trichotomosulcate   A pollen grain possessing three furrows on its distal face.

Tricolpate   A pollen grain possessing three meridionally arranged furrows.

Tricolporoidate   A pollen grain with three meridionally arranged furrows, each with a transverse furrow or pore.

Trilete   Y-shaped contact figure on the proximal surface of a spore.

Triradiate scar   Contact feature of a trilete spore.

Ubisch body   *See* Orbicle.

Vallecular canal   Air canals in the cortex of some sphenophyte stems that alternate with the vascular bundles.

Vascular segment   A strand of primary xylem that gives rise to leaf traces and is surrounded by a cylinder of secondary vascular tissue.

Zonate   A type of spore with furrows that encircle the equator.

Geologic Time Table

This geologic time table shows the chronostratigraphic names for Europe and North America. (Modified after a wall chart by Van Eysinga, 1975, with permission of Elsevier Publishing Co.)

GEOLOGIC TIME TABLE

STRATIGRAPHIC CLASSIFICATION

EON: PHANEROZOIC — **ERATHEM/ERA:** CENOZOIC

GEOLOGIC TIME (MILLION YEARS)	SYSTEM / PERIOD	SERIES	EPOCH	STAGE/AGE — GENERAL CLASSIFICATION	EUROPE — GENERAL CLASSIFICATION	EUROPE — LOCAL CLASSIFICATION	EUROPE — LOCAL CLASSIFICATION	NORTH AMERICA
0.01	Quaternary (Anthropogene)	Holocene (Recent)		Versilian				
0.1–0.5		Pleistocene	Upper	Tyrrhenian	Oldenburgian	Khvalynian / Khazarian / Singilian		Rancholabrean
0.6–1.0				Milazzian				Irvingtonian
			Late	Sicilian			Tiraspolian	Hallian
1.2–1.8			Lower	Emilian	Biharian	Bakunian		
			Early	Calabrian	Villafranchian	Apcheronian		Blancan
3		Pliocene	Upper	(Astian/Redonian)			Romanian	
			Late	Piacenzian		Akchagylian		Wheelerian
4	Neogene		Lower	Zanclean (Tabianian)	Ruscinian	Kimmerian	Dacian	Venturian / Repettian
5		Miocene	Early					
			Upper	Messinian	Turolian	Pontian / Meotian		Delmontian
10			Late	Tortonian (Helvetian)	Vallesian	Sarmatian	Pannonian (Oeningian)	Mohnian
	TERTIARY		Middle	Serravallian	Maremmian	Konkian / Karaganian / Tchokrakian	Badenian	Luisian / Relizian
15				Langhian	Vindobonian	Tarchanian / Kozachurian	Karpathian / Ottnangian	Clarendonian / Barstovian
			Lower	Burdigalian	(Girondian)	Sakaraulian	Eggenburgian	Saucesian / Hemingfordian
20			Early	Aquitanian		Caucasean	Egerian	Zemorrian
22.5								Arikareean

565

Geological time chart (stage/series/system correlation)

Age scale (Ma): 25, 30, 35, 40, 45, 50, 55, 60, 65, 70, 75, 80, 85, 90, 95, 100, 110, 118, 120, 130, 140, 141

North American stages (top): Arikareean, Whitneyan, Orellan, Chadronian, Duchesnean, Uintan, Bridgerian, Wasatchian, Clarkforkian, Tiffanian, Torrejonian, Dragonian, Puercan, Gulfian, Comanchean

Zemorrian — Refugian, Narizian, Ulatisian, Penutian, Bulitian, Ynezian; Upper, Lower (Late / Early); Upper

Egerian — (Tongrian), (Ilerdian), (Angoumian), (Salmurian), (Urgonian), (Virollian)

(Vitrollian), Lattorfian, Asschian, (Biarritzian), Cuisian, (Aturian), (Emscherian), (Provencian), (Ligerian), (Gault), (Wealden), (Purbeckian), (Tithonian)

Sannoisian, Ludian, Marinesian, Auversian, Wemmelian, Ledian, Bruxellian, Sparnacian, Landenian, Rognacian, Begudian, Fuvelian, Valdonnian, Vraconian, Clansayesian, Gargasian, Bedoulian

Chattian, Rupelian (Stampian), Bartonian, Priabonian, Lutetian, Ypresian, Thanetian, Montian, Danian, Maastrichtian, Campanian, Santonian, Coniacian, Turonian, Cenomanian, Albian, Aptian, Barremian, Hauterivian, Valanginian, Berriasian, Portlandian/Volgian

Subdivisions: Upper, Late, Lower, Early, Middle, Senonian, Neocomian, Malm

Series/System: Oligocene, Eocene, Paleocene — Palaeogene; Upper, Lower — Cretaceous; Early — Jurassic

Eras: TERTIARY, CENOZOIC, MESOZOIC, PHANEROZOIC

Geological time scale chart (Phanerozoic — Mesozoic and Palaeozoic)

Eon	Era	System	Epoch / Series	Stage (European / regional)	Stage (regional)	Stage (North American)	N. American subdivision	Facies / local names	Regional stage
PHANEROZOIC	MESOZOIC	Jurassic	Late / Malm	Oxfordian	Lusitanian	Corallian (M, L, E)		(Sequanian)(Rauracian)(Argovian)	
				Callovian					
		Middle / Dogger	Bathonian		(Vesulian)				
				Bajocian					
		Lower / Early / Lias	Aalenian / Toarcian						
				Pliensbachian	Charmouthian			(Domerian)(Carixian)	
				Sinemurian	Lotharingian				
				Hettangian					
		Triassic	Upper / Late	Rhaetian					
				Norian					
				Carnian				(Keuper)	
		Middle	Ladinian	Virglorian				(Muschelkalk)	
				Anisian					
		Lower / Early	Scythian	Werfenian				(Buntsandstein)	
	PALAEOZOIC	Permian	Upper / Late	Tatarian (Chideruan)	Thuringian	Ochoan		(Zechstein)	Djulfian / Penjabian
				Kazanian		Guadalupian			
			Middle	Kungurian	Saxonian	Leonardian			
			Lower / Early	Artinskian	Autunian	Wolfcampian		(Rotliegendes)	Induan / Olenikian
				Sakmarian				Uralian	
		Carboniferous	Upper / Late / Pennsylvanian	Stephanian (C, B, A)	Orenburgian	Virgilian	Upper	(Coal Measures)	
					Gzelian	Missourian	Late		
				Westphalian (D, C, B, A)	Moscovian	Desmoinesian	Middle		
						Atokan / Derryan	L / E		
				Namurian (C, B, A)	Bashkirian	Morrowan	Upper	(Millstone grit)	Springerian
			Lower / Early / Mississippian		Namurian	Springerian			Chesterian
					Visean	Meramecian	Late	Avonian (Culm)	
						Osagean	Lower		
					Tournaisian	Kinderhookian	Early		
		Devonian	Upper / Late / Chautauquan	Famennian	Strunian / Etroeungtian	Conewangoan		Breconian	Dasbergian / Hembergian
						Cassadagan		(Old Red Sandstone)	

Permian upper regional stages: Scythian, Smithian, Dienerian, Griesbachian

Age scale (Ma): 160, 170, 180, 190, 195, 200, 210, 220, 230, 240, 250, 251, 260, 270, 280, 290, 300, 310, 320, 325, 330, 340, 345, 350

Geologic time-scale correlation chart (Paleozoic / Phanerozoic)

Time scale (Ma, left margin): 360, 370, 380, 390, 395, 400, 410, 420, 423, 430, 435, 440, 450, 460, 470, 480, 490, 500, 510, 515, 520, 530, 540, 550

Era/Eon labels (vertical): PALEOZOIC — PHANEROZOIC

Devonian

Series	Stage names / regional correlations
Late / Upper	Chemungian; Fingerlakesian; Senecan; Frasnian; Old Red Sand Stone / Breconian; Nehdenian / Adorfian; (Coblencian)
Middle	Taghanican; Tioughiogan; Cazenovian; Onesquethawan; Erian; Givetian; Couvinian; Zlichovian; Eifelian
Lower / Early	Onondagan; Deerparkian; Oriskanyan; Helderbergian; Ulsterian; Emsian; Siegenian; Gedinnian; Pragian; Lochkovian; Dittonian; Downtonian

Silurian (Gothlandian)

Series	Stage names / regional correlations
Upper	Keyseran; Tonolowayan; Salinan; Cayugan; Pridolian; Kopaninian; Ludlovian; Whitecliffian; Leintwardinian; Bringewoodian; Eltonian; S a l o p i a n
	Lockportian; Cliftonian; Clintonian; Niagaran; Motolian; Wenlockian (U / M / L); Telychian; Fronian; Idwian; Himantian; Rhuddanian; Pusgillian; Onnian
Lower	Alexandrian; Medinan; Zelkovician; Kurnan; Landoverian; Valentian; Ashgillian; Longvillian; Costonian

Ordovician

Series	Stage names / regional correlations
Upper / Late	Richmondian; Maysvillian; Edenian; Trentonian; Blackriverian; Chazyan; Mowhawkian; Cincinnatian; Champlainian; Viruan; Harjuan; Caradocian; Llandeilian; Llanvirnian
Middle	Cassinian; Jeffersonian; Demingian; Gasconadian; Canadian; Ontikan; Oelandian; Litenian; Budnanian; Arenigian; Skiddavian; Olentian; Dolgellian
Lower / Early	Trempealeauan; Franconian; Dresbachian; Iruan; Tremadocian; Festiniogian; Maentwrogian

Cambrian

Series	Stage names / regional correlations
Upper	Croixian; Purtsean; (Potsdamian); Menevian; Shidertinian; Tuorian
Middle	Albertan; (Acadian); Solvan; Mayan; Amgan; Lenan
Lower	Waucoban; (Georgian); Caerfaian; Aldanian

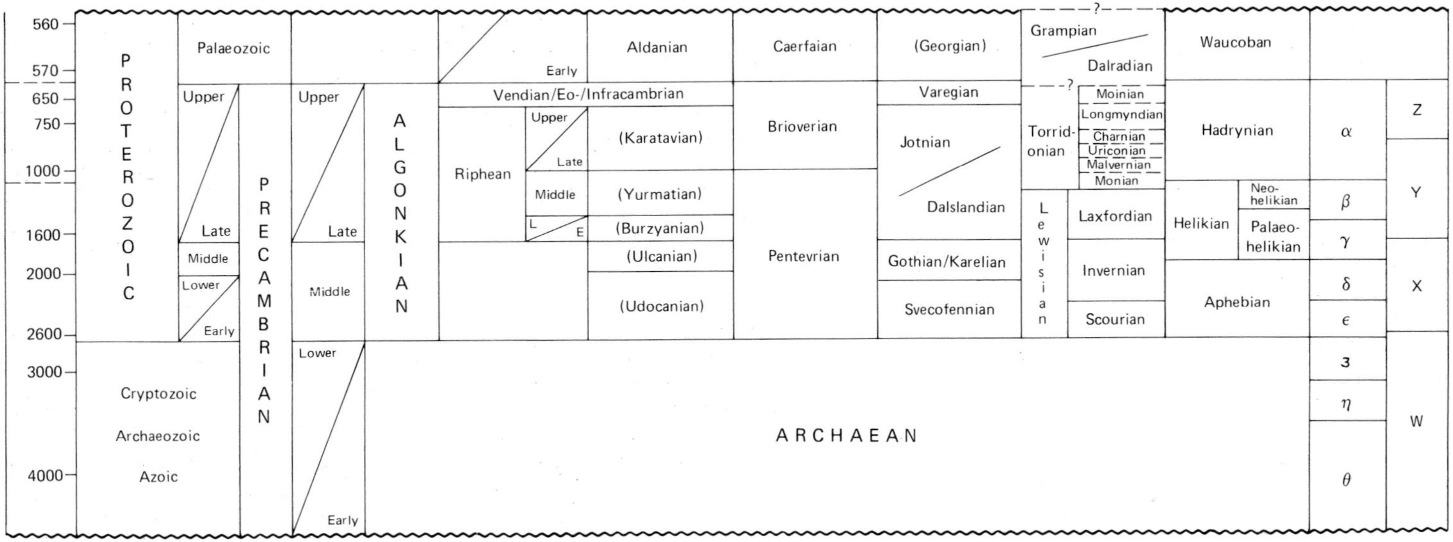

A stratigraphic correlation chart (rotated 90°). Its contents, read across the regional columns:

Age (Ma)	Period classifications
560	
570	PROTEROZOIC — Upper; PRECAMBRIAN — Late
650	
750	
1000	ALGONKIAN — Late / Middle
1600	Lower
2000	Early
2600	
3000	Cryptozoic
4000	Archaeozoic / Azoic

Column letters: Z, Y, X, W

Greek subdivisions: α, β, γ, δ, ε, 3, η, θ

Regional / stratigraphic terms:

- Palaeozoic — Waucoban
- Hadrynian — Neohelikian, Palaeohelikian; Helikian; Aphebian
- Vendian/Eo-/Infracambrian — Early
- Riphean — Upper/Late (Karatavian), Middle (Yurmatian), Lower/Early (Burzyanian), (Ulcanian), (Udocanian)
- Aldanian
- Caerfaian — Brioverian — Pentevrian
- (Georgian) — Varegian — Jotnian — Dalslandian — Gothian/Karelian — Svecofennian
- Grampian — Dalradian (Moinian, Longmyndian, Charnian, Uriconian, Malvernian, Monian) — Torridonian — Laxfordian — Lewisian — Invernian — Scourian

ARCHAEAN

PROTEROZOIC (ALGONKIAN) · PRECAMBRIAN

Appendix Two

Basic Palynological Terminology

POLLEN AND SPORE TETRAD CONFIGURATIONS

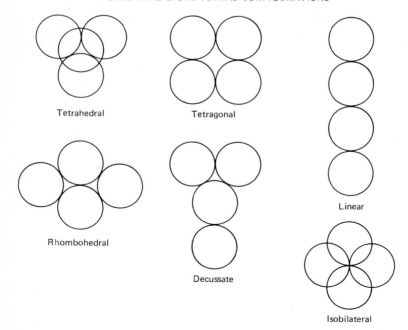

Tetrahedral

Tetragonal

Rhombohedral

Decussate

Linear

Isobilateral

TRILETE SPORE

Laesura

Proximal surface

Distal surface

TRICHOTOMOSULCATE POLLEN

Sulcus

Proximal surface

Distal surface

TRICOLPATE POLLEN

Colpus

Polar view

Equatorial view

MONOLETE SPORE

Laesura

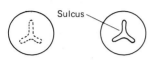

Proximal surface   Distal surface

MONOSACCATE POLLEN

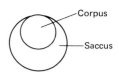

Corpus

Saccus

Equatorial view

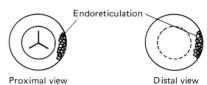

Endoreticulation

Proximal view   Distal view

BISACCATE POLLEN

Endoreticulations

Corpus

Saccus

Sulcus

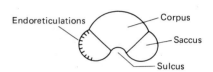

Equatorial view

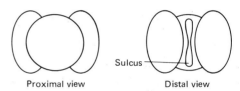

Sulcus

Proximal view   Distal view

Indexes

Taxonomic Index

Name and Subject Index